The Best of

NEW YORK

REVISED EDITION

Editor-in-Chief
Ruth Gardner

Chief Restaurant Critic and Editor
Edward Guiliano

Restaurant Reviewers
Jacqueline Friedrich, Colette Rossant, Ruth Spear, with contributions by
J.C. Suarès

Contributing Editors
Quick Bites and Hotels: Elizabeth Sahatjian; Nightlife: Rose Hartman;
Shops: Kathy Bishop plus Mary Arendt, Michel Blair, Julie Epstein,
Leonore Good, Joanna Levine, Ilana Locke, David Rubel, Bristol Voss;
Music, Dance, and Theater: Diane Solway; Sights: Kathy Henderson

Associate Editor
Kate Dalton

Prentice Hall Press Editor
Edith Jarolim

Series Editor
Colleen Dunn Bates

Coordination by
Alain Gayot

Directed by
André Gayot

Supervised by
Christian Millau

PRENTICE HALL PRESS ▪ NEW YORK

Other Gault Millau Guides Available
from Prentice Hall Press

The Best of Los Angeles
The Best of Washington, D.C.
The Best of San Francisco

Designed by Patricia Fabricant

Published by Prentice Hall Press
A Division of Simon & Schuster, Inc.
Gulf + Western Building
One Gulf + Western Plaza
New York, New York 10023

Please address all comments regarding The Best of New York to:
Gault Millau, Inc.
P.O. Box 361144
Los Angeles, CA 90036

Library of Congress Cataloging in Publication Data
The Best of New York / editor, Ruth Gardner; contributing
editors, Jonathan Burton . . . [et al.]; supervised by Christian Millau—
Rev. ed.
    p.   cm.
    Rev. ed. of: The best of New York / Christian Millau. Rev. ed. 1984.
    Includes index.
    ISBN 0-13-076076-5: $14.95
    1. New York (N.Y.)—Description—1981—Guide-books.   I. Gardner,
Ruth, 1950-   .   II. Millau, Christian. Best of New York.
F128.18.B43 1988
917.47'10443—dc19   87-30873
                                                                CIP

ISBN 0-13-076076-5

Thanks to the staff at Prentice Hall Press for their invaluable
aid in producing these Gault Millau guides.
Manufactured in the United States of America

CONTENTS

New York

POWERHOUSE CITY

The legend that is New York is self-fulfilling—the biggest, the brashest, the best. In the lyrics of its current unofficial anthem, "If you can make it there, you can make it anywhere." Midwestern jazzmen in the 30's knew this and so nicknamed New York City "the Big Apple." Creative artists have long regarded recognition in New York as the most coveted and tangible sign of success. Doctors, lawyers, anchor people, developers, restaurateurs, entrepreneurs—all eye New York and many cannot resist its pull. Some of those who do make it there become the subjects of Broadway shows, books, magazine features, movies, or television shows, thereby fueling and perpetuating the legend.

Feverishly hard work and long hours are part of the legend too. Visitors and returning natives regularly describe the rush of energy they feel when they arrive at one of the city's airports or terminals and head for its heart. Certainly the centuries of immigrants who have built New York—often the boldest, brightest and poorest of their native stock—embody its strong work ethic. As the old story goes, if the Martians landed in the Bronx on Monday but the subways ran on Tuesday, everyone would still go to work.

But this city that works hard also plays hard. New Yorkers like to reward themselves for their slavish labors with good times; they release some of the city's enormous energy by indulging in festivals, parades, elegant dinners, theater tickets, concerts, bending an elbow with compadres at the local tavern. They work as hard at enjoying their off-duty hours as they do on the job, much to the benefit of the visitor.

If you draw a 75-mile radius from New York's magnificent public library at 42nd St. and Fifth Ave. and inscribe a circle, you will have captured nearly ten percent of the population of the United States. It is this population, of course, that is the city's power and vitality—immense ethnic segments, fully assimilated families, the old guard, the new wave. And although New Yorkers are spread over five boroughs covering a vast area, those outside of Manhattan talk of a trip to the city just as they would if they lived in a small town hundreds of miles away. More remarkable still, "the city" usually refers only to a small part of the granite island of Manhattan, roughly the lower third, where the great majority of famous sights, nightspots, shops, restaurants, and buildings listed in this book are located.

This same piece of Manhattan is also the communications capital of the world: within walking distance from one another are found the executive headquarters of the national television networks, the major magazines, the book publishers, the radio networks, the record companies, the important newspapers with national and international impact, and, of course, the huge advertising industry—so called Madison Avenue—that shapes our opinions and determines our purchases. So is it the financial hub of the country and the most closely watched business center in the world. What happens on legendary Wall Street (a tiny, shadowy block) determines not only the financial success or failure of Americans, but of the entire globe.

But despite all their power and sophistication, New Yorkers are also provincial (some might say self-centered), forgetting how atypical their city is. Though it symbolizes America to the world, it is almost a country unto itself, as different from the rest of America as London or Hong Kong. The city is atypical as well in that in these changing times, it renews and rebuilds itself but has not changed fundamentally in centuries. Once the immigrants came from Eastern Europe, Italy, Ireland; now they come from Korea, Haiti, the Soviet Union. Once the Chrysler Building was the world's tallest, then the Empire State Building, then the World Trade Center, and now plans are proceeding for a 150-story building. It has, however, changed in one sense: the city's healthy economy was once based on a strong manufacturing industry, but now it is in step with the world-wide movement from developed to developing nations, and large-scale manufacturing is in a decline. New York has exchanged a great many blue collars for white collars; service-oriented industries, specialized manufacturing, and "paperwork factories" are now the foundation of the city's economy.

The sights that have become postcard clichés, the shops, the world-class restaurants: the list of greats in New York is remarkably long. In this guide we have tried to tally it candidly for you. Certainly the city has its flaws—its blighted neighborhoods, its dirty streets, its noisy subways, for example—but this is a guide to the city's best, an introduction to and celebration of the finest elements of the legend that is New York.

RESTAURANTS

Restaurants

A <u>CULINARY CROSSROADS</u>

If Brillat-Savarin could be lured from the grave (say with big bucks from one of New York's powerhouse publishers) to revise his seminal work on food, *The Physiology of Taste* (1825), his research and questing palate would soon lead him to New York City. It would be inevitable; modern Gotham is a culinary crossroads where people, products, and ideas travel en masse and often in style. A few weeks of eating in New York would give Brillat-Savarin a startling wealth of fresh material for his meditations on gastronomy.

The restaurant scene in New York has an unmatched vibrancy and diversity here that reflect the high energy of this city that never sleeps. How many other cities tally more than 16,000 restaurants? Where else can you get goat cheese ravioli at midnight, grilled tuna at 1 A.M., couscous at 2, shrimp lo mein at 3, pot au feu at 4, and a cheeseburger or steak anytime? Its denizens can ask with typical New Yorker pride, "How many other places have so many famous, world-class restaurants?" They have a point, and Brillat-Savarin would have to plan a lengthy stay.

The restaurant scene is an ever-changing landscape in America's largest city. New restaurants open daily and old (and sometimes not so old) ones close; chefs waltz from one kitchen to the next; addresses change amid construction and renovation. New Yorkers don't even shrug when a cozy storefront restaurant featuring the so-called cuisine of the American Southwest closes and re-opens two weeks later as an attractive place featuring Himalayan food, which in turn eight months later is recast as a zippy Japanese joint (true). No wonder the city has more professional restaurant critics than any other. Staying au courant is easier said than done, and a nightmare for anyone publishing a book such as this, with a lag of months between the finalizing of text and publication. But we have done our best to be timely and accurate, and trust our readers will understand the inevitable ravages of time.

Over the past few decades a revolution in American tastes and attitudes has occurred. Healthier foods, light foods, fish, increasingly diverse produce and preparations have all been embraced. Hamburgers, hot dogs, beer, and soft drinks are hardly threatened as national staples, but today many Americans travel and have been exposed to a tremendous range of wines, cuisines, and restaurants; thus they have become increasingly discriminating and demanding. Even stay-at-home New Yorkers have long insisted upon quality produce; Gothamites demand a higher percentage of grade-A chickens, prime meats, and the like than any other place in America. As chicken magnate and American folk hero Frank Perdue notes, "You don't go to Kansas City to get the best beef. You go to New York. You don't go to Maine to get the best lobsters. You go to New York." Add to this the astonishing increase in the availability of exotic fruits, vegetables, and fish in the past few years. The result: the level of restaurants in New York, especially in the middle ranks, has risen markedly in the last five years.

Consider these facts too. Several top French and Italian chefs and restaurateurs have relocated in New York, and with strong financial backing have launched dynamic and influential new restaurants. The Asian influx and influence have increased, and quality Japanese and Thai restaurants, in particular, have opened to warm receptions. Hotel dining has made a strong comeback. Many hotel chains have invested substantially in showcase eateries in New York, often hiring top European chefs as consultants or staff, and the results have been dramatic. Bistro fare is in at new and old restaurants. In particular there have been more than a dozen fine modern versions of classic French bistros that have opened to thronging crowds, and, in a kindred Italian vein, another dozen or so trattorias. Open-kitchen Californian and Southwestern restaurants and cuisines have become entrenched in the yuppie scene and influential in the New York restaurant scene at large. This last change points significantly to a respect for an emerging branch of authentic American cuisine, one differentiated from the traditions and histories of European or Asian cooking.

Why all this activity? The maturing of the baby boomers, the increase in discretionary income, and changes in eating habits and attitudes are all contributors. In New York, dining out is part of the daily life style of young urban professionals, and for two-income families, local restaurants are often the compensation for and decompression chamber after a high-pressured day at the office. Additionally, in New York, where rents are stratospheric and apartments microscopic, the restaurant has replaced the home as the place to entertain. Add to that the huge influx of tourists, booming business expense accounts, and a solid and traditional base of restaurant-goers, and it is easy to understand all the investment in restaurants and all the new openings.

Over the past two decades, Gault Millau has become as much a philosophy as a name. In France the Gault Millau guides and magazine are synonymous with, in Brillat-Savarin's phrase, the pursuit and pleasures of the table, publications dedicated to raising standards and awareness of fine dining. For this New York guide we composed a reviewing team of senior food writers who are at once familiar with and sympathetic to the Gault Millau philosophy and keenly aware of the world of restaurants in New York. Altogether the authors of more than a dozen books and hundreds of articles in national publications, the team visited and revisited restaurants, then debated and reconsidered relative strengths and weaknesses. We hope this professional collaboration has made this a truthful guide that will help you to explore and enjoy the restaurants of New York—and should Brillat-Savarin return, one he would value, too.

Edward Guiliano

SYMBOL SYSTEMS & PRICES

Restaurants are ranked in the same manner French students are graded, on a scale of one to 20. While thousands of satisfying New York restaurants would be rated below ten, with an eight or nine still a passing grade, for *The Best of New York* we have selected restaurants rated ten or higher; these are restaurants that for one or more reasons we can recommend. The rankings reflect primarily the quality of the cooking; decor, service, welcome, and atmosphere are explicitly commented on within the reviews. Restaurants that are ranked 13 and above are distinguished with toques (chef's hats) according to the following table:

    Exceptional 4 toques, for 19/20
    Excellent 3 toques, for 17/20 or 18/20
    Very good 2 toques, for 15/20 or 16/20
    Good 1 toque, for 13/20 or 14/20

These ranks are *relative*. One toque for 13/20 is a good but modest ranking for a highly-reputed restaurant, yet is highly complimentary for a small place without much culinary pretension.

Unless otherwise noted, the prices given are for a complete meal, including an appetizer, main course, dessert, and a half-bottle of wine per person. Naturally the prices are approximations; they have been checked and rechecked, but over time will have a tendency to rise. Menus and dishes we've described are also subject to the winds of change.

Note well that *prices do not include tax and tip*. In New York City a sales tax of 8.25% is added to every bill. Tipping, which constitutes the bulk of the service staff's wages, and thus should not be considered wholly optional, averages 15 to 20%, and in special circumstances and for special service is more. Many diners find it convenient to double the sales tax to arrive at a 16.5% gratuity. The number and quality of wines and beverages ordered, as well as the type of main course selected will significantly affect the bottom line of your check. Bear that in mind when reviewing our average prices, adjust accordingly, and add the tax and tip (say, roughly, another 25% on top) to come up with a more personalized and useful estimate than we can issue across the board. Remember, too, that in New York reservations are always suggested, and at many restaurants essential. For some they must be made weeks in advance.

Toque Tally

19/20

Le Cirque

18/20

Chanterelle   Lafayette

17/20

Le Bernardin	Lutèce
Le Périgord	The Quilted Giraffe

16/20

Arcadia	Nippon
Aurora	Parioli Romanissimo
La Réserve	The Sign of the Dove
Montrachet	

15/20

An American Place	La Caravelle
Arizona 206	La Côte Basque
Cellar in the Sky	La Grenouille
China Grill	La Tulipe
Dawat	Le Cygne
Felidia	Le Régence
The Four Seasons	Maurice
Gotham Bar & Grill	Mitsukoshi
Harlequin	Oyster Bar & Restaurant
Hubert's	Palio
Jams	Petrossian
John Clancy's Restaurant	Prunelle
King Fung	Terrace Restaurant

14/20

Andrée's Restaurant	The Carlyle Restaurant
Auntie Yuan Restaurant	Cavaliere
Bombay Palace	Chikubu
Brive	Georgine Carmella

Grand Palace
Il Bufalo
Il Cantinori
Il Mulino
Il Nido
Indochine
Kuruma zushi
Lola
Marcello
The Nice Restaurant
Pamir
Pesca
Primavera

The Polo
Quatorze
Rakel
Raphaël
Sabor
Sandro's
Shun Lee Palace
Sistina
Sofi
Tai Hong Lau
Union Square Cafe
Water's Edge

13/20

Agora
Amerigo's
Anatolia
Argenteuil
Arqua'
The Ballroom
Bangkok House
Barocco
Batons
Bellini
Bice
Bouley
Bud's
Café de Bruxelles
Café Luxembourg
Cafe Pierre
Caffe Roma
Canton
Cent' Anni
Chez Jacqueline
Chez Louis
Claire

The Coach House
Dabar
The Dolphin
Fu's
Gallagher's
Hatsuhana
Hawaii 5-0
Hulot's
Jane Street Seafood Cafe
Kitcho
La Gauloise
La Métairie (downtown)
La Ripaille
Lavin's
Le Chantilly
Le Festival
Le Palmier
L'Escale
L'Hostaria del Bongustaio
Lusardi's
Manducatis
Manhattan Chili Co.

Man Ray Bistrot
Maxim's
Mezzaluna
Mie
Orso
Paola's Restaurant
Peter Luger
Pig Heaven
Positano
Primola
Provence
Quaglino by Tino Fontana
Remi
René Pujol
The River Cafe
The Russian Tea Room

San Giusto
Scarlatti
The Sea Grill
Seryna
Shezan
Siracusa
Smith & Wollensky
Spark's Steakhouse
The Stanhope Dining Room
Tapis Rouge
Tommasso's
Trastevere
The Village Green
Wilkinson's Seafood Cafe
Windows on the World
    Restaurant

12/20

Alo Alo
American Harvest Restaurant
Au Troquet
The Black Sheep
Bravo Gianni
Bukhara
Café des Artistes
Cafe Destinn
Cafe du Parc
Chez Josephine
Cinco de Mayo
Coastal
Devon House
Elio's
Ennio and Michael Restaurant
Frank's
The Gibbon

Gloucester House
Greene Street Cafe
Inagiku
Island
Jacks
Keen's
La Bohême
La Bôite en Bois
La Colombe d'Or
La Métairie (uptown)
Lattanzi
Lello
Le Refuge
Le Relais
Manchu
Metropolis
Nightfalls

Odeon
Omen
One If By Land, Two If By Sea
Panda Garden
Pinocchio
Rao's
Rogers & Barbero
Sam's Cafe
Sant Ambroeus
Say Eng Look

Tatany Village
Tavern on the Green
Tenbrooks
Tommy Tang's
Toon's
Trattoria da Alfredo
Tre Scalini
'21'
Wong Kee

11/20

Akbar
The Barclay
Bistro Bamboche
Bridge Cafe
Cabana Carioca
Café Loup
Cedars of Lebanon
Chalet Swiss
Contrapunto
Cuisine de Saigon
Da Silvano
Dieci Ristorante
Erminia
Fandango
Gage and Tollner

Hyotan-Nippon
Il Palazzo
La Mirabelle
Le Veau D'or
Manhattan Ocean Club
Nicole Brasserie de Paris
The Palm
Petaluma
Raoul's
Rosa Mexicano
Sammy's Roumanian Restaurant
Sidewalker's
Toscana
20 Mott Street
Vanessa

10/20

Abyssinia
Barbetta
Blue Nile
Bon Temps Rouler
Carolina

Chapiteau
Dominick's
El Faro
El Rincón de España
Garvins

Il Valetto
Jezebel
Manganaro's
Mortimer's
Sante Fe

Singleton's Bar-B-Q
Sylvia's
Tastings
Ye Waverly Inn

The World's Cuisines

AFGHAN

Parmir

AMERICAN

American Harvest Restaurant
An American Place
Arcadia
Argenteuil
Arizona 206
The Barclay
Bon Temps Rouler
Bridge Cafe
Bud's
Cafe Destinn
Cafe Luxembourg
Carolina
Claire
The Coach House
Coastal
Gage and Tollner

Garvins
Gotham Bar & Grill
Greene Street Cafe
Hawaii 5-0
Jacks
Jams
Jezebel
Keen's
Lavin's
Manhattan Chile Company
Metropolis
Nightfall's
Odeon
The River Cafe
Rogers & Barbero
Sam's Cafe

Santa Fe
Sign of the Dove
Singleton's Bar-B-Q
Sofi
Sylvia's
Tastings

Tenbrooks
'21'
The Village Green
Water's Edge
Ye Waverly Inn

BELGIAN

Café de Bruxelles

BRAZILIAN

Cabana Carioca

CARIBBEAN

Lola

CHINESE

Auntie Yuan
Canton
Fu's
Grand Palace
King Fung
Manchu
The Nice Restaurant

Panda Garden
Pig Heaven
Say Eng Look
Shun Lee Palace
Tai Hong Lau
20 Mott Street
Wong Kee

CONTINENTAL

Cellar in the Sky

Devon House

Mortimer's
One If By Land, Two If By Sea
Sammy's Roumanian Restaurant

The Stanhope Dining Room
Windows on the World
   Restaurant

CUBAN

Sabor

ECLECTIC

Agora
Batons
China Grill
Fandango
The Four Seasons
The Gibbon
Hubert's

Il Bufalo
Island
The Quilted Giraffe
Tavern on the Green
Union Square Cafe
Vanessa

ETHIOPIAN

Abyssinia

Blue Nile

FRENCH

Aurora
Au Troquet
Bistro Bamboche
The Black Sheep
Bouley
Brive
Café des Artistes
Cafe du Parc
Café Loup

Cafe Pierre
The Carlyle Restaurant
Chanterelle
Chapiteau
Chez Jacqueline
Chez Josephine
Chez Louis
Hulot's
La Bohême

La Boîte en Bois
La Caravelle
La Colombe d'Or
La Côte Basque
Lafayette
La Gauloise
La Grenouille
La Métairie (downtown)
La Métairie (uptown)
La Mirabelle
La Petite Marmite
La Réserve
La Ripaille
La Tulipe
Le Bernardin
Le Chantilly
Le Cirque
Le Cygne
Le Festival
Le Palmier
Le Périgord
Le Refuge

Le Régence
Le Relais
L'Escale
Le Veau d'Or
Lutèce
Man Ray Bistrot
Maurice
Maxim's
Montrachet
Nicole Brasserie de Paris
Petrossian
The Polo
Provence
Prunelle
Quatorze
Rakel
Raoul's
Raphaël
René Pujol
Tapis Rouge
Terrace Restaurant

INDIAN

Akbar
Bombay Palace
Bukhara

Dabar
Dawat

ITALIAN

Alo Alo
Amerigo's
Arqua'
Barbetta
Barocco
Bellini

Bice
Bravo Gianni
Caffe Roma
Cavaliere
Cent' Anni
Contrapunto

Da Silvano
Dieci
Dominick's
Elio's
Ennio and Michael
Erminia
Felidia
Frank's
Georgine Carmella
Il Cantinori
Il Mulino
Il Nido
Il Palazzo
Il Valetto
Lattanzi
Lello
L'Hostaria del Bongustaio
Lusardi's
Manducatis
Manganaro's
Marcello
Mezzaluna
Orso

Palio
Paola's Restaurant
Parioli Romanissimo
Petaluma
Pinocchio
Positano
Primavera
Primola
Quaglino by Tino Fontana
Rao's
Remi
Sandro's
San Giusto
Sant Ambroeus
Scarlatti
Siracusa
Sistina
Tommasso's
Toscana
Trastevere
Trattoria da Alfredo
Tre Scalini

JAPANESE

Chikubu
Inagiku
Hatsuhana
Hyotan-Nippon
Kitcho
Kuruma zushi

Mie
Mitsukoshi
Nippon
Omen
Seryna
Tatany Village

MEXICAN

Cafe Marimba
Cinco de Mayo

Rosa Mexicano

MIDDLE EASTERN

Andrée's Restaurant

Cedars of Lebanon

PAKISTANI

Shezan

RUSSIAN

The Russian Tea Room

SEAFOOD

Claire
The Dolphin
Gloucester House
Jane Street Seafood Cafe
John Clancy's Restaurant
Le Bernardin
Le Festival

Manhattan Ocean Club
Pesca
The Oyster Bar & Restaurant
The Sea Grill
Sidewalker's
Wilkinson's Seafood Cafe

SPANISH

The Ballroom
El Faro

El Rincón de España
Harlequin

STEAK

Frank's
Gallagher's
The Palm

Peter Luger
Smith & Wollensky
Sparks

SWISS

Chalet Swiss

THAI

Bangkok House
Tommy Tang's
Toon's

TURKISH

Anatolia

VIETNAMESE

Cuisine de Saigon   Indochine

Below Houston Street

ABYSSINIA

35 Grand St. (Thompson St.)
226-5959
Ethiopian

10/20

Is ersatz Africa as good as the real thing? At Abyssinia, the Ethiopian restaurant in SoHo, it's good enough. The room is simply decorated with a large Ethiopian cross and several woven baskets hanging on the walls. Each table (also made of basket weaving) is covered with a dome of straw, which is removed as you sit down on three-legged stools, just as you would in an African village. The menu is divided into four categories: vegetarian, fish, poultry, and lamb. Everything is served on very thin white pancakes called "injera" which are used to pick up the food, replacing forks and knives. You will probably end up licking your fingers.

Doro wot is marinated chicken served in a thick, fiery red pepper sauce called berbère (you'll need plenty of beer to soothe your burning throat). The equally spicy beef stew has a nice touch of ginger, and the lamb dish, ye'beg alitcha, by far the best on the menu, is served in the same red sauce, but this time with the addition of turmeric, onions, and some rather exotic African spices. All the dishes are well-prepared, even if the chef skimps on the meat. The Ethiopian version of steak tartare is unusual and delightful and coupled with azefa wot, a lentil salad reminiscent of French bistro fare. The vegetables here are sadly overcooked, and the fish dishes are relatively unencumbered and an alternative for those who are not fond of hot and spicy cuisine. Dessert is fruit; forget the store-bought cakes. Enjoy a glass of Ethiopian honey wine instead, a nice touch to end the evening. A meal with beer costs $15-20 per person.
Mon.-Fri. 6 P.M. to 11 P.M., Sat. & Sun. 5 P.M. to midnight. AE.

THE AMERICAN HARVEST RESTAURANT

Vista International Hotel, 3 World Trade Center
938-9100

American

12/20

This Hilton showcase restaurant on the plaza level of the Vista Hotel gets an American salute for its concept—announced by the harvest table at the entrance. That plan "is to present the freshest of foods at their peak of flavor in American dishes." Thus, in August, when locally grown sweet corn comes to market, Martha's Vineyard green corn pudding is featured. In February citrus fruits from Florida and Texas are featured. The duck of the month for February comes (no, not à l'orange) with grapefruit.

Gimmicks aside, the menu is straightforward, but it is hard to put the gimmicks aside. Indeed, a perfectly sound baked red snapper comes, in February, with lemon orange sauce. Ditto for the tasty charcoal-broiled salmon unnecessarily bombarded with juniper berries, or broiled salmon served with lemon mayonnaise. For starters the ocean fresh bluepoint oysters always satisfy. Soups are fine, even interesting. And the Long Island duck variations are crisp and tasty, although you might not fancy your duck with, say, blueberries or rhubarb. The grilled or poached shrimp and the calf's liver with onions and avocado are recommended. The half-pound tenderloin steak wins the serious meat contest. Seasonal vegetables are usually prepared properly and are a bonus.

The all-American theme is everywhere evident in the

restaurant's five dining rooms, which are quiet and intimate. The rooms are separated by floor-to-ceiling glass vitrines featuring American arts and crafts exhibits. Service is hotel American, which means it can be pretty weak. The wine list too is heavily American, at least 60%, and with an American "Special Reserve" list of wines priced from $27 to $120. Markups are reasonable and there are drinkable wines available at $12. Among the all-American desserts are apple pie with cheddar cheese, or ice cream and a chocolate fudge layer cake, but like the entrées many old standards get a quirky dressing up here (in addition a heavy dose of sugar). You won't find tangerine cheesecake on many other dessert lists. Lunch averages $27 per person, and dinner $42 and up with a modest wine, plus tax and tip.

Breakfast Mon.-Fri. 7 A.M. to 10 A.M.; lunch Mon.-Fri. 11:30 A.M. to 2:30 P.M.; dinner Mon.-Sat. 6 P.M. to 10 P.M.; closed last two weeks before Labor Day. All major credit cards.

ARQUA'

281 Church St. (White St.)
334-1888
Italian

13 🎩

When Venice was a republic, the Doges periodically repaired to Arqua' Petrarca, a village near Padua, to discuss matters of state in a relaxing atmosphere. Arqua' was also the home of the Renaissance poet Petrarch and, more recently, of Ernaldo, this restaurant's chef. Restaurant Arqua', in trendy Tribeca, is a new world triumph for Italy. The decor, in what must have once been a nondescript industrial space, has cleverly been kept minimal—there is not even a single picture on the soaring Venetian pink walls to distract from the serious business of eating. The lighting is kind and the tables unusually well-spaced. And best of all, Arqua' is not just another restaurant cashing in on the vogue for Northern Italian food. It has a tight focus—the food of the Veneto, too little known here. The hallmarks are seafood, fresh pasta, polenta, simple preparation, relatively little fat, and the freshest ingredients, an ideal cuisine for eating considerations today.

The small, well-edited menu features, to start, the classic Venetian sgombretti in saor (marinated mackerel in a light sweet-and-sour sauce spiked with onion), a good stuffed artichoke, and many good homemade pastas, especially the pappardelle dei dogi with ricotta and radicchio, airy agnolotti filled with spinach in a light tomato sauce, and the mattonella d'Arqua', pasta layered with artichoke purée and brought together with bechamel. The special of polenta with sausages and wild mushrooms is outstanding and, when they are available, the whole baby octopuses are delicious. Various risotti are offered, most notably the famous Venetian black ink risotto, which you can get when seppie, tiny inkfish, are available from Italy. Only the too-buttery gnocchi with four herbs is less than successful.

Main courses, on the whole, come off less well than the starters; the kitchen seems to be overtaxed at peak hours. The sometimes downright curt service, occasionally overcooked fish, and inordinately long wait between courses would bear out this theory. Pollo al prosecco, chicken braised in the slightly sparkling wine of the Veneto with a paste of olives, mushrooms, and sweet peppers is a good main course choice. Try also the tender veal chop with sage. As for dessert, with tirami su on every Italian menu in town, one can afford to be picky. Arqua's is not special, though its lemony cheesecake is. Fruit is not a dessert option here. Prices are modest; about $28 per person for dinner.

Lunch Mon.-Fri. noon to 3 P.M.; dinner Mon.-Sat. 6 P.M. to 11:30 P.M. AE.

Barocco

301 Church St. (Walker St.)
431-1445

Italian

13 ♟

There are a few things you should know about Barocco: it hit the ground running, immediately attracting Bohemians with money and, later, the people who subsidize them—publishers, gallery owners, and parents. Its appetizers and pastas are better than its entrées; its portions are skimpy; its prices, high; and turnover, at least on weekends, is strongly encouraged. (Those who don't dig in their heels to slow down the pace will find themselves back on the street faster than you can say pappardelle al coniglio.) Still, Barocco is popular for very good reasons. It bills itself as a trattoria, and it effortlessly achieves an ambiance that is warm and relaxed but still electric with the excitement of people who know they are in the right place at the right time—and having a good time and a good meal to boot. Everyone's packed into a single room on the ground floor of a turn-of-the-century loft building. Typical of many warehouses-turned-restaurant, the room has high ceilings and is punctuated by tall Corinthian columns. The decor is minimal and the food simply prepared. And when the kitchen is under pressure, it's best to stick with pre-prepared or especially simple dishes.

The house bread, a crusty homemade loaf, is one of the best in town. They dress this up with garlic, call it fettunta, and give you two slices for $2, which would qualify as petty larceny were the dish not so delicious. Every other appetizer sampled was equally tasty, from grilled eggplant and red peppers, to a refreshing salad of translucent strips of fennel topped with Parmesan shards, to pencil-thin asparagus spears (listed under vegetables) served with butter and Parmesan. We'd happily argue in favor of any of the homemade pastas, from the aforementioned pappardelle al coniglio (with rabbit, black olives, and sun-dried tomatoes), to fettuccine with tomatoes and artichokes, to homey spinach lasagna, to delicate spinach ravioli (its ricotta-spinach filling is tinged with nutmeg, its light, fresh tomato sauce topped with shreds of fresh basil). As noted, entrées fare less well. Whole roasted snapper, with herbs and garlic, can be dry and bland. Roast pork—paper-thin slices of meat, served at room temperature and fanned out around a pile of broccoli rape—is somewhat better, but not a meal you eat with gusto. The à la carte roast potatoes, however, topped with deep-fried sage leaves and rosemary, are terrific. For dessert, there are good renditions of the standards—tirami su and ricotta cheesecake. The small, serviceable wine list is mostly Italian. Plan on spending $40 per person, with wine.
Dinner Mon.-Thurs. 6:30 P.M. to 11:30 P.M., Fri. & Sat. till midnight. AE, MC, V.

BON TEMPS ROULER

59 Reade St. (Broadway & Church St.)
513-1333
American/Cajun

10/20

The good times have rolled right by this place, which used to sizzle like the Cajun martinis it serves. The latter are still hot enough to fuel the Concorde, but this funky-looking place, with plastic beaded necklaces dripping from the lampshades and zaftig waitresses in skintight miniskirts and black lace stockings, just putt-putts along like an old jalopy. The original chef, Susan Trilling, has gone, and so have the crowds. Now, free hors d'oeuvre during happy hour attract loft-locals and Wall Streeters. Some even linger for dinner, which consists of rather forlorn renditions of Paul Prudhomme's new classics such as Cajun popcorn (the dipping sauce tastes as if it was made from his prepared mix, Cajun Magic), to blackened redfish (incinerated is more like it), to bland jambalaya (long on rice, short on chicken, sausages, and flavor). The famed alligator sausage is rarely available. Desserts, such as whiskey-laced bread pudding, apparently made from the Christmas-spiced muffins served with dinner, are as heavy as paperweights. Though we criticize, you can have a fun time here and eat satisfactorily. Dinner, with a Cajun martini and several beer chasers, costs about $30 a person.

Lunch Mon.-Fri. noon to 3 P.M.; buffet Mon. till 9 P.M.; dinner Tues.-Sat. 6 P.M. to 11:30 P.M. AE.

BOULEY

165 Duane St. (Hudson & Greenwich Sts.)
608-3852
French

13

It takes a combination of guts, confidence, and conceit to put your name up above the door of a restaurant. Thirty-four-year-old chef David Bouley has chosen to name his first restaurant after himself, and he'll have to live with that name and decision. At least the door is magnificent. A carved, curvilinear wood construction, it opens off Duane Square (a triangular park slice of TriBeCa) and into a strikingly handsome cloister of a restaurant. The setting has the feel of a European inn. Beige walls, vaulted ceilings, paintings, tiles, antiques, sunset lighting, Christofle forks, Limoges china—this top stage set evokes the inspirational countryside of Provence with unintentional hints of Southern Germany. Service and setting is black-tie all the way. The food doesn't match the level of the setting, but it has been inching up from a disappointing opening level in August 1987.

Expectations for food at this long-promised restaurant run high. Bouley worked in France for Bocuse, Girardet, Lenôtre, and Vergé, and in New York at Le Cirque before becoming the first chef and helping to establish very fine Montrachet. At Bouley, however, the dishes sound better than they taste. There is a crazy and inexplicable unevenness to the preparation. On two visits the clam ravioli is simply awful, rubbery and blah, the third (but middle) time it is much better. Twice the pot au feu is sublime, yet on a third occasion a miscalculation in the kitchen with salt signals disappointment. Once the millefeuille of smoked eel is a mess and is surrounded by lamentable coulis. Who wants to try it a second time to learn how good it can be? The tomato soup with tiny pink shrimp and accompanied by butter-fried bread spread with a purée of basil is wonderful, but who can trust tomatoes year 'round? What can be recommended without hesitation is the roasted pigeon, one breast served with a slice of grilled foie gras, the other stuffed into a cabbage leaf and accompanied with wild mushrooms and baby yellow zucchini. While this combination works, the curious marriage of lobster with red Sancerre won't work for everyone. The spit-roasted duckling with nine spices is recommended as are a number of salad appetizers. On the eight-course, $65 tasting menu, the only dish that was consistently underwhelming was the tiny rack and loin of lamb.

Meals begin with complimentary and generally tasty finger foods and end with a complimentary and generally so-so platter of petits fours. Desserts are distinguished by their striking presentations and their busy, ambitious, and usually successful combinations. Soufflés and sorbets are best. The pistachio opera cake with chocolate-ganache terrine served with a bitter-chocolate sorbet is dark, deep, and luscious. The mostly French wine offerings are sound but limited and wildly over priced. This place is pitched to the Wall Street crowd for lunch and the uptown taxi and limousine crowd for dinner. If prices were cut in half, we could get more excited about this young and potentially interesting restaurant. Jacket and tie are required for men. For dinner expect to pay $75 to $100 per person, plus tax and tip.

Lunch Mon.-Fri. noon to 2:30 P.M.; dinner Mon.-Sat. 6 P.M. to 11 P.M. All major credit cards.

BRIDGE CAFE

279 Water St. (Dover St.)
227-3344

American

11/20

Less would be more. This cozy place has enough going for it to be able to relax and have fun. But it doesn't. Instead, an overambitious kitchen defeats the combined charms of the look, feel, and location, which could not be more welcoming. Bridge Cafe is housed in a brick-red structure built in 1801. Huddled in the shadow of the Brooklyn Bridge, it greets the eye like a candle in the wilderness. Located a few blocks north of the South Street Seaport, it is the one sign of life in another kind of wilderness—the only bona fide restaurant anywhere near the theme park that Rowse built. Inside, the room is warm and relaxing; a bar spans one wall, and a dozen or so tables with red-and-white checked cloths fill the balance of the space without overcrowding it. There is an air of old New York here that never goes out of style. Today it attracts neighborhood families and couples for dinner, and Wall Streeters and city workers (including Hizzoner) for weekday meals and drinks (the roster of which includes a half dozen wines by the glass).

If only they'd leave well enough alone and stick with simple things such as burgers, salads, and fish from the nearby Fulton Fish Market. Instead, the kitchen eschews the simple in favor of overly complicated, overly seasoned dishes.

An appetizer of chicken quenelles, for example, consists of three tough pellets, at once fibrous and bland, on a flavorful fumet, itself marred by the needless addition of chopped chives and shredded red cabbage. Ask for a recommendation and you'll be pointed to the curried oysters appetizer with cucumber vinaigrette, or the chicken tenderloins with fermented black beans and garlic. Duck in green peppercorn sauce is not only overcooked, it's covered with shredded orange zests which make the whole dish taste like duck à l'orange. Pan-fried trout is similarly gussied up. A layer of salmon caviar, the berries of which are thicker than the fish, overwhelm the delicacy of the trout with saltiness. Sautéed Norwegian salmon or soft-shell crabs in season are better bets. Desserts, such as apple nut cake served with a warm rum sauce, are homey, hearty, and filling. Dinner, with wine, averages about $45 a person.

Lunch Mon.-Fri. 11:45 A.M. to 3 P.M.; dinner Mon.-Sat. 6 P.M. to midnight, Sun. 5 P.M. to 11 P.M.; brunch Sat. & Sun. noon to 3:30 P.M. AE, DC.

CANTON

45 Division St. (Market St. & the Bowery)
226-4441; 226-0921
Chinese

13

If not exactly chic, Canton's decor is a far cry from that of most Chinatown restaurants. It has a simple, uptown, Western-style interior (and is frequented by many Westerners.) The sea is Canton's decorative theme, and fish and seafood dishes are also the strength of the kitchen. You will get consistently well-prepared food here whether you are a regular or not, but you will eat better if you are known to the family. The regular menu is uninspired and you'll be in superb hands if you let Mrs. Leang—Eileen to regulars—suggest dishes prepared from ingredients found at the market that day, or that husband Larry is fine-tuning in the kitchen at the moment.

No, this is not your typical Chinatown restaurant. No, the cuisine is not Cantonese via Hong Kong. In fact, Larry learned to cook in Chinatown and cites refined French and Italian cuisines as continuing influences on his own. Stir-fried cooking is not the only rule here. To start, try a hand roll of lettuce stuffed variously with either squab or chicken or vegetables. Consider a main dish of boneless and herbed chicken with scallions, or a simple and excellent roast duck, cut into pieces you can manage easily with chopsticks. The stuffed duck—a command performance—is lovely. Lobster in a black bean sauce is recommended, but if you can get Larry to fix you a fish specially you'll be in for a treat. He prepares a sublime pike; its skin is removed and its meat served as light quenelles. Carp, that soft-finned freshwater fish, is something of a specialty and comes as light as air and as tasty as can be. Sea bass is also tamed by a master. Neither wine nor liquor is served, but plenty of people bring their own. Many people consider Canton to be tops, but sometimes people enter with such high expectations that they are disappointed. It surely is a good and appealing place to try. Dinner averages between $25 and $35 per person.

Lunch & dinner Wed.-Sun. noon to 10 P.M., Sat. till 11 P.M.; closed mid-July through mid-Aug. No credit cards.

CELLAR IN THE SKY WINDOWS ON THE WORLD

One World Trade Center, 107th Fl.
938-1111

Continental

15

This concept restaurant within the Windows on the World complex continues to be the finest of the World Trade Center's 22 or so restaurants. The concept is simple: one menu that changes every two weeks, one seating, one price ($70), and six courses designed around five wines. The wines are selected from a range of countries and the foods are similarly varied. Here you entrust yourself to fate as well as to the good professionals on hand, since you can't make on-the-spot selections and often have to book well in advance, not knowing what will be on the menu (though you can ask). Some wines are better than others, some dishes and preparations are better than others, some marriages of food and wine are better than others, so, obviously, some weeks the Cellar in the Sky is better than others. The range of dining experience runs from good (say a 13 on our scale), to excellent (say a 17). Unfortunately, it is unusual to pass through a range of dishes and wines without a disappointing course, and some of the pairings of food and wine are really problematic.

The show, however, is always very good. Thirty-six to 40 diners are pampered within a raised and glassed-in dining room surrounded by wine racks (the cellar). A classical guitarist contributes to the romantic setting. Each meal is composed of an appetizer, three courses, a cheese selection, and a dessert. One representative winter menu began with Veuve Clicquot Brut Champagne served with the chef's canapés, which were followed by lobster medallions in mustard vinaigrette with leek and caviar, then by ravioli of lamb and calf's feet in tomatoes and ginger butter. A 1984 Mondavi Chardonnay was served with freshly smoked salmon with tarragon sabayon. A1982 Volnay "Clos des Chênes" by Gaunoux accompanied marinated loin of venison with juniper berries and pink peppercorns. The cheese course consisted of Muenster on garlic croûtons and was accompa-

nied by a 1971 Château La Lagune. The dessert course was a Chinese spice soufflé with cinnamon ice cream. A 1977 Croft port was poured before the coffee and petits fours. The $70 price per person does not include tax or tip.
Mon.-Sat. 7:30 P.M. (one seating). All major credit cards.

CHANTERELLE

89 Grand St. (Green St.)
966-6960
French

18

That two kids from the Bronx have put together one of the city's finest French restaurants surely fuels the fires of fantasy for would-be or struggling restaurateurs. Culinary Institute of America-trained Chef David Waltuck and his wife, Karen, who is the professional presence out front, have succeeded in turning the small storefront restaurant they opened in SoHo in 1981 into a minimalist room with the most coveted tables in town. You must reserve weeks or months in advance and reconfirm the day prior to your reservation to be certain that one of the 30 to 36 mahogany chairs has your name on it. It is worth the effort, although it must be said that Chanterelle is not for everyone.

Its ambiance lies on the opposite end of the spectrum from bustling, crowded, charged Le Cirque. Here there is a starkness and precious civility; the food is the show, reverently so, but friendly and quiet conversation flows naturally, too. Salmon-beige walls, a gray rug, beautiful white tiles on the high ceiling, three early American chandeliers, beautifully appointed tables, and a desk and huge armoire facing the entrance create an Old World feeling of refined elegance that contrasts joltingly with the shabby street scenes outside the room's large windows.

The menu is limited and prix fixe ($58 or $73); however, it changes biweekly, fluctuating with the availability of products and with the seasons. Talented Chef Waltuck is not a couple-of-dishes wonder. He can do it all, with a few nouvelle American cuisine flourishes on one hand, and with much of the classic French style of a convert—including rich sauces and liberal use of salt—on the other. The curious result is a meal that is both creative and seemingly old-fashioned. Dishes we have enjoyed recently include the grilled seafood sausage appetizer, various seafood ravioli (e.g., salmon ravioli with cabbage and caviar, or ravioli filled with crab meat), soups such as crayfish bisque, red snapper with red butter as a main course, or tuna with tomato and coriander. The rabbit, usually served with a cream sauce and herbs, is recommended, as is the roast squab. We recently had a wonderful breast of Muscovy duck with sherry wine vinegar and wild mushrooms. The breast is grilled until

27

browned and crusted, then sliced, revealing a luscious slice of pale pink to rosy rare meat at its center. For heavy hitters the roast saddle of venison with black truffles is satisfying.

The bread here is the best in New York. The crusty dinner rolls originate in Long Island City, and are reheated before being served, but everything else short of the wine is homemade, including the walnut onion bread that accompanies the finest cheese tray in the city. The tray includes French, Italian, and American cheeses and is offered as part of the fixed price meal. It is rare to find a full-time wine steward, especially at such a small restaurant, but Michael Bilunas, young and serious, fills the role at Chanterelle. The wine list is mostly French with a few American selections. It is reasonably grand with seriously high prices, though there are some satisfying selections in the twenties and thirties. It has some good Burgundies from small producers, but the overall selections are a bit eclectic and obscure, even to very serious wine people. Apart from Champagne, it won't be easy to order a grand bottle known to the world for its consistent excellence. You may have to trust Mr. Bilunas. Desserts are all right but display a heavy hand with sugar. Three choices are usually offered, plus so-so complimentary petits fours at the close. Fruit tarts are fine, and ice creams and sherbets excellent. Jacket and tie are required for men. (Note: The current restaurant is scheduled to move to a nearby SoHo location in mid-1988.) At this spot for serious eating, both a white and red wine would seem appropriate; if so, your bill may top our ballpark figure of $100 per person, plus tax and tip.

Dinner Tues.-Sat. 6:30 P.M. to 10:30 P.M.; closed first week of Jan. and all of July. All major credit cards.

Cinco de Mayo

*349 West Broadway
(Broome St.)
226-5255*

Mexican

12/20

Differing in most aspects from the slew of mediocre, unauthentic Mexican eateries in New York, Cinco de Mayo offers good and often unusual cuisine, elegant and airy surroundings, and professional service. The restaurant is divided among three very different spaces; choose the front room with its bar if you want to be seen by the chic SoHo crowd, the back room if you're looking for intimacy, and the second floor balcony if you want to enjoy the Mexican harpist. Daily specials always include one or two soups and interesting additions to the entrées on the menu. Furthermore, the menu offers two regional specialties for each day of the week, so it could be disappointing to come on the wrong day if you want, say, camarones en pipian (Monday), fresh butterfly shrimp and chunks of potatoes and onions in a tangy sauce made with crème fraîche, coriander, ground pumpkin seeds, and a touch of green chile. Appetizers are delightful; even the ubiquitous guacamole has a creamy, chunky texture and a fresh, spicy taste. Don't shy away from taquitos de moronga, soft corn tortillas filled with minced blood pudding and fresh coriander; they are excellent and as authentic as you can get without flying due east of Mexico City, where the young chef, Jose Hurtado Prud'homme, was born. The enchiladas are freshly made and happily lack the overdose of sour cream and bean mush that has made the dish famous (and infamous). Try anything with mole. Cinco de Mayo's rich, delicious version of this classic Mexican sauce would dress up the most pedestrian dish. Another dish seldom touched by American tastebuds is a stew of tripe, chiles, and bits of vegetable called menudo norteño. Entrées from the grill are uneven; while the steak is tasty, the skewered shrimp served with dull rice lack flavor. Desserts are homemade but quite American, except for the flan de chocolat, a flourless, extremely dense chocolate cake flavored with Kahlua and served with whipped crème fraîche. Cinco de Mayo has separate lunch and brunch menus, lighter in fare and in price. The wines here are reasonably priced and mainly hail from Spain and California. The Mexican beers are highly recommended, as is the frozen Margarita. There's a Tudor City outpost of this restaurant as well (45 Tudor City Place; 661-5070). About $30 per person with drinks. *Mon.-Thurs. noon to 11 P.M., Fri. till midnight, Sat. 11 A.M. to midnight, Sun. 11 A.M. to 11 P.M. All major credit cards.*

EL RINCÓN DE ESPAÑA

226 Thompson St. (Bleecker & W. 3rd Sts.)
260-4950
Spanish

10/20

A very small, intimate, and dark restaurant in the Village, El Rincón de Espana is owned by Carlos Ventoso, a Spanish chef who makes a wonderful octopus dish (pulpo à la Carlos) that will send you reeling with its pungent taste of garlic. This is the sort of place best frequented when you're in a group and wish to be entertained—Senor Iñaki will strum Spanish and American songs with a flourish in front of your table. The appetizers here are disappointing; stay far away from entremeses variados, a mishmash of salty tuna, cold tomatoes, rigid and tasteless shrimp, and other nondescript, non-Spanish tidbits. If you must begin with something, order the chorizos, a spicy Spanish dried sausage, or the jamón con melon, a hearty country ham with melon. Any seafood entrée with salsa verde, a garlicky green herb sauce, is very good, but avoid the white sauce. Entrées come with a mediocre Spanish rice and an almost inedible iceberg lettuce salad. Most dishes here, as you might have gathered, are flavored with garlic; if you desire a bit of purity, try the tender grilled lamb chops or the grilled fillet of beef. Now for the specialties: yes, the paellas are good. They are chock-full of fresh seafood (and chicken in the paella Valenciana), well-seasoned, and quite authentic, although they lack the pungency of paella in Spain. With a swig of Rincón's very good Spanish red wines, however, you will be well satisfied. Desserts are ordinary, although the flan is homemade and pleasantly refreshing. The coffee here is as it should be: strong, robust, with a true Spanish spirit. Price per person with wine is $30.

Mon.-Thurs. noon to 11 P.M., Fri & Sat. noon to midnight, Sun. noon to 11 P.M. All major credit cards.

GEORGINE CARMELLA

165 Mulberry St. (Grand & Broome Sts.)
226-3999

Italian

14 🍴

This is the kind of restaurant food writers think twice about publicizing for fear of spoiling it; it's small, slightly out of the way, and the food is good—a contemporary interpretation of classic Italian food, at once recognizable and new. Georgine Cavaiola cooks with great style and authority, dishing up her exquisite food in a small storefront in Little Italy, still with its original pressed tin ceiling, tongue-in-groove wainscoting, and exposed steam risers, all painted an agreeable beige-peach. The lighting is pleasantly low; the crowd genteel. There is a welcoming basket of fresh flowers outside, no posters inside, and the opera music is just right. Service is low-key, professional, and caring. If we have a reservation about this place, it's that it tries a bit too hard to be the restrained antithesis to its Little Italy counterparts. (It is also expensive.)

A hint of what is in store is placed on your bread plate when you sit down; two very warm, dense, crusty pieces of fresh Italian bread, one plain, one gently garlicked, both with a thin melt of herbed mozzarella on top. Among the starters, try the nubbins of grilled littleneck clams, sweet with garlic and parsley, or the grilled eggplant with an elusive note of mint, served on a bed of arugula and perfectly set off with shavings of pecorino cheese. Another time the clams may be offered posillipo, in a silky tomato broth. Pasta dishes are excellent, especially the tagliolini in a flavorsome tomato sauce with basil, and the ravioli—plump, round, ricotta-filled pillows on a bed of spinach, dressed with sage butter and Parmesan cheese. The flavorsome risotto verde in its robe of puréed zucchini and spinach is outstanding. Veal scaloppine with wild mushrooms and cream is a good main course choice, as is a special of calf's liver veneziana, with sweet-tart onions. On occasion there is an inspired zuppa di pesce. The pan-roasted free-range chicken with garlic and vinegar is tasty but insufficient by itself, especially when the skin is removed. Most main courses come ungarnished, so you may want to order sautéed spinach or grilled radicchio on the side. A small selection of desserts is offered, including homemade cannelloni, fresh fruit, and a fabulous moist dark chocolate hazelnut torte. The wine list is exceptional and pricey; the Antinori Chianti Riserva at $32 is about the least expensive red and just fine with this food. Pinot Grigio, a decent white, is $24. Prosecco, the delightful, slightly sparkling white wine of the Veneto, is $6 a glass, as is the house red, Santa Madalena.

The management has cleverly designed two tasting menus for those who find the menu so appealing that they want to eat everything; one is composed of melon and prosciutto and four of the pastas; the Owner's Selection is a six-course tasting composed from the menu and daily specials. With both the entire table must participate. The menu can change frequently according to season and to the chef's whim. Dinner averages $56 before tax and tip; the pasta tasting is $42, the Owner's Selection, $62.

Dinner Tues.-Sun. 6 P.M. to 11 P.M. AE.

GRAND PALACE

94-98 Mott Street (Canal St.)
219-3088
Chinese

14

North of Canal, on Mott Street, you'll find a "new" Chinese restaurant: the Grand Palace. It deserves its name. You enter via a large stainless-steel façade, framed in red tiles with dark gray stripes. The dining room has a postmodern feeling with elaborate Art Deco ceiling lights, light pink walls, and mirrored columns. As you come in, you can contemplate the 18 Buddhas lined up against a green tiled wall, each a good luck charm. And a large Coke machine looms.

The menu is long, 12 pages, reflecting the latest changes in Chinatown fare. Shark's fin and bird's nest soups rate high among the new arrivals; here there are a dozen to choose from, one of the most interesting being a mixture of both shark's fin with crab meat and bird's nest. The broth is delicate and rich, the shredded shark's fin light and pungent. Other soups here have wild names like codfish maws with premier, or duck's juice with fish lip. Abalone is a star ingredient and is flown in fresh from California. It is served sliced, mixed with dry abalone sautéed in a light oyster sauce. Squabs are also featured, baked in port wine, deep-fried, braised with mushrooms, or just simply roasted with soy sauce, always served with their heads peeking out of the lettuce on which they rest. Among the seafood dishes, we recommend simple boiled sweet shrimp in their shells, served with soy sauce and shredded scallions. Crispy, crackling goose skin (tastier than Peking duck) must be ordered in advance; frog's legs are also in vogue and are served fried, steamed, or sautéed with garlic and ginger, so good they might make you renounce French cuisine. Dessert is sliced oranges. Price per person about $25.

Breakfast, lunch & dinner daily 8 A.M. to 10:30 P.M., dim sum daily from 8 A.M. to 3:30 P.M. AE (dinner only).

GREENE STREET CAFE

101 Greene St. (Prince & Spring Sts.)
925-2415
American

12/20

Greene Street is still a SoHo favorite. This enormous restaurant, with its jungle look and antique rattan furniture, is a very lively place that attracts locals who meet here for a drink at the bar and to listen to live music. Newly-arrived Chinese chef Pang has added his own touch to the menu with his fondness for New York nouvelle cuisine and, of course, a bit of the Orient. The excellent chicken consommé with enoki mushrooms has an unusually strong, rich chicken flavor. The lobster sausage served with artichokes in a herb mayonnaise is delicious. The escalope of salmon is lightly broiled and perfectly complimented by its vinegar and herb sauce. Unfortunately, you will still find a lot of the same old standybys, like goat cheese salad and seafood ravioli. Particularly avoid the fettuccine with smoked salmon and cream, which is too heavy and rich, or the warm bluepoint oysters with lemon butter and chevril, insipid and unpleasant. The entrées are also often sadly "déjà vu": red snapper (don't New York restaurants know any other fish?), loin of lamb (very good), and a breast of chicken with roasted garlic (too dry). And yet the fillet of salmon with three caviars is inspired, and the sirloin steak with roasted carrots and potatoes is juicy and tasty. Desserts are good, especially the excellent fruit tarts; the fresh fruits are beautifully served. The wine list is well-rounded, with some Europeans as well as wines from Australia and California. Prices are reasonable. Dinner per person, $40 with a drink.

Dinner Tues.-Thurs. 6 P.M. to 11:30 P.M., Fri. & Sat. till midnight, Sun. noon to 8 P.M. All major credit cards.

IL MULINO

With its well-spaced tables and chairs, one exposed brick wall, playing off papered walls, and a row of tall, stately

86 West Third St. (Sullivan & Thompson Sts.)
673-3783
Italian

14

plants that serve as a room divider, Il Mulino typifies the elegant Village-Soho restaurant trend. Lighting, pleasant, rosey, and atmospheric, is often so low you can barely read the menu. What you can read, you can be sure is good. The Italian kitchen here works very well.

Don't go too hungry to Il Mulino. The place can be crowded with passionate fans, and reservations are taken lightly—you may have to join the jam at the bar where the noise level approaches that of a large cocktail party. Once you're seated, however, flagging spirits will be quickly revived by the wonderful fried zucchini, crisp and greaseless, or the bruschetta, a tasty tomato-garlic toast that will be sped to your table. From there you can go on to the addictive boconccini, moist balls of buffalo mozzarella, flecked with roasted sweet peppers. Be sure to check out the pasta specials such as pappardelle (a broad ribbony pasta) in a gorgeously robust fresh tomato or sometimes a game sauce, or the unusual carbonara. Salmon with balsamic vinegar-slicked porcini mushrooms is a good main course choice, as is the veal chop fragrant with rosemary. Some entrées come quite naked, so ask if you need to order a veg or two. The house red wine, available by the glass, is a pleasing Cabernet Sauvignon from Italy. Fruit is always a good ending for Italian food; Il Mulino's fresh orange slices marinated in Grand Marnier and framboise are just right, ditto the poached pear with white wine and grappa. About $50 per person for lunch or dinner.
Lunch Mon.-Fri. noon to 3 P.M.; dinner Tues.-Sat. 5 P.M. to 11 P.M. AE.

KING FUNG

20 Elizabeth St. (Canal St.)
964-5256/57
Chinese

15

At the corner of Canal and Elizabeth Streets sits what is perhaps Chinatown's finest restaurant. The façade, lit by a row of red Chinese lanterns, has fan-shaped windows like the ones in the Imperial Summer House in Beijing, and two marble lions on pedestals. Inside, the walls are papered with beige and gold, discreetly illuminated, and adorned with the obligatory gold phoenix and fire-spitting dragon. The tables are laid with care. In front of each setting a silver chopstick-holder secures a long-handled spoon and your chopsticks; the spoon is to help you serve the dishes, set on a Lazy Susan.

The menu is long, with many shark's fin and bird's nest soups. But it also offers unusual thick soups, like shredded duck and fish maw soup in a rich brown stock, and numerous clear soups, the best one being the extraordinary double-boiled mushroom soup, transparent but with a strong mushroom flavor and tender black mushroom caps. The salt-baked squab, golden brown with crackling skin and dark, juicy meat, is superb. The steamed squab with ham is more delicate—the sauce creamy white, served with brilliant green Chinese broccoli. There is also stuffed squab and grilled squab... the list is endless. Among the chicken and duck dishes, the pan-fried boneless duck with lemon sauce is on par with the best nouvelle cuisine in America. Shredded duck with salted vegetables is beautifully presented in a crisp basket made of julienned taro which, when broken and eaten with the duck, rivals the best French baguette. Fish has star billing at King Fung. The fried whole flounder is magnificent. The fish fillets are deep-fried along with the bones; the fish is then re-formed and smothered with julienned scallions and ginger in a light soy sauce. Brilliant! Desserts anyone? The red bean cream with lotus seed is quite sweet but pleasantly light. Another good choice is mashed waterchestnut cream, sweet but with a strong nutty taste. About $25 per person.

Breakfast, lunch & dinner 8 A.M. to 11 P.M. AE, MC, V.

MONTRACHET

239 West Broadway (White St.)
219-2777
French

16 🍴

With the name Montrachet, you'd expect this restaurant to offer some luscious Burgundy wines and dishes—and it does. Established in 1985 in a Tribeca industrial space, it can be a little tricky for uptowners and out-of-towners to find the first time around. Its low-key, store-front entrance is a bit inconspicuous and certainly doesn't suggest the large restaurant beyond: a high-ceilinged, rectangular dining room with a mahogany and onyx bar that leads into another spacious, square dining room, that leads into yet another high-ceilinged dining room, this one used often for private parties. Soft colors—pale pinks and greens—and soft lights contribute to the comfortable, open, unpretentious feel of the dining spaces.

The food, prepared by chef Brian Whitmer, is very good and often excellent. Falstaffian owner and maître d' Drew Nieporent works the dining room like few New York professionals can, supervising a slick team of waiters all in black with slim, tucked-in ties. When it comes to wine, wine manager Daniel Johnnes is eager to help and has been developing an increasingly sophisticated list. There are 55 reliable wines printed on the menu card, mostly French but with a good selection from California; the prices are reasonable and ascend from $15 to $150. Things get really interesting on the supplemental list, where prices can be higher, vintages older, and uncommon selections enticing. Trust David or Drew.

Ordering is easy if you choose one of the two fixed menus, one at $29 and the other $45. The former is a bargain and an almost sure bet. It opens with a terrine of vegetables with tomato butter (which looks like a multicolored seven layer cake set in a light tomato sauce). A layer of eggplant and another two of red peppers signal the kitchen's occasional Provençal predilections, and the layer of goat cheese is a surprise and a delight. A main course of roasted duck with vegetables follows. It is simple and usually cooked flawlessly. The meal closes on a high note with a crème brûlée second only to Le Cirque's. There are always specials and plenty of temptations on the à la carte list. The parsley soup with belon oysters never disappoints, and the salad of roast pigeon and baby corn is sensational. If there is something to criticize on the menu, it's that many of the appetizers are salad-based and are accompanied by some version of a vinaigrette dressing. This can be a turn-off early in a meal for people serious about enjoying great wines, even when the appetizer is the excellent lamb's tongue salad with artichokes. The hot, fresh New York foie de canard with glazed shallots is a good alternative starter. For a main course, the red snapper with roasted peppers and lemon is cooked ever so well; the skin is slightly crisp and the meat as moist, tender, and flaky as you can imagine. The baby pheasant with orzo and olives is both an interesting and successful combination and a standout dish. If you like kidney, the roast kidney with Chiroubles wine (a light, fruity Beaujolais) is sensational. Nieporent certainly knows the trick for sending his customers off smiling and contented. One dessert after the next is excellent, and there are good digestifs and after-dinner drinks for anyone who desires a coup de grâce. About $48 per person with a modest wine, plus tax and tip.

Lunch Fri. noon to 3 P.M.; dinner Mon.-Sat. 6 P.M. to 11 P.M. AE.

THE NICE RESTAURANT

35 East Broadway
(Catherine & Market Sts.)
406-9776; 406-9510

Chinese

14

Nice is a vast playing field of a restaurant filled at peak hours with large Chinese families animatedly wolfing down some of the most attractive food to be found in Chinatown. The kitchen is Cantonese, but there are many dishes not found on the usual Chinese menu. A little book of photographs of various house specialties may help the uninitiated pick up where the waiter's spotty knowledge of English leaves off. Some of the food is ordinary, some quite special; because of the big turnover, everything is very fresh and prepared to order. Standards like spring rolls, moo shu pork, and the like are not offered; but there are moist and unusual shrimp paste rolls, spareribs barbecued and Peking-style (the latter cut from the chop and breaded), and a delicious salt-baked chicken. Chicken with black bean sauce and chili is a dish of great depth of flavor, the julienned meat full of fresh green pepper slivers. Roast suckling pig is presented as tender meat strips over a bed of delicious sweet-cooked soy beans, but too fat for anyone watching fat consumption. The fried dishes are exceptional, very light and dry. Service is prompt and efficient, but do make sure your waiter understands your order, since there are many items that sound alike on the vast menu. He will plunk down a number of sauces on your table and you may have to grab him for some explanation as to what is used with what. A dish of sectioned fresh oranges is provided gratis at the end of the meal.

The decor is stereotypical: a chartreuse ceiling is lit by the largest accumulation of imitation crystal this side of Las Vegas, and by two glaring gold dragons with blinking green and red eyes, respectively. Chinese children circulate playfully from table to table. Happily, the noise level is tempered by carpeting on the floor. With its moderate prices and animated atmosphere, Nice is worth several visits with the idea of some trial and error. The wait is never very long, but reservations are suggested, especially on Sunday. Because of the nature of Chinese food, assuming a party of four, and all you can eat, plus a beer, the average price per person is about $19.

Breakfast, lunch & dinner daily 8 A.M. to 10:30 P.M. AE.

THE ODEON

145 West Broadway
(Thomas St.)
233-0507

American

12/20

Call us undemocratic, but we think the Odeon was more exciting when it was impossible to get in; when the sheer exuberance of the trendsetting grand cafe made conversation impossible; when the crowd at the long bar with its tubular lights and neon-rimmed clock, was six-deep; when every table was crammed with artists, designers, writers, punk rockers, local judges, thrill-seeking Wall Streeters, and just-off-the-plane movie stars.

Now we're into the second generation and it shows. The original executive chef, talented Patrick Clark, left to open his own restaurant. The owners, with new ventures to distract them, are less visible and Gonzalo Figueroa now commands the kitchen. The crowd, though still around for late night supper, has moved on to Barocco and other spots.

Live music has been added from midnight to 2 o'clock or so on Mondays through Wednesdays, which brings back some excitement. Arrive for dinner now and you'll be greeted by a woman with a pineapple hairstyle, but you'll be forced to eavesdrop on a debate between a Vanna White look-alike sheathed in a leather minidress and her designer jean-clad beau over the merits of Finlandia vs. Dewar's vs. Budweiser. Cutting edge this is not. The food's not so interesting, either. Time was when your salad, with chickory, radicchio, red leaf lettuce and endive, would have tasted more freshly made. Yet do try the grilled salmon salad with mixed greens and vegetables. Humitas—fresh corn and coriander tomale with confit of duck—comes as a greenish slab of an appetizer with the corriander annihilating all other flavors. The three large eggplant ravioli are a better choice. Oversalting sometimes mars otherwise flavorful dishes, and chocolate mousse cake would never have been served stale. Such concerns aside, you can still get a pleasant dish here. Go for fettuccine with shrimp chardonnay sauce; the grilled brook trout with lemon, capers and avocado; the excellent calf's liver; the so-so grilled brochette of venison with chestnuts, prunes, Cremini mushrooms, Basmatic rice and a red wine sauce; or just plain and good steak with fries. A little time with the friendly waiters and waitresses should pay off with a solid recommendation of the day's best bets. The wine list is limited but good. Expect to pay $50 a person for dinner, with wine.

Lunch Mon.-Fri. noon to 3 P.M., Sun. noon to 3:30 P.M.; dinner nightly 7 P.M. to 12:30 A.M.; supper Sun.-Thurs. 1 A.M to 2:30 A.M., Fri. & Sat. till 3 A.M. All major credit cards.

OMEN

113 Thompson St. (Prince St.)
925-8923
Japanese

12/20

This SoHo outpost of a family business with two restaurants in Kyoto has been satisfying New Yorkers ever since it opened in 1981. It has a more rustic feeling than other Japanese restaurants in New York. The young Japanese staff is relaxed, and there's a non-reverential approach to Japanese eating at Omen. And the portions are prodigious.

As at its esteemed counterparts in Kyoto, people come to Omen for the specialty dish of the same name, an elaborate mating of assorted vegetables (spinach, scallions, burdock root, kelp) in a broth with dried flakes of bonito, ginger, sesame seeds, and wheat udon noodles. At $7.50 it's a meal in itself and a must for first-timers. You can't tell the delicious New York version from the Kyoto original. The menu is extensive, and everything is attractively presented and tasty, from tuna sashimi, to a specially marinated chicken, to a potpourri of pickles and relishes. Try the mussels in miso, the tuna steak with ginger, and the steamed acorn squash stuffed with tofu and vegetables. Vegetables continue to be a strength, tempura a relative weakness (though it need not be avoided). The casual dining room, up one flight of metal stairs from the street, is long and narrow with brick walls and wooden floors, and with a tatami room at the back. If you order more than the signature Omen, your bill will average about $28 per person, with beer or sake. *Dinner Tues.-Sun. 5:30 P.M. to 10:45 P.M. AE, DC.*

PROVENCE

38 MacDougal St. (Houston & Prince St.)
475-7500

French

13

This handsome Provençal bistro has been white hot since opening in SoHo on Bastille Day 1986, and deservedly so, because it delivers what it promises, including the proper and intoxicating smell of garlic. The food is authentic and sound if not sensational, the surroundings congenial, and the prices stunningly modest. The restaurant, the child of attractive owners Patricia and Michel Jean (a former captain at Le Cirque), is a pleasant evocation of sun-drenched Provence, where the young couple briefly owned a small inn near his hometown of Salon-de-Provence. Expansive French windows bordered in blue look out onto MacDougal Street; pale-yellow walls, dried flowers, handsome brass chandeliers, and a garden out back that seats 40 all contribute to an attractive country feeling. People don't complain about being crowded in the two indoor dining areas.

From an extensive handwritten menu and wine list patrons can order large bowls of a hot and powerful fish soup reminiscent of the kind that you'd drive miles to the Marseille waterfront to experience. On Fridays there's bouillaibaisse that also recalls the Riviera. There's a tempting eggplant and vegetable terrine with anchovy vinaigrette for a starter, as well as a pissaladière, the Provençal onion and anchovy tart. As a main course you can have poached seafood with aioli, a garlic mayonnaise, or perhaps poached sole with sea urchin butter. Rabbit is treated nicely here, both in terrine as an appetizer and as a paillard with mustard as a main course. As you might expect from a good bistro, you can get a decent roasted baby chicken washed in garlic, or a decent steak with French fries. Couscous is featured on Sundays. The sorbets and fruit tarts are O.K. desserts, and the crème brûlée, when the top isn't overly burnt, is testimony that friendly Michel Jean has learned his profession well. There are some good wines from Provence (Château Vignelaure is one suggestion for red, and Domaine Ott for a rosé) and plenty of viable French wines in the teens, twenties, and thirties. Lunch averages $22 and dinner, $30.

Lunch Tues.-Sun. noon to 3 P.M.; dinner Tues.-Thurs. 6 P.M. to 11 P.M., Fri. & Sat. till 11:30 P.M., Sun. 5:30 P.M. to 11 P.M. AE.

RAKEL

231 Varick St. (Clarkson St.)
929-1630
French

14

Among the new faces on the scene, Thomas Keller's certainly stands out. Still in his early thirties, Keller has worked at La Réserve and Restaurant Raphaël in New York and has *staged* his way through some of Paris's best kitchens, including Taillevent, Guy Savoy, Gérard Besson, and Toit de Passy. He emerges with distinction now, center stage, at Rakel. Despite forcing some food combinations and trying too hard with overly elaborate offerings, young, imaginative Keller should be encouraged and watched.

Rakel, where SoHo meets the Village, is co-owned by Keller and by Serge Raoul, who owns a charcuterie and a bistro a couple of blocks away on Prince Street. A vast room, separated into multi-level dining and drinking areas, its high ceilings are covered by a Delmas Howe *trompe l'oeil* mural of a cloudy sky. Martin Schreiber photos (one depicting a '38 pick-up in a Montana desert) and a commuter plane en route to Hawaii have been computerized and blown up onto giant canvases; a sprawling bar backed by mirrors and frames designed by craftsman Frank Siciliano; and, late at night, a movie screen pulled down for insomniac film festivals—the design scheme is completed by the pan-national, pan-generational mix of diners: men clad in cutting-edge suits and 60's pony-tails, groups of women who've seen it all and have come here to be fashionably resigned to life, young investment bankers, and foodies bent on scooping their confrères.

But the real drama is on the menu. Although the kitchen is at times spotty and service is with distressing regularity both negligent and awkward, exciting meals can be had. Taste your way through a complimentary cheese and onion quiche (perfect) or a complimentary sashimi roll of three fish to a delicious appetizer of three sautéed sweetbread slivers posed on a pile of deep-fried leeks (thin as angel hair pasta, and dressed in a sesame vinaigrette), and enjoy satisfying, delectable crab cakes. Then perhaps be bowled over by succulent rabbit served with savory rosemary, garlic, and

Parmesan-flavored tuiles, the layers of which are interspersed with confit of onions and rabbit liver mousse. Then sample roasted monkfish with a red pepper sauce and scattered garlic chips, or veal in a port sauce, or grilled tuna steaks resembling three perfectly shaped and cooked slices of duck breast (too heavily showered with black pepper, though), only to succumb to the marquise, two dense slabs of fudge-thick chocolate on pistachio sauce followed by complimentary lemon mini-tarts, almond tuiles, and meringue cookies. Next visit you can sample the cappuccino of wild mushroom consommé, the mosaique of foie gras and truffles, the pan-roasted duck breast and duck sausage on a bed of braised cabbage. And the thoroughly admirable wine list is full of tempting selections at reasonable prices. Dinner costs about $55 per person, with wine.

Lunch Mon.-Fri. noon to 2:15 P.M.; dinner Mon.-Thurs. 7 P.M. to 11 P.M., Fri. & Sat. till 11:30 P.M. All major credit cards.

RAOUL'S

180 Prince St. (Sullivan & Thompson Sts.)
966-3518
French

11/20

This is as close to an authentic neighborhood French bistro as you'll find in New York. When Serge Raoul opened the restaurant in 1974, people in the neighborhood started dropping in nightly for dinner. Many preferred eating at the bar. Nowadays Wall Street may have discovered the place, but the locals still drop by and expect to get a table. One of their tricks is to eat out back in the "garden" dining area (a glassed-in conservatory dining room popular for private parties), which requires walking through the kitchen (and having a chat with the gregarious chef). This place doesn't try to look good. The decor is classic New York—storefront, a long and narrow room with a bar up front, tin ceilings, a personal collection of photos and prints ("occasionally the clutter is rearranged or changed"), and booth seating. The seven booths are in great demand; there are also six banquette tables facing the bar.

The blackboard menu changes daily. Nothing is going to send you into gastronomic ecstasy, but neither are you going to go away hungry or with heartburn. Chilled sweetbread salad with homemade mayonnaise is a good appetizer, and there is a decent house foie gras d'oie. Steak au poivre is a standard, of course, and there's a duck breast with green peppers. Desserts are good, especially the gratin aux fruits and the regular fruit tarts. There are plenty of drinkable Bordeaux and Burgundy wines, and a handful of Californi-

ans as well; six 1978 Bordeaux go for $45 or less (the '78 Talbot is $39). About $45 per person for dinner.
Sun.-Thurs. 6:30 P.M. to 11:30 P.M., Fri. & Sat. till midnight. AE, MC, V.

SAMMY'S ROUMANIAN RESTAURANT

157 Chrystie St. (Delancey St.)
673-0330
Continental/Jewish

11/20

Sammy's only *looks* like it has been there forever. A run-down place in a run-down section of the Lower East Side, Sammy's still attracts crowds, who come by foot, car, bus, and limo for the quintessential melting pot old New York Jewish ambiance and food: chopped eggs and onions, chicken soup with noodles, chopped chicken livers, stuffed derma (kishka), sliced brains, Roumanian beef sausages (karnatzlach), stuffed cabbage, grilled meats covered with chopped garlic, potato pancakes, mashed potatoes with chicken fat, cholesterol, huge portions, schmaltz. Yes, there's still a container of milk, a jar of Fox's U-Bet chocolate syrup, and seltzer on every table so you can make you own egg cream. You can forget kosher here. You can forget Roumanian too. The fare—filling and honest but uneven and undistinguished—is generally Central European Jewish cooking. The smiling black chap in the kitchen turning out hot and hearty order after order doesn't appear to be replicating grandma's recipes from the old country, or displaying refined and interesting dishes such as those to be found in good restaurants in Roumania. He does all right, though, with Jewish soul food.

The storefront restaurant with low ceilings and dark walls is a collection of chairs and tables and people against a backdrop of noise and live singing and piano playing—assorted Jewish songs in English or Yiddish with an occasional Broadway tune for a surprise. And on occasion there is fiddle playing. This could be a tourist version of how things were, but for the moment it is still the real thing. If you haven't stuffed yourself, there's strudel and the like to finish you. There's a full bar too, with wines, beers, and the hard stuff. Tabs can be very low here, but for the real show count on about $35 per person.
Dinner Sun.-Fri. 4 P.M. to 11 P.M., Sat. till midnight. AE, DC, CB.

SAY ENG LOOK

The phrase "say eng look" means "four-five-six," a winning combination in mah-jongg, and this Shanghai cuisine restaurant has a long-standing reputation for dealing winners.

5 East Broadway (adjacent to Chatham Sq.)
732-0796

Chinese

12/20

Although it has slipped some in recent years, it remains one of the better choices in Chinatown, and an especially good spot to gather six or eight friends around a table. It doesn't operate at the frenetic pace of most Chinatown establishments, perhaps because the dining room is no longer jammed full. Service runs very hot and then a tad cold, but in general the level of sophistication at this restaurant is a notch above its neighbors, though still well removed from most uptown standards.

All the food served inside the red-and-black pagoda-theme dining room is sound and consistent, with sauces more elegant than the surroundings. Fried won ton and cold noodles with sesame (bland) are standard appetizers. Fillet of eel, scallops with crab, and king sea cucumber with shrimp seeds (a slimy delicacy) can usually be had, though perhaps the nod for fish goes to fried roll fish with bean curd sheet, firm and moist inside with a crisp, though not too crisp, light golden crust. About a dozen pieces of the roll fish are served in a dish bordered partly with a strip of salt, which lends an extra dimension to the fish. Tai-chi chicken remains a staple here, and the chunk chicken in spiced sauce with watercress and mushrooms is excellent. If you shy away from hot foods, this dish may still appeal to you; it's not too spicy. The sautéed watercress is sensational.

There are a good number of flops among the 122 dishes on the menu, but the roasted whole carp is another reliable choice. You can finish with an Italian gelato, much better than the industrial scoop of ice cream usually served in Chinese restaurants. The offering makes sense if you remember that Chinatown borders Little Italy: perhaps gelato can be considered Marco Polo's way of saying thanks. You must also try the Chinese wine featured on the overall respectable (and distinguished by Chinatown standards) wine list. The Beijing Long Yan is not just a curiosity but a pleasant dry white wine, balanced with modest acidity and a fresh floweriness that marries well with the restaurant's fish and chicken dishes. Lunch can be had for $10-15 dollars a person, and a more elaborate dinner with wine for $20-25. *Lunch and dinner Sun. to Thurs. 11:15 A.M. to 10:30 P.M., Fri. and Sat. to 11 P.M. AE, MC, V.*

TAI HONG LAU

70 Mott St. (Canal & Bayard Sts.)219-1431

Below street level and behind a stainless steel front (Chinatown's latest architectural fad) is Tai Hong Lau, an elegant dining room with an exciting menu. One of Tai Hong Lau's most popular dishes is minced clams and pork, sprinkled

Chinese

14

with cashew nuts and served with a mound of fresh crisp lettuce; you stuff it like a Mexican taco. Another surprising delicacy is a half pineapple shell filled with fluffy rice, pineapple chucks, tiny pieces of roast duck, crab meat, and vegetables—the contrasting flavors are tantalizing. The consommé of black mushrooms has an aroma of the earth; the cold country-style duck with not an ounce of fat is very tender. The best and most original dish to come out of Chinatown via Hong Kong is composed of tender pieces of beef sauteed with crisp, deep-fried, thinly-sliced Chinese crullers (fried dough). The faint taste of ginger combined with the crisp water chestnuts and crullers is superb. Shrimps are the restaurant's forte, and the golden fried shrimps served on a bed of shredded red cabbage with black sesame seeds are succulent. The most beautiful dish is winter melon treasure, a pale lime-colored dome made with steamed winter melon slices hiding pieces of lobster and assorted meats. Desserts, too, are Hong Kong sophisticated: a sweet peanut soup, and a water chestnut jello wrapped in crisp fried rice flour dough. About $20 per person.

Lunch & dinner daily 11 A.M. to 11 P.M. No credit cards.

Tapis Rouge

157 Duane St. (West Broadway & Hudson St.)
732-5555

French

13

The whole is greater than the sum of its parts. Add up all the little extras offered by this very engaging bistro in the heart of Tribeca and you feel a contentment somehow not undermined by the conventionality of some of the entrées, the decibel level of the dining room, and the rather high tariff for French home cooking. Mere quibbles. The little things that mean a lot start right at the door. You're greeted by a very gracious young lady whose politeness and sincerity are reprised by everyone else on the staff. She takes your coats and asks if you'd mind waiting for a "better table than the one that's available." Of course not. Especially when you spy a basket of homemade potato chips on the bar. Scrumptious. Inside, the dining room, which seats about 70, gleams like a jewel box of mirrors and black lacquer—a rather dressy setting for downtowners eating cassoulet but then there are plenty of wealthy suburbanites here too.

For menu contemplation comes a plate of amuse-gueules —a nice touch for a spiffy bistro. The delicious little squares of bacony quiche and puff pastry rounds topped with tomato provençale strike the right note for the hearty bourgeois cooking served here. Start with a well-seasoned terrine of venison, or artichoke hearts stuffed with smoked salmon mousse. Baby pheasant is good but the ratatouille served

43

with it is much more flavorful. So's the cassoulet, though it comes in such a small casserole there's hardly enough winey beans to accompany the ham, pork, and sausages. (Cassoulet is Saturday's special; the restaurant offers a different staple of the bourgeois repertoire each night of the week.) Whatever you do, order a "side" of French fries. They're excellent. Strawberry cheese cake or a block of hazelnut ice cream, decorated with fresh fruit, are refreshing desserts, followed by complimentary chocolate truffles and miniature langues de chats. Things are working well here, and if you should decide our rating could be a little higher, we wouldn't disagree. Dinner costs about $50 per person with wine, plus tax and tip.

Lunch Mon.-Fri. noon to 3 P.M.; dinner Mon.- Sat. 6 P.M. to 11:30 P.M. AE,V,MC

TENBROOKS

62 Reade St. (Broadway & Chambers Sts.)
349-5900

American

12/20

You don't have to worry about going far wrong at Tenbrooks so long as Mama is there, and she usually is. Mama Klein is a trim, elegant, no-nonsense, energetic lady of "a certain age." She's called "Mama" by the highly professional staff and by the City Hall and financial community regulars alike, but she's really Mama to Peter Klein, the co-owner, sometime chef, and sometime maître d'. Mama works the 50-seat dining room cum art gallery (gray rug, Formica tables, and a couple of rows of banquettes) and works the room like a pro, taking an order here, chatting there, directing staff somewhere else. Peter or sous-chef Richard Scofield do a good job in the kitchen, but Mama always seems to be back there eagle-eyeing and touching up the orders as they emerge. Moreover, she's in there in the morning preparing desserts.

The daily soup, pasta, and market fish are always good, and for a basic and inexpensive lunch there are good omelettes and hamburgers. The kitchen, however, is also up to more ambitious things. Try the jalapeño corn pancakes with sour cream chive sauce as an appetizer, or the grilled fennel sausage with mustard fruits. The menu and the wine list are updated seasonally, but tender, spicy crab cakes served with wild rice and, usually, broccoli, are always to be found as a main course. Lamb Louisiana with chili, garlic, and fennel is also a good bet, as is the grilled red tuna with ginger, soy and pepper glaze. If you have room for dessert, Mama recommends the triple-layer cheesecake or her chocolate whiskey torte. The 30-offering wine list is split between Californian and French wines, with a bottle or two of Australian or Italian thrown in; all fall in the $12 to $38 range and reflect

careful quality-price selectivity. Reservations at lunch are helpful. Figure about $25 per person, though it is possible at lunch to cut a few dollars off that.
Lunch & dinner Mon.-Fri. 11:45 A.M. to 11 P.M. AE, MC, V.

TOMMY TANG'S

323 Greenwich St. (Duane St.)
334-9190
Thai

12/20

From the looks of things, Tommy Tang's Hollywood fans have followed him to New York. The gold-chain, open-shirt, slouchy-linen-jacket set sips vintage Champagne and nibbles saté chicken with peanut sauce here. Investment bankers are here in full force, too. The artists and neighborhood folk (the two occasionally coincide, since the neighborhood is Tribeca) who used to hang out here when the place was a casual but ambitious restaurant called Exile, seem, well, exiled now that the understated European-cafe decor has been snazzed up with bed sheets painted in abstract turquoise and pink patterns. This is punk, trendy Thai. Safe Thai, too. And much, though by no means all, of it is very good.

Spicy, curry flavored fried won tons are delicious, as is Thai toast, deep-fried circles of bread topped with minced pork and shrimp. If a dish sounds sweet, watch out: striking the sweet-savory balance seems a problem here. Mee krob, the crispy noodles studded with shrimp, pork, sprouts, scallions, and cilantro is oversweet, as is Thai pasta, a cold noodle dish with garlic, black bean sauce, three peppers, cilantro, and shreds of chicken breast. It sounds delicious but tastes as musty and stale as if it had been in the refrigerator for two weeks. The original Tommy duck is a better main course option. Its honey-plumb sauce is sweet, too, but the duck, itself—steamed, baked, and deep-fried—is succulent and delectable. The desserts come from various pastry shops. If you haven't overdosed on sweetness, a good bet is banana ice cream, but hold the chocolate sauce. Expect to pay about $30 a person for dinner with drinks.
Lunch Mon.-Fri. 11:30 A.M. to 3 P.M.; dinner Mon.-Thurs. 6 P.M. to 11:30 P.M., Fri. & Sat. 6 P.M. to midnight. All major credit cards.

20 MOTT STREET RESTAURANT

Welcome to the dim sum circus. At lunchtime or earlier (8 A.M. to 3 P.M.) Chinese waitresses circle the floors of this bright, three-tiered restaurant with trolleys packed with inviting dishes. Some offerings are familiar, such as spring rolls (Chinese mushrooms, pork, and tofu in thick golden

20 Mott St. (Bowery &
Chatham Sq.)
964-0380

Chinese

11/20

deep-fried rolls), or wonton soup (here virtually a dish of ravioli in brodo with many soft stuffed wontons filling the soup bowl). Be on the lookout for golden fried crab claws, but consider carefully before ordering the steamed beef; in spite of the oiliness inside, the three meatballs often stick together and to the dish. The women wielding the carts barely speak English, so when an unfamiliar dish goes by ordering can become low-stake gambling. The waiters aren't much help either. It takes technique to break up the conversation they're usually holding among themselves; you may get a dour single word response, if any, to questions. In short, the service here on most days leaves a lot to be desired.

The food—be it dim sum or the more elaborate fare off the regular menu—doesn't, and it all arrives promptly, which are two of the reasons that people line up outside. The menu isn't much use. Every Chinese dish imaginable seems to be on it, either poorly described or not at all, and what comes out of the kitchen is often a surprise—a pleasant surprise. The Chinese regulars seem to know how to order, so if you point to their dishes you may do very well. You will certainly do well if you order duck. Recommended starters include melon soup and deep-fried assorted seafood roll. The lightly battered fried oysters are also distinguished; they reflect the kitchen's mastery of the ancient salt-cooking technique, culminates in either hot-oven baking or deep-frying. Try the shrimp in a shell for another good example. Seafood in a basket makes a good main dish, as does black fish with black pepper sauce. There's beer to get you through the meal, as well as a plum wine that is better than a dessert. Everything is inexpensive; $12 a person will set you in play and bring you to the cashier nicely; $15 or $20 will keep you at it indefinitely.
Lunch & dinner Sun.-Thurs. 8 A.M. to 1 A.M.; Fri. & Sat. to 2 A.M. All major credit cards.

Windows on the World Restaurant

One World Trade Center,
107th Fl.
938-1111

Continental

13

This place is tops literally if not gastronomically. A quarter of a mile above lower Manhattan, the view it offers takes the triteness out of the word spectacular. Heady and sensational vistas of the Manhattan skyline and waters, make you a winner here before you pick up a menu, and when you do you'll be able to choose surprisingly well. For a restaurant with 350 seats, the level of cooking is impressive. The room is, too. The huge space has been designed to afford intimacy and serenity. The populous professional staff is skilled at seeing that nothing intrudes upon your dining experience.

In addition to a full à la carte menu, six four-course dinners (prix-fixe by your choice of the entrée) are good values. You may dine, for example, on oysters on the half shell, followed by a leg of white veal with mushroom sauce and spinach polenta, followed by a seasonal salad, and finish off with cheesecake and coffee ($33.95). Or a dinner of chilled tomato bisque with diced avocado and basil, casserole of sea scallops and shrimp in Riesling sauce, plus a salad, and end with carrot cake with whipped cream and tea will run you $32.95. From the main menu, which is contemporary without being trendy, and which features fresh produce and timely preparation, the asparagus with venison carpaccio or the salmon and snapper (lightly grilled and served with orange and chive sauce) are two of the more appealing appetizers. Rack of lamb, sautéed paillard of chicken with grilled sea scallops, and medallion of veal tenderloin with morel sauce served with wild rice pancakes, are sound main courses. Try the warm bread pudding with apples topped with caramel sauce, or the cinnamon ice cream on a pear poached in red wine with ginger sauce for dessert.

As well as being a top tourist destination, Windows on the World is a lure for wine aficionados (and the site of a celebrated wine school). The wine offerings here are justly famous for both their breadth—though the strength of the list is California, then French wines—and reasonable prices. There are actually two lists. So not to confuse or overwhelm anyone, a regular wine list of about one hundred wines featuring dozens of wines in the $18-25 range, is presented. More intrepid souls may request the typewritten list of about 800 offerings. If you don't overindulge in wine, expect to spend $50 per person.
Dinner Mon.-Sat. 5 P.M. to 10 P.M.; brunch Sat. noon to 3 P.M., Sun. noon to 7 P.M. All major credit cards.

WONG KEE

113 Mott St. (Canal & Hester Sts.)
966-1160
Chinese

12/20

It's unlikely that you'll be disappointed at Wong Kee, although it is also likely that the food will not send you to heaven. What is certain, though, is that you will get your money's worth at this popular, sleek Cantonese style restaurant a half-block north of Canal Street—yes, the Little Italy side. Beyond a handsome stainless steel façade lies a bright, colorful dining room sitting about 100. At lunch you can be in and out comfortably in 15 minutes. Cannisters of chopsticks and forks grace the green formica tables, and, through a window-case of hanging Peking ducks, you can also see the kitchen.

Recommendations for appetizers are roast pork, roast duck, or barbecued spare ribs—all cold cut. For a main course try the chicken in sizzling platter, or the Wong Kee spiced chicken or pork. The chicken is cubed, breaded, and mixed with black beans, fresh garlic, hot pepper, and a sweet and pungent sauce. Order the Mong kee steak, the specialty of the house, and choice strips of steak come sizzling out of the kitchen, sautéed Cantonese-style. The tender, well cooked meat is served with broccoli and a thick sauce that displays overtones of both hot spice and sweetness. No beer or wine is served, though you can bring your own. No desserts either, which can be taken as an admirable sign of purity and integrity. The service is friendly, helpful, and hopping in this busy restaurant, one that is a Sunday afternoon favorite with locals and other New Yorkers alike. Meals average $10 per person, and at $15 you can overdose. *Lunch & dinner daily 11 A.M. to 10 P.M. No credit cards.*

Greenwich Village

AU TROQUET

328 West 12th St. (Hudson & Washington Sts.)
924-3413

French

12/20

This is the kind of out-of-the-way Village restaurant people enjoy discovering. It's far west on a dull corner where you wouldn't expect to find a restaurant, but look into the lace-curtained windows and you'll see a lovely "romantic" room with 14 tables. Antiques and flowers in addition to the oil paintings and watercolors by owner François Le Morzellec enhance the blue and yellow decor. French charm oozes everywhere (except perhaps when traditional French pop music is replaced by American country).

The food has its charms, too, but strengths is a better word, because the kitchen here is good and hearty, not elegant and flashy; it's one step up from bistro fare. The handwritten menu changes periodically and is predictably traditional. The fresh salmon marinated with basil is a very good appetizer, cool and flavorful. Snails with garlic butter and anise-flavored Ricard works well. There's usually an O.K. endive salad with Roquefort and a true soup that's been to school in France and working all day in the kitchen. Among the ten or so main courses nothing is irresistible, but

the lotte with endives and a curry sauce entertains with flavors. The rabbit dish that is usually offered (roasted with pears) is prepared well, but rabbit in New York just doesn't taste like rabbit does in Europe. Pigeon doesn't either, and once when it was called squab in a special it turned out to be a very nicely roasted Cornish hen. Spinach, carrots, and potatoes dauphinoise (nicely crusted on top with slices, cream, and nutmeg beneath) are usually the side vegetables and are passable. Grilled meats, fowl, or fish are generally safe bets. For dessert go with the daily tart; some of the other offerings such as the praline cake or the profiteroles can taste like they've been in the refrigerator too long. The mousse of wild strawberries is worth trying. For wines, your choice runs French with a few Californian on hand for good measure, but you'll be on shaky ground ordering. Vintages are cited but no producers, and there are no half bottles. Count on $40 per person sharing a bottle of wine.
Dinner Mon.-Sat. 6 P.M. to 11 P.M. AE, V.

BATONS

62 West 11th St. (Fifth & Sixth Aves.)
473-9510

Eclectic

13

Welcome to Santa Monica-by-Balducci. Here it is, the California food experience in New York's Greenwich Village. What that means is an open kitchen with wood-burning grill, a clay wood-burning oven (for designer pizza, of course), and an eclectic menu with French, Italian, and Oriental specialties on top of all the grilling and the farmer's basket of healthy vegetables. You can bistro lunch or graze up front in the big, gray bar—Cafe Batons—or can go all-out in the big gray dining room in the back with its huge atrium windows.

The most expensive item on the menu ($40) is the white Batons shirt with the restaurant's logo on the back. The young men and women serving you model it. They also casually deliver some appealing dishes. The bread is excellent, and the seven-inch pizzas, appetizers or meals by themselves, are good. Most of the concoctions work, such as a topping of lamb sausage with shiitake mushrooms, eggplant, tomato, mozzarella, and fontina. The crisp potato pancakes served with a dollop of crème fraîche and three caviars is a winning appetizer, as amusing as it is tasty. Sashimi or charred raw beef are simple, safe openers. There are always pastas, though not in the class of the grilled fish or meats. The duck ravioli with oyster mushrooms in a cream sauce with chives and sweet corn tastes a little like dark meat turkey in a sauce of mostly butter, cream, and chive. Stir-fried squab with Chinese vegetables and a yellow pepper sauce and wok-charred spicy blue-fin tuna with mango, tomato, and green onion sauce are choice representatives of this spot's successful attempts at a fusion cuisine. Or try the grilled snapper, chicken, or charred swordfish on bamboo skewers. The wine list is so-so, with reasonable prices for its Californian, French, and few Italian wines, but sometimes lacks such basic information as the producer's name for a Brunello or a date for a vintage Champagne. Desserts include fruit, an assortment of crèmes brûlées, and occasionally a fine apple tart with caramel, or even a goat cheese (what else?) cheesecake. Prices can vary depending upon how you compose your meal, but figure on $30-40 per person.

Lunch Mon.-Fri. noon to 2:30 P.M.; dinner Sun.-Thurs. 6 P.M. to 11 P.M., Fri. & Sat. till midnight; brunch Sun. noon to 3 P.M. except in July and Aug. AE, MC, V.

THE BLACK SHEEP

342 West 11th St.
(Washington St.)
242-1010
French

12/20

Once this was hot, then it was not. But it kept on true to itself, and we can recommend the Black Sheep as a good, steady restaurant for dinner, or a quaint spot for Sunday brunch. A black sheep sits at a table near the bar with its glass bubbling away with Champagne. The waiters are friendly and concerned and talk about the theater. The decor and food are both an attempt at French provincial.

The prix fixe menu (priced according to the entrée) begins as it has from day one, with a rustic table portion of crudités. Soup, pâté, or the daily appetizer special follow. A hot soup of two types of squash is simple and pure. Vegetables (eggplant, zucchini) on a hot pastry dough crust surrounded by a tomato coulis taste like a good French apple tart in vegetable drag. Main courses range from pasta, to grilled striped bass, to leg of lamb Provençal, to chicken stuffed under the skin with tarragon. The last is superb: moist, luscious, and well seasoned. The duck with apricots and prunes comes out a bit overcooked.

If you are there for brunch, go for the curried chicken salad with dill, raisins, and toasted almonds served in a croissant, or superb Amaretto whole-wheat French toast (made from Zito's bread) served with fresh berries. Desserts are very good, headed by a banana hazelnut cake served with a crusty top, true banana flavor, and an excellent, not-too-sweet whipped cream on the side. The double chocolate cake—virtually a deep, dark, tasty fudge—also comes with whipped cream. The wine list merits praise. It's extensive, with well-chosen French and American wines and a few from elsewhere, all with good prices ($10-90, plus the 1981 Opus I at $120). At $50, the 1970 Gruaud LaRose is a bargain. Five wines are offered by the glass. Dinner will run about $35-40 a person sharing a modest wine. A ten percent discount is given to customers paying cash.

Dinner Mon.-Thurs. 6 P.M. to 11 P.M., Fri. & Sat. till midnight, Sun. 6 P.M. to 10:30 P.M.; brunch Sun. noon to 4 P.M. All major credit cards.

CAFÉ DE BRUXELLES

118 Greenwich Ave. (13th St.)
206-1830
Belgian

13

This simple yet sophisticated cafe, with starched lace curtains and walls lacquered essence-of-bistro beige, did not start up under the best of circumstances. But with a new management it has righted itself to become a pleasant place to have a convivial dinner. Located on an odd triangle where Greenwich Avenue meets 13th Street, the restaurant is approximately the same shape, its small, cozy, but crowded bar joined by a long narrow space to a proper-sized room. Ask for a table by the window.

Mussels are a Belgian passion; the Café de Bruxelles's version of moules marinières—plump, steamed beauties in a delectable, garlicky white wine broth—is not only satisfying but would easily feed two. The bouillabaisse, chock-full of perfectly cooked shrimp, mussels, lobster, and shellfish, is one of the town's best renderings, rich and winey with accents of Pernod and garlic. Other Belgian specialties include waterzooi, a lemony, leek-fragrant stew, excellent in both the chicken and the fish version; and carbonnade flamande, tender chunks of beef flavored with onions and a smoky note of beer. A good first course or luncheon dish is the salade liègeoise of string beans, red onions, potatoes, and bacon, or a simple salad of endive and watercress with nubbins of smoked ham. If you're not planning to have steak/pommes frites for a main course, you might consider having those crisp golden fries on the side (the Belgians claim authorship and go crazy when you call the fries French). They are placed on your table in a cone of paper and meant to be dipped, in the Belgian manner, in mayonnaise.

On the dessert menu is a fabulous Belgian waffle with a scoop of vanilla ice cream and bittersweet hot Belgian chocolate sauce. Only a trencherman could manage it after the hearty cooking and generous portions of this restaurant. But don't despair; come for brunch (except in the summer months) when, for $6.75, you can devote yourself totally to this minor Belgian masterpiece. The house white wine, the slightly pétillant Vouvray, goes very well with this food; or

try Duvel, the malty Belgian beer. Dinner averages $29 per person.
Dinner Mon.-Thurs. 6 P.M. to 11 P.M., Fri. & Sat. 6 P.M. to midnight; brunch Sept. to May Sat. & Sun. noon to 3:30 P.M. AE, MC, V.

CAFÉ LOUP

18 East 13th St. (Fifth Ave. & University Pl.)
255-4746
French

11/20

A revitalized Union Square area may mean a new life for this small Bohemian bistro in the lower level of a Greenwich Village brownstone. Its current life, however, is just fine, thank you. Publishing types from Farrar, Straus, *Forbes*, the *Voice*, and *Women's Wear Daily* crowd in at lunch—and sometimes after work—for good, simple, and generally French food. The room is old Village: bar, stuccoed walls covered with vintage photographs by Brassaï, Brandt, Adams, Kertesz, et. al. In the evening it is transformed into a less businesslike, more intimate setting.

A dining area in the rear patio-garden has been added. The menu is relatively short and classic (mussels rémoulade, escargot, saucisson, steak au poivre, calf's brains, tournedos, liver, lamb chops with Provence herbs, and one or two fish dishes). The desserts have an American look and include key lime pie and Mississippi mud cake. The service is friendly and the wine list attractive. There are about 60 wines, half French, marked up reasonably by uptown standards. Figure $20 per person for lunch with a drink and $38 at dinner with a bottle of wine.
Lunch Mon.-Fri. noon to 3 P.M.; dinner Wed.-Sat. 6 P.M. to 11:30 P.M., Sun.-Tues. 6 P.M. to 10:30 P.M.; brunch Sun. noon to 3:30 P.M. All major credit cards.

CENT' ANNI

50 Carmine St. (Bleecker & Bedford Sts.)
989-9494
Italian

13 🍳

Cent' Anni means "one hundred years," as in "You should live to be a hundred," or "You should eat and live well for the next century." Good feelings abound in this small, bustling storefront restaurant, run by co-owner Franco Fassuoli (born in Tuscany). The food here can also be very good—lusty and a mix of the old and the new. The 15 tables in this minimalist room usually hold serious and fashionable folks in their 30's to 60's, and the place is often noisy and amazingly busy. There are plenty of staff members who speak Italian and who provide good-natured and attentive if not exactly refined service.

Your waiter will invariably propose "a nice appetizer," which inevitably turns out to be an assortment of offerings that are indeed nice, such as the combo of warmed radicchio with melted taleggio cheese, bocconcini (little mouthfuls of stewed veal), fagioli (white beans), and uccelletti (small birds). The cold seafood salad is a highly recommended opener. Soups are very good: zuppa ortolana, or "greengrocer's soup," is a striking baked soup of beans, cabbage, leeks, toast, cheese, and pancetta. The pastas are excellent and you can order half portions as appetizers or ask for a combination plate with several. Among the outstanding choices are cappellini con aragosta (angel hair pasta with a light tomato sauce with lobster meat and clams), and a pappardelle al coniglio (a broad noodle with a rabbit and game sauce). The restaurant is known for its veal chop salvia, a monstrous double cut chop of top quality veal which is broiled then sautéed in wine and fresh sage. Other recommended entrées are the roast loin of pork Florentine style (when it's not overcooked), the lobster combo Ligurian style, and a pleasing mixed grill (rabbit, lamb, sausage, and quail).

The desserts are a slight letdown. Fruit or cheese serve well. The cold zabaglione with berries is homemade, the rest are brought in and tend to run sweet, though chocolate lovers won't mind the chocolate cake. The wines, mostly Italian, are sound, and their prices modest if sometimes odd. There are good values, such as Capezzana Carmignano at $20. Wine service is lacking, and there's one all-purpose glass, even if you order a top French Champagne. Lunch averages $25 per person, and dinner $40.
Lunch Mon.-Fri. noon to 2:30 P.M.; dinner Mon.-Fri. 5:30 P.M. to 11:30 P.M., Sat. till 11:30, Sun. 5 P.M. to 11 P.M.; closed last ten days in July. AE.

CHAPITEAU

105 West 13th St. (Sixth Ave.)
929-8833
French

10/20

This place is hot. The heat, however, doesn't emanate from the kitchen, which turns out plain bistro fare. Owner Eric Demarchelier (also of Jean Lafitte and Demarchelier) has managed to attract the downtown fashion crowd, celebrities, and an English-as-a-second-language crew to his large restaurant. The room is casual, homey yet funky. Seven different designers brought forth seven different areas of architectural ruckus—from free-form plaster-of-Paris sculptures to intentionally cracked columns and crooked accoutrements. The with-it crowd dines late, and after 10:30, there's live entertainment—tango music, or French accordion, or jazz, or rock, or a French chanteuse. You don't change the channel, just the day.

Food is not the essence of Chapiteau. What's offered on its rows of tables with white linen and votive candles is eatable, but surely surpassed at several nearby bistros. Eggplant terrine, good; grilled tuna, fine if undistinguished; pasta, poor; pot-au-feu, hearty. The tell-tale sign is that the kitchen only barely manages to pull off the classic bistro offering of grilled chicken with French fries. You won't send anything back, but you'll forget the food as soon as the music starts. Even the desserts are on par with the other courses, and the mostly French wine list could use names of producers and vintage dates. Go with friends, have a good time, and expect to pay $30 per person.

Dinner nightly 6 P.M. to 1 A.M. All major credit cards.

CHEZ JACQUELINE

72 MacDougal St. (Bleecker & Houston Sts.)
505-0727

French

13

If you lived in a modest *arrondissement* of Paris, a restaurant not unlike Chez Jacqueline would no doubt be your *bistro du coin*, the place you'd fall into at night when you didn't want to cook, confident you'd get the same French home cooking you'd known all your life. Customers wander into this (what else?) lace-curtained bistro wearing everything from business suits to jeans, and, occasionally, bring the baby. Titou, co-owner and maître d', dressed casually without a tie and with sleeves rolled up, greets everyone like a friend, which is what most of the customers are. The tables are small, the decor pleasantly nonexistent. Only the lighting needs improving.

Jacqueline, who does most of the cooking, and her brother Titou, (who also cooks), are Niçois, which explains the touches of the cuisine of the sun. With your glass of wine you'll be offered pieces of feather-light, addictive pissaladière (a kind of pizza with onions, olives, and anchovies). The brandade de morue, an airy whip of salt cod, garlic, olive oil, and potato purée is probably the best in town. Pâté de campagne, a menu cliché elsewhere, is reinvented here with beautifully balanced flavors. That hard-to-find French Sunday dinner standby, blanquette de veau à l'ancienne, is absolute perfection, meltingly tender, the sauce not too gussied up with cream and egg yolk. Served with a timbale of rice, it's a real buy at $13.50. Gigot d'agneau happily paired with flageolets and garnished with a small mound of gratin dauphinoise and a grilled tomato niçoise was well-seasoned and rare as requested, but the flavor of the meat was compromised by having been held at a low warming temperature too long. The small, well-chosen menu includes veal kidneys in a creamy Dijon mustard sauce with Cognac; basquaise chicken prepared with tomatoes, green peppers, and onions; and the winey beef stew daube niçoise. For liquid accompaniment you needn't go beyond the house red or white wine, both well-chosen, inexpensive, and thoroughly enjoyable. If you go on a night when Jacqueline has made her buttery apple tart, don't miss it. Dinner about $30 per person.

Dinner Sun.-Thurs. 6 P.M to 11 P.M., Fri. & Sat. 6 P.M. to 11:30 P.M. AE.

THE COACH HOUSE

110 Waverly Pl. (off Washington Sq. West)
777-0303
American

13 🎩

"Folkloric" is what the French yuppies are thinking as they crane their necks to look at the brick walls, the red leather banquettes, the oil paintings of hunting scenes and still lifes of food. This is America. This restaurant is housed in a building constructed 150 years ago as a coach house for the Wanamaker family, and the fashionable French who reserve here have come to taste the vintage setting as well as the hefty portions of prime rib, the thick black bean soup, and the corn sticks, all of which have served owner Leon Lianides well over the past 40 years and which have (not without criticism) become the stuff of legend. But it is not only the curious French who eat here. The Coach House has always been a place to bring parents, grandparents, aunts and uncles—a place to impress recruiters from white shoe law firms. It also attracts a young business crowd, Greek expatriates, and food writers on their day off.

They come for the Lianides production at its best—which means sitting downstairs (and not in the converted hayloft) for cosseting Old World service, for the good crab cakes, and for "Continental" selections such as salmon served with the court bouillon in which it has been perfectly poached, Grand Marnier Bavarian cream, chocolate mousse cake, dacquoise, and a wine list that is extensive, reasonably priced, and thoughtfully put together. Of course there are downsides: some find Lianides chilly; at peak hours service can be hurried; and the chicken pot pie tastes like the chicken à la king made from a can of soup, leftovers, and store-bought pastry cups. But if you're wondering where to celebrate your grandmother's birthday, your search is over. Expect to pay $55 per person for dinner with wine.

Dinner Tues.-Sun. 5:30 P.M. to 10:30 P.M. All major credit cards.

CUISINE DE SAIGON

In a town not blessed with good Vietnamese restaurants, Cuisine de Saigon weighs in as a respectable middleweight. Some of the offerings are merely journeyman, but there are

154 West 13th St. (Sixth & Seventh Aves.)
255-6003

Vietnamese

11/20

some jabs at excellence. Leo Tran is usually out front to greet you as you enter the pleasant and separate bar of this long and narrow ground floor restaurant in a Village brownstone. He leads you through a passageway surrounded by the kitchen, where Marie Tran is responsible for the authentic Vietnamese cooking, and into the dining room. Peach walls, gray wall-to-wall carpeting, ceiling fans, original paintings by a Vietnamese artist—the room is pleasant enough and fills up with locals and groups out for a modestly priced, modestly exciting meal.

Spring rolls are touted as a house specialty, but this Vietnamese staple turns out to be unmemorable. The kindred shrimp roll on occasion turns out to be dominated by bean sprouts rather than shrimp, and like most of the appetizers may be greasier than we'd like. Steamed dumplings stuffed with pork and shrimp are all right, but soups are probably a better choice for a starter. The real temptation, however, is to get some of the good entrées on the table in a hurry and dig in Oriental-style. Shrimp wrap sugar cane (chao tom) is broiled shrimp fixed to a sugar cane stalk and served with rice paper, lettuce, and vegetables. Out of this you fashion a hand roll that is seasoned with accompanying sweet hoisin sauce. All of the broiled dishes come out fine, as does the steamed fish. Pasta via Saigon (bahn cuon) is an intriguing and excellent noodle dish. Light ravioli-like shells are stuffed with minced pork and mushrooms and served with a light, flavorful sauce that is the best of the three or four sauces served. Both the chicken and the shrimp crepe are dependable if undistinguished; the crepes themselves are prepared well. For meat eaters, lemon grass beef—strips of beef sautéed with lemon grass (a delicious, thin, scallion-like herb) served with a peanut curry sauce—is recommended. We are always tempted to skip dessert in Vietnamese restaurants, but decided to try the unusual steamed banana cake, which turns out to be a gooey, pudding-like thick medallion topped with coconut milk and peanuts. One order and one sweet bite should satisfy everyone's curiosity at a table for four. There are a handful of beers to choose from, and a balanced list of 25 generally inexpensive but sound wines. Dinner runs about $23 per person with wine.
Dinner nightly 5 P.M. to 11 P.M. All major credit cards.

DA SILVANO

For years Da Silvano was at the forefront of imaginative Italian cuisine in New York, but success has taken its toll. Three or four years ago, when the restaurant was remodeled,

*260 Sixth Ave. (Bleecker &
Houston Sts.)*
982-2343
Italian

11/20

the food took a plunge while the prices rose so sharply that its steady flock of food mavens drifted away. Suprisingly, however, the place remains packed, and many diners do come away satisfied with their lunch or dinner. The size of the tables at this rustic Tuscan eatery with an outdoor cafe may be conducive to intimate conversation, but you're always wondering whether it will be the wine bottle or the bread basket that will end up on the floor. The menu takes up only one page, but every night there are at least 18 specials. The antipasto giardiniera del giorno is well prepared, especially the braised tiny Italian artichokes cooked in olive oil with lots of garlic. The carpaccio is ordinary, but the panzella—a cold bread salad with roasted peppers, tomatoes, cucumbers, and onions—with its well-seasoned vinaigrette is delightful, as is the insalata di mare, a salad of calamari and mussels in the same vinaigrette. You'll want lots of bread to soak up the sauce.

The homemade pasta is good, though the sauces are disappointing. The spaghettini puttanesca lacks pungency and differs little from one of the specials, tagliatella checa, prepared sparingly with whole tomatoes and mozzarella. Furthermore, the waiters grate the Parmesan onto your pasta with a grudging smirk (well, at least it's real Parmesan). Among the main courses, the calf's liver with sage is somewhat drowned in a heavy wine sauce, but its accompanying polenta is good. The grigliata mista consists of a small lamb chop, a slice of kidney, and two skewers of liver and veal, dry and certainly not worth the $18.50. In fact, most dishes are overpriced and the service is woefully uneven, especially on weekends when you might find your companion finishing up while you're still waiting to be served. The short wine list features high-priced, good, but uninspiring Italian bottles. Desserts are the ubiquitous cream cakes, sorbets, and a plate of fresh fruit served with a scoop of ice cream. Fifty dollars per person without wine or drinks. *Lunch daily noon to 3 P.M., dinner Mon.-Thurs. 6 P.M. to 11:30 P.M., Fri. & Sat. till midnight, Sun. 5 P.M. to 11 P.M. AE.*

EL FARO

*823 Greenwich St. (Horatio
St.)*
929-8210

This culinary institution gets points for having been around so long. Its dark murals of flamenco dancers, its raffish decor, and the aroma of garlic give this out-of-the-way spot flavor. There's a big downside—the place is jammed with tourists, the wait for tables is interminable (no reservations accepted), the emphasis on turnover is frequently reinforced by the

Spanish

10/20

waiters, and the food is mediocre. Still, people flock to it and enjoy themselves. Whether or not the fare can be called authentically Spanish is open to question. It is, however, authentically Greenwich Village Spanish, from wilted salad, to chorizos, to mariscada (mixed sea food) in green sauces (parsley, onions, garlic, and olive oil), to paella, to chicken Villarroy (béchamel sauce separates the chicken breast from the baked breading). All those dishes tasted better in the late 60's when Craig Claiborne could tout the place for its "excellent Spanish kitchen." Today, the best food is a side dish: the fried potatoes. Most diners drink sangría by the pitcher ($12), and there is a short list of Spanish wines. Dinner costs about $25 a person, with wine.
Sun.-Thurs. 11 A.M. to midnight, Fri. & Sat. till 1 A.M. All major credit cards.

ENNIO AND MICHAEL RESTAURANT

504 LaGuardia Pl.
(Bleecker & Houston Sts.)
677-8577

Italian

12/20

This place is a long-standing find: a sleek and elegant Village restaurant serving up a reasonably refined Italian-American cuisine. People outside the Village, along with the locals, have discovered that they can enjoy themselves here and entertain impressively. Blond wood, grey tones, floral watercolors, white linen table-clothes: The room makes a stunning first impression. The main dining area lies beyond a wood bar facing a banquette and a handful of tables, and is terraced up two steps. Ennio Sammarone and/or Michael Savarese work the room where more people than just the waiters speak Italian.

If you pull Ennio or Michael over, either can probably crank the kitchen up a point or two for you, but we haven't tried. The fried zucchini (thin strips) are light and addictive (thankfully, the plate is well stacked). Stuffed artichoke or spiedini alla romana also get the nod as appetizers. The platter of roasted fresh peppers (in season) served with anchovies is touted, but the red peppers out of a jar aren't anything special. Hearty rigatoni alla matriciana is one of the better bets for pasta. The spaghetti puttanesca is tame and the pasta primavera is a joke (a few peas and some zucchini). For a main course, the scaloppine alla Sorrentia (veal sautéed with wine and topped with eggplant and mozzarella) is one of the most popular dishes. It's palatable, but the veal tends to be very thinly sliced and bland. Chicken all'arriatiata (golden brown pieces of chicken in a spicy garlic and vinegar sauce without a hint of oiliness) is another favorite and is more successful. The wine list could use some work, though most of Italy is represented and good special bottles can be found (by Gaja, Mastrobernardino, Antinori). There are plenty of pizzeria wines, but, curiously, no attractive Chiantis. Order the 1983 Montepulciano d'Abruzzo by Casal Thaulero, at $16 the best red wine value offered. Desserts are afterthoughts, except perhaps for Michael's special one—slivers of dark chocolate covered with hazelnut ice cream, topped with marinated strawberries, and a cold zabaglione, all served in a wine glass. Dinner about $36 a person, plus tax and tip.

Tues.-Fri. noon to 11 P.M., Sat. 5 P.M. to 11:30 P.M., Sun. 1 P.M. to 10 P.M. AE.

GARVINS

19 Waverly Pl. (Green & Mercer Sts.)
473-5261

American

10/20

Richard Garvin tries hard and is always up to something. We admire his dynamism, and we can recommend his restaurant and related enterprises, but not for the food (which continues to be risky but all right). Garvin has put together a handsome, romantic dining room with a 1900's look: there are tapestries, antiques, objets d'art, a baby grand piano, high ceilings, and a 28-foot bar (where you can order most dishes). Lately he has added an American touch to what was a Continental menu, so now you can get a mesquite-grilled breast of chicken with Cajun rice and tomato rémoulade. But the rule remains: keep it simple when ordering.

The sun-dried tomato salad with warm smoked mozzarella makes a good appetizer, and the roast duckling Valencia with almond rice, Grand Marnier, honey, and orange zest an acceptable follow-up. And there is always a large display of desserts to at least satisfy your eyes. Prices are reasonable here, especially for the 75 or so French and Californian wines. Adjoining the restaurant is Cafe Lido, Garvins' separate jazz room. You can make it an evening here. Lunch averages about $15, and dinner $32 a person.

Lunch & dinner daily 11:30 A.M. to 2 A.M. All major credit cards.

GOTHAM BAR & GRILL

12 East 12th St. (Fifth Ave. & University Pl.)
620-4020

American

15

Jerome Kretchmer is cleaning up at last. The city's Commissioner of Sanitation under John Lindsay, Kretchmer opened this place with a couple of partners in 1984. With its dismal, consultant-planned menu, offering a little of everything fashionable, Gotham #1 bombed. Take 2: Kretchmer found Alfred Portale, a culinary wunderkind with stellar credentials. A Culinary Institute of America grad, Portale has done stints with Maximin, Guérard, and Troisgros. When he took over Gotham's kitchens in the spring of 1985, the food became almost as exciting as the setting. That's no mean feat. Winner of the 1984 Restaurant and Hotel Design award for postmodern setting, the restaurant is a breathtaking transformation of some 5,000 square feet of formerly raw warehouse space (half a block deep) with palatial ceilings, Gotham takes the "see and be seen" excitement of restaurant going to the nth degree: everyone can make an entrance worthy of Loretta Young. The feel of the place, with its chintz-covered banquettes, parachute cloth-swaddled fixtures, and aqua trim, is alluring, contemporary, and urban.

The size of the room and the number of dinners served makes us nervous. Plenty must be prepared in advance, and Portale cannot eagle-eye everything coming out of the kitchen. That explains the occasional flop, but you will not find a better seafood salad than the one here: opalescent slices of squid, scallop, hunks of lobster, and mussels dressed in a vibrant vinaigrette, and served with chunks of avocado, which are a perfect counterpoint in both flavor and texture. Goat cheese ravioli are tasty little packets, about the size of large postage stamps, served in a parsley-flecked chicken broth. Grilled tuna is expertly cooked but somewhat dull. No matter. It's served with a fabulously delicious homemade lemon basil pasta. Squab, cooked rare, has a gamey richness. Its garnishes include wild mushrooms and Swiss chard but once again, the pasta steals the show: homemade spaetzle, tossed in mustard butter, is so good you want to eat it every night. Desserts are every bit as successful. Profiterole lovers should not miss these—stuffed with homemade pistachio and vanilla ice cream, bathed in a warm Belgian chocolate sauce. Ambitions and standards run high here. Expect to pay about $50 a person for dinner, with wine, plus tax and tip. *Lunch Mon.-Fri. noon to 2:15 P.M., dinner Mon.-Thurs. 6 P.M. to 10:45 P.M., Fri. & Sat. till 11:15 P.M., Sun. 5:30 P.M. to 9:45 P.M. All major credit cards.*

HARLEQUIN

569 Hudson St. (West 11th St.)
255-4950
Spanish

15

Harlequin is a revelation. Dedicated to alta cocina española (Spanish haute cuisine), it is easily the finest Spanish restaurant in New York City and probably in the United States. Since opening Harlequin in 1985, the husband and wife team of Ileana and (chef) José Bárcena have pledged themselves to offer "superbly prepared food in an 800-year-old Spanish tradition of warm hospitality." No doubt their successful efforts would be much more widely known and touted if their restaurant were in the expense-account lands of midtown or the Upper East Side rather than in the residential West Village. Ileana works the delightful room like a natural, loving to chat and knowing when not to, giving sound recommendations, and supervising her knowledgable and efficient staff.

Her husband's food stops conversation. Some dishes are arrestingly magnificent. As an appetizer the brilliant rendition of brandada de bacalao (salt cod with potatoes, olive oil, and garlic) is a must: served hot in a small baking dish, textured like a firm vegetable purée, all the flavors assert themselves subtly and harmoniously. The shrimp on a bed of two creams of garlic (one mild, one heady) is also recommended, as are the soups and the boquerones (fresh anchovy fillets in vinaigrette). Although not listed on the menu, angulas are often available, so if you have the stomach for these spaghetti-like white eels, order without hesitation. They are sensational, prepared in the traditional manner in an earthenware crock and cooked with sizzling olive oil and chopped garlic. Even the traditional wooden forks are provided. Chef Bárcena has a touch that is light but firm when necessary. Only his French-style dishes are without distinction. Need he try to prove he can cook French with the best of them, when he can make such paella—in our opinion the best in the city? The yellow rice with its saffron, garlic, tomato, and chicken stock flavors is cooked perfectly, and a cavalcade of seafoods—lobster, shrimp, crayfish, clams, mussels—join sausage, pork, and chicken in an exciting and hearty rendition of this popular Spanish dish. Meats, including game, are equally lusty. Also recommended: zortziko de pescados, the Basque fish stew, and the boneless duck with Chinchón liqueur and grapes. Desserts are fine but relatively weak. The worthy bizcocho de avellanas (hazelnut cake) is the best bet.

The wine offerings merit special kudos. The comprehensive listing of Spanish wines has been shrewdly and lovingly assembled. You'd have to go to a top restaurant in Madrid to find its equal. There are old and great wines, including "Spanish Pétrus," Vega Sicilia in the 1972, 1965, and 1960 vintages with prices, if you inquire, in the low hundreds. But generally the wine prices are modest. The CUNE Monopole 1983 at $18 is an excellent white wine choice. The Montecillo Viña Cumbrero 1982 at $12 is an adequate red. For a step up try the Lopez Heredia viñâ Tondonia Gran Reserva 1973 ($28), or 1970 ($48). And you can always order a good

French Champagne or red wine. Lunch averages $25 per person and dinner, $35.

Lunch daily noon to 3 P.M.; dinner nightly 5:30 P.M. to midnight; closed last two weeks in Aug. All major credit cards.

Hawaii 5-0

121 Ave. A (7th & 8th Sts.)
420-8590

American

13 ♟

Fresh tropical fruit punches and plastic bucket swivel seats aside, Hawaii 5-0 recalls nothing of the popular 60's TV series for which it is named. It is, instead, firmly entrenched in the 80's—the campy-nihilistic, mesquite-grilled, gentrified 80's. Smack in the middle of a neighborhood undergoing rapid transition, Hawaii 5-0 embodies its existing tensions. In theory, it caters to the artists who still live in this area, but are now being priced out of it. In practice, as the first and still the only serious restaurant in Alphabet City (as the developers dubbed the area), it substantiates the onset of yuppification.

Straddling both worlds, and distancing itself from Manhattan's restaurant mania, it maintains a low profile. It has no sign; its name is written in chalk on the window. Inside the decor is equally minimal—white linen tablecloths match the glacially bare white walls, providing a neutral backdrop against which the cutting-edge outfits and hairdos of the clientele may star.

The menu calls to mind Paul Prudhomme: "cajun" is a popular modifier and all entrées are mesquite-grilled. But they serve very good food here, and, despite the New Wave inclinations, the atmosphere could not be more welcoming or unpretentious. The best appetizer—and one that could easily prompt return visits—is a lovely garlic soufflé of cloudlike consistency with the wonderful, nutty flavor of roasted garlic. Almost as appealing are two deep-fried crab cakes studded with green peppers and served with a hot red pepper and mustard-spiked rémoulade. Grilled Cajun blackfish displays delicate, moist fish topped with toasted pecan butter and chopped pecans—satisfying, good food. What is billed as half-grilled chicken appears as two skinless, boneless chicken cutlets, cloaked in herbed breadcrumbs, and grilled. It is nicely done but the most humdrum of all offerings. Even the staff doesn't recommend it. For dessert, super-rich bourbon ice cream, sandwiched in fragile homemade lace cookies, is a knock-out. The restaurant has no liquor license. You may bring your own wine (or alcohol to mix with the fruit punches). Dinner costs about $25 a person, plus tax and tip.

Dinner Tues. & Wed. 7 P.M. to 11 P.M., Thurs.-Sat. till midnight. AE.

IL BUFALO

87 Seventh Ave. South (Barrow St.)
243-8000

Eclectic

14

There was considerable consternation among Villagers when another old-time Villager, the Buffalo Roadhouse (a dark, no-nonsense hamburger joint), closed suddenly several years ago. Consternation deepened when, several months later, the place reopened, flooded in sunlight, spruced up with white curtains, white linen and proffering an obscure name and a trendy, eclectic menu borrowing from France, Italy and California. The tariffs seemed borrowed from the Upper East Side. The good news is that Il Bufalo (formerly named Meridies) is the latest stop for chef Susan Sugarman (Wise Maria, Sabor) who serves up very good food, indeed, making this restaurant a welcome addition to the neighborhood.

In a clean, spare setting—earthenware urns suggest the southwest—Sugarman offers inventive, high quality fare. Not everything makes it, but much of it does. Just about every appetizer is a winner. Blue ribbons go to the 8-inch, thin-crusted pizza topped with asiago, Parmesan, fontina and fresh sage, to the large, grilled shiitake mushrooms, to the carpaccio on a bed of mâche, topped with thick curls of Parmesan, to the plump, juicy snails in a mouth-watering sauce of Pernod, shallots and butter, to a homemade duck sausage studded with apples and pine nuts. Success with pastas and entrées is less consistent. Potato/tomato gnocchi fare best; these are melt-in-the-mouth morsels served with deep fried sage leaves. Cold poached salmon is nicely accented by an herby crème fraîche sauce. Sautéed calf's liver with ginger, pancetta and onions is dull but is served with corn meal pancakes so delicious they make the whole proposition worthwhile. Speaking of cornmeal, Sugarman's fried polenta sticks which look and crunch like medium-thick French fries are terrific, and they come with brunch omelettes which are invariably tasty, unusual and interesting.

When the weather is fine, the whole world seems to congregate on the triangular patio featuring a long, curved stainless steel sculpture by Forrest Myers. (It's the sort of work that pits the art community against the local community.) The restaurant's wine list might also spark controversy. It's a welcome relief to find something other than a list thrown together by a major distributor. This list, however, was put together by a minor distributor and consists almost entirely of the bottlings of the obscure producers he represents—many from off years and all at high prices. It is, for example, a delight to find a red Sancerre on a Manhattan list. But not an '84. And not at $22.50 a bottle. Dinner, with a moderately priced wine, averages $45 a person.

Lunch and dinner daily noon to 3:00 P.M.; 6:00 P.M. to midnight. AE

IL CANTINORI

32 East 10th St.
(University Pl. &
Broadway)
673-6044

Italian

14

This spacious Village restaurant serves the real thing, true Italian food conceived, like the modern Italian language, in Tuscany. It is a relatively casual "rustic" restaurant whose owners and staff are very knowledgable about Italian food and wine. For a serious Italian (Tuscan) meal, Il Cantinori certainly ranks among the handful of contenders in New York. When it disappoints it is because the enthusiastic staff becomes overambitious and attempt more than they can handle. There is, for example, always a huge list of specials, in addition to the already substantial regular menu.

When you enter the front room with its stuccoed walls (there's a bar in the middle, opening into a big room in the back), you are treated to a lavish and colorful presentation of cold antipasti that may decide you on your first course before you take off your coat. The offerings range from marinated mushrooms, to zucchini with capers, to more unusual and elaborate preparations. The art and fashion crowds that have made Il Cantinori one of their clubhouses seem to prefer the special assortment of grilled vegetables for a starter. Of course there's risotto or pasta dishes (six regularly and usually about four specials) that can be had as appetizers or main courses. The pastas are a bit uneven, but can be very good. Consider the spaghetti with beans and mussels, or the rigatoni al buristo (blood sausage), or a classic puttanesca. Actually, you will do extremely well if you simply ask for spaghetti with tomato sauce. The roasted quail with polenta and tomato is an interesting entrée. Pheasant comes a bit dry by design and won't appeal to most. Osso buco is a safer choice. There's a fine tirami su for dessert, though you may opt for a dessert wine by the glass, vin santo or even picolit, with some traditional dry dessert biscuits. The Italian wine list has been built by people who care about small vineyards and producers and high quality. Try the Barbaresco Martinenga. Dinner runs about $48 per person.

Lunch daily noon to 3 P.M.; dinner Sun.-Thurs. 6 P.M. to 11:30 P.M., Fri. & Sat. till midnight; closed Sun. in July and Aug. AE, DC.

INDOCHINE

430 Lafayette St. (Astor Pl. & 4th St.)
505-5111

Vietnamese/ Cambodian

14

Indochine takes you back to the era of expatriates lolling in the palm-strewn lobby of a sultry hotel, while white-robed natives serve them icy gin with lots of lime. This large, well-lit, elegant restaurant sports painted palm fronds on the walls, real exotic flowers like bird of paradise and athurium, and dark green banquettes set against pure white tablecloths. Although contrived, it works. And so does the food, which is authentically Vietnamese. Located right across the street from the Public Theater on Lafayette Street, Indochine draws young actors (how do they afford it?) as well as theater-goers and New York "Euro-brats."

Efficient waitresses will suggest that you order by number, an amusing request considering the sophistication of the restaurant. But you'll soon understand why if you dare try to pronounce the names of any of the 47 dishes featured on the menu. The soups are rich and satisfying, especially the fish soup, a deep broth flavored with lemon grass and full of delicate noodles. Be forewarned about the spicy appetizers that are not marked as such; they are excellent and even refreshing, but they are hot, so eat them after the milder dishes you order. Steamed shrimp with fresh mint and lemon grass is highly seasoned but not hot, and the shrimps are large, tender, and delightfully fresh. Steamed ravioli are delicate and filled with minced pork, and the spring rolls are superb, especially goi cuon, rice paper filled with shrimp, vermicelli, and bean sprouts. Although very peppery, the beef salad is one of the best appetizers; the thinly-sliced beef is succulent and well-complemented by the sliced shallots, lemon grass, and vinegary sauce.

Main dishes are served Chinese-style, so you may taste several dishes in one evening. The steamed whole fish with ginger is flaky and delicate. Boneless chicken wings are enormous and stuffed with vermicelli and chopped chicken breast, and flavored with lemon grass. Although lemon grass figures in many of the dishes, each dish is distinct in flavor and many other seasonings are used as well. The brochettes of prawns and swordfish are delightfully simple, while the frog legs in coconut have a more complex, sweeter taste. Sticky rice is a must; the tasty brown rice, flavored with tiny bits of pork, offsets the clean bite of the spicier dishes. Desserts are good but no equal to the rest of the menu. To cool off, most diners go for the exotically-flavored sorbets.

The wine list is expensive but not terribly exciting, and besides, cold beer goes well with this cuisine. Average price is about $30 per person without drinks.
Daily 6 P.M. to midnight. AE.

JANE STREET SEAFOOD CAFE

31 Eighth Ave. (Jane St.)
242-0003, 243-9237

Seafood

13 ♟

A decade ago, before New Yorkers started pushing fish or seafood as a main course, this casual, New England-style fish house settled comfortably on the corner of one of Greenwich Village's most charming residential streets. Locals quickly started lining up. The draw was some of the freshest fish around, prepared in a range of styles, priced moderately, and served efficiently and with good fellowship. The restaurant succeeded, and not much has changed since then. The list of fish on the chalkboard has grown, and some trendy preparations such as a good blackened redfish served over a red pepper coulis have appeared. But the staples remain, such as linguini with mussels or clams, which you can always see on a nearby table.

The long room is cozy: brick walls, old wooden floors, a working fireplace, a 19th-century tin ceiling, and bare wood tables with small candles. The staff, male and female, are dressed in jeans and rugby shirts; pony tails are popular with both genders. Like the good actors they probably are, they can hit any mark or pace you desire, and smile the whole time.

The grainy and crisp Italian bread has always been very good here and arrives straightaway at your table with some complimentary coleslaw, carrots, and the like—all crunchy and well-matched with a creamy dressing. The Manhattan clam chowder is fine—chunky and spicy—but not great. The fried oysters, however, are very good, crispy on the outside and fresh and lush on the inside. Any of the sole dishes are worth considering—for example, broiled with slices of fresh tomato, herbs, and Parmesan cheese; or Portuguese, sautéed in garlic, butter and herbs, fresh tomatoes, and mushrooms, flambéed with sherry and served on a bed of brown rice.

There are about 75 choices of wine to wash that down. Most are good and reasonably priced, though the diner would be on easier and safer ground if vintages were included on the wine list. The desserts are simple and do the job, with a not overly sweet vanilla cheesecake deserving first consideration, though the chocolate truffle cake attracts the most attention. There are no "official" reservations here, so

people still line up outside in all weather. Son
minute phone call can peg the wait. Figure
person with a modest bottle of wine.
Dinner Mon.-Thurs. 5:30 P.M. to 11 P.M.; Fri.
midnight; Sun. 4 P.M. to 10 P.M. AE, MC, V.

JOHN CLANCY'S RESTAURANT

181 West 10th St. (Seventh Ave. South)
242-7350

Seafood

15

If you are in the mood for seafood and nothing but, then
run, don't walk, to John Clancy's Restaurant (no longer
owned by John Clancy, but by Samuel Rubin). Occupying
two floors of a century-old townhouse, John Clancy's is one
of the city's most reliable and best seafood restaurants. It's
especially noted for its mesquite-grilled seafoods, and deserves credit for being the first place in New York to
introduce the practice and for continuing to show trendy
others how it should be done. This is a charming restaurant
with a subdued elegance. The downstairs, with its low
ceiling and candlelit tables, is colored with quiet tones of
gray and white—white brick walls (bearing garden posters),
gray carpet, and white or grey bentwood chairs. Upstairs
there is an attractive and more intimate dining room.

Gravlax with a mustard dill sauce makes a silky cold
appetizer. Wild mushrooms in puff pastry or oysters New
Orleans (baked with clams, crab, and herbs) are two recommended hot appetizers. When available as a special, the
mussels steamed with spicy tomato and leek broth is very
good, though the mussels at times move beyond plumpness
into obesity. There are always a dozen interesting specials.
Half of the entrée offerings are prepared on the mesquite
grill, and thus come away enhanced with a light baptism of
woody smoke. The grilled swordfish on a skewer more than
justifies the visit. Barbecued jumbo shrimp is beguiling.
Accompanying vegetables, usually a broccoli purée, potatoes,
and/or rice, are serviceable but won't occupy your attention.
Desserts are huge and all-American, with a heavy dose of
chocolate (often four out of six possibilities), but all are good
to very good. A lemon meringue tart appears regularly and a
huge multi-layer English trifle always. The computerized
wine list is a gem. You won't have any difficulty choosing
well from the approximately 75 reasonably priced offerings
(the majority whites) ranging from Trefethen Riesling ($14)
to Roederer Cristal Champagne ($115). Expect to pay $50
per person.
Dinner Mon.-Sat. 6 P.M. to 11 P.M., Sun. 5 P.M. to 10
P.M.; lunch, phone for hours. All major credit cards.

₁ BOHÊME

24 Minetta Ln. (Sixth Ave.)
473-6447

French

12/20

Leave it to design-wizard Sam Lopata to fashion this bistro, which opened in December 1985, so that it appears to have been in the Village forever. With its wood-fired pizza oven, its white stucco walls, its Provençal pottery and fabrics, La Bohême would look quite at home in Arles, too—except maybe that the light fixtures made of painted colanders say New York, circa 1987. While students, tourists, and off-Broadway theater goers flock to this place, La Bohême is really a spot for Villagers. A convivial place in which to have a talk, a snack, or a full-fledged meal, La Bohême serves forth food that is as good as it needs to be. And that's just fine. Some regulars subsist on pizzas with a "side" of fries. The pizzas, in fact, are the best way to start a meal, the most popular choices being the vegetarian, La Bohême (with capers and anchovies), or Gitane (with snails). Steak/frites is fine—good beef cooked to order and topped with a pat of herb butter. Specials, too, can be satisfying, particularly the thin slices of medium rare leg of lamb arranged around a mix of goat cheese and spinach, or the salmon en croûte on a light, basil-scented sauce. The wine list is short, serviceable, and reasonably priced. Dinner, with wine, costs about $25 per person.

Dinner Tues.-Sat. 5:30 P.M. to midnight; June-Aug. Sun. 2 P.M. to midnight, Sept.-May Sun. noon to 11:30 P.M. AE.

LA GAULOISE

502 Ave. of the Americas (12th & 13th Sts.)
691-1363

French

13 🍳

One of the first of the new wave of chic French brasseries to hit New York, La Gauloise has become in a decade a trusted Village restaurant with hearty meals of exemplary honesty and regularity. Owner Jacques Allimann has created a handsome establishment decorated with Art Deco lamps, mahogany-bordered mirrors, and the obligatory banquettes, in which he delivers true bistro fare made from products of high quality.

Onion soup, oysters, escargots bourguignonne, pâté de campagne, choucroute (Wednesdays), bouillabaisse (Fridays), cassoulet (Sundays), grilled chicken, entrecôte béarnaise, and another dozen or so dishes one would expect to find in Paris at a good neighborhood bistro are there on the menu. The portions are hearty, and so what if now and again the chicken is dry and the veggies are only so-so, or if the saumon paillard with basil sauce is a little bland? Nothing is bad and most of the food is fine. The service is typically French bistro—sometimes charming and stunningly efficient, the staff can be at other times indifferent; some would say arrogant. The range of satisfying desserts should cement a solid meal. The lemon tart and crème brûlée are very good. The wines are also good—good selection, good years, good prices. They are mostly French (nice Burgundies), plus a handful of American offerings, and all are attractively priced from $18 to $110. Dinner with wine averages $40 a person. *Lunch Tues. to Sun. noon to 3:00 P.M.; dinner 5:45 P.M. to 11:30 P.M.; Sat. and Sun. brunch noon to 3 P.M.; closed three weeks in July. AE, MC, V.*

LA MÉTAIRIE

189 West 10th St. (West 4th St.)
989-0343
French

13

This charming place, which seats twenty in cramped quarters, looks as if Laura Ashley had been set loose in a chicken coop: candles flicker on teeny tables; a pitchfork is angled on a stuccoed wall; a caged dove coos; provençale paisleys cover tightly wedged banquettes; decorative dark wood beams give a rustic timbered look as do the white shutters and Dutch door opening onto 10th Street. You expect Snow White to come out of the kitchen. The food, however, is elemental and boldly flavored, particularly the couscous. This is, as it should be, a vivid and substantial dish. The grains are served on one side of the platter; a mix of muttony chunks of lamb, merguez (lamb sausage), chicken, carrots, and zucchini crowd the other. Ask for the harissa and use it with respect: it roars with garlic and heat. Garlic lovers will want to work up to the couscous with an appetizer of snails with vegetables (carrots, turnips) served with aioli (addictive garlic mayonnaise). Ask to keep the gravy boat. You'll finish the aioli with the very good rolls served here.

For more timid palates, La Métairie takes a more dulcet approach with citified selections such as sautéed foie gras with raspberry vinegar sauce, garnished with fresh raspberries and sliced Granny Smith apples, airy artichoke mousse with truffle sauce and deboned quail stuffed with a mix of liver and pork, served on a rich game sauce. La Métairie has spawned an Upper East Side offshoot at 1442 Third Avenue. Dinner, with a youthful, minor Bordeaux (the place could use a better and broader selection of red Rhones to go with the couscous), comes to about $50 a person.
Dinner Mon.-Thurs. 6:00 P.M. to 11:00 P.M., Fri. and Sat. to 11:30 P.M., Sun. 5:00 P.M. to 11:00 P.M. MC, V, AE.

LA RIPAILLE

605 Hudson St. (12th & Bethune Sts.)
255-4406

Behind an undistinguished facade, on a dreary strip of Hudson Street across from Abingdon Square, lies this appealing French restaurant that has been attracting West Villagers and pilgrims from uptown since the early 70's. The

French

13

attractive, somewhat rustic decor remains unchanged: a tiny bar, bare brick walls and stucco, lovely fresh flowers, an ancient grandfather clock, well-executed reproductions of medieval tapestries, and huge cross beams overhead. It is a cozy and charming room that seats 45. But while the food and ambiance are good, both have slipped a little over the years. Brothers and co-owners Patrick and Alain Laurent from Metz, France, made the restaurant, and may have spread themselves a little thin as of late, since they opened their successful second restaurant, L'Escale.

The large menu here changes daily, which is a tip-off that this kitchen pays more than lip service to its claims to be sensitive to what's good and available on the market. The strictly French fare is enticing. Much of the food is prepared in the classic style but always with nouvelle touches. The light mousse of broccoli with lemon butter usually heads the list of appetizers, and it belongs at the top. Another perennial is a creamy and flavorful fettucine with smoked salmon. The escargots come bathed in a tomato and basil cream. There is always a cold vegetable salad, and wild mushrooms are featured as appetizers when they are available. Among the hearty main courses, priced from $16.50 to $23, the salmon steak and the lamb chop are nicely grilled and seasoned, the former with mustard and the latter with fresh thyme. When rack of lamb is offered, it too is grilled and seasoned predictably but effectively with thyme and rosemary. Mustard is called upon again as sauce for an excellent kidney preparation. Should frogs' legs be on the menu, go for them in a garlic, parsley, and tomato sauce.

Classic crème caramel with a touch of orange is a fine and reliable dessert. The lemon tart is usually good, and if you have designs on the bombe glacée pralinée, know it is essentially a so-so slice of almond ice cream cake. The profiteroles are hit or miss. The French wine list is a serviceable one, and, of course, you can always drink Champagne. Figure $35 a person, but without Champagne.
Dinner Mon. to Sat. 5:30 P.M. to 11:30 P.M. All major credit cards.

LA TULIPE

104 West 13th St. (Sixth Ave.)
691-8860

It is said with regret but it must be said: this is a very good restaurant, but it is not the restaurant it was when it opened in 1979. The menu seems rigid, the flavors less vibrant. What seemed like growing pains in the restaurant's early days—frequently inept service, an overpriced, poorly composed wine list—suggest mismanagement now. For all that,

French

however, La Tulipe remains one of the city's best options for a civilized dinner; an intimate setting and refined, well-considered cooking manifesting a graciousness reflecting the aesthetics of the owners, Sally and John Darr.

La Tulipe occupies the ground floor of the Darrs' townhouse. A frosted glass door opens into a seductive bar-*cum*-waiting room. The small dining room is both simple and satisfying. Plum walls, dark brown corduroy banquettes, and a large mirror (which adds a sense of both lightness and space) combine to convey the feeling of confident well-being which strikes the right note for Darr's faithful renditions of haute bourgeoise cuisine. A mousse of smoked trout is among the best of the appetizers, but it's a child's portion. Langue valenciennoise, though not as compelling, is a toothsome jellyroll of interspersed layers of tongue and foie gras. Among the entrées, there is nothing to complain about in an off-the-menu special of navarin of lobster in a light-herb-and-tomato-infused cream sauce served over spaghetti, though it is hardly the best that this kitchen can turn out. Ballotine of chicken, stuffed with duck liver and foie gras, displays bland chicken and a mild livery taste. Happily, its light mushroom cream sauce is alive with the complex flavors of morel and shiitake mushrooms. Desserts continue to be excellent. The apple tart, the homemade ice creams in warm chocolate sauce, and the flourless chocolate cake are particular favorites. Note also that management attempts to observe two seatings—7 P.M. and 9 P.M. Opt for 7 P.M.; then you can linger. Those who reserve at 9 P.M. get seated late and served lickety-split. The prix fixe is $57 per person. That does not include wine, tax, or tip.

Dinner Tues.-Sun. 6:30 to 10 P.M. All major credit cards.

MANHATTAN CHILI CO.

302 Bleecker St. (Seventh Ave. & Grove Sts.)
206-7163

American

"Wish I had time for just one more bowl of chili," allegedly the dying words of Kit Carson, are printed on the cover of the Manhattan Chili Co.'s menu. Had Carson time for one more bowl, he might well have chosen this engaging Village restaurant opened by Michael McLaughlin (co-author of *The Silver Palate Cookbook*). Since chili is the kind of dish that inspires fanaticism, it is simply asking for trouble to claim that one place serves the best in the city. Suffice it to say that Manhattan Chili Co. is on anyone's short list of Manhattan's best chili purveyors. Its roster of chilis, however, is anything but short. Currently, the place serves ten: from the Real McCoy (no beans, no tomatoes, no bull), to Cincinnati-style (with lamb and hominy), to vegetarian, seafood, or venison with black beans, to the two most popular—Numero Uno and Texas Chain Gang (which gets real fire from jalapeños). The kitchen explores other Southwestern themes as well. Sure bets among the appetizers are the chunky guacamole with lots of red onion, tomato, and cilantro, or the zippy salsa, either plain (with tortilla chips) or with chèvre. A side order of Calico Corn Muffins, made with buttermilk, corn, jalapeño, and red peppers are delectable meals in themselves. Entrées other than chili which might convert even Carson include the chicken fajitas (grilled strips and onions served with salsa, guacamole, and warm flour tortillas), the spicy meat loaf, and the chicken tortilla pie. Sides are usually as good as the dishes they accompany—particularly the mustardy cole slaw and the rice salad with green and red peppers, olives, corn, kidney beans, and scallions.

The setting matches the cooking. It mixes the collegiate informality of Austin, Texas, with the colors of Taos (turquoise, pink, and bleached-out white) and a kind of tongue-in-cheek playfulness manifested by the neon jalapeño in the window and Elvis, the armadillo, on a counter by the bar. A small backyard patio for warm weather dining makes the place one of the nicest brunch options in town. The restaurant offers a number of wines by the glass. Its beer selection, however, is even longer. Try the Anchor Steam, which is almost impossible to find east of California. Dinner, with wine or drinks, costs about $25 per person. *Sun.-Thurs. noon to midnight, Fri. & Sat. till 1 A.M. All major credit cards.*

MIE

196 Second Ave. (12th & 13th Sts.)
674-7060

Japanese

13 🎩

Hidden in the basement of a Second Avenue tenement in the East Village, Mie is an oddity among the other ethnic Village restaurants, insofar as it is true to its roots. The entrance is "landscaped" with a stone path, rocks, and a semblance of a garden, just like many Tokyo restaurants. Mie's clientele is more often than not Japanese, plus a few die-hard Western aficionados. The sushi bar is surrounded by small tables and there's a larger room for parties of four or more. The rooms are discreetly decorated with wood benches and delicate wall lanterns, and the atmosphere is one of pleasant tranquility. The menu offers several dinners typical of most second-rate Japanese restaurants around the city, including sukiyaki, tempura, and teriyaki; these are to be avoided at all costs. Ditto for the sorry misinterpretation of a potato salad. But if you choose à la carte, the chef will know you're for real and the food will be good.

The sushi and sashimi are excellent, freshly prepared by an imaginative chef. If you sit at the sushi bar and befriend him, you are in for a treat. Yakiniku, thin slices of beef broiled with garlic and sancho pepper, are tender, rare, and will remind you of tuna. The fish teriyaki, marinated in soy sauce and spices, then lightly broiled and served with kombu sauce, is excellent. Mie has several noodle dishes made with udon (thick Japanese noodles). One features udon served in a casserole along with vegetables; large, barely-cooked shrimps; roast pork; and egg. The only dish on the menu that will satisfy a hearty appetite, it is wonderful on a cool night.

What makes Mie exceptional are the side dishes, such as yu-dofu, airy, silken bean curd served in a hot, tasty broth with excellent seaweed, or, in the summer, the same bean curd served cold in a bowl of ice water with shaved bonito and sliced fresh ginger. Another dish is chawan-mushi, the best egg custard served in New York, filled with tiny pieces of chicken, vegetables, shrimp, and gingko nuts—a sheer delight. Dessert is the usual fare of unripe melon, green tea ice cream, canned Mandarin oranges, and bean paste. The service is always pleasant. About $15 per person with wine, beer, or sake.

Tues.-Sun. 5:30 P.M. to 12:30 P.M. All major credit cards.

ONE IF BY LAND, TWO IF BY SEA

17 Barrow St. (Seventh Ave. & West 4th St.)
228-0822

Continental

12/20

If wishing alone could elevate the culinary standards of a restaurant, then we'd cast our first wish here. Currently the food is all right, and if you choose carefully you can eat and drink well, but the setting . . . wow. This place looks sensational, and is surely one of the most attractive and romantic restaurants in Manhattan. It is a restored 18th-century carriage house with bi-level dining, lots of space, some exposed brick walls, handsome paintings and furnishings (including red velvet banquettes and chairs and a warm patterned carpet), and a pretty garden outside in a courtyard. The humble street entrance doesn't prepare you for the interior: a pianist seated at a grand piano near the door greets you and entertains throughout the evening; regulars chat comfortably at a long bar, a few diners await their guests while having a drink at a low table near the fireplace, friendly waiters in black tie move suavely about. It is hard to imagine a date, a relative, or an out-of-town business guest who would not be flattered by a dinner here.

For that dinner, which might be considered an accessory to the atmosphere, the coquilles St. Jacques is a tasty appetizer. The soups, shrimp cocktail, pâtés, and salads all go down without much trouble—or impression. An individual beef Wellington is something of a house specialty as an entrée, and as it is not seen that often in New York, it merits attention—but don't expect the finest pastry wrapped about perfectly cooked beef. You won't go wrong with the simple charcoal-grilled meats. The veal chop is especially good and grilled to perfection. The waiters push the Long Island duck, which is O.K., but expect a big portion and some version of a sweet sauce. Vegetables are simply steamed, nicely under-cooked, crunchy, and innocuous. The desserts look all right and taste all right but are nothing special. The wine list, however, is a disgrace for an upscale restaurant like this. It's the product—down to the printing—of one of the bigger wine houses in New York: the result is a generally weak selection (though there are some good wines), no vintage listings at all, cutesy descriptions under each offering, and top, top prices. One If By Land is open for drinks from 4 P.M. to 4 A.M. Figure on $60 per person plus tax and tip. *Dinner Sun. to Thurs. 5:30 to midnight, Fri. & Sat. to 1:00 A.M. All major credit cards.*

SABOR

20 Cornelia St. (West 4th & Bleecker Sts.)
243-9579

Cuban

14 🍽️

Havana was never like this. Here two Americans, inspired cooks both but with only the most tenuous of Latin ties, dish up some of the best Cuban food around. Any of the escabeches—raw fish or shellfish "cooked"by being marinated in lime juice, then garnished with onion, celery, and capers—make pleasant starters, as do plump briny mussels in tomato sauce, spicy squid, and the frituras de malanga, a deep-fried starchy tuber served with two sweet hot sauces that set you pleasantly afire. For the main course you could not do better than the perfectly baked whole red snapper or succulent sautéed shrimp, both blanketed with Sabor's out-standing salsa verde.

Beef dishes include carne estofada, a pot roast with overtones of orange, and ropa vieja, chewy shredded beef exotic with hints of cloves and cinnamon. The classic accompaniments, rice and black beans, are fresh and blessed-ly unmushy, and to round things out be sure to ask for fried sweet plantains. For eight or more, Sabor will do a feast around a moist-meated, crisp-skinned, roast sucking pig. Dessert freaks will love the custardy key lime pie, the coco quemado (a tart of freshly grated coconut, sherry, and cinammon served warm), and the homemade ice creams. The coffee is wonderful, and great fresh fruit dark rum daiquiris will get you in the mood. Sabor is a drop-in place for neighborhood folk, but it's small so definitely reserve. Dinner runs about $26 per person; for the suckling pig feast, the charge is $40 per person, which includes appetizers, the pig, accompaniments, and coffee.

Dinner daily, Sun.-Thurs. 6 P.M. to 11 P.M.; Fri.-Sun. 6 P.M. to midnight. AE, MC, V.

SIRACUSA

65 Fourth Ave. (9th & 10th Sts.)
254-1940
Italian

13 🍳

Some say that the caponata served at this engaging takeout shop/wine bar/restaurant is better than the Sicilian original. It is certainly delicious with the vivid flavors of eggplant, capers, and peppers. In the daytime you could order the caponata "to go," but it's much nicer to sit in the plain, simply decorated dining room, with the actors from the nearby Public Theater as well as with neighborhood artists, designers, writers, and architects. It feels like a good place to be. Start with a non-Sicilian Bellini while listening to the "specials." Whatever they are, order a mixed appetizer, which is likely to bring the caponata (the moistest buffalo milk mozzarella on earth topped with sun-dried tomatoes), octopus salad, asparagus wrapped in prosciutto, disks of fried zucchini, fried cauliflower, and, perhaps, fresh sardines—if they're available and if you ask for them. With the occasional exception of triglia, a Mediterranean fish, all of the main courses are pasta. Don't miss the spaghetti with fennel sausage in a light tomato cream sauce jazzed up with hot pepper. Also satisfying are bow ties with fresh artichokes, fava beans, and peas in a light tomato sauce; and mezzaluna (large crescent-shaped ravioli) filled with ricotta, spinach, and mushrooms, accompanied by a thick tomato sauce. You will not go wrong if you order a strong Sicilian red, such as Regaleali ($18) to complement your food, but you'll blow it if you leave without sampling the homemade gelati, which may be the best in town. Taste all three—ricotta, espresso, and hazelnut. Then cap your meal with a glass of excellent dessert wine, Malvasia delle Lipari ($5). Prices mount quickly here and one person can easily spend $45 on dinner, plus tax and tip.

Lunch Mon.-Fri. noon to 3 P.M.; dinner Sun.-Thurs. 6 P.M. to 11 P.M., Fri. & Sat. to 11:30 P.M.; June-Aug. closed Sun. AE.

TATANY VILLAGE

This casual but elegant duplex restaurant occupying a land-mark brownstone on one of the Village's busy streets turns out first-rate sashimi, sushi, and tempura to an increasingly

62 Greenwich Ave.
(Seventh Ave.)
675-6195

Japanese

12/20

sophisticated clientele. At the tables, the dishes and combination platters are predictable and good, with cool, fresh fish and ethereally light deep-frying. There are no uptown banquet-style meals offered, but the standards are done well. If you want magic, sit at the sushi bar and win the confidence of one of the sushi chefs. Utilizing the pick of the freshest fish—which are often top local catches—and an artistry learned as an apprentice in Japan, he will expand your horizons. The chefs have learned English and how to accomodate New Yorkers. When they have a calm moment, a rarity at a frenetic sushi bar, they will delight in entertaining and educating your palate. Drink tea or Japanese beer with your meal (though you can order Champagne here), and expect a sweet plum wine to leave you with a pleasant aftertaste. There's an equally good and reliable Tatany under the same ownership on Third Avenue between 27th and 28th Streets. Expect to pay $15-25 per person.
Lunch Mon.-Fri. noon to 2:30 P.M,; dinner daily 5:30 P.M. to 10:30 P.M. AE, V.

TOON'S

417 Bleecker St. (Bank &
Bleecker Sts.)
924-6420; 243-9211

Thai

12/20

For Thai food or a moderately priced meal in general, spiffy and reliable Toon's is a good Village option. The entrance and bar are on Bank Street, but unless the restaurant is very crowded, you'll dine in the front room with huge windows looking out on Bleecker and Bank Streets, plants, and dramatically illuminated stalks of purple orchids. Tables are very close together, so if you haven't come with friends, you may end up making some new ones.

For starters, the shrimp fritters are good, though on occasion a bit oily, and ditto for the addictive zucchini fritters. The nuur satee is excellent; these strips of thinly-sliced steak marinated in coconut milk and Thai herbs are charboiled and served on a thin wooden skewer. The peanut sauce on the side is a yummy dressing. Good frogs' legs are available with different sauces such as garlic and pepper, basil leaf and chili pepper, and a red curry. You can get a nicely deep-fried whole fish here and a decent curry chicken (kang kai). Less fiery choices are the honey duck or the mee krob—the crisply fried rice stick noodles mixed with tamarind sauce and topped with shrimp and ocean sprouts. This ubiquitous Thai dish seems to taste different at every New York Thai restaurant, and here it is a bit sweet. Though many Thai dishes border on the violently hot, none here are lethal. A Thai beer helps. The tab runs only about $18-23 per person.

Dinner Mon.-Thurs. 5 P.M. to 11:30 P.M., Sat. till midnight, Sun. 4 P.M. to 11 P.M. AE, MC, V.

TRATTORIA DA ALFREDO

13 Eighth Ave. (12th St.)
929-4400
Italian

12/20

Theatrical Alfredo Viazzi, always nattily dressed with a jacket and ascot, is something of a West Village restaurant impressario. He has opened and closed several establishments, but his heart has always belonged to his long-running hit, Trattoria da Alfredo, to which he now devotes full attention. No absentee owner living off a past reputation, he seems always to be seated at the corner table near the bar. The author of several Italian cookbooks, Alfredo has also appeared as a star chef on public television. In March 1986 he moved his storefront landmark eatery up the block a couple of hundred yards into a handsome Village brownstone. The restaurant, which still seats only about 45 on its two floors, is now more elegant and homey (a brick wall, Pierre Deux wallpaper, wooden chairs and tables, attractive ornaments). The food has never been better.

For appetizers, the Roman style artichoke is perfection (if you don't mind using your fingers to enjoy the leaves); also appealing is the stuffed zucchini Genovese style, filled with chopped veal, sausage, herbs and cheese, then covered with a luscious tomato sauce and mozzarella cheese. The other appetizers (snails, clams, and stuffed mushrooms) are all fine, as are both the spinach and egg soup and the tortellini in broth. The latter gets our vote on a winter's evening. Trattoria da Alfredo earned its reputation on outstanding pastas and modest prices. The eleven pasta dishes daily are all recommended and all priced at $10 or less. The spaghettini puttanesca seems to have developed its own identity within the species, with the black olives and tomato sauce dominating the flavors of tuna and anchovy. The pastas can easily serve as a main course, but if you desire one of the handful of fish or meat dishes, try the fish stew Livorno style, or the mixed vegetables with sausage. There is a daily chicken and veal dish as well. The wine list is developing nicely; it's 90% Italian, with most prices in the teens. There are no vintages or houses listed, but they turn out to be better than one would expect. The house wines by the glass, especially the Vino Nobile de Montepulciano, are also recommended. Figure $20 for a meal with pasta as a main course and a single glass of wine, and $35 or so a person for a big meal with wine, plus tax and tip.
Lunch Mon. & Wed.-Sat. noon to 2 P.M.; dinner nightly 6 P.M. to 10 P.M. AE.

VANESSA

289 Bleecker St. (Seventh
Ave. South)
243-4225
Eclectic

11/20

Although the turn-of-the-century decor and grandiose floral arrangements haven't changed in years, Chef Anne Rosenzweig is long gone, replaced by Norio Morohashi, a Japanese French-trained chef who has worked at the Four Seasons and at several other restaurants on the East Coast. This chef and owner's intentions are not clear; the menu is rather long and a mixture of French, Italian, and Japanese cuisines. Take, for example, the appetizer of American wild mushrooms with light noodles and herb brandy. The pleurottes are sautéed in butter and served on top of Japanese rice noodles—is it Japanese or French? A successful marriage of the two? Not really. The slightly Italianate snails with tomatoes are cooked in cream with herbs and spices; indeed, most of the dishes are prepared with an overpowering cream. The Japanese buckwheat pasta is prepared in the same way as spaghetti, with flavorful sun-dried tomatoes, but is, again, made heavy by its creamy sauce. Try Vanessa's tasty soups instead of the pasta dishes.

The entrée choices are what you expect to find in any restaurant of this caliber: broiled swordfish, red snapper, medallion of veal, or Long Island duck. The dishes are cooked well but unimaginatively, except for the paillard of salmon, a thin slice of salmon sautéed in butter with caramelized onions and lobster butter. Desserts will not excite even a sworn sweet tooth; it is better to limit yourself to the excellent capuccino or espresso. The wine list is short but good and reasonably priced. Dinner here runs $40 with wine.

Lunch Thurs.-Fri. noon to 3:30 P.M., Sat. till 5 P.M.; dinner nightly 5:30 P.M. to midnight. All major credit cards.

THE VILLAGE GREEN

531 Hudson St. (Charles
St.)
255-1630
American

13 🍴

Unless you frequent the West Village, you probably won't know that this long-established, warm-and-cozy restaurant closed in 1986 and re-opened in June 1987 under new ownership and with a talented new chef. The handsome place, nestled in a 1827 townhouse, looks just like it always did. Upstairs, the bar and lounge with its fireplace and grand piano are warm and beckoning. Downstairs, the intimate brick-and-wood decor dining room seats 30. Some would call this a romantic spot, and perhaps it is if you do your romancing with your eyes alone. The room is small and the tables are sufficiently close together that you can pick up any conversation at will.

The chef does his romancing of course on the plates with contemporary American fare. Chef Tony Najiola, born in

Louisiana and a veteran of the kitchens at the River Cafe and La Réserve, offers a limited but changing menu. Several salads sampled with walnut oil dressing are very good. There's a special pasta of the day that in a half-portion serving succeeds as an appetizer. The spinach fettucini with scallops, coriander, pecans, walnuts, pine nuts, capers, and tomato is fine, as is the crispy sautéed foie gras. Fish, fowl, and meat are represented among the seven or eight entrées. The pan-roasted duck breast is a standout with ripe plums and a peppery stock. Also recommended are the roasted loin of mustard-smeared lamb stuffed with spinach, and a perfectly cooked tuna steak. Desserts do the trick, but little more. The hazelnut mocha mousse torte with its pecan shortbread and whipped cream gets our nod, though the cheesecake seems to get the popular vote.

The wine list is not long but will develop and already offers some desirable wines from California and Europe, including a mature '78 Chappelet Cabernet Sauvignon from Napa Valley. There is a fine digestif list in place, and a good Cognac or Armagnac can be enjoyed upstairs where late-night jazz is performed nightly except Sunday. The black-tied maitre d'hôtel and the rest of the service staff are friendly and professional. Dinner runs about $40 per person. *Dinner Tues.-Sat. 6 P.M. to 11:30 P.M., Sun. 6 P.M. to 9 P.M.; brunch Sun. noon to 3:30 P.M. All major credit cards.*

YE WAVERLY INN

16 Bank St. (Waverly Pl.)
929-4377; 243-9396
American

10/20

There are two chefs here at this Greenwich Village tribute to colonial Americana: William Thompson who has been in the kitchen since 1955 and William McDow, who has been cooking here since 1945. Both serve simple, honest fare which is perhaps a bit heavy, overcooked, and even over-seasoned by current standards. But what is most important to remember about this charming landmark is that customers continue to go away satisfied.

Chicken pot pie is a house specialty and merits considera-tion, along with Yankee pot roast, Southern fried chicken, and a barbequed rack of ribs as entrées. Seafood and fish specials are offered daily in increasing numbers. The price of a dinner is a revelation: about $12.75 will bring you a cup of soup, a choice of entrée, one vegetable, salad, homemade dessert, and coffee. That must impart as much satisfaction as the pecan pie. The restaurant's setting is as much a draw as the passable fare with yesteryear prices. Situated on the corner of one of the West Village's handsomest residential streets, the restaurant has four small dining rooms just below

street level in an old townhouse; they sport low ceilings and wooden booths, and there are two working fireplaces. In summer there are also tables in an outdoor garden. À la carte dinner with wine will run about $23 per person.
Lunch Mon-Fri. 11:45 A.M. to 2 P.M.; dinner Mon.-Thurs. 5:45 P.M. to 10 P.M., Fri. & Sat. till 11 P.M.; Sunday brunch, noon to 3:30 P.M., dinner 4:30 P.M. to 9 P.M. All major credit cards.

14th to 42nd Streets

THE BALLROOM

253 West 28th St. (Seventh & Eighth Aves.)
244-3005

Spanish

13 🎩

The talented Peruvian chef Felipe Rojas-Lombardi runs the Ballroom as a multifaceted restaurant-cabaret. The large front room has an enormous bar and small cafe tables where you can sit from 4 o'clock on eating tapas and drinking wine. Rojas-Lombardi has added a new dimension to these Spanish hors d'oeuvres by adding Peruvian delicacies such as fresh anchovies in grape leaves, escabeche of frogs' legs, and rabbit. This chef's imagination knows no limits, and you can make a dinner of tapas by choosing a careful combination of dishes. There are snails and red beans, or crunchy and spicy pigs' ears with pearl onions. The Ballroom empanadas, stuffed with meat or fish and spicy sausage, are some of the best in New York. Follow them with some succulent roasted kid and then perhaps yucca or braised morels. For dessert, the tapas bar offers several flans, fruit tarts, and cold compotes. Try the cremé catalane, a wonderful nutty flan.

The restaurant proper offers a more sedate menu that is neither Spanish nor Peruvian, but ersatz Continental and much too often uneven. The baked fennel or lightly fried yucca straws are good appetizers, but the salads are very ordinary. Chef Rojas-Lombardi serves Cornish hen with green peppercorns (uninspired), grilled duck that is sometimes tough, an excellent broiled rack of lamb, and sautéed sweetbreads. The Ballroom has an extensive wine list fairly priced. Average price per person $40.
Lunch & dinner Tues.-Fri. noon to 1 A.M., Sat. 4:30 P.M. to 1 A.M. All major credit cards.

CAFE DU PARC

106 East 19th St. (Park
Ave. & Irving Pl.)
777-7840
French

12/20

The theme song of this understated place might be, "I'm old-fashioned (and I don't mind it)," for this place seems a welcome throwback to simpler times. A narrow room with tempting desserts on a two-tiered cart as you enter, Cafe du Parc's cozy, romantic tone is created by exposed brick walls, etched glass partitions, candles, flowers, and tables spaced far enough apart to permit—even promote—conversation among the well-heeled neighborhood clientele. They lean back, talk, and take their time over dinner.

Dinner is a well-considered, if not spectacular, repast which might include homemade veal and duck sausage on a bed of salad greens; or a triangular puff pastry sandwich encasing shrimp and leeks in a chive-flecked butter sauce; or oversized, homemade ravioli filled with tangy goat cheese and prosciutto, in a light cream sauce flavored with sun-dried tomato; or a paillard of salmon served with a creditable choron sauce. Try the tart, refreshing lemon curd pie for dessert; it's much more restrained than the luscious chocolate mousse cake or bread pudding. If there's an overall criticism, it's that the food comes out of the kitchen tepid. Otherwise, this is a delightful, unpretentious neighborhood spot, half a block from the madding crowd at Canastel's. Dinner costs about $45 a person, with wine.

Lunch Mon.-Fri. noon to 2:30 P.M.; dinner Mon.-Thurs. 6 P.M. to 10:30 P.M., Fri. & Sat. 6 P.M. to 11 P.M. All major credit cards.

CAFFE ROMA

3 West 18th St. (Fifth
Ave.)
645-0875
Italian

13 🍳

Caffe Roma's postmodernism is characteristic of the eateries springing up all over the neighborhood (newly dubbed Sofi, for South of Flatiron). The immense loft-like dining room —awash in pink, with exposed brick, a large bar, high ceilings, and fake marble tables—usually contains a contingent of yuppies and celebrities, the prerequisite Californian waiters, and a noise level so high that even your waiter, bending down so close you can see his blue contact lenses, can't hear you. The menu is somewhat original (the owners have Chef Pier Luigi Manfroni from Perugia as consultant), and if you are patient (the service is slow), you're in for good food and a good time. Start with a salad of thinly sliced tiny raw artichokes topped with sliced Parmesan cheese in a light vinaigrette. The Italian country-style bread is excellent. The porcini mushroom soup with croûtons is so rich and flavorful, it's like drinking a good vintage wine. Caffe Roma specializes in carpaccio, but only the raw one is interesting.

The hot (!) carpaccio resembles second-rate deli roast beef, as do most of the beef dishes. The pasta is freshly cooked and the sauces are tasty if ordinary. The risotto is excellent, especially the mushroom risotto with radicchio.

Still, the restaurant's strength is fish. Grilled swordfish with olive oil is tender and moist, the vegetables crisp and fresh; Norwegian salmon has a delicate texture and is paired with a good mustard sauce. The salads are prettily arranged and tempting. Forget about dessert; just sip your espresso while eyeing the celebrities passing by. The extensive wine list is mostly Italian with some very good reds featured. Average price per person, $40.

Lunch Mon.-Fri. noon to 3 P.M.; dinner Sun.-Fri. 6 P.M. to 1 A.M., Sat. 7 P.M. to 1 A.M.; closed Sun. in summer. All major credit cards.

CEDARS OF LEBANON

39 East 30th St. (Madison & Park Aves.)
679-6755; 725-9251
Middle Eastern

11/20

Cedars of Lebanon has been around for more than 30 years, and for a long time it was the only Middle Eastern restaurant in Manhattan. The place will make you forget the sodden balls of meal you've ordered from the recent spawn of Middle Eastern fast food joints, thinking you were ordering falafel. And you won't spend that much more here for the real thing. Owners François and Antonio Hossri feature their authentic Lebanese cuisine in ambient, lively surroundings, with scenes of old Lebanon on the walls and belly dancing to live music on the weekend. Those biblical cedars in the restaurant's name are described on the cheery menu as "one of Lebanon's most precious possessions"; another, by implication, is Lebanese cooking, which the brothers Hossri attempt to serve up with a thorough, enjoyable pride. The restaurant, a rectangular room with silver wallpaper (an unsuccessful attempt at modernity), traditional red lights, chandeliers, and archetypical white arches, has a diner-like atmosphere.

As you sit down, a waiter will bring you small chunks of crunchy sour pickled turnips along with a plate of hot chilis; don't try them before ordering your beer, or your mouth may burn forever. The menu features more than a dozen appetizers. The hummus (mashed chick peas with sesame sauce) is flavored with cumin and is creamy. The baba ghanouj, mashed eggplant, has a marvelous smoky taste but a trifle too much tahini. Falafel here is perfect, tender and soft inside, with lots of parsley and a golden crust; but the stuffed vine leaves run a close second, with their slightly lemony filling of rice and a bit of lamb. If you're feeling adventurous, try the authentically Lebanese kibby nayeh, raw chopped lamb spiced with cumin and garlic and mixed with cracked wheat. Salads are refreshing and sometimes unusual, such as sliced brains in a lemony sauce; fava beans served hot with a lemon vinaigrette and pickles; and taboule, cracked wheat with an equal amount of chopped parsley and chopped tomatoes. Among the three soups on the menu, only the yogurt soup is worth a try; it comes with a very strong aroma of garlic and a touch of cumin and mint.

The entrées are a letdown. The shish kebab is overcooked, the rice watery, and the vegetables (a non-Lebanese addition) have a watery, frozen taste. The same is true for the baked kibby, large chunks of ground stewed lamb, served with cracked wheat and pine nuts. Your best bets are the stuffed vegetables, as the stuffing of rice, chopped lamb, cumin, and mint has a pleasant texture and a lively flavor. The desserts are a welcome surprise. The homemade baklava is filled with chopped nuts, and the crisp layers of phyllo are doused with just the right amount of honey and syrup. Other Lebanese desserts are just as good. Turkish and Lebanese coffees are delicious, but the American coffee is weak and the tea isn't freshly brewed. Drink beer with dinner, as the restaurant has a rather insipid wine list. Expect to pay $10 at lunch and $25 at dinner.

Lunch daily 11:45 A.M. to 3 P.M.; dinner 3 P.M. to midnight. All major credit cards.

CLAIRE

156 Seventh Ave. (19th & 20th Sts.)
255-1955

American/Seafood

13 🏆

Claire is a delight. It is a restaurateur's sleight-of-hand: the illusion of Key West in a most unlikely spot—an unpicturesque strip of Seventh Avenue in Chelsea directly across the street from a busy gas station. Inside it is restaurant-as-theater with a handsome, artfully laid out set by the great stage designer Robin Wagner. Blond wooden floors; walls in pastel blues, greens, and pinks; light wooden lattice room dividers and ceiling overhangs; mirrors; dramatic lighting; stunning flower arrangements and plants; plus a team of lazy tropical ceiling fans create a breezy and continually fresh Gulf environment. The staff in loose red-striped shirts are at once both laid back and efficient. Even the noticeable number of men eyeing each other across the table and room contribute to the Key West illusion.

All of this would be pretentious, of course, if the food wasn't legitimately good, and it is that at this offshoot of a (you guessed it) Key West original. When owners Claire and husband Marvin Paige opened in New York in 1982, they brought their head chef, Danny Choladda, with them from Florida. Danny's Thai background comes to the fore in several dishes (e.g., broiled fish "Thai style" with coconut curry sauce), and his bold handling of spices regularly reveals his culinary roots. Most appetizers are interesting: squid salad is chewy and sharply flavorful served in oil, garlic, and lime juice, and seasoned with bits of red pepper. Steamed mussels are very good in an onion-infused broth, as is seviche of fresh tuna, Gulf-style. Long Island oysters and a second choice of oysters depending on the market, such as the very tasty Skokomish Indian oysters from Washington state, have their partisans. The few pasta entrées, including rock shrimp marinara with linguini, are recommended, except that they'll keep you from ordering more from the list of 15 or so tempting fish and seafood main courses. The menu changes regularly, but there's always a varied range of broiled fish, a few types of pan-fried fish, and some blackened fish, two of which have a strong and deserved following here: blackened redfish New Orleans-style, and a Claire specialty, blackened bluefish, which is extra spicy. Vegetables are nothing to get excited about, but there are a few laudable meat entrées to balance the menu. The wine list has been shrewdly developed with an eye on the cost. Everything on the menu is reasonably priced, including the wines; most run in the teens. At $18 the William Hill Chardonnay, and at $18.50 the Burgess Cellars Chardonnay are highly recommended. It's hard to pass up dessert here: fresh key lime pie jumps off the menu and is fine; Mississippi mud cake with whiskey sauce is appealing as well. About $23 with wine for lunch, $38 for dinner.

Lunch daily noon to 5 P.M.; dinner Mon.-Fri. 5:30 to 1 A.M., Sat. & Sun. 6 P.M. to 1 A.M. AE, MC, V.

THE DOLPHIN

227 Lexington Ave. (33rd & 34th Sts.)
689-3010

Seafood

13

The no-nonsense Dolphin rates well among New York's better fish restaurants. Opened by Elio Rugova, an Albanian chef with an Italian background, its menu is both Italian and French. The large dining room, simply decorated, is pleasant if you avoid glancing at the garish paintings on the fake brick walls. Although the service is slow, once you do get the waiter's attention he will wheel out a table piled high with fresh seasonal fish from which you will choose your meal; it may be red snapper, turbot, salmon, blowfish, halibut, trout, or bass. The fish will then be cooked to order, filleted or whole, broiled or sautéed. Among the best fish on the menu is the superb broiled whole flounder. Marinated first in

Provençal herbs, shallots, and garlic, it is lightly broiled and moist. The red snapper is another good choice, as is the poached turbot or salmon, all of which come with an excellent Hollandaise sauce. All the fish are served with two vegetables and rice or potatoes.

Don't neglect the appetizers, however. The snails bourguignon are fat and juicy and filled with garlic in a hot butter sauce. The mussels, cooked in a light tomato sauce, are fresh tasting and well seasoned. The Dolphin offers a wide selection of clams and several kinds of oysters. The scungilli and calamari salad is excellent—tender pieces of octopus are marinated in a pungent vinaigrette and served on a fresh green salad with thinly-sliced onions. The New England clam chowder is rich but too starchy, and the clams are hard to find. It is a good idea to finish dinner with a salad; dessert is the restaurant's weak point. The house salad, a fresh mixture of watercress, Boston and romaine lettuce, plus some endive and arugula is tossed in an excellent Italian dressing. The Dolphin has a good, if ordinary, wine list. Most of the wines are reasonably priced. Dinner per person runs about $35.

Lunch Mon.-Fri. noon to 3 P.M.; dinner Mon.-Sat. 5 P.M. to 11 P.M., Sun. 5 P.M. to 10 P.M. AE, MC, V.

FRANK'S

431 West 14th St. (Ninth & Tenth Aves.)
243-1349
Italian/Steak

12/20

Frank's Restaurant deserves an award for tradition, despite the fact there never was a Frank. Established in 1912, this old-fashioned family-run restaurant continues to satisfy and keep to old practices. Not that it is frozen in time. Though papa George Molinari is still out front, Culinary Institute of America-trained George Jr. has been in the kitchen since 1980, and in 1987 a new 70-seat dining room was added upstairs. And these days you can order key lime pie for dessert. What would grandma say? *Mangia*, no doubt. Near the once-bustling meat market, Frank's still opens at 3 A.M. for "coffee and...," but the new dining room speaks to the new dinner crowd in an area where warehouses have been converted to pricey co-ops. The world is changing around Frank's, but the soul of Frank's remains pure—pasta, steak, casual service, good prices, and food the way it used to taste (to the degree that ingredients taste the way they used to). The downstairs dining room looks the same, too—old tile floors, long bar, pressed tin ceiling, a lazy fan, a lively local luncheon crowd who come for sliced steak, pot roast, omelettes, and deli-style sandwiches.

For dinner (or anytime), consider an appetizer portion of

good fresh pasta ($5). Give serious attention to the catch of the day and meat specials, but don't neglect the prime shell steak (unremarkable vegetables on the side), red snapper done Livornese-style, or a broiled veal chop. The meats are top quality, including tripe and sweetbreads, but it's the pasta you'll remember. You can mix and match just about anything here; no one will blink if you order an entrée as an appetizer. Wine has long been a tradition at Frank's, and the low mark-up on popular Italian and French wines and a few familiar Californian ones encourages consumption. You'll pay $12 to $30 per bottle. For the whole show, meaning lots of food on your plate, expect to pay about $35 per person for dinner.

Breakfast & lunch Mon.-Fri. 3 A.M. to 3 P.M.; dinner Mon.-Thurs. 5 P.M. to 10 P.M., Fri. & Sat. till 11 P.M. All major credit cards.

IL PALAZZO

18 West 18th St. (Fifth Ave.)
924-3800
Italian

11/20

Big, bustling, unconsciously hip Il Palazzo has been packed since the day it opened in 1987, without benefit or hinderance from the press. A throng of youngish, stylish creatures of both sexes are always standing near the bar drinking Champagne or beer and waiting for a table. And there are lots of tables. The huge room has two raised dining areas and a decor off the set of *Intolerance*—dark-green mock-marble columns rising to the high ceilings, walls made to look like weathered stone, big mirrors, tie-dyed banners. And the air tingles with energy and sexuality.

They turn out food in this place, lots of it, and the wonder is that it is just fine. Fried zucchini (three-inch strips) are crisp and not too oily. Order them straightaway with drinks from your friendly but harried waiter or waitress. The menu is a long one. The pasta is good and can be ordered in half-portions for starters. With antipasto palazzo (for two) you get hot shrimp, clams, eggplant, and mushrooms, some of which are good. There's a so-so carpaccio of beef with a good quality Parmesan on top. Consider various passable salads and some hearty risotti that can swing between appetizer and entrée. A perfectly grilled double veal chop comes with what seem to be wax tomatoes, but with very nicely grilled red and yellow peppers. Veal with vegetables is O.K., though the sauce is overly garlicky, perhaps stealing some from the otherwise tasty browned nuggets of chicken scarpariello. Some desserts are satisying, including delizia di palazzo, a chocolate and orange cake with a proper (not overly sweet) whipped cream. Ninety-five wines are offered;

the prices are good, if not all the wines themselves. Try the Brusco dei Barbi at $19, or go for Champagne like many in the crowd. Dinner averages $30-35 a person.

Lunch Mon.-Fri. noon to 3 P.M.; dinner Mon.-Sat. 5:30 P.M. to 1 A.M., Sun. 4:30 P.M. to 11 P.M.; brunch Sat. & Sun. noon to 4 P.M. All major credit cards.

KEENS

72 West 36th St. (Fifth & Sixth Aves.)
947-3636
American

12/20

General Manager Phil Nugent is an able curator of this worthy 1885 chophouse. He has preserved its treasures while bringing the operation in line with the times. This place in the garment center does steady lunch hour business (reservations a must), and with able Cheryl Kaneshiro as banquet manager, the private rooms are very active, especially with the wine trade. Work was done in 1981 to showcase the restaurant's venerable past. Ninety thousand pieces of memorabilia—including clay churchwarden pipes, theater posters and programs, photographs, early American prints and paintings, and front pages of turn-of-the-century newspapers – give the restaurant an early 1900's air. There are numerous dining rooms, upstairs and down. The street level tap room does good business at noon and at 5 P.M.

The mutton chop for which Keens is known continues to be larger than life—thick and flavorful, accompanied by its juice with just the right touch of mint. The rack of lamb is very good, as is the broiled veal chop with wild mushrooms. Fish and fowl balance the meat-and-potatoes offerings. Consider the sautéed shrimp with shiitake mushrooms, or the breast of duck with Stilton and walnuts. All the fare is hearty and filling, but you'll want an appetizer—perhaps a bowl of chowder, or snails and steamed clams in black bean sauce. Fresh oysters and clams are also available. Desserts include English puddings and the usual New York cheesecake. You might try the roasted pear with aged Stilton and plum purée. The wine offerings are more than sound. There are daily specials by the glass, and the 140 items on the list are updated weekly; many are priced attractively in the teens and twenties. About $28 per person for lunch and $40 for dinner, with wine, plus tax and tip.

Lunch Mon.-Fri. 11:45 A.M. to 3 P.M.; dinner Mon.-Sat. 5:30 P.M. to 11 P.M.; closed Sat. in summer. All major credit cards.

LA COLOMBE D'OR

Now in its second decade, the attractive Colombe d'Or is maintained with consistency by owners George and Helen

134 East 26th St.
(Lexington & Third Aves.)
689-0666

French

12/20

Studley. From the typed menu, which features French specialties from Provence and the Southwest of France, you can order acceptable food in pleasant surroundings. The long rooms with brick walls, tin ceilings, paintings, and provincial-print banquettes continue to be at once rustic and inviting. Local business types enjoy lunch here, and at dinner the chairs are filled with neighborhood people plus a very good dose of other-than-Manhattanites who want to say they've eaten at a good French restaurant in Manhattan, but who aren't willing to pay the prices most charge. In short, this place has found a niche.

Pissaladière (French onion tart), fish soup, or ratatouille merit consideration as a first course. The ratatouille, a warm Provençal vegetable stew with eggplant, zucchini, onion, herbs, and garlicky tomato, is vibrant, as is the soup (perhaps the only must on the menu). The bouillabaisse is the restaurant's best-known specialty; this idiosyncratic version comes with a tomato sauce topping. Other recommended entrées include a straightforward chicken with olives, or the hearty cassoulet (a stew of white beans with duck, sausages, ham, and whatever else might be on hand). There is also always a reliable and relatively simply-prepared fish or two on the menu, plus a steak, a duck, and a pasta—often with seafood topping—that are creditable if not glowing. Desserts are a step up. Try the raspberry tart if it is available, or the gâteau victoire. The short wine list is a good one. George has found some pleasant regional French wines with prices from $12 to $55, and he lays it on the line by checking off his favorites. For an inexpensive white he'd recommend an '85 Rully by Jaffelin ($16.50), and for a red an '84 Cahors by Château de Mercues ($12.75). Figure on about $24 per person for lunch and $38 for dinner.
Lunch Mon.-Fri. noon to 2:30 P.M., dinner Mon.-Sat. 6 P.M. to 11 P.M. All major credit cards.

LAVIN'S

23 West 39th St. (Fifth & Sixth Aves.)
921-1288

American

13 🍳

Built in 1915 by Andrew Carnegie as the "Grill Room of the Engineers Club," the long rectangular space was metamorphosed in 1980 by owner Richard Lavin into an attractive restaurant with lace curtains, bentwood charis, starched white tablecloths along with the original high ceilings and chestnut paneling. An active square bar up front features what was the first cruvinet wine dispenser in New York. Lavin's is known for pleasing food and extensive wine offerings. Though it can be crowded at lunch—it's the best restaurant in an area devoid of choices—it seems to gear up and operate at its best then.

Ingredients are superb here, so you can expect a top salmon tartare as an appetizer. New York State foie gras mousse with truffles is fine, and the mesquite carpaccio—a moist, smoky sliver of beef seared over mesquite—superb. The translucent tuna carpaccio served over a bed of marinated Japanese radish and carrot with lemon soy sauce is appealing. You *can* eat lightly here. Pasta, which can be had by the half portion for an appetizer or the full portion as a main course, is generally good. Try the linguini with shrimp and shiitake mushrooms; it is flavored with ginger, scallions, garlic, and sweet red peppers in a Chenin Blanc and butter sauce. Standout main courses include braised rabbit, grilled tuna, and grilled duck breast, all served with imaginative and winning accompaniments. You can forget about a light meal if you order dessert, and the excellent offerings are severely seductive, from bread pudding, to crème brûlée, to a flourless chocolate cake. Lunch averages $30 per person and dinner $45, plus standard tax and tip.

Mon.-Fri. noon to midnight. All major credit cards.

L'ESCALE

*43 East 20th St. (Park Ave.
South & Broadway)*
477-1180

French

13 🍴

Patrick Laurent, owner of La Ripaille, opened this pleasant bistro in 1986. In this informal (the walls are decorated with 40's French movie posters) and intimate atmosphere, you can meet friends and talk around a good bottle of wine without being disturbed. At lunchtime, L'Escale is full of local artists, photographers, and publishing types. Dinner is calmer. The food here is always good. The menu is true bistro, ranging from rabbit stew to cassoulet, couscous on certain nights, and the traditional steak/pommes frites which will instantly transport you to Paris. The Lyon saucisson, served with boiled potatoes doused in fruity olive oil, is well-seasoned, and salads, with leeks and fresh artichokes, are tasty and tossed in a piquant vinaigrette. Try the terrine d'aubergines, Chef Marcel Lattoni's own invention, an unusual pâté of eggplant accompanied by hot chèvre.

Among the entrées, the tender veal scaloppine with a strong mustard sauce is recommended. Chef Lattoni's ris de veau (sweetbreads) with port and capers has the distinct flavor of Normandy cooking. On Fridays and Saturdays, L'Escale serves an excellent bouillabaisse, generous with its chunks of fish and seafood and served with a strong, traditional rouille. Finishers are what you would find in

Paris: a chestnut dessert with ice cream, a good apple pie, a puckering lemon tart, and a delicious flan filled with dried prunes soaked in Armagnac. L'Escale has a well-balanced wine list, reasonably priced, and most wines are French. Average price per person with wine is about $35.
Lunch Mon.-Fri. noon to 3.P.M.; dinner Mon.-Sat. 6 P.M. to 11 P.M.; closed Sat. in summer. All major credit cards.

LE PALMIER

37 East 20th St. (Broadway & Park Ave. South)
477-6622

French

13

With Positano on the corner, L'Escale mid-block, and a Japanese steakhouse (with tableside swordplay) providing ethnic balance, the short block of East 20th Street between Broadway and Park Avenue South is becoming a new restaurant row in a re-emerging section of town. Le Palmier, owned by Raymond Abboud, opened in mid-1987 and may end up being the pick of some very nice choices on the block. David Shack is a chef to watch, and his appetizers and a few of his entrées are worth the taxi-ride to dinner. The attractive, airy room boasts a comfortable blond bar up front with a beguiling tropical fishtank behind it. The big dining area in back is post-manufacturing clean-up: sandblasted red brick walls, rosy mauve, gray, and white paint elsewhere, and a warm pastel carpet. Lest you forget the restaurant's name, large, thinly leaved, healthy palms abound, and as soon as you are seated a version of little palmiers—the French curled pastry—arrives at your table.

It's a stretch to call the good food here French, but that's at least its closest relative. Chef Shack, who learned his craft in New York (at the Terrace Restaurant, The Polo, Sign of the Dove, and Le Cirque before taking full charge of the kitchens at the swank private club, Doubles), builds sauces for his fusion cuisines with French technique. For starters, the coriander soup is tops, and the three cigars of wild mushroom canelloni with chive butter are excellent. The sea scallops provençale—grilled with oil and garlic and served with a spicy tomato in the center—are flavorful and prepared faultlessly. Only the thinly sliced salmon is ordinary. The fricassée of lobster with fresh pasta and slices of artichoke and vegetables is a standout main course. The sweetbreads with port wine and prunes are attractive as well. The veal chop with apples and Calvados is satisfying but straightforward and lacking the hit or even hint of Calvados.

Jean-Marc Rancher's desserts are ambitious, though overly concocted. The namesake le palmier, for example, is composed of coconut mousse with fresh dates and pineapple surrounded by an orange passion-fruit coulis. Instead choose the delicious L'Aurore, a hot gratin of pear and figs served with a custard sauce (requires 20 minutes). The wine list, as is too often the case with young restaurants, is young—in 1987 a 1986 Puligny Montrachet is already being offered—and features French and American wines by big producers such as Maufoux, Jadot, Drouhin and Mondavi. Let's hope it is not neglected as the restaurant grows to a higher level. About $42 a person for dinner.

Lunch Mon.-Fri. noon to 2:30 P.M.; dinner Mon.-Sat. 6 P.M. to 10:30 P.M. AE, DC.

LOLA

30 West 22nd St. (Fifth & Sixth Aves.)
675-6700

Caribbean

14

Lola is the brainchild of Eugene Fracchia, who used to own Pesca. The decor at Lola is simple, and the restaurant is an appealing setting for meeting a friend for drinks or dinner. While sipping an excellent Margarita at a small table near the handsome bar, try the cayenne ribbon onion rings, thread-like, transparent, and crisp. The deep-fried calamari with green chili sauce is another excellent hors d'oeuvre.

Back in the dining room, where Eugene has built a trompe l'oeil courtyard filled with flowers, you may choose from a menu that offers dishes from the Caribbean as well as South America, with a touch of Portuguese and Lola's own version of American cuisine. Douglas Farmer, Lola's chef, has an imaginative hand with vegetables, serving deep-fried parsnips, plantains mixed with red peppers, grilled baby artichokes, and a mixture of Chinese cabbage and acorn squash as accompaniments. The menu is divided between "small plates" (appetizer-size) and "large plates" (geared towards a full course). Especially good among the latter are crab and red snapper cakes, rich with crab meat, flavored with West Indian spices, tender, and served with a refreshing, not-too-sweet coleslaw. The West Indian shrimp and chicken curry, hot but not burning, is served with tasty wild rice waffles to soak up the sauce. For those who long for good fried chicken, the kind usually found only in the South, Lola's 100-spices Caribbean fried chicken with deep fried parsnips is out of this world. The honey chicken entrée here is equally compelling. Lola also serves grilled fish and meats, each prepared very originally. Highly recommended is a thick slice of calf's liver, grilled with a touch of jalapeño pepper and juniper-smoked bacon, and topped with chive butter.

Lola's atmosphere is a bit noisy, full of fun, right for the young and the not-so-young. The service is good, though the young waiters and waitresses can assume the role of overzealous travel agents full of personal recommendations.

Desserts are scrumptious. The dark chocolate cake, a mousse cake so rich you'll have to diet for a week, and a cinnamon brownie topped with homemade vanilla ice cream that tastes of the vanilla bean, are among the best. The poached Bartlett pear in poire eau-de-vie served with the apple crisp is also delicious. Average price about $40 per person.
Lunch Mon.-Fri. noon to 3 P.M.; dinner Mon.-Thurs. 6 P.M. to midnight, Fri. & Sat. till 1 A.M., Sun. 6 P.M. to 11 P.M. AE.

MANGANARO'S

488 Ninth Ave. (37th St.)
563-5331/2
Italian

10/20

If one of the old women serving the hot food likes you, she may give you the best rice ball, some extra Parmesan, or the freshly sliced, rather than recycled, bread. But if you hesitate between gnocchi and fettucine, off with your head! The capriciousness of the short, buxom, razor-eyed Italian cooks in baggy print dresses has probably held sway in this family-owned restaurant since it opened in 1893. Let's hope it stays that way. The Convention Center two avenues away and designer lofts up the ratty side streets threaten higher prices, tablecloths, maybe even waiters. So far the Dell 'Orto family has held out. The kids have punk hairdos (and are honing their cantankerousness), but Dad's up front supervising the Old World salumeria with its cold cuts, olive oils, and pastas. In back, at the tavola calda, timing is everything. Arrive before or after lunch and you breeze through the "cold" line for terrific heroes, good pasta salads, marinated mushrooms, roasted peppers and the like. At those hours you can also pause, without threat of the guillotine, to decide between hefty portions of the aforementioned gnocchi, meatballs, lasagna (regular or vegetarian), polenta, sausages, and various things "parmigiana." Arrive at the height of lunch hour and the wait is similar to that for a first-run movie. There are few seats at the communal tables, either counterside or upstairs in the less hectic but no less minimally decorated dining rooms, each of which is filled with about as good a cross section of New York as the Census Bureau could ever hope to find. A meal, with mineral water, beer, or wine, costs about $8 a person.
Breakfast, lunch & dinner Mon.-Sat. 8:30 A.M. to 7:00 P.M. AE, DC.

MAN RAY BISTROT

This handsome bistro next door to the Joyce Theater is a study in black and white, like the photographs and films of its namesake. The American Man Ray spent much of his life

*169 Eighth Ave. (18th &
19th Sts.)*
627-4220

French

13

in Paris, so the slick design is Paris Art Deco circa 1920-30, and numerous appointments are from the Paris Metro. The noise level, however, more often resembles the New York subway. With its marble floors and Italian marble wainscoting, bi-level dining and the like, the place is a bit showy in contrast with its simple bistro offerings.

But the food is good, hearty, and substantial. It looks at home served in filled dishes laid on paper tablecloths, and you won't go away hungry. Oysters are a good simple starter. Also recommended are sautéed bay scallops with escarole, confit of duck, or the merguez with chick peas (blackened lamb sausages that are at once sweet, hot, and dry). When available, the squash soup is a tasty alternative opener. Grilled salmon with leeks looks good and tastes fine. The grilled chicken with calamata olives is an attractive study in contrasts, as the dark, salty calamatas are mashed and coat the pale, moist meat. Cassoulet is a fine winter dish here, and you can get sound lamb chops, a decent steak (but only decent), and of course lots of French fries (thin and crispy). Simple desserts suffice, unless the good Paris Brest is available. The mostly French wine list is limited but affordable, with decent choices in the teens and twenties. Dinner runs about $30 per person with wine.

*Dinner daily 6 P.M. to midnight; late supper Fri. & Sat. till 2
A.M.; brunch Sun. 11:30 A.M. to 3:30 P.M. AE.*

PESCA

*23 East 22nd St.
(Broadway & Park Ave.
South)*
533-2293

Seafood

14

Pesca is one of Manhattan's premier seafood restaurants, blending the freshness and high quality one used to find in the old sawdust-on-the-floor places with the cooking styles and sophisticated atmosphere one now finds in some of the best contemporary restaurants. Pesca is generally crowded at lunch, but not so much at dinner, when live piano music combines with the excellent unobtrusive lighting to create a soft and lovely dining atmosphere that invites you to linger. The simple luxe of the decor is abetted by glowing peach enameled walls, a handsome stamped tin ceiling, and opulent bouquets of cardinal-red gladioli. Handsome primitive fish paintings and photographs contribute to the seafood theme.

For openers try the deep-fried calamari, light and greaseless and served in a zesty tomato basil sauce. Order it as a "table" dish because everyone is going to eat out of your plate anyway. Paper-thin carpaccio of fresh tuna crisscrossed with sweet mustard sauce is excellent. Cioppino, a California version of bouillabaisse, is chock-full of meaty fish, sweet lobster and other shellfish in a zesty, winey tomato broth. Broiled fillet of red snapper with a yellow tomato coulis and a spike of sweet red onion marmalade is outstanding; in fact, broiling is an art here: salmon steak, sea bass, and mahi-mahi (dolphin fish) emerge moist and perfectly cooked (which is to say, slightly underdone). There's a mahi-mahi with a sweet red pepper glaze, and a less successful one with green chilis poblanos (it had a bitter edge). A plate of buttery, delicious in-season vegetables accompanies main courses.

At lunch, the dishes to go for are the impeccable fresh oysters, a delightful tuna chili accompanied by fried sweet plantains, and Pesca's signature mussels cataplana, the mollusks steamed and served in the Portuguese manner in a tomato broth with chunks of sausage, garlic, and onion. Slowness of service between courses, early on a chronic, though understandable problem in a restaurant where everything must be cooked to order, seems to have been corrected. But the desserts, which were one of Pesca's sweetest temptations, seem to have fallen off. The wonderful astringent lemon tart, so delightful after a fish meal, is gone, replaced by a passion-fruit tart, which is little more than a sweet cookie covered with a canned fruit purée. A ricotta cheesecake was dry, crumbly, and undistinguished, and fresh fruit consisted of rock-hard melon and sour, unripe strawberries. All the other offerings involve chocolate, and the dated white chocolate mousse should be abandoned. Both lunch and dinner average about $41 per person.

Lunch Mon.-Fri. noon to 3 P.M.; dinner Mon.-Sat. 6 P.M. to 11 P.M., Sun. 6 P.M. to 10 P.M.; closed Sun. in summer. AE, DC.

POSITANO

250 Park Ave. South (20th St.)
777-6211
Italian

13 🍴

A cavernous former industrial space in an old neo-Gothic building has been cleverly converted by knowing Italian hands into an airy pink, white, and green restaurant-as-theater, full of noise and bustle and attractive, with-it young people. The food also happens to be good. The room has three levels: the upper dining tier, a mid-level tier devoted to the bar (which becomes ever more animated as neighborhood offices empty out), and the ground floor perimeter, set up with booths and twosomes by the windows. As the big room fills, the hubbub increases. If dining is your aim, the best place to isolate yourself is in one of the spacious and comfortable booths on the ground level.

Grilled vegetables (a special) are appealing. Sautéed mussels in tomato sauce with croûtons come in a flavorsome broth that begs to be dipped in, and sautéed baby calamari with fresh tomato, parsley, and olive oil are exceptionally good. Rather tasteless polenta with a gummy hunk of fontina on top is not redeemed by tasty nubbins of sautéed mushrooms. Zuppa di pesce is more pesce than zuppa—three pieces of bland, almost cheese-like white fish, a token clam, a few mussels, and a bit of sauce served on a flat plate.

There are several ravishing salads, and the pastas, which change from day to day, are all reliable. Main course offerings include rack of lamb with potatoes and mushrooms, grilled veal chop with roasted potatoes and vegetables, and a tasty boneless chicken sautéed with pancetta and onions in a light white wine sauce. In the dessert department, tirami su is a bit gooey, but the custard cake and the gelati are great. Service is amiable but casual; you will always be offered pepper with main courses, but you may be given a fork with a bowl of raspberries. Excellent wines by the glass from the Cruvinet include a rich, smooth red 1981 Merlot and a white Pinot Grigio Santa Margherita. About $30 per person at lunch, $40 per person at dinner.

Lunch Mon.-Fri. noon to 3 P.M.; dinner Mon.-Thurs. 5:30 P.M.to 11:30 P.M., Fri. & Sat. till 12:30 A.M. All major credit cards.

QUATORZE

240 West 14th St. (Seventh & Eighth Aves.)
206-7006
French

14 🍳

Primary colors are what they serve here in an authentic Alsatian brasserie/Paris bistro on New York's 14th Street. There are no attitudes in evidence; the plates are simple, the portions large, and the food very good. Owners Peter Meltzer and Mark DiGiulio have gone to some lengths to replicate a typical bistro decor, down to the Fernet Branca posters, *Le Figaro* in the newspaper rack, and a classic yellow menu card with "service non compris" printed on the side. The long, narrow, bright room has a red banquette, tile and wood floors, and a bar up front. The room is always crowded, busy, and crushingly noisy, but has a friendly *joie de vivre*. The entire menu is served at the bar, even if a table is available. It's that kind of place.

All of the staples of French bistro fare are available at Quatorze. You might start with a chicory salad with a warm bacon vinaigrette dressing, or a grilled boudin blanc (sausage) with béarnaise sauce, or an Alsatian onion tart. For a primary plate there's sautéed calf's liver in a shallot sauce, roast duck in a green peppercorn sauce, cassoulet, very fine Alsatian sauerkraut with pork and sausages (choucroute garnie), flounder fillet (grilled or meunière), superbly grilled and seasoned salmon, an enviable half a grilled chicken with herbs, and of course a steak with French fries. Desserts, big and not bad, include an apple tart and a properly done crème caramel. The wine list offers about three dozen French selections ranging in price from $12.50 to $60, all nicely appropriate to the food. The owners will probably be surprised by our rating; they'll probably say that they don't aspire to more than a thirteen, the one-toque level. Maybe so, but with a restaurant that succeeds so well with its good formula, and whose name means 14 in French, why not a 14? Expect to pay about $35 per person.

Lunch Mon.-Fri. noon to 2:30 P.M.; dinner daily 6 P.M. to midnight. AE.

ROGERS & BARBERO

149 Eighth Ave. (17th & 18th Sts.)
243-2020

American

12/20

This is one of the most pleasant and reliable eateries along the revitalized stretch in Chelsea near the Joyce Theater. Pat Rogers and Robert Barbero, who established their restaurant in 1983, aren't nuclear physicists, but they take their work seriously and succeed with a casual yet elegant place that works well within its sensible limits. The postmodern dining room is simple yet dramatic, with deep blue walls and pale wood relief.

The cuisine is imaginative but based upon traditional fare. Sometimes it misses, but the basics are pretty solid. The spinach and bacon salad with gorgonzola fritters is an excellent appetizer. The Maryland crab cakes with a Madeira sauce are moist, tasty, and spicy. A cooler appetizer is the juniper and dill-cured salmon with asparagus. The warm duck salad with papaya is good, if you like papaya, and when available the angel hair pasta with American caviar is a satisfying opener. Southern fried chicken with mashed potatoes and gravy is a solid main course. Steak is too, and the hamburgers, which are available on the lunch, brunch, and dinner menus, are very fine. Various fish and seafood dishes are offered, and if they have yet to distinguish themselves, they need not be avoided. There are plenty of choices and the menu changes several times a year. Among the good desserts, the bread pudding with bourbon sauce is excellent, and the "seriously chocolate cake" is serious. There is an intelligently planned and affordable list of American, French, and Italian wines ($12.50 to $90), with an assortment of wines by the glass, including ports and dessert wines. Expect to pay as little as $15 for lunch or brunch and up to about $35 for a full à la carte dinner.

Daily noon to 12:30 A.M. AE, MC, V.

SOFI

102 Fifth Ave. (15th St.)
463-8888

American

14 🍳

Sofi is one of the best of a crop of new restaurants in this nouveau chic South of Flatiron neighborhood, but like its confrères, it is restaurant as theater, with a stage set to make a strong first impression. The theater is a huge, high-flying affair with five giant faux-marble columns with Corinthian crowns; a narrow balcony, dark floors, embroidered chairs, and patterned carpet; and an elegant raised living room at the entrance near the bar. The cast is populated with Lavins— co-owner Richard Lavin (of Lavin's renown) and his son, Stephen, is maître d'. Michael Ballon and Dennis MacNeil wear the toques in the kitchen: the latter is executive chef and an alum of Lavin's and Alain Senderens in Paris and son of opera singer Cornell MacNeil. As the novelty of the set tires, you are then treated to a serious, clean, American cuisine, with heavy French and Italian influences. One winning meal might begin with fillet of skate with pesto and tomato salad (more like a vegetable stew in the center of the strips of lightly marinated fish), followed by a breast of quail in black bread sauce with mushrooms and foie gras, or an equally attractive roasted breast of Muscovy duck with tapenade, endive confit, and vermouth sauce. Any ice cream, and especially the hazelnut praline, lowers the curtain with high spirits.

Another winning meal might start with either the Gardener's salad or a half-portion of any of the excellent pasta, including the rigatoni stuffed with ricotta and Swiss chard in fresh tomato sauce. Fish dishes aren't yet consistent, though they are inviting and often good, so follow up with the splendid and colorful lobster Castlebay with julienned vegetables and a lobster sauce with dried ginger and shallots. The lobster is out of its shell and under a shower of crispy potatoes. They sucker you here with desserts at $8, $7, and $6, but they're delicious; end this repast with banana cream tart or perhaps something chocolate. You will get good service, and inviting wines at reasonable prices. Dinner averages about $50 a person, plus tax and tip.
Lunch Mon.-Fri. noon to 2:30 P.M.; dinner Mon.-Sat. 5:30-11 P.M. All major credit cards.

UNION SQUARE CAFE

21 East 16th St. (Fifth Ave. & Union Sq. West)
243-4020

Sometimes this place looks like a gastronomic salon: on a randomly chosen night you might find Hugh Johnson (*World Atlas of Wine*), Burton Anderson (*Vino*), and Angelo Gaja (*Mr. Barbaresco*) at one table; Richard Olney (*Simple French Food*) at another; a California winemaker and his local distributor at a third. What draws them to this two-year-old

Eclectic

14

spot? Union Square Cafe exudes the feel of being on the cutting edge of culinary New York, without any of the attendant ills—no hustle, no frenzy, and food that is good, contemporary, and interesting without being weird or sacrosanct. Smart young owner Danny Meyer was prescient enough to snag for his restaurant the name that would come to define the "new" neighborhood. He was also savvy enough to design his several rooms to be both smart and comfortable. The bar is an inviting place to sample the wines offered by the glass, or to try the variety of fresh oysters or a casual meal. There are three dining areas (the most popular being the main room, several steps below the bar), all with their cherry wood floors, hunter green wainscoting, ample space between tables, and servers who are attentive without being obtrusive. Though the U.S.C. has become a place to "see and be seen," it is also a place to eat.

The kitchen does have its weaknesses. But we have faith that the arrows are pointing upwards here and, in any event, the food is for the most part very good. Occasionally, it's excellent (at lunch, for example, you can get one of the best hamburgers in town, and the "sides" of garlic cottage fries and mashed turnips with crisped shallots are not to be missed). Mouthwatering starters include bruschetta (brown rice pancakes topped with shallot sour cream and three caviars), fried Ipswich clams, or calamari served with anchovy mayonnaise. Most of the pastas are delectable, favorites being bombolotti with eggplant and pancetta in a cognac-laced cream sauce, and "pappardelle" of zucchini—thin strips of vegetable tossed in a light tomato sauce. Grilled marinated filet mignon of tuna is one of the most popular entrées. It's not for everyone, though. A gargantuan slab of tuna, seared on the outside, sushi-raw within; its sheer size overwhelms. More restrained options include scallops (with their roe) arranged around a single perfect Spanish red shrimp on a sauce flavored with orange muscat; grilled salmon with Chinese mustard; glazed venison, cooked rare, served with a honey sauce; a sausage of duck foie gras; and tart, smoky red cabbage. Meyer is also a wine buff and prides himself on his extensive, ever-changing, reasonably priced list, including over half a dozen dessert wines available by the glass. Expect to pay $60 a person for dinner, with wine, $35 for a simpler lunch, plus tax and tip.

Lunch Mon.-Sat. noon to 3 P.M.; dinner Mon.-Thurs. 6 P.M. to 11 P.M., Fri. & Sat. till midnight. AE, MC, V.

East 42nd to 59th Streets

AKBAR

475 Park Ave. (57th &
58th Sts.)
838-1717
Indian

11/20

Akbar has been drawing the attention of the city's growing ranks of vegetarians, in part because of its central location. It has a subtly lit, low-key interior with airy white fretwork and well-spaced tables where you can always be accommodated. Service is sometimes lackadaisical and the piped-in sitar music can become monotonous, but you can put together quite a decent meal here if you order well. If you're interested in a vegetarian meal, ask about the day's special thali, a large metal plate which contains smaller bowls of three vegetables plus the spiced sautéed lentil staple (dal), a samosa (a spiced vegetable-stuffed pastry) served with rice pilaf, raita (a yogurt and cucumber side dish), and the Indian bread nan. It is good, very reasonably priced at $14.50, and you will be hard put to finish it, especially if you order as an accompaniment the onion kulcha (nan stuffed with onions). Or compose your own meal: aloo gobi, spiced cauliflower and potatoes, and the spicy okra called bhindi are the best choices, though on occasion they can be excessively oily. Any of the vegetable dishes eaten with the banarasi pilaf—made with saffron-infused bahsmati rice, vegetables, and nuts—make a filling, meatless meal with complete proteins. Tandoori chicken, marinated in yogurt and spices with a pleasant charred flavor from the heat of the tandoor (a clay oven), is another good bet, tender and moist. There is also boti kebab, skewered chunks of marinated lamb, or a chicken ginger kebab, and an unremarkable but pleasant Mogul dish of curried chicken with rice. Lamb vindaloo is hot, though the character of the spices does not come through. Akbar will also deliver nearby or by cab if you pay the fare. An average lunch is $17; dinner $15-20.
Lunch Mon.-Sat. 11:30 A.M. to 2:45 P.M.; dinner daily 5:30 P.M. to 10:45 P.M. All major credit cards.

ARGENTEUIL

253 East 52nd St. (Second
Ave.)
753-9273

Say it ain't so. Talented Leslie Revsin not pitching in the big leagues? Her exquisite sense of flavor and texture earned her a loyal following at her several stops along the way to Argenteuil. Now, presumably, Leslie has what she's always

American

13

wanted—a grand luxe setting in which to fully realize the talents and skills she's spent a decade and a half nurturing and honing. But it's just not happening. First, the setting is too Old Paris with its massive crystal chandelier, its tufted tea-rose velvet banquettes, its hunter green tapestried walls with powder blue and coral flowers. Revsin's cuisine was always spare, pure, clearly defined. The stark and workman-style artifacts from Urban Archaeology more suited her aesthetic than the expensive prettiness of Argenteuil. But forget setting. Leslie-niks come for this chef's unique way with food and, with the exception of her signature Roquefort beignets, *that* is what's not coming through.

The strongest dishes we sampled on the seasonally-adjusted menu would have been the weakest in the old days. Among such dishes is an appetizer that looks like a Georgia O'Keefe still life, a slice of cold roasted calf's liver accompanied by a mustard sauce and pepper pappadam. The flavors are firm and well-defined, but you don't understand the whole—it's not more than the sum of its parts, and you're eating more with curiosity than with gusto. The same better-on-paper feeling prevails with an entrée of veal and porcini mushrooms in a bay leaf sauce. The veal is moist and perfectly cooked, and the woodsy blend of bay leaf and mushroom comes through, but it's intellectual, not luscious. The next, middle level of dishes include dramatically presented oysters topped with wild mushrooms, artfully posed on smooth black pebbles; crisp goujonettes with celery rémoulade; grilled swordfish with gingered tomatoes; veal terrine with red peppers and wild mushrooms; a fancy, pricey ($22) meatloaf; sweetbreads with morels and shiitake mushrooms in a Madeira sauce; and homemade fettucine with lobster, mushrooms, and sun-dried tomatoes. "Glazed" fettucine is accompanied by a Stouffer-ish mix of mussels and dill. And dishes that should never have come out of the kitchen include a tired seafood terrine (garnished with only a teeny pinch of parsley—shrink-wrapped it would belong in the Horn & Hardart), and red snapper in wine sauce, too long under a hot lamp to be appetizing. Desserts, particularly a mold of strawberries, lemon chantilly and praline, and a flourless chocolate cake with (unnecessary) silver shavings are delectable, but desserts were never Revsin's strong point. There could be more changes in the offing. For now figure $35-40 per person.

Lunch Mon.-Fri. noon to 2:30 P.M.; dinner Mon.-Sat. 6 P.M. to 10:30 P.M. All major credit cards.

AURORA

60 East 49th St. (Madison & Park Aves.)
692-9292
French

16

The expensive ingredients are all correct at this brain-child restaurant created by transported French chef Gérard Pangaud, Joe Baum (creator of the Four Seasons and Windows on the World) and Milton Glazer (designer of half a dozen successful American restaurants), and everything runs together with cool efficency. Once you pass under the post-modern canopy, you will find yourself in a comfortable, wood-paneled dining room with large leather armchairs, elegant table settings and delicate, tasteful flowers. The crowd reflects the clubby atmosphere: Middle-aged businessmen with their clients and their dolled-up wives, young couples from Wall Street and an occasional bohemian just to take the edge off things.

The food is often excellent. The menu changes daily and reading it is a mouthwatering experience. For starters, the terrine of hare with walnuts or the short-smoked salmon with lentils are compelling. Only Gérard Pangaud can make lentils taste so good. The Belon oysters on poached quail eggs and sea roe are a masterpiece of airy freshness. The feuilletès of seven mushrooms, a sophisticated flaky pastry filled with a variety of wild and domestic mushrooms, creates a poignant meeting of earth and air.

Main courses are frequently no less exciting. It's difficult to choose between the excellent lobster poached with ginger, lime and Sauternes, and the yellow-fin tuna sautéed with endives and red shallot butter practically jumping with freshness. Even a simply boned roast pigeon becomes special with its savory garlic sauce, and the tournédos of beef served with a green mustard sauce and a little barquette filled with marrow vie with butter for tenderness.

O.K., this place can win raves, but it is too inconsistent, it offers up too many failed dishes to be counted at New York;s highest level. What will Pangaud do next? Is he content? Will the restaurant slowly sink a level or will he find new energy to carry it to an even higher rung? Think about it when you are enjoying dessert. And you must not, cannot, leave without having dessert. Perhaps try, the granite of Zinfandel with berries; for a heartier sweet, go for a warm tart or a simple baked apple infused with apricot sauce. If you are a chocolate lover, the warm chocolate mousse cake will bring you to your knees. Even the vanilla ice cream is the stuff of powerful memories. The wines are special too. The list is intelligently thought out with many, many intriguing bottles beckoning. Ask any of the highly knowledgable staff for advice. Now, if only the bill were not so special . . . it too can take away your breath (at those heights perhaps it's the lack of oxygen that does it). Figure $80 per person, plus tax and tip, plus the price of exploring beyond the basics of the wine list.

Lunch Mon.- Fri. noon to 2:30 P.M.; dinner Mon.-Sat. 5:30 P.M. to 10:30 P.M. All major credit cards.

THE BARCLAY

Hotel Inter-Continental, 111 East 48th St. (Park & Lexington Aves.)
421-0836

American

11/20

You could be anywhere in the world, in any good hotel. The expensive decor—club-like American circa 1900, with striking portraits plus a semi-private dining area on an upper level near a marble fireplace—is nevertheless rather gloomy. This excellent hotel chain often features fine restaurants, but here in New York the competition overwhelms the Barclay's sincere efforts. The menu, notable for its light fare and seafood, is nourishing but not memorable. Lunch is livelier than dinner; at night the restaurant is mainly inhabited by lonely guests or people here on business and careless of what they eat.

The menu is relatively short and will scare no one. Among the appetizers, the terrine of pheasant and duck liver is heavy and tastes more like a liver pâté. Its beet dressing is more interesting. When it's available, try the smoked lobster sausage with braised cabbage. The grilled Gulf shrimp, a bit sweet, are nevertheless tasty, especially with the accompanying shiitake mushrooms. The salads offered are cafeteria-style: iceberg lettuce, romaine, etc. The menu offers several soups; the duck consommé is excellent if the chef remembers to add the beets, and the chicken and sausage soup is hearty and spicy. Among the fish, avoid the Dover sole and choose the red snapper or the poached sea ray with virgin oil. Both dishes are well prepared and the fish is very fresh. The steak is tasteless, the broiled veal with onion marmalade tough and fatty, but you can opt for roast quail with excellent green lentils. The loin of venison with stuffed morels can be good as well. The desserts are nothing to write home about; the Hudson Valley caramel apple would entertain only an out-of-towner. But the wine list can add a spark to your meal—there are good choices among the nearly 200 offerings. The markups are high, though 50% of the wines are priced below $40. The 1949 Château Lafite Rothschild at $600 would no doubt make your meal memorable. Without the Lafite, expect to pay about $50 per person for dinner.

Breakfast daily 7 A.M. to 10:30 A.M.; lunch Mon.-Fri. 11:30 A.M. to 3 P.M.; dinner daily 5:30 P.M. to 11:30 P.M.; brunch Sun. 11:30 A.M. to 3 P.M. All major credit cards.

BICE

7 East 54th St. (Madison &
Fifth Aves.)
688-1999

Italian

13 ♟

Talk about hot—this place was sweltering when it opened mid-summer 1987. For the first week the air conditioning didn't work, but that did not prevent a fashionable throng from packing themselves into this big, handsome restaurant. And they've kept coming back, especially the couture crowd and associated made-up faces and hot celebs who give Bice (pronounced bee-chai) an identity. Bice's bootstrap up was that the rag trade knew owner Robert Ruggeri and his mother from their original restaurant in Milan, a commercial success and favorite with the fashion and fashionable crowd. Bill Blass, Calvin Klein, Oleg Cassini, and Gianfranco Ferré baptised the New York outpost with their regular presence.

The large, sleek room bespeaks snappy Milan design as well—long curved bar with white Italian marble, multi-level seating, expensive wood veneers against creamy walls, golden sycamore wood chairs, striped banquettes, deep green and beige plaid carpeting, bright lighting, and exquisite flower arrangements. The earthy Italian color scenes and the lighting create an upscale sense of vitality. And Bice is teeming with vitality. Everybody is in a rush, including the friendly but at times comically inefficient staff. The food is not so funny, just uneven. When it hits the mark it is excellent.

The Tuscan bean and pasta soup is garlicky and beguilingly bracing. All those models seem to enjoy the various salad antipasti, though components—from avocado to hearts of palm and parmigiano to tomato and basil—too often lack deep and pure flavors, and when olive oil is doled out, it seems to arrive either in floodgate quantities or in a mere trickle. The marinated swordfish carpaccio salad with varying vegetables, for example, never seems well oiled. On the other hand, the varying risotti (with seafood, black with baby squids, or with arugula, raddichio and bacon, for some examples) are generally all appealing. The homemade pasta offerings are a bit more problematic; the sauces are sometimes not up to the dough. At least their prices are in the low to-mid-teens and not in the higher (read: rip off) range increasingly found around town. This is not to say Bice is inexpensive. Not at all, but the delicious entrecôte Robespierre (thinly sliced and grilled beef) is well worth $19 as a main course. Properly grilled fish (salmon, swordfish, sole, sometimes red snapper), an inviting veal stew in a tomato-flavored sauce, roast rack of veal with new potatoes, grilled chicken and beefsteak alla Fiorentina (for two) are among the satisfying, if not exciting or original, main courses. Desserts are a let-down at present, excepting a cheese cake with warm raspberry sauce. The improving wine list is sound, and a good and reasonably priced Italian offering helps one wile away the time between courses. Or you can spend the time, like many others, smiling and nodding at familiar faces across the room. About $50 per person.

Lunch daily noon to 3 P.M., dinner daily 6 P.M. to 11:30 P.M. AE, DC.

BRIVE

405 East 58th St. (First Ave. & Sutton Pl.)
838-9393

French

14

Robert Pritsker obviously likes the neighborhood. From 1979 to 1982 he was owner of Dodin-Bouffant, out about as far east as one can go on 58th Street, and late in 1986 he returned to the same lovely townhouse as proprietor and executive chef of Brive. After opening with an eccentric and cutesy menu, things have settled down nicely at this romantic spot. Brive seats about 45; the dining room is narrow and opens into a small back room, beyond which lies a secluded alcove before a garden window. The appointments are handsome—Oriental carpets, antiques, burnt-orange walls, lovely flowers.

The single-page menu is short but not really limited. There are 11 entrées, five fish or shellfish dishes, and six meat or poultry dishes. Appetizers are included in the price of the entrées, but these prices can make you blink. If paying a lot of money for a meal preys on your mind while you're dining, then this isn't the place for you. That caveat aside, however, you won't be disappointed here. Try the rabbit chops "milanese," with parslied fettucine as an appetizer. The Seven Hills of Brive will catch your attention; this starter contains seven differently stuffed ravioli, the fillings ranging from artichoke or soft-shell crab to mussels or garlic. (Some hills are more worth climbing than others.) Lots of dishes will require some explanation, so you'll have to query the relatively formal, professional staff. Among the fish entrées, the swordfish with a plate of fried greens is recommended, as is the inspired "mi-cuit" salmon with the top half virtually raw, the bottom half cooked. The accompaniment is unusual but try it—pizza topped with anchovies, capers, red pepper, and marjoram. The menu changes, but the veal offerings never fail. The distinctive calf's liver "Dodin-Bouffant," breaded, topped with mustard seeds and black peppercorns, then sautéed, is worth trying. Add to that a progression of poultry breasts prepared superbly: on one menu it's chicken, the next squab, the next duck. You have few excuses for not eating very well.

The tarts, fresh berries, sorbets, ice creams, and chocolate cake all pass muster with distinction. The wine list has its merits as well. It is 65 bottles long, two-thirds French and one-third American, modestly marked up so that the wines ascend very regularly from $20 a bottle to $115 (for a '70 Ducru Beaucaillou). The list is a bit eclectic. The Bordeaux reds may be nicely aged and from good vintages, but there's nary a Pomerol to be found, and the only Margaux is the '79 Malescot St. Exupéry ($24). You won't know the producers of most of the Burgundies at all, and you'll probably not care after trying some of those wines. Prices will easily add up to $70 a person with a single bottle of wine, plus tax and tip. *Dinner Mon.-Sat. 6 P.M. to 10 P.M.; closed Aug. All major credit cards.*

BUKHARA

*148 East 48th St.
(Lexington & Third Aves.)
838-1811*

Indian

12/20

This restaurant, with cuisine described as the "frontier" food of northwest India, is a little hard to find initially, for the address is really the Helmsley Middletowne Hotel. The large, attractive dining room is done in Indian country style, plaster walls with lots of beaten brass and colorful woven wall hangings. Don't look for the usual Indian fare at this Indian equivalent of a grill. The cooking style, said to originate with semi-migrant tribes in Peshawar (now Pakistan), revolves around charcoal-grilling or roasting food that has been marinated in yogurt and spices. Every entrée on the limited menu reflects this, many made in the tandoor ovens which you can see behind a glass partition. Don't look for silverware either (though they will produce it if you ask), for here you are meant to eat with your fingers or use your bread to scoop up the delicious dal. Actually, it can be fun, rather like being at a barbecue, especially if you are a group of friends all doing the same thing. You prepare yourself by using the hot, moist handtowels handed around after you're seated, as well as the gigantic checkered cotton bib-*cum*-napkin you next receive. The latter will really come in handy; ask for a second one for your lap.

The tandoor chefs produce some terrific breads, including the astounding bukhara nan which is meant for your whole party to rip into; it's as big as a table, sprinkled with tasty onion seeds, and used for scooping, wrapping, dipping, and everything else you do when you don't have a knife and fork.

Or try also the khasta roti, a whole-wheat flatbread with toasted cumin seeds. One irresistible nan resembles a pizza; it's a flat bread loaded with garlic, tomatoes, and cheese. There are no appetizers as such on the menu, but nibbling on one of these fabulous breads, perhaps dipped into the mint-ginger chutney you will find on your table, does nicely. The best entrée is the chicken Bukhara, a whole bird marinated in yogurt, chili, garlic and ginger, then roasted in the tandoor so it is meltingly tender yet still moist. It is cut into parts so four can share this dish nicely, along with, say, the roasted leg of lamb or succulent, garlicky shrimp. Enjoy dal as a side dish. Beer is the ideal beverage for this food. Service is congenial if not always sharp. Desserts are limited, the best and most appropriate being a frozen orange crème served in a scooped-out orange shell. (For this you get a spoon.) Lunch and dinner menus are the same; ordering à la carte, you will average about $30 per person. There is a prix fixe lunch including tea or coffee for $14 per person.
Lunch daily noon to 3 P.M.; dinner daily 6 P.M. to 11 P.M. All major credit cards.

CHALET SUISSE

6 East 48th St. (Fifth Ave.)
355-0855

Swiss

11/20

Chalet Suisse is tucked away on 48th Street with an entrance that's difficult to find. The dark interior is dramatically defined by heavy white arches, and Swiss folk items adorn the walls. You can eat à la carte or go with the $37.50 prix fixe. Among the appetizers is a very good cervelat salad, quite vinegary. Marinated herring is just as tasty, and authentically prepared. Steer clear of the heavy onion pie and the bland pâté maison. The entrées represent a mixture of French and Italian Swiss cuisine, and the fish dishes are the best—try the red snapper, freshly prepared with a piquant, rather than sweet, dill sauce. Each entrée comes with a choice of rösti, spätzli or rice. Choose the spätzli, a small, irregular noodle which goes well with some of the heavier dishes. On the à la carte side a wonderful appetizer is bündnerfleisch, very fine slices of dried beef. Bratwurst and liver, and kidney à la Swiss in a wine sauce are both recommended. On a cold winter's night try a cheese fondue, a pleasant, simple dish to have after the movies or the theater. Desserts are what you'd expect: Swiss apple tart, carrot cake, mousse au chocolat and ice cream. Try instead a plate of Swiss cheeses, excellent if someone has remembered to take them out of the refrigerator at least an hour before dinner. There's a fair listing of wines on the expensive side. Average price per person, $45.

Lunch Mon.-Fri. noon to 2:30 P.M.; dinner 5 P.M. to 9:30 P.M.; closed Aug. AE.

CHEZ LOUIS

1016 Second Ave. (53rd & 54th Sts.)
752-1400

French

13

When young New York lawyer David Liederman dined at Troisgros in Roanne, he experienced a culinary epiphany that eventually made him give up the law to open a smart and stylish restaurant called Manhattan Market, one of the city's early bastions of nouvelle cuisine. Though the restaurant was a success, David went on to far greener pastures with his irresistible cookies, a foray which may or may not have contributed to the Market's subsequently uneven performance. It has now been reborn as Chez Louis (a frank homage—in name at least—to Antoine Magnin's legendary Chez Louis in Paris). Billed as hearty French bistro fare, the actual concentration here is on large portions of roasted and grilled foods. Hearty it is, but whether it's bistro is debatable; nevertheless, the small, appealing menu seems to have brought the old crowds back.

With the new name goes a new face. The black-and-white cityscapes of the former restaurant have been replaced by rather jarring red lacquer walls; the effect is bistro-simple in front and Chinese bordello in back. But the food can be quite good. For starters there is one of the best onion soups you'll ever eat, gratinéed, a bit sweet, rich, and supremely satisfying; or the ravishing baked wild mushrooms (for some reason billed as roasted) with mild, sweet roasted garlic— they are only occasionally overwhelmed by a too-intense smoky note from a brief sojourn over the oak-fired grill. Hors d'oeuvre variés consist of fresh pickled beets, roasted peppers, white bean salad, and so on, but somehow the naively fresh flavors that characterize their real French counterparts are missing. The roast chicken has quickly become Chez Louis's signature dish, a deceptively simple item never easy to find on the restaurant circuit, let alone this good. It is served with an outrageously rich and buttery potato pie—a thick crisp pancake (when it's not too greasy) with bits of garlic and parsley strewn on top. Two must share the pie at dinner, though it's offered as a half-portion at lunch. The roast poussin or squab chicken is the same though more diminutive, and comes with addictive, angel-hair-thin fried onion rings, which many tables order to nibble with drinks. If Muscovy duck is among the specials, don't miss it—moist, sweet, fatless, and perfectly cooked, also accompanied by the wonderful potato cake. Other trencherman dinner offerings include roast suckling pig, veal rib with roast vegetables, and roast prime rib steak. Fish specials are well presented; swordfish is moist and tasty. A changing variety of wines are featured, available by the glass as well as by the bottle, most well-chosen and fairly priced. Lunch averages $25 per person if you do not indulge in the marvelous but pricey foie gras to start with; dinner will run between $35 and $45 with the same caveat.

Lunch Mon.-Fri. 11:45 A.M. to 3 P.M.; dinner Mon.-Sat. 6 P.M. to midnight, Sun. 5 P.M. to 10 P.M. All major credit cards.

CHIKUBU

12 East 44th St. (Fifth & Madison Aves.)
818-0715

Japanese

14

For many years Chikubu was the restaurant always mentioned by Japanese people when asked for the best Japanese place in New York. Then located in a dismal setting on 62nd Street, the best and most imaginative food was served at the counter, but a Westerner could never get a seat there, and at the tables it was impossible to order the spectacular counter dishes without having a personal translator in tow. Much has changed at the new location, which is cleanly modern, if austere. You can sit at the tables and order any number of dishes from a regular menu that's in English as well as Japanese, or sit at the counter where the chef will create a meal for you if you say "omakase," meaning "the chef's choice." Then relax and enjoy.

Among the things that might appear when you say the magic word are a whole raw fish, its flesh chopped tartare-fashion with scallions and horseradish and reassembled minus the skin; miso soup with bits of poached chicken; morsels of octopus; an exquisite steamed dish of freshwater eel with burdock, lightly bound with egg white; a small whole grilled river fish with a green vinegar sauce; a tempura dish of shrimp balls and lotus root with mysterious and delicious batter-dipped flowers; fried bean curd in mirin broth; and a windup of delicious rice steamed with shrimps, clams, scallops, and pickled vegetables. You may also order regular sushi and sashimi, both at the counter and at the tables, but the surprise and invention of omakase is really an extraordinary experience.

And expensive. Here's how it works: you may specify the $60, $70, or $80 treatment. If you don't specify, you'll be given the $70, "unless you look high-class," in which case you'll get the $80 omakase you deserve. At a table, dinner will run between $50 and $60 per person. Lunch (talk about inscrutable) is a modest $13 to $15.

Lunch Mon.-Fri. 11:30 A.M. to 2 P.M.; dinner daily 5:30 P.M. to 10:30 P.M. AE, DC.

DAWAT

210 East 58th St. (Second
& Third Aves.)
355-7555

Indian

15

The word "dawat" means "an invitation to a feast" in Urdu, and that is the operative phrase at this airily attractive Indian restaurant with pretty pale turquoise and peach lacquered walls, discreet lighting, and comfortable banquettes. A glass-enclosed tandoor kitchen occupies one back corner, where a cheerful chef produces the naans, rotis, kulchas, parathas, and other tandoori dishes. Well-known cooking teacher/food writer/actress Madhur Jaffrey has designed the appealingly diverse menu, which includes a sprinkling of the tried-and-true—mulligatawny soup, samosas, and the like—and then a number of dishes with extraordinary flavor levels. The chances are overwhelmingly good that you will have an amazing meal.

The menu is a provocative read, best done leisurely over a drink while you nibble on the welcoming plate of airy pappadams dipped in the accompanying savory mint chutney. Starters include beautifully executed samosas and Jaffrey's baghari jinga, moist shrimp flavored with garlic, mustard seeds, and the highly aromatic curry leaves. Don't miss the dahi aloo poori, a mouthwatering mixture of small homemade crisps, diced potatoes, and chickpeas in a light yogurt and tamarind sauce. There are a number of good chicken dishes; outstanding is the reshmi kebab, meltingly tender cubes of chicken that have been marinated in yogurt and ginger, then roasted in the tandoor so that they arrive sizzling at your table. Positively super is Jaffrey's Parsee-style patra-ni-machhi, salmon smothered in a sublime fresh coriander chutney and steamed in a banana leaf. Keema matar is a tasty yet mild dish of ground lamb with peas, ginger, and browned onions. Vegetable dishes here are at a high level, not surprising for a country where vegetarianism has held sway for many centuries. Try the deliciously smooth sarson ka sag. It's a buttery purée of mustard greens, a Punjabi winter dish meant to be scooped up with the traditional flat cornmeal bread that comes with it. Or order the unusual moong dal of yellow peas cooked with spinach and flavored with fennel seeds; or bhindi masala, okra flavored with browned onions and dried mango; or the superlative baked eggplant with the elusive sweet-sour note of tamarind sauce. The vegetable biryani, rice baked with nubbins of vegetables, raisins, and nuts, is a wonderful complement to all these dishes.

Desserts are not Indian cuisine's strong suit, and are rendered unnecessary by the many sweet notes appearing in the food. Dawat, however, offers coconut or mango ice cream; the traditional Indian ice cream, kulfa; sweet cottage cheese dumplings; and lists a fruit salad sherbet which is rarely available. A refreshing cup of Darjeeling may be all you need. Dinner averages $30 per person, considerably less for a vegetarian meal.

Lunch Mon.-Sat. 11:30 A.M to 3 P.M.; dinner Sun.-Thurs. 5:30 P.M. to 11 P.M., Fri. & Sat. till 11:30 P.M. All major credit cards.

FELIDIA

243 East 58th St. (Second Ave.)
758-1479

Italian

15

An atmosphere of *joie de vivre* prevails at this elegant two-story restaurant, with its cheerful plants hanging from the balcony, and exposed brick walls lined with hundreds of bottles of wine. If you're one of the lucky ones, you'll be greeted by Felix, owner/chef Lydia Bastianich's husband, kissed on the hand, and shown to your table with such flourish that you can feel how good the food will be. Felix will then bring you his own toasted garlic bread to munch on while the waiters, never far behind, bring you the menu. Enthusiasm is the rule here, from Lydia's love of food to her maître d's mouth-watering descriptions of the day's special pasta.

Lydia is a master with pasta, as well as with her native Italian-Yugoslavian dishes from the region near Trieste. Broiled fresh porcini on a bed of polenta is unequaled in its earthy, authentic flavor. The fuzi with broccoli di rape or with duck sauce, and the papardelle integrale alla verdure (large flat pasta with vegetable sauce) are toothsome wonders. Among the three different vegetable salads served on a single plate, you will be refreshed by the pencil-thin asparagus with hard-boiled eggs in a lovely, delicate vinaigrette. The menu is awe-inspiring with specialties like roasted baby goat with fresh peas, tender calf's liver in a delicate wine sauce with lots of onion, Florentine tripe in a succulent fresh tomato sauce, Roman saltimbocca, and feather-light fried calamari. Lydia's veal chops, stuffed with savory broccoli di rape, are so thick they look like steak, and taste like veal fed on cream rather than on milk. Be forewarned, however, that the kitchen is a bit inconsistent, and the food on the heavy side in general.

The cook's hand with fish is as confident as it is with pasta. Her zuppa di pesce is light without being briny, and generously filled with chunks of fish and seafood. Try the red snapper with polenta or the monkfish with mustard sauce, both hearty and fresh-tasting. Dessert is a must, as Lydia's pastry chef vies with her for attention. The results (a raspberry tart or a mango mousse, for example), are very pleasing. Felidia has the most extensive Italian wine list in New York; treasures from every region of Italy are represented. About $50-60 per person, plus tax and tip.

Mon.-Fri. noon to midnight, Sat. 5 P.M. to midnight. All major credit cards.

THE FOUR SEASONS

99 East 52nd St. (Park & Lexington Aves.)
754-9494

Eclectic

15

The Four Seasons, an elegant restaurant located in New York's only Mies van der Rohe building, is still one of the best places in town for a business lunch or dinner. At lunch the grill is busy with financial and political power brokers deciding the city's fate, and publishers deciding what you'll read next. The spectacular dining room around the pool, with its atmosphere of luxurious discretion, has not changed in years but still makes a good impression, even if the food does not always live up to expectations. The menu changes every season, and some of Chef Seppi Renggli's creations are superb, such as curried mussels with papaya and melon, or the breast of pigeon with cranberries. The crayfish ravioli are light as air, but the delicate cream sauce falls flat and is uninspired. The Spa Cuisine, featuring dishes such as grilled fennel, leeks and raddichio salad, or wild mushroom won ton, is not as enjoyable as the classic menu. Even if you are on a diet, it's better to splurge for one night and indulge, for example, in the superb calf's liver with braised Maui onions, or a succulent pink roasted rack of lamb with tarragon. The Dover sole meunière is exceptionally fresh-tasting, and the côte de boeuf for two, a thick, juicy rib roast, is as tender as can be. The vegetables and salad are of the highest quality and beautifully prepared. Braised endives are tender and a good accompaniment to the crisp farmhouse duck au poivre.

For those of you with a sweet tooth, the Four Seasons' desserts are one of its greatest strengths. The chocolate cake cannot be bettered in preparation and richness. Luscious fresh fruit, such as raspberries with cream, are always available and are carefully selected. The Four Seasons has an impressive wine cellar with very expensive, high quality wines from Europe and California. Dinner runs about $80 per person.

Lunch, Pool Room, Mon.-Sat. noon to 2:30 P.M.; dinner 5:30 P.M. to 11:30 P.M.; after-theater 10 P.M. to 11:30 P.M. Lunch, Grill Room, noon to 2 P.M.; dinner 5:30 P.M. to 11:30 P.M. All major credit cards.

GLOUCESTER HOUSE

37 East 50th St. (Madison & Park Aves.)
755-7394

American/Seafood

12/20

Gloucester House stands like a fortress on 50th Street. Not much changes at this bastion for male executives entertaining their male clients; it is almost as if it is suspended in time. The house motto still seems to be "fine ingredients at astronomical prices." The decor remains "Cape Cod" as imagined by a city restaurant designer years ago: captain chairs at bare wood tables, and nautical motifs adding "atmosphere." Yet there is almost something refreshing about a masculine restaurant that works well (despite the poor service) and doesn't change for the sake of change.

If you order judiciously you can have a very fine meal. The soups (bisques, chowders, and broths) are not really up to snuff, so you'll do better by sticking to raw clams or oysters as appetizers. They are as fresh as you'll find, as are all the fish and seafood. Red snapper, striped bass, Dover sole, flounder, and their relatives are broiled to perfection, and if they were not served with overcooked vegetables (spinach is the exception) you'd forget the price. To accompany your meal you'll have to get by with a selection from an unremarkable list of American and French wines. At meal's end, the American desserts (apple pie, strawberry shortcake, etc.) tend to be overly sweet and served in portions big enough for two. The pecan pie served with a sugarless whipped cream will, however, surely satisfy any sweet tooth. Expect to pay $50-55 per person, plus the obligatory tax and tip.
Lunch Mon.-Fri. noon to 2:30 P.M.; dinner Mon.-Fri. 5:30 P.M. to 10:30 P.M.; Sat. noon to 10:30 P.M. All major credit cards.

HATSUHANA

17 East 48th St. (Madison & Park Aves.) and 237 Park Ave. (45th St.)
355-3345, 661-3400

Japanese

14

When Hatsuhana opened—about five years ago—it was hailed as the best sushi and sashimi restaurant in New York, the only one that would not adapt to the American palate. You could sit at the sushi bar and trust the sushi chef to lead you through an incredible experience, eating chopped tuna inside mountain potato, or small squares of seaweed still dotted with miniscule eggs. Gone today is the imaginative menu with dishes you never heard of. The sushi and sashimi are still excellent and of high quality but, all in all, predictable. Also worth tasting are the avocado salad with salmon caviar, the vegetable sushi and the broiled eel wrapped in paper-thin cucumber served with a sweet sauce. Makisushi from California, with its fake, rubbery crab, should be avoided at all costs.

Unfortunately, we have been spoiled; there are too many Japanese restaurants in New York offering the same fare.

However, if you are familiar with Japanese cuisine, can pronounce the names of dishes that you would like to have (that don't appear on the menu, such as uni—sea urchin— served on a shiso leaf), and have established a relationship with the sushi chef, you may still be surprised at how good Hatsuhana can be. Desserts here are the same as in most Japanese restaurants: green-tea or red-bean ice cream, fresh fruit (read: unripe melon) and yokan, a sweet paste. Hatsuhana has a full bar; sake followed by Japanese tea is *de rigueur*. Dinner is about $25 per person without liquor. *Lunch Mon.-Fri. 11:45 A.M. to 2:30 P.M., dinner 5:30 P.M. to 9:30 P.M. Open Sat. at 48th St. only for dinner. All major credit cards.*

Il Nido

251 East 53rd St. (2nd & 3rd Avenues)
753-8450

Italian

14

One of the first Manhattan restaurants to serve Northern Italian food in a serious setting, Il Nido still appeals to the diner with its Tuscan country decor of plaster walls and half timbering, comfortable banquettes and thick carpeting. The wine list still excites and the service is thoughtful. The food has always been first rate, with correspondingly high prices, although the static quality of the menu, unmitigated by some unsuccessful forays into the trend for lighter foods, left us without enthusiasm for Il Nido in the past. All that seems about to change. The lunch menu is still heavily skewed toward diner-type food—hearty, male dishes which may reflect the fact that the lunch crowd, at least, is composed mainly of businessmen, a traditionally conservative cadre— but if you pick wisely you can eat extremely well and even lightly. One new and ravishing dish one hopes is a herald of things to come, is the simply named insalata di pollo, which has nothing to do with chicken salad as any mortal knows it; it is, rather, a stunningly satisfying peasant dish of chunks of moist broiled chicken chunks, melting porcini mushrooms pignoli and mint in a reduced stock tinged with balsamic vinegar.

One of the nicest things about Il Nido is that you can ask to be fed, and the owner, Addi Giovanetti, and his capable staff will suggest a meal strategy, making a genuine effort to work around how you feel. And if how you feel is not on the menu, they will make anything in reason for you, a kind of personal service found in few restaurants today.

Il Nido has always served the best ravioli malfatti (literally "badly made ravioli," a lenten dish so-called for having no outer pasta), feather-light dumplings of cheese and spinach in a fresh tomato sauce. A half-portion makes a good starter.

The carpaccio (a combination of beef, raw salmon and artichokes) has the best green sauce around, but would do nicely without the artichokes. Crostini di polenta with mushrooms and nubbins of chicken liver is warming and satisfying as is capelli d'angelo, angels hair pasta with seafood. For main courses rely on any of the fish dishes or simply grilled meats such as the fine veal chop.

Desserts have never played a big role in the Italian kitchen, a fact that is only too sadly underlined in many of the city's Italian restaurants. Here do try and save some room for the excellent homemade gelati, served with a knockout sauce of wild cherries—the tantalizing bittersweet chocolate and the coconut are especially good. An airy creation of mocha, almond and crushed meringue is worth a day's fast. Fresh raspberries and zabaglione, offered when good berries are available, is a fitting ending that will set you back at least $10.

The lunch and dinner menus are essentially the same, prices being about 20 percent higher at dinner. Reservations a must. Lunch averages $40 per person, dinner about $60.

Light cold dishes, many of the pastas, takeout and the superb gelati are available in a different mode at the new racing-car sleek Il Nido Cafe, open all day (except Sunday) around the corner at 875 Third Avenue (53rd Street). *Lunch Mon.-Sat. noon to 2:30 P.M.; dinner Mon.-Sat. 5:30 P.M. to 10:30 P.M. Closed Sunday. All major credit cards.*

INAGIKU

Waldorf-Astoria Hotel, 11 East 49th St. (Park & Lexington Aves.)
355-0440

Japanese

12/20

Inagiku is a Japanese restaurant that recalls a 15th-century shrine, but without the grace of an open-air garden or beauty of flowering plum trees. The golden walls bring some life to this rather dull and heavy-handed dining room, located in the basement of the Waldorf-Astoria. The tokonoma (the altar found in all Japanese homes) boasts a skillful flower arrangement and a magnificent lacquered box. Waitresses in lovely blue-and-red kimonos glide silently among the noisy tables, attentive to your slightest wish. Inagiku is primarily a tempura restaurant, and at the central tempura bar a crowd of chefs in superb maroon *happi* coats and black straw hats fry seafood, vegetables, and even flowers with amazing dexterity.

In the main restaurant, dinner may be chosen from a sample of three suggested menus: A, B, and C. "A" is the only one worth trying, as it offers choices of both sashimi and sushi, plus tempura or tender steak cooked on a large, red-hot stone. However, if you feel secure, it would be much better to switch to à la carte, or to go for the kaiseki dinner, a ten-course meal composed around the season, the chef's mood, and your waiter's judgment. If you have convinced him that you are fearless, you are in for an exciting experience.

For appetizers, try the satsuma-age (minced fish and crab meat mixed with vegetables, lightly steamed and then deep-fried), or the very delicate chawan-mushi (egg custard with tiny morsels of fish, chicken, and gingko nuts). The beef tataki (thin slices of tender beef quickly seared) is served with a tasty ponzu sauce. Another good appetizer is hirame usuzukuri, paper-thin slices of fluke served with soy sauce and grated pink radish. The tempura Inagiku is excellent, as is the very popular ishiyaki steak, cooked on a large stone with vegetables and bean curd. Dessert is what you'd expect in a New York Japanese restaurant: melon, oranges, or green tea ice cream. Dessert in the kaiseki dinner is usually a delightful small cake of sweet azuki bean wrapped in transparent sweet seaweed jelly. The restaurant has a small but fairly representative wine list, Kirin beer, and two excellent sakes, one quite dry and one medium dry. Lunch will run around $30, dinner around $45, plus tax and tip. *Lunch Mon.-Fri. noon to 2:30 P.M.; dinner daily 5:30 P.M. to 10 P.M. All major credit cards.*

LA CÔTE BASQUE

5 East 55th St. (Fifth Ave.)
688-6525

French

15

If restaurants are theater, La Côte Basque is the Comédie Française performing Feydeau. A museum piece, yes, but fun for all that and anything but stuffy. Now, eight years after Jean Jacques Rachou took over Henri Soulé's legendary rooms—sprucing up Bernard Lamotte's murals, expanding the dining area, showcasing his own style of French cooking—the restaurant is regarded as a new classic, as stylish today as it was in 1980, consistently lively and smart.

The Lamotte murals set the mood. Trompe l'oeil shutters open onto sunny seascapes of fishing boats and quayside cafes of the harbor town of St. Jean de Luz. Back tables "overlook" a pretty marina. Merriment arises from the sense that outdoors has moved inside, and the raffishness of a fishing port adds adrenalin to the sleek-red-banquette-and-crisp-white-linen urbanity of haute East Side dining. No spa-style grilled tuna served here. The food is opulence, shameless opulence. Pâtés in every shape, design, and flavor. Foie gras, quenelles, rack of lamb, roasted duck, all garnished to a fare-thee-well, complete with balletic tableside carving, flambéeing, sautéeing, and saucing. When it all works, it's grand theater and a lustrous and happy escape from the aerodynamic 80's, simultaneously celebratory, romantic, and delicious. Often, however, it doesn't all come together. Dishes arrive from the kitchen tepid. Flavors are often mute. Sauces taste the same. Cooked-to-order may be a memory. The cold platters, such as artichoke vinaigrette, taste of the refrigerator—as if they were assembled hours earlier. And those tableside service carts seem decorative rather than functional. La Côte Basque is a classic institution, a restaurant people feel strongly about. . . one way or the other.

The best appetizer may be the unshowy fish soup. Aromatic, vividly flavored, filled with shrimps and scallops, it comes with a luscious garlic mayonnaise. Lobster terrine, however, gives a more accurate portrait of the chef's aesthetic. A pretty mosaic of shellfish, green beans, and tomato, its numerous garnishes steal the show: there's a pile of shredded carrots, another of celeri rémoulade, still another of green beans, and a minor work of art fashioned by layering an artichoke bottom with carrot curls and radish slices, the two bound with an egg-based sauce. That's Rachou. So is an appetizer of quenelle mousseline Nantua, an airy mousse of pike posed atop a three-toned sauce depicting a flower pot and plant. The dominant flavor is not shellfish, however, but long-cooked onion. A creamy, piquant green peppercorn sauce is delicious with perfectly roasted duck. Rack of lamb is treated simply—seasoned with thyme and served with pan juices. Both dishes come with a superb wild mushroom custard which some restaurants might single out and serve as an appetizer for $8. Less successful choices include quail in a soggy pastry crust with a commercial-tasting, overly-salted sauce, and a lavish preparation of scallops and lobster in sauce Nantua. The sauce is tradition exemplified, but the lobster is tough and overcooked. The best desserts are the individual soufflés, particularly the chocolate with chocolate sauce and Grand Marnier with raspberry sauce. It's a pity this French classic doesn't have a better wine list. This one, with its inflated prices, its mistakes (Côte Rôtie in the Burgundy section), its omissions of vintages and producers, wouldn't win friends in the most modest bistro. But even with its flaws, La Côte Basque is engaging and worth the price of admission. The fixed price at lunch is $29 and $48 at dinner, but with wine and maybe a supplement, you must figure $65-75 a person.

Lunch Mon.-Sat. noon to 2:30 P.M.; dinner 6 P.M. to 10:30 P.M. All major credit cards.

LAFAYETTE

*Drake Hotel, 65 East 56th
St. (Park Ave.)*
832-1565

French

18

When this elegant restaurant quietly opened in the Drake Hotel in the summer of 1986, curious gastronomes wandered in and left entranced. The marvelous cooking was a revelation; New York had a new star. The restaurant has had a few wobbles on the high wire, but has achieved a level consistently close to those opening showcase performances.

The menu is the work of consulting chef Louis Outhier, whose L'Oasis in La Napoule, on the Riviera, was long among France's elite restaurants. Outhier's brilliant disciple, Alsatian Jean-Georges Vongerichten, executes the menu to perfection in a kitchen that looks out onto the dining room from behind a glass wall. Young Vongerichten worked in other Outhier satellites, including those in Bangkok and Boston. His talents are prodigious and his remarkable touch with spices reflects his time in Southeast Asia. He's a chef to watch, and we look forward to the time when he has more opportunities to explore local produce and his own imagination, rather than replicating dishes made famous by Outhier.

There are $55 and $65 fixed price menus (minimum two persons) that change with the seasons, and plentiful à la carte offerings. Among the hot hors d'oeuvre, the shirred egg in its shell topped with vodka cream and beluga caviar is both distinctive and pleasant. The combination of fresh New York State foie gras and a chef from Alsace yields a couple of winners, including the foie gras in thin layers of almond pastry, moistened by a chilled consommé with vin de paille, and in winter a classic brioche of foie gras. The ravioli of frog's legs with sautéed watercress and the crab bouillon with crab-stuffed pasta both show a different range of skills and palette of flavors. Sweetwater shrimp with a Thai herb sauce is another recommended appetizer. Among main courses, the sliced steamed lobster with red pasta and a coral sauce is hot stuff, literally. Thai seasonings and some chili peppers add the fire, Maine lobster the elegance. As might be expected from a Mediterranean seaside chef, numerous fish dishes are innovative and excellent, as are the various preparations of pigeon and duck, such as barbary duck steak with sesame seeds, mango crepes, or sliced breast of duck with ginger and kumquat sauce. Wonderful things are done with rabbit as well. Among meatier dishes, the medallions of truffled lamb with a purée of leeks is very good, as is the rack of lamb with goat cheese.

Pastry chef Jean-Marc Burillier's desserts are all correct if not thrilling, and you get the grand show, dessert trolley and all. The homemade sorbets and ice creams are very fine, the soufflés commonplace. After a formidable meal a caramel ice cream or an eau-de-vie de poire sorbet are sometimes more appealing than a fine chestnut mousse cake or a grand (chocolate) opéra. The French and American wine list is a young one without great merits yet, but is serviceable at a price.

The room is big and plush in the international hotel mode, done in shades of salmon; it's spacious and comfortable but has an overall heaviness. It's a downer to many. The excitement here is clearly on the plates. Meals can be extraordinary, and we're taking a leap to reward those stellar occasions. Reservations are necessary, and if you see empty tables, it's by order of the Swiss hotel management; space is seemingly held back for hotel guests. Figure $50 per person for lunch and $100 for dinner, and you'll be in a workable range.

Lunch Mon.-Fri. noon to 2:30 P.M.; dinner 6 P.M. to 10:30 P.M.; closed Aug. All major credit cards.

LA GRENOUILLE

3 East 52nd St. (Fifth Ave.)
752-1495

French

15 🍳

If you want a glowing evening with noble accoutrements—flowers, art, and food—consider this once up, then down, and now solid old French restaurant. The bouquets in every nook and on every table are glorious, bigger than you've ever imagined and like something out of a Renoir. Artwork abounds too—still lifes, landscapes, and portraits by both original owner/chef Charles Masson and Bernard Lamotte, whose studio was on the third floor of the Grenouille carriage house. Nowadays the royal Masson legacy has been passed down from Charles senior to his wife Gisèle and their two sons Charles and Philippe.

On your way in you'll pass a tiered table displaying hors d'oeuvre—pink pâtés dotted with circles of black olives, quenelles crisscrossed with strips of green vegetables, salads. The menu lists both classic dishes, which have been served since the Massons first opened in 1962, and an ever-changing list of newer offerings. Charles Masson's preference for fresh ingredients led him to utilize many regional foods, such as blue crabs from Maryland, or sweet Vidalia onions from Georgia for the onion tarts (which are perfection). Fall 1987 chef Gerard Chotard was imported from Paris where he worked at Le Vivarois and Archestrate; he's expected to carry on the traditions here as well as introduce modifications.

Regulars come nightly for the sole grillée, which, served with a delicate mustard sauce, is sublime. But consider the specials. In the spirit of adventure order the grilled salmon instead, cooked quickly in a lemony sauce with braised baby fennel. For an appetizer try the quenelles lyonnaise (perfectly poached pike dumplings), the fish soup with little mousse-lines, or the chaud-froid of salmon, light as air. Savants order the crab cakes as a first course (usually served as an entrée): soft-shell and blue crab croquettes are served with a crème fraîche (from a farm in Pennsylvania) and a baby's breath of aneth. The ravioli are also good, especially the ones made of truffles and leeks, in a morel mushroom sauce.

For an entrée the frogs' legs deserve endless mention, cooked à la provençale with garlic butter. Or try the range-fed chicken poached for hours in a bouillion of leeks, carrot, clove-dotted onions, coarse black pepper, and lettuce leaves, served with the same vegetables cooked separately in a similar perfume. The confit of duck is a great take on traditional pot au feu, a duckling cooked with ribs of beef, oxtail, and vegetables. The sautéed Maine lobster is gorgeous, served with red cabbage and saffron, and the grilled sea bass in green peppercorn sauce is also recommended, as is the fillet of lamb with vegetable tian. If you want to linger in the intimate elegance of Grenouille's dining room, feel secure in trying the desserts. Some of the best, such as the Granny Smith apple tart served with pecan ice cream, have to be ordered in advance. All the sorbets and ice creams are made in-house and reflect the inspiration of the day's market—fresh boysenberries, loganberries, and huckleberries wind up in a mixed berry soufflé, or pistachios turn up in a soufflé served with a green tea sauce. Also recommended— the Grand Marnier or the chocolate soufflés. The wine list includes many outstanding vintages. For a moderately priced wine, Madame Masson recommends a 1985 Sauvignon Blanc from Arbor Crest (Oregon) for $20; Chablis Premier Cru, Baron Patrick for $40; or for a red, Château Grand Puy Lacoste 1979 for $55. Reservations are necessary and should be reconfirmed. Dinner is prix fixe at $62 per person, lunch prix fixe at $36, so with a modest wine figure $78 and $40 respectively, plus tax and tip.

Lunch Tues.-Sat. noon to 2:30 P.M.; dinner 6 P.M. to 11:30 P.M.; closed Aug. AE, V.

LE CHANTILLY

106 East 57th St. (Park & Lexington Aves.)

The luxury liner comforts of classical French dining are enjoying a comeback: for many the pendulum has swung away from restaurants as noisy and crowded as Filene's basement. The timing was right, then, when in the spring of

751-2931
French

13

1986 Camille Dulac (formerly of La Gauloise) joined with chef Roland Chenus in refurbishing this spiritual descendent of Henri Soulé's Le Pavillon, in which both Dulac and Chenus worked. Le Chantilly continues to draw Pavillon's crowd (minus the dukes, the senators, and the stars), but it is also attracting young business types. Dulac and Chenus have modernized both the room and the menu to give a contemporary gloss to a classical structure. The room works; the kitchen is not quite as successful, though it does not disappoint. Misty murals of the château of Chantilly seem to blend into dulcet pale green walls. Banquettes and chairs upholstered in hunter green tapestry with a floral pattern contribute to the graceful, feminine tone. The kitchen's output arrives with sound predictability—from the somewhat bitter and resistant terrine of duck foie gras, to ravioli stuffed with diced snails, tomato, and shiitake mushrooms, to noisettes of lamb sautéed with dill and green peppercorns, to lobster broiled with Thai herbs, to Muscovy duck with a lime and bitter orange sauce, to desserts such as St. Honoré, mocha layer cake, and strawberry tart. If you are looking for cruise ship comforts, this may be the place for you. Figure $65 per person for dinner with wine.

Lunch Mon.-Sat. noon to 3:30 P.M.; dinner 6 P.M. to 11:30 P.M.; closed Sat. & Sun. in Aug. All major credit cards.

LE CYGNE

55 East 54th St. (Madison Ave.)
759-5941
French

15

At the end of its second decade, a goodly period for a New York restaurant, Le Cygne is keeping up with the times admirably well. When owners Michel Crouzillat and Gérard Gallian moved their restaurant to the brownstone next door to their original restaurant, they expanded into three dining rooms over two floors and had things entirely redone. The main room is serene postmodern: muted lighting and toned-down peach and gray walls, misty wildflower murals, and bountiful bouquets. Upstairs, the macho executive wine room retains a medieval feel with its wood beams, clay-tiled floors, and brick walls.

Pierre Baran, chef here since 1986, has a keen understanding of game and charcuterie (shown by his rustic but appetizing country-style pâté) which provides a good foundation for his cooking. But this is not heavy food; there's a spring-like prevalence of duck and fish on the menu. Start with his special mosaique de saumon et sea bass in aspic, in which the oft-abused salmon (clobbered with sauces, grilled till charred, poached into early retirement) is treated with genteel respect—its delicate, sweetish taste offset by the slightly meatier presence of sea bass, and the whole thing glazed in an unpolluted aspic. Or try the canard fumé (smoked breast of duck served in thin slices), or the casserole of snails with wild mushrooms. For an entrée consider râble de lapin, prime saddle of rabbit stuffed with apricots and herbs and served in a light pool of strong mustard sauce. Fresh lobster with ravioli is a wonderful dish. The ravioli, stuffed with seafood and lobster, fills the center of the plate, and more lobster is arranged around it, with a roseate lobster-based sauce. For more countrified dishes try the caneton rôti aux baies sauvages—roast duck cooked to perfection so that the fat is drained away, and served with wild berries that taste like they were picked that day. You can also order small frogs' legs sautéed in a smooth garlic butter, monkfish in saffron sauce, or Dover sole either broiled or sautéed. Venison, pheasant, and mallard duck are available in season. If none of the above strike your fancy, the maître d' might recommend mignon de veau—a loin of pink veal with wild mushrooms.

Do save some room for dessert. The soufflé au citron is first-rate, the lemon tempered by a sweet dark raspberry sauce. A rich dark chocolate cake is served with a nicely tart orange sauce. Le Cygne has an extensive wine collection, developed over the years. Monsieur Gallian recommends a number of moderately-priced selections, including for white Sancerre-Clos de la Perrière 1985 ($21), and for red Château de Sales 1981 ($29) and Mercurey-Clos des Myglands 1981 ($27). Ever-popular with the well-suited, Le Cygne not only requires reservations but "gladly appreciates cancellations, even on short notice." Expect to pay $45 per person for lunch, and $65 per person for dinner, plus tax and tip. *Lunch Mon.-Fri. noon to 2:30 P.M.; dinner Mon.-Fri. 6 P.M. to 10:30 P.M., Sat. till 11 P.M.; closed Aug. All major credit cards.*

LELLO

65 East 54th St. (Madison & Park Aves.)
751-1555

Italian

12/20

Hey, so this place has been coasting a while. If you want a posh midtown restaurant with Northern and Southern Italian offerings that you won't have to scratch your head over, you got it. Velvet walls, banquettes, chandeliers, mirrors, subdued lighting (read dark), formal tableware, tacky adornments, businessmen; you know the setting. You know the menu, too (which is almost identical to that of sister restaurant Scarlatti). Yes, it can be boring, and the specials are nothing to get excited about, but once in a while this is just the right spot. The produce is always good and the preparation sound. The carpaccio is a fine starter, fresh clams have it all over the tired baked casino rendition, and the soups are O.K., especially the angel hair in broth. There's plenty to choose from. The meats and vegetables tend to be overcooked, so try to get in a word with your waiter. Scampi ribelli (baked in mozzarella) is interesting, and most of the seafood sauces are good. Try a grilled fish with oil and garlic; it's very tasty. The desserts are serious and good, and there are plenty of Italian wines that will please you. Prices and pretenses can run pretty high at what in the end is a good restaurant. Expect to pay at least $35 for lunch and $50 per person for dinner, plus tax and tip.

Lunch Mon.-Fri. noon to 3 P.M.; dinner Mon.-Sat. 5:30 to 10:30 P.M. All major credit cards.

MITSUKOSHI

461 Park Ave. (57th St.)
935-6444

Japanese

15

This excellent restaurant ensconced beneath an elegant Japanese clothing store has many fans who think its sushi is the best around, and judging from the number of Japanese businessmen who eagerly descend its every flight of stairs every day, they might be right. All seafood is absolutely top quality, defty handled, and you pay for it. There are three dining areas: a small, spanking-clean, three-chef sushi bar seating only ten (you can reserve and it does a SRO business at lunchtime); a soothing, softly-lit central area where you can dine on comfortable upholstered chairs or just have drinks; and the main dining room, now more inviting since it has been done over with softer illumination.

You can have sushi or sashimi either at the sushi bar or as a platter at a table, choosing from the house assortment, all-tuna sushi, or a sushi/sashimi combination. Futomaki sushi are slices of a large jellyroll like creation of seaweed, fish, and rice, delicious but a bit hard to eat gracefully. Appetizers include a smaller sampling of sashimi, beef negimaki, and airy tempura. Yamakake is grated Japanese potato on raw tuna fillets. Whatever the grilled fish of the day is, it will be perfectly grilled and moist. Shabu-shabu, something like a Mongolian hot pot, in which diners cook their own slices of lean beef and vegetables in simmering broth, is convivial and delicious. For quality and artistry Mitsukoshi sushi and sashimi could be the straight edge against which all others are measured. There is infinite variety in sushi—a body of classic executions and then those which follow the fancies of the individual chef. You might start with a yellowtail-scallion handroll, proceeding through incredibly sweet baby Gulf shrimp, smoked eel, and the sensuous sea urchin roe, choosing what appeals from the pristine display before you. Then, when you tire of pointing, ask the chef nearest you for his specials; you'll both be pleased. Service is excellent, as you might imagine. Sushi at the bar priced by the piece, averaging $30 per person at lunch, $38 at dinner. The regular menu runs $25 for lunch, $30 for dinner.

Lunch Mon.-Sat. noon to 2 P.M.; dinner 6 P.M. to 10 P.M. All major credit cards.

LE PÉRIGORD

405 East 52nd St. (First Ave.)
755-6244
French

17

You must try your hardest not to eat too much of the homemade bread at Périgord; it is so incredibly good you may not have room for the dazzling dishes of Antoine Bouterin, a brilliant young chef ranked *maitre cuisinier* (best chef) in France in 1980 and getting better all the time. That the address is a bit far east does not trouble the large contingent of regulars one bit. They come for Bouterin's cooking, which at its best has a singular French balance of form and content, hominess and elegance, without ever being pretentious. His nouvelle escapades are softer now, mellowed by classicism, but the exuberant creativity is still there. It would be hard to go wrong even if you closed your eyes and ordered whatever dish your finger fell on.

One of the most memorable openers is the light vegetable tart in a sheer lime-perfumed beurre blanc. Foie gras and sauterne jelly, served cold or hot, with capers, is outstanding. Soupe au pistou, a delicious and satisfying country soup which almost never appears on menus here, shares billing with a sublime cream of garlic soup, wonderfully comforting on a cold day; call a couple of hours ahead to order it. Alluring smoky grilled lobster with a counterpoint of pleurottes (meaty oyster mushrooms) on a chiffonnade of green cabbage surrounded by a sheer fumet of wild mushrooms, is one of the headiest dishes on the menu. Though Bouterin still has a curious tendency to over-truffle some dishes, he is not all dazzle; if you choose to have simple sole it will be broiled to perfection and served with a dab of mustard butter. The carpaccio chaud, quickly seared and served on a crispy potato pancake in which nestle bits of truffle one day, leek another, was light and tasty though puzzlingly underseasoned. Dieting could be painless with a menu special of red snapper and scallops cooked en papillote, with no fat of any kind, and the house's exquisitely fresh and appealing salad.

George Briguet, a familiar face to old La Grenouille denizens, makes everyone feel like an honored guest. The service is considerate and utterly professional. Here is the place to try some great wines: the cellar is very good, the prices emminently reasonable at a restaurant of this class, and it's hard to imagine food more deserving of them. One excellent moderately-priced choice is the Château Bel Air '83. The dessert cart has a number of appealing classics like tarte tatin and oeufs à la neige (and your waiter is always happy to oblige you with a taste of as many of them as you wish). The traditional luxe room is nothing to get excited about, but clever new lighting makes the most of the low ceiling, and the velvet-covered banquettes are comfortable. Lunch averages $35 per person; dinner, prix fixe, $44-62, plus tax, tip, and as much as you dare for wine.
Lunch Mon.-Fri. noon to 3 P.M.; dinner Mon.-Sat. 5:30 P.M.to 10:30 P.M. All major credit cards.

LUTÈCE

249 East 50th St. (Second & Third Aves.)
752-2225/26

French

17

Hail Lutéce, for 25 years the standard-bearer for haute cuisine in America. Lutèce *is* chef-owner André Soltner, and it is impossible to award him too much credit. Year in and year out he mans the ovens and walks the floors of his restaurant, setting a standard of performance against which all other top restaurants in America are compared. It's a no-win situation, yet most people walk away from Lutèce nodding their approval, and that's fairly remarkable, considering that this favored temple of haute cuisine is a relatively modest restaurant, not very big, not very fancy, neither intimate nor really exciting; it is simply a fine restaurant that works and works.

Why doesn't Lutèce earn four toques instead of three? It's true that Soltner can and does perform at that level—he'd be our choice for a single, all-out meal in America provided he put his heart into it—but Lutèce dishes out more than one standard of cooking. Most dinners served in the recently spruced-up downstairs garden dining room (with slate floors and white latticework) as well as upstairs (in the brownstone's more formal little dining room) fall below the level of intoxicating excellence. Now that Soltner's longtime aide de camp, chef de cuisine Christian Bertrand, has left to open the suburban restaurant he has been planning for years, it may have a few more temporary hiccups (though Bertrand's replacement, Jean-Michel Bergougnoux, is highly regarded). If Soltner could only clone himself. . . or fully recharge his burned-out cells. The menu at Lutèce, frankly, is on the tired side: if you ate there a decade ago, you'll be familiar with its classic offerings—though admittedly they are lighter today and some novel ingredients and nouvelle touches have been introduced.

We have, of course, eaten wonderfully well at 249 East 50th Street, and the $32 prix fixe lunch and the $53 dinner are great bargains compared with prices at some other places. As at the other truly great restaurants of the world, most of the cooking is done at the last minute and all of the ingredients are the finest that can be had. The bread is superb, the Alsatian specialties compelling. The onion tart at lunch, the foie gras en brioche, snails à l'alsacienne, choucroute (blond sauerkraut) with pork and sausages, fresh trout in a cream sauce, dishes accompanied by noodles (also an Alsatian specialty), all define the genre. The marinated salmon and also the cold shrimp terrine are great appetizer standbys. Order the special crab and potato pancakes if they're available, and you'll know what all the fuss has been about. The light, flavorful mussel soup is something of a miracle. The kitchen manages fish deftly, so take your pick—perhaps the salmon or bass (for four) en croûte or the special feuilleté of the day, which are beyond the range of most restaurants. The puff pastry is perfection. Sweetbreads with capers are attractive, as is the standout spring lamb, braised and slowly simmered with garlic cloves, carrots, onions, tomatoes, turnips, celery, and bay leaves and served with irreproachable noodles.

Detractors of Lutèce point to its occasional inconsistencies and failed dishes—and always to the service, which can be cold to first-timers and cool to everyone else. The service staff are old-time French and deserve chastisement. They perform soundly but are smug. Once we asked for a sharper knife, and the waiter crossed the blades of two butter knives a few times and then handed us one. Another time we heard waiters complaining openly in French about the people they were serving. The all-French wine list is arrogantly below standard. There are great bottles, including rare, old, and expensive ones, and 250 wines overall, but there are wines listed without vintage or producer, wines listed but missing, wines by big commercial outfits, wines from off-vintages, and wines of unexciting or questionable quality. Maybe 15 years ago a list like this was acceptable or even impressive; today it sends oenophiles elsewhere. Desserts, however, go a long way toward sending diners off in gastronomic bliss. The tarte tatin is a classic, and other worthy temptations include luscious and ever-changing fresh berries from around the world, fruit pies, hot and cold soufflés, ice cream, sorbet, and a satisfying and moist chocolate cake highlighted with orange. Book weeks in advance. You can pay $40 a person for lunch, and get away with $65 at dinner (plus tax and tip), but since this is one of the temples where you should worship without inhibition, expect to pay about $100 or more a person at dinner.

Lunch Tues.-Fri. noon to 2 P.M.; dinner Mon.-Sat. 5:30 P.M. to 9:45 P.M. AE, DC, CB.

NIPPON

*155 East 52nd St.
(Lexington Ave.)
758-0226*

Japanese

16

A tatami-lined floor in a quiet room, silk cushions around a black lacquered table, whispering waitresses in traditional kimonos: this is the setting of one of the private rooms at the Nippon restaurant. The Nippon is among the city's finest eating places, at its best with Japanese ceremonial dinners, such as a traditional seven-course Kaiseki menu. The force behind the Nippon is Nobuyoshi Kuraoka, a short, gentle Japanese man whose knowledge and love of Japanese food is equal only to his respect for Americans whom he believes can enjoy real Japanese delicacies. Mr. Kuraoka has imported the finest sushi and sashimi chefs from Japan. The pleasure of sitting at the cypress sushi bar in front of a chef whose dexterity will transform a piece of cucumber into a well filled with yamakake (chopped raw tuna mixed with grated mountain potato and wasabi, and garnished with salmon caviar) is beyond words. The beauty of the dish simply hints at its extraordinary taste. Chimmi is another wonder: seaweed imported from Japan with fish roe still attached to its briny tendrils.

Hot appetizers include shishamo, small broiled smelts, and sake kawayaki, smoked salmon skin soaked in sake, then broiled until delicately crisp; both are superb. Another appetizer worth trying is composed of slivers of sautéed duck breast served with a light soy sauce and tender broiled scallions which will make you wonder why you ever ate duck any other way. Transparent slices of raw fluke, arranged like the petals of a pink anemone with vinegared grated ginger and fennel, are delicate and fresh tasting. Fresh tuna, Norwegian smoked salmon, and yellow-tail set on small black trays can be followed by exquisite tempura tsutsumiage— deep-fried bay scallops wrapped in a small purse of diaphanous dough and served with fried burdock and gingko nuts.

The Nippon's chefs invented a superb and widely imitated roast beef salad: thin slices of roast beef barely cooked, served on a bed of Japanese greenery in a sesame vinaigrette.

Mr. Kuraoka also introduced New York to the kobachi: six small dishes to eat while drinking sake. The dishes depend on the chef's mood and the season. The soups here are delicate and unusual; among them, homasui, a clam consommé with sculptured vegetables, seaweed strands, and clams, is the best by far. Una-ju, broiled eel kabayaki, served in a lacquered box over rice and with a piquant sauce, is a Japanese fantasy. Desserts, too, are unusual. Try the small round Japanese cake made of rich marzipan; inside you will find a slightly tart, glazed green plum. There are also melon, green-tea, and azuki bean paste with vanilla ice cream, and fresh fruit. Nippon's sake collection is grand compared to that of other Japanese restaurants. This restaurant appeals to connoisseurs of subtle Japanese cuisine, and its ambitious formal dinners propel it a rank above the city's several superb sushi-sashimi based establishments. Expect to pay $50 per person.

Lunch Mon.-Fri. noon to 2:30 P.M.; dinner Mon.-Sat. 5:30 P.M. to 10 P.M. All major credit cards.

PRUNELLE

18 East 54th St. (Fifth Ave.)
759-6410
French

15

This heavyweight with chic decor and serious clientele will never be the champion, but it belongs in the ring with the top rank of French contenders in New York. Prunelle is owned and operated by two seasoned professionals who hail from France: skier, sailor, and New York restaurant network organizer Jacky Ruette, and chef Pascal Dirringer. An efficient staff which actually seems happy works one of the prettiest dining rooms in town. Its stunning Art Deco design, gorgeous flower arrangements, and subdued lighting help create an atmosphere of low-key elegance. When the restaurant opened in 1983, its pricey fixed lunch and dinner menu convinced people they were paying, literally, for the decor. Today the $34 lunch or $52 dinner doesn't raise many eyebrows.

The Dirringer team performs at a high level—though the seafood appetizer, the smoked fish, and the gravlax of salmon are hardly inspired. Concentrate on the light lobster ravioli, the sweetbreads with leeks, or the tasty snails with basil. Among the entrées, seafood is a clear winner. Monkfish, Dover sole, swordfish, or lobster are cooked properly and served with various baby vegetables and light but flavorful sauces. A wonderful and unusual luncheon entrée is a moist cheese soufflé with dried tomatoes. The perfectly cooked rack of lamb, the buttery Black Angus steak, or the crisp duck confit are good meat dishes and are served in big, old-fashioned portions. The dessert cart is appealing albeit not overly imaginative. The apple tart and most other fruit tarts are recommended, as are lemon selections (soufflé, meringue tart) and the rich chocolate cake. The essentially French wine list is extensive, with 40 of the 220 choices priced under $30. Jacket and tie are required for men, and reservations are in order for everyone. Even with one of the less expensive wines, prepare to pay $45 per person at lunch and $70 at dinner, plus tax and tip.

Lunch Mon.-Fri. noon to 3 P.M.; dinner daily 5:30 P.M. to 11 P.M. All major credit cards.

OYSTER BAR & RESTAURANT

Grand Central Station (Lower level) 42nd St. & Vanderbilt Ave.
490-6650/51; 490-6653 (saloon)

American/Seafood

15

This place has to be seen to be believed. The cavernous main dining room in Grand Central Station just off a main entrance to the train tracks boasts acres of tables under a colossal vaulted ceiling of sand-colored tiles. A look at what is on those tables will reveal a wide selection of some of the freshest fish to be found in America. "What we serve today was swimming yesterday" might be the motto for what has become in the last decade a renowned New York restaurant. A couple of thousand meals are served here each weekday, a mere level away from the comic frenzy of dashing commuters and thundering trains of Grand Central Station. This is New York with all of its extremes—and it is very good indeed.

The menu is a bit long. It is redone daily to include the day's catch, which averages about 30 creatures fished out of the sea, stream, lake, or river: grouper, lotte, mahi-mahi, pompano, sturgeon, tilefish, wolfish, just name it. A dozen or so varieties of oysters are sold by the piece—all are as fresh as can be, and generally make exquisite appetizers. The milky New England clam chowder gets the nod over the Manhattan version, with Maryland she crab soup for the curious. With fish this fresh, a simple preparation (grilled, fried, meunière) often flatters the fish most and is a safe choice. Any of the pan-roasted shellfish, done following the Oyster Bar's classic preparation, is delicious. And in a city where standout bouillabaisse is becoming widely available, here it is uncommonly good. The all-American wine list offers plenty of excellent, nicely priced choices kicking in at about $10 a bottle and burning out at $55. The hundred or so wines have been judiciously selected, but it will take many visits to the Oyster Bar before you'll find a really exciting American wine. Daily wine specials are cited on the menu as well. The good, hefty desserts weigh in as all-Americans, too: apple pies and tarts, cheesecake, carrot cake, rice pudding, fresh fruits, and the obligatory assortment of chocolate concoctions.

If the fast-paced, noisy playing fields of the main dining room are not to your liking, there's a separate den of a saloon with a nautical motif that's a tad less noisy and on a slightly more human scale. If you are alone or in a hurry, you can eat along the Oyster Bar counters and watch the cooks shucking oysters and preparing the oyster stews. As incredible as it may sound for a restaurant of this size, reservations are a necessity for lunch. Figure on $45 a person.

Lunch & dinner Mon.-Fri. 11:30 A.M. to 9:30 P.M. (last seating). All major credit cards.

THE PALM

837 Second Ave. (44th St.)
687-2953

American/Steak

11/20

Walking across the sawdust-strewn floor of this steakhouse, you will feel you are in an aggressively staged scene from a 1950's that never was. No 50's patron would stand for the rudeness and crudeness of the grimy and gloomy 80's Palm, yet this contemporary crowd doesn't seem to expect more. There is no menu. The waiters rattle off only the most traditional dishes such as lobsters (boiled, broiled), steaks, rib roast. If you want something else, you must then ask for more information. You might hear about the veal chops (very good) or double lamb chops. Vegetables are represented solely by a dish of creamed spinach as watery as it used to be 20 years ago. If ordered broiled, the four-pound lobsters are too often dry; boiled, they are a moist, fresh sea feast. Sirloin? Large and tender but not always very flavorful. On the other hand, rib roast, about three inches thick, is magnificent, with its deep-roasted brown outside becoming pink and then juicy red as you near its center—by far the best dish on the menu. Stale, overdone fried potato chips, served with fried onions, is the traditional side order here. A salad made from oil-drenched iceberg lettuce and soapy tomato wedges is to be avoided. "Just like it always was," is the explanation. After the rib roast go to Patisserie Lanciani for dessert and coffee or go home. It must be said, however, that many people enjoy the Palm and consider it one of New York's top steakhouses. There is a full bar with a short wine list with Californian wines and some not too great French ones. Good beer on tap. Palm Two, across from Palm #1 on the east side of Second Avenue, is a faithful replica. Price per person with drinks, $60.

Lunch Mon.-Fri. 11:30 A.M. to 5 P.M., dinner Mon.-Sat. 5 P.M. to 11:30 P.M. All major credit cards.

THE QUILTED GIRAFFE

A.T.&T. Building, 550 Madison Ave. (55th & 56th Sts.)
593-1221

Eclectic

17 🦒🦒🦒

The Quilted Giraffe is so pretentious that it would be comical were it not for the huge bill presented at the end of the meal. It's hard to laugh when you're about to drop three hundred bucks for a dinner for two. But that's putting the cart before the horse; let's start from the top. Once upon a time there lived a Quilted Giraffe in a handsome midtown townhouse on Second Avenue. Said Giraffe gave birth to a Casual Quilted Giraffe that lived in a restaurant that looked like a designer cookie shop, located in the arcade of the A.T.&T. building. The prices were anything but casual, and the place got clobbered by would-be critics on all fronts. The offspring died in infancy, but owners, Susan and Barry Wine, moved the Quilted Giraffe into its high-tech digs. Remnants of the troubled Casual Quilted live on in the fixed price lunches ($40 and $65). At lunch we've been able to order such things as celery soup with lobster, seared beef with endive, fettucine with lobster and poached chicken, grilled vegetable salad, swordfish served cold with basil-scented tomato compote, tuna steak, broiled rack of lamb with Chinese mustard, as well as some concoctions that are more or less unintentional culinary lampoons. The good food has a solid chance to attract big business account customers for a midday meal. Things are like old times in the evening, though, minus some of the charm and intimacy.

At dinnertime, tables wear tablecloths and all the serving people in their black dinner jackets look uncomfortable— and their discomfort is contagious. Everything on the menu is described to you by those hovering penguins, including the cheeses. "This cheese gets its blue-green veining from the mold in the caves in which it ages" (Roquefort). This is only one clue that the management considers everyone unknown to them an innocent, or perhaps an idiot. An underlying contempt for the diner is manifested in all this fussing and description. Instead of feeling cosseted and well cared for, you feel abused. So what's all the fuss been about? The food—which at dinnertime is excellent. It can be ordered from a $75 prix fixe menu—though many of the famous specialties bear a hefty supplement—or via a $100 tasting menu.

Choosing a tasting menu not only gives you a chance to try a lot of things but is the best way to escape paying the $30 surcharge for the caviar beggar's purses on the regular menu. The most extravagant item here (actually developed in France by François Clerc at La Vieille Fontaine in Maison-Laffitte decades ago), they consist of a dollop of fine beluga caviar dropped into a little sack that looks just like a moneybag. You should try this appetizer once, thereafter try the spicy breast of duck with relishes and/or the veal kidneys with homemade white fettucine. The wild mushroom and truffle soup is marvelous. The house smoked salmon is fresh Norwegian, nicely cured on the premises.

Inventiveness prevails over the entrées and desserts as well, and few could ever fault Barry Wine (who is the executive chef as well as co-owner) for lack of originality. The lobster and scallops in sauternes sauce is cooked with, "instead of white wine, sauternes, which is a much sweeter wine, which gives it a very nice flavor more in harmony with the seafood," quoteth the waiter. Calf's liver is given new life here: slices are coated with a breading made of crushed pine nuts, pistachios, and almonds, sautéed until the crust gets brown and served with a sherry-vinegar sauce. The coating on the rack of lamb—a Chinese mustard sauce—is similarly divine. Veal scaloppine with soft polenta and truffles is quite good, even if the word soft is redundant for this yellow Italianate version of congealed cream of wheat.

For dessert consider bypassing the good and tempting cheese cart even though it comes with the package (unless you desire a lecture) and head straight for the ginger mousse Napoleon with glazed pear. The filling is dreamily light, the pastry as flaky as ancient parchment. Other desserts are all-American, such as delectable pecan squares, or hazelnut waffles with vanilla ice cream. The computerized wine list is outstanding, displaying depth, breadth, shrewd selections, and Tiffany price tags. Dinner reservations are necessary, the sooner the better. Jacket and tie are required for gentlemen at all times except Saturday lunch. Expect to pay $70 for lunch and $100-150 for dinner, plus tax and tip.
Lunch Tues.-Sat. 11:30 A.M. to 3 P.M.; dinner Mon.-Sat. 5:30 P.M. to 10:30 P.M. AE, MC, V.

Rosa Mexicano

1063 First Ave. (58th St.)
753-7407

This upscale Mexican eatery with pink stuccoed walls and arches, machine-carved wood chairs, and an open grill in the front room (the livelier of the two dining areas) could be located in Anywheresville, U.S.A. The crowd it attracts

Mexican

11/20

seems to consist of citizens in good standing from the same town. Generally considered one of the best Mexican restaurant in the city—which may be damning with faint praise—Rosa Mexicano often promises more than it delivers. The executive chef, Josefina Howard, is trained, knowledgeable, and creative, and it is reasonable to expect a lot from her kitchen. Her menu, which introduces such dishes as menudo (a spicy tripe stew) and pozole (a stew based on pork and hominy), not usually seen around town, fuels expectations.

But for all its potential, Rosa Mexicano can be disappointing. Even the made-to-order guacamole is an anticlimax. Though it is still made tableside from separate bowls of crinkly-skinned avocados, chopped onions, chiles, cilantro, and tomatoes, it is fine but no longer stellar, and the waiters seem to ignore requests for "spicy" as opposed to "mild." However, one of the tastiest appetizers, taquito de tinga poblana, shows what the kitchen is capable of doing. Coarse tortillas with the distinctive taste of masa harina enwrap a fiery blend of shredded pork, smoked chipotle chile, onions, and tomatoes. Enchiladas filled with chicken are a notch above average due to a mole sauce that is more subtle than the one-note, fudgy moles usually encountered in New York. Mixiote de tlaxcala, a traditional method of cooking meats in agave leaves, is here accomplished with parchment. Chicken or lamb is coated with chiles, spices, and beer, placed in the parchment, and oven-braised. Much ado about nothing, it seems, for the chicken thigh is often as dry as terry cloth. The small wine list is largely ignored in favor of Mexican beers, classic Margaritas, and the house Margarita with pomegranate juice. Dinner for one, with beer or drinks, comes to about $45.

Lunch Mon.-Sat. noon to 3:30 P.M., dinner nightly 5 P.M. to midnight.; buffet Sun. noon to 3 P.M. All major credit cards.

SANDRO'S

420 East 59th St. (First Ave. & Sutton Pl.)
355-5150

Italian

14

Take a look at Sandro. If he doesn't inspire confidence, nothing will. This tall, robust chef of Rabelaisian proportions and appetite has limitless energy in the kitchen (and elsewhere, it seems, since by his own account he has had six wives). Brought to Manhattan from his restaurant in Castelli, near Rome, by restaurant impresario Tony May (Palio, La Camelia), Sandro is the perfect emissary to win hearts and minds to the gastronomic specialties of the Roman kitchen. Certainly the reason to dine here is to savor his uncompromising renditions of that lusty cuisine.

Start with carciofi alla giudia (artichokes Jewish-style).

Deep-fried in corn oil until they flower like roses, the baby artichokes are delicious and addictive artichoke chips. Equally irresistible is the fried ricotta. Moist and creamy on the inside, its egg and breadcrumb coating is crisp and greaseless, its fresh, light tomato sauce a zingy accompaniment. Pungent salads of puntarelle clear the palate for hearty stews and roasts. Roast pork Roman style, seasoned with wild fennel, garlic, and fresh rosemary and doused with olive oil is so delectable it could be banned by the Vatican. Oxtail stew with celery, carrots, onion, and pancetta is equally brawny and delicious. When Sandro errs it's either on the side of blandness (a "special" salad of tepid salt cod and disks of polenta) or on the side of pleasing the general public with pan-Italian standards (veal marsala and company) which interest neither him nor the consumer—although his carpaccio with julienned vegetables, lots of lemon, olive oil, and slivers of Parmesan is about as good as this dish gets.

Now for the downside: location and tariff. First, Sandro's is located on the ground floor of a highrise that is both unfortunate in its look (anonymous) and in its location (way, way east). As for the prices, a plate of pasta for $16 or lamb stew for $22 still seem daunting. In a perfect world Tony May would transfer the rustic and handpainted plates and mugs, the communal table (a fabulous, if underutilized, concept), and Sandro's homemade grappas (they're actually sweet and flavored with fruits such as pear, strawberry, and banana) to a more centrally located and casual home, scale down the prices, eliminate the veal marsala and *let Sandro be Sandro*. Dinner, with a moderately priced wine, averages $60 per person, plus normal tax and tip.

Lunch Mon.-Fri. noon to 3 P.M.; dinner Mon.-Sat. 5 P.M. to 11 P.M. All major credit cards.

SAN GIUSTO

935 Second Ave. (49th & 50th Sts.)
319-0900

Italian

13 🍳

San Giusto was born of two Italians: a chef, Gino Martincich, and a maître d', Bruno Viscovich. Both come from the same Italian enclave of Yugoslavia, and both have not only a great love of fine cuisine, but take immense pleasure in seeing their guests enjoy the food. San Giusto is an elegant restaurant with excellent service and the careful, jovial Bruno is everywhere at once. The best way to order is to put yourself in his hands and let him order for you. He may start you off with prosciutto e peperoni gialli, the best homemade prosciutto in New York, served with marinated yellow peppers that melt in your mouth; or with airy mozzarella fritta; or, when in season, carciofo ripieno, a whole stuffed artichoke, redolent of garlic and Parmesan cheese with strong olive oil. Gino is a giant when it comes to risotto and there are several on the menu. Risotto with mushrooms (or white truffles) is creamy and rich with the flavor of earthy fungi. The gnocchi with meat ragout or with fresh tomato sauce brings cries of sheer delight from the customers. Among the fish and seafood dishes, the best are large, tender sautéed shrimps in a garlic butter with some sherry, and a poached salmon coated with fresh tomato coulis. If you are in the mood for meat, the roasted squab with polenta in a light herb sauce is succulent, as is the breast of chicken with white truffles. The sweet Italian sausages cooked with porcini mushrooms and polenta is a hearty combination that will take you back to the Italian countryside. Every night there are specials. If you are offered risotto with black ink, don't turn it down! Enjoy it with one of San Giusto's salads or a whole escarole head smothered in fragrant olive oil and garlic. Desserts are heavy Italian; consider the sorbets or the fresh fruit. The wine list is extensive, well-composed, and reasonably priced. Price per person with wine is $50.

Lunch Mon.-Sat. noon to 3 P.M.; dinner Mon.-Thurs. 5 P.M. to 11 P.M., Fri. & Sat. till 11:30 P.M. All major credit cards.

SCARLATTI

34 East 52nd St. (Madison & Park Aves.)
753-2444

Italian

13

Good restaurants are often an extension of a person or a family; Scarlatti *is* owner and host Raphael "Lello" Arpaia. After succeeding with Restaurant Lello, he launched his idea of a *luxe* counterpart to a solid, traditional, upscale midtown French restaurant. Without host Lello in the room, though, Scarlatti is all posh and glitzy surface; it loses its room-filling personality. The Art Nouveau reception area contrasts (to say the least) with the music of Scarlatti. This place is really heavy Italian opera.

Lello can crank the kitchen up a notch for you, and can enchant with specials. The produce here is good, and the large printed menu includes specialties from many Italian regions: the familiar antipasti, soups, pastas, rice dishes, fish, chicken, veal, or other meat dishes, as well as grilled meats. You might start with crostini di mozzarella, the luscious seafood salad (cool slivers of squid and shrimp and other seafood items), or a half-portion of a good pasta, perhaps the malfatti con carciofi (artichokes). Veal medallions with garlic, tomato, and mushrooms is something of a house specialty as a main course. A good shrimp scampi ribelli (baked in mozzarella), or a healthy veal chop are alternatives. Decent if unremarkable wines go along with all this, and good desserts are on hand, including a zabaglione prepared at your table by a captain who separates the eggs, whisks them over a flame, and delivers the hot froth to you. This place is large part show, with steady if unspectacular cuisine and Broadway prices. Lunch will run at least $35 and dinner $45 per person.

Lunch Mon.-Fri. noon to 3 P.M.; dinner Mon.-Thurs. 5:30 P.M. to 10:30 P.M., Fri. & Sat. till 11 P.M. All major credit cards.

SERYNA

11 East 53rd St. (Madison Ave.)
980-9393
Japanese

13

Discreetly planted in one of Madison Avenue's highrises, Seryna is packed at lunch with Japanese businessmen, their American clients, and advertising execs watching their weight. At night the restaurant is quieter and the service more pleasant. Although this eatery has a good sashimi bar, it only serves sashimi and sushi as an appetizer or an afterthought. The restaurant's forte is steak of the highest quality, cut paper-thin and served raw, accompanied by a delicate dipping sauce made with soy, garlic, and apples. Ishiyaki steak, tender filet mignon sizzled on a hot stone that absorbs all the fat, is another specialty. Served with two dipping sauces, a hot chili sauce or a garlic soy sauce, the meat is superb, but the portion is small, so it's advisable to order a soup and an appetizer as well, or you may find yourself wanting pizza an hour after you finish dinner.

Shabu-shabu, a dish served in most Japanese restaurants, has panache here. More paper-thin slices of beef plus various vegetables and noodles come to the table arranged next to a copper pot of steaming hot broth. You poach the beef to your taste and dip it in sesame sauce; the vegetables are then added to the broth with the noodles and dipped in a soy and lime sauce. Among the appetizers, the chawan-mushi, a lightly steamed egg custard filled with delicious chunks of chicken, shrimp, and gingko nuts, should not be missed. The crab kohra-age is also good—a huge crab shell stuffed with crab meat in a light white sauce, then fried. The crab, like most dishes on the menu, is served with a tangy sauce. One of the nicest side dishes is shiso rice, steamed rice which has been spiced with salted Japanese plums, sesame seeds, crushed bonito, and chopped shiso leaves (a very fragrant member of the mint family). Dessert offerings are sparse; you can stick to melon and ice cream. The restaurant offers several sakes and a short and expensive wine list. Dinner for one with wine runs $45-50.

Lunch Mon.-Fri. noon to 2 P.M.; dinner Mon.-Fri. 5:30 P.M. to midnight, Sat. 6 P.M. to midnight. All major credit cards.

SHUN LEE PALACE

155 East 55th St. (Third & Lexington Aves.)
371-8844

Chinese

14 👨‍🍳

This is a good uptown Chinese restaurant's answer to Western elegance. The spacious dining room is tightly packed with tables, its walls covered with ancient Chinese motifs and beautiful paintings. The table is set European-style and the maître d' wears evening clothes. With all the waiters rushing about, it's hard to imagine why the service is slow.

The food can be excellent. There are reliable nightly specials reflecting both Cantonese and Szechuan cuisine. The cold appetizers are more interesting than the hot ones. Start with crunchy honey-glazed walnuts, followed by slices of lean and smoky cold duck served with a pungent Hunan sauce. Won tons floating in a rich duck broth are light and tasty, though the hot-and-sour soup belongs in a cafeteria. Shun Lee Palace has a few unusual dishes, such as stir-fried sweetbreads with hot peppers, and frogs' legs with black Chinese mushrooms and scallions in a ginger sauce with black beans, similar to the French version and you won't miss the garlic. The Szechuan tripe with scallions and pork is served in a hot and peppery sauce with a faint touch of vinegar. The menu offers several well-prepared, standard Chinese dishes of poultry and fish, and a few noodle dishes.

It's a good idea to ask the waiter to describe the sauces when ordering, as the restaurant has a tendency to serve too many dishes with the same brown sauce. Be forewarned, too, that the chef may at times have a heavy hand with monosodium glutamate. The menu lists several desserts, but they are rarely available. You'll have better luck with something off the extensive wine list. The overall high quality and ambiance have their justifiable price: here it averages about $40 per person.
Lunch daily noon to 3 P.M.; dinner nightly 3 P.M. until about 11 P.M. AE, DC.

SMITH & WOLLENSKY

201 East 49th St. (Third Ave.)
753-1530

American/Steak

13 👨‍🍳

After he purchased the old Manny Wolf's steakhouse in 1977, it took Alan Stillman some time to bring things up to bearable standards. He changed the name, renovated the several dining rooms and the bar, and produced a sort of tailored impersonation of a steakhouse. Even the waiters have manners. People who don't like sawdust under their shoes frequent this place and sing its praises. It also attracts a sports-minded crowd. Certainly for steak and chops (and maybe Ester's pecan pie) Smith & Wollensky is fine, and you can get O.K. grilled fish and humongous lobsters.

Lately what has distinguished S&W and made it a destination restaurant is its sensational wine list. It seems people who order $25 steaks don't drink cheap wines. There are great old vintages and big bottles here from France and California. There are good values at the high price end: Haut Brion '61 and Pétrus '66 are $255, and some of the '82 Bordeaux—perhaps listed prematurely among the 550 offerings—are at prices below current retail. Closer to earth are the bottles and bottles of Robert Mondavi cabernet the restaurant sells, starting at $27 for the 1981 and working up to $155 for an unfined '68. Waiters are versed in wine etiquette, and there is a full-time cellar master on hand to chew the grape with sophisticated palates. Expect to pay $45 or so per person, without a rare wine.

Mon.-Fri. noon to midnight, Sat. & Sun. 5 P.M. to midnight. All major credit cards.

SPARKS STEAKHOUSE

210 East 46th St. (Second & Third Aves.)
687-4855

American/Steak

13

When mobster Paul Castellano was rubbed out on the street in front of Sparks, it was not a bad thing for business. If anything, it added to the macho, larger-than-life image of this big joint. The large dining rooms continue to be filled with he-man business types doing some serious eating here at lunch: they return from the suburbs with the family on weekends or for dinner.

In terms of fine dining, this is not it. But there is no faulting the unadorned prime sirloin or the juicy filet mignon, the lamb chops, or the charred veal chop. Within the genre of old-style New York steakhouse there are a handful of prime choices, and Sparks is one of them. Recently there has been more than a lip-service commitment here to fish as well. You can now always get half-a-dozen fish fillets. Grilled swordfish or tuna steaks are good, and red snapper and trout are prepared effectively. And of course there is always lobster, which comes in three sizes that could be dubbed not-so-small, pretty big, and man-eating. Appetizers are pretty standard. Naturally, you eat cheesecake for dessert, or perhaps chocolate-covered tartuffo ice cream. The award-winning wine list is enormous, and even if you don't subscribe to *The Wine Spectator*, you'll be able to spot familiar and inviting names and vintages. Bullet-proof vests are not required. Expect to pay $55 or so per person.

Lunch Mon.-Fri. noon to 3 P.M.; dinner Mon.-Thurs. 5 P.M. to 11 P.M., Fri. & Sat. till 11:30 P.M. All major credit cards.

TOSCANA

200 East 54th St. (Second & Third Aves.)
371-8144
Italian

11/20

The excitement here is largely architectural. After a comfortable and successful 11 years on the corner of 54th and Second, in mid-1987 Toscana moved a couple hundred feet to a 7,700 square-feet space in the "lipstick building," the elliptical Philip Johnson and John Burgee structure. Everything inside the relocated restaurant is striking Milan high style: curvilinear pearwood and Carrara marble floor, walls of imitation gray slate, a lofty skylight decorated with undulating blue-green glass strips, asymmetrical (and uncomfortable) chairs made of burlwood and black leather. The room is asymetrical as well. Up front there is a bar and grill that features light Tuscan fare (soups, salads, pasta, grilled light entrées). The big dining room in the back is the place for hearty main courses.

This is one of those places where you know you could eat well if only the waiters would steer you to the right dishes. But to them, everything is wonderful. We'll try to do better. Thick and hearty Tuscan bean soup makes a good beginning, and the carpaccio of beef with shards of Parmesan cheese is a safe choice. The marinated salmon and smoked raw swordfish are odd appetizers to find on an Italian menu, and not worth exploring. The vitello tonato *is*—extra thick veal with a tuna cream sauce. The pricey pasta could be much better, but as a curiosity try the ravioli à la fornariana, a single ravioli stuffed with raw egg, asparagus, and artichoke, served with raw vegetable sauce. The risotto with provola (a Tuscan cheese) and escarole could use some more escarole, and the fish stew with shallots barely suggests a stew. Fillet of veal with baby vegetables and lamb sautéed in olive oil with thyme, served on a thin crust of potatoes, are passable; sweetbreads prove very good. Desserts, no. The wine list, Italian with some American wines and French Champagnes, is sound. Prices to match the decor. Expect to pay $50-60 for lunch or dinner in the main dining room, and less up front. *Lunch daily noon to 3 P.M.; dinner Mon.-Sat. 5:30 P.M. to 10:30 P.M. All major credit cards.*

TRE SCALINI

230 East 58th St. (Second & Third Aves.)
688-6888
Italian

12/20

You'd think by now the management would have gotten around to renovating or redecorating the suffocating dining room. The long, narrow, lugubrious room lined with mirrors, green plants, and overbearing bouquets of flowers is, however, filled with middle-aged women with bouffant hairdos, men smoking fat cigars, and noise.

The menu is Italian of the old school. The carpaccio is tender and served here with thin slices of excellent Parmesan. Bresaola, thin slices of air-dried beef, is delicious with the restaurant's Italian bread, and the insalata di funghi tartufati, although short on truffles, is fragrant with fresh mushrooms. Tre Scalini has several salads, but avoid the insalata mista or Cesare, both of which belong in a Midwestern steakhouse. Insist on arugola, served with an excellent vinaigrette. Pastas are ordinary, but the risotto verde is worth the wait. Fish dishes are uneven; the Dover sole is bland but the striped bass alla cartoccio is tasty. A top dish on the menu is the scallopina alla Tre Scalini (small, tender, well-seasoned veal). The veal paillard is to be avoided at all costs. Choose rather the chicken cacciatore, good if not spectacular. Desserts are heavy except for the not-overly-sweet zabaglione. Tre Scalini needs a lighter hand in the kitchen and even the slightest hint of imagination, but it must be said this place has a steady clientele and many satisfied diners. About $55-60 per person without wine or drinks.

Lunch Mon.-Fri. noon to 3 P.M.; dinner Mon.-Sat. 5:30 P.M. to midnight. All major credit cards.

West 42nd to 59th Streets

BARBETTA

321 West 46th St. (Eighth & Ninth Aves.)
436-9171

Italian

10/20

Octogenarian Barbetta continues to seduce, though not always via her culinary charms. One of the theater district's longest-running restaurants (since 1906), it turns out dish after dish of Northern Italian standards, many featuring the cuisine of the Piedmont, to a receptive and not too demanding audience. The place has a style about it, and a sort of aging elegance. In 1962 Bryn-Mawr graduate Laura Maiolglio took Barbetta over from her father, the founder, and put her art history degree to work on the 1874 and 1881 townhouses that comprise the restaurant. She furnished them opulently, but perhaps her biggest success is the restaurant's charming garden with its century-old trees and rainbow flowers. Its wrought-iron tables covered with linen are rightfully in demand for fair weather dining.

In 1987 Gino Chiesa was promoted to chef and keeper of the established lunch, pre-theater ($34), and à la carte dinner menus. Perhaps he'll be able to bring about a somewhat lighter cuisine. Right now the room and the menu are ready for a major face-lift, and the lackadaisical staff needs a boot in the pants. The "Grande Antipasto Piemontese" on the menu lets you start off with a huge assortment of cold dishes, some worth trying. In the fall, when the white truffles are in season, you can have fettucine topped with shaved truffles or fonduta con tartufi; otherwise, the risotto Piedmontese is a good choice. In summer the cold minestrone soup is both hearty and refreshing. There are passable fish dishes as entrées, and nice, attractive game dishes in season. The more standard the item, generally the more standard the taste. For dessert the chocolate mousse, the zuppa inglese, or fruit are all right. The wine list has some appealing choices—though the list is not well-maintained and vintage dates are wrong too often. Try some of the Piedmont wines (Gavi, Barbaresco, Barolo) from the 350 plus choices given, or perhaps even the Barbera Maiolglio 1974 at $45 from owner Maioglio's own vineyard. Lunch averages $35 and dinner $45 per person.

Lunch Mon.-Sat. noon to 2 P.M.; dinner Mon.-Sat. 5 P.M. to midnight. All major credit cards.

BELLINI

777 Seventh Ave. (50th & 51st Sts.)
265-7770
Italian

13 🍳

Bellini is a good restaurant for pre- and post-theater dining in a district without top competition. Offered here is an affordable ($35) Venetian menu with the famed bean and noodle soup (so-so with an overdose of cheese), and a wonderful calf's liver with onions and polenta—surely the equal of the rendition at the Venice original, Harry's Bar. So, a toque is in order, but beyond that we have our doubts.

This noisy, elbow-to-elbow bright rectangle of a place with marble floors attracts an 18-karat crowd. Everyone starts with a glass of Champagne or the namesake Bellini ($8), the peach liqueur concoction with sparkling wine that on neutral turf would lose every time in a shootout with Champagne. Bruno Dussin manages the staff of young waiters in formal get-up. The food is in the Cipriani simple home-cooking tradition, with about 30% unique to Bellini, and prepared by a young kitchen staff scheduled to float periodically between the various Cipriani outlets.

The appetizer of asparagus ravioli with herbs is fair, though overly dry, as are the papardelle. The three reigning risotto—one day's offering might be milanese, asparagus, and Sibilia—are good though timidly flavored beyond the moist rice (and cost $20 each). The lamb chops and the veal are very thinly sliced and have nothing on a straightforward carpaccio à la Cipriani. Desserts, however, are very good, from a specialty rendition of lemon meringue to a dark chocolate cake that is rich, dense, and dependable. There's a good wine list with plenty of bottles in the twenties. Lunch is slightly less expensive than dinner, especially if you opt for a surprisingly available club sandwich or a hamburger (each $12), but expect to pay at least $50-60 a person for dinner, plus tax and tip.

Lunch Mon.-Sat. noon to 4 P.M.; dinner Mon.-Sun. 6 P.M. to 11 P.M., Sun. till 10 P.M. AE, MC, V.

BOMBAY PALACE

30 West 52nd St. (Fifth & Sixth Aves.)
541-7777

Indian

The turbaned doorman, Kripal, by now an institution, still sweeps you out of your car and not only into the restaurant but into the Raj. He is only one of the many reasons why the Bombay Palace stands apart. Another is the food. Punjabi or Mughlai food is more delicate than the usual run-of-the-mill Indian food; ghee (clarified butter) rather than oil is the cooking medium, and complex, elusive tastes rather than fiery hotness are the hallmark. On all these points Bombay Palace scores well; the food reveals personal, inventive touches not seen elsewhere. Flavors come through as they are meant to, allowing you to appreciate the complex taste levels and contrasts characteristic of this cuisine. Mattar panir is a fine vegetarian dish of squares of chewy homemade cottage cheese braised with peas, onion, and tomato. The Indian bread onion kulcha, often sodden and doughy elsewhere, here is light and puffy. Roghan josh (mildly spiced lamb curry with yogurt) is one of the most popular dishes, as are tandoor chicken, lamb, or prawns, carried aloft on a sizzling platter to your table. Chicken makhani or butter chicken (shredded tandoori chicken in a buttery tomato sauce with hints of ginger and garlic, garnished with chopped coriander), and the jhinga masala (spicy shrimp) are outstanding. Many dishes, like the flavorsome keema matar (ground meat with peas) are garnished with crispy fried caramelized onions that add an extra delicious note. Do start with a drink as an excuse to nibble on the delicious samosas, pakoras, and spicy papadum.

The Indian kitchen generally offers a very limited range of desserts, sweets being eaten by Indians rather as snacks throughout the day. For diehards, however, there is kulfi, the Indian "ice cream" made with condensed milk and chopped almonds and pistachios. Or you can try mango ice cream or, if you have room, Indian rice pudding with almonds and rose water. Beer or a light white wine goes well with Indian food. On hot days try the lassi, a cooling yogurt drink which you may have in any desired degree of sweetness, as well as salted or plain. At lunchtime, a buffet is set out on the second floor, and you can eat all the salads, curries, and grills you want for $9.95. There is also a four-course executive lunch for $16.95. Lunch averages about $12, and dinner about $20. *Lunch daily noon to 3 P.M.; dinner Mon.-Sat. 5:30 P.M. to 11 P.M., Sun. 5:30 P.M. to 10 P.M. All major credit cards.*

CABANA CARIOCA

123 West 45th St. (Sixth & Seventh Aves.)
581-8088
Brazilian

11/20

This folkloric Brazilian restaurant gets points for sheer fun, for value, and for being a bona fide New York institution. A block east of the heart of the theater district, Cabana Carioca is, literally, the one bright spot on one of the seedier streets in midtown: its façade is lemon yellow, and, inside, the bannister of a shabby staircase is painted in vibrant primary colors. The second floor dining room (that's where the action is) is jammed with the broadest cross section of New Yorkers to be found outside of the U.N. The small bar is lined with regulars downing massive portions of mixed grill, feijoada (Brazil's national dish of black bean stew and fixings), pork, and steak. Caipirinha, a Brazilian cocktail made from Cachaça (local rum), lime juice, and sugar, is a fine way to whet the appetite. Move on to a traditional soup. The best, caldo verde, is a thick potato-based broth with collard greens and sausage disks. Sopa alentejana is a watery but vividly garlicky soup made more substantial by virtue of the egg that has been poached in its broth, and the slices of bread that have absorbed its savory juices. Feijoada, the best bet among the entrées, is offered nightly. A substantial bucket is filled with beans, rich sausage, beef ribs, and whatever other meat comes up in the ladle. Rice is served alongside along with a number of condiments, including sliced oranges; a sharp relish made of tomato, vinegar, and onions; and manioc flour, which looks and tastes like finely ground stale bread crumbs. Shrimp Paulista, cooked with white wine and garlic, is fair. A mixed grill with sausage, lamb, and pork is a he-man's delight, but the meat tends to be overcooked. Brahma, the Brazilian beer, is rather boring and not worth the $2.75 price. Opt for one of the Portuguese wines or stick with the caipirinha. Dinner with drinks (and leftovers) comes to about $20 per person, plus tax and tip.
Daily noon to 11 P.M. All major credit cards.

CAROLINA

The TKTS booth on 47th Street ought to sell half-price seats for long-run restaurants that have lost their punch and

355 West 46th St. (Eighth & Ninth Aves.)
245-0058
American

10/20

their following. Then it might make good sense to reserve at Carolina. A trendsetting restaurant which played to SRO crowds when it opened about five years ago, Carolina now appears so bored with its regional American repertoire that it blatantly cuts corners, pre-cooks dishes, and plays for a convention crowd rather than for a savvy New York audience. The food's acceptable, but the restaurant's location—on the theater district's restaurant row—is the key to its survival. Appetizers appear in a New York minute and suffer for the evident pre-preparation: the corn soufflé, which is not a soufflé at all, but a custard, is slightly watery and bland except for occasional hints of jalapeño; dried out cheese and parsley sausages and even drier ribs would probably be tasty and satisfying if they had any juice or flavor left. Crab cakes, too, are bland and tepid. Key lime pie exemplifies the "convention" mentality approach to seasoning: the pie lacks a citrus bite and is oversweet. There are satisfied customers here and presumably they are satisfied with the most popular items on the menu—corn chowder, Hell's Kitchen chili, hot smoked barbecued ribs, and swordfish grilled over a wood fire (not bad). Mud cake and apple crisp head the list of desserts. There are about 70 American wines and they are marked up modestly. Try the Beringer Napa Chardonnay 1985 ($17). Opt for the romantic, candle-lit back room with its mirrors and skylight—you'll enjoy eating the atmosphere. Without a TKTS discount, dinner comes to about $45 per person, with wine or beer.
Lunch Mon.-Fri. noon to 3 P.M.; dinner Mon. 5:30 P.M. to 10 P.M., Tues.-Sat. 5:30 to 11:45 P.M., Sun. 3 P.M. to 9 P.M.; closed Sun. in summer. All major credit cards.

CHEZ JOSEPHINE

414 West 42nd St. (Ninth & Tenth Aves.)
594-1925
French

12/20

It's difficult to imagine anyone not liking this flamboyant bistro that recalls Paris's Montmartre and New York's Harlem of the 20's and 30's. It is dedicated to Josephine Baker, the world-renowned chanteuse and star of *La Revue Nègre*, and owned by one of her "rainbow tribe" of 13 adopted children. Jean Claude Baker, one of the warmest and most endearing hosts around, pays homage to Josephine's early years in Paris (1925-30) with numerous vintage posters and paintings of the singer (in various stages of artistic undress) from the Folies Bergères and Casino de Paris. The hundred-year-old grand piano was once used by Miss Baker as a rehearsal piano in Harlem; Jean Claude has restored it and splendid pianists now entertain on it during dinner and late into the night.

143

The cooking is hearty, a blend of Paris bistro fare with the down-home cooking of Miss Baker's early years. Since the arrival of young French chef Frank Ruidavet in the summer of 1987, the food has vastly improved. The Chinese ravioli with roasted pignoli, fresh dill, and goat cheese is a pleasant appetizer, though it is a bit chewy and dry and the dill is only a sprig on the side. The warm endive salad with Roquefort and walnuts stands out as an appetizer. The boudin noir (blood sausage) with red cabbage, onions, apples, and French fries is first-rate, except that the French fries (like the sweet potato fries) are a bit oily. Seared Black Angus strip steak is tasty and cooked to perfection; it comes with excellent julienned vegetables and French fries. Lobster cassoulet with shrimps, scallops, black beans, and seafood sausage is also recommended. Desserts are good, including fruit tarts and the chocolate-covered tartuffo ice cream, and the wine list is balanced and affordable, with a couple of good half bottles. Out west on a renewed stretch of 42nd Street, Chez Josephine surely should rate high if you're looking for a place to go before or after the theater. Dinner averages about $35-40 per person.

Lunch Mon.-Fri. 11:30 A.M. to 2:30 P.M.; dinner Mon.-Sat. 5:00 P.M. to midnight. AE, MC, V.

CHINA GRILL

60 West 53rd St. (Sixth Ave.)
333-7788

Eclectic

15

As we go to press, China Grill is enjoying its first few weeks of excitement and adoration. It's clear that this high-energy, high-quality, over-sized brasserie will be successful and influential. It's an original run by an original, Kenji Seki, part owner and maitre d'. Kenji, who has lived in France and in California, gained fame as the host of Wolfgang Puck's excellent Chinois on Main in Santa Monica. Ten Chinois staffers headed east with Kenji, including four chefs who are old hands at masterfully combining French, Californian and Oriental cooking. Count on Kenji and crew to add a dynamic new element and level of excellence to New York's restaurant scene.

The huge, slickly elegant restaurant is carved out of a space in the CBS building previously occupied by four separate restaurants. It is a post-modern study in black and white. With high ceilings painted in black, white moon-shield lights overhead, black walls, bleached white wood floors and white table cloths, each side of the restaurant that runs from 52nd to 53rd Streets is a mirror image of the other. Each half contains two dining areas, one raised slightly, and a long bar where you can be served a complete meal. The mirror dining areas, seating about 200 in all, hinge in the middle at an open kitchen. Pulsating, upbeat, modern music fills the room where a young, frequently pony-tailed service staff of both sexes figuratively dance the kitchen's wonders to your table.

Sautéed foie gras with pineapple is superb; tempura sashimi—tuna quickly battered, then deep fried, sliced, and served with a Champagne and sea urchin sauce—is sublime. The grilled quail appetizer served in a nest of crispy noodles is delicious and spectacular to look at. The always artful presentations add to the excitement of the meal. Dishes are generally served Chinese style, so you can sample plate after plate around the table with either the chopsticks or knife and fork provided. The chicken salad appetizer is a worthy choice among such other appetizers as Beijing oysters, grilled marinated lamb salad with spicy pepper garlic sauce (garlic is liberally used in many dishes), Chardonnay steamed mussels in black bean and sake, and China Grill exotic vegetables with Oriental dressings.

Main course range from sizzling whole fish with ginger served with ponzu sauce, to grilled free-range chicken with toasted garlic and grilled mushrooms, to a roasted veal chop with Oriental mushrooms. The grilled squab served on a bed of crispy noodles in a luscious shiitake-plum sauce might be the pick of the menu. Only the lamb chops marinated in jade sauce disappoint slightly after such fine antecedents. Desserts are freshly inviting, including the small napoleons of exotic fruits with passion-fruit juice or the warm noodles in honey cream with sautéed apples and golden raisins. The chocolate fans, one with pistachio cream and the other with chocolate sabayon, don't work quite as well, but nothing tops the frozen vanilla mousse with warm poached blueberries in a fruit nage containing anisette and tarragon. The wine list is superb. It is not enormous but contains only top quality wines in top vintages from Europe and California and includes many scarce wines on allocation. About $40 per person for dinner.

Lunch daily 11:30 A.M. to 3 P.M., dinner daily 5:30 P.M. to 11:30 P.M. All major credit cards.

DARBAR

44 West 56th St. (Fifth & Sixth Aves.)
432-7227

This is one of New York's perennial finds. The food is delicious, consistent, and rewarding; the setting's lovely; the service, conscientious. Yet Darbar has never been a "scene." It has never attracted a particular crowd. It remains, despite its obvious charms, to be discovered. Enter this little jewel in midtown Manhattan and you leave behind the teeming

Indian

streets of Gotham for a civilized place with terra cotta ultrasuede walls decorated with plaques, carpets, tapestries, and hammered copper trays. A dramatic curved staircase leads to a second story dining area, but the most appealing tables are on the first floor, separated into discreet booths by carved wood partitions anchored by brass poles. The menu is enticing. You want to order everything. The best appetizers are the vegetable pakoras (perfectly fried spinach fritters), onion bhajia (a web of thinly-sliced onions, deep-fried in a flour batter), and channe kichaat (a cold mound of chick peas, potatoes, and onions). All are good by themselves as well as being appropriate foils for the intriguing condiments, such as the mint dipping sauce which comes on light, refreshing, and cooling, and then packs a fiery wallop. The mingling of sweet and/or cool flavors with searing hot ones continues with murgh madras, chicken pieces cooked with cinnamon and lemon and a "special hot sauce" which is, to say the least, uncompromising. Another winner is josh vindaloo, a lamb stew cooked with potatoes in a hot curry sauce. Saag panir, cubes of fresh mild cheese blended with creamy spinach, coriander, and "mild spices" is a soothing counterpart to the more aggressively flavored dishes, as is the patiala pillau, a simple dish of scented basmati rice. Sampling several of the breads is a must. The pappadam is textbook; the onion kulcha, a flatbread stuffed with onions, is superb; lajawab paratha, stuffed with shredded chicken, spices, and herbs, a close second. The only disappointments are the dry tandoori chicken (murgh tikka) and the wine list, which offers very little at very high prices. Order beer and expect to pay about $30 for dinner per person, plus tax and tip. *Lunch Mon.-Fri. noon to 2:30 P.M.; dinner Sun.-Thurs. 5:30 P.M. to 11 P.M., Fri. & Sat. till 11:30 P.M.; Sat. & Sun. buffet noon to 3 P.M. All major credit cards.*

GALLAGHER'S

228 West 52nd St.
(Broadway & Eighth Ave.)
245-5336

American/Steak

Nothing proves the adage, "If it ain't busted, don't fix it," better than New York steakhouses. They just keep feeding satisfied customers the same fare, done in the same way, and served in the same huge portions as 50 years ago. Not much has changed at Gallagher's, a theater district stalwart that proudly packs in businessmen at lunch and the Broadway crowd at night. Entering this former speakeasy you'll pass by a glass-enclosed aging refrigerator where more than 600 prime sirloin strips are on view, and arrive in the large wood-paneled dining room with walls covered with photos of famous New York politicians, athletes, and actors—vintage New York nostalgia.

You won't have to look at the menu to know that clams or oysters on the half shell are a good starter. There's an open kitchen with a charcoal broiler where meat, fish, and poultry are cooked over hickory logs; you might try your oysters grilled. You can order a jumbo shrimp cocktail so truly jumbo that it would be a parody of the appetizer, except that this is the original. You can have lobster if you want to pass on meat, or a nicely grilled swordfish steak. There's roast prime rib of beef, too. But face it, you came here to experience the gluttony of a serious, monstrous steak. Order a simple baked potato on the side or perhaps some French fried onion rings, expect overcooked greens if you insist on ordering beans or spinach, and finish up with a hefty piece of cheesecake or a chocolate mousse cake. You'll be able to find an increasing number of acceptable American wines to wash this all down. Per ounce of food, the tab here isn't that high: about $35 per person for lunch and $45 for dinner, without tax or tip and with a modest wine.

Lunch daily noon to 3 P.M.; dinner 3 P.M. to midnight. All major credit cards.

JEZEBEL

630 Ninth Ave. (45th St.)
582-1045
American/Soul food

10/20

This is steam table soul food at gourmet prices. You're paying for the packaging—the setting and the scene. Dinner is theater. And in the theater district, playing to a theater crowd, dinner—not what's on your plate but what's around you—had better be one helluva show. The performance starts at the nondescript entrance, with only a small, well-camouflaged plaque saying "Jezebel." But inside, the decor is New Orleans bordello out of *Pretty Baby*, with seven-foot-high palms, orange birds of paradise in antique vases, white wicker furniture, crystal chandeliers, lawn swings, settees, antique shawls draped from the ceilings, mirrored columns, movie posters, jelly glasses for water, and zombie waitresses who seem part of some cabalistic order (headed by Jezebel?), though the piano player seems live enough. They tell you seatings are at 6 P.M. and 9 P.M., but that's for outsiders. Regulars can arrive whenever. If forced, opt for 9 P.M.; that's when things start to swing. The crowd is dominated by actors, directors, and large groups of acting students who take turns in the lawn swings, table-hop, and sing along to the Berlin, Ellington, and Fats Waller tunes. The scene at least is worth the price of the meal.

Whether the result of ritual or management, kitchen timing is nonexistent. If you want to stick around for awhile, stall the kitchen by ordering a cocktail. If you order immediately, you'll get appetizers by return mail and entrées before you've finished the first course. On the other hand, when you're there for a pre-theater dinner and want things in a hurry, you are sometimes left drumming your fingers on the table. What you'll get sooner or later are appetizers such as rib bits and shrimp sautéed in garlic, either of which might be handed out free in a bar during happy hour. For main courses, the fried chicken, smothered chicken, pork chops, curried goat and the like are akin to versions served in places that would only charge $6.95 for the package, and include yams, greens, black-eyed peas, and okra. The deep-fried whole fish have a following. For dessert, the bread pudding has it over most choices, including a lamentable strawberry shortcake. Expect to pay $40 for dinner, sharing an over-priced bottle of cheap wine, plus $1 for your coat. *Mon.-Sat. 6 P.M. to midnight. AE.*

KITCHO

22 West 46th St. (Fifth & Sixth Aves.)
575-8880

Japanese

13 ⌖

"Yokoso" (welcome) says the hostess as you enter this homey Japanese restaurant. Although Kitcho could do with a fresh coat of paint and a new carpet, the hushed comfort and friendliness of the tatami rooms outdo any shortcomings in the decor. The menu is sound and serviceable, but if you befriend the motherly, kimono-clad waitresses, you may get an unusual and tasty appetizer such as suzuko, red caviar with grated white radish, or refreshing iced bean curd with soy sauce. Among several inspiring dishes you will find wonderful rice in broth, a rare dish for New York. Sake-cha, rice and salmon in broth, is soothing and redolent of seaweed. Another standout is the kaiseki offering: a seven- to nine-course dinner which will reflect the season, your own tastes, and the waitress's intimate knowledge of the chef's mood on a particular evening. You may try such exotic dishes as shrimp broiled in front of you on a heated stone, delicate sushi served with an extraordinary piquant plum sauce, a soup called Shining Moon (made with turtle meat and mountain potato), and kamamechi, the best rice that Japanese cuisine has to offer. Prepared with shrimp, chicken, vegetables, and gingko nuts, cooked and served in a beautiful cast-iron pot set in wood, this rice dish is sophisticated yet supremely delicate. You can choose among several sakes; the waitress will ask you if you prefer it dry or slightly sweet. . . such courtesy! The restaurant has a fairly safe wine list, several beers, and excellent smoky tea. When making reservations for a kaiseki dinner be sure to ask for a tatami room. The price for a kaiseki dinner varies between $60-80; however, this does include the drinks.

Lunch Mon.-Fri. noon to 2:30 P.M.; dinner Mon.-Fri. 6 P.M. to 10:30 P.M., Sun. 5 P.M. to 10:30 P.M. AE, DC.

KURUMA ZUSHI

18 West 56th St. (Fifth & Sixth Aves.)
541-9039

Japanese

14

We were fans of Kuruma zushi when it was the best "secret" sushi address in town, situated over a noodle parlor and reached by a narrow staircase and a sliding door almost impossible to find. Diminutive, with a tiny sushi counter, the only thing not small was the bill, which the clientele (mostly Japanese) gladly paid for the luminous freshness of the fish and lapidary skill of the three chefs. Spurred by success, Kuruma zushi moved and in doing so, went temporarily off track in attempting to cash in on the then-new trend for combining Japanese and French cooking styles. Bizarre concoctions such as hamachi Hollandaise and chicken teriyaki with peach nearly caused this excellent establishment to founder. Now, at yet another location, the restaurant is back to doing what it does best—serving first-rate sushi, sashimi, and simple Japanese dinners.

The new restaurant has a simple Oriental decor with an ample sushi bar in back, a few tables, and a private tatami room into which are carried possibly the most ravishingly beautiful sushi platters ever seen. The chefs bellow greetings, farewells, and calls for the bill in tones that would do the Old Vic proud. Perhaps no other Japanese restaurant in town offers the variety of fish found here; the sushi menu lists 39 items, including all the usual fish, though of course not all may be available on any one day. All the sushi and sashimi are well-cut and simply presented, with a minimum of razzle-dazzle. The rice in the sushi has a slightly sweet presence that is very agreeable. At the tables you may have chicken or beef teriyaki or broiled fish. Sushi items are priced by the piece; dinner will run about $50 per person without drinks, depending, of course, on one's appetite, with a $20 dinner-time minimum per person at the counter. Expect to spend a similar amount for lunch at the counter, or take advantage of the three fixed price soup-and-sushi lunches offered at $10, $13, and $16.

Lunch Mon.-Fri. noon to 2:30 P.M.; dinner Mon.-Sat. 5:30 P.M. to 10 P.M. All major credit cards.

LA CARAVELLE

33 West 55th St. (Fifth & Sixth Aves.)
586-4252

French

15

La Caravelle could never exist anywhere but in New York. It's not a transplanted French restaurant, it's the quintessential New York French restaurant—the kind you used to see in 60's movies with Jack Lemmon. From the heavily accented and very serious (but benign) owner who greets you, to the tall and graying maître d' with impeccable manners, to the white tablecloths and dim lights, to the china and the glimmering silverware, to the Henry Pagès postwar murals of Paris, to the very good food (which has not succumbed to trends or the dictates of the food chroniclers), this is a fine restaurant. It caters to old, monied regulars.

In his mid-30's, chef Michael Romano still has the burning enthusiasm he did eight years ago when he joined La Caravelle. His salade Caravelle is made of whatever greens he can get fresh at the time, such as young oak leaves and French white chicory, plus foie gras and lobster. The foie gras plate changes all the time. Crab Caravelle is crab meat with herbs, cognac, and dressing; it is excellent. Also good is a tiny saddle of very young lamb, roasted and served in thin slices over a sauce made with its juice and with a salad of white chicory, chanterelles, fresh basil purée, wine, and lamb juice tossed together and cooked quickly. Other successful combinations: hot oysters and lettuce with a Champagne-spiked butter sauce, a poached salmon roll stuffed with spinach and served with a fragrant chive sauce, and any of the terrines (lobster with leeks, vegetables with a green herb sauce).

The Caravelle classic quenelles are superb: ground pike, crab meat, and truffle dumplings are first poached, then put into a closed cassolette with chopped lobster and lobster sauce. The sauce boils and the fragrant steam expands the quenelles. By the time the dish is brought to the table and its cover opened to release the sweet steam, the dumplings have become as light and airy as a soufflé. The duck is another treat. A roast Pekin comes with any number of different garnishes, sometimes a silver cassolette with a baked apple in a light royale, sometimes topped with cherries. Yet another entrée to try is the fillet of veal, which nests in a lively circle of crab meat and artichokes, sprinkled with young chives. A meltingly gentle sauce of veal and lobster is pooled underneath. Among the top desserts are the tarts and tartelettes, as well as the soufflés and mousses (for chocolate lovers there is a chocolate swirl mousse with pale white peaches, a chocolate soufflé with mint, and a mint soufflé with chocolate sauce). There's an extensive range and list of wines, and for a moderately priced selection, consider the white Saint Véran-Maconnais 1985 ($25), or the red Givry Châlonnais 1981

Louis Latour ($22). Lunch and dinner are prix fixe at $40 and $60 per person respectively, so add another $10-20 to that for wine, plus tip and tax.
Lunch Mon.-Fri. noon to 2:30 P.M.; dinner Mon.-Sat. 6 P.M. to 10:30 P.M.; closed Aug. All major credit cards.

LA RÉSERVE

4 West 49th St. (Fifth Ave.)
247-2993
French

16 👨‍🍳

What a difference a chef makes. When Jean-Louis Missud opened this handsome cafe in 1983, the kitchen was earnest and unpredictable. A couple of chefs did the waltz. Then in March 1985 a young Burgundian named André Gaillard came on board from La Côte Basque. It took some months for Gaillard to retool the menu, and even longer for the young chef to hit his stride, but for the past year all has come together wonderfully well. In a town where new restaurants burst onto the scene to crowds of curious and condemning customers, only to fade from favor within the year, La Réserve has followed a steadily upward path to the top ranks of New York restaurants. The restaurant's two dining rooms (featuring attractive fabric-covered banquettes, comfortable chairs, large paintings of waterfowl, and beautiful chandeliers) as well as the private party room are nowadays filled with a range of relaxed and serious diners.

As at most truly top restaurants, virtually all of the dishes here are recommended, though some dishes and other components of the restaurant need strengthening. The cold appetizers are all generally straightforward and good, such as the salmon and scallops marinated in lime juice and thyme. The hot hors d'oeuvre, however, are one of the restaurant's strengths. At least three dishes are round-trippers. The salad of grilled quail with hazelnut vinaigrette comes with one perfectly grilled and largely deboned quail on a bed of greens, with three soft-boiled quail eggs surrounding the nest. The foie de canard flavored with passion fruit works, with its fresh sautéed New York State foie a sure-fire hit. The salmon Napoleon with chives is a stunning presentation. The delicious millefeuilles topped with a glossy green and brown marble is picture perfect, and if it were on the dessert cart, you'd order it straightaway. As an appetizer, though, this may not be the finest showcase for salmon; still, it's a satisfying one. The bass with carrot and lemon grass butter is a good dish, broiled nicely and flavored lightly. The more elaborate poached Dover sole with artichoke mousse is the standout fish dish, with the mousse spread between fillets of fish and embellished with slivers of vegetables and truffles served in a beurre blanc and accompanied by tiny lobster-filled ravioli. Lobster is a key ingredient in the ragoût of pasta with seafood and vegetables, one of the least distinguished main courses on the menu. It's really a passable mixed seafood plate with a nice sauce featuring a ball of so-so fresh noodles in the middle. Instead of that, go for the sweetbreads with a sweet red pepper sauce, the rack of lamb, or one of the specials.

The service is veteran European professional, and the desserts are good but not great, except on occasion. The basket of sherbets and fresh fruits with its spun sugar dressing is lovely to look at and also to eat. The fruit tarts are less so, but the excellent dacquoise makes up for them. The wines and wine service are another matter. For a restaurant of this caliber, the list should be better. It is 90% French, 10% Californian, and seemingly prepared and printed by one of the bigger New York importers. There are plenty of 1970, 1976, and 1979 Bordeaux, but at big prices. Don't expect many attractive offerings under $30 in that section. The Burgundies feature Jadot wines and a few other big negotiants; not much exciting there or elsewhere. The house wines are regrettable, so you are stuck—but, then, try going to Alsace for inexpensive white. Even if you count out a hundred or more dollars for one of the good red Bordeaux, you get it served in a Burgundy balloon glass. Let's hope help is on the way. The menu is prix fixe: $29 for lunch, $35 for pre-theater, and $44 for dinner, so with wine and an odd supplement you'll be up to about $60 per person for dinner, plus tax and tip.

Lunch Mon.-Fri. noon to 3 P.M.; dinner Mon.-Sat. 5:30 P.M. to 11 P.M. All major credit cards.

LATTANZI

361 West 46th St. (Eighth & Ninth Aves.) 315-0980

Italian

12/20

The latest outpost of the amazing Lattanzi family restaurant empire (this one is run by brother Vittorio) is in the theater district, a good address to have. A snug, low-ceilinged spot with brick walls, cloth-covered hanging lamps, and piped-in opera, Lattanzi offers some enjoyable dishes at reasonable prices. Everything is prepared to order, even during the pre-theater crunch, by a kitchen staff of no less than nine to ensure that you will be out on time. After 8 P.M. a small transformation takes place; while the regular menu is still in effect, with its offerings of simple, well-prepared dishes like homemade fettuccine with peas and mushrooms in cream, spaghetti with white clam sauce, roasted half-chicken with fresh rosemary and garlic, and veal chop with fresh mushrooms, a second menu featuring classic Roman Jewish food is offered. This is simple, straightforward food, the best-known dish probably being artichokes Jewish style, peeled, flattened, and deep-fried in boiling olive oil laced with garlic cloves and seasoned with salt and pepper. In Italy special large artichokes, tender and chokeless, are used for this ancient preparation: they emerge as totally edible bronze flowers. Because American globe artichokes are too fibrous, Lattanzi uses baby ones, which imitate the taste if not the appearance of the originals. An interesting opener on the Jewish menu is caponata Ebraica, which is an unusual combination of the marinated eggplant dish, mozzarella in carrozza, and a deep-fried ball of rice with tomato sauce. The caponata with its elusive sweet edge is the secret recipe of Vittorio's Aunt Maria and may just be the best you have ever tasted anywhere.

All the Lattanzi establishments do fish well. Ask for the fish of the day, which may be red snapper with shrimps, clams, and mussels in a fragrant thick red tomato sauce. On the Jewish menu, the red snapper with raisins and vinegar harkens back to the old Venetian sweet-sour fish preparations. Desserts are unremarkable; the house wine a pleasant Chianti. Dinner averages $32 on the regular menu, $25 on the Jewish menu; figure $22 per person at lunch, plus tax and tip.

Lunch Mon.-Fri. noon to 2:30 P.M.; dinner Mon. 5 P.M. to 10 P.M., Tues.-Thurs. 5:30 P.M. to 11 P.M., Fri. & Sat. 5:30 P.M. to midnight. AE.

LE BERNARDIN

155 West 51st St. (Sixth & Seventh Aves.)
489-1515

French/Seafood

17

There is no question that Gilbert Le Coze is one of the most talented chefs in New York today. Whether the New York version of his and his sister Maguy's Paris restaurant (which was sold to Guy Savoy) merits the stars, the breathless adjectives, the slavering adulation, and the boulevardiers-of-the-world, panting for tables, who stormed Le Bernardin (and its chef) immediately upon opening is more problematic. There is certainly much to admire, yet there are flaws as well. One thing is sure, however; all the excitement surrounding the restaurant's opening and the brilliant performance in its kitchen raised the consciousness of a smug city about fish. People were stunned by the layers of flavor in simply done food, and in one burst, Le Bernardin spurred other top New York restaurants to new heights of awareness and performance.

Le Bernardin speaks grand luxe at once. Its walls covered in muted blue-and-gray paisley fabric, its street-side windows draped with filmy cream curtains, its table lamps and floral displays, and its glass and wood frame partitions sectioning the open room into discrete dining and drinking areas make it feel like the lobby of a genteel, conservative, and fabulously expensive hotel. (It's a setting that some adore and others find cold.) Only the oils of fishing scenes suggest the restaurant's theme—seafood.

If management knows you, Maguy or the maître d', Richard, greet you affably. Strangers are treated with a cold but not unfriendly French formality. If that bothers you, remember you are in New York, where regulars make a restaurant. They are indeed friends and treated as such. Service in general here may be flippant and inattentive or, on happier and more frequent occasions, professional, observant, and conscientious. The dashing Le Coze himself will often work the dining room.

The food is variable, ranging from superb to sometimes only fair, and of course some find the menu limited. While we find we can be critical, we must be fair and confess that, on the whole, the place delivers an unforgettable experience and when at its best, the food preparation is brilliant. Always superb is the quality of the fish and seafood. In fact, Le Coze has raised the standard of products available across the board by insisting on the best. Sushi lovers will adore the carpaccio of tuna; oyster hounds justifiably go nuts over oysters cooked with truffles and artistically arranged on a bed of seaweed. But the otherwise delectable fricassee of shellfish, a pungent mix of clams, mussels, oysters, and scallops in a tomato-infused broth, is undermined by grittiness. Inconsistency prevents out-and-out raves for the baked sea urchins, which are at times divine—a nuanced and sensuous blend of sea urchin and butter—at other times bland as egg yolks, and an embarrassment to the person who'd loved them before and insisted new guests try them. Similarly, roast monkfish with savoy cabbage and chunk bacon is, on one try, a terrific combination of perfectly cooked fish contrasting nicely with the earthiness of the cabbage and the bacon. On other occasions it's prohibitively salty, as is pavé of salmon with mint. In the disturbingly soupy escalope of salmon with sorrel (Troisgros), scallops of salmon float on an otherwise delicious sauce of salmon fumet, sorrel, and cream. Successful and satisfying, if not quite worth all the ballyhoo, is a preparation of poached skate in brown butter, and one of sautéed strips of red snapper, simply dressed with basil and olive oil. Theme desserts such as a half dozen variations on "pear"—offering sorbets, mousses, and tartelettes—work best. A chocolate mousse cake and a pretty chocolate mille-feuille with pistachio cream and chocolate sauce are good but hardly outstanding. The caramel dessert plate, on the other hand, is sensational. The wine list is priced high. Book well in advance. The fixed price at lunch is $35 a person; dinner is $60, but your tab (with tax and tip) will run much higher than that.

Lunch Mon.-Sat. noon to 2:15 P.M.; dinner Mon.-Fri. 6 P.M. to 10:30 P.M., Sat. 5 P.M. to 10:30 P.M. AE, MC, V.

MANHATTAN OCEAN CLUB

57 West 58th St. (Fifth & Sixth Aves.)
371-7777

American/Seafood

11/20

The trouble with Manhattan Ocean Club is that it costs twice as much as it is worth. This is a slick restaurant, with columns that remind you of Mediterranean ruins; metal rails that bring cruise ships to mind; and diffuse, warm lighting that suggests a summer evening on the docks of the Piraeus. There are Picasso plates in display cases downstairs and Picasso paintings upstairs.

Naturally, the fish is fresh—very fresh—and prepared with a minimum of fanfare, indeed very little of anything to enhance its taste. So while on the surface it seems healthy as can be, in fact it's dull. The food has in fact been improving here, but you are still mostly paying for the swank setting. You might start with an appetizer of littleneck clams or bluepoint oysters (no way to mess those up). Or you can order the steamed asparagus or artichoke, which are served up with a wonderful, prickly mustard vinaigrette. Stay away from the arugula salad; it comes floating in dressing, covered with shredded tomatoes and pieces of bacon. If you ask the waiter what comes with the main course, his standard answer is, "You get the piece of fish and the slice of lemon, and everything else is à la carte." You have your choice of steamed or creamed spinach and sautéed mixed vegetables and rice, among other things. All bland. The choice of broiled fish varies according to what's available that day: Maine lobster, "stolen" blackened redfish, red snapper, sole, soft-shell crab, shark, pompano, sea trout, halibut, etc. The steamed lobster is acceptable. Swordfish steak, underboiled and supposedly prepared in a pepper sauce, looks healthy and chunky, but has no personality. The red snapper was a nonentity all its life. For $25, you can get the five soft-shell crabs, breaded and deep-fried. The restaurant ought to have a rebate system where you could, say, kick two crabs back and get $10 off on your bottle of wine.

The wine list is computerized and contains a number of good, reasonable Californian wines and a few safe French ones. There is a dessert cart with some acceptable desserts. Try the chocolate cake or the raspberry tart. But forget the white chocolate Grand Marnier cake; it's all show and no substance.

The service, when available, is ceremonious. The waiters might forget to serve you the tiny soda breads they keep in baskets by the captain's station, or forget to clean off the table for half an hour or more. One waiter announced as he was serving us brewed decaffeinated espresso that this was the only restaurant in New York where it was available (which is nonsense). The same waiter told us that he had jotted down the "suggested gratuity" amount on the bill. He assured us that it was restaurant policy, except in the case of the "regulars." Dinner $65 per person, before the suggested gratuity.

Lunch & dinner Mon.-Fri. noon to midnight; dinner Sat. & Sun. 5 P.M. to midnight. All major credit cards.

MAURICE

Parker Meridien Hotel, 118 West 57th St. (Sixth & Seventh Aves.)
245-7788

French

15

Maurice represents French elegance, smooth and haughty French service, and exquisite French food. Soaring ceilings, mirrored wall panels alternating with floral murals, and magnificent flower-filled vases filled with flowers provide an apt backdrop for the authentic French cuisine and excellent people-watching.

The appetizer list on the dinner menu is very tempting. Eating warm oysters wrapped in lettuce leaves with truffles gives credence to the claim that oysters are an aphrodisiac. Ravioli filled with scallops and served with zucchini and thyme flowers are almost transparent, and so delicately seasoned that each flavor comes through. Chef Christian Delouvrier's vegetable soup with cabbage and foie gras is, in a word, divine.

The kitchen has an extraordinary touch with fish and shellfish, and by some culinary miracle the strange flavor combinations work. Roasted Maine lobster is yoked with a vanilla wine sauce, which marries nicely with the sweetness of the lobster meat. The filet de Saint Pierre, cooked in rock salt and served with a confit of tomatoes, has a wonderful taste of the sea. Meats and poultry are given almost equal attention. Calf's liver cooked in wine vinegar is pink and tender; roasted squab with small firm lentils is fragrant with herbs; and extra lean duck is spiced with coriander, saffron, and cumin, unusual in its Oriental flavor. (But the chef doesn't apply his magic to the sirloin steak with shallots or the tournedos Rossini; they are uninspired.)

Maurice's dazzles with desserts, which are among New York's more irresistible displays. The millefeuilles aux framboises is a dream of lightness; the thin, hot caramelized apple tart will make you forget you ever liked grandma's pies; and the lemon soufflé is superbly light. The wine cellar is good but quite expensive. At lunch the service is a bit harried and the food duller and not as carefully prepared as at dinner. Average price $60 per person for dinner, plus tax and tip.

Breakfast Mon.-Fri. 7:30 A.M. to 9:45 A.M.; lunch Mon.-Fri. noon to 2:15 P.M.; dinner Mon.-Fri. 6 P.M. to 10:45 P.M., Sat. 5 P.M. to 10:45 P.M., Sun. 5 P.M. to 10 P.M. All major credit cards.

NICOLE BRASSERIE DE PARIS

Omni Park Central Hotel, 870 Seventh Ave. (56th St.)
765-5108
French

11/20

Hotel restaurants are a contrary lot. Unlike most new restaurants, which take months to iron out wrinkles and years to build up a clientele, restaurants owned by hotels tend to open in all their glory—no doubt with the highly paid executive chef and outside consultant eagle-eyeing everything and everyone—and then fall off lazily. That appears to be what is going on at Nicole, a spot that still has a lot going for it. The handsome decor here is Alsatian brasserie via Paris: Art Nouveau designs and accoutrements such as an antique bar and pastry cart, four-color marble floor, faux marbre and trompe l'oeil walls, and bentwood chairs. The open kitchen is a nod to California. The location is superb. You can see the back of Carnegie Hall from your seat, and Lincoln Center, the theater district, Rockefeller Center, and Fifth Avenue shopping are within easy walking distance. So with its location, appealing atmosphere, and wide-open hours, Nicole is a good choice for pre- or post-concert or theater meals, or light meals at odd hours, as well as all-out lunches or dinners. And then there is the food.

If you choose well, you can eat well, although some dishes vary from visit to visit. The traditional brasserie dishes are usually sound. Consider the cassoulet (lamb, duck, and garlic sausage stewed with white beans and tomato) or the old reliable entrecôte (sirloin steak) with French fries. Among the bistro fare, the onion soup has proven uneven: once it is excellent, hot, flavorful, and crowned with cheese gratinée crust that must be broken with a spoon; the next time the topping is an anemic floating cheese cross and the broth a bit undernourished. The couscous is minor league as well. It looks good, and the portion is large, but the grains have not been worked well. Salads are very large, and make a good meal if you handle the dressing yourself; if not, you wind up with something resembling flavored industrial mayonnaise. The veal paillard is a sound, simple, and reliable choice, as is the Dover sole—nothing extraordinary but nothing regrettable. Among the more ambitious dishes, the won ton ravioli stuffed with snails and wild mushrooms in a basil sauce looks inviting, but at times the won ton are either over- or undercooked, and the basil sauce is more like an inelegant coulis. There's a general inconsistency in cooking pasta. Though hardly a staple in either Alsace or Paris, the crab cakes with curried tomatoes or Louisiana sauce is an attractive main course. The desserts are so-so, though they look appealing, while the beverage list is very good. As you would expect in a good European brasserie, there is a nice range of beers, and the wine list featuring French and Californian wines is fine, with a number of bottles priced in the teens plus nine premium wines offered by the glass. Price for lunch is about $25 and for dinner, $35, plus tax and tip. *Lunch Mon.-Sat. 11:30 A.M. to 3:30 P.M., dinner daily 5:30 P.M. to midnight; light menu daily 3:30 P.M. to midnight; brunch buffet Sun. noon to 3 P.M. (not in summer). All major credit cards.*

ORSO

322 West 46th St. (Eighth & Ninth Aves.)
489-7212

Italian

13

There's got to be something right about a restaurant that serves decent food, with amiable service, in a pleasant setting where you can eat, drink, and philosophize late into the night. The people-watching's not bad either; Gene Shalit's here for pre-theater dinner, Frank Rich's name is in the reservation book for nine; Donna McKechnie strides in after curtain call, and table-hopping editors from *Time* discuss the to-ings and fro-ings of art critic Robert Hughes.

The action takes place in the bar and in two small dining rooms, the latter with a skylight and an open kitchen. Mottled mauve, cream, and gray walls are cluttered with photos of the known (D.H. Lawrence, Olivier) and the unknown. Handpainted Italian china and pitchers by Vietri make artistic backdrops for the fresh and satisfying food. For a light meal, you can't beat the small pizzas—salads, actually —with crusts more brittle and thinner than matzos. The copious toppings generally fall off, but the ingredients are fine and make for tasty eating. Pizza alla Siciliana, for example, is a cornucopia of roasted peppers, raw Paris mushrooms, black olives, tomato, onion, garlic, and fresh basil. Pastas, such as tagliatelle with peppers, leeks, mushrooms, butter, and Parmesan, make more substantial and equally savory meals. For a truly hefty repast, try the densely packed homemade sausages of veal and lamb, distinctively flavored with anise. The wine list is more than reasonably priced, and there's not an unappealing selection on it. In all, this is a truly inviting, genial, and engaging trattoria. A leisurely dinner, sharing a moderately priced bottle of wine, will run about $40 a person.

Sun., Mon., Tues., Thurs. & Fri. noon to 11:45 P.M., Wed. & Sat. 11:30 A.M to 11:45 P.M. MC, V.

PALIO

151 West 51st St. (Sixth & Seventh Aves.)
245-4850

Italian

15

Palio is nothing if not controversial. This is Tony May (Sandro's, La Camelia) at his most expansive—and expensive. Detractors and admirers alike fault the prices, which are among the highest in the city, and the service, which is often negligent. Debate starts with the dining room (cold vs. handsome) and continues with the food (confusing and boring vs. provocative and delicious). Most would agree that the ground floor entrance is spectacular. The small room is completely enveloped by Sandro Chia's vivid mural of Palio, the famed horse race which runs through the city of Siena. A marble and stainless steel bar occupies the center of the room, an appropriately sleek hub of activity for the sleek international crowd of CEO's and lawyers who stop at the bar for a post-work or pre-prandial drink or a light supper of, say, artichoke lasagna ($9.50), or polenta and sausages ($8.50).

The second floor dining room is a plush, vast expanse, separated into three sections by wine racks. Black lacquer chairs and brown leather banquettes continue the polished midtown feel. The fragile grissini introduce the theme of food, scoring one for the Palio-adherents. Andrea Hellrigl (a.k.a. da Merano) of Italy's Villa Mozart is the executive chef. You won't find a cliché on his menu. And you will join the ranks of Palio's admirers if you order the seafood salad, a sparkling presentation of squid, mussels, and scallops, lightly doused with good olive oil and garnished with shavings of bottarga. More soothing than mother's mashed potatoes— and a lot more elegant—are two soupspoon-sized dollops of ricotta dumplings, set on a light cheese sauce and garnished with slivers of white truffle. Squid, again, is perfectly cooked and nicely complemented by a light, garlicky tomato sauce and flat disks of polenta. The sweetness of cinnamon mars the otherwise delectable pumpkin ravioli, tossed in butter and fresh Parmesan. Orrecchiete with broccoli rape is simply good food. Nothing wrong with that, but at $18 a portion you expect to see stars. On the whole, appetizers and pastas fare better than entrées. Gamey rabbit is nicely set off by red cabbage, but the pomegranate seeds add nothing. Rollatine of salmon, covered with crumbled sun-dried tomatoes, is an interesting exercise in contrasts, the fresh, moist flavor of salmon juxtaposed with the earthy, parched flavor of the tomatoes. But the seafood salad more effectively explored the same theme. It's hard to argue with detractors about the desserts, unless you're a fan of black polenta pudding. There are better chocolate mousses in town and no shortage of tirami sus. Palio serves a pre- and post-theater menu at $35 a person. Dinner with wine regularly costs about $65 per person, plus tax and tip.

Lunch Mon.-Fri. noon to 2:30 P.M.; dinner Mon.-Sat. 5:30 P.M. to 11 P.M. All major credit cards.

PETROSSIAN

182 West 58th St. (Seventh Ave.) 245-2214

French

15

In a restaurant bearing any other name the black, gray, and pink Art Deco decor would be showy, but at an establishment synonymous with the finest caviar to be found, what's more indulgently appropriate than gray mink and kid leather banquettes, Erté etched mirrors, Lalique appointments, and a long, long Angolan and Finnish granite bar running the length of the back wall? Here with a flute of Veuve Clicquot Champagne in hand (or a glass of chilled vodka) you feel like a welcome extra on the set of *Life Styles of the Rich and Famous.*

As a restaurant, Petrossian starts with a huge lift. Its core ingredients are its own superb beluga, ossetra, and sevruga caviars, its renowned foie gras, and its excellent North Atlantic smoked salmon. True afficionados of those fragile fish eggs enjoy them at Petrossian au naturel, without chopped onions, eggs, or sour cream. Ditto for the salmon and for the foie gras. You can, of course, order some variations on their themes, such as ravioles of smoked salmon in a Champagne sauce, or a fantastic green salad with foie gras. Among the more conventional (some would say classic French) offerings, the roasted breast of duck with honey and fresh raspberries is fine, as are the medallions of lamb sautéed with sprigs of fresh rosemary. The thickly sliced, seared fresh tuna is very good, and perhaps the pick of the à la carte selections is the classic red snapper with julienne of vegetables.

Top honors among the desserts—all done on the premises —go to the apple or pear tarts, unless you are a chocolate freak, then the rich chocolate cake prevails. Chocolate doesn't go overly well with Champagne, but everything else on the menu does, and the wine list is filled with top bubbles. A few wines are available.

You get a taste of the basics on the reasonably priced pre-theater ($32) and post-theater ($29) menus. And should you crave more, there's always the Petrossian gourmet boutique adjacent to the dining room. Lunch runs $40 per person and dinner about $60, though those little eggs can run up the bill in a hurry.

Lunch Mon.-Sat. 11:30 A.M. to 3 P.M.; dinner 6 P.M. to 10:30 P.M.; supper 10:30 P.M. to midnight; cold menu midnight to 1 A.M. All major credit cards.

RAPHAËL

33 West 54th St. (Fifth & Sixth Aves.)
582-8993

French

14

In its decade of existence this intimate restaurant has developed a solid reputation and following, especially among the French business community. Occupying the narrow ground floor of that dying breed, the midtown townhouse, Raphaël seats only about 40 people in a rustic, château-like setting. One wall is brick with a cozy fireplace, the opposite is comprised of a handpainted floral motif, and the back wall opens onto a pretty little garden. This a comfortable, sedate setting, in which owners Mira and Raphaël (thus the name) Edery supervise a small but steady team of French professionals, featuring Arnauld Briand in the kitchen.

Like the room and the staff, the menu is petite and not very flashy, but good and reliable. The one typed page of offerings changes every few weeks to exploit the seasonal market, but the bulk of the menu never changes radically. For starters the super-light mousse of chicken livers with marmalade of onions is tasty. The baked snails appetizer is an interesting variation on a French standard. Instead of the all-powerful garlic and butter, in this dish a basil coulis blankets four snails, and at the center a small puff pastry shell, stuffed with two or more snails, sits on a tomato purée. The red snapper ravioli with light tarragon sauce looks appealing on paper and is touted by the maître d', but in practice the delicate fish is often overwhelmed by the tarragon flavor. For a main course there is always a breast of duck, which is all right, but the accompanying sauce, which changes periodically, tends toward the heavy side and can overwhelm the meat. Perhaps the best choice is one of the many incarnations of veal chop, thick and moist inside and generally grilled to perfection. Vegetables are fine, and a side saucer of noodles with sliced strips of carrot mixed in is a clever and effective accompaniment. The pick of the desserts is the warm apple tart, which must be ordered at the beginning of the meal. The wine list is in harmony with the menu. It contains about 90 selections, mostly French but with a handful of Americans, and runs from $16 to $225. There are some good bottles to be had, such as the Guigal Côtes du Rhône 1983 at $19, or the Gruaud LaRose 1970 at $85, but there are too many off vintages and too many predictable wines from big importers and producers to excite sophisticated wine palates. About $40 at lunch and $45-50 at dinner per person with wine, plus tax and tip.

Lunch Mon.-Fri. noon to 2:30 P.M.; dinner Mon.-Fri. 6 P.M. to 10 P.M., Sat. till 11 P.M.; closed Sat. during Aug. All major credit cards.

RENÉ PUJOL

321 West 51st St. (Eighth & Ninth Aves.)
246-3023

French

13 🍳

This good, conservative French restaurant in the theater district continues to attract hordes of theater-goers as well as tourists looking for a not-too-too-expensive, solid French place to eat. And rightfully so, because it delivers on all fronts. Or rather René delivers, along with his family, notably son-in-law Claude Franques in the kitchen as well as daughter Nicole Franques and wife Monique Pujol out front. Chef Franques has been firing up the ovens here for 14 years. Before that he learned his knack for peeling potatoes on rotation at top-echelon restaurants in France (Troisgros, Pic, Bocuse, Chapel, and Guy Savoy). Working out of a large modern kitchen, he prepares a duck terrine, fresh salmon with anise, and a salade de crustacés (a green salad with a vinaigrette topping covered with sautéed lobster and julienne of vegetables) that are among the most popular appetizers. The grilled tuna steak is a commendable fish entrée, as is the poached salmon (if you can avoid the Hollandaise sauce—it's good but an old-fashioned killer). The kitchen has a propensity for traditional bourgeois dishes such as boeuf bourguignon and rognon de veau. The desserts are fine, but none are extraordinary, though the marquis au chocolat with a vanilla sauce usually sends away satisfied customers.

The wine list (and cellar) is a very good one. Beyond the dozen California wines there for goodwill is a large and comprehensive French assortment, with especially strong Burgundies. Unlike so many New York restaurants that serve wines right off the truck, at René Pujol the inventories have been built up carefully over the years, so that properly aged wines at civilized prices are offered. The majority of the Bordeaux and Burgundy wines on the current list are from the best vintages of the mid-to-late 70's. The French country dining room is appealing (stucco and brick walls, false wood beams, copper pots and bric-à-brac) and made more cozy in winter by the glowing fireplace. A comfortable bar and dining room upstairs hosts private parties of up to 50. Lunch averages $26, and dinner $36 per person without wine ($20-40 average per bottle), plus tax and service.

Lunch Mon.-Fri. noon to 3 P.M.; dinner Mon.-Sat. 5 P.M. to 11:30 P.M.; closed July. All major credit cards.

THE RUSSIAN TEA ROOM

150 West 57th St. (Sixth & Seventh Aves.)
265-0947

Russian

13

In fickle New York, where "in" dining places change with the hemlines, the "RTR" has a record for longevity and popularity that is the envy of its competition. Since its early days, when homesick Russian ballet dancers hungry for blinis and sour cream formed the nucleus of patrons, its show biz clientele has been one of the RTR's biggest attractions. The best time to people-watch is at lunch or after the theater, but make sure you have a reservation, or you may be dining peacefully in Siberia upstairs. In the days when the Russian Tea Room was a quiet little restaurant, the waiters were all Russian and you could always get a table. But that was before the power lunch and the $50 theater ticket. Now the waiters have first names like Akmed and Pedro, and the restaurant caters to two clearly different clienteles. There are the regulars—movers and shakers of show business, who inhabit their assigned tables day after day and order appetizers for lunch that get computed onto their monthly bills—and a constant flow of intimidated out-of-towners who wait patiently in line.

The decor is pleasant and idiosyncratic—deep green walls, red banquettes, brightly shining samovars, and Christmas decorations that got left up longer and longer each year until they became part of the decor. French chef Jacques Pepin has been hired as a consultant to gradually introduce "lighter, more contemporary fare" to complement the old standbys, and French chef Patrick Pinon (formerly of New York's Maxims) took to the ovens here in autumn 1987. So, promising developments are possible. You can trust the house specialties: the mainstay peasant soups like borscht (cold in summer, hot in winter), roszolnick (a hearty chicken and vegetable soup), and the steaming barley mushroom soup that, when eaten with flaky meat-filled pirozhki, is a meal in itself. The Wednesday special is Siberian pelmeny, a kind of delicate ravioli served in a rich consommé. The unctious eggplant orientale, a puréed merger of eggplant, onions, green peppers, and tomato is zesty and filling and eaten with black bread. Of course there are the matjes herring, smoked salmon, and the like. And where better to enjoy the great choice of caviar and blini with one of the 20 vodkas offered? Crepes appear in many guises, such as the familiar blinchiki (filled with cottage cheese and slathered with sour cream and perhaps a dollop of red caviar) and the nalistniki (filled with pâté and mushrooms). Main courses include the marinated and skewered lamb karsky shash-lik, luli kebab (ground lamb patties broiled on skewers), and a beef Stroganoff too rich for some people's tastes. The best entrée is the moistly buttery chicken cutlet Kiev.

For dessert try kissel, a sweetened cranberry purée served with cream and sugar. The late supper menu features satisfying cold veal cutlets on black bread, steak tartare, smoked Irish salmon, and, of all things, cinnamon toast, just right with a glass of tea sweetened in the Russian manner with cherry jam. Dinner runs about $40 per person, lunch $24.

Lunch Mon.-Fri. 11:30 A.M. to 4:30 P.M.; dinner nightly 4:30 P.M. to 9:30 P.M.; supper nightly 9:30 P.M. to 11:30 P.M.; brunch Sat. & Sun. 11 A.M. to 4:30 P.M. All major credit cards.

THE SEA GRILL

Rockefeller Plaza, 19 West 49th St. (Fifth & Sixth Aves.)
246-9201

Let's be thankful for what we've got—a good, upscale seafood restaurant at one of the great tourist, shopper, and business crossroads of the world. It could have been much worse. In fact, the establishment in 1984 of such a fine restaurant adjacent to the Rockefeller Center skating rink symbolizes the significant increase in the quality of restaurants in New York during the 80's. Access to The Sea Grill is via a glass elevator that takes you down from street level on

American/Seafood

13

49th Street. The restaurant is on the south side of what is the ice rink in winter (and a garden and host of umbrellas in summer). The spacious dining room is a bit big-hotel without the hotel slick: marble fountains, pools, skylights, thousands of bottles of wine beyond glass walls, an open kitchen with refrigerated fish on display, and soft seashore colors in the carpeting and upholstered armchairs. Oversized tables with white tablecloths are set apart and on several levels.

As starters, the cold courses—oysters, cherrystone clams, salmon carpaccio, or squid salad—taste as if they just came out of the ocean. Soups and chowders are more problematic, either bland or overpowered with cayenne or Calvados. A favorite hot appetizer is Maryland crab cakes, and they can be had as a main course. Soft-shell crabs, on the other hand, should be avoided at all times—what ruinous preparation. The best entrées are the "regional dishes," all fish or seafood based. Their nouvelle American accompaniments seem to always work, e.g., gingered red snapper with kumquats, pea pods, and sweet peppers. (What American region is that from?) As you might expect from the restaurant's name, fish, lobster, and shellfish as well as such non-fish staples as veal and steak are grilled over hardwood coals. You might also expect that they would be prepared flawlessly. The fish, however, too often suffers from overcharring. The meats fare better, in particular a tender and flavorful breast of pheasant with cranberries and pears. The desserts, most of which are out on display, are adequate, with top honors or at least first preference going to a tangy key lime pie. The Prometheus chocolate cake will take care of chocolate addicts for some time. The wine list is extensive (150 choices) and all-American. Jackets are required for men. For lunch or dinner figure $55 per person with a shared bottle of one of the many appealing American wines, plus tax and tip. There is also a $29.50 pre-theater dinner.

Lunch Mon.-Sat. noon to 3 P.M.; dinner 5:30 P.M. to 11 P.M. All major credit cards.

SHEZAN

8 West 58th St. (Fifth & Sixth Aves.)
371-1414

The only quality Pakistani restaurant in New York, Shezan is hidden away in the basement of a building across from the Plaza Hotel. The decor, realized by a top architect, is a surprise in its simplicity, with its light gray carpeted

Pakistani

13

walls on which hang magnificent antique cooking and weaving utensils. Bear in mind that Pakistani cuisine differs from its Indian cousin. Although it features curries, the food is not as spicy, and displays a marked Middle Eastern influence. The beautifully dressed waiters will push the sampling menu for $38 per person. The selection is interesting, but you get a tiny portion of everything.

Baingan bhurta, a delicately spiced eggplant appetizer, is first roasted, then gently sautéed, and is a far cry from the ordinary roasted eggplant. Samosas (turnovers filled with vegetables or chopped beef and fried until golden brown) are crisp and not at all greasy. Soups are Shezan's strong point. Yakhni, a rich chicken consommé graced with fresh coriander and carrot shreds, can compare to a French consommé. The mulligatawny soup is a must on a cool evening. The menu is divided into several sections: tandoori charcoal barbecues and grills (tandoor means "clay oven"), seafood dishes, and salam (curries and vegetables dishes). The barbecued dishes include sheesh kebabs (similar to the Middle Eastern variety—skewers of lamb broiled to perfection), grilled sweet river shrimp, and fresh fish. A particularly interesting dish is a stew of lamb kidneys and sweetbreads, cooked in a tandoor oven with yogurt, crushed ginger root, fresh cumin, and herbs, excellent on a bed of basmati rice. The six curries here will not scorch. Saag gosht, tender chunks of lamb cooked with fresh spinach, fresh coriander, garlic, and other spices is excellent. The keema aloo, a mixture of chopped beef, cumin, and potatoes is too starchy and reminds us of second-rate Italian meatballs. Vegetable dishes such as lentils or basmati rice with sautéed vegetables are good if slightly overcooked. The dessert list features shahi turka, very thin textured bread sweetened with saffron and sprinkled with pistachio nuts, delicate and not too sweet. The ice cream has a rich flavor of fresh milk and cream mixed with nuts and cardamom, unusual and refreshing. Shezan has a good, reasonably priced wine list, very good strong jasmine tea, and a wide selection of blends of coffee. Dinner with drinks runs about $45 per person. *Lunch Mon.-Sat. noon to 3 P.M.; dinner Mon.-Sat. 5:30 P.M. to 11 P.M., Sun. 5 P.M. to 10 P.M. All major credit cards.*

TASTINGS

Freshness. Tastings, the ground floor restaurant of the International Wine Center, has lost whatever freshness it

144 West 55th St. (Sixth & Seventh Aves.)
757-1160

American

10/20

once had. The International Wine Center holds tastings and classes upstairs, and this restaurant was one of the first in New York to model itself after a London wine bar, and to offer wines by the glass—the bottles of which were attached to a Cruvinet, a machine designed to keep opened wine fresh by replacing the poured liquid with a blanket of nitrogen. Time revealed the limitations of the Cruvinet; wines did not remain fresh longer than two weeks. As for the restaurant, it has similarly fallen victim to the ravages of time. Now its main selling point is its proximity to several Manhattan institutions which have retained their appeal— Carnegie Hall and City Center—as well as to a number of massive midtown office buildings. Its location, therefore, makes for an almost captive lunch, pre-, and post-theater audience. The decor in this mid-19th-century carriage house is loosely British—hunter green and brick walls, posters, and shelves with great bottles of wine, now empty.

The menu features stylish ingredients which the kitchen mangles in the execution: a flan of eggplant, zucchini, and red pepper has too much gelatin and no flavor save a bitter middle palate (wine school upstairs, remember?). The crawfish salad in tomato-cognac mayonnaise is over-the-hill, and the chicken breast sautéed with wild mushrooms and escarole tastes like a bad stir-fry. Even opting for simple items has its perils: a plate of four cheeses with a bunch of grapes and some slices of pear is pricey at $12.50. But the wine list is great, however mediocre the food. You can't go wrong with an after-theater glass of 1976 Graham's Malvedos ($6). Dinner will average about $35 a person, with wine.

Lunch Mon.- Fri. noon to 2:30 P.M.; dinner Mon.-Sat. 5:30 P.M. to 11 P.M., Sun. 5 P.M. to 10 P.M.; closed Sun. in summer. All major credit cards.

'21'

21 West 52nd St. (Fifth & Sixth Aves.)
582-7200

American/French

12/20

Early in 1987 the new owners of this legendary club closed the 60-odd-year-old restaurant down for a couple of months of cleaning and renovation, fired some of the old staff, and hired some hot-shot chefs. Some $9.5 million later, the place looks better—cleaner and more plush, like a museum. The expensive art added to the already fine American collection justifies the notion. The irony is that the food still isn't very good, except for a few safe choices, and although

'21' is not what it used to be, it's not what it could be, either.

In the old days a party of four could count on one of the four appetizers or main courses arriving late. The kitchen and staff seem to have retained that skill. Prices, formerly, were absurd. This was the home, after all, of the famed '21' burger that cost $20.50. Now they've changed the roll, played around with different cuts of meat, stuffed a frozen pat of herb butter inside to add flavor and keep the inside medium rare during cooking, and . . . raised the price to $22.75. Prices are now obscene, with onion rings at $1 a piece, and lamb chops $5 a bite. Ann Rosenzweig and Ken Aresky were brought in from Arcadia to run the revised version and promptly hired the redoubtable Alain Sailhac, most recently of Le Cirque, as executive chef. He is first-rate, with 38 years in top kitchens behind him. The lesson to be learned here is *no one* can turn out 700 outstanding meals a day.

The renovation resulted in a comfortable and elegant upstairs where there was once only Siberia. In the evening, the upstairs menu is essentially French. Downstairs in the famed and idiotic bar, and at lunch upstairs, you get the upgraded version of the old menu. Nevertheless here you will see a bit of the Rosenzweig influence: the grilled calf's liver with bacon has been replaced by seared calves' liver and red onion marmalade. And there's an open face variation on Arcadia's lobster club sandwich. The oysters remain excellent. Upstairs you can get good sautéed foie gras served with crispy noodles so sharp it feels as though you're eating pins. You can get a dry pheasant, so-so ravioli, decent lamb, and a curious duck stew; a number of the new combinations don't make it yet. Desserts upstairs or down are undistinguished, except for what at the moment is the world's worst rice pudding, and for the affront of $7.50 extra for petit fours. This place is on a long shakedown cruise and eventually the food should improve a notch, including the currently flawed and former signature dish, chicken hash. The wine list, thank goodness, is excellent, with Bordeaux and Burgundies aged and purchased in a bygone era at '21'. There is a $37.50 pre-theater menu (without wine), but figure between $75 and $100 a person for dinner.

Lunch Mon.-Fri. noon to 3 P.M.; dinner Mon.-Sat. 5:30 P.M. to midnight. All major credit cards.

Upper East Side

AGORA

1550 Third Ave. (87th St.)
369-6983

Eclectic

13 ♟

Agora is a gorgeous 1890's ice cream parlor imported from Haverstraw, New York, in 1971 and reassembled on the corner of Third Avenue and 87th Street. Its mahogany walls and beams, brilliant onyx bar, stained glass, and chandeliers are so perfect that the restaurant has been used as a movie set. Local regulars of days gone by saw Agora as a place to bring the kids for a good, simple meal. Tommy and Jennifer could always be bribed to sit still with promises of raspberry floats, but it's a sign of the changing times that the regulars who come here now are more likely to bring their business associates and agents. Owners Paul and George Gorra (cousins) like to keep things simple and honest. Hence the homemade country pâté is actually made in-house—by the ebullient chef Zoltan DeBari. The buffalo mozzarella served with bresaola (thin slices of dried beef) and roasted peppers is actually made from the milk of Italian buffalos. The gazpacho is excellent. Crisp chunks of celery and scallion float in a garden-fresh tomato soup whose peppery kiss will linger long after you've finished. Sour cherry and yogurt soup, a Hungarian specialty, is a beautiful fuschia color. For an entrée you have your choice of Cajun (blackened redfish, grilled lobster, crab cakes New Orleans), Italian-ish (a number of pastas and veal dishes), or French-American (lots of seafood and Chateaubriand). There is also a Japanese bent here, as DeBari loves the arrangement and simplicity of Japanese cooking (or not-cooking), and serves a very good chicken enoki and teriyaki, and a japonaise skewered swordfish with shiitake mushrooms that has a very strong, athletic flavor. The tricolored fusilli with fiddlehead ferns, pine nuts, and chèvre proved unbelievably rich. The angel hair pasta with two salmon and sturgeon caviar is a better bet.

Chef DeBari feels obligated to do predictable things like "Surf and Turf," but he does so with a distinctive, devilish twist. Adding half a lobster to a Black Angus steak, he pronounced it "Demi-Surf and Turf." A semi-circular raw bar right by the entrance of the restaurant is piled high with the daily catches: king crab legs, crayfish, cold poached salmon, Nova Scotia and Scottish smoked salmon, oysters (bluepoint, kumumodo, flower), and cold lobster. There's also frutti di mare—cold seafood salad.

Dessert remains stellar and the most consistent course, and commands its own two-foot menu. In addition to dishing out a wonderful plethora of ice cream—such as sundaes with liqueurs; shakes and floats with coconut, rum, peach, mocha fudge, or various chocolate ice creams; and a King Kongian banana split—a lot of baking is done on the premises. Homemade cakes are kept fresh in the pantry instead of out in the air, so be sure to ask about them. Tarts are kept on a sparkling bed of ice looking like oversized mums and marigolds. Price per person averages $25.
Lunch & dinner daily 11:30 A.M. to 12:45 A.M. All major credit cards.

ALO ALO

1030 Third Ave. (61st St.)
838-4343
Italian

12/20

The circular bar in this slightly chic, glass-walled corner restaurant serves as a backdrop for young shoppers from Bloomingdale's who need some refreshment after dealing with the crowds and the credit cards. The diners, dwarfed by the theatrical kitsch (a Dino DeLaurentis production) of the airy dining room, are more sedate and serious, although the noise level tends to be high. The space is big enough so that seating is not a problem, and Alo Alo is an easy, cheerful kind of a place to fall into. One of its best traits is the daylight that pours in through the soaring windows that face, in back, a vest-pocket park complete with a waterfall of sorts.

The cuisine at Alo Alo (the accent is on the second word) is sprightly and sometimes surprisingly good. Antipasti are not unusual—herbed wild mushroom salad, mozzarella with roasted peppers, unripe tomatoes—but the carpaccio served with arugula and thin shavings of Parmesan is delightful. Its mix of sweet delicate beef, salty cheese, and tart greenery works exceptionally well. There's a daily risotto, and another special might be fennel salad with mandarin sections, also refreshing. As for entrées, the pastas are serviceable, from the simple, al dente spinach gnocchi in a tomato and cream sauce (with a nod in memory of Campbell's Soup), to the tarocchi with fennel, shrimp, and clams. Chef Marc Weisberg favors vegetable sauces, which the svelte Bloomie's crowd appreciates. Still, we wonder if there isn't a hardworking microwave back there in the kitchen. If you're not in the mood for pasta, try the calf's liver. It is tender and pink inside, and served with sautéed leeks and delicious timbales of polenta imbued with a sauce redolent of sage. The broiled red snapper is also worth a try, but keep away from the tonno sott'olio, a messy, salty combination of tuna, olives, and string beans. Service here equals pushy actor-types, very young and often friendly, but the food comes quickly. The desserts, from Sant Ambroeus, include raspberry or apple tart and a luscious St. Honoré. A pasta lunch with a glass of wine will run about $20 before taxes and tip, dinner about $35.

Lunch daily noon to 3 P.M.; limited menu 3 P.M. to 6 P.M.; dinner 6 P.M. to 11:45 P.M. All major credit cards.

An American Place

969 Lexington Ave. (70th & 71st Sts.)
517-7660

American

15

At the least, An American Place will offer you an intellectual dining experience grounded in history and culture. The menu celebrates Americana in a unique style. You'll find unusual dishes whose roots master chef Larry Forgione has traced to colonial times, as well as regional dishes. Forgione has a supersleuth's eye for American ingredients, and a surgeon's hands for sewing things together. A poet's imagination is at work here as well, but sometimes the results are failed poems. The American-friendly staff is serious about the food and the exclusively American wines offered. No question will receive less than a full and thoughtful response. This was all relatively exciting a few years ago when Forgione, to his great credit, was raising people's consciousness about a new style of American cuisine. But some of the excitement is gone, though this remains a very good restaurant. The look of the dining room was never a strong point and, not withstanding the addition of some Robert Motherwell paintings, a new paint job, and new cane chairs, it continues to be bland and sedate.

For starters, the signature dish is the terrine of America's three smoked fish (salmon, whitefish, and sturgeon) with their respective caviars. The colorful contrast, splendid seasoning, and layers of delicious fish make this a hit. The Pennsylvania Dutch potato pancakes with grilled, lightly smoked salmon is very good, too. Unfortunately, you only get two little coins of pancakes with three tasty strips of salmon; you could eat a dozen. There's usually a pasta dish, which generally delivers more looks than taste, but why would you go here for pasta anyway? The regularly changing single-page typed menu usually contains a breast of free-range chicken with varying sauces, one time avocados and asparagus in a fresh basil sauce, another time black chanterelle sauce with creamy pasta and excellent grilled leeks. If the grilled marinated quail with Ozark country ham served over buttery whipped potatoes is on the menu, go for it. The ham is nothing special, but the quail, which has a crisp honeyed skin and is as boneless as you'll ever find, is superb. Big red meats are always to be found, from buffalo steak to roast loin of lamb. The latter sometimes comes filled with spinach and an overpowering goat cheese.

Desserts have improved markedly. They are big and filling, so forget elegance and dig into a chocolate devil's food cake that is 50% fudge. The banana betty and apple pandowdy are favorites, and old-fashioned fresh berry short-cake takes the cake. The wine list is mostly Californian with a few New York and Washington State wines. The backlist of vintages is a strength, but in the end this is not a truly exciting American list. Fixed price for dinner is $58, so with wine and coffee figure at least $70 a person, plus tax and tip. *Dinner nightly 5:45 P.M. to 11 P.M. All major credit cards.*

ANATOLIA

1422 Third Ave. (81st St.)
517-6262

Turkish

13 🍳

It's here, the gourmand's dream: a restaurant where one can, if so inclined, make a meal of dish after dish of delicious appetizers. Restaurant addicts won't be able to resist the appealing simplicity and freshness of tomato, red onion, olive, lemon, garlic, feta, dill, leek, eggplant, and yogurt in dozens of combinations and permutations. This is a place to loosen your tie (or better, wear none) and *eat*. The Turks claim to know a thousand ways to prepare eggplant, and the offerings here are among the best; the soguk memzeler or cold appetizers include pan-fried eggplant disks with a tangy garlic and yogurt sauce; sublime patlikan ezme, a garlicky, parsley-dotted purée of grilled eggplant (which is delicious, though not as smoky as we'd like); and the imam bayeldi, roasted baby eggplant stuffed with tomato, garlic, and onion. There's a hot version stuffed with ground beef, peppers, and tomatoes, and the prices are so easy you can try them all. Don't miss the Turkish bean salad, piyazi, firm white beans tossed with olives, tomatoes, and onions in a light lemony dressing. Skip the baby octopus salad (rubbery and bland), and the dull sautéed leeks, and save room for the hot appetizers, the most outstanding of which are the pan-fried cubes of liver topped with spiced red onions, the zucchini fritters oozing feta and dill, the skewer of batter-dipped mussels with a lemony pistachio sauce, and a lovely thin Turkish open-faced pie like a pizza, with spiced ground beef, arugula, and tomatoes. Or you can restrain yourself, eat just one or two of the appetizers, and select a main course such as lamb shank with lemon sauce; skewers of grilled swordfish; grilled quail in grape leaves, served with a currant-and-pine-nut-studded pilaf; shish kebab; or stuffed Cornish game hen. The lotte in parchment is beautifully fragrant but needs more cooking. If you still have room for dessert, a lovely tray will be brought out from which you can select various types of baklava, a yogurt cake with sour cherry sauce, or rice pudding. The Turkish coffee will make you sit up straight; tell the server in the gold-bullioned jacket how you like it—very sweet or medium.

The decor is modern taverna: marble-topped tables, garden chairs, improbable gold-touched Corinthian columns, and a touch of neon here and there. The banquette arrangement makes seating a bit cheek-to-jowl, and with the blaring jazz and yuppie-puppy clientele this may not be the place to take your mother-in-law for dinner unless she's a swinger. The service staff is attentive and pleasant and food arrives with astonishing promptness. Two red wines available by the glass. For an inexpensive bottle try the Jadot Beaujolais Village, or the Italian white Principessa Gavi. Dinner, before tax and tip, averages $25 or so per person.

Dinner daily 6 P.M. to 11:30 P.M. AE, MC, V.

ANDRÉE'S RESTAURANT

354 East 74th St. (First & Second Aves.)
249-6619

Middle Eastern/ Mediterranean

14

Taking up the ground floor of a charming New York townhouse, Andrée's gets as close to serving a Middle Eastern home-cooked meal as is possible without a palm-reading grandmother in the kitchen. The long, narrow, rather ordinary dining room is always crowded, the service is slow, and the food is excellent. Andrée, the gracious owner/cook, serves a cuisine so expansive that every country of the Mediterranean is represented, from Lebanon to France and Italy.

The taramosalata, a Greek "caviar" made from fish roe, is prepared in the Egyptian manner with bread as its base. It is smooth and piquant without being too salty. Merguez with cheese, a new addition to the menu, napped with a fresh tomato coulis and seasoned with cumin, is a wonderful appetizer. So are the stuffed vine leaves, kobeba, baba ghannoush, and hommos. Andrée also makes mulkheyyah with rice, a deliciously fragrant herb soup served in every Cairo cafe. Tunisian couscous with fish is unusual and very tasty, especially with its accompanying harissa (hot sauce). You should discover for yourself the crispy skin and juicy

pink meat of the carré d'agneau Méditerranée, a rack of lamb coated with garlic and fresh herbs. The red snapper à l'égyptienne, baked with potatoes, peppers, tomatoes, and onions in a saffron broth, is hearty and refined at the same time and a favorite among the faithful clientele. The vegetarian in your party will delight in the moussaka rajan: layers of eggplant and cheese with a rich bechamel sauce. Desserts are mostly French and excellent, but don't leave without tasting the pistachio baklava, small cakes made with phyllo and lots of butter and stuffed with high quality pistachio nuts. The khochaf (a fruit salad) is mediocre, as is the basboussa, a semolina pastry with almonds. Choose rather the delectable crème caramel. The new wine list is expansive—from Californian wines to excellent French—all at fairly reasonable prices. Figure $38 per person for dinner.
Mon.-Sat. 6 P.M. to 10 P.M. All major credit cards.

ARCADIA

21 East 62nd St. (Fifth & Madison Aves.)
223-2900

American

16

Though Arcadia is small and narrow, a soothingly sylvan mural by artist Paul Davis gives airiness and dimension to this popular place, where the diminutive chef Anne Rosenzweig developed her very personal, consistently superb renderings of essentially down-home food. But Ms. Rosenzweig's heavy involvement in '21' and her consulting activities require a caveat emptor: she is no longer regularly firing up the ovens at Arcadia, and though there has not been a noticeable drop-off in quality, there is a suspended question mark in the air. The low ceiling and cheek-by-jowl banquette arrangement can produce a fair din when the restaurant is packed, which it almost always is. The menu, small and select, changes seasonally and has been miraculously edited of clinkers; everything on it is familiar yet with an unexpected twist. In Rosenzweig's thoughtful, complex renderings, flavors may be repeated like musical themes, building in intensity, as in the toothsome tortellini made of a pumpkin pasta filled with pumpkin and Parmesan served in a creamy sauce rich with strands of ham and Swiss chard. For an elegant opener, corn cakes, a takeoff on blini, accompany dabs of ossetra and golden whitefish caviars and crème fraîche. In cold weather don't miss the spicy grilled duck sausages surrounded by roasted chestnuts and sautéed apple slices.

Hearty grilled leeks in delicate puff pastry bedded down in onion purée and wreathed by a thin beurre blanc with chives is a heavenly lunchtime starter. The lunchtime star, a substantial lobster club sandwich with bacon, tomato, and lettuce on French bread, is appealing as a concept but hard to eat gracefully. And with a food like lobster, where delicacy is all, the point is lost in such hearty BLT company. At dinner, warmed figs with Gorgonzola and walnuts on a bed of greens, a meltingly good wild mushroom tart, and grilled leeks in puff pastry swathed in a chive butter sauce with onion confit make provocative appetizers. A stellar main course choice is the moist, sweet, chimney-smoked lobster, fragrant with tarragon butter, accompanied one time by squash-and-potato fritters, crusty-celery root fritters another. The meat, with a tantalizing hint of smoke, is removed from the shell, cut, and replaced for ease in eating. Flawless duck breast fillets punctuated by cracklings is paired with savoy cabbage and kasha. In winter a venison fillet, tender from its sojourn in poivrade marinade, is hearty and warming. Loin of veal with stewed tomatoes and onions, accompanied by scalloped potatoes, is another good choice.

Desserts are irresistible, from the house specialty (billed as chocolate bread pudding, but really a rich, warm, chocolate-permeated brioche cake served in brandy custard sauce), to the lemon curd tart swathed in raspberry sauce (it has just the right degree of astringency). Or try a simple plate of perfect fruit, enhanced by an intense grapefruit sorbet; an opulent tuile filled with lemon curd mousse; or the pear timbales dressed with caramel sauce and served with homemade sugar cookies. The wine list, while small, is nicely varied and fairly priced. When you reserve, which you must do as far ahead as possible, specify the main room; the tables added to the front bar room are continually grazed by the passing parade. Jacket and tie required. Prix fixe at dinner is $55; about $28 per person at lunch. Wine will add another $10, $20, or more to that, plus tax and tip.

Lunch Mon.-Fri. noon to 2:30 P.M. (two sittings, noon and 1:45 P.M.); dinner Mon.-Sat. 6 P.M. to 10 P.M. All major credit cards.

ARIZONA 206

206 East 60th St. (Third Ave.)
838-0440
American

15

The blasé bartender clangs the Soleri bell to signal the waitress to pick up her frozen Margaritas, and what's astonishing is the tone of the bell is high enough to be heard above the blaring rock. The waitress (in pink Oxford shirt and khaki pants) responds, elbowing her way through the three-deep crowd of Burberry coats and tooled leather jackets at the bar. More Soleri bells are strategically placed in the small après-ski-style lounge area, where diners with reservations usually have to wait a solid half hour for their tables. Still, the bells instantly evoke the American Southwest, and magically transform this former Austrian dining room into Tucson, Phoenix, or Anywhere, Arizona.

Why suffer the wait, the noise, the smoke, the tiny seats, and the overcrowding? Brendan Walsh, that's why. One of the most talented chefs in the city has elected to make this hectic obstacle course his culinary showcase. He turns out food so innovative, exciting, and delicious that you can't help submitting to Caramba-like riotousness to sample what he's up to. At times he misses, but usually he's stunning. Combining Southwest staples (chilis, masa harina, cilantro, beans) with French technique, Walsh devises dishes that are precise, delectable, and inventive. His popular goat cheese ravioli, consisting of pasta lightly flavored with masa harina, demonstrates Walsh's subtlety with this distinctive flour. Three of the ravioli are filled with tangy goat cheese and are set on a two-tone sauce; the first is lime green and made of Anaheim chili; the second is a russet sauce made of earthy, roasted Ancho chilis. Cornmeal pizza displays the same masa nuance and is topped with grilled fennel, leek, and eggplant. Cornbread-coated oysters are deep-fried and placed back into shells which have been filled with a vibrant salsa of tomato, chilis, and cilantro. Walsh's mastery continues with flour tortillas with tomatillo sauce, warm lobster salad on a grilled pepper brioche, smoked duck with a jalapeño-tamarind sauce, chile relleno stuffed with goat cheese, venison black bean chili, and spa-light grilled salmon with tomatillo and chayote relish. Desserts, prepared by other hands, are hit and miss. Winners include chocolate macadamia nut cake and ice cream cake on a warm chocolate sauce. Downright weird was a concoction of beaten egg whites and pignoli nuts on an anise crème anglaise. Arizona 206 has expanded, claiming space in #204 for a cafe serving tapas-sized portions of selected items. Dinner for one in the restaurant costs about $60, with wine.

Lunch Mon.-Sat. noon to 3 P.M.; dinner Mon.-Thurs. 6 P.M. to 10:30 P.M., Fri. & Sat. till 11 P.M.; cafe Mon.-Sat. noon to midnight. All major credit cards.

AUNTIE YUAN RESTAURANT

This is definitely not your usual Chinese restaurant. Conspicuously absent, for one thing, is that unerring benchmark of other good Chinese restaurants, Oriental customers.

1191A First Ave. (65th St.)
744-4040
Chinese

14 🍳

Though the food preparation at Auntie Yuan is Chinese, many of the ingredients (such as quail, salmon, and mussels) are Western, as are many of the waiters. Instead of the usual garish (or nondescript) decor and bright lights, this tranquil dining room is sleekly black, with overhead pinlights illuminating a flower here, a snow-white tablecloth there. The captains in black tie assist you in planning the meal you'd like; no columns A and B here.

Two welcoming giveaways, the julienned carrot and white radish in chili pepper dressing, and shredded Chinese cabbage in a coriander-sesame oil vinaigrette, are so good you must force yourself to save room for appetizers such as vegetable dumplings, turnip pastries, or mussels in black bean sauce. Skip the dry, doughy scallion pancakes, a Chinese street snack that has no place at table. The Peking duck is one among the city's best, with shiny, brittle skin you eat sandwiched with a scallion and hoisin sauce in a rice pancake, before biting into the moist, sweet meat.

Seafood is handled particularly well, especially the steamed salmon or flour with fermented black beans and ginger. Other good bets: shrimp with ginger and garlic, and the not-too-sweet orange beef. Vegetarians can have a field day with the pan-fried vegetables with noodles and the homestyle eggplant. There is an ambitious wine list geared more toward social climbers than toward Chinese food; stick to tea or beer, though Champagne or a spicy wine from Alsace could elevate your dining experience. Sherbet is, appropriately, the only dessert offered, the apple flavor being especially good. Figure on $35 per person for dinner, about $20 at lunch.

Lunch & dinner daily 11:45 A.M. to midnight. AE.

BANGKOK HOUSE

1485 First Ave. (78th St.)
249-5700

Thai

13 🍳

People at home with Chinese and fans of Indian often go wacky over Thai cuisine, which incorporates flavors you know with some you don't in what seem to be endlessly new combinations. Comfortable captain's chairs, spacious tables with glass topping pretty batik squares, attractive drawings, fresh flower arrangements, and good lighting supplemented by votive candles combine to give Bangkok House a relaxed atmosphere in spite of the fact that it can be noisy when very full. Soothing deep purple walls and dark carpeting make the narrow space appear deceptively small; actually the main room is almost half a block long, and there's a nice smaller room annexed as well, so seating is rarely a problem (except on Saturday nights).

The gentle staff is charming and your meals will arrive with alacrity, but don't expect too much help in choosing what to eat. Do plan to eat as the Thai do, sharing as you would in a Chinese place. Appetizers to try include bamboo-skewered marinated lean beef satays served with the traditional cucumber salad; tiny, delicate Thai spring rolls; and the outstanding peek-gai, lightly fried chicken wings (stuffed with a savory mixture of ground pork, black mushrooms, and scallions) which you dip in plum sauce. Pla-pa-muok, a citrusy salad of squid with red onion and lemon grass, or pla-koong, shrimp similarly prepared, are excitingly hot and flavorsome.

Don't miss a specialty "for Thai people," not on the menu, steamed mixed seafood or a steamed fish, the foil packet cut open under your nose to release smells so tantalizing that two adjacent tables will sit up and sniff the air. When available, try hoi-pad-king, stir-fried sea scallops tossed with ginger and scallions. Gang-gai is an interesting sautéed sliced chicken breast with coconut milk and bamboo shoots in a fiery red curry. Whatever else you have, don't miss pad Thai, a deeply satisfying tangle of rice noodles stir-fried with shrimp and scallions with the intriguing note of ground peanuts. For a further example of Thai talent with noodles, try the addictive mee krob, sweet crisp noodles with shrimp, pickled garlic, and tamarind sauce.

The diversified nine-page menu is nicely balanced between dishes that are mild and flavorful, very hot and spicy, or absolutely incendiary—helpfully flagged on the menu. Singha (the light Thai beer) and plain rice will brake the burn. The house white wine goes nicely with this food, too. Three desserts are offered: a custard, green tea or red bean ice cream, and, in deference to American tastes, chocolate mousse, totally inappropriate to this cuisine. As sweet notes appear in many dishes, consider finishing with Thai salad—lettuce, cucumber, and bean sprouts in an intriguing peanut dressing. Reservations accepted for parties of four or more. Average price per person, when two or more share dishes, is between $17 and $20.

Dinner daily 5 P.M. to 11 P.M. All major credit cards.

BISTRO BAMBOCHE

Bistro Bamboche is your regular little neigborhood restaurant which offers no surprises except that most of the time

*1582 York Ave. (83rd &
84th Sts.)*
249-4002
French

11/20

the food is good. Run by a Polish couple, Yolanda, the wife, is the cook and Gregory Warankow, the husband, maître d'. The long rectangular room has only about 15 closely packed tables covered with flowered tablecloths, exposed brick walls, and lovely etchings. There's a regular menu and a prix fixe menu at $28 per person, the latter including a choice of appetizer, followed by salad, then several entrées and dessert. There are specials every night. Among the appetizers, the blinis au caviar are tiny buckwheat pancakes topped with crème fraîche and caviar. The sorrel soup is excellent, slightly bitter and rich; the mussel soup is too heavy, as Yolanda has a heavy hand with cream. The fresh leaf salad has a pleasant dressing. Among the entrées you'll have better luck with the fish and seafood than with the meat and poultry. The papillote of salmon with vegetables is not only lovely to look at but tastes very fresh. The poulet farci taste more like a first class airplane meal, and the sweetbreads are overcooked. But the butterflied veal chop with asparagus was superb, which shows that with time Yolanda may surprise us all. Bistro Bamboche's forte is the apricot soufflé, light, tart, magnificent. The other desserts, a tulipane and a tarte aux pommes, are not worth writing to Paris about. Bistro Bamboche has a limited but quite good wine list, reasonably priced and equally divided between French and Californian. Price per person $42.
Tues.-Sun. 6 P.M. to midnight. AE.

BRAVO GIANNI

*230 East 63rd St. (Second
& Third Aves.)*
752-7272
Italian

12/20

This restaurant is one man's domain and he runs it like a wolf pack. Top dog Gianni either welcomes you or ignores you, and everyone else in the restaurant (mostly a middle-aged, well-dressed group) follows suit. The first time you go there you'll wonder why you're being shunned, but if you keep returning anyway, one evening owner Gianni will do a characteristic about-face and come to the door to greet you personally. Then the reception in the dining room will be a lot different, too.

The food here is all right—classic, lusty, and made with good produce. People come here for the clubbiness and the spectacle as much as to eat. The pastas can be good. Try the tortellini in cream sauce, or the tiny raviolis (pansoti) in a walnut sauce that's cut with garlic (and just in time, too). The house's light tomato sauce, fragrant with herbs, is good on almost anything. But for the most part the entrées lack luster. The red snapper, served with capers, is notable, as is the squid in white wine sauce. The scampi looks healthy—huge prawns swimming in garlic butter—but is overdone. The veal is best as a chop topped with vegetables, which liven up the taste. For dessert, be swank and order zabaglione —far superior to the regulation cheesecake and chocolate mousse—and espresso. Being part of this film premiere crowd will cost you about $50 per person for dinner. *Lunch Mon.-Fri. noon to 2:30 P.M.; dinner Mon.-Sat. 5:30 P.M. to midnight. All major credit cards.*

THE CARLYLE RESTAURANT

35 East 76th St. (Madison Ave.)
744-1600

French

14

The elegant and comfortable dining room of the Carlyle Hotel may be one of the prettiest rooms in Manhattan. Beautifully decorated in the classic Georgian style, with tête-de-nègre linen velvet upholstered walls, discreet chinoiserie touches, a thick carpet, comfortable chairs, and a center banquette surmounted with a fabulous flower arrangement, it manages to be both elegant and cozy. Light comes from well-placed spots and is softened by pink-shaded wall sconces. Consider eating breakfast in this lovely setting with its buffet laden with fruit; all kinds of breads, muffins and rolls; scrambled eggs in a chafing dish; bacon; sausages; and so on. Coffee comes discreetly but non-stop. At all three meals the clientele is as attractive as the room.

The menu is essentially classic French (and quite good) but the nouvelle overtones in presentation and garniture do not prevent some dishes from being extremely rich, so order carefully and ask questions about sauces if you want to avoid something that sounds as innocent as "warm oysters with leek julienne," which turns up in a beurre blanc. At lunch there is beautifully poached cold Norwegian salmon, pristine Dover sole, and rich and delicious ravioli with wild mushrooms and shrimp. At both meals hearty eaters will like the lamb chops with rosti potatoes, weight watchers the veal medallions with finely julienned vegetables on lettuce leaves. Other dinner offerings include a fine breast of duck with white peaches, and a rich lobster stew with basil. This is a good place to order a soufflé for dessert. The wine list is extensive, with a good range of prices from moderate to expensive. The food is uniformly expensive, the service impeccable. Expect to pay $50 and up per person at dinner, plus tax and tip, and $40 at lunch; there is a prix fixe of $27.50 for Sunday brunch. *Breakfast Mon.-Sat. 7 A.M. to 11 A.M., Sunday 8 A.M. to 10:30 A.M.; lunch Mon.-Sat. noon to 2:30 P.M.; dinner daily*

6 P.M. to 11 P.M.; Sunday brunch noon to 3 P.M. All major credit cards.

CAFE PIERRE

Hotel Pierre, 2 East 61st St.
(Fifth Ave.)
940-8185
French

13 ♨

Cafe Pierre falls into the category of new and improved hotel restaurants supposed to evoke the grand old style of the 30's and 40's. The walls are covered in satin and the tables are roomy; it's a combination of mirrored-modern and tea-room baroque. For breakfast your uncle can still get creamed chipped beef, though the Pierre's "alternative" guide for dieters (items are starred) features low-cal bran muffins (promise?), berries, and yogurt. You can also get scrambled eggs made of EggBeaters for $5.50. At lunch the food gets brighter. Start with a delicious shrimp piquante, or a juicy filet mignon on a vegetable torte, and then have lobster and mango salad or lamb cutlets in mustard. There's also a roast wild turkey salad with lingonberries, but the most extravagant choice would be the beignets of sweetbreads on a purée of spinach, with truffle sauce.

At dinner try such appetizers as poached baby chicken filled with mousse and sherry sauce, and duck liver parfait with a currant brioche. For entrées, try the first-rate duck ravioli, salmon with wild mushrooms, or loin of venison. Though clearly not among the Pierre's "alternatives," the lemon mousse with raspberry Louis and the chocolate profiteroles with mint, white chocolate, and raspberry ice cream are worth being bad for. The restaurant boasts a list of 500 wines. Lunch for one will range from $20 (table d'hôte) to $25 (à la carte). Dinner will run about $65 per person, plus tax and tip.
Breakfast daily 7 A.M. to 11 A.M.; lunch daily noon to 2:30 P.M.; dinner nightly 6 P.M. to 10:30 P.M.; supper nightly 10:30 P.M. to 11:30 P.M. All major credit cards.

CONTRAPUNTO

200 East 60th St. (Third
Ave.)
751-8616
Italian

11/20

The knee bone's connected to the thigh bone. And in the corporate body of the Santo group (Dr. Santo also owns Sign of the Dove), Contrapunto, the second-story pastaria on 60th and Third, is connected to Yellowfingers (ground floor), is connected to Arizona 206 (one door east). Like Bloomingdale's across the street, the Santo complex offers a series of adjoining boutiques, each exploiting a different contemporary gastronomic fashion in an atmosphere as frenzied, noisy, and crowded as the BMT at rush hour—albeit somewhat cleaner, brighter, and more cheerful.

The fashion at Contrapunto is pasta. Indeed, the menu "prologue" describes the restaurant's fare as more than mere fashion—and more than mere food: it's a "philosophy," the tenets of which consist in serving the "finest, unusual pasta dishes not generally found elsewhere. . . the dishes are balanced in form and size so that splitting is inadvisable. . . split orders will be charged $10 *extra*" (their emphasis). Predictably, the pastas are neither so unusual (or contrapuntal), nor so balanced, nor so exquisite as to defy portion adjustment to suit customer preferences. They're O.K., however, making Contrapunto a pleasant option for the Bloomie's shoppers and Third Avenue moviegoers who wait in the corridor for tables to open up as docilely as they'd line up to pay for a Norma Kamali dress or to buy tickets for Woody Allen's new one.

If your tastes run to the rustic, choose the focaccia, a thick bready rendition topped with roasted peppers and tomatoes. Slightly wilted braised hearts of radicchio gain nothing by cooking but, abetted by strips of fresh mozzarella and strands of arugula, make a satisfying appetizer. Simpler is better when it comes to the 20-plus selections of pasta. Cansonsei tre herbe, large pasta pockets filled with spinach, parsley, ricotta, and Parmesan and tinged with nutmeg, are fresh and delicious served with a basil butter sauce. Capelli bergino, on the other hand, is a hodgepodge of ingredients and flavors, comprising sun-dried tomatoes, fresh artichokes, diced scallions, slightly cooked domestic mushrooms, chives, Parmesan, and butter, all showered over angel's hair pasta. Less would be more. The gelati—chocolate, banana, vanilla—is so-so, but the house red is just fine. Expect to pay about $30 per person for dinner, with house wine, plus tax and tip. *Lunch Mon.-Sat. noon to 5 P.M.; dinner nightly 5 P.M. to midnight. All major credit cards.*

DEVON HOUSE LTD.

1316 Madison Ave. (93rd St.)
860-8294
Continental

12/20

To charge $55 per person for a prix fixe menu you need more than sincerity, good intentions, pretty flower arrangements, and a glass of port with the cheese course. But those are what Devon House Ltd. has going for it, except its iffy premise—the attempt to create the fantasy of "dining out" in the home of English gentry. Devon House Ltd. occupies the ground floor of a lovely brownstone. Diners ring the front door bell to gain admittance. Inside, there are two small dining rooms with a half dozen or so tables apiece. The rooms look like they're in a private home—or a posh doctor's office—right

down to the coffee-table books angled on window sills and the bowl of dried flower petals on the mantel of the fireplace. In this setting, the presence of so many separate tables seems artificial, a feeling underscored by the fact that diners feel obliged to whisper to their companions, rather than disturb the near-silence that prevails. And therein lies the rub. There's no sense of occasion here. You're not at home; you're not in someone else's home; and you don't feel you're in a restaurant, either. The premise would need fabulous food to bring it to life, but none of the Continental fare with Jamaican overtones served here is fabulous—not the skillful but uninteresting rabbit terrine, not the snails in somewhat soupy cream sauce, not the pheasant in brown sauce flavored with rosemary and sage, not the Jamaican-style salmon which tastes as if it were brushed with Matouk's Calypso Sauce. Worthy of consideration are the sweetbreads in puff pastry, the rack of lamb, and the breast of chicken stuffed with shrimp and leeks and flavored with Pernod. Desserts are brought in from a good bakery, Bonté. Wine is reasonable: Stratford Chardonnay is $19, '82 Vosne-Romanée from Daniel Rion is $32. Your dinner check will average $65 per person, with wine but without tax or tip.
Dinner Mon.-Sat. 6 P.M. to 11 P.M. All major credit cards.

DIECI RISTORANTE

568 First Ave. (81st St.)628-6565
Italian

11/20

Walking into Dieci is like walking into an exclusive club. Here the membership consists mostly of neighborhood regulars, but the smugness is the same. The kitchen, though prolific, sometimes has trouble dealing with delicate foods. The best appetizers are those left somewhat unadulterated: mozzarella served with roasted peppers, prosciutto with melon. Polenta with raisins, sautéed mushrooms, and Madeira sauce sounds promising, but the raisins overpower the mushrooms and do battle with the Madeira. Better to stick with linguini with clam sauce (white or red), or the capellini (angel hair) with vegetables for a pasta course. Caviar served with the heavy penne is completely wasted. And porcini mushrooms get no respect for their delicate flavor.

Keep to the simple entrées as well. Grilled swordfish steak with anchovies, garlic, and capers comes with a red sauce on the side so you can protect the fish from its intrusion. Veal chops are described on the menu as "pounded" and "flattened"; believe it. Filet mignon, grilled to your liking, is better. But boneless baby pheasant served for two is slightly overcooked, and you'll wish they'd just let you do it yourself.

When you order wine, be careful not to order the Brunello di Montalcino Biondi Santi 1925, or you'll be stuck with a $6,500 tab. There's enough to choose from in a lower price range. If you ask, they may recommend Pinot Griglio Franco de Amatis for $19, or Gavi di Gavi, Villa Broglia for $32. You can eat dinner here for $39 a person (without the Biondi Santi).

Dinner daily 5:30 P.M. to 11:30 P.M.; closed Sun. July & Aug. AE, MC, V.

ELIO'S

1621 Second Ave. (84th & 85th Sts.)
772-2242
Italian

12/20

With its welcoming globe lights, wood paneling and wainscoting, pretty flower arrangements, and animated crush of patrons, Elio's is like a neighborhood club, an "in" place in which to see and be seen, people-watch and table hop. Elio Guaitolini used to be a partner at Parma, and the menus of the two restaurants greatly resemble each other. Here the bill of fare is by and large predictable, with a few items not offered at the other establishments founded by the ex-Parma (and previously ex-Elaine's) family. You will eat well if not grandly. Vitello tonnato is artfully presented in a properly dense yet silky tuna sauce, though on occasion the veal seems to have sojourned in the refrigerator too long. There is an unremarkable seafood salad, bruschetta alla romana, a good seafood risotto, the usual clams raw or oreganata, and the usual pastas. But listen to the specials (if you can—the noise level is such that unless your waiter shouts you may or may not hear them). They can be quite superior, notably the eggplant rollatini. Splendid steamed mussels in a rich, garlicky white wine broth would be wholly successful were they not mined with mastodon-tooth sized garlic cloves which should have been left in the kitchen. Eat one by mistake today and you'll eat alone tomorrow. Main courses include veal in all expected guises (scaloppine, piccata, and marsala)—a decent chop, nice quality, well executed. A cut above is the noisette with sage. Tasty chicken scarpariello has a nice balance of garlic and wine. Fish, which varies from day to day, is cooked with respect, and saffroned zuppa di pesce with lobster is satisfying.

Service is brisk and efficient. The wine list has been given a lot of thought and offers a good selection of popular, well-priced Italian wines like Barolo, Dolcetto, and Pino Grigio, as well as less familiar ones and some interesting wines from older Italian vintages. Desserts fare better than in the usual Italian restaurant, thanks to the fine hand of Elio's

partner, Anne Isaak. The vanilla cheesecake is very good and the thin lemon tart, refreshingly intense and acidic on a buttery pâte brisée, is one of the best of its kind. Reservations are a must during peak hours (7 P.M. to 10 P.M.) and on weekends; dress is casual-chic. Dinner averages $35 per person with a modest wine.
Dinner nightly 5:30 P.M. to midnight. AE, V, MC.

ERMINIA

250 East 83rd St. (Second & Third Aves.)
879-4284
Italian

11/20

When it comes to charm, it's hard to beat this place. The smell of a wood fire in this tiny candlelit room with its walls of exposed brick or thick-planked wood combine to make a setting that is romantic, rustic, and warm without seeming calculated. Regrettably, romance isn't high on the menu, at least not for food lovers. Few dishes are good enough to inspire even minor infatuation. The Lattanzi family, which also owns Trastevere and Lattanzi (in the theater district) owns this place and has named it after mama. She deserves better.

Ermina specializes in pastas and grilled foods. But even if you stick to those options—which is advisable—dinner is still a hit-or-miss proposition. Nothing is bad; most, however, is just average. What is billed as smoked carpaccio, for example, is a bland, utterly standard piece of meat with a handful of capers and a couple of shards of Parmesan tossed on almost as an afterthought. Artichokes Jewish-style spend a long time cooking in olive oil. Tasty, to be sure, but nothing like the traditional version in which the leaves crisp up and fan out like deliciously charred flower petals. The best dish on the menu proves to be the orrecchiete with a savory mix of sausage and broccoli. Vermicelli pizzaiolo displays full flavors of garlic, capers, tomato, and olives. (Puttanesca, anyone?) It benefits from a generous sprinkling of Parmesan (which must be requested). Various grilled skewers (meat, poultry, shellfish) tend to be overcooked and taste mostly of having been grilled over wood. There is a very restricted wine list. Ronco di Gnemiz whites and the Taurasi (a red) are recommended. Jackets required. Dinner easily costs $50 a person, with wine.
Dinner Mon.-Sat. 5 P.M. to 11 P.M. AE.

FU'S

1395 Second Ave. (72nd & 73rd Sts.)
517-9670

Done up in a formal contemporary style, rather like a nightclub, popular Fu's is part of the uptown trend in Chinese dining. Unlike some downtown counterparts, where you feel lucky to get what you ordered, here sincerely

Chinese

13

helpful captains and the hostess Gloria Chu will expound on any dish on the menu and help you put your meal together. While no one branch of Chinese cuisine could be said to dominate here, there is an appealing contemporary note in the way food is flavored and presented—fresh and attractive, never mired in overly thick sauces. Appetizers include delicate steamed dumplings of shrimp, or pork with coriander and ginger, plus the crunchier, fried half-moon type, both with delicious dipping sauces. The succulent regular barbecued ribs, or the honey-glazed babies, little more than a mouthful on each, will disappear from your table in record time. A special worth noting is the calamari in black bean sauce with hot red and green peppers. Cold appetizers include sesame noodles (perhaps a little too heavy on the peanut butter) and good hot-and-sour cabbage.

Though we could complain that many of the specialties are fried (no matter how expertly), Fu's version of spa cuisine, their "forgotten menu" of easy-to-eat low-fat dishes such as delicate steamed shrimp dumplings, or steamed shrimp or whole flounder in a blizzard of scallions, parsley, and ginger, more than make up for it. Moo shu vegetable is a crunchy and flavorful meatless version of the well-known pork dish.

The wait after appetizers for the main round of dishes can be considerable on crowded nights; nevertheless, Mrs. Chu runs a tight ship and we rarely see service as deft as here; the Peking duck appears in its burnished entirety and is magically prepared for eating almost instantaneously. Other dishes worth noting are the crispy orange beef and the lemon chicken, moist breast meat coated with water chestnut flour and lightly fried before saucing. Shrimp with a garlic and scallion sauce was outstanding. For dessert there is ice cream, fresh fruit, the usual lichees and kumquats, and unneccessary cheesecake. Skip the wine list and go for Kirin beer or tea (although the latter is oddly served in demitasse cups and is frequently cold—you are never permitted to pour tea yourself as you require it). Though the cooking is well above the ordinary, we wonder about Fu's claims that MSG is omitted on request and that food is prepared to order. A takeout order, requested without MSG, was ready in ten minutes and gave two sensitive diners that unmistakable headache. The kitchen needs a better exhaust system (the place really gets smoky with all that frying). About $25 per person when four or more share.

Daily noon to midnight; dim sum brunch Sat. & Sun. noon to 4 P.M. All major credit cards.

THE GIBBON

*24 East 80th St (Fifth &
Madison Aves.)*
861-4001
**Eclectic/Japanese/
French**

12/20

When nouvelle cuisine chefs began applying the Japanese aesthetic to French food, Gibbon chef Ikuo Kamata took an ambitious further step by frankly combining the salient features of both. The result is intriguing and highly pleasing aesthetically, if not always uniformly exciting. You enter the restaurant, in an elegant townhouse just off Fifth Avenue, through a small cozy bar area with a brick fireplace. You may go through to the snug downstairs dining room, or ascend to the more formal parlor floor with its antique Japanese and Chinese screens and paintings, and deep carpeting.

The best starters are those purely or nearly Japanese in origin; beautifully presented sashimi of moist, fresh tuna, yellowtail, and fluke, especially pleasant to eat here without the usual sushi bar hubbub; taffeta-crisp tempura; or plump steamed New Zealand mussels in a supernal garlic and bean paste broth. Among the entrées, sautéed sea scallops, briny and flavorsome in a lemon garlic butter, are an excellent choice. So is sakura-mushi, slices of salmon rolled around green buckwheat noodles, served hot or cold with a vibrant ginger and scallion sauce. Negima, asparagus, and spring onions rolled in thin slices of beef are a tasty and pretty notion as long as the meat is charred rather than steamed. In season, baby soft-shell crabs delicately sautéed with soy, shallot, and ginger are Kamata at his best. Though the presentation of all dishes is exquisite and imaginative, a consistent level of flavor excitement is somehow missing. The graceful edible wild-rice-flour cup has more flavor than does the tasteless grass it holds, and certainly more than the unimaginative string beans it accompanies. Yet the Gibbon has a solid following among well-heeled Upper East Siders who seem content with this safe foray into the mysteries of the East. The staff is pleasant and attentive, and there is a good selection of French and Californian wines well-chosen to accompany this food. Lunch averages $25 per person, dinner $45.
*Lunch Mon.-Fri. noon to 2 P.M.; dinner Mon.-Sat. 6 P.M. to
10 P.M. All major credit cards.*

HUBERTS

575 Park Ave. (63rd St.)
673-3711

Karen Hubert and her husband, chef Len Allison, have been satisfying diners with good, imaginatively rendered food and excellent wines since their Brooklyn restaurant days in the 70's. Theirs is an evolving fusion cuisine capitalizing on the market and on the vitality and ethnic variety that is New York City. On the one hand they've rethought many

Eclectic

15

standard regional American recipes; they've also embraced Japanese and other cuisines as well. In early 1988 they moved their restaurant again, from their Gramercy Park location to the old Perigord Park space. Adam Tihany designed a large and tasteful Americana room with beautiful cherrywood and mahogany tones, handsome furniture, and American arts-and-crafts touches, such as Vermont pottery. There's a large sitting room and small bar near the entrance.

Because the fixed price ($55) menu changes continually and the move will generate changes for some time, perhaps including à la carte offerings (and higher prices?), we can only cite characteristic dishes we have enjoyed, such as the grilled tuna appetizer surrounded by an exotic symphony of sauce, the red snapper with potato sticks, the cool seviche, or the shrimp appetizer served over crushed cucumbers. The grilled rabbit sausages with herbs served with mole sauce has been a satisfying opener here for years. Pan-blackened salmon with a white horseradish sauce is very good, as is the pan-fried duck. Venison with carrot noodles is only so-so, but the rack of lamb with goat cheese lasagna and spinach is excellent. The chops and medallions are pink and tender, the contrasting lasagna creamy and luxuriant. Vegetables in general are more than afterthoughts—yellow squash, sugar-snap peas, carrots, wild rice, onions, zucchini, asparagus, and sweet potato purée all enliven the plate to the eye and to the palate. The bread is good, as are almost all of the desserts, from almond brittle ice cream or red currant sherbert, to plum or lemon tarts or a chocolate fudge cake with whiskey sauce. The award-winning wine list with 250 offerings (mostly Californian and French with a few Italian selections) is a model of good taste, knowledge, and reasonable pricing. Service is earnest, friendly, and generally effective. For dinner, expect to pay $70 a person, and more if you want to sample a second bottle of wine.

Lunch Mon.-Fri. noon to 2:30 P.M., dinner Mon.-Sat. 5 P.M. to 10:30 P.M. AE, MC, V.

HULOT'S

1007 Lexington Ave. (72nd & 73rd Sts.)
794-9800

Hulot's is a French bistro on Lexington Avenue in the 70's, which is a neighborhood full of nannies pushing imported strollers by day and blond professionals scouting out places to eat by night. At Hulot's, well-dressed people sit on chintz banquettes and imported bistro chairs and get served French workers' food. Narrow as an arrow, with a compact open kitchen at center right, the simple decor consists of posters

French

advertising Jacques Tati's film *M. Hulot*, for which the restaurant is named. Try to sit up front, near the window, or in the rear; the twofers opposite the kitchen can feel a bit frenetic. Small cavils aside, eating here is quite enjoyable.

The French family food served here is grounded in tradition, and based on the weather and what is best and freshest at market. On a blustery day the soup may be a cosseting carrot, or curried purée of zucchini. For lunch in May, a marvelous vichyssoise appears. Simple, satisfying lunches include a good omelette basquaise, firm outside, properly runny within, with a garniture of the zesty tomato, green pepper, and onion filling; croque monsieur (a gentleman's ham-and-cheese sandwich served on wonderfully crusty bread) garnished with salad; fresh chicken salad dressed with a mustard mayonnaise; and unusual skate wings with pesto. Start dinner with a wedge of first-rate leek tart—sweet red peppers felicitously combined with a stuffing of mild goat cheese—or a simple salad of lentils, or cucumbers with savory eggplant purée. Or have pasta, handled here with great finesse; versions with scallops, with sweet red peppers in a white wine sauce, or with fennel and Parmesan are all good.

Hulot's offers a sound roast chicken with rosemary. Calf's liver fans will delight in Hulot's quickly sautéed version with shallots, simply dressed with a reduction of pan juices and sherry vinegar. Thin, moistly pink slices of leg of lamb, garnished with dauphinoise potatoes, is always a good choice at dinner. A fish sauté provençal graces salmon one day, lotte another. A variety of vegetable garnishes are especially tasty, always giving an extra interest to the main course. The young staff is efficient but sometimes a bit grumpy, a condition that may be brought about by negotiating the narrow aisle. (Nevertheless, there's something very considerate about the way they take your order. "...And you will have?" they say, and wait until you're sure you've made the right choice.) The house red, a Duboeuf Beaujolais, complements the food nicely, as does the house white, also Duboeuf's. The wine list as a whole is limited and undistinguished. There's a competent pastry chef somewhere in the wings; Hulot's fruit tarts, which run from raspberry to apple to fine astringent lemon, are an effective finish. The tender, buttery tarte tatin is sinful. Lunch averages $25 per person; dinner, $35.

Lunch Mon.-Fri. noon to 2:15 P.M.; dinner daily 6 P.M. to 10:30 P.M. All major credit cards.

HYOTAN-NIPPON

119 East 59th St. (Park &
Lexington Aves.)
751-7690

Japanese

11/20

Nobuyshi Kuraoka opened his second restaurant (he owns the Nippon) to cater to American tastes. Calorie-counting, natural foods, broiled dishes, and the drama of chefs doing their thing in front of the diners all figure in this concept. Even Hyotan's decor reflects "energized" Japanese cuisine. An enormous, amoeba-shaped wooden counter dominates the dining room, along with a large tank of frolicking lobsters. Chefs are always busy cooking, broiling, tempura-frying, or preparing sashimi, like Kabuki actors in the throes of a colorful dance.

The menu is several pages long. Salads are uneventful variations on iceberg with Japanese dressing. For dieters there are many sautéed vegetables, and for vegetarians, a special Zen (what else?) lunch. Appetizers will perk you up; a very good one is aigamo-hasamiyaki, perfectly broiled seasoned duck. Just be sure that the sauce is served on the side, as it is overly sweet. Among the usual meat dishes of teriyaki, sukiyaki and yakitori, the only one worth serious consideration is veal à la Hyotan, tender pieces of veal sautéed with fresh shiitake mushrooms. Fish and seafood dishes are surprisingly well-prepared. Hirame kara-age, gently fried flounder served with soy sauce, has an honest taste, and the broiled eel served with a piquant sauce is tangy and satisfying. Bento meals, the best bet at this restaurant, are served in beautiful lacquered boxes with compartments filled with delightful cold dishes such as sashimi, sushi, salad, vegetables, pickles, and a surprise. The desserts are the usual fare: melon, ice cream, and yoka. Average price per person with a drink is $28.
Lunch Mon.-Fri. noon to 2:30 P.M.; dinner Mon.-Thurs. 5:30 P.M. to 10 P.M., Fri. & Sat. till 10:30 P.M. All major credit cards.

IL VALLETTO

133 East 61st St.
(Lexington & Park Aves.)
838-3939

Italian

10/20

This successful restaurant has changed hands recently, upon the retirement of the venerable chef and host Luigi Nanni, who gave New York some of the best and most authentic dishes of the Abruzzes. Nanni's cooking wooed and held a solid following; what his absence will mean in the long run remains to be seen, but at the moment we feel like we're in a classroom with the teacher absent. Waiters josh each other loudly and scream requests and commands in various Latin tongues, and the captain recites specials in the hope you'll say yes to one of them, and seems bored and distracted if you would rather peruse the menu. (When Nanni used to whisk the menu away and feed you, you *knew* you were in for a treat.) The large dining room, once plush, now seems a bit seedy. Its lighting is especially in need of a serious overhaul; bright naked candle bulbs went out long ago. If possible stake out a table in the contrastingly elegant little dining room just beyond the bar; it's cozy and pleasant there.

The bruschetta is irresistible, fresh toasted bread piled with garlicky diced tomatoes, basil, and herbs, but you may not get it unless you ask. Baked stuffed clams are still as moist, flavorful, and tender as when turned out by Nanni. The eggplant alla siciliana with its delicate ricotta and spinach stuffing under a blanket of mozzarella and tomato sauce is delicious.The popular special, bow-tie pasta tossed with diced tomatoes, zucchini, eggplant, and fresh basil is still tasty, but overly rich and soupy. Lemony seafood salad with tender rings of calamari and shrimp is good and fresh but unremarkable. Linguini with garlicky white clam sauce is a winner, properly al dente, the clams fresh and tender (though overpriced at $18.50). Chicken scarpariello, usually sautéed nuggets of chicken in a garlicky wine sauce, consists of too-large pieces of chicken, cooked too long, and though it looks pretty it is short on sauce. Osso buco, the Thursday special, lacks that melting quality that characterizes its best readings. Steamed/sautéed zucchini accompanies main courses and is first-rate. Desserts? A nice baked pear, fresh fruit salad, berries in season, zabaglione. The O.K. Antinori Chianti classico is at $25 one of the least expensive wines available. About $50 per person for dinner, $35 at lunch. *Lunch Mon.-Fri. noon to 3 P.M.; dinner Mon.-Sat. 5:30 P.M. to midnight. All major credit cards.*

ISLAND

1305 Madison Ave. (92nd & 93rd Sts.)
996-1200

Eclectic

12/20

They are choking on their hipness at Island. The jean-clad waiter with the Chico Marx hair is so impressed with himself he sings out the night's specials over his shoulder, three tables away from his purported audience. He can't resist a pirouette out of sheer delight with his own performance. The maître d' is so blasé he blithely keeps two women standing for a "deuce" to open up, assuring them the larger (empty) tables must wait for parties of four. No sooner has he squeezed them in by a structural column than he promptly fills a four-seater with a couple right out of a William Hamilton cartoon.

What does Island mean? An island of noise, as opposed to calm? An island in the stream of uptown traffic? A treasure island for the owners? The owners explain that the name describes the style of cooking (Mediterranean, including the off-shore islands) as well as where the clientele spends the winter. Nothing about the look or feel of the place, however, suggests any kind of island. Not Corsica. Not Virgin Gorda. Not Shelter or Block. This is a long, narrowish room divided into a bar area (with a half dozen or so tables) and a main dining room. The walls are a creamy off-white and are dotted with mirrors. There are marble-topped tables and bistro chairs. Neutral good taste, like the clothes of the clientele.

The menu is eclectic, offering a little of everything fashionable. Grilled vegetables, grilled chèvre, grilled fish, grilled meat, radicchio, mache, pasta, and the top of the pops in desserts—crème brûlée, tarte tatin, tirami su. Some monikers are confusing. An appetizer of "tarama" for example, is described as a purée of sun-dried tuna eggs, bread, capers, and onions. Not to put too fine a point on it, but it's that fish that defines tarama. There's no point asking about individual items. The music's too loud and the waiter is too busy, and he thinks questions are occasions for comedy anyway. Explaining the pasta of the day—orecchiette—he smirks, "little ears" and wiggles his index finger under his flop of curls. Well, the little ears of pasta are just fine—with plum tomatoes, potatoes, and wilted arugula. Just add a hefty dose of Parmesan. And the grilled rabbit, brushed with mustard and fresh basil, is both tasty and spa-like; it feeds fashionably and keeps customers in size sixes. The wine list is consistent with everything else; there are some good selections, but it's next to impossible to find them on the uninformative list. You can, if you care, go look at the bottles for yourself. Or order a martini. As the juggernaut of gentrification rolls inexorably uptown it will deposit a thousand formula-hip Islands along the way. Whether this one can distinguish itself from the pack remains to be seen. Dinner averages $50 per person.

Lunch Mon.-Sat. noon to 3 P.M., Sun. till 4 P.M.; dinner nightly 6 P.M. to 11 P.M.; late night supper nightly 11 P.M. to midnight. AE.

JACKS

1022 Lexington Ave. (73rd St.)
628-5300

The Upper East Side area around 72nd Street, chronically short of good, not-too-formal eateries, gave smart little Jacks its vote virtually from the day it opened. Jacks is the brainchild of Ed Safdie, who made a spa food success story out of the Sonoma Mission Inn in California. You enter a tiny street-level space dominated by a cozy mahogany bar

American

12/20

whose domain, in mild weather, extends to tiny tables outside. A circular staircase leads to the second floor and the dining room proper, where the most has been made of a very narrow space. Many of the tables are pleasantly situated near big windows, through which one can watch the passing parade at lunch. At night, dark walls and candles create a soothing atmosphere with an edge of elegance hampered only by the unnecessary, piped-in 50's music. A thoughtful menu gives a calorie count for the fixed items. The good range of food includes spa specialties such as grilled shiitake mushrooms, paillard of chicken, steamed asparagus with tomatoes and endive, and the signature barbecued marinated Gulf shrimp served warm on a bed of zesty greens, to such other signatures of spa fare as baby grilled coho salmon and hearty, tender medallions of venison in black currant sauce. Vegetable garnishes are in miniature but attractive and varied, and there are always several interesting, non-rabbit food salads. Having thus been prudent, you can indulge in the delicious warm apple crumb cake à la mode or chocolate mud pie for dessert. There's a good selection of Californian wines. Dinner runs about $50 per person, lunch about $25. *Lunch noon to 3 P.M.; dinner Mon.-Sat. 6 P.M. to 10:30 P.M.; Sunday brunch noon to 3:45 P.M. All major credit cards.*

JAMS

*154 East 79th St.
(Lexington & Third Aves.)*
772-6800

American

15

New Yorkers got a serious exposure to California cooking when West Coast chef Jonathan Waxman and co-owner Melvyn Master opened Jams in February 1984. Whether the attractive flagship restaurant will retain its high quality now that the dynamic duo have gone west (Bud's), south (Hulot's), and across the seas (London) remains to be seen. For now Jams is holding. You enter on the street level and walk though a terrazo-floored downstairs dining room, examine the attractive open kitchen, and perhaps climb a flight of stairs to the second floor dining area with its white walls, colorful abstract paintings, and comfortable tables. The menu, which changes frequently, is so genuinely appealing that choosing becomes difficult. Everything sounds wonderful and almost always delivers, reflecting Mr. Waxman's unerring instincts in his choice of primary ingredients and mix of tastes and textures. The parsley-caper vinaigrette that dresses the greens is the perfect complement for an opener of grilled duck sausage, its richness tempered with hash-brown potatoes. Fresh pasta is simple and satisfying in a Madeira cream sauce, pristine salmon fillet with a julienne of celery root is dressed with a light creamy mustard sauce, and sea bass is enlivened with roasted red and yellow peppers and niçoise olives. Cornmeal-coated catfish is Americana incarnate, deftly sautéed, garnished with apple fritters, and served with a lemon/basil mayonnaise. You'd be hard put to find any chicken better than Jams' grilled free-range chicken served with more delicious crisp slender French fries than you can possibly eat. A garnish of wine-poached pears lends succulent marinated pork loin paired with delicious potato cakes an appropriate fruity touch. Don't miss the red pepper pancakes crowned with yellow whitefish caviar and golden red caviar. One hopes another favorite, crab cakes with corn and tomato salsa, will return in colder weather. Among the alluring desserts is an astringent lime meringue tart and the Heath Bar ice cream with a praline topping. The large wine list has a good range of prices ($12 to $200) and includes some interesting California vintages. Dinner averages $60 per person.

Dinner Sun.-Thurs. 6 P.M. to 11 P.M., Fri. & Sat. 6 P.M. to 11:30 P.M. All major credit cards.

LA MÉTAIRIE

1442 Third Ave. (81st & 82nd Sts.)
988-1800
French

12/20

Here the farm's gone upscale. Owner Sylvain Fareri has brought a brand-new version of his cosy Greenwich Village haven to the Upper East Side, and this one's a little more like a brasserie—breezier and faster-paced. The restaurant's name, taken from medieval French, refers to the sweet country farms of the old days, where fat ducks waddled past haystacks and doves cooed from the trees. But the duck's more at home downtown. Uptown there's white linen and crystal on the tables and uptown chef Joel Huchet has added things like Hawaiian tuna and more elaborate preparations such as homemade ravioli with sea scallop filling (disappointing), and an endive and raw oyster salad with lime juice. The bouillabaisse comes highly recommended for a main course, as does the pigeon en cocotte. In winter Huchet touts his choucroute. Grilling over *feu de bois* is something of a specialty here, and the rib of Black Angus large enough to serve two is sound. Vegetables are unmemorable except for a superb and elegant garlic flan. The bistrot dessert are all right, but without great distinction, though the caramel mousse in a chocolate casing overpowered by a sharp, bitter orange flavor should be avoided. Dinner reservations are cancelled if not confirmed before 5 P.M. Dinner should run about $50 a person, plus tax and tip, and a bit less at lunch.

*Lunch Mon.-Fri. noon to 3 P.M.; dinner Mon.-Sat. 6 P.M. to
midnight, Sun. 5 P.M. to midnight. AE, MC, V.*

LE CIRQUE

*58 East 65th St. (Park &
Madison Aves.)*
794-9292

French

19

Early in May 1987 Le Cirque moved up in class. Already by
broad consensus one of a handful of premier restaurants in
the United States, it has earned its way to the head of the
class. The occasion that marked the restaurant's extraordinary emergence was the issuance of a revamped menu, the
first under its brilliant new French chef, Daniel Boulud. It
took Boulud, his two talented sous-chefs, Cambodian Sottha
Khunn and Frenchman Marc Poisdevin, six months to ease
into command of the kitchen but when the Boulud team was
ready to make its statement, it made a stunning one. These
chefs introduced a level of innovation, including a dimension
of lightness, that probes the limits of haute cuisine as we now
know it, while maintaining Le Cirque's traditions and
traditional fare at its finest. Even Le Cirque's European
captains—members of an esteemed, arched-eyebrow profession never caught nonplussed—were amazed.

True to its name, which is French for "the circus," Le
Cirque is larger than life. Hangout for the rich and famous,
clubhouse for the world's great chefs, mecca for New York's
movers and shakers while being a chic but unpretentious
neighborhood eatery, it is a spectacle and a phenomenon of
the 80's. Monkey murals provide a touch of circus whimsey
to this elegant, grand room, which is filled with excesses,
including people—Europeans, South Americans, and New
Yorkers buzz about. Mind you, the glitter, frenzy, and
electricity of this place is not for everyone: many high-level
business types find it tough to unwind here after a hectic
day, and resent the elbow-to-elbow conditions (even if one of
those elbows leads to a face that stops traffic). On the other
hand, Le Cirque is the ultimate pick-me-up for legions of
well-coiffured and bejeweled ladies, and despite inevitable
power surges, it's often a thrilling experience for the rest of
us.

The ringmaster at this megawatt circus is a great one:
owner Sirio Maccioni. Born in Italy—Tuscany, he would
say—and trained in top European establishments, he is
driven to make his restaurant the best he possibly can. He
sees and worries about everything. When he stops, you'll
know Le Cirque has peaked and is on its way down. Watch
him eye all that's going on in the dining room, watch his
face light up when someone offers a tribute, and watch him

195

kiss the hand of a parting lady, sharing some of the room's electricity and making her feel like a princess, whether she is or not.

Dining at Le Cirque is like dining nowhere else. In these days of limited menus, Le Cirque is a throwback. You can eat superbly every day for a month and never order the same thing, something that cannot be said for any other top restaurant in America. On the dinner menu are 15 cold hors d'oeuvre, six hot hors d'oeuvre, six soups, 44 entrées, plus an average of 12 specials. And if you don't see it listed, you can still ask for it. One of the restaurant's most popular dishes, pasta primavera, does not appear on the menu or as a special. Nevertheless, be sure to order it.

It used to be something of a joke and commentary on the sad state of New York City's Italian restaurants to cite Le Cirque, whose menu is almost exclusively French, as the town's best Italian restaurant. It wasn't much of an exaggeration, though, and nowadays Le Cirque can be called the city's best French restaurant, the city's best bistro, and the city's best fish restaurant: full bistro and fish menus are buried within Le Cirque's masterlist. These days bistro fare is hot, but no bistro around can top the quality of Le Cirque's roasted chicken with lemon, garlic, herbs, and olive oil; its veal kidney grilled with bacon and herb butter; its calf's liver sautéed with mustard sauce and braised celery; its lamb stew with tossed pasta in basil; or its renowned bouillabaisse or courageous bollito misto, the Italian version of pot-au-feu.

Chef Boulud—who hails from Lyon and trained at Roger Vergé's Moulin de Mougins before commanding a hotel kitchen in New York—believes that currently fish is his greatest strength, and based upon two of his newest creations, we cannot disagree. Sea scallops black tie is unforgettable: moist, poached scallops are dressed to the hilt with thin slices of black truffles sandwiched inside each scallop and grated on top. The sweetness and texture of the scallop is a shockingly fine companion for the usually overpowering truffle. And Boulud's black sea bass wrapped in thin slices of potato and served with a Barolo wine sauce, a variation on an established French theme, is thrilling.

Relentless experimentation goes on in the kitchen, and new and stunningly exciting dishes are whisked into the dining room with breath-taking regularity. Among other remarkable dishes are the carpaccio of red snapper; the otherworldly pasta with white truffles (when in season . . . and Le Cirque gets the first and the finest); variations on a sublime fresh New York State foie gras—sautéed and served with black pepper and grapes or in a terrine, say; or the lobster ravioli on a bed of spinach.

Influence as well as originality is one of the characteristics of a great restaurant, and here too Le Cirque is distinguished. It is a proven breeding ground for top chefs and restaurateurs. For Europeans, Le Cirque is probably America's most famous quality restaurant, an obligatory stop for chefs from all over America and Europe. (Europeans used to say you go to Le Cirque for the people, now they are humbled by the food.) It's clear, too, that Le Cirque's legendary dessert, crème brûlée, inspired the emergence of the old Catalan standard in New York City, across America, and over to Europe and Japan. At Paul Bocuse's restaurant in France it's called crème brûlée "Sirio" in homage to the great restaurateur Maccione.

Indeed, from its earliest days one of the keys to Le Cirque's success has been its justified reputation for having the finest selection of desserts in New York. Those beautiful high society ladies who lunch on a salad or grilled fish still cannot resist a fork of this or a spoon of that seductive sweet. In recent years Le Cirque has become a destination for another reason: its world-class wine offerings. More than 500 wines are always listed (65% French, 20% American, 15% Italian), and many more are aging among the 50,000 plus bottle inventory. You can close your eyes and point and be sure you'll hit a quality wine. Prices are good for a restaurant of this class, with more than 150 wines priced in the teens, twenties, or thirties. On the other hand, if you just closed a million or billion dollar deal and want to splurge, you'll be able to order great and rare Bordeaux and Burgundies in top vintages going back to the 19th century. And of course Champagne flows at Le Cirque like sparkling water. Viewed from multiple perspectives, this place has to be called extraordinary. Jacket and tie are required, as are reservations. The $29.95 fixed price lunch is a remarkable value, but for dinner don't inhibit yourself: expect to spend $100 per person.

Lunch Mon.-Sat. noon to 2:30 P.M.; dinner 6 P.M. to 10:30 P.M.; closed first three weeks in July. AE, DC.

LE FESTIVAL

134 East 61st St.
(Lexington Ave.)
838-7987

Le Festival doesn't feel like a festival. It is a good restaurant, but it lacks soul, identity, and joie de vivre. The lightness of the cuisine is counterweighted by the anonymous heaviness of the decor. This second restaurant of Jean-Jacques Rachou

French/Seafood

13

of La Côte Basque fame is an all-seafood affair. The luncheon menu costs $24 and dinner $40, but there are enough premiums for lobster, sole, fresh berries, etc. to render the menu in effect à la carte.

With the La Côte Basque connection, you'd think the Mediterranean fish soup with saffron would be a winning first course. It's not. The raw fish appetizers are better: three individual tartars of different fish with herbs and lemon, sea scallops with olive oil and basil, and renditions of salmon or snapper with herbs. The seafood casserole is an appealing hot appetizer. Lobster, shrimp, scallops, and mussels are served in a small silver pot with lobster sauce. Or try the ravioli stuffed with seafood and wild mushrooms. Six to eight fish are available for a main course. The poached skatefish with dark butter sauce with capers is a good choice; the others come close to the mark without ever actually hitting it. Desserts are all right; the wine list could list some more vintages, and could use some less expensive bottles. The Louis Latour Chardonnay from the Ardèche at $18 is a frugal selection. In the end, however, Le Festival has its charms and strengths, but don't make the mistake—and it is hard not to—of bringing Côte Basque expectations to it. Expect to pay $38 per person for lunch and $60 for dinner, plus tax and tip.
Lunch Mon.-Sat. noon to 2:30 P.M.; dinner Mon.-Fri. 5:30 P.M. to 10:30 P.M., Sat. till 11 P.M. All major credit cards.

LE REFUGE

166 East 82nd St.
(Lexington & Third Aves.)
861-4505

French

12/20

Le Refuge was first situated in a narrow brick-walled establishment on 83rd Street (which now houses Trastevere), and it was then as it is now one of the few neighborhood restaurants where good, simple French home cooking could be had in a not-too-fussy atmosphere. It quickly built up a solid neighborhood following, moved to its present, spacious quarters, and remains, happily, a pleasantly rustic yet smart neighborhood restaurant. This is a neighborhood crowd, but dressy. There are no culinary pyrotechnics on the small menu, and if you won't be thrilled, still, the food is consistent and you will eat well. The chef, Pierre St. Denis, has locked into a number of nouvelle executions, some more or less successful than others. You can't blame him for sticking to what works for his clientele, but dishes once new now seem a tad old hat.

The vegetable terrine salad with hot goat cheese is delicious but oddly too filling as a dinner starter; snails in a pastry shell is a better choice. The rouille accompanying the bouillabaisse is terrific. The veal with wild mushrooms and the duck are good main course choices. For dessert there is fruit sherbet, a good little chocolate cake, nice fruits with mint, and a dacquoise if you go for rich cakes. Le Refuge is particularly pleasant at lunch, a good address to keep in mind if you're doing the Metropolitan Museum or uptown galleries. There are several good omelettes and salads, and the sole meunière with a salad makes a perfect light lunch. Lunch will run about $23 per person, and dinner (with a bottle of the recommended Château des Tours Brouilly '85) between $35-40.

Lunch Mon.-Sat. noon to 3 P.M., Sun. noon to 4 P.M.; dinner Mon.-Sat. 6 P.M. to 11 P.M., Sun. 5 P.M. to 9:30 P.M. No credit cards.

LE RÉGENCE

Hotel Plaza Athénée, 37 East 64th St. (Madison & Park Aves.)
606-4647; 734-9100

French

15 🍴

This restaurant's majestic (as in Versailles) dining room makes a stronger and longer-lasting impression than the good food served in it. The room would make a fine movie set for some courtly period piece out of Hollywood—sea foam colors, gleaming crystal chandeliers, wall sconces, ceiling painted with clouds, smashing flowers, and posh, leather-cushioned Louis XV chairs, so solid that it takes a waiter to help petit diners adjust their seat. The room has hours going for it as well. It's available for a power breakfast, or a Sunday lunch or dinner, which can't be said for other restaurants of its class.

In its four years, Le Régence has had good and bad luck with chefs, attracting, then losing, some top French ones. Some consistency has been added by bringing in as consultants Jo, Michel, and Philippe Rostang (father and two sons), owners of Michelin two-star restaurants on the Riviera and in Paris. Theoretically one of the three is in New York ten days a month. They had good luck with fellow countryman Jean-Michel Bergougnoux serving up their recipes and menu as the resident chef, but within a year he left for Lutèce. Now 25-year-old Rostang protégé Richard Adam has been brought in to handle the ovens on a daily basis, and it will take time for him to prove himself and to master the seasonal menu changes. The restaurant continues nicely all the same, with balanced offerings adapted to American produce. The menu includes a fixed price three-course $57.50 dinner, a $30 lunch, plus à la carte listings.

Tiny soft-shell crabs (when available) are prepared superbly and vie with a delicate lobster ravioli, moist with fish stock, and usually served on a bed of spinach as a lovely prelude. Or you can have a lobster consommé with tiny fresh goat cheese ravioli. The fresh salmon tart with cream, onions, and dill, and the warm lobster salad with baby carrots and basil are highly recommended. And there's always pricey caviar or foie gras to start, at lunch. Grilled red snapper with butter and leeks, and a breaded fillet of pompano with olives and fennel, are both worthy of serious consideration for a main or fish course. There is a passable fillet of lamb and an intriguing roasted squab dish accompanied by a light garlic flan. The squab (baby pigeon), coppery, with its skin lacquered with vinegar and honey, is quartered and comes moist and medium rare (unless you stipulate otherwise). Wine to go along with all this will set you back some, unless you opt for the Louis Latour Chardonnay from the Ardèche (white) or the Château Vignelaure (red). The desserts won't divert your attention from the posh surroundings or the monied old folks nearby, but they're reasonably inviting, especially the cold chestnut soufflé with praline sauce and caramelized hazelnuts. Figure on $45 a person for lunch, $75 for dinner.

Breakfast daily 7 A.M. to 10 A.M.; lunch daily noon to 2:30 P.M.; dinner daily 6 P.M. to 9:30 P.M. All major credit cards.

LE RELAIS

712 Madison Ave. (63rd & 64th Sts.)
751-5108
French

12/20

One of the relatively few Upper East Side places with sidewalk seating, this appealing restaurant decorated with mirrors and old engravings quickly became the neighborhood headquarters for well-heeled youth at play. At almost any hour you can see pretty young things clustered around the bar or relaxing at the miniscule tables outside. This is also one of the few places where at off hours you can sit down with coffee and the paper and not be looked at askance. Though it can be uncomfortably noisy when full (the wooden floor is uncarpeted), the animated crowd that frequents Le Relais doesn't seem to mind. The cuisine, while quite adequate, is unremarkable, the menu featuring the kind of bistro standbys you'd have found 20 years ago at a dozen similar places in France. For openers at lunch there is lentil salad with a zesty ravigote sauce, pâté, and celery root rémoulade in season. Main courses include a pasta, leg of lamb classically paired with flageolets, trout with almonds, and Le Relais' ever-popular salade Eleonore, a good, moist, chunky chicken salad. At dinner, snails in a puff pastry shell join the menu along with duckling à l'orange, steak au poivre, and herbed roast chicken. Desserts include crème caramel, oeufs à la neige, chocolate mousse, and a wonderful

lemon tart. Average tab at dinner runs $29 per person; at lunch, $23, plus tax and tip.
Lunch Mon.-Fri. noon to 3 P.M., Sat. till 3:30 P.M., Sun. 12:30 P.M. to 3:30 P.M.; dinner Mon.-Fri. 6:30 P.M. to 11 P.M., Sat. & Sun. 7 P.M. to 11 P.M. AE, MC, V.

LE VEAU D'OR

129 East 60th St. (Park & Lexington Aves.)
838-8133
French

11/20

Let food fashions come and go. This outpost of Paris, circa 1950, changeth not. It has, instead, become an institution attracting a broad generational mix of well-heeled New Yorkers, including Dr. Ruth Westheimer, who, like many who dine here, arrives with most of her family in tow. What attracts are reasonable prices, stability, and ineffable charm. Le Veau d'Or is a small restaurant, a complex of alcoves in which every centimeter counts. Tables are wedged together in front of red leather banquettes. Walls are obscured under a clutter of a French ephemera: street signs, travel posters of the great châteaux, black-and-white glossies of flower markets, meat markets, and Frenchmen eating French bread. The glory that is France is celebrated in maps, castles, and cattle embossed in gold on large mirrors—all bracketing the portrait of the restaurant's namesake, the golden calf, asleep under a fluffy quilt—*le veau dort*, a pun as whimsical and good-natured as the restaurant itself.

The food is pure culinary nostalgia—down-home Parisian cooking as it is writ in the texts, from crunchy céleri rémoulade to snails in garlic butter to sauté de veau niçoise (a homey stew of cubed meat, tomatoes, and green olives), to squab cooked in a casserole with bacon, mushrooms, and pearl onions. Textbook, too, are the desserts, including a somewhat chalky chocolate mousse, and vanilla ice cream-filled profiteroles. Surprisingly, the most reasonably priced wines are from California, such as Domaine Chandon Brut ($24) and an '82 Jordan Cabernet Sauvignon ($30). Dinner for one with wine costs approximately $38.
Lunch Mon.-Sat. noon to 2:30 P.M.; dinner Mon.-Sat. 6 P.M. to 10:15 P.M. AE.

L'HOSTARIA DEL BONGUSTAIO

108 East 60th St. (Park & Lexington Aves.)
751-3530

In a city saturated with upwardly-mobile Italian restaurants, it is nice to know there's one where you can eat well but where no one's nose will be out of joint if you're in the mood for just a dish of pasta and a salad. And when the restaurant is not only well-located (it's a lunch haven for Bloomingdale shoppers) but sunny and pretty, it becomes a good place to know about. Tiles, earthenware plates, and

Italian

13

flowery fabric give L'Hostaria an easy, Mediterranean kind of sophisticated comfort. Service is considerate, professional, and pleasant. There are a dizzying 19 pasta dishes on the menu, some of the more unusual being orrechiette in an arugula-spiked tomato sauce, penne all' arancia with bitter-orange and herb overtones, and an excellent green gnocchi with zucchini and almonds. The creamy pesto, offered on several types of pasta, owes its unusual texture to the tiny dice of potatoes it contains. Pasta can be had by the half-portion and for a light, waistline-conscious lunch precede it with the lemony salad of fresh mushrooms, celery, and shards of aged Parmesan, or the insalata mare, in which conch, octopus, squid, and shrimp are lightly bathed in superb olive oil and lemon. If pasta doesn't appeal, there are ten risotti from which to choose. Try the wine-poached salmon, veal scaloppine with peas and artichokes, or anything that involves red snapper. The wine list has a number of good, modestly priced offerings. Desserts are nothing to rave about, but there are always fresh berries. Dinner about $35 per person.

Lunch Mon.-Fri. noon to 3 P.M.; dinner Mon.-Sat. 5:30 P.M. to 10:30 P.M. All major credit cards.

LUSARDI'S

1494 Second Ave. (77th & 78th Sts.)
249-2020

Italian

13

In the same way that the offspring of Pavillion have been fruitful and multiplied, the Italian contingent that began with Parma, son of Elaine's, has been setting up around town—at Nicola, Elio's, and now the Lusardi brothers. Each has its casual but well-dressed côterie and a smattering of celebs of one persuasion or another, and they all serve many similar dishes. It is interesting to observe the subtle differences in execution—it's kind of like eating at the homes of a large family whose members all cook.

Lusardi's gets first ranking in the finesse of its execution (after an earlier unevenness) of many of the standard menu items. Take the chicken scarpariello, for example: every restaurant in the "family" serves the small pieces of chicken with garlic and white wine. But at Lusardi's the sauce is reduced to an exquisite, lustrous glaze. The veal chop valdostana, butterflied and thinly layered with prosciutto and a melt of fontina cheese, is faultless. Among the openers, try grilled peppers, or, when available, the carpaccio of venison, served with sweet shards of aged Parmesan. Fusilli with pesto or any of the pasta specials, such as angel hair with tomatoes and basil, are good. Only the bruschetta suffers from being made with pallid, unripe winter tomatoes,

and while well conceived should not be served when true tomatoes are unavailable. Among main courses, a special of sweet-and-sour chicken with raisins and pine nuts was unusual, the fegato veneziano was buttery soft, sweet with onions, and pink as requested. From a wine list impressive for this genre of restaurant, the Gattinara Travaglini is a good, well-priced red. For dessert there are the usual berries in season, a forgettable commercial tartufo, and a truly extraordinary tirami su served in a huge stemmed glass. Either Mauro or Luigi, who are hard to tell apart, is always on hand to keep an eye on things, and the staff is gracious and professional—none of those Italian restaurant theatrics, thank you. Dinner averages $30 per person.
Lunch Mon.-Fri. noon to 3 P.M.; dinner nightly 5 P.M. to midnight. AE, DC, V.

MANCHU

1394 Third Ave. (79th St.)
734-5335
Chinese

12/20

This is one of the most popular restaurants above East 79th Street. It does so much trade in home delivery that it provides a bench outside for the delivery boys. The clientele is mostly young, and the food, mostly Mandarin and Szechuan, but with some Cantonese dishes. Good sweet-and-sour pork, chicken, shrimp, and whole flounder, as well as a Cantonese lobster can be had here. Try the lobster supreme (listed under Manchu Specialties): fresh lobster meat sautéed with garlic sauce on one side and white sauce on the other. Four flavors beef is named, we've been told, as much for the four colors of the vegetables—yellow baby corn, bright green snow peas, carmine red pepper, and creamy white bamboo shoots—as for the complex flavors of its spicy Hunan sauce. General's duck, a spicy dish of boneless duck sautéed with black mushrooms, sweet red pepper, and bamboo shoots, is outstanding. Other recommended choices include asparagus in white sauce with jumbo shrimp, and asparagus with beef and chicken in a rich brown sauce. All the food is fresh here, untouched by MSG, and you can have your choice of white or brown rice. To show its modern bent, Manchu offers Häagen-Dazs ice cream for dessert, as well as Tofutti. Prices average $18 per person, without Chinese beer.
Lunch & dinner Mon.-Thurs. 11:30 A.M. to 11:30 P.M., Fri.-Sun. till midnight. AE, MC, V.

MARCELLO

The disturbing noise level which plagued this otherwise outstanding restaurant in its first year has now been some-

1354 First Ave. (73rd St.)
744-4400

Italian

14

what reduced by expensive ceiling baffles, but the din on crowded evenings can still make conversation difficult. The decor is low-key rose and beige contemporary, the rear wall dominated by a handsome floor-to-ceiling photographic mural of Florence, cleverly arranged to appear three-dimensional. The fleet-footed staff is exceptionally professional and helpful; your captain always seems to have an eye on your table. Order the fried zucchini as soon as you sit down; it is among the best around, and makes a splendid nibble with a glass of the house red or white Frescobaldi while you peruse the menu. If the food seems familiar, it is because the chef (and co-owner) was previously berthed at Nanni Il Valetto and Sign of the Dove. Here Gianvito Fanizza has clearly come into his own. The pastas are all first-rate; you might ask about the night's "trittico," a fresh pasta trio which changes frequently according to availabilities and which can include angel hair with fresh peas, porcini and pancetta or with delicate sea urchin sauce; tortellini of porcini mushroom and ricotta in a sheer tomato sauce; and, when fresh basil is around, pesto-swathed shells. The mixed seafood pasta is another good bet. The pastas are rather pricey, but many can be had in half-portions. Best among the seafood dishes are the red snapper with wine and tomatoes, zuppa di pesce, and mustard-sharpened Dover sole. Chicken grilled simply over a wood fire, perfumed with rosemary, and served with a side of grilled young fennel, is absolute perfection. The tomato, onion, and pepper garnished Milanese chop is excellent, as are tender veal scallops with chestnuts in a lustrous white wine glaze. There's a good veal paillard, too. Marcello is very proud of his wine list and rightly so—there are over 200 listings, 30 from the Piedmont alone.

Almost every Italian restaurant worth its name has a tirami su these days, a dessert of espresso-soaked sponge with mascarpone, whipped cream, and some kind of chocolate topping. Marcello's ethereal version, made with split ladyfingers and thoroughly dusted with cocoa, is worth every calorie. As a simple alternative, there are fresh raspberries. About $35 per person.

Dinner Mon.-Sat. 5 P.M. to midnight, Sun. 5 P.M. to 11 P.M. All major credit cards.

MAXIM'S

If you're out to impress your in-laws from Westchester, take them to Maxim's. A New York clone of the original Paris

*680 Madison Ave. (61st
St.)*
751-5111
French

13 🍳

restaurant and nightclub frequented by tout-Paris for over three-quarters of a century, it's owned by designer Pierre Cardin. Your in-laws will like the look of the place: its name done in dancing red letters in joie de vivre upper case, plus a glorious array of flowers and vases, gleaming silver railings, glowing wood, and Art Nouveau-styled glass. A leafy carpet that runs from here to there will goggle their eyes when they look down, trying to figure out what is on the menu, which is written only in French.

With chef Patrick Pinon gone to the Russian Tea Room the menu, which despite seasonal additions is a little stagnant, may get some new input with experienced Jean Luc Garrigues coming over from La Grenouille. If you choose well you can eat well. To start, try a little Russian beluga caviar at $52 a moundlet, or the quail eggs and caviar tarts (a close second at $30) topped with a thumbnail-sized bit of sour cream and chives. Rolled sole with herbs and the Norwegian smoked salmon taste impersonal. Salade Maxim's is a wasteful assemblage of roast breast of pigeon, lobster, scallops, and foie gras over lettuce with a vinaigrette, and the various temperatures of the ingredients (from lukewarm to January) is unsettling. The orange-flavored consommé of duck is spiked with port. The Billy By, a cream of mussels soup, is recommended by the waiters. It says on the menu that it's served hot or cold; add the suffix "ish" to those words. Like the clientele, some of the entrées are dressed to impress. The medallion of venison with orange sauce and black currants, and hearts of beef with shallots are both nice; fresh duck foie gras with endives is sublime. So are the tranches de turbot with little rolls of blanched cabbage leaves and prawns, and the breast of duck served with pink grapefruit. The sole Albert (named for the notoriously inventive chef of those original days) is quite good, filleted with bread crumbs and served with duxelles, prawns, and lobster in a vermouth sauce. The waiter calls it "typical, typical Maxim's." The bread, by the way, is always stale.

Desserts are a little more lyrical. Désir de Roy are profiteroles with ice cream and a waterfall of chocolate sauce. If your company's attention is fading, order them the $9 crêpes flambées with raspberries: whoomp! They can always dance them off to Maxim's orchestra, so long as they're properly dressed; Saturday is black tie. One can eat here for about $60.

Dinner Tues.-Sat. 6 P.M. to midnight. AE, DC, MC.

MEZZALUNA

*1295 Third Ave. (74th &
75th Sts.)*
535-9600
Italian

13 🍳

The Upper East Side hardly lacks fashionable, casual Italian restaurants where you can reserve and be seated more or less at the appointed hour. Nevertheless, much of the populace of this well-heeled neighborhood, including young upscale Italians, line up here (overcrowding begins around 7:45 P.M.) and wait, wait, wait, because Mezzaluna takes no reservations for the 46 seats squeezed around its marble-topped tables. (It's not so crowded at lunch and the food is just as good.) What makes the waiting easier is the engaging look and feel of this up-to-the-minute trattoria. It has a narrow storefront with a split-level dining area, one wall completely obscured by 77 drawings, paintings, and collages from students in a Florentine art school who'd been asked to create a "work" exploring the theme of Mezzaluna, referring to both the crescent-shaped vegetable cutter as well as the moon at half-cycle. The other wall is dominated by a breakfront filled with handmade, handpainted Italian ceramics, a long bar, and—at the rear—a wood-fired pizza oven that stokes up at lunchtime and again at 10:30 P.M.

The fashionable pizzas—four cheeses, for example, or primavera (assorted vegetables)—are good bets, as are any of the pastas. Skip the appetizers such as the bland shrimp and white bean salad, and the rather mushy hot seafood salad. The homey, delicious pastas are far more satisfying, from the pansotti (dumplings stuffed with a blend of ricotta and light pesto and sauced with butter, Parmesan, and fried fresh sage leaves), to orrecchiette (with diced potatoes, arugula, and light tomato sauce), to "designer" pasta such as black linguine (the color comes from cuttlefish ink) with a feisty arrabiata sauce—a dish that is as beautiful as it is toothsome. For dessert, tirami su or fresh fruit tart are good standbys. The wine list is short and serviceable and you can't go wrong with an '83 Avignonesi ($24). Expect to pay $35 per person, with wine, plus tax and tip.

Lunch Mon.-Fri. noon to 3 P.M., Sat. & Sun. noon to 3 P.M.; dinner Mon.-Fri. 6 P.M. to 1 A.M., Sat. & Sun. 6:30 P.M. to 1 A.M. No credit cards.

MORTIMER'S

*1057 Lexington Ave. (75th
St.)*
861-2481

The main room of this society bistro may be a sea of empty tables when you enter, but unless you are known through friendship or fame to the proprietor, don't expect to be given one; those without rank automatically go to the side room. Though the official policy is "no reservations" except for parties of five or more, Mr. Bernbaum, the owner, makes no

Continental

10/20

bones about choosing to hold tables for his personal friends, making Mortimer's a de facto private club that fills extra tables with walk-ins. At lunch the regulars love the freshly made melba toast, the paillard of chicken, the really good red cabbage slaw, and don't seem to mind salmon croquettes burnt outside and raw within, dry salade niçoise (the potato salad is good), or linguini so al dente as to be unbendable. Though a food consultant added some imaginative numbers like gravlax and Senegalese soup, by and large the food is predictable, designed to be eaten without interrupting conversation beyond a quaff of Perrier to wash down the overcooked calf's liver or the dry twinburgers. At dinner there is nicely roasted chicken, roast beef with Yorkshire pudding, quail in season, and a quite good crème brûlée. The room has its charm, lots of wood and mirrors, and well-spaced tables to allow gossiping eavesdrop-free. Sunday brunch is an important event. Figure $30-40 per person for dinner.

Lunch Mon.-Fri. noon to 3:30 P.M., Sat. & Sun. till 4:30 P.M.; dinner nightly 6 P.M. to midnight; supper nightly midnight to 2 A.M. All major credit cards.

PAMIR

1437 Second Ave. (74th & 75th Sts.)
734-3791

Afghan

14

Walking into Pamir is like walking into a Kabulian bric-à-brac shop: the lights are dim and the walls covered with shawls and rugs from Afghanistan and Pakistan. You sit down at one of the closely-spaced tables and a sweet mosaic of aromas—sharp spices, a tease of mint—dances over to greet you. This enchanting little oasis, created by the Bayat brothers, teems with activity every night.

Afghan cooking is earthier than its Indian counterpart. Of the appetizers, sambosa goushti—deep-fried dumplings of ground beef and chickpeas, served with an "Afghan sauce" that tastes like spicy ketchup—stands out. The best deal is the Pamir combination. Though you're offered a choice of three appetizers, they often give you all four: a scallion turnover with yogurt (bulanee gandana), a ground beef and potato turnover (bulanee kachalou), scallion dumplings (aushak), and the sambosa goushti. This group comes with a salad, however, that's as disappointing as it is inevitable—the supermarket lettuce and tomatoes are served with all the main dishes as well.

The best entrées are the marinated kebabs—kofta (chicken), and Pamir, an assortment of four different meats (lamb chunks, lamb chops, ground beef, and chicken). Chalaw sabsi, a spinach stew with spicy sauce, and chalaw bedenjan, sautéed eggplant with yogurt, are the best vegetarian dishes. But stick with Afghani tea for a finisher—the desserts are heavy and strange, dominated by pistachios and too much sugar. Our only question (given Pamir's predilection for using good ole USDA ground beef) is, where's the lamb? Did you ever see an Afghani walking a herd of cows? Figure on $25 or so per person, plus tax and tip.

Dinner Tues.-Sun. 5 P.M. to 11 P.M. MC, V.

PANDA GARDEN

1606 Second Ave. (83rd St.)
288-0400
Chinese

12/20

In a spacious and unassuming room the size of a banquet hall, with a wall made up entirely of lace-curtained windows and vigorous plants jungling up the corners, Hunan and Szechuan specialties are cooked with a verve and skill unusual for a restaurant this size. The best appetizers are the steamed dumplings, served in a blazingly hot oil sauce; shredded pieces of fresh Chinese cabbage with a red oil sauce; fried crispy shrimp balls, a little greasy (which is sometimes nice); and paper-wrapped chicken. The hot-and-sour soup is a veritable song of flavors. The house special soup is a light broth filled with chunks of chicken, shrimp, and vegetables and is a meal in itself.

The best entrées are listed under "Chef's Specialties." Try the orange beef (chunks of high-class steak sautéed with an orange sauce) or the house special beef, which is a spicy mixture of steak and hot pepper sauce, served with crisp, cool watercress. General Tso's chicken, a common dish at better-quality places, is excellent. Crispy prawns with walnuts again with a tangy sauce, is also good. But the dish that's the most fun to eat here is the neptunes in bird's nest: noodles are moulded into a basket and fried until they're stiff, then the middle is filled with seafood. By the time you get through the seafood the heat and moisture have softened the noodles, and they're a delicious way to finish. Among the non-specials, which are almost as good if a bit less elaborate, are the scallops with black bean sauce, which taste better than the shrimps served with the same sauce. An often abused common dish, cold noodles in sesame sauce, is unusually notable: the sauce is creamy and full of nutty bite, the wheat noodles cooked al dente and served with a proper abundance of scallion greens. On a slow day it feels like the waiting room of Grand Central Station here, but the food is good and the portions are enormous. Average price per person, for a full meal, is $15.

Lunch & dinner noon to 11 P.M. AE, MC, V.

PAOLA'S RESTAURANT

*347 East 85th St. (First &
Second Aves.)*
794-1890

Italian

13

Paola's is a small romantic place on the Upper East Side, frequented by the civilized folk who live on East End Avenue. WASPy women in elegant out-of-date clothes and inherited jewelry, and men who were born into Brooks Brothers suits (and look like they run the company that owns the company you work for) sit quietly while the waiters—who are a bit on the snobbish side—work up and down the narrow aisle with oversized plates. The walls are covered with lots of little mirrors, a design which makes the place look bigger, and affords the bric-à-brac (candles, porcelain, flowers) a little breathing room.

The food here is very good by New York Italian restaurant standards, but sometimes it's a little pale. Start with the mozzarella fresca (with vegetables), the brodetto di cozze e vongole (steamed mussels and clams with white wine and tomatoes), or the crostino (toasted bread with prosciutto, mushrooms, mozzarella, and peas). The linguini with shad roe, though a bit rich, is recommended; the lobster, salmon, and wild mushroom ravioli is very good. The best buy, the gnocchi (dumplings with tomatoes, basil, and bacon) are so big that they can only be described as burly. For the second course stay away from the lamb chops, which are too small, and instead try the veal scaloppine, either pizzaiola (with olives and red peppers), or al marsala (with mushrooms and Marsala wine). Or ask for the fish of the day. The mixed grill of veal chop, lamb chop, liver, sausage, chicken, and scampi is the most expensive item on the menu, and ordering it will gain you instant status (watch your waiter perk up). But it also happens to be a wonderful dish. Chocolate mousse tartufo with crème de cacao is a fine dessert. Owner/chef Paola Marracino recommends Luna di Feldi for a white wine ($26), or the red Aglianico ($30). Dinner averages $38 per person.
Dinner daily 5:30 P.M. to 11 P.M. AE.

PARIOLI ROMANISSIMO

*24 East 81st St. (Fifth &
Madison Aves.)*
288-2391

Italian

16

Parioli's new digs in an elegant townhouse just off Fifth Avenue will give you the immediate sense of being in for a special treat. A small bar for cooling your heels or throat offers huge macadamia nuts as a nibble. Soothing peach-stippled lacquer walls, carpeting, and a handsome garden room in the rear all speak of a quiet opulence. There's a sense of privacy (no one even *stares* at Paul Newman), almost as if you were a guest at a dinner party. The clientele and the waiters—middle-aged and elegant—look like they're from a Giorgio Armani fashion show. The serious staff function

209

quietly on a level one usually finds only in the better European restaurants—no flash, no tableside dazzle, just unobtrusive, good service. In the Grand Room of this class building, Rubrio Ross oversees his classy restaurant with a practiced hand.

The dishes are clearly Italian in inspiration, but so refined, and there's not a cliché in the lot. There are nine veal dishes alone, each mouthwatering. The 21-day-old chicken, hovering between squabhood and adolescence, its blushing flesh delicate and juicy, its sheer skin crisp as silk, is absolute perfection. There are superb pastas, to be shared by two as an appetizer, or enjoyed by one as a main course: subtly refined trenette in a wild mushroom sauce; fedelini with a sauce of tomatoes, prosciutto, and jalapeños, a thrill of flavor and heat; and delicate wild mushroom ravioli in a light butter basil sauce. There is also an unusual carpaccio of thinnest baby lamb slices, quickly charred without, tender and raw within, is served with delicious caramelized shallots and a cream of roasted red peppers. Buffalo mozzarella is superb with deliciously sweet home-roasted peppers and arugula.

Scaloppine alla zingara is tenderest veal transformed with succulent anchovies, capers, and mushrooms. A rosemary-scented rack of roast veal with a broccoli purée (which must be ordered for two) is extraordinary, a baby rack of lamb with the sweet-tart tang of mustard fruits, exquisite. Be warned that most main courses come absolutely unadorned, and you must be prepared to raise your already hefty bill by the cost of one or more à la carte vegetables. The pleasing dessert assortment includes a perfect raspberry tart, a heady excess in a pool of raspberry purée and so recently made its paper-thin pâte feuilletée crust is still paper-crisp; an excellent macedonia of fresh fruits; and a light cheesecake. Or you may wish to have a selection from the truly staggering assortment of cheeses (we counted 47 one night). This may require another bottle of wine. Parioli's wine list is extensive; you can pay as much or as little as you want. The house recommends some moderately-priced ones, including the white Pomino from Frescobaldi ($28.50) or Pinot Chardonnay from Jermann ($24.50), and the red Vino Nobile di Montepulciano by Fassati 1979 ($39.50) or I Sodi San Nicolo from Castellare ($32.50). All this luxe comes dear, but how can you put a price on near-perfection? Don't expect to get out for less than $150-175 per couple, which includes a modest wine, but not tip and taxes.
Dinner Tues.-Sat. 6 P.M. to 11:30 P.M. AE, DC.

PETALUMA

1356 First Ave. (73rd St.)
772-8800

Italian

11/20

A theatrical pastel California-Southwest-oceanliner architectural hybrid, Petaluma's spacious interior attracts one of the most diverse crowds you'll see in a Manhattan eatery—young and social singles, female and male duos, the retirement crowd, families who like a place where the varying taste of individual members can all be satisfied. The brainchild of Elio Guaitolini of sister restaurant Elio's, Petaluma is sort of a modern-day Left Bank cafe into which you can fall at almost any hour; the elegant bar has been brilliantly positioned so as to cater to the singles crowd without interfering with diners. Likewise the exposed kitchen, which does not intrude on the privacy of the raised dining area.

Petaluma's menu is now its strong suit, reworked from an earlier version in which it seemed every second item was fried. It is a moderately-priced, diversified grazing food place bolstered with a small but good assortment of more substantial fare, designed to attract yuppies who'd rather snack, and oldsters who prefer to eat lightly or taste several dishes at once. At lunch you can get a burger and fries, grilled tuna or duck breast salad, grilled veal sausages with black bean chili, good Maryland crab cakes, or various pastas or pizzas. Mozzarella in carozza, small batter-dipped mozzarella and Italian bread sandwiches, are ravishing to look at under a tangle of skinny fried zucchini around a pool of tomato sauce, but are too salty and capered. There are a number of pastas, all acceptable, none brilliant. Salmon and swordfish are treated impeccably, as is a free-range chicken with roasted peppers. Many people go for the individual dinner plate-sized pizzas available on both menus, pizzas with the kind of crispy thin crust characteristic of a wood-burning oven. The Margharita with mozzarella, tomato sauce, and basil, and the four-seasons with prosciutto, artichokes, and mushrooms are two of the best, though the toppings are skimpy. The vanilla cheesecake for dessert is underwhelming; the chocolate cake good but too rich an ending. Service ranges from professional to inept—the young lady who uses her fingers to pull a piece of tart onto a plate. Classy wines and vintage port are inappropriate to this food; stick to the good inexpensive house offerings or one of the terrific selection of beers. About $22 per person at lunch, $35 at dinner. If you just want a pizza and a glass of wine, however, you might get by with $16 or so.
Lunch daily 11:30 A.M. to 3 P.M.; dinner Mon.-Sat. 5 P.M. to midnight, Sun. 5 P.M. to 11 P.M. AE.

PIG HEAVEN

1540 Second Ave. (80th &
81st Sts.)
744-4887

Chinese

13 ♟

Pig Heaven, one in David Keh's triumvirate, is the new
haunt for uptown chic crowds who want to experience
Chinatown without leaving their turf. Sam Lopata, David's
architect, surrounds us with the pink walls of a nursery
barnyard—150 little pink dancing pigs overlooking a large
yellow moon and a neon cartoon of a tipsy pig presiding over
a white tiled bar. Roast ducks, chickens, and suckling pigs
(the restaurant's specialties) peer at you from behind a
glass-enclosed barbecue grill. The menu is suprisingly authentic and Keh's chefs (there are several) do not compro-
mise. The spicy, tangy shredded pig's ears make a crunchy,
excellent appetizer, followed by an array of dim sum,
steamed and fried dumplings and scallion pancakes. The
small dumplings steamed in a bamboo basket are exquisitely
light, as are the unusual turnip cakes. If pork is not your cup
of Chinese tea, the vegetarian rolls are as good as in
Chinatown.

As its name implies, Pig Heaven serves up great
Cantonese-style suckling pig and roast pork. Tender and
sweet, with crackling skin, both dishes will have you gleeful-
ly licking your fingers. The menu also features several
Szechuan dishes such as pork with pickled vegetables or with
garlic sauce, and braised pig's feet. Unfortunately, these
dishes are not consistently good. Stick to three glass chicken,
lightly sautéed with fresh ginger, garlic, wine, soy sauce, and
vinegar, or a whole braised carp with hot bean sauce. Just
beware of the hundreds of fish bones! Double-fried bean
curd, crisp outside and light as air inside, is the best
non-meat dish. The mussels in casserole with transparent
mung beans is also a hit. The French and American desserts
should be avoided. The restaurant serves wine, and on
Saturdays and Sundays, Pig Heaven offers a Chinese breakfast
of dumplings, congee (rice soup with pork and pickles), and
suckling pig. About $30 per person.
*Mon.-Fri. noon to midnight, Fri. & Sat. till 1 A.M.; breakfast
Sat. & Sun. 11 A.M. to 3 P.M. AE, DC.*

PINOCCHIO

170 East 81st St. (Second
& Third Aves.)
650-1513

Italian

12/20

Pinocchio is an appealing family restaurant that has expanded its quarters from the storefront of one antique East Side
tenement building to the storefronts of two. Peeking their
noses through the heavy curtains in the front windows to
greet you are various antique wooden Pinocchios. A lot of
people consider this their special place, though for some it's
no longer special—ordinary and reminiscent of a past dis-
covery. It's a romantic kind of dark—spare, elegant and real,

no frou-frou or pretense—but enlivened by the sounds and bustle of staff and guests.

The changing, handwritten menu offers, at its best, a solid, well-wrought example of Northern Italian cooking, with stately sauces and lively meats. Start off with the special crostini nostri: muscular cheese melted over carmine pimento strips and strong anchovies, layered onto a good slice of crusty bread. Or try the carpaccio; the pâté of veal, artichoke, bacon, and brandy; the hot Genoa salami served under grated cheese; or the sautéed and stuffed mushroom caps, which, with their fragrant mushroom and herb stuffing and gratinée tops, are so good you'll want many more than the allotted two. Pinocchio's pastas are best for what's in them: the ardent veal and indefatigable ham in the green and white paglia e fieno; the tart capers and bacon pieces in the (sometimes too rich) cream sauce, spiked with a whiff of sharp cheese, in the penne palermitana. Other recommended pastas are the fettucine al porcini, and the Norwegian salmon puttanesca. For entrées you might order a special fish dish, since that's the only way you can sample the otherwise unlisted trout poached in red wine and butter sauce, or any of the salmon dishes. The liver torinese is stellar, and there are good lamb chops milanese, and veal piccata.

Italian desserts can be delightful or fall flat (we're thinking of some rather pallid versions of cheesecake), and here you'd better stick with the best. Zabaglione is served cold over ripe berries, or it's slid into a glass and laced with hot espresso in café nonno. Budino al caffé is mocha mousse and bittersweet dark chocolate bits; a macaroon soaked in mocha lurks like a seductress in the bottom of the sundae glass. Something magic is done to the espresso here to make it strong yet never bitter; its cap of amber froth has its own staying power. Dinner runs about $38 per person.
Lunch Mon.-Sat. 12:00 P.M. to 2:00 P.M.; dinner Mon.-Sat. 5 P.M. to 11 P.M.; closed July & Aug. AE.

THE POLO

Westbury Hotel, 840 Madison Ave. (69th & 70th Sts.)
535-9141; 535-2000

French

14 ⌂

Hotel dining in New York is back, and the Polo is one of the restaurants that brought it back. When it opened in 1982 it drew a lot of attention for its opulent English club-style setting, its high prices, but most of all for its heavy-hitting French food—classic yet nouvelle with the Provençal influence of consultant Roger Vergé of the famed Moulin de Mougins on the French Riviera. Vergé-trained chef Patrice Boëly established the kitchen, but in many ways the Westbury's former general manager Pierre Constant put the restaurant on the gastronomic map. He left in 1987, but the talented Boëly is still in command, and the restaurant remains true and consistent to its standards and offerings—that is to say what was once innovative and distinctive is now establishment. And one wonders where everyone in the dining room has gone at 10:30 P.M. on a Saturday evening. Upstairs to bed?

Walk past the portrait of Prince Charles in the vestibule and into the handsome, solid dining room with its dark mahogany walls and horsey prints and slide into a plush banquette or leather club chair for some hearty fare. The appetizer portions tend to be as large as main courses. The menu changes four times a year, but the excellent sautéed slice of fresh foie gras served with artichoke bottoms and a vinegar sauce is usually available as an appetizer. Another starter, the stuffed brioche with scallops and a cream crayfish sauce, tastes better than it looks. The various fresh herbs in the fish entrées—for example, the salmon or red snapper—show a Provençal influence. Meats are top quality and generally display the light touch evident in the fish dishes. Quail is good, as is the grilled chicken with curry and Indian potatoes. There is an O.K. deer steak that is surrounded, like most meat dishes, with a symphony of vegetables. A most memorable entrée is a huge and strong-tasting portion of calf's sweetbreads, served with snowpeas and a foie gras sauce with port wine.

Service is black tie and effective, but with a European-American indifference. An old-fashioned dessert trolley offers some standard delicacies. The wine list is 75% French and 25% American, and though it contains nothing surprising or overly exciting, it is sound and has a few exceptional values for the well-informed. The Polo has wine by the glass, a handsome bar, and a pianist most evenings. Dinner averages $60 per person, lunch or brunch can be had for half that.

Breakfast daily 7 A.M. to 10 A.M.; lunch noon to 2:30 P.M.; dinner 6:30 P.M. to 10:30 P.M. All major credit cards.

PRIMAVERA

1578 First Ave. (82nd St.)
861-8608

Italian

14

Primavera was one of the first uptown restaurants to abandon tomato sauce and serve pricey Northern Italian cuisine in a romantic setting. It developed a solid following very quickly, and became an "in" place with a fashionable crowd that gets dressed up to come here. Since the move to larger and more elegant quarters on the corner, what was once a classy bistro has become an unabashedly fancy restaurant, albeit still charming, and one that performs appealingly. That the quality and good service has remained constant is due to the instincts and watchful eye of its creator, Nicola Civetta. Hors d'oeuvre are fairly predictable, and you would do better to start with a half-portion of pasta. Tortellini with ham and peas, agnelloti, pasta primavera, or linguini studded with fresh vegetable morsels in a sauce brought nicely together with a bit of cream and Parmesan are all good bets. Baked clams are pasty, as are the stuffed mushrooms.

Primavera customers can be fairly evenly divided between people who go to see and be seen, and those who go because they are addicted to the roasted marinated kid that started out as a sometime special and developed a passionate following. It's like lamb, but better and sweeter, occasionally a bit tough, but mostly bone-gnawingly succulent and redolent of rosemary. Nicola's fresh fruit plate, which he himself used to carve into fanciful and delightful shapes as a "gift" to special patrons, also became so popular it is now a staple. Other restaurants should take note. Service is professional and attentive, though occasionally there is a long wait for the main course. The wine list is imposing, but great Bordeaux are not entirely appropriate to the food. Stick to wines like the Pinot Grigio Santa Margherita or the Gattinara. Dinner will run between $40-50 per person.
Dinner daily 5:30 P.M. to midnight. All major credit cards.

PRIMOLA

1226 Second Ave. (64th & 65th Sts.)
758-1775
Italian

13 🍳

The newest outpost of the gang of Elaine's and then Parma is the lively, spirited Primola. Bustling at night with enthusiastic regulars, Primola is enough off the beaten path to offer a deliciously tranquil lunch. Co-owner and maître d' Djuliano Zuliani, who has an encyclopedic memory for names and faces, is everywhere, welcoming, seating, keeping an eye on dishes as they are served.

Decor is spare, that is to say, nonexistent: there's a natural wood floor, some inoffensive posters and watercolors, a welcoming bar which can be a bit raucous on crowded nights, and an appealing display of hors d'oeuvre and desserts. Food is skillfully prepared. Besides listed items on the ambitious menu there are numerous specials like rigatoni isolana, homemade pasta and tender eggplant in a vivid tomato sauce, or homemade ravioli filled with a flavorsome, well-seasoned spinach ricotta mixture in a fresh tomato basil sauce. Other good starters are the toothsome sautéed sliced artichokes or salmon marinated with fennel. Excellent quality veal appears as scaloppine, piccata, or with wild mushrooms. Pink, moist charcoal-grilled lamb chops are also good. Seafood is skillfully handled as well at Primola. The whole roasted sea bass for two and grilled baby snapper sauced with a reduction of balsamic vinegar are simple and perfect. Vegetable accompaniments are no mere afterthought: the grilled fennel and endive accompanying the fish is first-rate. Desserts include pleasant homemade ice creams, berry tarts, the ubiquitous ricotta cheesecake, and crème brûlée. Lunch runs around $22 per person; dinner about $35.

Lunch Mon.-Fri. noon to 2:30 P.M.; dinner daily 5 P.M.to midnight. AE, DC.

QUAGLINO BY TINO FONTANA

Sherry-Netherland Hotel, 781 Fifth Avenue (59th & 60th Sts.)
759-9020

Italian

13

Scene 1: lunch on the last day of August, 1987, in the cosmopolitan restaurant Harry Cipriani. The place is oh-so-very chic. No one seems to mind the noise and tables so small and crowded that the details of a nasty divorce can be heard close at hand. The pasta isn't so good, but no one notices either. Scene 2: dinner the same day in the same dining room. Since lunch the restaurant has changed its name, management, and chef. "Where's Harry?" people ask. Tino Fontana—restaurateur, caterer, and consultant from Northern Italy—is now in charge.

The next day people learn from the front pages of *The New York Times* as well as Italian dailies that celebrated Arrigo (Harry) Cipriani and his son, Giuseppe, of Harry's Bar in Venice and recently Bellini in New York, have been sacked with military suddenness from their two-year-old restaurant by the management of Trusthouse Forte, the international hotel chain that financed it. Scene 3: lunch and dinner one month later in Quaglino by Tino Fontana. The society folk are gone, the green cloth wall coverings and other design features are untouched, the same low seats and small seats remain, but they are largely empty.

Perhaps because the kitchen does not have to cope with a press of diners, the food is a notch better than it was under Cipriani. Or perhaps Mr. Fontana's team, which trained in Milan for their raid, is better than the earlier hired hands. Still, they are not top-notch or renowned, and $18 to $25 plates of pasta don't beckon off-the-street drop-ins. The pasta is good, notably a plate of rectangular, flat noodle stracci served with an asparagus cream sauce. With the recent influx of contemporary Northern Italian restaurants in New York, risotto has taken on new meaning and life. All of a sudden it is everywhere, and the native versions offered up at Quaglino are good. Recommended à la carte entrées include an interwoven combination of sole and salmon in a basil sauce, and a veal scallop in a rich stock sauce accompanied by an asparagus purée. Desserts are rich, creamy, and heavy. If you don't feel like sorbet or fruit, stick to the authentic espresso or finish your good but high-priced bottle of Italian wine. Trusthouse Forte can surely afford a half-empty restaurant, and hotel and condominium residents are no doubt pleased with the breakfast hours and room service; nevertheless, one can not help wondering about Quaglino's future. There are two tasting menus at diner, $40 or $50, and a lunch menu fixed daily at about $30, but overall expect to pay top prices here, $50 to $75 a person for dinner, and only slightly less for lunch.

Breakfast daily from 7 A.M. to 10 A.M.; lunch daily from noon to 3 P.M.; dinner daily from 6 P.M. to 10:45 P.M. All major credit cards.

RAO'S

455 East 114th St.
(Pleasant Ave.)
534-9625
Italian

12/20

Where is it most difficult to book a table in New York? Chanterelle? Le Bernardin? Nope. Rao's. The wait for one of the eight tables in this reverse-chic, old-time bar-and-grill of a restaurant averages two to three months, and that's only because reservations generally aren't taken any further in advance. "For my own sister, I had to wait three months for a table," the barman of eleven years said with a straight face. Now in its second century, Rao's looks like it belongs in a 1930s movie, and some of the types who frequent it could get parts as extras in a minute. The singular and often big-name cast that frequents this cozy corner restaurant in East Harlem eye Vincent Rao as soon as they enter. The octogenarian is in his kitchen wearing a cowboy hat and cooking the Southern Italian/American food he has been turning out for decades with wife Anna and a few assistants at his side. Able nephew Frank Pellegrino is the host and manages the place.

Frankie pulls up a chair to your table and takes your order: "Everything is good," he says and provides engaging rhapsodic descriptions of dishes when prompted. A more apt broad description of the offerings is, "There's nothing bad." For starters, the seafood salad is more than not bad, it's cool, lush, chewy and flavorful. Lobster, crabmeat, rings of squid, octopus bits, conch meat, scungilli are tossed with celery, lemon juice, olive oil and parsley. Roast red pepper salad, with or without anchovies, is another good starter. Among the pasta, the garlicky linguine with clam sauce is recommended, as is the macaroni tossed with broccoli. For a main course, try the "famous" lemon chicken or the he-man dish of pork chops. There are veal, beef or pork pizzaiola, and many familiar preparations. Desserts are weak, and when you ask the engaging bartender for the wine list, he replies, "I'm the wine list." The half-dozen white and half-dozen red wines he recites belong in a pizzeria, but he'll steer you to the one or two best bottles. Everyone under the low black ceiling or behind the bar with the year-round Christmas decorations will steer you well. And you can even steer yourself well to Rao's and park your car safely outside. Frankie has everything under control. Prices as well, which run about $28-35 a person.

Dinner Mon.-Fri. 6 P.M. to 10 P.M. No credit cards.

REMI

323 East 79th St. (First & Second Aves.)
744-4272

Italian

13 ♟

This handsome, noisy, and bustling Venice-by-the-Upper-East-Side ristorante has been packing people in since it opened in March 1987. It's proof that New York can always use another good little Italian restaurant with appealing pastas and some good fish and meat dishes. Indeed, people book days in advance, and wait at a small and crowded bar for a seat at one of the three rows of tables in the long rectangular dining room. "Remi" is the Italian word for a gondolier's oars, and architect and co-owner Adam Tihany has decorated with a Venetian motif, using real oars (crossed and set in three large, recessed light boxes on the ceiling) and Venetian glass from the island of Murano. The walls are lined with blue-and-white banquettes, and a six-inch band of mirror permits diners facing the wall to glimpse much of the room.

The young staff are attired in blue-striped shirts and sometimes have trouble negotiating the tiny-aisled passageways to deliver chef and co-owner Francesco Antonucci's dishes. Antonucci trained in Milan at El Toulá, and worked in New York at the former ddl Bistrot and at Alo Alo. A little tasty and gratis dish such as goat cheese, mozzarella, and tomato with garlic on bread (variations on the theme of bruschetta) helps the drinks and the wait, which can be long before and between courses. There are excellent Italian wines with good prices to muse over (from Livio Felluga's Pinot Grigio 1985 near the bottom of the scale at $21, to Gaja's Barbaresco 1982 near the top at $50) and three great Champagnes (Veuve Clicquot vintage, Roederer Cristal, and the ubiquitous Dom Pérignon). Among the appealing antipasti, the bresaola in salsa senape (paper-thin sheets of sun-cured beef on a bed of bitter arugula, with swirls of

mustard sauce on the side) is a hit. The salads are made with good ingredients but are nothing extraordinary. The surprise in the radicchio e grana con polenta salad is that the polenta in this Venetian restaurant is not outstanding. Ditto for the risotto, theoretically a house speciality. It is good with asparagus or alla parmigiana, but it doesn't make you nostalgic for Piazza San Marco. The five or six pastas offered are all good and out of the ordinary. Corkscrew fusilli with smoked bacon and radicchio served in a light tomato sauce is particularly successful, though the Venice connection seems dubious. In fact radicchio, especially grilled, is one of the restaurant's strengths. It accompanies a fair veal paillard along with the regrettable polenta. Rack of lamb perfumed by garlic is a better choice. The fish dishes are undistinguished, but can be ordered with confidence. The desserts fall into the familiar Italian restaurant pattern of looking better than they taste. The crème brûlée is too thin and actually too firmly creamy. The tirami su (literally, "pick me up") tastes good, but is dusted with an avalanche of cocoa. The dessert list wisely begins with frutta di stagione (seasonal fruit). If your taste runs to grappa, that Italian firewater, this is the place to indulge. More than 25 selections are available. Prices at this high energy spot run about $35 a person, plus tax and tip.
Dinner daily 6 P.M. to 11:30 P.M. AE.

SANT AMBROEUS

1000 Madison Ave. (77th & 78th Sts.)
570-2214
Italian

12/20

The sleek but unassuming front of Sant Ambroeus is a pastry and gelato shop that might possibly make you think you're in Milan. Walk past the stunning pastries and appealing salads to the back and you will see well-dressed East Siders eating in great style, nestled in a little jewel-box of a dining spot, the unusual ceiling draped in white like a boudoir. Sant Ambroeus is a pricey but pleasing spot to breakfast, lunch, have tea, dine or just relax after you've done the nearby gallery circuit. The antipasti hold no surprises but are all good: air-dried bresaola, prosciutto with melon, vitello tonnato; only the sea food salad is curiously bland. An arugula salad with shards of aged Parmesan is overpriced at $10.50. The pastas are uniformly good, especially trenette al pesto (white gnocchi swathed in a pesto tomato sauce) and spaghetti bolognese. The buttery risotto is first-rate. Any of these with the house salad makes a perfect light meal at any time. (You may have a half-portion of pasta, but you'll be charged $2 extra.) Fillet of sole, veal picatta, and lamb chops with rosemary are all faultless. There is a simple list of

219

Italian wines, but most people just order the excellent house red or white.

Save some room for the desserts, which are culled from the excellent gelati and pastries for which Sant Ambroeus is renowned, notably colibri, a delectable sorbet and fresh fruit combination, and the rich chestnut delizia. The coffee and capuccino are wonderful. This goodness and chic-ness is dear: expect to pay about $30 per person at lunch, $45 at dinner.
Breakfast daily 9:30 A.M. to 11:30 A.M.; lunch daily noon to 4 P.M.; tea daily 3:30 P.M. to 6 P.M.; dinner Mon.-Sat. 6:30 P.M. to 10 P.M. AE, MC, V.

SINGLETON'S BAR-B-Q

346 Lenox Ave. (127th & 128th Sts.)
369-6101
American/Soul food

10/20

Singleton's claims to be the only open barbecue pit in New York that uses hickory chips. Located in the heart of Harlem, it is considered a venerable institution among rib aficionados. Safe and easy to get to, the restaurant has a thriving takeout business and also several tables covered with oil cloth. A pleasant waitress will take your order, and you are expected to order the works. Very large beef barbecued ribs are crisp at the edges, meaty, and succulent; pork ribs are smaller but just as tender. The ribs are served with a barbecue sauce which the owner claims is a family secret recipe from the heart of Virginia. Here you can also experience crunchy, crisp pig ears and feet, smothered pork chops, and the best ham hock north of mammie's kitchen. Each order comes with two vegetables and a tossed salad. Best among the side orders are a rich baked macaroni and cheese, tangy collard greens, and tender black-eyed peas. Forget about the salad. For dessert, choose the homemade sweet potato pie—every mouthful will make you wish you were born a Southerner. There is no bar and no drinks; bring your own beer. Price per person about $10.
Daily 10 A.M. to 3 A.M. No credit cards.

THE SIGN OF THE DOVE

1110 Third Ave. (65th St.)
861-8080
American

16

The yellow three-story building with white trim that houses Sign of the Dove has been a landmark on Third Avenue for many years. For a long time there were too many hanging plants, the tables were badly arranged, and the food was uninspired. Happily, all this has changed. In the hands of Clark Wolf, the well-known food consultant with magic hands, the building's façade is now pink, the hanging plants have disappeared, the tables are now set far apart, the flowers are beautiful, and the food is excellent.

The menu is prix fixe at $55 and changes with the seasons, although some dishes are available all year round. The menu, devised by Wolf and chef Andrew D'Amico, has a light touch of the Far East. The ravioli stuffed with duck confit and shiitake, topped with a fricassée of wild mushrooms, is superb; the tender duck is not masked by the transparent buttery cream sauce. Among the salads, the best one is warm roasted quail on a bed of tender-leafed raw baby spinach, artichoke hearts, and a poached quail egg sprinkled with a tart vinaigrette. The chef likes to mix his fish, and the marriage of red snapper and sea bass is a great success. The fried strips of fish are placed on top of homemade pasta sautéed in rosemary and wine. The originality of the menu is brought forth in a simple dish of tenderloin of beef poached in its own broth and served with vegetables and coarse sea salt mixed with chopped scallions. The chef has a wonderful touch in mixing tastes and textures, such as aioli with red pepper purée, veal with sweet garlic custard, and venison with polenta. Desserts are equally inspired. The crème brûlée is flavored with orange and candied orange peel and its caramel topping is like a mirror; the millefeuille is composed of delicate layers of paper-thin crunchy dough filled with fresh fruit and served with a sabayon sauce; the chocolate plate will satisfy any chocolate-lover's craving. The wine list is impressive with first-class wines from all over the world; prices are reasonable when you consider their quality. Service is excellent and unobtrusive. Monday through Friday there is a prix fixe menu from 5:30 P.M. to 6 P.M. for $32 which includes entrée, dessert, and coffee. After six the prix fixe jumps to $55 for a full meal. Lunch is à la carte; expect to pay about $35, and tag on another $10-20 per person for a modest wine at either meal.
Lunch Tues.-Sat. noon to 2:30 P.M., Sun. 11:30 to 3 P.M.; dinner Mon.-Sat. 5:30 P.M. to 10 P.M., Sun. 6 P.M. to 10 P.M. All major credit cards.

SISTINA

1555 Second Ave. (80th & 81st Sts.)
861-7660

Italian

14

From the looks of things, the Upper East Side can assimilate an inexhaustible number of polished, expensive Italian restaurants. This is one of them, and it's packed every night. The blond wood façade, the bentwood chairs, the central casting Italian waiters (who swoop gracefully to relieve you of your wine bottle in mid-pour and who describe each dish as "Fantastico!" kissing their finger tips in the mere contemplation of such deliciousness) are all familiar. And it's just fine because the food, for the most part, is as satisfying as the waiters lead you to expect, although much of your time is taken up in deciphering the menu, with its opaque titles for dishes such as Pollo Alla Sisto IV and Scampi Sopresa. You'll never go hungry, however. The very good bruschetta (chopped tomatoes and chopped basil on toast) and tiny slivers of fried zucchini which immediately appear whet your appetite for a fine pasta such as tagliatelle del capo cuoco (thin strands of noodle tossed with porcini mushrooms in a light, creamy tomato sauce) or pappardelle with porcini, arugula, and prosciutto. These are better starters than the somewhat lackluster seafood salad and the palatable grilled buffalo-milk mozzarella which, after the bruschetta, seems redundant with its topping of chopped tomatoes, basil, and extra virgin olive oil. If there's dentice (red mullet from the Adriatic or the Mediterranean), order it; it's deliciously basted with olive oil, balsamic vinegar, garlic, and chopped Italian parsley. For all the pomposity of the title, Pollo alla Sisto IV turns out to be game hen, split and grilled with rosemary. It's on the dry side but tasty all the same— particularly with a bottle of Lungarotti's Rubesco Riserva ($32). Expect to pay $40 per person for dinner, with a half share of a good wine.

Lunch Mon.-Fri. noon to 2:30 P.M.; dinner Mon.-Sat. 5 P.M. to midnight, Sun. 5 P.M. to 11 P.M.; no lunch in summer. AE.

THE STANHOPE DINING ROOM

Stanhope Hotel, 995 Fifth Ave. (81st St.)
288-5800

Continental

13 🍴

With a German developer's zillion-dollar face-lift and a stint by Michel Fitoussi in the kitchen, the Stanhope is making a bid to join the ranks of the city's top hotel dining rooms. Fitoussi, whose undeniable culinary brilliance runs amok at times, reworked the menu and kitchen here in 1987 before decamping for a similar renovation job at Regine's. At the Stanhope the spun sugar is green, in the form of an apple, which floats on a raspberry coulis and is filled with lime mousse. Clever, pretty, but do you want to eat it? Or the chocolate-covered dates or marzipan ice cream? Apparently excess has its audience, willing to start with tuna tartare with quail eggs and caviar, truffle soup en croûte, and a forgettable lobster mousse on coral sauce with a julienne of sugar snap peas. Ravioli of lamb in an intense curry sauce garnished with chickpeas and spinach is a better choice. From there you can play it safe with loin of veal with cream of tarragon sauce, garnished with puffs of potato purée and a rather dated bundle of asparagus, or really send your cholesterol soaring with rabbit kidneys bordelaise with a ragoût of escargots. Two ploys to keep in mind: ask about the fish specials (you may be rewarded with a winner like the pompano baked under a rock salt crust, a miracle of moistness) and note the legend on the menu which says any entrée can be broiled. At lunch one can stay elegantly slender with Spanish red shrimp and purée of ratatouille, lobster salad with marinated avocado, or a nice fillet of sole enlivened with sesame seeds and cucumber sauce. An appetizer of ravioli of wild mushrooms with tomato coulis is a must.

The dining room is elegant and tranquil, exquisitely appointed, yet low-key and comfortable, with pale wood paneling, chandeliers in the grand hotel manner, and tables set well apart—the perfect place for a moneyed or amorous exchange. This is definitely a place where women can wear hats; gentlemen are required to wear ties and jackets. The upper level serving staff is very professional; entrées arrive importantly, set before you under silver serving domes by tuxedoed waiters. Once the Lucullan contents are consumed, however, the busboy may stack dirty plates on his arm like a diner waitress. Lunch (with an $18 minimum) averages $45 per person including a glass of wine; dinner carries a prix fixe of $55 before wine, so figure at least $65-75 sharing a modest bottle, plus tax and tip.
Lunch Mon.-Fri. noon to 3 P.M.; dinner daily 6 P.M. to 11 P.M.; brunch Sat. & Sun. 11:30 A.M. to 3 P.M. All major credit cards.

SYLVIA'S

328 Lenox Ave. (126th & 127th Sts.)
534-9348
American/Soul food

10/20

Sylvia's brings hungry New Yorkers up to Harlem for breakfast with a down-home Southern touch. Imagine eggs, sunny side up or down, with thick slices of sausage redolent of rosemary and thyme, and smooth grits served with fried chicken or pork chops. The best is yet to come: plump hot cakes with butter and syrup always served with a side order of hot sausages, bacon, or that same fried chicken. Sylvia's specialties include smothered chicken, greasy and spicy, with the best home fries in Manhattan, and short ribs of beef in brown gravy (the meat falls off the bone) with onions and green peppers, accompanied by a hot biscuit to soak up the sauce. You may need an Alka Seltzer later, but the pain is worth it! There is a full bar with beer, hard liquor, and wine by the glass. Lunch or dinner run around $10 per person.
Breakfast, lunch & dinner Mon.-Sat. 7:30 A.M. to 10:30 P.M., Sun. 1 P.M. to 7 P.M. No credit cards.

TRASTEVERE

309 East 83rd St. (Second Ave.)
734-6343
Italian

13 ♟

The Lattanzi family seems to specialize in adorable little restaurants the size of shoe repair shops. This one, named after the economically poor but trattoria-rich section of Rome, was the first. Now there is Trastevere II, Erminia, Lattanzi, and Trastevere (III) in Forest Hills, Queens. One wonders whether the food might not be even better were the family to lease a larger space and concentrate their culinary skills in a single kitchen. The food here does not quite live up to its early repute, or to the charm of the minuscule room with its brick walls, huge oil paintings, and taped top-of-the-pops of Italian opera. The menu is short—too short, in fact, even though amplified by several specials, to offer an appetizing variety of tastes. Too many of the sauces sound the same, and even when they don't *sound* the same, they end up *tasting* the same. That aside, this is a good restaurant and many of the dishes make for satisfying eating. Garlic is the preferred flavoring, and it is displayed to very good effect in a mixed vegetable appetizer with artichoke hearts, roasted red peppers, broccoli vinaigrette, and mushrooms. It's even more pronounced in a fine capellini puttanesca, which also boasts the vivid flavors of capers, black olives, and plum tomatoes. Linguine with white clam sauce is a little too al dente and a soupy rendition. Chicken alla romana is too salty, and its sauce is too reminiscent of the puttanesca; though it adds rosemary, red and yellow peppers, and onions, the theme is really garlic and capers. The wine list is even shorter than the menu. A good bet is the '83 Brusco dei Barbi ($26). Sharing a bottle of that, dinner will cost about $35 a person, plus the normal tax and tip.
Dinner nightly 5 P.M. to 11 P.M.; closed Sun. in summer. AE.

WILKINSON'S SEAFOOD CAFE

1573 York Ave. (83rd & 84th Sts.)
535-5454
American/Seafood

13 ♟

This stylish bistro with smoked-glass lamps, attractive brick walls, and handsome trompe l'oeil flower niches sports a long mahogany bar where casually well-dressed East Siders gather nightly. The tone is definitely conservative; no mad singles scene here. Wilkinson's features good seafood dishes. The tender, greaseless calamari fritti, served with a silken tomato sauce redolent of tarragon and garnished with fried parsley, is a sophisticated new reading of this old Italian standby. The other nouvelle-ish combos work, too—warmed oysters in orange butter, mussels in a white wine reduction, and, when in season, soft-shell crabs, deftly sautéed and dressed in lime butter. Sea bass in a sake sauce dotted with fermented black bean sauce is outstanding. Grilled swordfish is moist and tender, simply glazed with butter and lemon. If someone in your party doesn't feel like seafood, there is a grilled veal chop in a mustard sauce and, in season, a port-glazed, marinated, broiled quail bedded down in a nest of spinach.

There's a recently expanded, medium-sized wine list; you will do well with the house red and white, both pleasant, well-rounded Loire Valley wines. Desserts are irresistible, especially the cheesecake in hazelnut sauce, and the fudgy chocolate mousse cake served in a puddle of rasberry purée, and topped with whipped cream. About $38 per person with wine.

Dinner Mon.-Sat. 6 P.M. to 10:30 P.M., Sun. 5:30 P.M. to 9 P.M. AE, MC, V.

SAM'S CAFE

1406 Third Ave. (80th St.)
988-5300

American

12/20

Sam's Cafe has its star owner, Mariel Hemingway (who rarely, if ever, makes an appearance), while Eric Crisman (co-owner and husband) and chef Mark Ostrowsky actually run this good restaurant. Its two dining rooms are pleasant, each in a different way. The front room, on Third Avenue, seems to be reserved for the younger crowd, while the back room is for those adventurous oldies who want to experience a good meal in an "in" spot. The latter clientele will enjoy the skylight, gabled ceiling, and quilts adorning the walls, all lending a country feeling to the place, and aided by the friendly service.

The escargots and scallops in a spirited garlic sauce, and the thick slice of foie gras on a bed of wild mushrooms in port wine are two excellent appetizers. The fresh salad with barely-broiled goat cheese is an authentic version of a usually tired dish. Ostrowsky's smoked salmon with fried capers has a lovely tang. Among the entrées, the grilled duck breast with Chinese vegetables is pungent and light. The grilled tuna is the best fish on the menu—rare in the center, charcoal broiled on the outside, and served with an excellent hoisin sauce. In season the soft shell crabs with rice sausage is superb. When dinner is over and it is time for dessert, you'll be surprised by the coconut pineapple tart, made without dairy products or sugar. Its wonderful refreshing taste will happily conclude the evening. The wine list is extensive, with some excellent California wines. Prices are in the medium range. Dinner per person with drinks runs $38.

*Dinner Mon.-Sat. 6 P.M. to midnight., Sun. 5:30 P.M. to 10
P.M.; closed Sun. in summer. All major credit cards.*

Upper West Side

BLUE NILE

103 West 77th St.
(Columbus Ave.)
580-3232

Ethiopian

10/20

An intriguing, intimate restaurant that caters to a youthful
clientele, the Blue Nile features authentic Ethiopian cuisine.
The dining room, located below ground on a quiet Upper
West Side street, is windowless but folksy, with its woven
straw tables low to the ground and its various artifacts from
the Egyptian delta adorning the walls. You sit on squat
three-legged stools and eat with your hands. The ebony
waitresses are colorfully costumed but slow on the uptake—
you may have to call out several times for a beer, which is the
recommended drink for this spicy food.

Ethiopian food should certainly be sampled and savored,
but for many once is enough. The dishes, most in stew form,
are arranged on metal platters lined with the national staple,
a flavorless, spongy white flour pancake (injera). Additional,
folded sheets of injera are provided in lieu of Western
utensils. Eating here can be a fun, messy, exotic business.
Dishes to try are headed by a spicy beef tartare (kitfo).
There's also tibs wot, beef stewed in a hot sauce. The more
people you are with the more dishes you'll be able to order
and dip into, literally. Consider the kale and potatoes with
spices (yegomen wot), the hottest chicken in town (doro
wot), or a chickpea purée (shuro wot). Avoid the Western
desserts. The management here also runs a sister restaurant
in SoHo, Abyssinia. It's a toss-up between them, though
some feel the food is better uptown. A meal here will run
$15-20 per person.
*Lunch Tues.-Sun. noon to 3 P.M.; dinner Sun.-Thurs. 5 P.M.
to 11 P.M., Fri. & Sat. till midnight. AE.*

BUD'S

359 Columbus Ave. (77th
St.)
724-2100

Subtitled "An American Bistrot," casual Bud's is the standard bearer on the Upper West Side for so-called California
cuisine. Owned by Jonathan Waxman and Melvyn Master
(Jam's, Hulot's), it is a corner storefront with tall French
doors and windows and dining on two levels indoors: in
good weather, there's sidewalk dining along busy Columbus

226

American

13

Avenue, where you can find some clothing stores still open after you've finished dinner. Inside the theme may be California (palms, bright tropical colors, staff in T-shirts), but the crowd is Upper West Side. This cramped, crowded and thunderously noisy place has become a neighborhood eatery, and there is no mistaking the look of the clientele—not Village, not Midtown, not Upper East Side.

The soup of the day usually is a good choice, especially when it is the thick and luscious apple and acorn squash with a dab of crème fraîche. Black bean soup generally appears on the photocopied, single-page menu. Avocado-and-mussel salad in a cilantro pesto with purple coleslaw is a fine appetizer, as is deep-fried squid with caper and basil mayonnaise. A few steps below the main level is an open kitchen where mesquite grilling enhances many of the main courses, including a pork chop, chicken, yellow-fin tuna, and a very nice Mahi-Mahi prepared Yucatan style with plantain fritters and orange butter. There's more fish than meat (the grilled quail is recommended on chef Manny Goodman's menu), and the sautéed Mako shark with corn and poblano peppers and beer-batter onion rings is excellent. Order a single plate of shoestring potatoes for a party of four; they come looking like a haystack and tasting like potato chips. Desserts are sweet—the key lime pie too sweet, the dark chocolate cake with praline and crème anglaise more in harmony. The wine list is short, young, and only passable, but one of the picks of the list is the ever-satisfying Sonoma Cutrer "Russian River" Chardonnay. About $35 per person. *Dinner Mon.-Sat. 6 P.M. to 11:30 P.M.; Sun. brunch noon to 8 P.M. All major credit cards.*

CAFÉ DES ARTISTES

1 West 67th St. (Central Park West & Columbus Ave.)
877-3500
French

12/20

This is still one of the prettiest spots in town, especially at lunch, when the sun streams in and highlights the opulent window plantings. The exquisite Howard Chandler Christie murals have been carefully restored and are as lush as ever, and you will be decently fed if you can work your way through the menu, a hodgepodge of culinary buzzwords in a particularly irritating format. Owner and restaurant consultant George Lang has a desperate need of his own services here. What's the sense of offering tripes with prunes in July, on the same menu with seviche?

The pumpernickel and rye in the bread basket is a bit tired, like much of the food. The gravlax is fine, the charcuterie assortment superior, and the oysters fresh. Soft-shell crabs said to be sautéed with almond butter are in fact blanketed

with almond slivers, very dated, and who in his or her right mind would want calf's liver with avocado? The roasted leg of lamb with flageolets is nicely pink, the beans tasty. Grilled salmon is dry and inappropriately garnished with grainy cauliflower purée. In asparagus season there's a separate menu for the stalks, which are offered vinaigrette, with eggs, and so forth. Salmon replaces ham in the Cafe's version of eggs Benedict, a nice or killer lunch dish, depending on whether you are watching your cholesterol. Desserts include a delicious sour cream apple pie with walnuts, a pleasant key lime pie, and some refreshing fruit sherbets. The house Ilona torte will please chocolate addicts. Fresh apple slices with walnuts and doux de montagne cheese is an inspired alternative. The wine list has several well-priced wines including a Châteauneuf-du-Pape at $16. Or try the basket selection, a group of unlisted wines that change frequently and are offered for the same price. They are actually trundled to the table in metal baskets, and you can choose from a dozen American and French reds and whites. The restaurant is extremely popular, always filled, and you must reserve well in advance. The management recommends booking one week in advance for dinner before or after a Lincoln Center event, two weeks for dinner on Friday or Saturday. Average dinner cost per person is $45; for lunch, about $32.
Lunch Mon.-Fri. noon to 3 P.M.; dinner Mon.-Sat. 5:30 P.M. to midnight, Sun. 5 P.M. to 11 P.M.; brunch Sat. noon to 3 P.M., Sun. 10 A.M. to 3 P.M. All major credit cards.

CAFE DESTINN

70 West 68th St. (Central Park West & Columbus Ave.)
496-2144

American

11/20

Cafe Destinn is a good choice if you're on your way to Lincoln Center. The decor of this West Side townhouse restaurant is simple, with intimate tables, a skylight, and a few hanging flowerpots. The wood-burning fireplace facing the bar at the entrance and a small garden in the back add to the charm. Opened a couple of years ago by two opera buffs (Destinn was a buxom, boisterous Hungarian prima donna), the cafe features a cuisine that is basically American/Californian nouvelle with a dash of Italian. Naturally you'll be served by young, good-looking, unemployed actors. Chef Neil Kleinberg is a Brooklynite who worked at the Water Club before taking over this ambitious kitchen.

Among the few appetizers on the menu (there are additional specials offered every day), the pasta campagnola with uncooked tomato sauce, mozarella, and basil deserves praise for its freshness and rustic authenticity. Try bruschetta, toasted country bread soaked in olive oil with sausage, peppers, and black olives, another peasant dish that allows the mellow flavors to shine through. The grilled boudin blanc with savory cabbage is a good choice if you are going to hear Wagner; it will sustain you, awake or asleep, all evening. Kleinberg makes meaty but mild crab cakes served with an unusual corn salad. The risotto with shrimp, saffron, and vegetables could be more buttery, but it's a hit among the restaurant's habitués. Try the grilled marinated free-range chicken and hope it is served with roasted spring onions, a major delicacy here. The menu, like the opera, is seasonal. Most of the unexceptional desserts are store bought, except for the ice creams and sherbets; nevertheless the poached pear served with marscapone is delightful. The wine list is heavy with California and is reasonably priced. Lunch will run between $10-12 per person with a glass a wine; dinner $25-30.

Lunch Mon.-Fri. noon to 2:30 P.M.; dinner Sun. & Mon. 5:30 P.M. to 10:30 P.M., Tues.-Thurs. till 11 P.M., Fri. & Sat. till 11:30 P.M.; brunch Sat. & Sun. 11:30 A.M. to 3 P.M. AE, MC, V.

CAFE LUXEMBOURG

200 West 70th St. (Amsterdam & West End Aves.) 873-7411

American/French

13

With Cafe Luxembourg's talented executive chef, Patrick Clark, recently gone to open his own restaurant, and since the Odeon dropped several notches after Clark's departure from there, it would not be unfair to assume that the inevitable changes here will not be for the better. Why then talk about the delectable ravioli stuffed with a duxelle of shiitake mushrooms, garnished with grilled whole shiitake mushrooms and sliced duck breast, and served on a sauce of mushroom juice reduction? Why mention the snails with black beans and croûtons in garlic and cilantro butter? The grilled red snapper in a red pepper vinaigrette? Such dishes demand creativity, skill, and split-second timing. Unless and until savvy Keith McNally, one of the owners, finds another star waiting-to-happen, stick with the foolproof country salad of chicory, Roquefort, lardons, garlic croûtons, and mustard vinaigrette, or good steak and pommes frites. Those who admired the cassoulet in the past probably will like it still. And certainly the setting, which attempts to recreate the charms of an Art Deco bistro in 30's Paris, continues to please. The restaurant's proximity to Lincoln Center and its $25 prix fixe pre-theater menu (served between 5:30 and 6:30 P.M.) draw a literate, prosperous crowd. The group that comes after eight is worth the price of a show—a mix of sleek New Yorkers from either side of Central Park and funky downtowners, some still sporting Grace Jones hairdos, others aggressively wearing visored painters caps but ordering '79 Clicquot Rosé ($75). Dinner costs about $60 a person, with wine.

Dinner Mon.-Thurs. 5:30 P.M. to 12:30 A.M., Fri. and Sat. till 1:30 A.M., Sun. 6 P.M. to 12:30 A.M.; brunch Sun. 11 A.M to 2:30 P.M. All major credit cards.

CAVALIERE

108 West 73rd St.
(Amsterdam & Columbus Aves.)
799-8282

Italian

14

On the ground level of a house in a pleasant block of West Side brownstones, Cavaliere is a series of discoveries. The well-designed entry room, locus of the bar and small dining area, opens into the handsome, mirrored-ceiling main dining room, airy but intimate, with the single rose spotlighted on the mantle enigmatically revealing the origin of the restaurant's name. In back is another ravishingly pretty small skylit room, used only on weekends (a perfect place for a party). Cool, sleek, blond-wood chairs, pale gray tweed banquettes, attractive flower arrangements add to the cosseting, festive feeling. The waiters, in formal dress softened with jaunty red bow ties, are a crackerjack professional team. The food has improved considerably since Anne Rosenzweig of Arcadia and '21' fame was brought in as a consultant. The menu she has come up with is a lightened, smartened version of Italian food, simple, yet sophisticated, with the kind of invention grounded in classic cooking she's known for.

Calamari friti, on every Italian menu in town, here are rescued from banality first by the impeccable frying and secondly by a toothsome pesto marinara sauce. Hair-thin sesame fried zucchini are first rate. Even ubiquitous tortellini are royally reborn when served up with mushrooms in a delicious marsala cream sauce. Garlic bread awash with pesto and Parmesan sauce is tasty but too rich for an appetizer, and the mozzarella rolled with red peppers and olive paste is a visual dud. But simple arugula endive salad in a marvelous balsamic vinaigrette with a sweet garlicky note is first rate. Melting roasted baby eggplant slices and sweet red pepper with a tomato garlic sauce are offered as an appetizer, and appear in a reprise in a gorgeous main dish of grilled shrimp, their tails aloft. Veal chop with roasted shallot, a red wine sauce and roasted garlic potatoes is another winning main dish. Both grilled swordfish on a bed of fresh tomatoes with a minty overtone and the grilled salmon with a lemon-pepper aioli on a bed of grilled zucchini merit raves. Also good are the roast chicken with rosemary butter and a warm potato-and-caper salad. The wine list features many well chosen and well priced wines, mostly Italian such as the Nebbiolo d'Alba at $18. Save room for dessert because among the rather ordinary offerings on the slightly silly trolley there is a chocolate amaretto torte topped with a dollop of espresso mousse that gives sin new meaning. Otherwise go for the fresh fruit tart. The $26 prix fix theater dinner from 5 to 6:30 P.M. is a good buy as it includes many of the recommended items. Afterwards it's only a short walk to Lincoln Center. Dinner averages about $36 per person with a modest wine.

Daily noon to midnight, Fri. & Sat. till 1 A.M. All major credit cards.

COASTAL

300 Amsterdam Ave.
(74th St.)
769-3988

American

12/20

When the noise of the honking taxis and grunting buses on Amsterdam Avenue vies with the clatter of plates and chatter of diners, and when tables "turn" once an hour, you know you're not in for a Lucullan experience. Coastal—brought to you by the boys who gave you Memphis and 107 West—is a formula restaurant, but it gives as good as it gets. A lot of expense evidently has been spared on its decor, which is minimal, stark, and high tech—track lights, blond wood, lots of floor-to-ceiling windows, turquoise trim, and vague outlines (in gray, white, and turquoise) of portions of the American coast. But when it comes to food, the ingredients are fresh and good, their integrity is respected in the cooking, and the prices are reasonable.

Satisfying appetizers include a plate of grilled marinated eggplant, asparagus, peppers, tomatoes, and fennel, or a yuppie shrimp cocktail in which four shrimp are posed on a mound of good, chunky guacamole and zesty salsa, surrounded by tortilla chips. Broiled tilefish and grilled grouper are both moist, medium rare, and perfectly fresh. To accompany the simply cooked fish you may choose one of six sauces served in small ramequins: béarnaise, concassé of tomato, scallion and basil, beurre blanc, pear mango salsa, hollandaise, and Provençale. The waiters believe "one flavor fits all" and will recommend any sauce with any fish. Be forewarned, however, that some of the fish are brushed with a sweet teriyaki sauce before grilling. It's fine, it's tasty, but it wars against the "side" sauces. Homemade ice cream such as chocolate with Grand Marnier, amaretto, and "sin" (coffee and marsala) are as good as you'll find in the designer ice cream outposts along nearby Columbus Avenue. Eating them here will spare you a second long line—those who arrive after 8 P.M. have to wait for a table. Dinner, with a modest wine, runs about $35 per person.

Dinner daily 6 P.M. to 11:30 P.M. AE.

FANDANGO

305 West End Ave. (74th & 75th Sts.)
877-1500
Eclectic

11/20

Granted, Fandango is a spinoff of another restaurant—Batons. Originality, therefore, is not its strongest suit. But its owners might do well to take to heart Polonius's homily—to thine own self be true. Most of Fandango's flaws stem from trying to tailor itself to fit the latest culinary or decorative fashion. Located on West End Avenue, which is rich in city lore, Fandango ignores the legacy of both its area and space in favor of the standard lower Manhattan conversion of warehouse into restaurant. It is a vast, multi-leveled expanse punctuated by structural columns, an occasional Art Deco flourish, or a flamboyant floral display. And while much of the food is tasty, the failures seem due to inexperience taxed by an over-ambitious repertoire.

Each dish on the menu reflects as many cultural influences as the U.N.'s General Assembly. Consider these three: grilled tuna with black bean marmalade, golden aioli, and winter melon vinaigrette; roasted baby corn and red pepper pancakes with whipped crème fraîche, American salmon roe caviar, and sea urchin butter sauce; and ravioli filled with scallops, artichokes, mache, jicama, lemon grass, and chive butter sauce. The dishes are too busy and the roster of choices too extensive for the kitchen to handle—though it's evident that people back there are trying. The ravioli are too pasty, though the chive butter sauce is expertly done. Similarly, the cited pancakes were enjoyable, albeit a bit tough, and the billed sea urchin was nowhere in evidence. Wild mushroom and lamb dumplings are spicy and satisfying, but hold the sauce, which is overreduced and as concentrated in flavor as a bouillon cube. Another dish, roast duck, is overcooked, though the scallion crepe garnish is delicious. The best dishes are the simplest: wonderful home-made potato chips, lavish salads, or a clear duck consommé with chopped chives, sliced red peppers, and dumplings. Opt for cinnamon or chocolate with Jack Daniels ice cream for dessert. Expect to pay about $45 per person for dinner, with wine.

Dinner Mon.-Fri. 6 P.M. to midnight, Sat. & Sun. till 12:30 P.M.; brunch Sun. noon to 5 P.M. All major credit cards.

LA BOÎTE EN BOIS

*5 West 68th St. (Central
Park West & Columbus
Ave.)*
874-2705

French

12/20

This is a modest French provincial restaurant, like the ones that thrived in New York before the advent of nouvelle cuisine and superstar chefs whose country houses rate a spread in *People*. On entering, you step down into a lace-curtained anteroom that houses the coat check, and then into a dining room that's not much larger, decorated with gladiolas. There you're greeted by the patron Jean-Claude Coutable—a delicate little man in a dark gray suit and a blue tie.

Old World charm and authenticity bear repeating, and among the clientele are Upper West Side regulars for whom this is an elevator ride away. The food is honest and substantial. Start with the string bean salad with preserved duck, the warm sausage cooked with lentils, or the casserole of mussels in cream sauce. For an entrée try the snapper baked in parchment paper with basil butter, shrimps and scallops in puff pastry, or the veal kidneys in red wine. Jean Claude recommends the red St. Nicholas de Bourgueil ($21), or the white Du Bois Duphin ($25) wines. Crème caramel à l'orange is your best bet for dessert. Lunch is prix fixe at $20 per person; dinner will run about $50.
Lunch Mon.-Fri. noon to 3 P.M.; dinner daily 6 P.M. to 11:30 P.M. No credit cards.

LA MIRABELLE

*333 West 86th St.
(Riverside Dr. & West End
Ave.)*
496-0458

French

11/20

This place is as unpretentious as can be. Located on the ground floor of a residential hotel, La Mirabelle consists of several connecting rooms with pink walls trimmed in white, small tables with crisp linen, waitresses direct from the French provinces, and bistro classics from coquille St. Jacques to entrecôte bercy and crème caramel. La Mirabelle could be a real charmer, but when it comes right down to it, the food's pretty standard. You will enjoy your meal, but don't expect an epiphany. The fresh asparagus are thick as carrots—albeit nicely cooked and served with a creditable vinaigrette; the escargots bourguignonne and the soft shell crabs Provençale are no better or worse than those served in a thousand other places; the rabbit basquaise is seriously overcooked. But the Upper West Side crowd doesn't seem to mind. The place is full of lawyers talking cases and career changes, and aging actors still discussing showcases in third-floor walk-up acting studios. A modest place, with modest ambitions, La Mirabelle charges, by today's standards, modest prices. Dinner, with an inexpensive Mâcon or Beaujolais, comes to about $30 a person.
Dinner Mon.-Thurs. 6 P.M. to 10 P.M.; Fri. & Sat. till 10:30 P.M. AE, V, MC.

METROPOLIS

444 Columbus Ave. (81st & 82nd Sts.)

American

12/20

When the Upper West Side wanted to compete with SoHo it turned to Metropolis, the loft-like restaurant on Columbus Avenue in a turn-of-the-century building. The gigantic space, sporting an atrium, a skylight, and full grown trees, has managed to retain a certain intimacy despite its size and its mirrored walls. The tables, decorated with terra cotta pots filled with flowers, are well-spaced so that you can sustain a conversation with your companion—unless you're more interested in the crowd or in the dexterity of the waiters juggling silver-domed orders.

The menu is long and is photocopied every day with the specials added so you don't have to listen to a long litany from your waiter. The Italian onion and bread soup with roasted peppers has a rich broth, lots of onion, and a strong pepper taste which counterbalances the sweetness of the onions. The sautéed pleurottes and shiitake mushrooms served with semolina and buckwheat gnocchi is quite original. The pleurottes are tender and soft while the shiitake are firmer and served in a sauce of reduced beef broth, but the real originality of the dish lies in the gnocchi (one large one), which has a wonderful nutty taste and is neither dry nor overcooked. The raclette of fresh mozarella with roasted peppers, eggplant, and pesto croûton is not as successful. The menu offers several pastas. The hazelnut-and-ricotta-filled tortelloni have a nutty flavor which offers a strong contrast with the slices of sun-dried tomatoes, but we feel it could use more pepper or stronger spices. The portions are also small, and the pasta dishes can easily be ordered as appetizers. All the entrées are roasted or grilled over hardwood. The roast leg of lamb is pink, tender, and well-spiced with chives, and the potatoes au gratin, thin slices of potatoes cooked in cream, have a crunchy crust and just melt in your mouth. The kitchen overuses peppers and sun-dried tomatoes here; a good exception is the grilled salmon with asparagus, served with a leek and sorrel sauce. The thick salmon steak is broiled crisp on the outside, tender and moist inside. Unfortunately, the sauce is under-spiced. Usually quite dry, swordfish here is moistened with a very good orange and olive sauce, and has a delicious added touch of cumin.

Leave room for desserts, which are wonderful. The lemon timbale with ricotta is a beautiful mold in a sea of blueberry juice and has just the right amount of tartness. A hot fudge cake with ice cream should make you come back for more, and the mint brownie sundae puts all other sundaes to shame. The wine list is short, but includes a good selection

from all over the world. Prices are reasonable. Wine by the glass offers a good Chianti Classico and an excellent dry Chardonnay. Be warned that the service is amateurish. Price per person with wine runs about $40.
Daily 5:30 P.M. to midnight. All major credit cards.

SANTA FE

72 West 69th St.
(Columbus Ave. & Central Park West)
724-0822
American

10/20

This attractive renovated townhouse on a side street off Columbus will satisfy the strongest yuppie love for Southwest chic. You'll find the requisite salmon-pink walls, Indian artifacts, handsome chairs, and candles on each table that allow you (barely) to read the menu while flattering your complexions; all this may make you forget that the food here is uninteresting and often simply tasteless. You might as well fill yourself up with nachos (here crisp tortillas served with chopped beef, onions, and hot peppers) while drinking a fairly good Margarita or a Mexican beer. The guacamole is insipid, and the seviche, while fresh, needs some punch. Avoid the special combinations—they are heaped on a plate and you can only guess at what you're eating. Among the specialties, the red snapper is acceptable, as is the salmon fillet with avocado cream. The fish dishes in general are O.K. The tacos al carbon is to be avoided at all costs: overcooked roast beef rolled in a soft floured tortilla and topped with what looks like cheese but tastes like cardboard. Still, the place fills some people's gastronomic urges for Tex-Mex. Desserts are not homemade and are better forgotten. Dinner per person $28 with beer.
Lunch & dinner daily noon to midnight. AE, MC, V.

SIDEWALKERS

12 West 72nd St. (Central Park West)
799-6070
American/Seafood

11/20

The word on the street is that you go to Sidewalkers once a year for crabs. Maybe, but obviously a lot of people go once a year, because its three dining rooms (seating 25, 60, and 125 respectively) are filled with diners at paper-covered tables, wearing the ubiquitous bibs and cracking crabs to their hearts' delight. Maryland crab cakes can be had as appetizers, and Maryland spiced or garlic crabs are among the standout entrées. On Sunday and Monday, there's an "all you can eat crab-bash," which at $14.95 is a good deal; included are (you guessed it) crabs, cole slaw, French fries, onion rings, and dessert. But the menu at Sidewalkers is extensive and goes well beyond the featured crustaceans. Steamers (for two) makes a good alternative appetizer, and steamed spiced

shrimp a good entrée. Seafood, including fresh fish, is prepared over a mesquite grill; try the Texas barbequed shrimp. Desserts are sound and substantial, and the mostly American and French wines are moderately priced, including the Sanford Vin Gris (California) at $14 a bottle, and the Clinton Seyval Blanc (New York State) at $12. Dinner averages $25-30 a person with a modest wine.
Mon.-Sun. 5 P.M. to 11 P.M., Fri. & Sat. till 11:30 P.M. All major credit cards.

TAVERN ON THE GREEN

Central Park West & 67th St.
873-3200
Eclectic

12/20

After years of pretentious and mediocre food, restaurant showman Warner Leroy has finally gotten, in George Masraff, a chef worthy of Manhattan's biggest dining extravaganza. The glitz is somewhat played down now—confined to the Tiffany lamps, the rococo ceiling, and the Venetian chandeliers of the Crystal Room, and the 350,000 twinkle lights that make every evening a Christmas fairyland. Now all the Tavern needs is a serving staff that brings to such splendor a modicum of expertise. You may be treated grandly or seated and ignored. Though orders are written on a computerized form, you may or may not get what you asked for. It also seems few on the staff can speak knowledgably about the food, which can be quite good—and considering the huge number of meals served daily at this top tourist attraction, the quality of the offerings is impressive. When you book (reservations are recommended but walk-in seating is often available, especially at lunch), specify the cozier Chestnut room or the more glittery Crystal Room, a pretty winter palace enclosure. In fine weather dining on the terrace can be lovely, when the wind does not carry souvenirs from the nearby carriage horses.

The menus have been put together with great care and range from simple to elaborate, trendy to traditional, hearty French to grazing food, hot and cold dishes, fish and shellfish, pastas, grills, sandwiches, and salads. It would be the rare diner who could not find something appealing here. Lunch and dinner menus offer openers that include baked goat cheese with a salad of field greens in walnut vinaigrette, and lobster "purses," crisp phyllo pastry filled with succulent lobster in a rich aurora sauce. The linguini with crab, basil, and tomato with the same sauce is excellent. Entrées include a homey veal blanquette, Saint Pierre (white fish fillets with roasted shallots), and a roasted duckling. Sweets lovers will adore the mouthwatering dessert selection: there's a chocolate truffle cake, a buttery and paper-thin hot apple tart, a gratin of tropical fruits crème brûlée, and all kinds of ice cream sundaes and fresh fruit sorbets. The huge and excellent wine list runs the gamut from a modest DuBoeuf Beaujolais to a $1,000 Lafite. In addition, there is a neat little prix fixe pre-theater menu featuring roast baby chicken, grilled salmon steak, poached sole, or roast beef for a first course, plus dessert and coffee. Offered between 5:30 P.M. and 6:15 P.M. Monday through Friday, it's a great buy for $14.50, with two or three items carrying a small supplement. Tavern on the Green is clearly on its way back and up, and that's good news for New York City. Average lunch price is about $20, dinner about $33, though the many tantalizing wines may run that price up into the three digits in a hurry.

Lunch Mon.-Fri. 11:30 A.M. to 3:30 P.M.; dinner Mon.-Fri. 5:30 P.M. to midnight, Sat. & Sun. 10 A.M. to 1 A.M. All major credit cards.

TERRACE RESTAURANT

400 West 119th St. (in Butler Hall, corner Morningside Dr.)
666-9490

French

15

Terrace is at the top of a Columbia University building and has a breathtaking view of Manhattan, both rivers included. The room is elegant, romantic, intimate, and softly-lit. Its chef, Dominique Payradeau, is a young man who has again turned the restaurant around, making it very French but using local ingredients and his own lively imagination.

Among the appetizers, try the mousse de truite fumée, a delicious light mousse of smoked trout with a cream sauce, and the salade de foie gras gourmande, thin slices of American foie gras on top of a tepid salad of very thin French string beans tossed in a honey vinaigrette. Even more glamorous are the escargots aux noix, fat escargots sautéed in a rich meat stock with warm walnuts, served in a small ramequin. A truly original dish is the crevettes roses with herb butter—large, fresh broiled prawns served on top of real homemade pasta. If you prefer soup to begin your meal, try the bisque de homard, smooth as velvet, spiced with Armagnac, and full of cream. There are several special entrées every night, although the à la carte menu has some very tempting dishes. The medallions of fresh salmon with two caviars is not only very good but looks like a magnificent still life. Simplicity is the essence of the steamed imported fillet of sole accompanied by tiny steamed vegetables. Payrandeau's boned quails are tender and tasty, sautéed with shallots and ginger, and sprinkled with fresh herbs. The ginger sauce adds even more zest. The sweetbreads, sautéed in port and served with truffles and pommes de terre

237

dauphine, are delicately spiced and not overcooked. You can also find braised endives and lightly steamed fresh leaf spinach.

For a finish you may choose from assorted domestic and imported cheeses with seasonal fresh fruit. The numerous desserts from the wagon include a scrumptious chocolate cake, fruit tarts made with transparent flaky pastry, and a sinfully rich, deeply satisfying, incredibly light chocolate mousse. The wine list is laudable. Prices run about $50 per person.

Lunch Tues.-Fri. noon to 2:30 P.M.; dinner Tues.-Sat. 6 P.M. to 10 P.M.; closed mid-July to mid-Aug. All major credit cards.

Other Boroughs

AMERIGO'S

*3587 East Tremont Ave.
(Lafayette Ave.), the Bronx
792-3600*

Italian

13 🍳

People come from all over to this Bronx standby in a good section with good parking. If you are in the Bronx already, and near the Throg's Neck Bridge, by all means make a little detour and try to get a table at this suburban-style, old-fashioned, good Italian-American restaurant. It's another matter altogether to contemplate a trip up from Manhattan. Tony and Anna Cortese own what started out as Amerigo Coppola's pizzeria in 1934. Today their place contains two big dining rooms, one slightly more "elegant" than the other, but with your basic fancy Italian restaurant decor and waiters (male and female) in black tie. The less formal room usually contains families and casually-dressed regulars who think nothing about introducing a two-year-old to Amerigo's. They've probably been stuffing themselves here since they were two.

Portions are enormous. You know the menu, everything's on it: appetizers, soups, 31 pastas, fish, meats (including 14 veal preparations), and, of course, the daily specials. The pastas are excellent. You can't order a half portion as an appetizer, though two people can split a regular portion. The paglia e fieno alla molisana is terrific—green and white fettucine noodles in a savory cream and cheese sauce. Stellar capellini (angel hair pasta) alla provincale (olives, onions, capers) is a house specialty. A rich fettucine Alfredo or verdant seasonal spaghetti al pesto earn a place on the table, as do most of the other hearty and flavorful pasta dishes.

Steaks, chops, and lobster are also touted here, and the armies that get fed here appear very well nourished. Veal scaloppine alla Amerigo's is big and tasty, with a layer of eggplant over the veal and a layer of not-so-impressive cheese over the eggplant; everything bathed in a pure tomato sauce. And the breaded veal cutlet alla Milanese is dried out and akin to something you'd find on the shelf of a stationery store. Another house specialty is osso buco—a big shin of veal stewed in wine, herbs, tomatoes, onions, carrots, and garlic—with meat that properly falls away from the shank. It's a passable version but is accompanied by a risotto that has very little up on Uncle Ben's rice. Side vegetables tend to be overcooked and overspiced with garlic.

Ninety-five percent of the roughly 150 wines offered are Italian and run from pizzeria wines to distinguished offerings from top producers from all over Italy. Prices are good, and there are some special values to be found (for example, Lungoretti Rubesco '79 at $19.75). You'll wind up pouring your own refills; in general service is weak. Desserts, most of which are brought in, are filling but humdrum. The home-made Italian cheesecake tends to be overly dry and bland. Espresso comes with the obligatory lemon peel and a pouring-capped bottle of anisette. The anisette is distilled in Kentucky—what more need be said about this restaurant that prides itself on using the finest ingredients. About $35 per person, with wine.
Wed.-Mon. noon to 11 P.M., Fri. & Sat. till 1 A.M.; closed first two weeks of Aug. All major credit cards.

DOMINICK'S

*2335 Arthur Ave. (186th & 187th Sts.), the Bronx
733-2807*

Italian

10/20

The line every night is long and one wonders, why? This restaurant is a legend in the Bronx and might have been excellent 20 years ago, but more recently it has expanded and the food is uninteresting. Nevertheless, people still champion Dominick's lusty Southern Italian cooking, gargantuan portions, and yesteryear prices. It has a remarkable and remarkably satisfied following, who sit elbow to elbow amid communal dining and imitation wood paneled walls. There is no menu, and if this is your first time here, don't be intimidated by the waiter who will try to get rid of you as soon as possible. Ask questions. The steaks are the best, charcoal broiled. The pastas are the worst; watery, over-cooked, with sauce that is totally unspiced—sad because this is one of the last of the old guard of basic pasta houses. You'll probably order pasta anyway, so try one of the exceptions, the usually tasty homemade fettucine with fresh mushrooms in a cream sauce. The cold antipasto is not worth ordering, as it consists of iceberg lettuce, domestic Parmesan or provolone, two slices of salami and, if you're lucky, some anchovies. The grilled pork chops are dry, but braised they are not too tough. The fish soup is good, but be sure you ask for it very hot—if not you'll get it tepid. Go for the bread, it's excellent; forget the desserts, they all weigh a ton. The house wine is barely drinkable; stay with beer. This place is a scene. Price per person, about $22.

Lunch & dinner Mon.-Sat. noon to 10 P.M., Fri. noon to 11 P.M., Sun 1 P.M. to 9 P.M. No credit cards.

GAGE AND TOLLNER

372 Fulton St. (Smith St.), Brooklyn
(718) 875-5181
American

11/20

Gage and Tollner is one of New York's oldest restaurants; it claims continuous operation in downtown Brooklyn since 1880. This restaurant's architecture is a handsome example of the style of that period: dark wood paneling, large mirrors, a stamped tin ceiling, and the original lamp fixtures. Here the power brokers of Brooklyn and downtown Manhattan hobnob with each other at well-spaced tables. The waiters, sporting insignias stating the number of years they've been working here, are well-acquainted with the restaurant's regulars. The menu hasn't changed in ages: excellent fresh clams and oysters, well-seasoned clam chowder, steamed oysters, broiled oysters, fried oysters, creamy oyster stew. The same preparations hold for bay scallops and shrimps. The crab meat à la Virginia is a good choice if you're in the mood for a crustacean, but the broiled fish of the day is always a sure bet. The so-called tartar sauce, however, tastes as if it came out of a jar and is overly sweet. The vegetables are overcooked, except for the broiled mushrooms and the asparagus when in season. Don't even think about ordering chicken (tasteless) or the omelette (dry); try instead the English mutton chop with sausage for a taste of old-fashioned fare. Desserts are all-American, such as the rich, smooth Nesselrode pie. Beers and decent Californian wines are available. Price per person around $25-30.

Mon.-Fri. noon to 9:30 P.M., Sat. 4 P.M. to 10:30 P.M., Sun. 2 P.M. to 9 P.M. All major credit cards.

MANDUCATIS

13-27 Jackson Ave. (47th Ave.), Long Island City
(718) 729-4602

Ida's pasta. That's why Manhattanites schlep to this godforsaken intersection in Queens—a blight of shut-down gas stations, squat buildings with bricked-up windows, and several deservedly obscure subway stations. But the thought of Ida's pasta brightens up the whole scene. Behind the pool

Italian

13

hall façade, and in an uninspiring (or downright ugly) setting of orange brickface, five-and-dime chandeliers with electric "candles," vaguely obscene food posters, grade "C" Italian bread, and grated Parmesan in glass shakers, there is homemade fettucine with Ida's hearty but subtle bolognese (gently simmered ground beef with tomatoes, pine nuts, and carrots), homemade spaghetti with sun-dried tomatoes, and Ida's ricotta gnocchi (which needs Parmesan to give it zip).

Ida Cerbone and her husband Vincenzo opened this Neapolitan outpost eight years ago. Manducatis, they explain to the untutored, is the second person plural of the Latin verb "to eat." And when you come to Manducatis, you eat cheaply, copiously, and well. And not just pasta. There's also greaseless, crunchy fried seppia ("like large calamari"); sparkling scungilli salad full of garlic, oregano, and parsley; swordfish Manducatis (breadcrumbs, scallions, and mushrooms); gutsy eggplant rollatini; and garlicky, room temperature broccoli, not a second overcooked. Though some of the fare is humdrum, there's enough plain good eating here to make the place a magnet for hungry Manhattanites as well as for prowling oenophiles—for Vincenzo is a wine buff with hidden treasures in his cellar and a, well, generous spirit (i.e., no corkage fee) for those who have a special bottle to share. Droves of gold-chained locals come too, cramming the back room (the one with the fireplace) and spilling over into less desirable seats in the front rooms on weekend nights. Everyone comes for huge platters of Ida's pasta, for a nice 1982 Cappezzano Carmignano ($20), service that's as friendly and unpretentious as any dreamed up by Frank Capra, and prices that recall the 1950's. Dinner, with wine (when in doubt, let Vincenzo choose), costs about $25 per person.

Lunch Mon.-Fri. noon to 3 P.M.; dinner Mon.-Fri. 5 P.M. to 10 P.M., Sat. till 11 P.M.; occasionally open Sun.; closed last two weeks in Aug. No credit cards.

NIGHTFALLS

7612 Third Ave. (76th & 77th Sts.), Bay Ridge, Brooklyn
(718) 748-8700

American

12/20

Nightfalls, which opened in 1983, added elegance and sophistication to Bay Ridge's restaurant row. It's a stunning restaurant, two joined brownstones designed in the post-modern style by Voorsanger & Mills, it is located in two joined brownstones. A handsome outside brick terrace garden-dining room features a 36-foot wall of falling water, a terra cotta interior, Roman villa columns, and an exciting upstairs bar atrium.

The regional American cuisine does not quite measure up

to the setting, but we're rooting for executive chef Maria Pirozzi to come into her own. The food is already fine and intriguing, and this is a great place for Sunday brunch and a steal at lunch ($7.95 prix fixe). For appetizers (yes, plural), consider potato pancakes with sour cream and salmon caviar or beer-batter coconut shrimp. You might try intriguing medallions of lobster in a phyllo nest with a Kentucky bourbon sauce, or, if that seems too strong a contrast, consider California snails sautéed with mushrooms, garlic, and parsley. There are a handful of so-so pasta offerings, but fish and seafood are done very well. Sautéed jumbo shrimp and bay scallops in a lobster cream sauce ($14.95) or fillet of lemon sole wrapped in smoked salmon and leeks with a key lime and lemon sauce ($11.50) are two good bets. Also touted is the fillet of veal stuffed with black peppered ham and fresh mozzarella with two sauces. Certainly the menu isn't ordinary, though sometimes less is more. At times things work and at other times they don't—you can always get a plain steak.

Desserts are O.K., especially if you like chocolate mousse. The wines are more than O.K.; there are about 125 European and American selections reasonably priced. A good Vocoret Chablis is $20. Dinner is about $35 per person, and lunch and brunch cost half that.
Daily noon to 11 P.M. All major credit cards.

PETER LUGER

178 Broadway (Driggs Ave.), Brooklyn
(718) 387-7400
Steak

13 🎩

Having celebrated its 100th birthday in 1987, Peter Luger is today an institution and a New York landmark located in a somewhat rundown neighborhood across the Williamsburg bridge. A favorite of Wall Streeters and lawyers, it is packed at lunch with men gorging themselves on excellent quality, humongous steaks, large orders of French fries or hash browns, overcooked spinach, and cheesecake. In the evening these same businessmen, this time casually dressed, reappear with their families to eat more steak served with thick slices of tomatoes and onions. The two-story restaurant (try to reserve for the downstairs dining room) sports well-worn oak tabletops, wood-handled knives and forks, and waiters who have worked in this restaurant for years. The steaks, basted with butter and tender and juicy, are always cooked rare—if you order medium or well done you will be frowned upon, and service will be terrible. Order a steak for one if you are two and a steak for two if you are three. Seriously. The menu also offers two-inches-thick loin lamb chops and thick slabs of roast prime rib of beef, both of which are as good as the steaks. A doggie bag is provided if you cannot quite wipe your plate clean.

There is a limited wine list, mostly Californian with some recently added French and Italian wines. Everyone seems to partake, however, of the good selection of imported and domestic beers. A word of caution: don't park you car on the street, park it in the adjacent lot or ask the doorman to park it for you. Taxis back to Manhattan are also available. Dinner for two runs about $80 with drinks.
Lunch Mon.-Sat. 11:30 A.M. to 3 P.M.; dinner Mon.-Thurs. 3 P.M. to 9:45 P.M., Fri. & Sat. till 10:45 P.M., Sun. 1 P.M. to 9:45 P.M. No credit cards.

THE RIVER CAFE

1 Water Street (under pediment of the Brooklyn Bridge)
(718) 522-5200
American

13

When Larry Forgione left the kitchen here we thought the River Cafe would return to being just another pretty face, content to rest on "location," offering its drop-dead view of the Manhattan skyline. Not so. It is true that the view tends to make the River Cafe an "occasion" restaurant—a place for New Yorkers to observe significant birthdays and anniversaries. The decor of the dining room is deliberately understated, directing all eyes to the sweeping vista across the Hudson, of boats plying the waters from the Statue of Liberty up to the Citicorp Building. A piano player tinkles Porter and Gershwin. A bar crowd toasts the sunset. The River Cafe may seem to be trying to be too many things to too many people in the overeager fashion of a restaurant "in the boondocks," yet it works because the kitchen too is still ambitious. Under chef Charles Palmer (Culinary Institute of America, La Côte Basque), the River Cafe turns out imaginative, well-conceived dishes—though perhaps not with the consistency that it should.

Simple appetizers are sure bets; try the impeccably fresh oysters with a mignonette sauce or one of the sprightly seasonal salads. Perhaps the best appetizer is a somewhat more complicated preparation: seared sea scallops on a light red pepper sauce encircling a custardy leek-and-potato-flan. Also satisfying are home-smoked salmon with blue corn blinis and a ham made of home-smoked leg of lamb, the latter distinguished for its garnishes—peppery cheddar cornbread, roasted red peppers, salad with chunks of avocado. Main courses are equally ambitious but slightly less successful. (They're all good, but they don't transport you to culinary heaven.) Seared red snapper in shellfish sauce is overcrisp and dry, the sauce, bland. There's nothing at all wrong with grilled squab with home-smoked bacon and pepper salad, or with pheasant breast with wild mushroom sauce; it's just that they're more exciting on paper than on the plate. The best desserts are the bittersweet chocolate mousse terrine, a triple-threat chocoholic's dream—layers of chocolate cake interspersed with chocolate mousse, decorated with chocolate truffles—and a spicy crème brûlée. They try hard at this place; the service is more than competent, and the wine list is exceptional (it offers a broad spectrum with attractive options in all price ranges, and it's notable for old Californian wines). Prices, in general, invite criticism however. Fixed price for dinner is $48 per person, and an à la carte lunch will run about the same, plus wine, tax and tips. *Lunch Mon.-Fri. noon to 2:30 P.M.; dinner Sun.-Thurs. 6:30 P.M. to 11 P.M., Fri. & Sat. 7 P.M. to 11:30 P.M.; brunch Sat. noon to 2:30 P.M., Sun. 11:30 A.M. to 2:30 P.M. All major credit cards.*

TOMMASSO'S

1464 86th St. (14th & 15th Aves.), Brooklyn
(718) 236-9883

Italian

13

"Tommasso's is not a restaurant; it's an extension of our kitchen," claim two food-and-wine writers. Admittedly, they've become family. Their books are on Tommasso's crammed food and wine bookshelves by the bar; they've extended Tommasso's already considerable collection of grappas with samples they've brought back from Italy; they attend staff Christmas parties. Still, Tommasso's in the Bensonhurst section of Brooklyn is a long walk from the kitchen of a Manhattan apartment. To have become family, therefore, they must have indulged more than once in Tommasso's fresh homemade mozzarella, accompanied by piles of roasted red peppers bathed in olive oil and garlic. They must've feasted well on the same delicious mozzarella, this time in carrozza, and topped with a sauce spiked with chopped gaeta olives and capers. And thousands of succulent clams oreganato must have, in Oscar Hammerstein's words, galloped down their gullets. Tommasso's is one of New York's best-kept open secrets. It's a funky destination—a place to eat copiously, raid the wine cellar (Tommasso's list is not only incredible in extent but in price; a '77 Taurasi Riserva, for example, costs $26), and to listen to Tommasso himself sing opera at the upright piano by the bar.

Tommasso plans to change his menu. He wants to make it more Neapolitan than it already is. But even if that takes more time than he expects, and even if you're not yet a member of the family, you can still enjoy incomparable pasta e fagioli ("Fazool!" Tommasso corrects), linguine with red clam sauce, and light potato gnocchi. Meat and poultry dishes are slightly less successful. Chicken with a piquant olive, parsley, garlic, and white wine sauce is a bit over-cooked, as is breaded veal cutlet with a fine caper sauce. But when Tommasso insists that you make room for his Marsala-rich zabaglione, just whisked in copper bowls, all seems right with the world. No matter that many of the other diners look like targets for federal investigations. Or that conversation barely misses a beat when a birthday cake is brought out for a three-year-old named Phaedre. What may stop the conversation is the check. You can eat and drink yourself into stupefaction for $40 a person.

Dinner Tues.-Thurs. 4 P.M. to 11 P.M., Fri. & Sat. till midnight, Sun. 1 P.M. to 10 P.M. All major credit cards.

WATER'S EDGE

44th Dr. & the East River, Long Island City, Queens
(718) 482-0033

American

14

For a few years now the Water's Edge barge has been moored on the East River at Long Island City. Here you can dine while gazing at the most magical view on the East Coast. The jeweled towers of Manhattan illuminated at night make you feel you're in another world, especially if you get there to see the sun set behind the sparkling Citicorp building. The Water's Edge was purchased in 1986 by the Sommersteins, well-known Long Island caterers. Since then, unfortunately, the old barge feeling has disappeared. The magic towers still gleam at night but the dining room, refurbished in a somewhat more expansive suburban style, has too many extras: a piano player, flowers on the bar, and small lights on each table whose reflections on the windows upstage the view. Fortunately, the food is revitalized and good.

The cuisine is American with Continental tendencies and the menu is carefully thought out and executed. Waiters are attentive if not always on the ball. The bar makes good Margaritas, and the wine list has improved. Norwegian gravlax, large thin slices of tender salmon, is served with a mustard dill sauce that manages to allow the fresh taste of the salmon to come through. Oysters are elegantly presented and very fresh; they come accompanied by a vinegar sauce redolent of chopped shallots instead of nasty horseradish. They also come glazed with sliced sautéed leeks and topped with wild mushrooms. Chef Gregory Godon has a wonderful hand with soups, which always taste homemade. The lobster dishes are superb, especially one served with braised kale. The fillet of Dover sole sautéed in hazelnut butter is delicate and tasty, with al dente vegetables gracefully garnishing the plate. While Chef Godon's chicken dishes are not a bit dull, they are overly complex, with both American

245

and Oriental spices fighting for attention. Stay with the fish, always well-prepared—avoiding, however, anything that sounds Japanese. Dessert can be surprising: excellent home-made sorbets in countless flavors, a very good crème brûlée, and a too rich chocolate cake which is the chef's pride. The view remains the best dessert and can be enjoyed while sipping a good espresso. Figure $45 per person for dinner. *Lunch Sun.-Fri. noon to 3 P.M.; dinner daily 6 P.M. to 11 P.M. All major credit cards.*

QUICK BITES

BETWEEN THE ACTS

If there is one trait that characterizes that unique species, the native New Yorker, it's an unexcelled talent for noshing that begins with the first bite of bagel and cream cheese in early morning and progresses happily through several hours of heavy duty snacking. Call it street fare, finger food, or between-meal sinning—in addition to more formal dining establishments the city obliges its insatiable food lovers with a paradise of casual eateries, from pizzerias and barbecued rib shacks to outdoor cafes, ice cream parlors, and all-night diners where truckers and club-hopping fashionables rub elbows at dawn over platters of steaks and pommes frites. You'll find the range of culinary diversions as tantalizing as a spice market on a windy day, so go ahead and indulge yourself—just like Manhattanites have been doing for years.

Barbecue

DALLAS B-B-Q
27 West 72nd St. (Central Park West & Columbus Ave.)873-2004

If you don't mind the clatter of the few hundred other diners who nightly pack into this mammoth-sized eatery, you can indulge in one of the best food bargains in town. The decor is strictly old warehouse, with towering ceilings and tightly packed vinyl tables, but the early bird special makes the confusion worthwhile: two people for dinner before 6:30 P.M. Monday through Saturday, or before 5 P.M. on Sundays, can each feast on chicken soup, half a barbecued chicken, cornbread, and potatoes for just $6.95 for both. If you come later the prices are just a couple of dollars more for the same menu. Or you can choose tender baby back ribs, beef ribs the size of an elephant's midsection, and an oversized loaf of fried onion rings (skip the soggy vegetable tempura). Don't expect real barbecue in this place—the sauce is too mild and the country singer's probably from Hoboken, but the prices are right and the waiters good-natured. Dinner for two (after the early bird special hours) is about $25 with beer. Or you can take out food for that next concert picnic in nearby Central Park. There's another location at 21 University Place (674-4450).
Sun.-Thurs. noon to midnight, Fri. & Sat. till 1 A.M. All major credit cards.

SMOKEY'S REAL PIT BARBEQUE

230 Ninth Ave. (24th St.)
924-8181

This vinyl and plastic Chelsea way station for the famished serves some of the best tasting baby back ribs and chicken this side of the Mason-Dixon line, topped by a rich, thick barbecue sauce that comes in your choice of mild, medium, or the devil's own hot. There's also spicy chicken wings, hot links, syrupy baked beans, and crispy deep-fried potato skin chips. Save room for Smokey's chocolate wafer icebox cake. For about $25 for two with beer, you'll be stuffed to the ribs. *Mon.-Fri. 11 A.M. to 10 P.M., Sat. & Sun. noon to 10 P.M. No credit cards.*

WYLIE'S RIBS & CO.

891 First Ave. (50th St.)
751-0700

You say your out-of-town friend plays nose tackle for the Dallas Cowboys and he's hungry? No problem—join the crowd of bright young singles and healthy-looking families who spill out onto the sidewalk of this no-nonsense rib house. And it's worth the wait, too, for meltingly tender baby back ribs, hefty beef ribs, and barbecued chicken that's moist and juicy. The pitcher on your table isn't sangria—it's extra barbecue sauce, and regulars even drizzle some on top of Wylie's much-touted "brick" of fried onion rings. Forgettable steak fries and coleslaw accompany your entrée. About $30 for a he-man portioned dinner for two. There's another location at 59 West 56th Street (757-7910), open daily 11:30 A.M. to midnight. Here you'll find an airy outdoor cafe for summer dining, along with gorgeous slabs of prime rib, meaty short ribs, and an oil-soaked aberration known as fried zucchini loaf that only a vegetarian could love. *Daily 11:30 A.M. to 12:30 A.M. All major credit cards.*

Cafes

ALL STATE CAFE

250 West 72nd St.
(Broadway & West End Ave.)
874-1883

Brick walls, a lively jukebox, plus a roaring fire in winter are a few of the many modest charms that make this cafe a perennial favorite for hungry Upper West Siders. Actors and literary types conduct serious conversations at the bar, then sit down at one of the small wood-topped tables for a hearty and inexpensive meal. The food is filling and tasty and you can't beat the $4.75 tab for a luncheon special that includes a bowl of soup or salad followed by sautéed calf's liver, grilled bluefish, or a scallion and cheddar cheese omelette. A plentiful weekend brunch with a Bloody Mary thrown in runs a humble $4.75.

Daily 11:30 A.M. to 1 A.M. No credit cards.

AMERICAN FESTIVAL CAFE

20 West 50th St. (at Rockefeller Center)
246-6699

The regal beauty of Rockefeller Center and its guardian, the statue of Prometheus, are noteworthy surroundings for the Festival Cafe, one of New York's most beloved traditions. In winter, diners can gaze out through the glass walls onto a Currier and Ives vision of ice skaters on the surrounding rink; in summer, the rink turns into a colorful patio of umbrellas and tables for outdoor dining. The view is the real star—the American cuisine is acceptable, but don't expect any showstoppers. For breakfast, homemade muffins, tender ham steaks, pancakes, waffles, and buttery French toast are always good choices. Lunch and dinner offer specialties like Thomas Jefferson's chicken hash, Maine lobster gazpacho, overcooked skewers of seafood doused in herbs, free-range chicken with mustard, and a treacherous array of limp pasta dishes. Bring the kids at Christmas for breakfast with Santa and you'll understand what the magic of this place is all about. About $10 per person for breakfast. Lunch and dinner will average from $20 to $30 per person with a glass of wine. *Mon.-Sat. 7:30 A.M. to 10:30 P.M., Sun. 11 A.M. to 9 P.M. All major credit cards.*

ARIZONA 206 CAFE

206 East 60th St. (Second & Third Aves.)
838-0440

This charming, airy cafe sparkles with the same dazzling glow that young chef Brendan Walsh creates at his stellar Arizona 206 Restaurant next door. The atmosphere is casual and contemporary, with bleached wooden tables, warm lighting, a vast open grill which sends forth luscious aromas of seared meat and poultry, plus an attractive crowd of trendy diners who always seem to be having a great time. And no wonder, for Chef Walsh's innovative, Southwestern-style fare is some of the most provocative and mouthwatering food in town. The menu consists of an ever-changing variety of marinated, grilled, and smoked foods accompanied by tantalizing chutneys and homemade preserves; the items are served in small portions that range from $6 to $14 per plate, so you can pick as few or as many as you like to make up a full meal. Take, for example, the juicy grilled squab, or the seafood nuzzled with fruit and an incendiary dollop of chile oil, marvelously spicy skirt steak tortillas, or barbecued

oyster tacos. As for dessert, try the cooling cactus pear sorbet, outrageously rich ice cream cake made with mango and coconut ice cream, or the dark and deadly baked chocolate mousse cake. If this is what they eat like in Arizona, we should all take a trip to Tuscon. (See the restaurant section for a review of Arizona 206 Restaurant.)
Mon.-Sat. noon to midnight. All major credit cards.

BEACH CAFE

1326 Second Ave. (70th St.)
988-7299

This relaxing cafe/gallery is a soothing spot in which to linger over lunch, drinks, or a casual supper. Cheery paintings of seascapes, brick walls, wood paneling, soft classical music, and an efficient staff are on hand, along with generally well-prepared, if unimaginative, food. At lunch there's the usual roster of hamburgers, quiches, omelettes, main dish salads, and a few Italian dishes. At night the menu offers more Italian with some passable pasta selections such as tortellini with tomato cream sauce and angel hair pasta with a choice of sauces. Lunch for one with a glass of wine is about $12.
Sun.-Thurs. 11:30 A.M. to 1 A.M., Fri. & Sat. till 1:30 A.M. AE.

BEGGAR'S BANQUET

125 West 43rd St. (Sixth & Seventh Aves.)
997-0959

This unpretentious, popular midtown eatery is a good choice for lunch or before-theater supper. Friendly service and a casual, pub-like atmosphere attract hordes of regulars from the business district, who come for simple, well-prepared fare in a relaxed setting. A basket of homemade honey and whole-wheat bread on the table will get you in the proper mood for a lusty bowl of chili, stew, or soup (Italian lentil, pistou, or cold cucumber and beet). In addition there are superior quiches such as ham, broccoli and cheddar, or Provençal, plus a worthy assortment of salads and good sandwiches. Desserts are delicious (try the Scotch chocolate cake or the New Orleans rum pudding with hard sauce). For dinner the kitchen turns out platters of shrimp stuffed with crab meat and a perfectly acceptable, if uninspired, rendering of chicken piccata. Lunch for two with a glass of wine is about $20; dinner for two with wine comes to under $40.
Mon.-Sat. 11:30 A.M. to 8:45 P.M. AE, DC.

BETWEEN THE BREAD

This handsome cafe with its elegant indoor garden-style dining room serves more substantial American fare than the

145 West 55th St. (Sixth & Seventh Aves.)
581-1189

Between the Bread salad and sandwich bistro on the East Side (at 141 East 56th Street). Adjacent to its own takeout muffin bakery, this very popular lunch spot attracts a crowd straight out of central casting—handsome L.A. show biz types, publishing people, and well-dressed businessmen. They stop by regularly for such marvelous fare as chicken pot pie in a tender shortbread crust, perfectly grilled fresh salmon over fettuccine with champagne sauce, or a superb array of salads and desserts like crumbly oatmeal pecan tart. The muffins are adored all over Gotham, and many customers walk next door after their meal to pick up a half dozen of the bran or cranberry walnut ones for the next day's breakfast. For interesting, well-prepared food with a tab that won't tug at your purse strings, this charming restaurant should not be missed. About $12 per person without wine. *Mon.-Sat. noon to 10 P.M.; closed Sat. in summer. All major credit cards.*

CAFFÉ DANTE

79-81 MacDougal St. (West Houston & Bleecker Sts.)
982-5275

Espresso aficionados make the Dante part of their daily routine for some of the most bracing, well-made demitasse this side of the Trastevere. A good selection of teas, hot chocolate, cappuccino, iced drinks, and pastries are available. In summer, you can sit outside at tiny tables and people-watch for hours. Even if you're not hungry, you'll want to try one of the lovely sandwiches made with crisp rolls and top-quality imported Italian cold meats and cheeses.
Sun.-Thurs. 10 A.M. to 2 A.M., Fri. & Sat. till 3 A.M. No credit cards.

CAFE LA FORTUNA

69 West 71st St. (Central Park West & Columbus Ave.)
724-5846

Within a few blocks of Lincoln Center, join the locals at this cozy subterranean nook for the best espresso on the Upper West Side. There's a soothing pace here, enhanced by the decor of vintage opera records and yellowed photos of Tristams and Aidas peering at you sadly from the walls. A better-than-decent selection of pastries are on hand—anise cookies, chocolate cakes, and rum-scented zuppa inglese—all at remarkably low prices ($2 for a wedge of velvety Italian cheesecake). For sipping choose from fragrant teas, fruit drinks, and frothy hot chocolate. In summer the garden terrace is open, and it's worth the half-hour wait in line to relax over iced cappuccino topped with a scoop of excellent homemade gelato.
Sun.-Thurs. 1 A.M. to 1 P.M., Fri. & Sat. till 2 A.M. No credit cards.

CAFE MADELEINE

403 West 43rd St. (Ninth Ave.)
246-2993

You'll find your favorite columnist along with most of the *New York Times* staff lunching at this charming petite cafe with its lacy white curtains and immaculate country look. In warm weather the patio garden is a serene spot in which to linger over a pleasing slice of country pâté, a bowlful of herb-flecked mussels marinière, or pistou. The salads are perky and generously studded with nuggets of Roquefort cheese and walnuts, or various crisp vegetable combinations. Simple grilled fish and roast duck are good choices for heartier appetites. About $30 for a simple meal for two with wine.
Daily noon to midnight. AE, MC, V.

CAFE MORTIMER

1057 Lexington Ave. (75th St.)
517-6400

You would never guess by the friendly ambience that this cheery cafe is the offspring of New York's most disdainfully exclusive dining salon, Mortimer's. The stunning walnut bar, handsome beige tiled walls, and soothing menu of good sandwiches, individual pizzas, and soups make this a popular spot where tired shoppers repair for a light luncheon or an afternoon coffee break. The appetizers and desserts are from Mortimer's—never big on culinary inspiration—so stick with simple items like artichokes in vinaigrette or gravlax for appetizers, and the satiny crème brûlée to polish off the meal. About $15 per person for lunch.
Lunch Sun.-Fri. noon to 4:30 P.M.; dinner 5 P.M. to midnight. All major credit cards.

CAFE REGGIO

119 MacDougal St. (West 3rd & Bleecker Sts.)
475-9557

The Cavallacci family opened this shrine to coffee and companionship in 1927, and they've been going strong ever since. There are plaster busts of Verdi and Wagner in the niches of the smoke-darkened walls, and a faintly seedy air that is vintage Fellini. Sip a satiny rich cup of espresso, frothy cappuccino, or a devastating hot chocolate whirled with whipped cream while you study what passes for Bohemia these days in the tamed streets of the Village. For nibbling, there are tasty prosciutto and cheese sandwiches, Italian pastries, homemade Italian slush, and Rome by Night, which turns out to be some rather dull combination of yogurt and fresh fruits.
Sun.-Thurs. 10 A.M. to 2 A.M., Fri. & Sat. till 4 A.M. No credit cards.

CAFE UN DEUX TROIS

123 West 44th St. (Sixth Ave. & Broadway)
354-4148

Imagine a brasserie decorated to look like a Parisian railway station and you'll have a good idea of the design at Un Deux Trois, with its ponderous chandeliers, neo-Gothic colonnades, and food that falls short of what a good snack bar can do. Too bad, because with just a little effort the owners could have a first-rate theater district eatery to be proud of, instead of an ordinary people-watching mob scene. The stunning Tiffany glass paneled bar is always popular, the service cheerfully efficient, and you're provided with crayons to doodle on the paper tablecloth while you wait. Be prepared for disappointment: incredibly overcooked and sandy mussels, tough cubes of skewered beef with a bland peanut sauce, oily fried chicken strip, and an eminently mediocre cassoulet. On the plus side there's a fair pepper steak served with some of the best pommes frites in New York, passable duck breast stuffed with spinach, good vinaigrette over crispy salad greens, and perfect calf's liver with a rosy pink center. Stay away from the charlottes and much-touted profiteroles. If you must order dessert, try the poached pear with ice cream and chocolate sauce. About $40 per person for dinner with house wine.
Mon.-Fri. 7:30 A.M. to midnight, Sat. & Sun. 10:30 A.M. to midnight. AE, MC, V.

CAMELBACK AND CENTRAL

1403 Second Ave. (73rd St.)
249-8380

Another rubber-stamped version of high tech decor meets nouvelle American food with predictably clichéd results. Uncomfortable steel chairs, Art Deco bar, and pretty fresh flowers on every table create a semi-romantic mood for the doddering clientele who mostly live nearby. You'll know the lunch menu already: the usual array of salads, quiches, and good, meaty burgers. At dinner stick with simple items like the crisp roast duck with black currant sauce, or grilled veal chops, rather than the virtually inedible oriental concoctions. About $17 for lunch for two; dinner for two will be $40 without wine.
Mon.-Sat. 11:30 A.M. to midnight, Sun. 11:30 A.M. to 11 P.M. All major credit cards.

CANTINA

Imagine being served Mexican food in a hospital—bland, soggy, and precisely the kind of insipid fare you'll find at the Cantina. In summer tourists at the sidewalk tables linger over

221 Columbus Ave. (70th St.)
873-2606

passable nachos and pretty decent Margaritas before they continue on to tackle the trendy boutiques. The taco and enchilada combination plates are filling, but mediocre at best. More exotic specialties like Mexican-style shrimp and red snapper inevitably come to the table cold and over-cooked. Around 6 P.M. on weeknights the bar starts to throng with yuppies, who come for the friendly atmosphere and efficient service rather than any serious singles watching. The portions are enormous, and the prices are too high, but you've got one of the best ringside seats around to survey the Columbus Avenue scene. Dinner for two with Margaritas is about $45.
Daily 11:30 A.M. to 1 A.M. AE, MC, V.

CENTRAL FALLS

478 West Broadway (Houston St.)
475-3333

After a morning of gallery-hopping in SoHo, pamper your-self with a lingering weekend brunch at this pretty spot. For decor, the white walls of this converted loft display changing exhibitions of paintings and photographs by artists like Joan Mitchell or Weegee. The gleaming mahogany bar, soothing live chamber music performed by well-known musicians, and a fashionable crowd of soigné uptowners make up for a menu that's reliable but a bit short on imagination. The blueberry pancakes are light and fluffy, someone in the kitchen knows how to make a great creamy omelette, and the frittata with smoked salmon and fresh vegetables is enticing. The dinner menu is a rubber-stamped version of every other trendy restaurant in town—smoked mozzarella and tasteless fresh tomatoes for salad, nicely seared fresh swordfish with key lime butter, and overcooked sea scallops with linguine. Brunch for two with wine or mixed drinks, about $25.
Daily 11:30 A.M. to 2 A.M. AE, DC, CB.

CLOISTER CAFE

238 East 9th St. (Second & Third Aves.)
777-9128

Artists, writers, and a steady clientele of regulars from all over Greenwich Village pass through here daily for the atmosphere and frothy café au lait served in bowl-sized china cups. In winter there's a cozy fire blazing, while in summer everybody moves outdoors to the brick courtyard that boasts a pretty fountain and fish pond. The food falls into the usual omelette/burger/chicken routine, but at $6.95 for the din-ner specials, no one complains too loudly. Still, the desserts are good quality, and the setting makes this cafe a worthy spot to tarry for a while. About $4.50 for dessert and coffee.

Sun.-Fri. 11:30 A.M. to 12:30 A.M., Fri. & Sat. till 1:30 A.M. No credit cards.

COTTONWOOD CAFE

415 Bleecker St. (Eighth Ave.)
924-6271

You may never mistake this place for a roadhouse in Galveston, but the Tex-Mex specialties here are tasty, abundant, and easy on the wallet. Cowboy posters and Lone Star memorabilia festoon the walls; live music and good, friendly service more than make up for the tiny tables jammed with neighborhood regulars. Start with wonderfully tender fried chicken livers or fiery chili. When you're ready to get down to serious eating, try the saucy ribs smoked over mesquite, or half a barbecued chicken, honest-to-goodness homemade mashed potatoes, and crunchy fried okra. You can avoid the overdone chicken-fried steak with pasty gravy and the underseasoned pork chops. The bar fixes a great frozen Margarita to ice it all down, and for $12 per person for dinner, you'll go home well-fed.
Mon.-Sat. 5 P.M. to 11:45 P.M., Sun. till 11 P.M.; brunch Sat. & Sun. 10 A.M. to 3 P.M. No credit cards.

DDL BISTRO

Trump Tower, 725 Fifth Ave. (56th & 57th Sts.)
832-1555

Pass by the tiers of unaffordable boutiques, slack-jawed tourists, and the ennui-stricken pianist serenading passers-by in the foyer of this marble and gilt shopping mall and head down to the lower level. There you'll encounter a cozy but pricey bistro with comfy red leather banquettes and chairs and marble-topped tables, plus a handsome crew of bow-tie clad waiters and waitresses waiting to pamper a colorful, Eurochic clientele. The food is appetizing, freshly prepared, and bright with seasonal ingredients such as fusilli nourished with juicy ripe tomatoes and basil, assorted antipastos, an excellent salad of roasted goat cheese with polenta, and superbly light gnocci in a tomato and Gorgonzola sauce. For dessert gianduja mousse cake is a heavenly mixture of chocolate and hazelnuts. Lunch for one will run a whopping $35 for the simple bistro fare—this is big-spender turf with a vengeance.
Mon.-Sat. 11:30 A.M. to 4 P.M., Sun. noon to 4 P.M. All major credit cards.

DEMARCHELIER

808 Lexington Ave. (62nd St.)
223-0047

At noon groups of ladies arrive in droves from Bergdorf's to lunch at this charming outpost of French politesse; at night these women come with their husbands in tow. Rich wood paneling, a handsome antique bar, sidewalk seating, an intimate back room salon, and waiters who will cater to every whim are just a few of the many charming qualities that draw a steady clientele to this delightfully old-fashioned bistro. Alas, the cuisine is insipid and at times downright inedible, from the lackluster house pâté and limp salads, to a passable saucisson chaud, dry, overcooked broiled salmon, and tough entrecôte of beef. After suffering through dinner, you'll at least be rewarded with some surprisingly good classic bistro desserts such as a silken crème caramel and a fruit-laden tarte tatin. About $25 per person for lunch with a glass of wine.

Lunch Mon.-Sat. noon to 3 P.M.; dinner 6 P.M. to 11 P.M. All major credit cards.

ELEPHANT AND CASTLE

183 Prince St. (Sullivan St.)
260-3600

While trendy SoHo restaurants come and go, this cozy spot is always crowded with local artists, out-of-work actors, and svelte uptowners down here boutiquing for the day. Ceiling fans, small wooden tables, and white paneled windows add a grandmother's kitchen touch of friendly warmth, and the service is efficient and cheery. The interesting menu ranges from day to night choices: for breakfast there's creamy oatmeal with golden raisins and hazelnuts, scrambled eggs with curried sour cream, and crisp Indian bread as well as 20 omelettes—goat cheese with fresh and sun-dried tomatoes is lavishly cheesy. The Elephantburger for a pricey $6.95 is worth the money for this charcoal-grilled beauty that's topped with curried sour cream, bacon, cheddar, tomato, and scallions; for more spartan tastes the kitchen makes a terrific Caesar salad. Desserts are a big draw and tend toward the rich and gooey: towering sundaes like the Kaffee Klatsch or Magnificent Obsession, satiny Indian pudding, or dessert crepes filled with ice cream and hot fudge. Dinner for two with a glass of wine and dessert will cost $25.

Sun.-Thurs. 8 A.M. to midnight, Fri. & Sat. till 1 A.M. All major credit cards.

FRONT PORCH

253 West 11th St. (West 4th St.)
675-8083

Be it ever so humble, there's no place for humble, old-fashioned cooking like this cozy nook in the Village. Green curtains hanging from the windows and a score of tiny glass-topped tables create the look of a cafe somewhere in the cornbelt. The menu features good quality soups, salads, omelettes, and sandwiches simply prepared and modestly priced to attract a loyal following of young students and would-be thespians. You're invited to sample the soups before choosing from such worthies as Mom's chicken or silky fresh cream of mushroom. Try a crumbly wedge of meatloaf savory with herbs, or the spicy rich chili stuffed into pita bread with cheddar cheese. A bowl of juicy, sweet, fresh peach pudding drenched in cream for dessert will make you feel as if you just had dinner at a country church supper. Other locations at 2272 Broadway (877-5220), and 119 East 18th Street (473-7940). About $8 per person for lunch. *Daily noon to 11:30. No credit cards.*

GIANNI'S

South Street Seaport, 15 Fulton St. (Water St.) 608-7300

If people-watching is your favorite hobby, you'll be in spectators' heaven at this teeming sidewalk cafe where pin-striped Wall Streeters rub elbows with tourists in running shorts. The vaguely northern Italian menu will probably fill but not thrill you: tangy garlic bread steeped in a creamy Gorgonzola pesto, overcooked pastas like fettucine in a bland lobster cream sauce, and an array of seafood salads. A better choice are the snapping fresh fish entrées like grilled tuna or swordfish. For dessert, the smooth tirami su of ladyfingers, mascarpone mousse, and amaretto is one of New York's finest examples of this trendy dessert. On Friday and Saturday nights a Gatsbyish crowd of well-heeled singles show up for dancing. About $30 per person for dinner with wine.
Mon.-Thurs. 11:30 A.M. to 11 P.M., Fri. & Sat. noon to midnight, Sun. noon to 11 P.M. All major credit cards.

HARD ROCK CAFE

221 West 57th St. (Seventh Ave. & Broadway) 489-6565

Only preteens and an adult with the torture quotient of Torquemada would come here a second time. Pass beneath the fins of a vintage Caddy plastered against the building and you'll enter a rock 'n' roll theme park gone mad. Beatle tickets and Elvis memorabilia on the walls, a guitar-shaped bar, and waitresses "slam dancing" to music played to the screech level of a departing SST are just part of the fun you've got in store after waiting outdoors in line for three hours to get in. The great surprise is that the food is pretty decent—if your waitress ever hears your order—mammoth burgers in sesame buns, Pig Sandwiches made with juicy roast pork, and fresh salads, all to be washed down with a creamy milkshake or float. While you're traveling down memory lane with the Everly Brothers on tape you can overload on a fudge-laced ice cream sundae or any of several other gooey rich desserts. It should sweeten your mood

before your teenager hits you up for a sweatshirt or other expensive trinket *so* conveniently located in the gift shop right by the exit.
Daily 11 A.M. to 4 A.M. AE, MC, V.

JIM MCMULLEN

1341 Third Ave. (76th & 77th Sts.)
861-4700

Few people are indifferent to this quintessential Upper East Side boîte where the cashmere and pearls show up nightly. The atmosphere is modish but intimate, with pretty lace curtains, wood paneling, flowers on each table, and an impeccably groomed, handsome young crowd who come for the preppy singles' scene and the cliquish bonhomie that is host Jim McMullen's forte. As for the cuisine, it's as whitewashed and limp as the surroundings—omelettes, good sandwiches, overdone seafood dishes, tender but tasteless calf's liver, and a lovely chicken pot pie. This is the place to come when you're in the mood for dinner at the country club. About $15 per person for lunch with a glass of wine.
Daily 11:30 A.M. to 1:30 A.M. AE.

J.S. VANDAM

150 Varick St. (Vandam St.)
929-7466

Now that Tribeca is only slightly less chic than SoHo, you might meet your uptown dentist hobnobbing with art gallery and film types at this frenzied bar scene. The vaguely club-like atmosphere of sagging red leather banquettes and dark wood is sadly inappropriate, for the rafter-ringing pace here is anything but sedate. Since no one wanders in till after 10 P.M., when it's too late to think about serious dining anyway, the barely passable food does less harm than it would to more ravenous appetites. Salads and appetizers are the best here: baked polenta with goat cheese on crispy greens, golden beer-batter shrimp, and crunchy rings of fried calamari make wonderful nibbles. The fettuccine with sweetbreads needs seasoning, but the grilled swordfish piccata has just the right tang of lemon butter. Simple items like nicely seared steak au poivre and veal chops will amply fuel you for dancing the night away at the club Heartbreak, just down the street. About $35 per person for dinner with wine.
Nightly 4 P.M. to 4 A.M. All major credit cards.

KLEINE KONDITOREI

Once an Eastern European enclave, this area of New York known as Yorkville has lost nearly all of its ethnic trappings. Happily, Kleine is still going strong as a dear relic of

234 East 86th St. (Second & Third Aves.)
737-7130

Germanic gusto. Beef roulade, schnitzel, sauerbraten, goulash, herring, and other rich specialties saturated in butter and heavy cream sauces will drive you willingly back to salad and yogurt for a few days. A better time to visit is during afternoon coffee break, when you can indulge your Teutonic fancy in such toothsome confections as chocolate and whipped cream Black Forest cake, gulgelhupf, marzipan cherry cake, sachertorte, apple strudel, and cups of marvelous Viennese coffee. Complete dinners cost under $20.
Sun.-Thurs. 10 A.M. to midnight, Fri. & Sat till 1 A.M. AE, DC.

O'NEAL'S BALOON

48 West 63rd St. (Columbus Ave.)
399-2353

You'll probably get heartburn after eating the fatty hamburgers and soggy French fries, but you'll enjoy every minute of it at this good-natured, turn-of-the-century tavern. Conveniently located across the street from Lincoln Center, the before- and after-curtain scene here is rowdy, animated, and a great place to people-watch. Some excellent beers on tap; they'll mellow the blow to your appetite from the dying salads and club sandwiches, gravy-soaked chicken pot pies, and lasagna that's been hanging around since the days of Mayor LaGuardia. A simple dinner for two with beer will run $25.
Daily 7 A.M. to midnight. All major credit cards.

POPOVER CAFE

551 Amsterdam Ave. (87th St.)
595-8555

Don't let the Salvation Army decor and health food trappings fool you. This Upper West Side eatery serves better-than-your-favorite-truck-stop breakfasts and luscious overstuffed sandwiches. Start your meal off by noshing on a popover—a gigantic golden-crusted balloon made of eggs and flour. The extensive breakfast offerings include puffy omelettes filled with fresh mushrooms, cheddar cheese, horseradish, and other tasty tidbits; "cappuccino eggs," steamed under the cappuccino jet to clouds of yellow fluff, and perfectly made cheese grits. At other times of the day you can join all the hungry young actors and dancers who frequent the place for hefty eight-ounce burgers made of beef and veal, mammoth main dish salads, and tasty combination sandwiches. There is a good range of coffees and herbal teas for sipping, but someone in the kitchen should learn how to make an espresso that doesn't taste like dishwater. About $12 per person for lunch with beer.
Mon.-Fri. 8:30 A.M. to 11 P.M., Sat. 10 A.M. to 11 P.M., Sun. 10 A.M. to 10 P.M. AE.

SOHO KITCHEN AND BAR

*103 Greene St. (Prince &
Spring Sts.)*
925-1866

This large, multilevel restaurant with its rambling 120-foot bar is wealthy both in space and culinary talent. Dramatic lighting, attention-getting artwork, a black-as-midnight ceiling, and rock music loud enough to shatter cement are a few of the more dubious charms of SoHo Kitchen. Just shrug them off philosophically and concentrate instead on the food: savory pizzas generously garnished with sausage, sun-dried tomatoes, and cheese, crackling crisp French fries, chicken wings, and ho-hum pastas. Along with these snacks comes one of the most inspired wine selections in New York: over 110 different selections (including 14 Champagnes) are available daily by the glass for sipping and comparative tasting among the many budding young oenophiles who frequent this notable SoHo place. After 10:30 P.M. there is a 25% discount on all Champagnes. About $20 per person for a light supper with two glasses of wine.
Mon.-Thurs. 4:30 P.M. to 12:30 P.M., Fri. till 1:30 A.M., Sat. noon to 1:30 A.M. AE, V, MC.

SUCCESS LA CÔTE BASQUE

*1032 Lexington Ave. (73rd
& 74th Sts.)*
535-3311

Superb French pastries and a pleasant, countrified ambience make this Lexington Avenue cafe an inviting spot any time of day. For breakfast there are wonderfully flaky croissants, ethereal Danish pastries, and bitter French coffee. The luncheon menu offers a good selection of pâtés, salads, soups, and quiches. The chocolate ganache cake and coupe Swan Lake, a frothy confection of meringue, ice cream, and fresh fruit, will revive the spirits of even the most bone-weary midtown shopper. About $12 per person for lunch with dessert.
Daily 7:30 A.M. to 7 P.M., Sun. in summer till 3 P.M. AE, DC.

WEST SIDE STOREY

*700 Columbus Ave. (95th
St.)*
749-1900

Depending upon who's cooking the food that particular day at this inviting neighborhood restaurant, it will have an American, Thai, or French character, but in all cases the results are superb. On the increasingly trendy Upper West Side this neighborhood eatery offers interesting food, efficient service, and a relaxed atmosphere for both families and the budding yuppies who live nearby. There is a sit-down counter and comfortable booths with upholstered banquettes; try to arrive before 8 P.M. unless you don't mind waiting up to an hour in line. Saffron chicken broth punctuated with smoked chicken and tortellini is a good way to begin the meal. For entrées there are spicy chicken gai yang with a potent Thai hot sauce, crispy whole sea bass with black bean sauce, excellent homemade raviolis, plus interesting salads and vegetarian dishes. A lovely dinner in a cordial setting will run about $45 for two with wine and espresso.

Mon.-Sat. 7 A.M. to 11 P.M., Sun. 8 A.M. to 11 P.M. No credit cards.

Delis

CARNEGIE DELICATESSEN

854 Seventh Ave. (54th & 55th Sts.)
757-2245

Ever since Woody Allen filmed *Broadway Danny Rose* in this hallowed New York landmark just off the theater district, the question running through every serious nosher's mind has been, "But is the pastrami still lean?" Happy to report it is, and the corned beef is still a fine specimen of cured meat. Despite its wisecracking waiters, cramped tables, and cigar smoke, everyone still loves the place, even if the sandwiches are way overpriced and the chicken in a pot lacks some of its former luster. A deli lunch will cost between $10-12.

Daily 6:30 A.M. to 3:30 A.M. No credit cards.

NEW YORK DELICATESSEN

104 West 57th St. (Sixth & Seventh Aves.)
541-8320

The bold and brassy authentic Art Deco setting is probably the best thing this tacky deli has going for it, unless you like fatty corned beef. Once a Horn and Hardart automat, both the restaurant and most of its dubious-looking clientele have seen better days, but you'll have fun noshing here anyway. Have some brisket, munch on the creamy coleslaw, and you'll soon start humming a Gershwin tune.

Open daily 24 hours. All major credit cards.

SECOND AVENUE KOSHER DELICATESSEN

156 Second Ave. (10th St.)
677-0606

Got a craving for chicken in a pot, or the most mouth-watering stuffed cabbage this side of Tel Aviv? Just hop in a taxi and head for the Lower East Side, where you'll find New York's best kosher deli. Owner Abe Lebewohl has perfectly captured the frantic hustle and bustle of a turn-of-the-

century eatery with delicious kosher food; the nostalgic atmosphere comes complete with cramped booths and pickles at every table, and waitresses who could be your dear Aunt Bessie ordering you to finish every spoonful of the divine chicken and matzo ball soup. In addition, there's zesty mushroom and barley soup, kasha, kishka (stuffed beef intestine), kugel (noodle pudding), silky smooth chopped liver, and cholent (a casserole of beef, potatoes, beans, and barley). Each year at Passover Abe sells more than 3,000 pieces of his excellent gefilte fish. If you ask him what's in the recipe, he'll hold you spellbound for hours as he passionately discourses on whether to use whitefish or carp. About $25 for a sumptuous deli feast for two.
Daily 8 A.M. to 11:30 P.M. No credit cards.

Fast Food

THE BIG KITCHEN

*World Trade Center,
Concourse Level
938-1153*

When this complex of restaurants first opened on the concourse level of the Twin Towers, it was hailed as a culinary feat: eight marvelous food stands serving an incredible variety of wholesome and tasty food at moderate prices in a relaxed atmosphere. Wall Streeters came in droves, the tourists loved it, and soon even uptowners who rarely traveled lower than Bloomingdale's were trekking down to the Big Kitchen for lunch. Sadly, the quality of the food has plummeted severely over the last couple of years. While it is still possible to find a few decent items among the many disasters, you'll end up spending a fortune before you do so on the likes of soggy tacos, woebegone barbecued chicken, fatty ribs, mediocre deli sandwiches, and the greasy-fried-rice-and-egg-roll school of Chinese cooking.
Mon.-Fri. 7 A.M. to 7 P.M., Sat. 9 A.M. to 5 P.M. All major credit cards.

DOSANKO

*135 East 45th St. (Third &
Lexington Aves.)
697-2967*

Every day at noontime you'll find thousands of New Yorkers chomping happily on gyozas (delicate pork or shrimp dumplings) at one of the many Dosankos that abound in midtown. These popular Japanese fast-food establishments are strictly no-frills in the design department, with garish formica tables and too-bright lighting, but the food can be as delicate as a cherry blossom. Besides the light and tasty dumplings, there is superb fried chicken for less than $4 a basket, great noodle dishes, and aromatic soups laden with bright green vegetables and bits of meat. Japanese wines and beers, tea, and coffee are available for sipping with your meal. About $6 per person for lunch or dinner. Takeout service available at several locations. Check the phone book for the nearest location.

Mon.-Fri. 11 A.M. to 9:30 P.M., Sat. & Sun. noon to 8 P.M. No credit cards.

Ice Cream

AGORA

1550 Third Ave. (87th St.) 369-6983

Agora is the Greek word for marketplace, and this Upper East Side boutique is indeed a shopper's paradise: half of the establishment is a swank clothing store for men and women, and the other half a charming ice cream parlor and restaurant. The stunning black onyx soda fountain dates from the late 1900's, and the decor is a handsome blend of stained glass, frosted mirrors, chandeliers, and gorgeously carved mahogany cabinets. This delightful environment is a serene setting for some superb soda fountain treats made with the creamiest ice cream in town (all 21 excellent varieties). The ice cream sodas and sundaes are made with the best ingredients—fresh fruits, heavy cream, buttery toppings, and a host of different liqueurs. If you want to feel like a child again, this is the place to come to. (See the restaurant section for a more complete review of the food here.)

Mon.-Thurs. 11:30 A.M. to 11:30 P.M., Fri. & Sat. till 1 A.M., Sun. noon to 11:30 P.M. All major credit cards.

DIMITRI'S CAFE

156 Spring St. (West Broadway) 334-9239

This tiny gray and white cafe is a popular spot for SoHo shoppers who come to revive their flagging spirits with a calorie-loaded treat. Ben & Jerry's ice cream from Vermont is the main attraction here, and you can choose from such flavors as Cherry Garcia (chocolate with cherries), Heath Bar Crunch, or Oreo Mint. There's good espresso and some worthy pastries on hand as well, such as the densely nutty pecan pie or feather-light cheesecake.

Daily 8 A.M. to midnight. No credit cards.

LE GLACIER

1022A Madison Ave. (78th & 79th Sts.)
772-3870

A wide assortment of frozen products are on hand at this inviting spot to appease every kind of sweet tooth from dieters' to splurgers'. There's low-calorie glacés made of fresh fruit, bean curd-based Tofutti, 16 flavors of Sedutto's ice cream, plus outstanding frozen yogurt that comes in vanilla, raspberry, peach, and strawberry. Join the school kids and Madison Avenue shoppers who throng here every afternoon for some delightfully sweet licks.
Mon.-Sat. 11 A.M. to 10 P.M., Sun. noon to 11 P.M. No credit cards.

MINTER'S ICE CREAM KITCHEN

South Street Seaport, Pier 17
608-2037

After your umpteenth stroll through the maze of pricey tourist shops at South Street Seaport, you deserve something luscious and creamy, even if the calories will set you back a month of diet lunches. Walk up to the third level of Pier 17 where the sweet smell of vanilla, chocolate, and coffee will lead you directly to Minter's. This attractive ice cream booth offers super-rich homemade ice cream made directly on the premises in 16 tantalizing flavors like kahlúa and cream or triple chocolate. There's a wide range of goodies on hand for mixing into your cone—brownies, crumbled Heath Bars, and fresh strawberries—as well as enormous crispy waffles filled with ice cream, then dipped in chocolate and nuts for a double dose of decadence.
Sun.-Thurs. 10 A.M. to midnight, Fri. & Sat. till 1 or 2 A.M. No credit cards.

OLD-FASHIONED MR. JENNINGS

12 West 55th St. (Fifth & Sixth Aves.)
582-2238

This deliciously prim ice cream parlor has been frequented for years by women of a certain age (the blue-rinse set). It serves the same purpose as a neighborhood saloon does for their husbands. Mr. Jennings himself is always around like a good bartender to lend a sympathetic ear and help settle such important questions as whether to choose the chicken salad today or stick with the tuna on whole-wheat, and doesn't this nasty weather call for a butterscotch sundae? Most of Mr. Jennings' customers do have a sweet tooth, and he obliges them and even the occasional stranger who wanders in with a roster of lovely old-fashioned ice cream treats such as extra thick shakes, sodas, banana splits topped with hand-whipped cream, and creamy hot fudge or fruits in season. Freshly made salads and sandwiches round out the

menu for lunch and light suppers.
Mon.-Fri. 11 A.M. to 8 P.M., Sat. 11 A.M. to 7 P.M. No credit cards.

PEPPERMINT PARK

1225 First Ave. (66th St.)
288-5054

Homemade ice cream and chocolates along with sand-wiches, crepes, and salads make up the menu at this attract-ive, modern ice cream parlor decked out in crisp peppermint green. The ice cream comes in 50 flavors—big as far as the imagination goes, but definitely on the mediocre side as far as quality and taste are concerned. Forget you ever heard of such abominations as strawberry cheese or Dutch apple ice cream. Still, this spot is pleasant enough to warrant a visit. Other locations in Madison Square Garden (736-4070) and at 666 Fifth Avenue (581-5938).
Mon.-Thurs. 10 A.M. to midnight, Fri. till 1 A.M., Sat. till 2 A.M., Sun. 11 A.M. to midnight. AE, DC.

SANT AMBROEUS

1000 Madison Ave. (77th St.)
570-2211

Everything at this New York branch of a famed Milanese pastry shop is precious, expensive, and ostentatiously baroque—from the ornate dining room (open for breakfast, lunch, and dinner) to the jewel-like pastries, beribboned and decorated like a June bride, to the well-heeled European clientele hobnobbing at the espresso bar over crusty panini sandwiches of ham and mozzarella. If you're dressed for all this pretense, have a seat at a table; if not, take out a serving of truly superb gelato in such magnificent flavors as hazelnut, zabaglione, or cappuccino. On the lighter side there are sparkling fresh fruit sorbets that change according to the season. The price for a fashionably small serving of gelato or sorbet is $1.50. (This *is* a full-fledged restaurant; for a more complete review see the restaurant section.)
Mon.-Sat. 9:30 A.M. to 10:30 P.M., Sun. 10:30 A.M. to 7 P.M. AE, MC, V.

SERENDIPITY 3

225 East 60th St. (Second & Third. Aves.)
838-3531

As its name implies, Serendipity is a charming hodgepodge —expensive toy boutique, ice cream parlor, casual restau-rant, and for more than two decades New York's favorite dessert hangout after the movies. The young waiters all look like Peter Pan and the white-on-white decor with its marble tables and wire chairs add to the feeling that you've just entered a Victorian sugarplum fantasy. As for the menu, there are better-than-average burgers, omelettes, and salads,

but most regulars come here mainly for the colossal sundaes and banana splits made with excellent ice cream and butter-rich toppings, especially the incomparable hot fudge sauce. There are some great iced drinks on hand for sipping (try the frozen hot chocolate or espresso), plus a few good pastries for that inevitable heretic in the crowd.
Sun.-Thurs. 11:30 A.M. to 12:30 P.M., Fri. till 1 A.M., Sat. till 2 A.M. All major credit cards.

Late Night

Brasserie

100 East 53rd St. (Park & Lexington Aves.)
751-4840

Busy as an airport lounge during Christmas, the Brasserie is filled into the dead of night with show biz types, middle-aged night owls, and all kinds of loyal customers who think it's normal to eat steak and fries at five in the morning. The 24-hour menu is slightly French in the simple tradition of omelettes, quiches, grilled meats, onion soup gratinée, crisp Monte Cristo sandwiches, and a decent choucroute that is hearty enough to chase away the most persistent midnight hunger pangs. About $12 per person for a light meal without wine.
Open daily 24 hours. All major credit cards.

Corner Bistro

331 West 4th St. (Jane St.)
242-9502

A notch above your basic bar and burger joint, the Corner Bistro is always crowded with the mixed jam of people who live or work in the West Village. The vintage jukebox is well-stocked, the tables scarred with graffiti, and nobody minds squeezing into the hard wooden booths for beer, Irish coffee, and macho bowls of chili or "bistro burgers" made with good beef, cheese, bacon, onion, lettuce, and tomato wedged between the two halves of a toasted bun. About $7 per person.
Daily 11:30 A.M. to 4 A.M. No credit cards.

Empire Diner

210 Tenth Ave. (22nd St.)
243-2736

At 4 A.M. on a Friday or Saturday night, this Art Deco railway car blazes with megavolt energy as the city's most rabid club-hoppers stop by for breakfast. The menu offers glorified diner dishes—omelettes, club sandwiches, chili, burgers, brownies, hot fudge sundaes. Much of the food is

only passable and wouldn't cut the mustard in a regular restaurant. But lots of leggy models love the place, some stockbroker types think it's wild, and for a saving grace, Miss Bea plays a mean piano from 11 A.M. to 3 P.M. (other pianists entertain during dinner and until 4 A.M. on Saturday nights). About $10 per person.
Open daily 24 hours. AE.

FLORENT

69 Gansevoort St.
(Greenwich & Washington Sts.)
989-5779

Smack in the middle of the city's meatpacking district, this place used to be a tumbledown diner until an adventuresome Frenchman rashly decided to convert it into a bistro. Thank goodness for his astute daydreams, for ever since opening day Florent has been good news for New Yorkers of all incomes, ages, and tastes. The noise level is deafening, the small wooden tables are placed too close together, and you'll probably end up squashed on a stool at the long formica counter—but it's all great fun. The best hours to come are between 3 A.M. and 5 A.M., when the crowd is a mix of modishly dressed club crawlers and Hulk-sized butchers wearing aprons. There are three different menus for breakfast, lunch, and dinner. The food is essentially Franco-diner cuisine: simple, hearty choices like grilled chicken, boudin, steak and pomme frites, escargot in garlic sauce, and steamed mussels in wine. At 2:30 A.M. breakfast begins, and there's a good assortment of eggs, omelettes, breakfast steaks, burgers, and wonderfully light pancakes ($1.95 for a generous stack) that are close to crêpes in texture. You can bring your toddler here for dinner, and your date for late night supper. About $15 per person for dinner, $6 per person for breakfast.
Open daily 24 hours. No credit cards.

KIEV

117 Second Ave. (7th St.)
674-4040

Where else would you satisfy a craving for stuffed cabbage at 5 A.M. but the Kiev? This family-operated, East European coffee shop attracts a large local following who come for the blintzes, scrambled eggs with kielbasa, and delicious slabs of French toast made with challah. The portions are generous and prices prewar, all of which makes this place a popular student hangout. About $5 per person.
Open daily 24 hours. No credit cards.

LOX AROUND THE CLOCK

This punk deli has a decor that fashion pundits call "demolition chic" or homage to a junkyard, take your pick. Conveniently located near some of the major clubs like Limelight,

676 Ave. of the Americas
(21st St.)
691-3535

Private Eyes, and the Palladium, LATC boasts a 35-foot bar, video jukebox with seven monitors, and a 24-hour menu that includes your basic Jewish standards like stuffed cabbage, bagels, blintzes, and, of course, lox (and it's good!). For dinner, there's fresh fish and a few boring chicken dishes which will make you wish you had ordered the chopped liver instead. About $14 per person with a glass of wine.
Mon.-Wed. 7 A.M. to 4 A.M., Thurs.-Sun. open 24 hours.
AE.

MARKET DINER

572 Eleventh Ave. (43rd St.)
244-6033

This classic diner decorated in the formica and aluminum school of design is number one on the list of good, cheap eating for taxi drivers, policemen, truck drivers, and anyone in the mood for old-fashioned home cooking—from ham and eggs with a stack of pancakes for breakfast to Yankee pot roast, chicken pot pie, and meatloaf for dinner. For an added inducement, the parking is free, something as rare in New York as the low $10 per person tab you'll pay here for dinner. Another location at 256 West Street (925-0856).
Open daily 24 hours. MC, V.

103 SECOND AVENUE

103 Second Ave. (6th St.)
533-0769

About 3 A.M. on any given morning, this bright and cheerful East Village spot is one of the hottest scenes in town, with fashion industry and club people, musicians and night owls from all over in rakish attendance. The jukebox is tremendous, the dress outlandish, and on weekends there's a long wait for a seat at one of the butcher block tables. The total effect is an atmosphere that's bright and friendly, and the service is good, too. The menu offers round-the-clock items including sandwiches, burgers, omelettes, vegetarian casseroles, and an assortment of decent pies, cakes, and desserts. The daily dinner specials usually include some zingy Mexican platters like carne asado or cheese crisp tacos. About $15 per person for dinner with wine or beer.
Open daily 24 hours. No credit cards.

RESTAURANT

63 Carmine St. (Seventh Ave. South)
675-3312

Restaurant is one of those devastatingly "in" places that deliberately has no sign outside—the idea is that you're either a member of the owner's family or a regular. This place attracts the fashion victim set: designers, models and their groupies, assorted artists, decorators, and a few stray yuppies. The walls are painted with multicolored maps of the world, and the ceiling is a constellation of stars—the world is the Restaurant and the Restaurant is the world, if you want to get philosophical about it. The food is a cliché of California cuisine specialties such as calamari with green tomatillo sauce, grilled tuna with mango, shrimp with artichoke, and salmon sashimi. But everything is fresh and made with a proper light touch, so that nobody's size 4 figure runs the risk of getting ruined. The kitchen closes at 12:30 A.M. About $30 per person for dinner with wine. *Sun.-Thurs. 6:30 P.M. to about 3 A.M., Fri. & Sat. till about 5 A.M., closed Sun. in summer. AE.*

SILVER STAR RESTAURANT

1238 Second Ave. (65th St.)
249-4250

More than just another Greek coffee shop, the Silver Star is well-known in the neighborhood and to eagle-eyed bargain hunters who drop in regularly for tasty fresh seafood at moderate prices. Conveniently located near the major first-run movie houses on the East Side, the decor is vaguely nautical, and there's an enclosed outdoor area that's almost always full. The food ranges from Greek specialties like pasticcio and moussaka to live lobsters, soft shell crabs, and a fish of the day. In addition, there are burgers, sandwiches, omelettes, grilled steaks and chops, salads, and just about any food item known to Western man available on the menu. The full bar includes all the basics as well as ouzo and retsina. If you must order dessert, go for the fruit salad instead of all those elaborate cakes and pastries which invariably taste like Styrofoam topped with artificial cream. About $11 per person for dinner.
Open daily 24 hours. All major credit cards.

TEXARKANA

64 West 10th St. (Sixth Ave.)
254-5800

A few years ago this West Village spot was hotter than a chili pepper and well-respected among food mavens for its snappy Creole and Cajun cookery. Today the heat has dimmed to a dull glow as the kitchen suffers from a midlife crisis and the service gets even slower, if that's possible. The best time to come here is late at night when the mood is more intimate and friendly people mill around the bar. For food, charred barbecued pork, dirty rice, blackened redfish, fried chicken, pickled shrimp, gumbo, and a variety of Southern specialties are available. The walls are a light salmon color interspersed with western artifacts. The crowd likes to dress in Calvin Klein, and the tab for this gussied-up roadhouse fare is heftier than a steer ready for market. About $30 per person. *Sun.-Thurs. 6 P.M. to midnight, Fri. & Sat. till 4 A.M. AE.*

Pizza

AMERICAN PIE

434 Amsterdam Ave. (81st St.)
877-6740

A couple of years ago the Mantone family was contentedly serving zesty stuffed pizzas from a humble West Side takeout shop. Now they've moved and revamped into a postmodernist nuova pizzeria that's all glitter and no taste. Ignore, if you can, the jello-colored decor and uncomfortable plastic banquettes and take deep draughts of the tomato-and-cheese filled aromas that announce there's still good fare to be found in these too precious environs. Plump calzones, piping hot lasagnas, and a stupefying selection of pizzas made with either whole-wheat or white crust plus impeccably fresh ingredients are the main attractions. Pizza fillings range from tried-and-true favorites like tomato with mozzarella and sausage, to outlandish specimens like barbecue beef and cajun, made with poultry or seafood and hot spices. Prices range from $4.50 for a four-inch individual pie, to about $20 for a ten-inch version with "the works" on top. For more high-calorie fun, there are fudgy banana splits, sundaes, and a batch of nasty-tasting sweet pies for dessert.
Sun.-Thurs. 11 A.M. to 11 P.M., Fri. & Sat. till 1 A.M. AE.

FAMOUS RAY'S PIZZA

465 Ave. of the Americas (11th St.)
243-2253

Despite many other pretenders to the throne, this is the one, the only, the original Ray's Pizza and consistently rates as one of the best pizzerias in the city. Try a slice at $1.25 for a hefty wedge, or indulge in one of Ray's 18-inch whoppers that begin at a modest $9.50 for a basic pie.
Daily 9 A.M.. to 2 A.M., Fri. & Sat. till 3 A.M. No credit cards.

JOHN'S

278 Bleecker St. (Seventh Ave.)
243-1680

After more than half a century on the same spot in Greenwich Village, New York's best-loved pizzeria just gets better with age. Maybe it's the coal-fired oven that deliciously chars the thin crust, the mounds of fragrant fresh garlic that top off every piece, or the first-rate ingredients like crumbly sweet Italian sausage, green peppers, and fresh mushrooms. Most likely, it's the combination of all of those things that makes for a truly excellent rendering of pizza at its simple best. Prices start at $6.75 for a basic 14-inch pie. A second location uptown at 408 East 64th Street (935-2895). *Mon.-Sat. 11:30 A.M. to 11:30 P.M., Sun. noon to 11:30 P.M. No credit cards.*

PIZZAPIAZZA

785 Broadway (10th St.)
505-0977

This pretty-in-pink-and-green Village restaurant is a popular gathering spot for local business people, neighborhood regulars, and weekend shoppers. Soft sculpture cacti and pastel checked tablecloths give the place a light, modern feeling, and the staff is courteous and efficient. Individual deep dish pizzas on crispy whole-wheat crust in combinations that range from the bountiful to the outrageous are the attraction here, from the "All-white" with its savory topping of four cheeses and onions, to such rare birds as Chicken Mexicano with tortilla chips. Burgers, main dish salads, pastas, and soups are also available. The bargain $4.95 luncheon special on weekdays features a small pizza or pasta, soup or salad, and beverage. The excellent double fudge chocolate cake for dessert is a must.
Daily 11:45 A.M. to 11:30 P.M. AE, MC, V.

PIZZERIA UNO

391 Ave. of the Americas (8th St.)
242-5230

This marvelous pizzeria offers hefty Chicago-style deep-dish pies in three different sizes. A handsome, young crowd are on hand around the clock at this pretty eatery with its dark green banquettes, black and white tiled floors, and chandeliers. The pizzas are baked on a conveyor belt in a three-story oven and arrive at your table steaming with generous pools of melted cheese and tasty toppings. Try the Uno with extra cheese, sausage, pepperoni, mushrooms, onions, and green peppers. There's sangria by the pitcher to wash it all down, and a nice assortment of beers as well. There's also a worthwhile luncheon special on weekdays for $3.75 which includes an individual pizza, plus soup or salad. Pizzas can be taken out fully or partially baked, or frozen.
Mon.-Thurs. 11:30 A.M. to midnight, Fri. & Sat. till 2 A.M., Sun. noon to midnight. MC, V.

TRATTORIA PINO

981 Third Ave. (58th & 59th Sts.)
759-1220

Cozily ensconced near Bloomingdale's and a string of first-run movie theaters, this cheery trattoria serves a good variety of pizzas deliciously charred with the flavor of a genuine wood-burning oven. The setting is standard issue:

Tiffany lamps and brick walls and hanging plants, but relaxing, particularly if you ask for a table in the back away from the uproar of Third Avenue. In addition to pizzas, there are well-made pasta dishes featuring a choice of six sauces such as perky tomato with eggplant or a redolent seafood sauce. About $20 for two for a pizza dinner with a glass of wine.

Mon.-Sat. 11:30 A.M. to 11 P.M., Sun. 1 P.M. to 11 P.M. All major credit cards.

Sandwiches

BETWEEN THE BREAD

141 East 56th St.
(Lexington & Third Aves.)
888-0449

This self-service eatery offers some of the most imaginative and sumptuous sandwiches in Gotham. Step up to the sparkling glass counter to order your choice for a tasty lunch or casual supper. There are clunky white bowls overflowing with salads, baskets of irresistible just-baked muffins, and all manner of good things for sandwich fixings: applewood-smoked chicken, roast lamb with herb butter on black bread, smoked mozzarella and roasted red peppers on Italian bread, plus cheeses and imported hams galore to suit every taste. Desserts are worth every devastating calorie, from dark, luscious brownies to Southern pecan pie. Sandwiches range from $4.50 to $8.95. For more ambitious fare plus an elegant ambience, visit the Cafe Between the Bread, 145 West 55th (581-1189).

Mon.-Fri. 7:30 A.M. to 8 P.M., Sat. 8 A.M. to 3 P.M. All major credit cards.

JACKSON HOLE BURGER SHOP

232 East 64th St. (Second & Third Aves.)
371-7187

Remember the good old days when it was no crime to admit you loved red meat? This no-frills eatery will bring tears of joy to your eyes with its gutsy, eight-ounce burgers that are as juicy as they are huge. While purists will opt for just a slice of onion on top, you can add your choice of mozzarella, Swiss, or blue cheese along with bacon, ham, or even mushrooms for some tasty counterpoint to the excellent quality beef. The French fries are the usual frozen sticks and the onion rings soggy, but you still won't walk out unhappy. Burgers range from $3.25 to $7.

Mon.-Sat. 10:30 A.M. to 1 A.M., Sun. noon to midnight. No credit cards.

MANGANARO'S HERO BOY RESTAURANT

492 Ninth Ave. (38th St.)
947-7325

Call them heros, subs, or grinders, but under any guise these torpedo-sized monsters, overstuffed with hearty Italian cold cuts, are among the toast of New York sandwiches. The environment is a little run-down and the roster of hot Italian dishes that flesh out the menu are pretty lackluster, but the aroma of imported cheeses, fresh bread, and olives is as intoxicating as a summer picnic in Florence. Sandwiches range from individual heros to order-in-advance specialties like the six-foot Champion, which feeds up to 40 hungry people at a single chomp. (For a more complete review, see the restaurant section.)
Mon.-Sat. 7 A.M. to 7:30 P.M. AE, DC.

MANGIA

54 West 56th St. (Fifth & Sixth Aves.)
582-3061

This handsome takeout sandwich shop and coffee bar serves arguably the most intriguing and well-prepared sandwiches in New York, along with a cornucopia of excellent breads and pastries. Baskets laden with muffins and changing still lifes of fruit and vegetables beckon from the large storefront window as the usual lunchtime throng of junior clerks line up for takeout food. For sandwich fixings, there are over 60 different cheeses to choose from (including Mangia's own homemade mozzarella), along with tasty hams, salamis, perfectly rare roast beef, roasted chicken, turkey, and smoky roasted eggplant with tomato. To accompany these dishes there are potatoes, pasta, and some colorful vegetable salads which are always tempting and freshly made. Even a high-minded stoic would find the marvelous selection of muffins, intensely rich brownies, pound cakes, and crumbly scones irresistible, cleverly assembled as they are right near the cash register. About $8 per person for lunch. Delivery service available.
Mon.-Fri. 8 A.M. to 7 P.M., Sat. 10 A.M. to 6 P.M., closed Sat. in summer. AE, DC.

NATHAN'S FAMOUS

1482 Broadway, Times Sq. (43rd St.)
382-0620

At the turn of the century, long before golden arches and whoppers became the dominant icons of the fast food business, Nathan Handwerker was stuffing ground beef into sausage casings at his tiny snack bar on Coney Island. His customers liked these so-called "Coneys" so much that in a few years Nathan's hot dogs had becomes as much a New

York institution as the Brooklyn Dodgers. Happily, the legend survives today at several Nathan's outposts in both the metropolitan area and as far away as California. At the sprawling Times Square location these plump, fragrantly-spiced links sell for $1.49 apiece—steep when you consider the original price was a nickel, but still a bargain for these pedigreed all-beef hot dogs. In addition, there are hamburgers, pizza, corn on the cob, chili, fried chicken, seafood, raw clams on the half shell, and terrific French fries as well as domestic beers and soft drinks. The ambience is tacky—what is politely known as Times Square picturesque—and everything is self-service, with table seating as well as stand-up counters. Meats, sandwiches, and, of course, franks can all be taken out.
Open daily 24 hours. No credit cards.

NYBORG NELSON

Citicorp Center, 153 East 53rd St. (Third & Lexington Aves.) 223-0700

This inviting sandwich and takeout shop excels in Scandinavian delicacies. Choose from smoked fish (herring, salmon, trout), creamy Scandinavian cheeses, dainty open-faced sandwiches, and a deliciously cured gravlax. Meat lovers will opt for the well-made beef hash or maybe something from the good assortment of hams and cold cuts that are available. For an afternoon kaffee klatsch, there is a tempting array of Viennese pastries and desserts. Takeout service available. A Scandinavian sandwich and a glass of wine will cost about $8.
Mon.-Fri. noon to 9 P.M., Sat. noon to 7 P.M., Sun. noon to 6 P.M. All major credit cards.

Tea Rooms/Pastries

THE BARCLAY TERRACE

Hotel Intercontinental, 111 East 48th St. (Lexington & Park Aves.) 755-5900

If you've ever wondered what the executive dining room of an investment bank looks like, just stroll over to the Hotel Intercontinental, where the parrots still shriek from their cage in the lobby as they did in the old days when this was the Barclay. The Terrace is the room set aside for tea, and this clubby salon offers an atmosphere that is as sedately poised as the Queen Mother, with its red leather banquettes, lovely floral arrangements, paintings by John Singer Sargent, and voices that never rise above a patrician whisper. Individual Rosenthal china pots are used for the afternoon tea, which costs $9.75 per person. It's accompanied by barely passable finger sandwiches and scones served with whipped cream and jam, followed by mediocre pastries that change daily. There's a choice of eight different teas, but the Barclay blend, a Darjeeling tea, outshines all the others. It is available for purchase in eight-ounce tins from the maître d'hotel. *Tea Mon.-Fri. 3 P.M. to 5:30 P.M. All major credit cards.*

CHEZ LAURENCE PATISSERIE

245 Madison Ave. (38th St.)
683-0284

In the mornings, workers from nearby offices line up for takeout or grab a seat at this buoyant midtown cafe. The room has the feel of a Paris cafe with its white tiled walls, small marble tables, and surly black-attired waitresses who will grudgingly serve you steaming cups of cappuccino and exceptional croissants, brioche, and Danish pastries. The pies, tortes, and cakes are as luscious as they look, and there are some unusual creations like the lampion (individual rounds made with almond paste) or the sugar-coated mally tranche (made of slices of brioche dough), both standouts on the list. A typical lunch menu of salads, sandwiches, and soups round out the daily fare. The best time to come here is the afternoon for a restful pot of tea or coffee, along with a pastry. About $7 per person.
Mon.-Fri. 7 A.M. to 6:30 P.M. No credit cards.

ECLAIR

141 West 72nd St. (Columbus & Amsterdam Aves.)
873-7700

Wander into Eclair any time of the day and you'll find elderly Middle Europeans talking politics over slices of opera torte and prune-filled Danish. This Upper West Side bakery and restaurant is well-known among diehard dessert lovers for its authentic Austro-Hungarian style pastry. Steer clear of the obligatory croissants and artificial-tasting pound cake and order what the regulars do: sachertorte with a mound of whipped cream, Black Forest or Grand Marnier cake, chocolate mousse-filled Princess torte, and the buttery Danish that comes with assorted fillings. Although a full menu is offered from breakfast to dinner, the desserts are what has made this place so popular for more than a quarter of a century. About $5 per person.
Daily 8 A.M. to midnight. No credit cards.

HELMSLEY PALACE HOTEL

The Beaux-Arts grandeur of the Gold Room may not be your cup of tea if you're looking for a simple, unassuming place to relax. This opulent salon with its ornate arched

455 Madison Ave. (50th & 51st Sts.)
888-7000

ceiling, painted friezes, and golden-tufted settees was once the music room of financier Henry Vuillard, and it is every bit as elegant now as it was in its turn-of-the-century heyday. The tea service here is formal, with individual courses served in sequence, beginning with an excellent array of Fortnum & Mason teas, followed by so-so sandwiches, scones with cream and fruit preserves, and ending with slices of excellent fruitcake and moist chocolate fudgecake. Tea is also served on Saturdays in the bright and cheery Madison Room. About $15 per person.
Tea daily 2 P.M. to 5 P.M. All major credit cards.

THE KING'S ANGEL

115 East 74th St. (Park & Lexington Aves.)
879-4320

The soothing tea service offered at the Parish House of the Church of the Resurrection is as restorative to the soul as to the stomach. The rector's administrative assistant, a charming Englishwoman, bakes the traditional tea foods herself to go along with what she calls "a proper cup of tea." The nominal charge of $4.50 a person for tea includes scones with strawberry jam and cream (Devon when it's available), lemon curds, fruit tarts, shortbread, and a dozen different types of teas. On cool days, tea is served in the Parish House with its cozy fireplace and amply-stuffed furniture. In balmy weather the tea is served outdoors.
Tea Sun. 3 P.M. to 5 P.M. Closed July, Aug., & Sept. No credit cards.

LE SALON

Stanhope Hotel, Fifth Ave. & 81st St.
288-5800

At last, this old doyenne of the horsey set has gotten a much-needed facelift, and she looks positively charming. The new tea salon is a light and gracefully spacious room with green-and-white striped wallpaper, French Impressionist paintings, and small tables covered with Spanish lace tablecloths. Afternoon tea served on lovely Limoges china is unfortunately a lot more show than substance. The $15 per person prix fixe includes a choice of 16 different teas, bland finger sandwiches, scones with strawberry jam, and a variety of fruit tarts and pastries that even the Automat would reject as insipid. This is the place to come with your maiden aunt or former schoolteacher, perhaps after a shopping frenzy when you're too exhausted to know what you're eating.
Tea daily 2 P.M. to 5:30 P.M. All major credit cards.

LES DELICES GUY PASCAL

When Guy Pascal, the former pastry chef and part-owner of La Côte Basque, decided to strike out on his own, he opened this cheery, thimble-sized cafe and stocked it with some of

939 First Ave. (51st &
52nd Sts.)
371-4144

the most exquisite pastries this side of Provence. The tables are covered with pretty French country fabric, the waitresses know their mousse from their crème chantilly, and the glass cases are artfully arranged with gorgeous cakes, glistening fruit tarts, cups of chocolate mousse, and exquisite little cookies. Come in the morning for a breakfast of café au lait with fragrant apple turnovers, brioche, Danish, pecan rolls, or almond crescents. During lunch and for light suppers there are soups, salads, quiches, pâtés, and saucissions en croute. The justly popular Delice cake is $2.75 for a single serving, and is a splendid construction of layers of almond meringue, chocolate mousse, whipped cream, and mocha butter cream sprinkled with toasted almonds. About $7 per person. Another location at 1231 Madison Avenue (289-5300), plus a cluttered, overcrowded concession at Zabar's. *Daily 8 A.M. to 9 P.M.; closed Sun. in summer. AE, DC.*

THE MAYFAIR LOUNGE

Park Ave. & 65th St.,
Mayfair Regent Hotel
288-0800

With its handsome floral centerpieces, gleaming oval tea tables, sunken court, and warm gold-with-burgundy color scheme, the Mayfair Lounge offers its tea service with a grace and good taste unmatched in the city. Seven different varieties of Indian, Chinese, and herbal teas are served in delicate china pots, each one covered with a pretty tea cozy. Simple but delicious finger sandwiches are on hand for discreet nibbling, along with feather-light scones served with cream and preserves, ladylike cakes, cookies, and assorted ice cream desserts. This is a charming place to linger the afternoon away over a wonderfully scented brew and light conversation. About $11 per person.
Tea daily 3 P.M. to 5:30 P.M. All major credit cards.

PALM COURT

Plaza Hotel, Fifth Ave. &
59th St.
759-3000

An hour at the Palm Court is usually all it takes for most people to start hoping that the Marx Brothers will suddenly appear and break up the dripping sentimentality of it all. Potted palms in every corner, green and floral chintz seats, fragile china teacups, plus a piano and violin duet playing waltz tunes—the entire effect is a ponderous recreation of a Viennese coffeehouse. An inviting assortment of tea foods are well-prepared and attractively presented: freshly baked scones served with Devonshire cream; open-faced sandwiches studded with smoked salmon, pâtés, hams, and cold meats; dainty pastries; and ice cream. It's all very enchanting, though a bit too contrived. About $15 per person.

Tea Mon.-Fri. 3:30 P.M. to 6 P.M., Sat. & Sun. 4 P.M. to 6 P.M. All major credit cards.

PATISSERIE LANCIANI

177 Prince St. (Sullivan & Thompson Sts.)
477-2788

This delightful cafe and pastry shop in SoHo, with its spare gray walls and black tables, is the new sister establishment to the highly successful Lanciani's in Greenwich Village (271 West Fourth Street; 929-0739). Locals line up early for breakfast croissants, pain au chocolate, Danish pastries, and puffy beignets, those irresistible fritters of deep-fried dough which are a specialty of New Orleans. The pastry cases offer a rapturous array of sweets that range from velvety chocolate mousse to wafer-thin crusted fruit tarts, nut tortes, and fruit-laden pies. For sipping there is a lengthy choice of wines, Champagnes, and liqueurs, as well as espresso, cappuccino, and old-fashioned lemonade. About $6 per person. *Tues.-Sat. 8 A.M. to midnight, Sun. 9 A.M. to 9 P.M. AE.*

RUMPLEMAYER'S

46 Central Park South (59th St.)
755-5800

This marshmallow fluff tea room all decked out in pink may remind you of those soda shops in 50's movies where teenagers Annette and Frankie would smooch over malts. The decor is rife with fake marble, cute stuffed animals, and enormous mirrors in which you can watch yourself dribbling hot fudge sauce. This is a good place to take children for wonderful hot chocolate with real whipped cream, shakes, sodas (try the lemon ice cream soda), and sundaes of all kinds. There are also soups, salads, and sandwiches available. About $14 per person.
Daily 7 A.M. to 12:30 A.M. All major credit cards.

ST. HONORÉ PATISSERIE

235 East 57th St. (Second Ave.)
355-6478

This authentic French pâtisserie/cafe is a charming oasis for frazzled midtown shoppers who troop in regularly for lunch before returning to the battlegrounds. In an exchange of chefs with its sister shop in Paris, St. Honoré's new pastry chef is a sixth-generation Parisian baker who daily creates a whipped cream fantasy world of elegant desserts—tarts, individual pastries, cakes, cookies, and liqueur-enhanced gâteaux like Armagnac rose cake, and "Top hat" made of raspberry mousseline. At breakfast, besides the excellent croissants there are flaky petit Danish, pain au lait, and butter raisin buns. The lunch menu offers a traditional assortment of cold meats, pâtés, salads, and smoked trout, and there are some interesting nouvelle cuisine platters for dinner. About $14 per person for lunch.

Mon.-Fri. 8 A.M. to 7 P.M., Sat. & Sun. 11 A.M. to 5 P.M.
AE, MC, V.

THE WELL-BRED LOAF

1612 Third Ave. (90th &
91st Sts.)
534-6951

The Well-Bred Loaf bakery supplies most of those extra-large chocolate chip cookies, brownies, and pound cakes you find at delis and greengrocers throughout the city. Their retail shop on Third Avenue is a hangout for hungry-looking young locals, who come to this casual cafe for whale-sized servings of outrageously good, old-fashioned desserts. There are chocolate cupcakes with billowing chocolate icing, carrot cakes, crumbly fresh muffins, pies, breads, and scones to eat in or take out, plus a never-ending supply of cookies and brownies that taste much better than their prepackaged counterparts. You can even watch the bakers icing made-to-order wedding and birthday cakes while you go into calorie overload. About $6 per person.

Mon.-Fri. 7:30 A.M. to 8 P.M., Sat. 8:30 A.M. to 5 P.M.,
Sun. 9 A.M. to 3 P.M. No credit cards.

NIGHTLIFE

ALL NIGHT LONG

If you live in or are visiting the city that never sleeps, as long as you have the energy, there's something going on, no matter what the hour. And in New York's extraordinary number of clubs (both intimate and large), bars, and restaurants, you'll find a contingent of dauntless creatures who dash from one hot spot to another at a pace unmatched elsewhere. They come in all shapes, sizes, and colors, and always seem to be in the right place at the right time. And just when you think you've discovered the last word in clubs, there'll always be a new one to whet your appetite. From week to week, it's almost impossible to keep up with the hottest new nightspot—as soon as you get to know the doormen, the place goes out of business—but a sure bet is to follow the crowds. If there's a line outside (during the week, of course) you can bet that's the current "in" place for late-nighters.

For those not interested in making the latest 2 A.M. dance scene, New York offers up an unparalleled panoply of sophisticated nightlife, from serene piano bars to swinging jazz clubs. Whether you're seeking a view-drenched cocktail, a rowdy pub, a good laugh, or live music, you'll find it in New York.

Bars

BEACH CAFE

1326 Second Ave. (70th St.)
988-7299

If you wear a blue Oxford shirt, gray suit, striped blue tie, and work on Wall Street or in advertising, you'll feel right at home here. There's always an attractive, fresh-faced crowd of locals who meet under the ceiling fans at the old wood bar to exchange stories about new and lost loves, drink a Chiquita Bulldog (a potent banana drink), and admire the beach motif art for sale on the walls.
Sun.-Thurs. 11:30 A.M. to 2 A.M., Fri. & Sat. till 3 A.M. AE.

BOWLMOR LANES

Bowling is the name of the game here, and there's lots of loud music and one bartender to divert your attention from it. Celebs and regular folks hang out together at this shabby,

110 University Pl. (12th St.)
255-8188

low-lit watering hole, with 44 lanes evenly divided between the second and third floors. Come for the drinks or come for the bowling, but come especially for the people you'll meet and the fun you'll have.
Sun.-Thurs. 10 A.M. to 1 A.M., Fri. & Sat. till 4 A.M. No credit cards.

CAFE 43

147 West 43rd St. (Sixth Ave. & Broadway)
869-4200

Fixtures of brass and fluted glass, barbershop tiles on the floor, a vast, high-ceilinged cafe, and etched glass panels separating the seating areas make up Cafe 43. At the marble-topped bar, the pre- and post-theater crowd orders wine by the glass from a selection of two dozen. Every Wednesday there's jazz between 5 P.M. and 9 P.M., with more on Friday from noon to 3 P.M.; the musicians change weekly. There's also dinner theater upstairs on Monday, starting at 7 P.M.
Mon. 11:30 A.M. to 8 P.M., Tues.-Fri. 11:30 A.M. to 11:30 P.M., Sat. 5 P.M. to 11:30 P.M. All major credit cards.

CARAMBA!!

684 Broadway (West 3rd St.)
420-9817

At this downtown branch of the Caramba Mexican empire, you enter by way of an expansive bar—and dive into a fiesta of attractive but definitely yuppified pin-striped Upper East Side professionals guzzling margarita slushes that come in three sizes: small (3 1/2 oz.), medium (12 oz.), and gargantuan (26 oz.). Those in the know come to drink instead of eating the disappointing Mexican food. A deafening noise level makes earplugs a must.
Sun.-Thurs. noon to midnight, Fri. & Sat. till 1 A.M. All major credit cards.

CITY LIGHTS BAR

1 World Trade Center, 107th Fl.
938-1111

Hold a drink, listen to soft music, and view the city from an extraordinary perspective. Once you've enjoyed drinks from this height, you may become hooked.
Mon.-Sat. 3 P.M. to 1 A.M. Sun. 4 P.M. to 9 P.M. Cover charge varies. All major credit cards.

COSTELLO'S

225 East 44th St. (Second & Third Aves.)
599-9614

This is a serious drinking man's bar whose clientele makes it newsworthy. *Daily News* columnist Jimmy Breslin has been a regular here, but as he is soon to switch to *New York Newsday*, you'd better look fast.
Mon.-Fri. 11:30 A.M. to 2 A.M. All major credit cards.

DOBSON'S

341 Columbus Ave. (76th St.)
362-0100

Dobson's is a spacious bar where a casual crowd drops in after work for reasonably priced food and frozen drinks. Sidewalk seating allows for people-watching and sunning when the weather is good.
Daily 11:30 A.M. to 12:30 A.M., Fri. & Sat. till 1:30 A.M. AE, MC, V.

ERNIE'S

2150 Broadway (76th St.)
496-1588

This large, spacious, well-lit West Side restaurant and bar has a deafening noise level created by a crowd that comes for North Italian pastas and pizzas or to hang out at the large bar. As soon as the weather is warm, you can sit at tables outside. It seems as if it's always New Year's Eve in this popular hangar-sized establishment.
Daily noon to 4 P.M. & 5:30 P.M. to midnight. All major credit cards.

HARD ROCK CAFE

221 West 57th St. (Seventh Ave. & Broadway)
489-6565

No matter what the hour, throngs of yuppies and tourists wait patiently to get into the Hard Rock Cafe, the New York version of the legendary London restaurant and bar. Inside you'll find a deafening sound system that doesn't seem to affect the young trendies packed around the guitar-shaped bar drinking endless bottles of beer. There's a rock-and-roll memorabilia museum featuring 100 gold records and Chubby Checkers's boots.
Daily 11:30 A.M. to 4 A.M. All major credit cards.

HARVEY'S CHELSEA RESTAURANT

108 West 18th St. (Sixth Ave.)
243-5644

When you enter this old restored Chelsea saloon, you'll feel as if you've entered an earlier era. The room glows with rich mahogany woodwork, and the etched glass behind the bar is especially striking. It's a great after-work meeting place, filled with affable three-piece-suiters, local artists, and photographers. In the back room you'll find good English and American pub food.
Sun.-Thurs. noon to midnight, Fri. & Sat. till 1 A.M. AE.

GRAMERCY PARK HOTEL BAR

2 Lexington Ave. (21st & 22nd Sts.)
475-4320

Overlooking Gramercy Park, this once opulent, now slightly seedy piano bar is where you'll find neighborhood regulars and eccentric guests discussing the restoration of this charming neighborhood. A calm oasis that is never crowded, but often interesting.
Daily 11 A.M. to 1:30 A.M. All major credit cards.

JOE ALLEN

326 West 46th St. (Eighth & Ninth Aves.)
581-6464

In an atmosphere punctuated by theatrical posters, gingham-topped tables, blackboard menus, and the sound of piped-in Ethel Merman, girls with silken hair and men with glossy smiles who long to work on Broadway gather at the lengthy bar, drinking sweet Bass ale. And if you're interested, you'll probably spot a few celebs dining on roast beef and salad. *Daily noon to 2 A.M. MC, V.*

LANDMARK TAVERN

626 Eleventh Ave. (46th St.)
757-8595

This beautiful classic Irish tavern, built in 1868, features a working fireplace, potbellied stove, mahogany bar, and tin ceiling, and offers charm and a hearty bill of fare. Neighborhood regulars and tourists visiting the nearby Intrepid come by for a Saturday or Sunday brunch featuring Irish oatmeal pancakes. It's also popular with a pre- and post-theater crowd. *Daily noon to midnight, Fri. & Sat. till 1 A.M. AE.*

LE SALOON

1920 Broadway (64th St.)
874-1500

If you thrive on deafening music, a colorful crowd of theater-goers, tourists, actors, and aspiring actor-waiters, head to Le Saloon, conveniently located just across the street from Lincoln Center. If you go just before or after the show, be prepared for a long wait for a seat at the bar. *Daily 11:30 A.M. to 4 A.M. All major credit cards.*

LION'S HEAD

59 Christopher St. (Seventh Ave. South)
929-0670

Anyone who ever thought he was a poet—even for a minute—owes it to himself to pay a visit to the Lion's Head, one of the most famous writers' bars in the city. Its dark and cozy interior is punctuated by book jackets lining the walls, a jukebox playing oldies but goodies, a congenial bartender, and a macho yet artsy Village crowd discussing art and politics. You can drink good tap beers (McSorley's, Guinness) and sit at the bar, or continue to the more cozy back room for an eclectic menu featuring everything from hamburgers to roast duck with black currants. *Daily noon to 4 A.M. AE, V.*

MAXWELL'S PLUM

1181 First Ave. (64th St.)
628-2100

Maxwell's Plum is a must for anyone's first visit to New York, or for those who like restaurants as theater. While show biz types and full-fledged celebrities get preferential treatment in the back dining room, locals and BBQs (the Brooklyn, Bronx, and Queens crowd) pack the front room's

slightly elevated bar. Maxwell's Plum was the brainchild of Warner Le Roy, whose razzle-dazzle Hollywood origins are all too obvious in the decor: Art Nouveau treasures mixed with pseudo-antiques (circa 1969), etched mirrors, and stained glass ceilings.
Daily noon to 2:30 A.M. All major credit cards.

JIM MCMULLEN

1341 Third Ave. (76th & 77th Sts.)
861-4700

Attractive women (models and otherwise) hoping to make contact with basketball, football, and tennis players, and Robert Redford look-alikes congregate at this lively bar, the perfect setting for meeting a Mr. or Ms. Right. It's always crowded and is a must for seeing and being seen. Regulars at Jim McMullen tend to consume tank-car quantities of liquor—providing they can get the overworked bartenders' attention. If you get hungry, there are three dining rooms.
Daily 11:30 A.M. to 4 A.M. AE.

MCSORLEY'S OLD ALE HOUSE

15 East 7th St. (Second & Third Aves.)
473-9148

McSorley's Old Ale House, the oldest bar in the city, has the most convivial bartenders in town. Until 1970, only men were allowed in to enjoy steins of McSorley's draft ale, hard-boiled eggs, sandwiches, and animated conversation. Today a solid college crowd mingles with local old-timers sitting around the potbellied stove.
Daily 11 A.M. to 1 A.M. No credit cards.

MERIKEN

189 Seventh Ave. (21st St.)
620-9684

Meriken is a young, trendy restaurant and bar that features Japanese food, a New Wave decor, and the works of local artists. Don't leave without trying the house specialty, Windex. It's a potent combination of Grand Marnier, vodka, and blue Curaçao.
Nightly 6 P.M. to midnight. AE, DC.

OAK ROOM

Algonquin Hotel, 59 West 44th St. (Fifth & Sixth Aves.)
840-6800

You are nearly sure to run into a few literary types in the lobby of Algonquin, with its sedate atmosphere of a traditional men's club. Relax over drinks ensconced in an oversized chair, or if you prefer a more intimate space, sit in the dimly lit adjoining Blue Bar.
Daily noon to midnight. All major credit cards.

ODEON

It's still the ultimate downtown/upscale destination south of Canal, and a favorite hangout for artists, art dealers, Wall

145 West Broadway
(Thomas St.)
233-0507

Street types, and young SoHo-ers dressed in up-to-the-minute, androgynous chic. Housed on premises abandoned by a cafeteria, there's a 30's feeling about Odeon: a terrazzo floor, white hanging globes, dated background music, a mural of New York, racks of newspapers, and chrome chairs with plastic covered cushions. The place jumps, but you can still hold a conversation with your date.
Daily noon to 4 A.M. All major credit cards.

PETE'S TAVERN

129 East 18th St. (Irving Pl.)
473-7676

The menus, matches, and signs tell you this is the tavern that "O. Henry made famous." Established in 1864, it's also the oldest original tavern in New York. Its simple setting and relaxed atmosphere (and outdoor cafe in summer) is an antidote to the hustle and bustle of New York.
Daily 9:30 A.M. to 2 A.M., Fri. & Sat. till 3 A.M. All major credit cards.

P.J. CLARK'S

915 Third Ave. (55th St.)
355-8857

Dwarfed among neighborhood skyscrapers, P.J. Clark's is one of New York's last great saloons. Made famous in the film *The Lost Weekend*, this bar and restaurant is packed with celebrities and Joe Schmoes alike—bankers, account executives, artists; everybody seems to end up here sooner or later. There's an ornate cut-glass and mahogany bar, an extensive list of imported beers, and a fabulous nonstop jukebox with oldies by Sinatra and Peggy Lee.
Daily noon to 4 A.M. AE, DC.

PRINCE STREET BAR/RESTAURANT

125 Prince St. (Wooster St.)
228-8130

There are no signature touches by a hot interior designer in this place. Instead, you'll find mismatched mirrors, maroon walls, and ceiling fans. SoHo residents and tourists enjoy a menu ranging from ceviche to Indonesian dishes. Take a break from gallery- or boutique-hopping with a warming brandy in winter or a refreshing piña colada in summer.
Daily 11:30 A.M. to 2 A.M., Fri. & Sat. till 3 A.M. No credit cards.

REDBAR

116 First Ave. (7th St.)
No phone

This corner bar, not far from St. Mark's Place, has no sign or distinguishing marks outside and resembles an abandoned diner. A diverse crowd ranging from preppies to purple-haired punks crowd this place after dark.
Daily 4 P.M. to 4 A.M. No credit cards.

287

RICK'S 181 LOUNGE

181 Eighth Ave. (19th St.)
691-9845

Against a witty decor punctuated by a pink and white cloud-edged bar and lots of mirrors, a young, attractive staff dressed in black dashes back and forth serving Tex-Mex food to local Chelsea residents and dance aficionados (the Joyce Theater is across the street). For fun decor there are birdbath-size strawberry Margaritas, plastic daiquiri drinks, plastic palm trees, and blue marlin swizzle sticks. Live bands play two sets a night.
Daily 4 P.M. to 4 A.M. No minimum. AE.

SWELL'S

1439 York Ave. (76th St.)
879-0900

You'll have to knock to get into this popular, clubby bar filled with yuppies and trust-fund babies. Prints of race horses cover the walls and backgammon sets are available to patrons, typically dressed in Polo shirts, jeans, and penny loafers. Fifties music as well as the Beastie Boys keep these pretty people on their toes.
Mon.-Wed. 6:30 P.M. to 3 A.M., Thurs.-Sat. till 4 A.M. All major credit cards.

TOP OF THE SIXES

666 Fifth Ave. (53rd St.)
757-6662

This skyscraper cafe and bar offers a spectacular view of New York City. You can have the view and a drink too, and there's entertainment Tuesday through Saturday.
Mon.-Fri. 11:30 A.M. to midnight, Sat. till 1 A.M. All major credit cards.

UZIE'S

1444 Third Ave. (82nd St.)
744-8020

Although some of the beautiful people have moved on, there is still a well-heeled crowd of Europeans and New Yorkers who enjoy having a drink here or dining on Northern Italian cuisine in a sexy, subtlely lit atmosphere.
Nightly 6 P.M. to 12:30 A.M. AE, DC.

Cabarets & Comedy

ASTI

13 East 12th St. (Fifth Ave. & University Pl.)
741-9105

If you feel like being part of the entertainment at Asti, just join in with the waiters and regulars singing opera classics and Broadway tunes. Check out the old pictures of divas and male singers that cover the walls, and indulge in the friendly service. Asti is an ideal place to visit when you and your friends want to spend a nostalgic evening out on the town. *Tues.-Thurs. 5 P.M. to 12:30 A.M., Fri. & Sat. 5 P.M. to 1 A.M.; closed July & Aug. No cover charge. All major credit cards.*

THE BALLROOM

253 West 28th St. (Eighth Ave.)
244-3005

In its new, expanded quarters, this former SoHo cabaret/restaurant presents all sorts of entertainment—from legendary ladies like Peggy Lee to temporary ladies like Charles Pierce. Not to be missed is an early evening concert by the superb Blossom Dearie. Up front is a roomy two-tiered bar with an overhead rack of smoked hams and sausages where those who enjoy the early evening habit of Spanish hors d'oeuvres (tapas) and wine can load up on such specialties like eggplant, snails, and baby squid.
Shows Tues. 9 P.M., Wed.-Sat. 6:30 P.M., 9 P.M. & 11 P.M. Cover charge varies. Two-drink minimum. All major credit cards.

CAROLINE'S ON EIGHTH AVENUE

333 Eighth Ave. (26th & 27th Sts.)
924-3499

Caroline's is a handsome club filled with good-looking, fun-loving people from all walks of life. In the early 80's, Caroline's became the first headliner club in the nation where a new breed of young comedians were able to perform hour-long (or more) sets (call ahead for info on who's scheduled). With the opening of a new Caroline's at the South Street Seaport, the original club now showcases developing comedians who are ripe for TV exposure. You can munch on Chinese appetizers of shrimp toast and the like while watching late-night comedy. The crowd is sophisticated but varied; you're apt to hear French lisps mingling with Brooklyn accents.
Wed.-Sat. 5 P.M. to 3 A.M. Cover charge varies. Two-drink minimum. AE, MC, V.

CHIPPENDALES

1110 First Ave. (61st St.)
935-6060

Men with bursting biceps perform a sexy striptease for a vociferous females-only clientele. To show their appreciation for the energetic young performers with megawatt smiles, the audience unabashedly stuffs dollar bills into the dancers' minuscule G-strings. The men thank them with kisses, and

the women respond in kind with a fair amount of manhandling. After the show, the boys sell some pretty interesting souvenirs, including au naturel playing cards.
Shows Wed.-Sat. 8:30 P.M. AE.

DANGERFIELD'S

1118 First Ave. (61st St.)
593-1650

Although the brilliant Rodney Dangerfield no longer performs at his namesake comedy club, there are enough promising newcomers to provide laugh-provoking talent throughout the week. Definitely a fun place.
Shows Sun.-Thurs. 9:15 P.M., Fri. 9 P.M. & 11:30 P.M., Sat. 8 P.M., 10:30 P.M. & 12:30 P.M. Cover charge varies. Minimum $7. All major credit cards.

THE DUPLEX

55 Grove St. (Seventh Ave. South & Bleecker St.)
255-5438

On Saturday night at this dynamic Greenwich Village fixture, come join the crowd of tomorrow's stars who gather around the downstairs piano bar. Who knows who'll get discovered next in this place where Woody Allen, Joan Rivers, and Rodney Dangerfield got their start in show business.
Shows Mon.-Thurs. 8 P.M. & 10 P.M., Fri. & Sat. 8 P.M., 10 P.M. & midnight, Sun. 3 P.M., 5:30 P.M., 8 P.M. & 10 P.M. Cover charge varies. Two-drink minimum. No credit cards.

FREDDY'S

308 East 49th St. (First & Second Aves.)
888-1633

Christine Horgensen made a comeback at Freddy's, and female impersonator Charles Pierce has frequently gotten top billing here. Nowadays you can hear the likes of singer Maureen McGovern.
Shows nightly 8:30 P.M. & 11 P.M.; closed in summer. Cover charge varies. AE.

PALSSON'S

158 West 72nd St. (Broadway & Columbus Ave.)
595-7400

Nestled among food joints, this delightful cabaret has been packing the house for five years with a hilarious show biz revue. On what is probably the smallest stage in town, four actors sing, dance, and savage the contemporary Broadway scene in a fast-paced, quick-change parody entitled *Forbidden Broadway*.
Shows Sun. & Tues.-Thurs. 8:30 P.M., Fri. & Sat. 8:30 P.M. & 11:30 P.M. All major credit cards.

Dancing & Nightclubs

THE BAJA

246A Columbus Ave. (71st
& 72nd Sts.)
724-8890

Founded by ten young Wall Streeters, the Baja is a small, unpretentious, unintimidating, relaxed club that does not promote exclusivity. The mostly early 20's crowd works in the financial district and hates to journey back downtown for a night out. They give the Baja the casual, comfortable feel of a college frat basement. The dance floor is large, and the music is fast-paced, with a good sounding mix of 60's rock and Motown greats. If you can remember the song titles, the DJ takes requests.
Tues.-Sat. 9:30 P.M. to 4 A.M. Cover charge $5 Tues. &
Wed., $10 Thurs.-Sat. AE.

BIG KAHUNA

622 Broadway (Bleecker &
Houston Sts.)
460-9633

The Big Kahuna—the name means "witch doctor" in Hawaiian—is a small nightclub catering to Wall Streeters who stop here on their way home. A few tropical drinks and the crowd breaks loose, dancing on the picnic tables, throwing Frisbees, and generally having a good time. Got the munchies? Barbecue-style fare is served through the snack bar window. And if your suit gets too hot, buy yourself a new pair of Bermudas at the nightclub's boutique.
Sun.-Wed. 5 P.M. to 2 A.M., Thurs.-Sat. 5 P.M. to 4 A.M.
Cover charge $5 after 9 P.M. No credit cards except in the shop.

CBGB

315 Bowery (Bleecker St.)
982-4052

If you've wondered where all the punk rockers are, they're hanging out at CBGB adorned with leather jackets, tatoos, multi-colored hair, and heavy-metal jewelry. Although its exposed beams and splintered wood posts make this Lower East Side club look like a run-down stable, it makes up for its decrepit state with a terrific sound system and the best up-and-coming avant-garde rock and "severe punk" groups around.
Nightly 8:30 P.M. to 2:30 A.M. No credit cards.

THE CHINA CLUB

Walking down a long flight of steps, you'll discover an intimate space (capacity 250) painted Chinese blue, com-

2130 Broadway (75th St.)
877-1166

plete with hand painted Oriental murals, fish tanks, and dragon sculptures. This is one of the few uptown spots that remains packed into the wee hours, and it's a music industry favorite. Don't be surprised if David Bowie, Julian Lennon, or Stevie Wonder suddenly appear on the stage for a surprise performance. You can dance or simply listen to up-and-coming rock talents showcased nightly at 12:30 A.M.
Nightly 10 P.M. to 4 A.M. Cover charge $10 Sun.-Thurs., $15 Fri. & Sat. AE, MC, V.

HEARTBREAK

179 Varick St. (Houston St.)
691-2388

By day Heartbreak is an authentic 50's diner, functioning as a luncheonette and serving people who work in the printing industry. But when the dinner hour passes, most of the tables are pushed aside, and you can dance all night long to 50's and 60's music. On Mondays there's a live band and, more often than not, a lot of bona-fide celebs—like Cher and Liza—dancing in the crowd. On Tuesdays, the works of contemporary photographers are flashed on a large overhead screen.
Nightly 9:30 P.M. to 4:30 A.M. Cover charge $15. No credit cards.

LIMELIGHT

660 Ave. of the Americas (20th & 21st Sts.)
807-7850

Since it is housed in what was formerly an Episcopal church dating from the mid-19th century, the Limelight attracted notorious publicity when it opened a few years ago. Things have cooled down a bit, but inside all the holy trappings of this three-floored desecrated church are still intact, from the stained glass windows to chapels that have been converted into secluded hideaways. The crowded dance floor still uses the original pews, a laser beam shoots out from the altar, a church organ descends from the ceiling, and a giant screen flashes stop-motion videos. In the past, at least, Limelight has been a popular haunt for stars as diverse as Billy Idol and Molly Ringwald, who relax in the library, which serves as a VIP room far away from the very loud and conventional music (almost all Top 40) and the crowd of 2,000 below. Occasionally, live performers hold theme parties and fashion shows.
Nightly 10 P.M. to 4 A.M. Cover charge $15 Sun.-Thurs. $18, Fri. & Sat. AE.

MADAM ROSA

Reminiscent of a dark Parisian boite, Madam Rosa is in a small basement fronting an alley in Tribeca. Although it's

St. John's Ln. (Canal & Beach Sts.)
219-2207

difficult to find, it's worth the effort. The club is divided into two rooms, one with a horseshoe-shaped bar, the other with a dance floor and disc jockey. The music ranges from rap and soul to blues and funk. On most nights you'll find artists, musicians, filmmakers, models, photographers, and an occasional celebrity, like John Lurie, Matt Dillon, or Jean-Michel Basquiat. And when you're tired of looking at the black-clad crowd, check out the slide projections and paintings on view.

Wed.-Sat. 11 P.M. to 4 A.M. Live music Wed. & Thurs. from midnight. Cover charge $5.

NELL'S

246 West 14th St. (Seventh & Eighth Aves.)
675-1567

The club of the moment (at least when we went to press) is Nell's, the best reason we can think of for venturing west on 14th Street. Co-owned by English actress Nell Campbell, the captivating star of *The Rocky Horror Picture Show*, Nell's is an old-English-style club complete with dark oil paintings, crystal chandeliers, and mirrors in different shapes and sizes. If you can get past the fickle doormen, who are so picky (or nearsighted) that even Cher was turned away, or if you buy a $200 membership (available only to a select few), you'll be ushered into a large room filled with slender young men ensconced on red Victorian couches next to women in leather micro-miniskirts and Sade-inspired hoop earrings. Revelers in black tie drink Champagne at a long wooden bar, while folks like Bianca Jagger, Robert DeNiro, and Sting enjoy a paparazzi-free dinner in the back booths. Downstairs there are two more bars, more enveloping couches and armchairs, and an understated room for dancing. Avoid the weekends, when the crowd outside is unbearable.

Nightly 10 P.M. to 4 A.M. Cover charge $5 Sun.-Thurs., $10 Fri. & Sat. All major credit cards for dinner only.

THE PALLADIUM

126 East 14th St. (Fourth & Third Aves.)
473-7171

The Palladium is owned by Steve Rubell and Ian Schlager of Studio 54 notoriety. Redesigned by leading Japanese architect Arata Isozaki, the huge theater on East 14th Street is a visual extravaganza featuring large-scale murals and environmental installations by some of the city's hottest young artists, including Keith Haring and Jean-Michel Basquiat. The dance floor is huge, with the latest in disco technology and banks of video screens flashing fabulous images. Stockbrokers dance within feet of funky downtown types. Because of its size, it can be the best of clubs or the worst of clubs. Although the Mike Todd Room is usually reserved for private parties, if you can get in, it's the best place to hang out. It's presided over by Anita Sarko, the Queen of the DJ's, spinning fabulous music all night long. With gauzy white cloths thrown over minuscule tables topped with candelabra and walls covered with mirrors of all shapes and sizes, the Mike Todd Room is a Hollywood fantasy come true. *Wed.–Sun. 10 P.M. to 4 A.M. Cover charge $15 Wed. & Thurs., $18 Fri. & Sat.*

PRIVATE EYES

12 West 21st St. (Fifth & Sixth Aves.)
206-7770

Though much smaller than the other leading clubs (with a capacity of only 500), Private Eyes has a sleek, high-tech atmosphere highlighted by a gigantic tiled bar in the center of the room. The club emphasizes video and has a video jockey (a VJ), 32 monitors, and two giant screens showing seven or eight different movies or rock videos simultaneously. On Private Party Nights, you'll have to persuade the inscrutable club doorman to let you into one of these exclusive events. If you're dressed distinctively enough, you may get a chance to mingle with record producers and rock stars. *Tues.–Sat. 10 P.M. to 4 A.M. Cover charge varies. AE.*

PYRAMID CLUB

101 Ave. A (6th & 7th Sts.)
420-1590

At the Pyramid, downtown's most consistently different club, you'll find an eclectic mix of East Village nonconformists. When not dancing on the minuscule floor, you can watch such murder mysteries as *Dial M for Model* on the video screens. The audience, a young crowd dressed primarily in oversized 50's T-shirts, is as much fun to watch as the performance. The tongue-in-cheek atmosphere is heightened by a tropical decor of hand-painted animals and graffiti-covered walls. It's particularly lively on Sunday nights. *Daily 4 P.M. to 4 A.M. Cover charge $10. No credit cards.*

THE RED PARROT

617 West 57th St.
(Eleventh & Twelfth Aves.)
247-1530

The city-block-long Red Parrot draws a dressy crowd (no jeans, please). A 15-piece orchestra features 40's and 50's classics on Friday and Saturday nights, with contemporary music played during the band's breaks. Spacious areas off the dance floor with comfortable sofas arranged as conversation pits make The Red Parrot is one of the easier dance clubs to socialize in. It's worth a trip once, if only to see the striking red parrots watching the action from their large cage.

Wed.-Sat. 10 P.M. to 4 A.M. Cover charge varies. No credit cards.

REGINE'S

502 Park Ave. (59th St.)
826-0990

Although this French disco still manages to hold onto its glamour, it's no longer the "in" spot, unless Queen of the Night Regine shows up to host a fabulous dinner party. Most of the patrons consist of (aging) men with expense accounts and expensive modelettes who smile just a little too much. There is a small neon dance floor and lots of mirrors. If you have dinner ($49.50), you get free admission to the disco. *Nightly 7:30 P.M. to 4 A.M. Cover charge $15 weeknights, $25 Fri. & Sat. All major credit cards.*

THE RITZ

119 East 11th St. (Third & Fourth Aves.)
254-2800

The Ritz is a two-tiered barnlike rock/New Wave club sporting a 40- by 50-foot dance floor and stage on the first level, surrounded by an Art Deco balcony. The Ritz books both well-known names (such as B.B. King and Robin Trower) and unknown talents, including many of the new British bands. An oasis for restless young people who are seriously into music. *Nightly 10 P.M. to 4 A.M. Cover charge varies. No credit cards.*

ROSELAND

239 West 52nd St. (Broadway)
247-0200

The shoes of famous dancers still adorn the entrance of this newly renovated legend. A 700-seat restaurant and bar await dance aficionados who like to nourish themselves between bouts of ballroom and disco dancing. *Thurs.-Sun. 2:30 P.M. to 5 A.M. Cover charge varies. AE, V.*

S.O.B.'S

204 Varick St. (West Houston St.)
243-4940

S.O.B.'s is a high-energy club featuring live bands from Brazil, Africa, and the Caribbean. On Fridays and Saturdays its packed with a casually dressed international crowd dancing "belly to belly" to beating drums. Go there dressed to dance; the music won't let you stay in your seat. *Tues.-Thurs. 7 P.M. to 2 A.M., Fri. & Sat. till 4 A.M. Cover charge varies. Two-drink minimum at tables. All major credit cards.*

STRINGFELLOW'S

35 East 21st St. (Park Ave. & Broadway)
254-2444

Stringfellow's, like its two successful sister clubs in London, is owned by Peter Stringfellow, a garrulous, spiky-haired blond who wears extravagant clothes and a butterfly earring. Inside there's a pink marble-topped bar, glorious flower arrangements, lots of mirrors, and sexy waitresses in extremely revealing chiffon tutus. There are lots of singles in the crowd, and a sprinkling of expense-account men trying to impress fickle, overdressed chicklettes with overpriced bottles of Champagne. At 11 P.M., to the sound of the *1812 Overture*, the wall separating the disco from the restaurant rises and the dancing begins.
Sun.-Thurs. 8 P.M. to 3 A.M., Fri. & Sat. till 4:30 A.M. Cover charge $10 Mon.-Thurs. after 11 P.M., $20 Fri. & Sat. after 10 P.M. All major credit cards.

THE SURF CLUB

2415 East 91st St. (First & York Aves.)
410-1360

The Surf Club, opened by the Beaver brothers, is a true WASP nest. A very preppy crowd can be found beyond the portals of this club, plus lots of gazebos, parasols, and surfboards. After a few glasses of Champagne, the Upper East Side crowd becomes less and less inhibited.
Tues.-Sat. 9 P.M. to 4 A.M. Cover charge $5. All major credit cards.

THE TUNNEL

220 Twelfth Ave. (entrance on 27th St.)
244-6444

A definite must on any club-goer's schedule is the 15,000-square-foot Tunnel housed on the desolate West Side. This popular club has massive brick walls, exposed steel beams, and arched chambers that lead into the darkness of abandoned railroad tracks. Small rooms lining the Tunnel offer temporary respite from a deafening sound system and a crowded dance floor and bar. The Basement (downstairs, natch) is open to the public when it isn't being used for private parties. In it are a bar, couches arranged in conversational pits, a smaller dance floor, and paintings of questionable taste decorating the walls. Still, The Tunnel has a lot of electricity and conscious style. Many of the patrons sport hair in colors not found in nature; the young women wear leather and lace stockings; the young men, basic black, Italian-style. Habitués of all the arts and both sexes keep late hours, so there is no point in going early.
Club and Basement open nightly 9 P.M. to 3 A.M. Cover charge varies.

Jazz

CAFE LIDO

19 Waverly Pl. (Washington Square & Broadway)
533-4151

In addition to excellent acoustics, Cafe Lido offers a spacious, classically elegant setting—filled with flowers, chandeliers, European posters, and salmon-pink walls—for enjoying swing jazz. There's also a cafe-style menu of tasty tidbits at affordable prices.
Music Tues.-Thurs. from 8 P.M. No cover. No minimum. AE, MC, V.

FAT TUESDAY'S

190 Third Ave. (17th St.)
533-7900

Fat Tuesday's is a popular singles hangout (especially the bar and the street-level restaurant) with well-known contemporary musicians downstairs. A knowledgeable jazz crowd fills the comfortable, elegant space, and the acoustics are quite good.
Shows Tues.-Thurs. 8 P.M. & 10 P.M., Fri. & Sat. 8 P.M., 10 P.M. & midnight. Cover charge varies. Minimum varies. AE, MC, V.

GREGORY'S

1149 First Ave. (63rd St.)
371-2220

This 20-seat jazz oasis is dark, relaxed, and enveloping—so small that it's impossible to sit more than 15 feet from the piano (unless you're in one of the 30 extra seats in the glassed-in porch that looks out onto First Ave.). Try to catch the witty piano playing of Brooks Kerr on Sunday evenings.
Nightly 5 P.M. to 3 A.M. Cover charge varies. No music charge at the bar; $4.50 at tables. Two-drink minimum. All major credit cards.

MICHAEL'S PUB

211 East 55th St. (Second & Third Aves.)
758-2272

Michael's Pub features old-fashioned jazz for a nostalgic, conservative, middle-aged crowd. It's also known as Woody Allen's pub, because he occasionally plays clarinet here on Mondays. But if you come on a Monday, don't go to the last set; it lasts less than half an hour.
Shows Mon.-Sat. 9 P.M. & 11 P.M. No cover charge. Minimum $10. All major credit cards.

MIKELL'S
760 Columbus Ave. (97th St.)
864-8832

Such greats as Whitney Houston and Art Blakey have played in this West Side club in front of a crowd of neighborhood people and European imports who have one thing in common—a love of good jazz.
Nightly 4 P.M. to 4 A.M. Cover charge varies. Two-drink minimum. All major credit cards.

RED BLAZER TOO
349 West 46th St. (Eighth & Ninth Aves.)
262-3112

Nostalgia rules at this large, always busy, friendly club, which has revived the big-band sound. The Dixieland here on weekends is tops. Red Blazer Too draws a mix of young sophisticates and an older crowd that wants to relive the days of Benny Goodman and Fred Astaire.
Nightly 9 P.M. to 1 A.M. No cover charge. No minimum. AE, DC.

SWEET BASIL
88 Seventh Ave. South (Bleecker St.)
242-1785

With its hanging plants and its glass façade, Sweet Basil is one of the more attractive jazz clubs around town. Its wide range of top jazz groups—from mainstream small combos to avant-garde big bands—ensures a constant crowd of jazz lovers.
Nightly 9 P.M. to 3 A.M. Cover charge varies. Minimum $6. AE, MC, V.

SWEETWATER'S
170 Amsterdam Ave. (68th St.)
873-4100

Located in the Lincoln Center area, this striking multi-level, mirrored cabaret/bar/restaurant could have been designed by the same architect as the center itself. Jazz performers play for an attractive, affluent crowd that takes dressing up very seriously.
Shows Mon.-Sat. 10 P.M. & midnight, Sun. 8:30 P.M. & 10:30 P.M. Cover charge $10 Mon.-Thurs., $15 Fri. & Sat. Minimum $10. All major credit cards.

THE VILLAGE GATE
160 Bleecker St. (Thompson St.)
475-5120

In addition to presenting many top names from the jazz world, this popular club has lately been presenting off-Broadway revues. One of the best shows in town is its "Salsa Meets Jazz" series—each Monday, a top Latin bandleader appears with a top jazz soloist. The downstairs showroom is spacious, and there's an area in back for dancing. The crowd is made up of unpretentious music aficionados of all ages. For those who prefer their jazz in the background, a pianist and bassist play in the upstairs bar/cafe for a young Village-*cum*-tourist crowd.

Nightly 9:30 P.M. to 2:30 A.M. Cover charge varies.
Minimum $6. Fri. & Sat. No credit cards.

VILLAGE VANGUARD

178 Seventh Ave. South
(11th St.)
255-4037

For more than 30 years this dark, smoky basement has featured all the jazz greats—including Miles Davis, John Coltrane, and Pharoah Sanders. Musicians love this place as much as customers—there is no hustling for drinks and no ringing cash registers. On any given night a performance can turn into a lively jam session. Monday night regulars Mel Lewis and the Jazz Orchestra are becoming a New York jazz tradition.

Shows nightly 9:30 P.M., 11:30 P.M. & 1 A.M. Cover charge $8.50. One-drink miniumum. No credit cards.

THE WEST END

2911 Broadway (113th &
114th Sts.)
666-9160

Featuring a huge circular bar, a beer-covered floor, and video shows on TV screens, this famous bar, rib joint, and jazz club attracts a crowd of boisterous students from nearby Columbia University. There's always a good local band playing jazz or other good music, 14 types of beer on tap, and more than 70 varieties in stock. The pizza is edible, and there are low-priced barbecue dishes. There's a minimum but no cover in the music room, and on Monday night you can see live comedy at the West End as well.

Music Tues.-Sun. from 9 P.M. No cover charge. Three-drink minimum. MC, V.

Music

CHELSEA PLACE

147 Eighth Ave. (17th St.)
924-8413

When you first enter Chelsea Place, you'll think you're at the wrong address. The front room has all the appearances of an antique shop, but five steps further, past the swinging door, you'll feel like you've stepped into a speakeasy. There are flashing lights, dancing in the aisles, and non-stop hard-rocking blues à la Tina Turner. The room is crowded, smoky, noisy, and friendly. For those who crave something more intimate, try the upstairs area, where there are mirrored walls and tables surrounding a sleek white bar. It's all a bit touristy, but a good time is guaranteed.

Nightly 5:30 P.M. to 4 A.M. Cover charge $10 Mon.-Thur., $15 Fri. & Sat. All major credit cards.

LONE STAR CAFE

61 Fifth Ave. (13th St.)
242-1664

The Lone Star offers continuous top-notch country and western music. A casually dressed, beer-drinking crowd ranging from business people to college students packs the bar or tiny tables to hear the entertainment. This is the top chili-loving cowboy oasis in the city, and you don't have to be Texan to feel like one here. Don't think you've had too many beers when you spot an enormous iguana posed outside on top of the cafe (of course it isn't real; they don't get that big even in Texas), or when soul singer James Brown turns up as the headliner in this cowboy setting.
Nightly 7:30 P.M. to 3 A.M., Fri. & Sat. till 4 A.M. Cover charge varies. All major credit cards.

O'LUNNEY'S

915 Second Ave. (48th & 49th Sts.)
751-5470

If you love country music that keeps your foot tapping and makes you want to "swing your partner," this place is for you. After a hard day on the job, the down-home food and cool beer will restore your spirits. The crowd is young, loud, and there to have fun.
Daily 9 A.M. to 4 A.M. Cover charge $3. Minimum at tables $3. All major credit cards.

TRAMPS

125 East 15th St. (Irving Pl.)
777-5077

This friendly rock and blues club is still the best place to see Buster Poindexter (alter ego of former New York Dolls singer David Johansen) and his four-piece band, the Banshees of Blue, as well as great old blues singers on weekends. Young bands often play on Thursdays, when NYU's radio station sponsors a $5 admission.
Nightly 10 P.M. to 4 A.M. Cover charge $10 Fri. & Sat. Two drink minimum. No credit cards.

Piano Bars

BEEKMAN TOWER

3 Mitchell Pl. (First Ave. & 49th St.)
355-7300

From the top of this vintage 1928 tower, the view unfolds from the north along the East River and south past the U.N. and the Empire State Building all the way to downtown. Day turns to night before your eyes, sometimes with a mesmerizing sunset. Try to get a seat on the terrace—the pianist sounds just as good out there, and the view of New York City is not to be missed.

Pianist Tues.-Sat. 9 P.M. to 2 A.M. No cover charge. All major credit cards.

BEMELMAN'S BAR

Carlyle Hotel, 35 East 76th St. (Madison Ave.)
744-1600

Named for the painter of classic murals, this intimate bar attracts a relaxed crowd who enjoys the voice and piano of Barbara Carroll year-round.

Pianist Tues.-Sat. from 9:45 P.M. Cover charge $5. All major credit cards.

BRADLEY'S

70 University Pl. (10th & 11th Sts.)
228-6440

If listening to some of the best jazz piano/bass duos in New York is your predilection, head to this long, dark-paneled room to hear the likes of Tommy Flanagan and Kenny Barron. Reasonably priced food is served in the back room until 12:30 A.M., and the bar is usually quite lively.

Shows nightly 9:45 P.M., 11 P.M., 12:30 A.M. & 2 A.M. Minimum at tables $5. All major credit cards.

CAFE CARLYLE

Carlyle Hotel, 35 East 76th St. (Madison Ave.)
744-1600

For a taste of cafe society, visit Cafe Carlyle to hear pianist-in-residence Bobby Short perform stylish renditions of Cole Porter, Gershwin, and Hart. Since 1968, Short has amassed an incredible number of sophisticated admirers. Especially pleasant are the comfortable, cozy, aqua banquettes next to the romantic pastel murals painted by Vertes. In Short's absence, such greats as George Shearing and Peter Niro perform.

Shows nightly, 10 P.M. & midnight. Cover charge $20. All major credit cards.

CHEZ JOSEPHINE

414 West 42nd St. (Ninth & Tenth Aves.)
594-1925

Chez Josephine is a bistro named for the legendary singer of the 1920's, Josephine Baker. Its exuberant owner, Jean Claude Baker (Josephine's unofficially adopted son), has created a rococo atmosphere highlighted by red velvet curtains and banquettes, a brilliant blue tin ceiling, a long zinc bar, and posters and paintings showing the singer in various stages of scanty dress. On any given night, an eclectic crowd—including models, writers, a sprinkling of celebrities, international businessmen, and actors—fills the long, narrow restaurant. Be forewarned: You may enjoy the show so much that you might decide to ditch your theater tickets.

You can linger at the bar drinking Champagne (or whatever) and listening to show tunes hammered out by two sensational piano players.
Tues.-Sat. 5:30 P.M. to 11:30 P.M., Sun. 4 P.M. to 10:30 P.M. AE, MC, V.

THE HORS D'OEUVERIE

1 World Trade Center, 107th Fl.
938-1111

Getting a bit bored with the view from your hotel? For a unique perspective of the city, disembark on the 107th floor of the World Trade Center and enter a gorgeous, multileveled, internationally minded cocktail lounge. In between potent martinis you can snack on fresh oysters, sushi, and Spanish sausage. There's a mellow jazz trio alternating with a pianist, with dancing on a postage-stamp-sized floor. Jackets are required but reservations are not, though there's often a wait for seats.
Daily 3 P.M. to 1 A.M. Jazz ensemble Mon.-Sat. 7:30 P.M. to 12:30 A.M., Sun. 4 P.M. to 9 P.M. Cover charge $2.95 after 7:30 P.M. No minimum. All major credit cards.

KNICKERBOCKER SALOON

33 University Pl. (Fifth & Sixth Aves.)
228-8490

World War II posters and original Hirschfield drawings decorate the walls of this neighborhood bar and restaurant, where locals, Europeans, and NYU students gather to enjoy fine jazz piano/bass combos. Such greats as Sir Roland Hanna and Ron Carter play in this upbeat atmosphere against a low murmur of conversation.
Nightly 9:30 P.M. to 1:30 A.M., Fri. & Sat. till 4 A.M. Cover charge varies in restaurant. Minimum $7 at bar tables. AE, MC, V.

ONE FIFTH AVENUE

1 Fifth Ave. (8th St.)
260-3434

Although this was once the watering hole of the madly stylish, today you can find a noisy crowd of young singles and couples who hang out at the long bar or sit in the front room listening to jazz trios and imagining they are aboard an ocean liner (courtesy of the Art Deco-style porthole photos of the sea).
Daily noon to 1:45 A.M., Fri. & Sat. till 2:45 A.M. Minimum $6.50 Fri. & Sat. All major credit cards.

ONE IF BY LAND, TWO IF BY SEA

A sophisticated crowd comes to this delightful carriage house for dinner and to listen to the show tunes played in the handsome bar. The front room is a relaxing amalgam of

17 Barrow St. (Seventh Ave. South)
255-8649

brick walls, rust-colored velvet banquettes, Spanish chandeliers, masses of spectacular flowers, and American primitive paintings. Though the guests are super-chic, casual dress is permitted. If you're lucky, you might catch Joseph Papp, Pat Lawford Kennedy, or Diana Ross dining in the back.
Mon. & Tues. 8 P.M. to 1 A.M. Wed.-Sun. 6 P.M. to 4 A.M. No cover charge. All major credit cards.

PEACOCK ALLEY

Waldorf-Astoria Hotel, 49th St. & Park Ave.
355-3000

Peacock Alley is a New York institution, situated next to a two-ton, nine-foot-tall bronze clock that's topped with a miniature Statue of Liberty. An international crowd gathers around what was Cole Porter's personal piano to hear some fine music played with style by Jimmy Lyon; Lynn Richards sings after 10 P.M., and Penny Brook fills in on Sundays and Mondays.
Sun. & Mon., 8:30 P.M. to 12:30 A.M., Tues.-Sat. 6 P.M. to 2 A.M. No cover charge. All major credit cards.

REGENCY LOUNGE

Hotel Regency, 61st St. & Park Ave.
759-4100

The intimate Regency Lounge is filled with men in Saville Row suits who speak four languages, and who have with them willowy beauties sheathed in the latest fashion. The alternating pianists play second fiddle to the chic crowd.
Nightly 6 P.M. to 1:45 A.M. No cover. All major credit cards.

THE RIVER CAFE

1 Water Street (beneath the Brooklyn Bridge), Brooklyn
(718) 522-5200

Poised below the Brooklyn Bridge, this barge restaurant with piano bar and cocktail lounge offers a breathtaking view of lower Manhattan and the East River. This romantic rendezvous is elegantly simple: wooden floors, fresh flowers, and one wall made entirely of glass. Reserve well in advance if you're eating, and ask for a seat next to a window.
Nightly 8 P.M. to 1:30 A.M. No cover charge. AE, DC, CB.

VILLAGE CORNER

142 LaGuardia Pl.
(Bleecker St.)
473-9762

If you don't mind a seedy decor (well, at least it's authentic), you'll be compensated by the fine playing of Lance Hayward. On Wednesdays and Thursdays Jim Roberts takes over with music from the 30's. You can eat burgers, chili, and cheesecake and drink beer by the mug, bottle, or pitcher. Many of the regulars are flashy young downtowners, leftovers from the now-defunct Danceteria.
Music nightly 9:30 P.M. to 2 A.M. No cover. No minimum. No credit cards.

VILLAGE GREEN

531 Hudson St. (West 10th & Charles Sts.)
255-1650

This stunning West Village townhouse features a dark, romantic restaurant downstairs and a lounge upstairs decorated with mirrors, fireplaces, and flattering lighting. West Villagers and uptowners gather around the piano while Murray Grand sings his own songs and plays contemporary favorites.

Tues.-Thurs. 8 P.M. to 1 A.M., Fri. & Sat. 9 P.M. to 2 A.M. No cover. AE, MC, V.

HOTELS

GRACIOUS HOSPITALITY

Amid all the frenzied activity of never-ending urban renewal projects, many of New York's finest city blocks have become tractor-and-crane wastelands. New skyscrapers rise daily as the formerly contained business district rapidly engulfs more and more residential neighborhoods. Such projects as the gentrification of Times Square have demonstrated the positive and negative aspects of reconstruction: the boon of vital new resources which can reawaken a deteriorated area must be weighed against the tendency to tear down priceless monuments (such as the Helen Hayes Theater) in the rush of progress.

Against this backdrop of turmoil, New York hotels have intelligently adopted the role of serene, welcoming oases in the storm. Well-staffed, constantly refurbished and maintained, Manhattan lodgings are in general more attractive and appealing now than ever before, venerable grande dames and brash newcomers alike. A European style of personalized attention, including 24-hour concierge service, is the direction for many luxury and first class hotels such as the recently remodeled Drake and the new Plaza Athénée. With the number of visitors to the city steadily rising, due to the recent opening of the Jacob Javits Convention Center, and the ranks of business travelers and sophisticated tourists from Europe and Asia swelling, many more superb accommodations are in the offing, such as Maxime's de Paris Hotel (it will be run by Robert Berger of Parker Meridien fame), which will replace the old Gotham on 55th and Fifth, and the Grand Bay Hotel at the new Equitable Center.

At the moderate and economy end of the spectrum, our best advice is to select with care and insist on viewing the accommodations before accepting the room. The listings include good hotels in every price range, from elegant suites to dormitory-style accommodations for young people. The prices listed are before taxes; weekend packages are for doubles per night, unless otherwise noted.

Luxury

CARLYLE

As discreet as a Swiss bank, the Carlyle exudes an atmosphere of privilege, good breeding, and elegance that will

35 East 76th St. (Madison Ave.)
744-1600

make you feel like you've arrived for high mass. Dowagers resplendent in heirloom jewelry, old money gentry, and millionaire CEO's frequent this unremittingly posh oasis for service that is as silken and polished as the dialogue of a Noel Coward play. The rooms are gracious and luxuriously furnished with one-of-a-kind accessories and antiques in every chamber. For the moment, the Carlyle continues to receive the concensus nod as New York's finest. In the Cafe Carlyle Bobby Short still performs his ineffable magic as if this world of noblesse oblige will go on forever. . . perhaps it will.

Singles $200-255, doubles $220-275, suites $425-1,000. *All major credit cards.*

HOTEL INTER-CONTINENTAL

111 East 48th St. (Park & Lexington Aves.)
755-5900

If Old World refinement combined with super-efficient amenities are what make a good hotel, the Inter-continental deserves a Distinguished Service Award. Typical of the Inter-continental chain, this establishment prides itself on its genteel luxury and understated elegance, along with service that is keenly professional and friendly. The rooms are comfortable, spacious, and furnished in excellent taste. In fact, good taste seems to be the modus operandi for everything here—the recently refurbished Barclay and Terrace restaurants, the attractive lobby, and an outstanding level of professional, personalized service that makes a stay here as refreshing as a week on the Aegean. The long list of services include a hair salon; 24-hour concierge and room service; secretarial, translation, and interpretation services; wheel chairs and other amenities for the handicapped; a men's clothing shop; and last but not least, a branch of Caswell-Massey where you can buy everything from cucumber soap to black tar chewing gum.

Singles $175-215, doubles $205-245, suites $285-3,000, weekend packages $139-175.
All major credit cards.

MAYFAIR REGENT

610 Park Ave. (65th St.)
288-0800

The quintessence of civility, this most European of New York's hotels takes pride in a style of hospitality that is gracious and imperturbable. The establishment is small and exclusive, and its loyal following a heady mixture of diplomats, fur-clad socialites, and wealthy jet-setters who come for the highly individualized attention and soothing, relaxed atmosphere. Antiques abound, tastefully of course, in the lovely lobby and salon lounge where breakfast, lunch, and cocktails are served amid flowers and swaying palms, and in the pretty rooms that overlook Park Avenue. Always luxurious, never showy, this is a place of caviar days and Champagne nights.

Singles $210-230, doubles $230-270, suites $320-1,200, weekend packages $440.

All major credit cards.

OMNI BERKSHIRE PLACE

21 East 52nd St. (Madison Ave.)
753-5800;
(800) THE-OMNI

What a pleasure to linger in the atrium lobby of the Berkshire with its stunning floral arrangements, pastel decor, and smart contemporary furniture. Conveniently located in midtown near major shops and the business district, this quietly elegant hotel offers personalized and impeccable service combined with an air of subdued luxury that most travelers will find enchanting. The rooms are spacious, airy, and comfortable; complimentary coffee and newspapers await all guests, and to work off the excesses of New York dining, the hotel provides an off-premises health club.

Singles $185-235, doubles $205-265, suites $400-1,700, weekend packages $160.

All major credit cards.

PARKER MERIDIEN

118 West 56th St. (Sixth & Seventh Aves.)
245-5000

The lobby of the Parker Meridien will make you think you're in Hollywood, with flashy California entertainers and moguls checking in at all hours of the day. This establishment is geared to the nouveau riche, and the pace here is fast, efficient, and noticeably extravagant, from the Aubusson tapestries and travertine marble floors of the foyer to the lavish penthouse health club where every form of exercise equipment known to modern man is available—along with a running track, racquetball courts, and heated swimming pool for all those bikini-clad starlets. The not-so-large contemporary style rooms and suites provide excellent views of Central Park, and the hotel is conveniently located near the Fifth Avenue shopping blitz. In the highly-esteemed Meridien dining room, chef Christian Delouvrier offers superb interpretations of nouvelle cuisine.

Singles $180-235, doubles $205-260, suites $275-650, weekend packages $150-190.
All major credit cards.

PIERRE

2 East 61st St. (Fifth Ave.)
838-8000

Most of the Pierre's predominantly European clientele look like passengers on the Orient Express—eccentric, old-money tycoons and their dowager wives dressed in good, solid tweeds and feather hats. This small, clubby establishment has many permanent residents, which may account for its calm, cozily elegant pace and almost dreamy atmosphere—time doesn't march, but rather waltzes by regally at the Pierre. The service, however, is crackerjack efficient, as if each guest were served by lifelong family retainers. The rooms and lobby wear the subdued elegance of traditional European antiques and gleaming mahogany. The Rotunda room serves tea, and for those daring couples who wish to indulge in a discreet two-step or fox trot, the Cafe Pierre Lounge offers piano music nightly.

Singles $240-335, doubles $265-355, suites $475-1,100, weekend packages $210-485.
All major credit cards.

PLAZA ATHÉNÉE

37 East 64th St. (Madison
& Park Aves.)
734-9100

The grand opulence and elegance of the Plaza Athénée would make it a perfect site for the next royal wedding. For us mere commoners, this new hotel strives for, and superbly achieves, an extremely high level of performance. The lobby is a crystal and marble fantasy with massive floral arrangements, potted palms, and Louis XVI furniture. The multilingual staff includes three concierges as well as an excellently trained corps well-versed in the vagaries of its *très soigné*, predominately European guests. Rooms are luxurious; several come equipped with kitchens. Under the expert hands of the world-renowned chef Jo Rostand and his sons, the dining room, Le Régence, serves excellent French haute cuisine. Like its sister hotel in Paris, this magnificent establishment, owned and managed by Trusthouse Forte, is a lustrous addition to city life at its elegant best. Weekend packages include Champagne and continental breakfast.

Singles $245-285, doubles $275-315, suites $550-1,800, weekend packages $210-275.
All major credit cards.

REGENCY

*540 Park Ave. (60th &
61st St.)*
759-4100

At the Regency you'll find leather-clad rock stars squeezing into the elevator alongside hordes of elderly matrons who look amazingly like Miss Marple or the maiden aunt in an English domestic comedy. Eccentric, doddering, jet-setting, flamboyant, corporate stuffed-shirt—just name any type of well-heeled traveler and sooner or later you'll encounter the species wandering through this gilt and velvet playground. The rooms are furnished in Regency decor with pretty green and salmon accents, while the lobby contains enough marble and gilt accessories to redo Versailles. As an antidote for all this fuss, the service is warm and extremely efficient. The 540 Park Avenue restaurant originated the concept of the power breakfast; on any weekday morning, you'll find members of New York's business community swapping fortunes over kippered herring and eggs.

Singles $175-235, doubles $195-255, suites $425-925, weekend packages $370-420.
All major credit cards.

RITZ CARLTON

*112 Central Park South
(Sixth & Seventh Aves.)*
757-1900

Imagine a sojourn in an impeccably maintained English country manor house and you'll have a good impression of what it's like to stay at the Ritz. Self-assured, clubby, and always very chic, this establishment attracts a sophisticated international clientele. With a new manager on board late in 1987, the hotel's somewhat tarnished tiara should once again sparkle. The handsome lobby and rooms are decorated with English antiques graced with touches of chintz, and pretty seasonal flowers add a cheery, pastel accent. The dignified Jockey Club Bar is well-known as one of those elite watering holes where power brokers wheel and deal over Campari and sodas. Poised, self-confident, and excellently staffed, the Ritz is a precious jewel among New York lodgings.

Singles & doubles $225-325, suites $575-800, weekend packages $155-195.
All major credit cards.

STANHOPE

995 Fifth Ave. (81st St.)
288-5800

Just about every aspect of this hotel has changed (including its name, formerly the American Stanhope) after its recent $30 million renovation. The Laura Ashley decor is gone, and so too is the comfortable cozy atmosphere that made you feel like you were visiting a friend's country home. Instead, the new look is elegant, austere, and very French with sparkling Baccarat chandeliers and European antiques in the lobby,

Impressionist art on the walls, and gratis Chanel toiletries in every bathroom. The rooms are ornately furnished with masses of heavy drapery and Louis XVI furniture, and a Mercedes limousine is available to chauffeur guests around town. Located directly across the avenue from the Metropolitan Museum, the Stanhope has thankfully retained its pretty-as-a-picture outdoor cafe, one of New York's most popular and delightful settings for people-watching.

Singles & doubles $250-325, suites $350-775, weekend packages $250.
All major credit cards.

UNITED NATIONS PLAZA HOTEL

1 U.N. Plaza (44th St.)
355-3400

This handsome contemporary hotel built by the noted architect Kevin Roche has won architectural awards ever since it opened a decade ago. And no wonder, for the United Nations Plaza Hotel is not only visually impressive, but is also one of New York's most vibrant and sophisticated hotels. You'll find scores of ambassadors and diplomats here with their entourages, as well as wealthy travelers who like this hotel's get-away-from-it-all location across from the East River. The lavishly appointed rooms don't begin until the 28th floor (there are offices beneath that) and these lofty heights offer stunning views of the Manhattan skyline. The lobby is all green Italian marble, chrome, and mirrors. The total effect is that of a millionaire's fun house, but the guests find it chic. The top floors house tennis courts, an indoor swimming pool, and an exercise center where any day of the week you just might encounter a foreign diplomat pumping iron. The Ambassador Grill serves an ambitious menu of modern American cuisine complemented by the rugged country cooking of Gascony. This is a place where power and privilege hold court with politics to create an aura that is luxurious, high-pressured, and, for many, fascinating.

Singles $180-215, doubles $200-235, suites $400-1,100, weekend packages $120.
All major credit cards.

WALDORF TOWERS

100 East 50th St. (Park Ave.)
355-3100

The Waldorf Towers would make a great location for a whodunit movie, with its private elevators and driveways, brusque security guards, and privacy-seeking clientele—a head of state, this year's biggest rock star, eccentric nobility, and every President since Hoover. The style here could be called "dowager elegance." Most of the rooms are one-of-a-kind suites outfitted with ornate wallpaper, period antiques, dimly lit chandeliers, and lots of gilt and plush velvet. Butler and maid service is available for your private dining room, and the excellent staff provide the kind of perfectly executed service that would make Jeeves green with envy.

Singles, doubles, $260-300; suites, $350 to $3,000 for the four-bedroom Presidential suite.

All major credit cards.

WESTBURY

15 East 69th St. (Madison Ave.)
535-2000

You need only pass a few hours in the lobby of the Westbury to get a bird's eye view of what is *au courant* in the world of fashion, glamour, and good taste. One of New York's choicest lodgings, this establishment caters primarily to a sophisticated European clientele and international celebrities who know precisely what they want from a hotel. The Westbury services the demands of these experienced travelers with subtle grace, refinement, and poise. The rooms are delightfully furnished in a French Provençal style with exquisite touches such as silk pastel wallpaper. The Westbury Lounge, with its dark mahogany bar and paisley seats, is a haven for beautifully dressed women and their dapper escorts. Its charm, warmth, and intimacy make this lodging a perennial first choice for people who seek the finest in quality.

Singles $210-230, doubles $210-250, suites $350-850, weekend packages $150.

All major credit cards.

First Class

DRAKE SWISÔTEL

400 Park Ave. (56th St.)
421-0900

Designer Adam Tihany has helped transform the Drake into one of New York's most attractive and gracious lodgings. The lobby of this bright jewel in the first class Swisôtel chain features warm woods, brass, pretty etched glass, plus the Swisôtel's signature gold fish bowl brimming with heavenly Swiss chocolates. The ample rooms are pleasant and pretty with European and oriental touches, as well as refrigerators for the more practical sensibilities. The sophisticated customers include business executives, jet setters, and entertainers like Phil Donahue, who conducts interviews from his suite. The Restaurant Lafayette, under the guidance of internationally renowned chef Louis Outhier, is one of the city's finest dining salons with its superb Mediterranean French cuisine. The Drake's service is impeccable and the staff friendly, courteous, and always willing to help; it's a perfect combination of civility, intimacy, and discreet luxury.

Singles $185-235, doubles $205-235, suites $380-700, weekend packages $220.
All major credit cards.

ESSEX HOUSE

*160 Central Park South
(Sixth & Seventh Aves.)
247-0300*

A bustling, handsome hotel, with a superb Central Park location, the Essex is one of those pleasant but nondescript establishments that attract a wide range of well-to-do, if not especially demanding, clients from harried business executives to starry-eyed honeymooners. Wood paneling, fresh flowers, and chandeliers enliven the lobby, and the efficient staff are helpful and friendly. The rooms are spacious and well maintained; many offer exceptional vistas of the park. Despite its large size, the Essex runs a very tight ship, and your stay here will be comfortable and always first-rate. Interesting weekend package plans include movies, meals, Champagne, and bicycles.

Singles $180-245, doubles $205-270, suites $350-1,750, weekend packages $159-349.
All major credit cards.

GRAND HYATT

*Park Ave. at Grand Central
883-1234*

A Concorde could easily land in the lobby of the Grand Hyatt with its vast open spaces, and corridors as wide as runways. As in the other hotels in the Hyatt chain, the decor is chilly and austere in a style mistakenly called contemporary—meaning, of course, loads of glass, marble, and chrome. Baseball and other sports teams stay here, along with business travelers and tourists who want efficiency, not personality, in their lodgings. The lobby features a splashing waterfall, delicate blooming trees, and a jungleland of tropical flora. The rooms are airy and comfortable, but hardly memorable. In all, this is the kind of smoothly run, antiseptic, modern hotel that you forget about the moment you leave.

Singles $175-245, doubles $220-245, suites $350-1,100, weekend packages $125-155.
All major credit cards.

313

HELMSLEY PALACE

455 Madison Ave. (50th St.)
888-7000

Texas oil barons stay here. Hollywood show business types thrive here. Post-debs take tea here. But you'll barely ever find a truly sophisticated American or European traveler here. The Palace is Queen Leona's supreme indulgence, her gold and marble testimonial to the fact that money cannot buy good taste. Once the private home of financier Henry Vuillard, the hotel has become as much of a tourist attraction of late as that other monument to materialism, Trump Tower. The rooms are gilt-edged and lavishly ornate in a style that can only be categorized as Leona baroque. Still, a large, experienced and courteous staff is available at all hours, and certainly the location is perfect—should your limo break down it's an easy walk to midtown boutiques, businesses, and Rockefeller Center.

Singles $205-255, doubles $225-275, suites $375-2,000, weekend packages $170.
All major credit cards.

LOWELL HOTEL

28 East 63rd St. (Park & Madison Aves.)
838-1400

It is impossible not to fall in love with the Lowell. Intimate, cozy, and fashionable in the manner of an impeccably tailored couturier suit, this establishment caters to many English guests as well as independent minded Americans who seek elegance, discretion, and highly-personalized service. Most rooms feature woodburning fireplaces and kitchenettes. The Pembroke Room serves cinnamon toast and watercress sandwiches on bone china at their afternoon tea service. And where else but in this bastion of civility would you find a library for all those *veddy* literate guests?

Singles $180-200, doubles $220-290, suites $340-600.
All major credit cards.

MARRIOTT MARQUIS

1535 Broadway (45th St.)
398-1900

The Marriott Marquis is one of those brazen new buildings that have sprung up all over the theater district as part of the recent Times Square gentrification program. This gargantuan hotel, with more than 1,800 rooms, opened in 1985 on the sight of the once glorious Helen Hayes Theater (sadly destroyed to make way for "progress"). It has been a hit with tourists, if not locals, ever since. The eighth floor atrium lobby is a chrome and glass amusement park replete with theme tropical flora and fauna; getting hold of one of the tubular glass-enclosed elevators, straight from the set of Mel Brooks' *High Anxiety,* is one of the many distractions. The oversized rooms are smart and expensively furnished, with two telephones per room. When you're ready to leave, you can take advantage of video checkout: You settle your account from your room, via the television screen. But then human warmth or contact is not a strong suit in this impersonal, user-hostile establishment. The View, the revolving roof top restaurant and lounge, will remind you of all the other rotating dining rooms you've endured on business trips. Still, if you can't connect with anyone else here, you can always work on yourself. A well-equipped health club has all the goodies—sauna, whirlpool, and exercise gear. And this is the only New York hotel with a theater, The Marriott, on the premises; its highly polished productions divert the resident conventioneer crowd. Some weekend packages include breakfast, Champagne, and theater tickets.

Singles $220-270, doubles $230-280, suites $425-3,500, weekend packages $130-399.
All major credit cards.

MORGANS

237 Madison Ave. (38th St.)
686-0300

Take the social network of former Studio 54 owners Steve Rubell and Ian Schrager, the avant garde taste of designer Andree Putnam, and the culinary expertise of chef Larry Forgione—the result is Morgans, one of New York's newest and most willfully eccentric hotels. In its new incarnation, the former Executive Hotel is intimate and dramatically furnished: stereo cassette systems gleam in high-tech splendor from the essentially tiny, cramped rooms. Morgans approaches the hostelry business with humor and boldness; there is no lobby, no concierge, the bathroom sinks are made of stainless steel, and the trademark Putnam decor used throughout the hotel is a severe palette of gray, black, and white—minimalist and chic. Who stays at Morgans? A star-studded clientele like Cher and Margaux Hemingway, along with world-weary international types who find the congenial, casual staff and the offbeat touches a fresh and welcome approach. Staying at Morgans is like having a share in the house in the Hamptons—fashionable, loaded with pretty young things . . . in fact, a bit like Studio 54 in its heyday, only now you can spend the night in a bed.

Singles $155-190, doubles $170-205, suites $270-380, weekend packages $115.
AE.

NEW YORK HELMSLEY

It's easy to mistake the Helmsely for an expensive car dealership. The U-shaped driveway is perpetually clogged with Jaguars, the lobby is all stainless steel columns and

212 East 42nd St. (Second
& Third Aves.)
490-8900

brass, and the staff follows you around as if they were magnetically attached. Formerly the New York Harley, this is now the high level executive link in the Helmsley chain, and the indomitable Queen Leona has made sure that every aspect of this establishment is efficient and modern in a nondescript, contemporary fashion. The rooms are spacious and airy, filled with loads of free toiletries, as well as magnifying mirrors and bathroom scales to assess the latest New York culinary damages. The scene in the lobby bar is a mixture of singles on the make, and businessmen with happy-face nametags.

Singles $155-200, doubles $175-220, suites $330, weekend packages $115.

All major credit cards.

PARK LANE

36 Central Park South
(Fifth & Sixth Aves.)
371-4000

The aura of new money and impersonality that wafts through the Park Lane seems to attract business guests, globe-trotting travelers, and honeymooners who can easily hide out in complete privacy amidst the large-scale glitter and plush. The rooms are pleasantly furnished in a range of Old World styles; at the top levels the suites provide sweeping vistas of Central Park below. The experienced, multi-lingual staff is polite, courteous, and will help you find your way through the marble and chandeliered confusion of the lobby.

Singles $175-235, doubles $195-255, suites $300-735, weekend packages $145.

All major credit cards.

PLAZA

768 Fifth Ave. (59th St.)
759-3000

New York without the Plaza is as unthinkable as Rogers without Hammerstein. However frumpy and stodgy this grande dame may be, the Plaza is still the city's monument to romance. For proof, just step into the lobby (politely elbowing past the hordes of tourists in Bermuda shorts looking for the restrooms)—the impression that you have stepped back into the Gilded Age is as rich and vivid as an exciting perfume.

The Plaza perches like an island unto itself directly facing Fifth Avenue and 59th Street on one end, and Central Park on the other, a superb location if ever there was one. This immense edifice is like a medieval cathedral: narrow corridors, blind hallways, and never a busboy in sight to dispel the rarified atmosphere (or to direct stymied guests to the elevators). The rooms tend toward the small and chintzy, although the many suites offer more attractive and spacious amenities. New York's old guard families spend a good part of their lives here, whether at the Palm Court for tea with Mumsy, the Oak Bar for hustling business deals with other corporate swells, clinking cocktail glasses at the Oyster Bar, or celebrating births, wedding, and deb parties in the ballroom. It's all very Social Register, and great fun if you belong. But even if you don't, your stay here will always be much more than a night in a hotel; charming at times, outrageous at others, but never dull—a perfect image of New York itself.

Singles $150-380, doubles $225-410, suites $450-1,000, weekend packages $170-415.

All major credit cards.

ST.-REGIS SHERATON
2 East 55th St. (Fifth Ave.)
753-4500

The gracious ambiance and Old World decorum of the St. Regis make this lovely accommodation a choice for top level business executives and discriminating, middle-aged patrons. Built by John Jacob Astor in a style of fin-de-siecle opulence, this establishment still glows with the luster of a gentler age. Rooms are pleasant and airy. The lobby is a mundane hodgepodge of the faintly antique, but the marvelous "Old King Cole" tableau in the dining salon, painted by Maxfield Parrish, makes up for any latter-day decorating sins. Its excellent location near Fifth Avenue shops attracts many guests who come for a week's shopping blitz.

Singles $195-250, doubles $195-280, suites $300-375, weekend packages $125-245.

All major credit cards.

SHERRY NETHERLAND
781 Fifth Ave. (59th St.)
355-2800

The hauteur of the Sherry Netherland would give a Sherpa guide respiratory problems, but when you're looking for the rarified elegance of the past, this is the place to come. The rooms are spacious and handsomely furnished with subtle good taste. Service is always courteous and personalized, both to the many permanent residents and overnight travelers. Off the lobby, the recently opened Harry Cipriani's bar has brightly restored the drop dead glamour that once upon a time meant cocktails at the Netherland. The excellent location and civilized, courtly ambiance attract a loyal following who would never stay anywhere else.

Singles & doubles $175-250, suites $280-450.

All major credit cards.

VISTA INTERNATIONAL HOTEL

3 World Trade Center
938-9100

You'll find more briefcases in the lobby of the Vista than at Mark Cross, for this is a hotel catering to business executives bound for Wall Street, as well as tourists who enjoy vacationing off the beaten track. Located in the heart of the financial district, this is one of those contemporary glass-and-chrome monoliths that pulsates with efficiency and all kinds of modern amenities geared to fast-track guests. The rooms are comfortable and handsomely furnished, with many affording spectacular views of Lower Manhattan and New York Harbor. There are free guided tours of nearby points of interest, such as SoHo and Chinatown, along with such creature comforts as an executive fitness center equipped with sauna and massage, heated indoor pool, jogging track, and tennis and racquetball courts. Conference and meeting rooms are available, and the business service center offers Standard & Poor's Marketscope, secretarial help, and Telex facilities. You'll encounter native New Yorkers from all over the city who willingly trek downtown for the pleasures of dining in the splendid American Harvest and Greenhouse Restaurant where American cuisine is presented with flair and imagination.

Singles $170-235, doubles $195-260, suites $360-1,210, weekend packages $158-258.
All major credit cards.

WALDORF-ASTORIA

301 Park Ave. (49th & 50th Sts.)
355-3000

The Waldorf is finally learning how to age gracefully rather than plummet headlong into disarray as it was doing a few years back. An ongoing restoration of the original Art Deco decor has brought back a great deal of the glamour and beauty that this great hotel displayed in its heyday. The lobby is still choked with gawking tourists, business executives, and geriatric travelers who honeymooned here 40 years ago, but the staff works valiantly, and service is smooth, if slow. The 1,692 rooms vary considerably, from ones resembling large closets to rambling suites with Texas-sized bathrooms. Tucked away from the frantic crowd madly shopping and eating on the lobby level, the chic Waldorf Towers has its own entrance and an Old World elegance undiminished by time.

Singles $145-250, doubles $175-280, suites $340-770, weekend packages $230-270.
All major credit cards.

Comfortable

BEVERLY HOTEL

125 East 50th St.
(Lexington Ave.)
753-2700;
(800) 223-0945

This quiet, family-owned establishment is a fine choice for travelers who crave serenity and personalized care, thanks in large part to the services of the resident concierge. The clientele is a mixture of business executives, families, and, when the General Assembly is in session, U.N. delegates. Most of the attractively furnished rooms are suites and junior suites featuring fully equipped kitchenettes. One noticeable flaw: the outside noise level can be outrageous, so ask for a room on the upper floors, or turn up the volume on your Walkman.

Singles $129, doubles $139, suites $160-245, weekend packages $76-96.
All major credit cards.

BLACKSTONE

50 East 58th St. (Park &
Madison Aves.)
355-4200

Unless you know where to look, you'll probably walk right past the Blackstone, with its nondescript entrance. Conveniently located near major boutiques and businesses, this is a reliable place to stay: the service is always good and the rooms are well-maintained, if small. Lots of Europeans stay here, as do business executives who take their free morning edition of the *New York Times* with them to breakfast.

Singles $84-89, doubles $104-140, suites $140-225.
All major credit cards.

DORAL INN

49th St. & Lexington Ave.
755-1200;
(800) 223-5823

This is a friendly and comfortable establishment whose welcoming ambiance is matched by attractive accommodations. Each of the 700 rooms at the Doral have been renovated in a clean, contemporary style. There is a new fitness center, squash courts, saunas, self-service laundry, coffee shop, restaurant, and a proficient, multilingual staff. Its popular location (across the street from the Waldorf) draws large tour groups, so be prepared for long lines at the registration desk and overcrowded elevators.

Singles $102-120, doubles $116-134, suites $200-600, weekend packages $90.
All major credit cards.

319

DORSET

30 West 54th St. (Fifth & Sixth Aves.)
247-7300

Although the staid Dorset may never win any hostelry awards, it does offer agreeable accommodations and a worthy location just off Fifth Avenue by the Museum of Modern Art. The wood-paneled lobby and pastel rooms are somber, but quietly elegant, like many of the mostly middle-aged guests who enjoy the serenity and moderate prices. A dining room and cafe bar are on the premises.
    Singles $135-195, doubles $155-215, suites $265-475.
All major credit cards.

GOLDEN TULIP BARBIZON HOTEL

140 East 63rd St. (Lexington Ave.)
838-5700

The Barbizon is a delightful secret closely guarded by a steady roster of selective clients. Formerly a residential hotel for women, it has been renovated with charming results. Warm pastel walls, pink marble floors, and lots of fresh flowers give the lobby a younger than springtime look. Most rooms are on the small side, but are adequate and pleasantly furnished; 12 new tower apartments offer more luxurious living, plus terraces with superb views of the cityscape. Downstairs, the restaurant, cafe, and bar do a brisk business with guests and exhausted shoppers from Bloomingdale's, located just a few blocks away.
    Singles $99-135, doubles $160-195, suites $295-375, weekend packages $99.
All major credit cards.

HALLORAN HOUSE

525 Lexington Ave. (49th St.)
755-4000;
(800) 223-0939

The Halloran House offers a nice combination of modern amenities and traditional charm. The lobby has the look of a private club, with its handsome leather furniture and oak paneling. The oversized rooms combine old-fashioned spaciousness with such up-to-date features as closet safes, color televisions with bedside remote, extension telephones in the bathrooms, and a special television channel for viewing your messages and itemized bills. A new health club and swimming pool are being built at the present time. The weekend package includes chocolates and a full breakfast.
    Singles $140-155, doubles $155-170, suites $350 and up, weekend packages $124.
All major credit cards.

HELMSLEY WINDSOR

100 West 58th St. (Sixth Ave.)

If the ongoing renovation of the Helmsley Windsor is portent of things to come, Leona Helmsley must be working with a better decorator. Gradually disappearing are her

320

265-2100;
(800) 221-4982

signature flowered bedspreads and billowing curtains. Ask for a newly decorated room and you'll get soothing pastel walls and pretty, contemporary decor, along with a staff whose fear of the Queen makes them efficient, if not particularly cheery. The location is convenient to Central Park and Carnegie Hall.

Singles $115-125, doubles $125-135, suites $195-310, weekend packages $89-119.
All major credit cards.

LEXINGTON

Lexington Ave. & 48th St.
755-4400;
(800) 448-4471

As of this writing the Lexington has half-completed a major renovation of the lobby and rooms. Gone are the pink Spanish courtyard foyer and orange rooms. Instead, the new decor is soothing pink and green pastels, although the rooms (many come with refrigerators) are still small. Conveniently located in midtown and staffed by a friendly, multilingual group, this establishment is popular with United Nations visitors and airline crew members. A new lobby bar and lounge is a welcome addition to the Lexington.

Singles $125, doubles $140, suites $250-350.
All major credit cards.

LOEWS SUMMIT

51st St. & Lexington Ave.
752-7000

Short on style, long on efficiency—sometimes you can't have everything. The Loews Summit is one of an increasing number of lodgings geared to corporate executives. The decor is what passes for contemporary these days, meaning lots of boring earth tones. But if you don't mind that look, you'll find such amenities as mini-refrigerators and extra telephones in the rooms, as well as an up-to-date health club with Nautilus equipment, a Jacuzzi, and a sauna. The staff is dedicated and conscientious in the brisk, impersonal style of everything you'll encounter here. Steer clear of the even-numbered rooms—they face the roaring confusion of Lexington Avenue below.

Singles $125-145, doubles $135-155, suites $230-345, weekend packages $89.
All major credit cards.

LOMBARDY

11 East 56th St. (Park &
Lexington Aves.)

Thankfully the dreary old lobby of this small hotel is about to be renovated. The big plus of the Lombardy is its location—a hop, skip, and a jump away from Tiffany's and other midtown shops. The studio-apartment rooms are

753-8600;
(800) 223-5254

pleasant and come equipped with kitchen facilities. The multilingual staff provides friendly and helpful service—all in all, an acceptable, if uninspired place to stay.

Singles $135, doubles $150, suites $270-425.

All major credit cards.

MADISON TOWERS HOTEL

Madison Ave. & 38th St.
685-3700;
(800) 225-4340

In the serene Murray Hill section of town, the Madison Towers offers a welcome that's both charming and unpretentious. This small, intimate hotel combines Old World, European ambiance, and personal attention with prices as sensible as a sturdy pair of walking shoes. The rooms are cozy and prettily decorated, the coffee shop makes a decent breakfast, and the Whaler Bar boasts a roaring fireplace in winter, and a good piano player all year round.

Singles $105-125, doubles $120-140, suites $125-300, weekend packages $80.

All major credit cards.

MAYFLOWER

15 Central Park West (61st St.)
265-0060;
(800) 223-4164

An affable, easy-going oasis amidst the nouveau riche bustle of the Upper West Side, the Mayflower is so close to Lincoln Center that if you open your window, you may just hear a violin concerto. Attractive rooms (ask for one with a park view) and a friendly staff make this a good choice. At the overpriced Conservatory Restaurant, you'll dine with marathon runners, clarinetists, and other performing artists who frequent this hotel. The weekend package includes breakfast.

Singles $115-145, doubles $130-170, suites $210-250, weekend packages $104-152.

All major credit cards.

MILFORD PLAZA

270 West 45th St. (Eighth Ave.)
869-3600;
(800) 221-2690

If staying at Grand Central Station sounds like fun, park your suitcases at the Milford Plaza. Enjoy the roar of the glitzy lobby, crowded with airline flight crews, senior citizen groups, and gawking tourists. The rooms are cramped and dull to look at, although the new bathrooms and carpeting have helped brighten the decor. The staff can be surly at times (who wouldn't be in all this bedlam?), but the moderate rates and the convenient Times Square location make it a bearable choice. The weekend package includes cocktail, dinner, and a continental breakfast.

Singles $85-125, doubles $100-140, suites $200-375, weekend packages $92.

All major credit cards.

NEW YORK HILTON

1335 Ave. of the Americas
(53rd & 54th Sts.)
586-7000

With its more than 2,000 rooms and amenities galore, this establishment is one of those sprawling, nondescript mega-hotels which functions like a city unto itself. The rooms are airy and spacious, particularly in the Executive Towers where a 24-hour concierge, private lounge, complimentary hors d'oeuvres, and continental breakfast are among the perks of the day. Two floors of non-smoking rooms, accommodations for handicapped guests, bars, lounges, a disco, a coffee shop, a dining salon, a beauty salon, a multilingual staff, a *Wall Street Journal* business station with services like dictation, typewriters, and Dow Jones averages—all insure that your stay will be comfortable and well-pampered. The weekend package includes cocktails and Sunday brunch.

Singles $145-205, doubles $170-230, suites $375-500, weekend packages $228.

All major credit cards.

NEW YORK PENTA HOTEL

Seventh Ave. & 33rd St.
736-5000;
(800) 223-8585

The Penta is a marvelous gem of a place designed by Stanford White and immortalized by Glen Miller when it was the Statler—remember Pennsylvania 6-5000? It's the closest hotel (five blocks) to the new Jacob Javits Center, and a recent $20 million refurbishment of the premises has added a worthy trove of facilities geared to the business executive. The rooms are pleasantly redecorated in a contemporary motif, the lobby sports a newly glowing peaches and cream complexion, and tennis and racquetball courts, a health club, and a swimming pool are soon to come. A bit of history, efficiency, and a friendly, helpful staff—you can't ask for much more.

Singles $99-185, doubles $199-210, suites $250-850, weekend packages $99.

All major credit cards.

NOVOTEL

226 West 52nd St.
(Broadway)
315-0100

Built piggyback style atop a pre-existing storehouse, the Novotel is another new addition to the ongoing renovation of Times Square. You know the look by now—glass, brass, chrome, and stainless steel, and all the antiseptic comforts that are the signature of contemporary, big-city hotels. The seventh lobby floor is nearly always thronged with corporate types and well-dressed tourists about to venture out to Broadway shops and matinees. On the floors above, the guest rooms are spacious and airy with bright furnishings (many offer fine views of the Hudson River and cityscape). Other creature comforts include a rather ordinary gift shop, a booth

323

for theater tickets, a brasserie, and the Wine Bar to indulge your oenological passions with tastings of Champagnes and wines by the glass. Some weekend packages include breakfast and a wine tasting.

Singles $135-165, doubles $145-175, suites $350-600, weekend packages $115-200.

All major credit cards.

OMNI PARK CENTRAL

Seventh Ave. & 56th St.
247-8000;
(800) THE-OMNI

Another member of the Omni-vorous hotel chain, this is a good place to stay when you don't want much more than a clean and comfortable place to hang your hat. This enormous hotel has wall-to-wall guests at any hour of the day—flight crews, conventioneers, and sightseers from the Plains states. The 1,450 rooms have recently been redecorated, and may put you in mind of your doctor's office. There's a new bar/lounge and an ambitious French bistro restaurant that's about as authentic as airplane ethnic food.

Singles $135-175, doubles $175-215, suites $199, weekend packages $105.

All major credit cards.

RAMADA INN

48th St. & Eighth Ave.
581-7000;
(800) 272-6232

Ramada Inns are the fast-food chains of the hotel business; don't expect any sophisticated touches just because this one happens to be located in New York. What you do get is a clean room, a location near the theater district, and, in the summer, an outdoor rooftop swimming pool where you can cool off all your frustrations.

Singles $95-125, doubles $107-137.

All major credit cards.

ST. MORITZ ON THE PARK

50 Central Park South
(Sixth Ave.)
755-5800

The St. Moritz is like the expensive dress you've stuck in the back of your closet: too good to throw away, but hopelessly out of fashion. The small, but well-maintained rooms are frumpy in that deadly dull style known to seasoned travelers as "hotel antique." In warm weather, you can escape to the outdoor cafe and gaze at Central Park across the street. Off the lobby, wander into the bubble gum pink room known as Rumplemeyer's: this vintage ice cream parlor replete with stuffed animals, ice cream sodas, and little girls in white dresses will make you weep for the nostalgia of it all.

Singles $130-200, doubles $150-200, suites $225-400, weekend packages $118-168.

All major credit cards.

SALISBURY

123 West 57th St. (Sixth & Seventh Aves.)
246-1300

Cozy and pleasant, the Salisbury is a welcome find, with its friendly ambiance, proximity to Carnegie Hall, and sensible prices. The rooms are adequately sized, cheery, and full of light. The coffee shop off the lobby serves better than average food at less than average prices.

Singles $84-94, doubles $94-104, suites $159-275, weekend packages $69-119.
All major credit cards.

SHERATON CENTRE

52nd St. & Seventh Ave.
581-1000;
(800) 223-6550

Formerly the Americana, the Sheraton Centre is one of New York's most popular convention and tourist hotels—central casting couldn't have filled the lobby with more predictable types. The 1,835 rooms (for guests and pets) are comfortable and spacious; the top five floors known as the Sheraton Towers are tonier and more elegant, with butler service available as well. The buffet lunch at the Caffe Fontana is stupefying in its variety, if not in its quality. Guests have swimming pool privileges at the sister Sheraton City Squire across the street.

Singles $125-175; doubles $150-200, suites $360-500, weekend packages $108 (summer only).
All major credit cards.

SHERATON CITY SQUIRE HOTEL

790 Seventh Ave. (51st St.)
581-3300;
(800) 325-3535

The City Squire has successfully risen from its lowly origins as a motel to become one of the more agreeable places to stay in the theater district. The rooms are well-maintained and pleasant (some have skyline views), and on-premises are a beauty/barber shop, restaurant, and coffee shop. Minibus service is provided to all city airports. For a final worthy touch, there's a glass-enclosed swimming pool open year-round.

Singles $110-170, doubles $135-195, suites $280-380, weekend packages $99 (summer only).
All major credit cards.

SHOREHAM

33 West 55th St. (Fifth & Sixth Aves.)
247-6700

A new marble lobby can't disguise the fact that the Shoreham is for spartan tastes only. Well-situated a few steps away from Fifth Avenue, this establishment offers clean, modern rooms (all equipped with pantry units) at moderate prices. Caution: bring earplugs. The noise level from street construction below combined with the ancient air conditioning units will make an insomniac of even the soundest of sleepers.

Singles $80-85, doubles $90-100, suites $120-135, weekend packages $59-72.
All major credit cards.

TUDOR

304 East 42nd St. (Second Ave.)
986-8800;
(800) 221-1253

Amid the gracefully aging apartment complex of Tudor City near the United Nations, this serene establishment offers agreeable accommodations to an international clientele. The cramped rooms are furnished without much taste, but all are clean and comfortable. Rooms are equipped with color televisions, private baths, and telephones.

Singles & doubles $95-110, triples $140, suites $160-175.
All major credit cards.

WARWICK

54th St. & Ave. of the Americas
247-2700;
(800) 223-4099

The Beatles stayed here when they were in town, and we've had a fondness for the place ever since. The lads' zaniness clearly did not preclude a fondness for the creature comforts: the Warwick, built in 1927 by William Randolph Hearst, has always been carefully maintained, tastefully furnished, and courteously staffed. Each of the 500 large rooms has spacious closets and double windows to filter out the street noise. The Sir Walter Raleigh Restaurant, hair salon, and same-day laundry valet provide good service, and the Sixth Avenue location is convenient for executives and Fifth Avenue shopping tourists alike.

Singles $135-175, doubles $150-190, suites $225-400, weekend packages $105-125 (include chocolates and continental breakfast).
All major credit cards.

Small & Charming

ALGONQUIN HOTEL

59 West 44th St. (Fifth & Sixth Aves.)
840-6800

The conversations you'll overhear in the lobby may not be as scintillating as in the days of Dorothy Parker and the Round Table, but the Algonquin is still one of the most popular gathering spots for visiting artists, writers, and other creative types. The atmosphere in the handsome lobby, with its traditional furnishings and unhurried, civilized pace, is more that of a private club than a hotel. At lunch, publishers and editors congregate in the dining rooms for cafeteria-quality food at haute-cuisine prices—no one complains because it's the literary scene that brought them there anyway. Most travelers find the hominess of the conservative, tastefully furnished rooms a welcome relief from the banality of many newer hotels. At night the Oak Room turns into a cabaret that features a changing roster of some of the most spellbinding lyricists in the country.

Singles $118-126, doubles $126-134, suites $242-510.
All major credit cards.

BEDFORD

118 East 40th St.
(Lexington & Park Aves.)
697-4800;
(800) 221-6881

An agreeable, European-style hotel in the middle of the garment district, the Bedford is a decent home away from home for buyers and fashion industry moguls. The 200 large rooms are pleasantly decorated and equipped with kitchen facilities. A concierge is on hand, in-house laundry service is available, and the staff is friendly and helpful—all this plus sensible rates, too.

Singles $99-140, doubles $120-150, suites $140-200, weekend packages vary.
All major credit cards.

CHELSEA HOTEL

222 West 23rd St. (Seventh & Eighth Aves.)
243-3700

A stay at the Chelsea is like a pilgrimage to the Poet's Corner at Westminster Abbey—dark, dreary, and haunted by the spirits of dearly departed literary and artistic luminaries. Dylan Thomas, Arthur Miller, Brendan Behan, Mark Twain, and, lest we forget, Sid Vicious, all hung their hats here at one time or another. Likewise, today's clientele are mainly artists, writers, and creative souls from the world over. The rooms are comfortable but badly in need of refurbishment. Still, what they lack in decor they make up in size, soundproof walls, and in many rooms, woodburning fireplaces.

Singles $65-95, doubles $80-95, suites $145-175.
All major credit cards.

DORAL PARK AVENUE

70 Park Ave. (38th St.)
687-7050

This gracious hotel winningly combines big city sophistication with the intimate charm of a small *pension* in the French countryside. The elaborate appearance of the rotunda lobby is mollified by the cozy decor of the 203 newly redecorated rooms with their pretty pastel tones and contemporary furnishings. The handsome dining room and friendly bar are frequented by the well-dressed, privacy-seeking clientele who are the hotel's stock-in-trade. Although not the bargain it used to be, this lodging is well worth a visit.

Singles $155-175, doubles $175-195, suites $350-475, weekend packages $119.50.
All major credit cards.

DORAL TUSCANY

*120 East 39th St.
(Lexington & Park Aves.)
686-1600*

In contrast with the impersonal treatment endemic to today's sprawling contemporary hotels, the Doral Tuscany offers the civilized, tranquil charms of a gentler age. One of many small hotels located south of Grand Central, this establishment has a steadfast, international clientele who are loyal to this "biggest little hotel" in New York. Major refurnishing of the decor has improved the Doral's appearance considerably. The lobby now sports an airy, pastel look, and the 150 rooms (all equipped with refrigerators) are attractively furnished in a variety of tasteful motifs. A new bar and restaurant complement the many amenities this pleasant hotel has been providing for years.

Singles $175-195, doubles $200-215, suites $350-800, weekend packages $110.
All major credit cards.

ELYSÉE

*60 East 54th St. (Park &
Madison Aves.)
753-1066*

The Elysée attracts the kind of clientele who look as if they write mystery stories for a living—tweed-suited, slightly eccentric in their mannerisms, and in search of privacy amid big city chaos. This small and gracious midtown hotel offers both serenity and amiable service at reasonable rates. The rooms are comfortable and their formerly neon hues have recently given way to more soothing colors. The Monkey Bar contains enough primate imagery to make even Tarzan feel at home.

Singles $125-175, doubles $140-190, suites $250-500.
All major credit cards.

HELMSLEY MIDDLETOWNE

*148 East 48th St.
(Lexington & Third Aves.)
755-3000;
(800) 221-4982*

Formerly an apartment house, the Helmsley Middletown still has a residential quality that can be calming to frazzled nerves. The 192 rooms are furnished in Early Leona, that is, the Queen's usual floral bedspreads and curtains; all come with kitchenettes and some with terraces. The hotel offers minibus service to major airports, a beauty salon, and a friendly, professional staff who will make your stay as pleasant as a visit to an efficient friend.

Singles $115-125, doubles $125-135, suites $185-215, weekend packages $89.

All major credit cards.

KITANO

66 Park Ave. (38th St.)
685-0022

The gracious welcome of a Japanese host is a unique experience for even a seasoned traveler. A stay at the Kitano is not simply another night at a hotel, but an experience as soothing and restful as a languorous bath. The simple furnishings and lovely, subdued decor in the lobby and rooms create a mood of unruffled calm, which is strengthened by the professionalism of the staff. There are two Japanese suites with tatami (straw) sitting rooms, as well as traditional bathtubs and decor. Try Hakubei, the Kitano's Japanese restaurant, for sushi and other authentically prepared specialties.

Singles $105-140, doubles $130-140, suites $190-300.

All major credit cards.

MADISON AVENUE HOTEL

25 East 77th St. (Madison Ave.)
744-4300

What was, until recently, modest Hyde Park Hotel is currently undergoing major renovation, and its new name clues you in to the changes. *Intime* and terribly chic, the Madison Avenue Hotel is part of a growing trend toward smaller lodgings which offer individualized service and decor that is not standard hotel-issue. The large rooms, 150 of them, feature lacquer furniture and attractive pastel accents. Most rooms and all suites have high-tech kitchenettes, each with a microwave oven. The location is serenely luxurious—a few steps away from expensive boutiques, galleries, museums, and Central Park. Adjacent to the lobby, the Sant Ambroeus offers elegant Italian pastries, gelati, and espresso to a gorgeous St. Tropez-tanned crowd.

Singles $155-165, doubles $175-185, suites $300-500, weekend packages $220.

All major credit cards.

SHERATON PARK AVENUE

45 Park Ave. (37th St.)
685-7676

Who would ever expect a Sheraton Hotel to have as much grace and personality as this lovely charmer? A recent $6.5 million refurbishment has rendered the premises dashing. The rooms have been handsomely furnished in a traditional, European decor (many have fireplaces). The popular dining room draws both guests and local business people, and lively jazz sessions attract music buffs to the lounge on weekends. A new rooftop garden offers one of the most delightful aeries in town.

Singles $165-245, doubles $200-270, suites $360-500, weekend packages $115-140.

All major credit cards.

SURREY HOTEL

20 East 76th St. (Madison Ave.)
288-3700

Quiet good taste is the byword at the Surrey, from its soignée location on a tree-lined street near the Whitney Museum to its pleasant, large rooms (all come with kitchenettes), and the tranquil gentility which permeates this small, established hotel. The recent renovation of the lobby and rooms have added a fresh sparkle to the surroundings, but the attentive, Old World courtesy of the staff remains as reliable and welcome as ever.

Singles $170-190, doubles $215-235, suites $375 and up, weekend packages $130-250.

All major credit cards.

WYNDHAM

42 West 58th St. (Fifth & Sixth Aves.)
753-3500

The Wyndham lobby, with its comfy sofas, greenery, and earth-toned furnishings, is probably the most agreeable nook you'll find outside of your mother's parlor. Choose from 200 spacious and attractive rooms, some with cold pantries. Close to Central Park and Fifth Avenue shops, this intimate lodging is a jewel prized by loyal clients who relish privacy, smooth service, and a friendly, dedicated staff.

Singles $95-105, doubles $105-115, suites $150-180.

All major credit cards.

Economy

CENTURY PARAMOUNT

235 West 46th St. (Broadway & Eighth Ave.)
764-5500

For reasonable rates and safe, clean lodgings in the theater district, the Century Paramount is a good bet. The 600 rooms are cramped and rather stuffy, and the combination of thin walls, old windows, and rusty air conditioners makes for a noisy setting at best. However, the rooms are well-maintained, with private baths and color televisions in each unit. A coffee shop is conveniently located adjacent to the lobby.

Singles $70-90, doubles $80-100.

All major credit cards.

COMFORT INN MURRAY HILL

42 West 35th St. (Fifth & Sixth Aves.)
947-0200

When the Quality International hotel group recently spent $4.5 million refurbishing the premises, they transformed the old Murray Hill Hotel into a charming, European-style lodging with excellent amenities at affordable rates. Close to Jacob Javits Convention Center, the hotel's 115 rooms are decorated in soft pastels and contemporary furnishings, along with color televisions and air conditioning. Complimentary coffee and Danish for breakfast are nice eye-openers. The staff is crackerjack efficient and eager to please.

Singles $90-110, doubles $105-125, weekend packages $75-85.

All major credit cards.

EDISON

228 West 47th St.
(Broadway & Eighth Ave.)
840-5000;
(800) 223-1900

Another accommodation worth considering if you want to stay in the Times Square district is the sprawling Edison. Its 1,000 rooms are large and spotless with good-sized closets, color televisions, and quiet air conditioners. The hotel cafe, cocktail lounge, and lobby bustle with tourists sporting vinyl suitcases and I Love the Big Apple buttons.

Singles $70-78, doubles $80-88, suites $95.

All major credit cards.

ESPLANADE

305 West End Ave. (74th St.)
874-5000

A stone's throw from pretty Riverside Park and close to Lincoln Center, the gracefully aging Esplanade is old fashioned in its courtesy as well as in its rates. The spacious, pleasantly decorated rooms have kitchenettes, air conditioners, and cable television, and the conscientious staff will cater to your every whim—eventually. Adjacent to the lobby the *très chic* restaurant Fandango consistently wins rave reviews for its superb nouvelle American cuisine.

Singles $75-80, doubles $99 and up, suites $99-109.

All major credit cards.

INTERNATIONAL HOUSE

Overlooking the Hudson River, the International House is a non-profit institution built by John D. Rockfeller in 1924. It's open to graduate-level students, researchers, trainees,

500 Riverside Dr. (123rd St.)
316-8400

interns, faculty members, and visiting scholars. Rooms are available from mid-May through August, and accommodations, though spartan, are clean and safe. All student rooms are singles and the guest rooms can be rented as either singles or doubles. Showers, cafeteria, aerobics room, laundry, dry cleaner, TV rooms, and a gym are just a few of the many amenities that make this a popular student lodging.

Student rooms $25. Guest rooms: singles $35-55, doubles $45-65. Monthly rates available.
Cash or traveler's checks only.

INTERNATIONAL STUDENT CENTER

38 West 88th St. (Central Park West)
787-8806

Conveniently located near Central Park, the International Student Center is a youth hostel for foreign student travelers only (ages 18-30). The ISC offers dormitory accommodations at $8 per night, with a seven night maximum stay during the summer. Another location at 210 West 55th Street (757-8030). Both establishments have shower facilities.
Cash or traveler's checks only.

PICKWICK ARMS

230 East 51st St. (Second & Third Aves.)
355-0300

Savvy budget-minded travelers have patronized the Pickwick Arms for years, with good reason—the prices are rock bottom, the rooms are clean and equipped with air conditioning and cable television, and the location, a pretty midtown street on the East Side, is quite good. The accommodations range from rooms without bath to large studios with kitchenettes, and you'll find the service efficient and friendly. Daily payment required in advance.

Singles $34-46, doubles $60-75.
All major credit cards.

WALES

1295 Madison Ave. (92nd St.)
876-6000

Built in 1900, the tiny Wales is one of New York's oldest ongoing hotels, and many loyal clients would never stay anywhere else. All the rooms have private baths (some suites available with kitchenettes) and the accommodations are tidy and comfortable, if their decor is purely functional. Since it's off the beaten track of most hotels, you'll find the rates extremely reasonable. Sarabeth's Kitchen, adjacent to the lobby, serves some of the finest breakfasts and pastries in town.

Singles $65-70, doubles $65-70, suites $80-115.
All major credit cards.

WELLINGTON

Seventh Ave. & 55th St.
247-3900

The Wellington is your generic brand hotel—low rates and mediocre quality, but it does get the job done. The rooms are clean and well-maintained, with ample closet space. Tour groups and clothing buyers lugging their sample suitcases choke the lobby day and night, so checkout can be a nightmare. The upper level "tower rooms" offer better amenities at higher rates.

Singles $71-86, doubles $84-96, suites $125-165. *All major credit cards.*

WENTWORTH

59 West 46th St. (Fifth & Sixth Aves.)
719-2300;
(800) 223-1900

The Wentworth's proximity to the fashion district makes this lodging a natural stopping place for buyers from all over the world—there's even a jewelry exchange in the lobby so you can buy your diamonds along with the morning paper. The 195 large rooms are well kept and decorated with pretty floral bedspreads and curtains. With its high housekeeping standards and courteous, prompt service, this hotel is a good choice for any cost-conscious traveler.

Singles $65-75, doubles $75-105, suites $110-150. *All major credit cards.*

SHOPS

WHAT'S YOUR PLEASURE?

As the saying goes, "When the going gets rough, the tough go shopping." Hence New York City, a tough city if there ever was one, is one of the world's great shopping capitals. Each year more and more stores appear in Manhattan, and droves of new shoppers cart into the city. The old guard heads for Fifth Ave. and Madison Ave., still as elegant as ever. The young-in-spirit flash their credit cards in the upwardly mobile boutiques on Columbus Ave. on the Upper West Side and in SoHo downtown. And as the Lower East Side becomes gentrified, style-conscious trend-setters seek out its ultra-hip shops. Shoppers needn't travel to Japan, China, Europe, Mexico, and points beyond—the best of the world's products, from food to fashion, can be found right here on this crowded island.

Antiques

THE MANHATTAN ART & ANTIQUES CENTER

1050 Second Ave. (55th St.)
355-4400

One of New York City's richest and most exotic shopping experiences. Collectors on the prowl for better-quality items at less-than-Madison-Avenue prices will fare well here. Fabergé, Tiffany, Lalique, Hummel, Cartier, Baccarat—all are casually displayed in one center. There are dealers offering English furniture, American quilts, Ming and Tung pottery, and Satsuma pieces; in total some 104 dealers display their wares on three large floors. Keep a sharp lookout; some of the best shops are squirreled away around corners. The center offers expert packing, crating, and shipping, and is open seven days a week (but be sure to check with the individual galleries).
Mon.-Sat. 10:30 A.M. to 6:30 P.M., Sun. noon to 6 P.M.

ACCESSORIES & COLLECTIBLES

BARDITH I

1015 Madison Ave. (79th St.)
737-6699

This boutique's large selection of porcelain and china plates arrest the eye and attest to the owner's good taste. Collectors have long flocked here seeking 18th- and 19th-century English ware.
Mon.-Fri. 11 A.M. to 5:30 P.M.; closed Sat. in summer.

CHARLOTTE MOSS

131 East 70th St.
(Lexington & Park Aves.)
772-3320

If all of New York's interior designers were to agree on one thing, they would probably say that the accessories at Charlotte Moss are just right for capturing the English country look. Her on-target selections of prints, bird cages, bows, tassels, boxes and candlesticks make admirable and elegant statements by themselves or grouped.
Mon.-Fri. 11 A.M. to 5:30 P.M.

FUNCHIES, BUNKERS, GAKS & GLEEKS

1050 Second Ave. (55th St.)
980-9418

Its name may sound silly, but Funchies, Bunkers, Gaks & Gleeks is a delightful gallery with an authoritative collection of toys and nostalgia. Though the shop seems whimsical and its owner free as a breeze, beneath the apparent chaos is strong order. Items are organized by color, material, or subject; ask to see the album that catalogs hundreds of patchwork quilts. The counters are covered with regiments of soldiers, windup toys, mechanical banks, chocolate molds and the like, and the place is especially good for duck and goose decoys.
Mon.-Sat. 10:30 A.M. to 5:30 P.M., Sun. noon to 6 P.M.

LEO KAPLAN LTD.

967 Madison Ave. (75th & 76th Sts.)
249-6766

Specializing in four categories of accessories—Art Nouveau glass, 18th-century English pottery and porcelain, antique and contemporary paperweights, and Fabergé and Russian works of art—this family-owned business has a grand reputation as well as a grand assortment of quality items. Warm, personal attention makes separating you from your funds easy and pleasant.
Mon.-Sat. 10 A.M. to 5:30 P.M.

RITA FORD MUSIC BOXES

19 East 65th St. (Madison & Fifth Aves.)
535-6717

This store has been a favorite and an internationally known source for automatic music boxes for many years. Rita Ford offers a large inventory of affordable, jewelled, and intricately adorned antique and contemporary music boxes of all sizes and shapes. The most popular boxes are the antique Swiss, German, and French ones. Hand-crafted carousels are also favorites. Both the shopper in search of unusual gifts and the collector will find children's items, jewel boxes, and gold-encrusted wonders. The prices range from a paltry $13.50 to a shocking $75,000.
Mon.-Sat. 9 A.M. to 5 P.M.

RITA SACKS

1050 Second Ave. (55th St.)
421-8132

In this elegant, well-organized store, you'll find quality objects, including Art Nouveau, Art Deco, signed glass, and 20th-century costume jewelry. Rita is a cordial host who makes wonderful conversation, especially when it concerns her special hobby, collecting fakes.
Mon.-Sat. 10:30 A.M. to 6:30 P.M., Sun. noon to 6 P.M.

AMERICAN

AMERICAN HURRAH ANTIQUES

766 Madison Ave. (66th St.)
535-1930

With the ever-increasing interest in Americana at an all-time high, a family-owned and -operated business with a friendly atmosphere *and* authentic merchandise is a treasured contact. American Hurrah is one of those establishments. For almost two decades, the owners have taken their hobby of collecting bits and pieces of America's history and built it into a business. They personally select, repair, and restore each item. And double hurrahs for the selection of patchwork quilts, American Indian art, folk art, and paintings.
Tues.-Sat. 11 A.M. to 6 P.M.; closed Sat. in summer.

LAURA FISHER

1050 Second Ave., 2nd Fl. (55th St.)
838-2596

Laura Fisher, author of a reference book entitled *Quilts of Illusion*, is an authority on Americana. Her American gallery is a fantastic assemblage of baskets, tables, and such folk art as needlework, decoys, primitives, hooked rugs, quilts, and coverlets. She arranges for quilt repair and restoration and searches for antique textiles. Many of her items are found in major corporate collections.
Mon.-Sat. noon to 6 P.M.

THOMAS SCHWENKE INC.

956 Madison Ave. (75th St.)
772-7222

Since 1969, Schwenke has made available to the serious collector fine examples of American Federal furniture. Seek here for Chippendale, Heppelwhite, Sheraton, and even Pilgrim furniture, and you shall find it, all of the finest quality. There are William and Mary styles as well. Child's Gallery (772-6606), which shares the space, specializes in American paintings, prints, drawings, and watercolors.
Tues.-Sat. 11 A.M. to 6 P.M.; closed Aug.

ART DECO & ART NOUVEAU

ARTISAN ANTIQUES

*989 Second Ave. (52nd &
53rd Sts.)
751-5214*

This store houses the largest collection of French Art Deco lighting in the world. You'll find 1920's Art Deco frosted glass and metal chandeliers in profusion, along with wall sconces, lamps, period furniture, statues, and bronzes, most of which were imported here over 30 years ago. In the manner of Lalique, the lighting fixtures are beveled, shaped, etched, and raised.
Mon.-Sat. 10 A.M. to 6 P.M.

DELORENZO

*958 Madison Ave. (75th &
76th Sts.)
249-7575*

Objects rare, unique, and definitely in the French Art Deco tradition are carefully displayed in this well-known Madison Avenue store. The handsome collection of Art Deco sits side by side with more curvaceous European and Art Nouveau designs. All attest to the highly tuned taste of owner Delorenzo. For the serious collector of this genre, a visit is a must.
Mon.-Sat. 10 A.M. to 6 P.M.; closed Sat. in summer.

LILLIAN NASSAU LTD.

*220 East 57th St. (Second
& Third Aves.)
759-6062*

Carrying on the family tradition established years ago by his mother Lillian, Paul Nassau runs the store that's known to house one of the most extensive collections of Tiffany glass in the world. Plus, there are beautiful bronzes, European art pottery, and a broad range of Art Nouveau and Art Deco furniture.
*Mon.-Fri. 10 A.M. to 5 P.M., Sat. 10:30 A.M. to 5 P.M.;
closed Sat. in summer.*

MINNA ROSENBLATT LTD.

*844 Madison Ave. (69th
St.)
288-0250*

This tiny shop, with its beautiful glowing Tiffany and Art Nouveau shades, all precisely and tastefully displayed at staggered heights, has a profusion of glass. Stained glass reached a zenith of perfection in the Art Nouveau period, and Minna Rosenblatt presides over some of the best selections of this remarkable, decorative glass.
Mon.-Sat. 10 A.M. to 5:30 P.M.

PHILIP CHASEN GALLERY

This small shop beckons to passersby with a superb and colorful selection of Art Nouveau and Art Deco, including Tiffany, Galle, and Lalique. The owner and his associates are

1050 Second Ave. (55th
St.)
319-3233

knowledgeable and friendly. Other works to note are Han-
del, Rookwood, and Icart etchings.
*Mon.-Fri. 10:30 A.M. to 5:30 P.M., Sat. 1 P.M. to 5:30
P.M.*

PRIMAVERA

808 Madison Ave. (68th
St.)
288-1569

Primavera was one of the first stores in New York to
specialize in Art Deco; today many of its items have been
loaned or sold to major museums. Visitors will find pieces by
leading Deco designers on view. A fine collection of jewelry
is combined with a judicious selection of furniture. Its SoHo
gallery (at 133 Prince Street; 254-0137) specializes in 50's
decorations, postwar industrial design, and American mod-
ernistic jewelry.
Mon.-Fri. 11 A.M. to 6 P.M.

AUCTION HOUSES

It's one thing to wander through an antique store, perusing this and that;
it's quite another to feel the quickened pace of the auctioneer's cadence.
Unlike retail stores, auction houses do not buy property for resale; they
act as agents only. You'll find lively action and interesting antiques for
sale—going once, going twice—at New York's handful of top-drawer
auction houses.

CHRISTIE'S

502 Park Ave. (59th St.)
546-1000

Christie's has been selling fine art at auction for over 220
years. With offices worldwide, this venerable name in
auctioneering holds sales several times a week. Even the
doorman, Gil, has become a celebrity in his own right.
*Mon.-Fri. 9:00 A.M. to 5 P.M., Sun. 9:30 A.M. to 5 P.M.;
closed Sat. & Sun. in summer.*

CHRISTIE'S EAST

219 East 67th St. (Second
& Third Aves.)
606-0400

Christie's subsidiary auctions off less expensive merchandise
—furniture, art, glass, china, and paintings. Like its parent
company, it prints a catalog prior to the auction, and a sale
here is equally exciting and interesting.
*Mon.-Fri. 9:30 A.M. to 5 P.M., Sat. & Sun. 9:30 A.M. to 5
P.M. depending on auction; closed Sat. & Sun. in summer.*

PHILLIPS FINE ART AUCTIONEERS

406 East 79th St. (First & York Aves.)
570-4830

Located near the East River, this gallery has a substantial business worldwide. Offering a diverse set of auctions, it features mainly high-quality decorative arts, furniture, and paintings.
Mon.-Fri. 9 A.M. to 5 P.M.

SOTHEBY PARKE BERNET INC.

1334 York Ave. (72nd St.)
606-7000

A handsome building houses this important gallery, a coalition of Sotheby's and the former Madison Avenue Parke Bernet. Sotheby's is perhaps New York's most famous auction gallery in terms of gross sales; the media readily publicizes major purchases. Auctions are held frequently, and by category—for instance, rugs, silver, or furniture from a particular estate, country, or period. The sales are always lively and brisk; buyers are fierce in their acquisitiveness and determination. Viewing the auction collector at work is a theatrical experience: go for the drama of it all.
Mon.-Fri. 10 A.M. to 5 P.M.

SOTHEBY'S ARCADE AUCTIONS

1334 York Ave. (72nd St.)
606-7147

In addition to Sotheby's regularly scheduled specialized auctions, more than 30 Sotheby's Arcade Auctions are held during the year. These auctions, generally every other week, are an excellent venue for buying and selling less expensive collector's items and estate property.
Mon.-Sat. 9 A.M. to 4:30 P.M; closed Sat. in summer.

WILLIAM DOYLE GALLERIES

175 East 87th St. (Lexington & Third Aves.)
427-2730

According to sales, Doyle, an American-owned firm, is the third largest house in New York. For some reason, most likely the clientele, it can have some extraordinarily high prices. Watch for unusual estates that blend glamorous names with beautiful merchandise. Exhibitions are held on Mondays, Tuesdays, Wednesdays, and Saturdays.
Mon. 9 A.M. to 7:30 P.M., Tues. 9 A.M. to 5 P.M., Sat. 10 A.M. to 3 P.M., Sun. noon to 5 P.M.

CLOCKS

CLOCK HUTT LTD.

1050 Second Ave. (55th St.)
759-2395

This gallery has over 1,200 square feet of space, yet it still manages to overflow with an astonishing array of clocks that spill onto the promenade of the Manhattan Art and Antiques Center. The Hutt family has been in this business for some

21 years, and are known for their meticulous repairs. They have the largest collection of 18th- and 19th-century European and American clocks in New York.
Mon.-Sat. 10:30 A.M. to 5:30 P.M., Sun. noon to 5:30 P.M.

OLDIES, GOLDIES & MOLDIES

1609 Second Ave. (83rd & 84th Sts.)
737-3935

Until recently the bulk of this store's inventory was Victorian and turn-of-the-century objects, along with an extensive collection of memorabilia. Now it's clocks, and you'll find all kinds of them—neon, radio, you name it. Ronald Reagan purchased one here in 1986. Wide variety and warm, personal attention are good reasons to shop here.
Mon.-Fri. noon to 8 P.M., Sat. 11 A.M. to 7 P.M., Sun. 11 A.M. to 6 P.M.

BERGER-COLE ANTIQUE CLOCKS

29 East 12th St. (University Pl. & Fifth Ave.)
929-1830

You can purchase almost any kind of clock here, but the bulk of the business is in clock restoration and repair. Dealers, museums, and private collectors attest to Mr. Berger's expertise. Don't hesitate to entrust your cherished timepiece to his care.
Tues.-Fri. noon to 6 P.M., Sat. noon to 4 P.M.; or by appointment.

ENGLISH

ARTHUR ACKERMANN & SON INC.

50 East 57th St. (Park & Madison Aves.)
753-5292

Long established at this address between Madison and Fifth, Arthur Ackermann & Son has a reputation as the undisputed leader in resources for 18th-century English furniture. The gallery is still a place to find extraordinary equestrian delights mingled with English accessories and fine furnishings. If you have trouble findng English antiques in England, come here.
Mon.-Fri. 9 A.M. to 5 P.M., Sat. 9 A.M. to 4 P.M.; closed Sat. July & Aug.

JUDITH AMDUR ANTIQUES

950 Lexington Ave. (69th & 70th Sts.)
472-2691

There are no adjoining doors between this Amdur shop and Amdur Antiques on 1129 Lexington Ave. (879-0652), but they are definitely his and hers antique stores. Each one is filled with small English furniture and accessories, including trays, tables, candlesticks, vases—beautiful objects of a diversified nature.
Mon.-Sat. 11 A.M. to 6 P.M. (both stores)

FLORIAN PAPP INC.

*962 Madison Ave. (75th &
76th Sts.)
288-6770*

A visit to Florian Papp is a must for any serious collector. Specializing in 18th-century English furniture, this store was the first antique store of its kind to open in New York, and it remains one of the very best today. Since the start of the century, it has offered such quality decorative pieces as grandfather clocks and gleaming mirrors, as well a fine assortment of American and Colonial pieces.
*Mon.-Fri. 9:30 A.M. to 5:30 P.M., Sat. 10 A.M. to 5 P.M.;
closed Sat. in summer.*

KENTSHIRE GALLERIES LTD.

*37 East 12th St.
(University Pl. &
Broadway)
673-6644*

Kentshire has added a new collector's gallery for antique collectibles in cut crystal, porcelain, silver, and tortoise shell from the Georgian, Regency, and later periods. The larger, elegant gallery still has its usual magnificent wood furniture, floor after floor of gleaming old antiques—all in all, a remarkable selection, and in excellent condition. Prices are high, but so is the quality.
*Mon.-Fri. 9 A.M. to 5 P.M., Sat. 9:30 A.M. to 2 P.M.;
closed Sat. in summer.*

TILLER & KING LTD.

*1058 Madison Ave. (80th
St.)
988-2861*

For authentic 18th- and 19th-century English and American furniture, visit Tiller and King. Accessories of all types emphasize a deft collection of beautiful furnishings. Period lamps are the store's specialty.
Mon.-Sat. 10 A.M. to 5:30 P.M.; closed Sat. July & Aug.

EUROPEAN

BETTY JANE BART ANTIQUES

*1225 Madison Ave. (88th
& 89th Sts.)
410-2702*

Open for only six years, this tiny shop, tucked away inconspicuously in the middle of the block, deals in marvelous 17th- and 18th-century European antiques. Betty specializes in Italian and Spanish items, but carries some French pieces as well. She favors furniture and things whimsical, such as puppets and amusing bird cages. Her painted furniture (with its original paint) is eminently collectible, as are her many decorative screens, although they do sell quickly.
Mon.-Sat. 11 A.M. to 5 P.M., closed Fri. & Sat. in summer.

KURT GLUCKSELIG ANTIQUES INC.

This 108-year gallery was originally established in Austria. Owner Kurt Gluckselig currently sits on the Board of Directors of the Appraisers Association of America. His store

1050 Second Ave. (55th
St.)
758-1805

specializes in 16th- to 19th-century porcelain, French furni-
ture, and paintings, and customers include the Metropolitan
Museum of Art.
Mon.-Sat. 10:30 A.M. to 5:15 P.M.; closed Sat. in summer.

LINDA HORN ANTIQUES & DECORATIVE OBJECTS

1015 Madison Ave. (78th
& 79th Sts.)
772-1122

Displayed in a fairytale setting, the antiques in this new
location are romantically reminiscent of the turn of the
century. The former New York store was painted to resemble the ruins of Pompeii; this one, full of trompe l'oeil by
Russian artist Ilya Schevel, evokes the atmosphere of a
garden. The store features dramatic selections favored by
Linda Horn—a grouping of some 300 bulldogs atop a
massive chest, and animal forms everywhere: snakes, frogs,
toads, even a bat sconce.
Mon.-Sat. 10 A.M. to 6 P.M.; closed Sat. July & Aug.

THE LITTLE ANTIQUE SHOP

44 East 11th St.
(University Pl. &
Broadway)
673-5173

Large, larger, and largely wonderful is a way to describe the
highly unusual, highly decorative, and often highly priced
objects that are glamorously displayed throughout this "little
antique shop." The name belies the truth, and the quality
and unique aura of many of the pieces command attention.
This is an eclectic collection of impressive quality, with
particularly outstanding Oriental pieces.
Mon.-Fri. 9 A.M. to 5 P.M.

PIERRE DEUX

367 Bleecker St. (Charles
St.)
243-7740
870 Madison Ave. (71st
St.)
570-9343

Les deux Pierre Deux have long been famous for introducing
America to the charms of rustic French provincial style.
Pierre Deux's antique furniture is now being reproduced for
a mass market, but it still retains its simple purity, whether
stripped or stained. Here you will find a potpourri of
furniture, accessories, and fabrics, all affordable.
Mon.-Sat. 10 A.M. to 6 P.M.; closed Sat. July & Aug.

*Mon.-Sat. 10 A.M. to 6 P.M., Sat. 10 A.M. to 5 P.M; closed
Sat. July & Aug.*

ORIENTAL

ART ASIA INC.

Twenty-seven years in the business assure us that the collectibles that fill this shop are chosen with a practiced eye.
Jewelry from the Orient, Indian miniatures, fine chests, and

1086 Madison Ave. (81st &
82nd Sts.)
249-7250

reasonably priced porcelains are available as room accents. The store's bounty is decorative and definitely mixable with items from different periods.

Mon.-Sat. 10 A.M. to 6 P.M., Sun. noon to 6 P.M.

DORIS LESLIE BLAU INC.

15 East 57th St. (Fifth &
Madison Aves.)
759-3715

The Blau gallery is stocked with Oriental and European tapestries and rugs of exemplary quality and distinction. For over 15 years, the owner has specialized in rare rugs, carpets, and textilles from the 17th to the early 20th centuries. Here one finds antique floor coverings of all types—Turkish, Caucasian, European, Indian, Chinese, and, of course, Persian.

By appointment only.

E & J FRANKEL LTD.

1020 Madison Ave. (79th
& 80th Sts.)
879-5733

A skilled eye for collecting, a wide range of items, and undisputed scholarship combine to create an unusually attractive Chinese and Japanese art gallery. There are splendid bronzes, delicate jewelry, furniture and paintings of excellent design and quality, and lovely robes, instruments, and jade—artifacts dating from the year 5000 B.C. to the present.

Mon.-Sat. 10 A.M. to 5 P.M.

FLYING CRANES ANTIQUES

1050 Second Ave. (55th
St.)
223-4600

Curator Clifford Schaefer regularly assists *Metropolitan Home*'s Dr. Swatch with answers about Oriental art objects. Indeed, Japanese collectors who are familiar with his reputation regularly come—from Japan—to his New York gallery for fine 18th- and 19th-century Japanese furniture, ivories, and silver.

Mon.-Fri. 11 A.M. to 6 P.M., Sat. 11 A.M. to 5:45 P.M.

KOREANA ART & ANTIQUES

963 Madison Ave. (75th &
76th Sts.)
249-0400

Displayed in room settings, Korean art and antiques are tastefully arranged, as if in a home. The owner, an artist and collector, has carried out authentic Korean designs in the displays. There is a wide selection of woods, paintings, and ceramics as well, dating from the 18th and 19th centuries.

Mon.-Sat. 10 A.M. to 6 P.M.

REPAIRS

If it is expensive to buy antiques, so too is it to have them repaired. But many beautiful items are worth the cost, and we've found a few places for you to take your valuables without fear of their becoming further damaged.

CERAMICS

SANO STUDIO

767 Lexington Ave., 4th Fl.
(60th & 61st Sts.)
759-6131

For over a decade, repairs have been skillfully made by owner Jadwiga Baran, who repairs all types of ceramics for prices that range from $25 to $2,500 and up. Ask for a free estimate; for a fee of $25, she'll also provide insurance appraisals.
Mon.-Fri. 9:30 A.M. to 5 P.M.

HESS REPAIRS

200 Park Ave. South, 15th
Fl. (17th St.)
260-2255

Bernie Hirsch has spent over 40 years doing repairs, many for our city's museums. Jobs start at $17.50. This family of Russian immigrants works together closely on all projects.
Mon.-Fri. 10:30 A.M. to 4 P.M.

CHANDELIERS

ANTHONY BAZZA RESTORATIONS

315 East 62nd St. (First &
Second Aves.)
755-1179

Mr. Bazza will clean, refurbish, and rewire such metals as iron, brass, and tin, as well as crystal chandeliers. He can replace silver chandeliers and polish copper and brass; he also custom makes chandeliers. All services have waiting lists several months long, but it's worth the wait.
Mon.-Fri. 8 A.M. to 4 P.M.

GEM MONOGRAM

623 Broadway (Houston &
Bleecker Sts.)
674-8960

Gem will clean crystal chandeliers in your home. It provides a full range of services for glass and metal fixtures, including replating brass, silver, or gold, and the staff can replace broken metal ends. There's a wait for all work except cleaning.
Mon.-Fri. 9 A.M. to 5 P.M.

FURNITURE

SOTHEBY'S RESTORATION

440 East 91st St. (First &
York Aves.)
860-5446

This division of Sotheby Parke Bernet is a workshop for conservation and restoration of fine furniture, including a full-time metal foundry and a finishing center for japanning, lacquering, gilding, and polishing. Sotheby's has only one requirement: that the piece, whether furniture or a work of art, be at least 100 years old. Work can be done at the client's home. On-site work runs $300 for a half-day and $550 for a

347

full day; an estimate costs $50 (whether you bring the piece in or have them visit) and is deducted from the cost of the restoration. Sotheby's can also refer you elsewhere for metal, glass, and porcelain repairs.
Mon.-Fri. 8 A.M. to 4 P.M.

Beauty & Health

APOTHECARY

BIGELOW PHARMACY

414 Ave. of the Americas (8th & 9th Sts.)
533-2700

This pharmacy hasn't budged from this location since 1838, which makes it one of the oldest apothecaries in the country —and an official New York landmark. No wonder—the fine oak showcases, light and gas fixtures, stained glass, and mosaic floor are all original and lovely. The merchandise is far from cobwebby; in fact, the inventory changes constantly. In addition to reliable pharmaceuticals, makeup artists are available to do makeovers for free with purchases of at least $25 worth of skin products.
Mon.-Fri. 7:30 A.M. to 9 P.M., Sat. 8:30 A.M. to 7 P.M., Sun. 9 A.M. to 5:30 P.M.

CASWELL-MASSEY

518 Lexington Ave. (48th St.)
755-2254

Though established in 1752, this midtown apothecary is no musty old shop. With its cut glass jars, mirrors, and dark wood cases, the U.S.'s oldest chemist and perfume company is still going strong. Many of the items come from all over the world. You'll find oils, fragrances, potpourri, rice powder, face powder, huge sponges, loofahs, whale nail files, and even assorted flavors of snuff. The selection of soaps is extensive, to say the least, and includes ones made with rainwater, seaweed, lettuce, and tomato. The almond cream soap and cucumber products are famous. The shop still stocks straight razors from France and pomander balls similar to those used in the 17th century. Other locations at Herald Center, 1 Herald Square (244-0411), and South Street Seaport (608-5401).
Mon.-Fri. 10 A.M. to 7 P.M., Sat. 10 A.M. to 8 P.M., Sun. noon to 5 P.M.

KIEHL'S PHARMACY INC.

109 Third Ave. (13th & 14th Sts.)
677-3171

Visiting this wonderful little apothecary is like stepping back into time. Magical colored potions and powerfully scented dried flowers and herbs make this an exotic health and beauty wonderland. There are also rose water eau de toilettes with petals at the bottom, mystical henna, and an incredible collection of homemade skin-care products to treat everything from dry skin to dandruff. White-aproned pharmacists will prepare and suggest a natural treatment for almost any beauty ailment. Prices are comparable to those of any department-store beauty counter line, yet you get so much more.
Mon.-Fri. 10 A.M. to 6 P.M., Sat. 10 A.M. to 4:30 P.M.

BEAUTY & HAIR SALONS

ASTOR PLACE HAIR DESIGNERS

2 Astor Pl. (Broadway)
475-9854

Walk down to the Village and stroll along Astor Place, and chances are you'll see a line that stretches out a shop door, into the street, and around the corner. Amazingly enough, that queue is for a haircut. Not any haircut, either, but one of the infamous and cheap—only eight to ten bucks—Astor Place cuts. Yuppies, punks, and grandparents alike all stop here. If you don't instruct the barbers, expect a generic cut. But the mere suggestion of freedom and creative juices run wild: crewcuts and mohawks are among the more mundane.
Mon.-Sat. 8 A.M. to 8 P.M., Sun. 9 A.M. to 6 P.M.

BRUNO LE SALON

16 West 57th St., 3rd Fl.
(Fifth & Sixth Aves.)
581-2760

You are greeted by an electronic message board and a human receptionist behind the desk. Suddenly, you hear a name called over the P.A. system and a person arrives from nowhere to whisk you away to a private cubicle. No, this isn't some futuristic bureaucratic office, but an efficient and chic salon run by the Italian master hairstylist Bruno himself. The stylists don't believe in imposing their own styles on you, but rather create a look that's free and manageable, and most important, one that you feel comfortable with.
Mon.-Sat. 9 A.M. to 6 P.M., Thurs. till 7 P.M., Sat. 9 A.M. to 4 P.M.

CHRISTINE VALMY

Below the hustle and bustle of Fifth Avenue lies this calm, small salon dedicated solely to the care of skin of all shades for both men and women. There's a wide range of facial

767 Fifth Ave., Concourse Level (58th & 59th Sts.)
752-0303

treatments, including the patented skin-renewal treatment for teenagers and adults, which alternates between machines and the internationally renowned Valmy homeopathic skin-care products. After an in-depth skin analysis, a specialist will blend the Valmy products in the minilab on the premises, creating a home skin-care program that's exactly right for you. Other services offered include full- and mini-body massages, manicures, pedicures, and makeup lessons. An all-inclusive Valmy day (even lunch is served) is $200. Two other locations at 1 Rockefeller Plaza and 101 West 57th Street, 2nd Floor.
Mon. & Tues. 10 A.M. to 6 P.M., Wed. & Fri. 10 A.M. to 7 P.M., Thurs. 11 A.M. to 7 P.M., Sat. 9 A.M. to 5 P.M.

ELIZABETH ARDEN SALON

691 Fifth Ave. (54th St.)
407-1000

You can definitely leave this salon a different woman. It is best known for its "Maine Chance" day, named after Elizabeth Arden's former resort in Maine—a six- to seven-hour experience in which you'll be remade from crown to toe, starting with an exercise class and continuing with a body massage, face treatment, hair styling, manicure, pedicure, light lunch, and makeover. Total cost is $208; you must book several months in advance for a Saturday. Or try a half-day package: Miracle Morning (massage, face treatment, hair, and manicure) or Visible Difference (face treatment, hair, manicure, and makeup lesson), both for $156. Individual services are also available à la carte, including body waxing, makeup lessons, and a deep cleansing, non-depilatory paraffin bath. There are seven floors, five of service and two of merchandise that ranges from Arden's own makeup to quality sportswear and haute couture.
Mon.-Sat. 9 A.M. to 5:30 P.M., Thurs. till 8 P.M.

GEORGETTE KLINGER

501 Madison Ave. (76th St.)
838-3200

Georgette Klinger offers pampering services that include facials, massages, hair and scalp treatments, and makeovers. The facials are luxurious 90-minute treatments where a specialist cleans and massages your face, prepares a steaming pot of camomile and a potpourri of other therapeutic herbs, clears your face of blemishes, and finally treats you with two masks designed for your particular skin type. Klinger also offers manicures and pedicures as well as exercise and nutrition classes. Another location at 978 Madison Avenue (744-6900).
Mon.-Fri. 9 A.M. to 6 P.M., Tues. & Thurs. till 8 P.M., Sat. 9 A.M. to 5 P.M.

KENNETH

19 East 54th St. (Fifth &
Madison Aves.)
752-1800

Kenneth is as different from ordinary salons as New York is from Des Moines. The attention, pampering, and professionalism that Kenneth offers his clients is apparent from the moment the chauffeur picks you up and whisks you to the exquisitely decorated townhouse to be greeted by name by the doorman and the rest of the staff. And all this before you've changed into a dressing gown and been escorted to your stylist. The four floors contain two main rooms where the 22 stylists work, as well as numerous well-appointed private rooms. You may have your manicure where and when you choose, because the manicurist assigned to you will follow you from floor to floor depending on the other services you are taking advantage of. When you're all finished, you can be made up by one of two makeup artists using Kenneth's own line of cosmetics. There is a separate men's salon on the main floor. All the services, except coloring, are available in your own home.
Mon.-Fri. 9 A.M. to 6 P.M., Wed. till 9 P.M.

MAKE-UP CENTER

150 West 55th St. (Sixth
& Seventh Aves.)
977-9494

Enter this store and get a glimpse of Broadway. Located across the street from City Center and right near the theater district, the Make-Up Center is frequented by many artists who purchase this makeup for both professional and personal use. Well-known theatrical makeup by Bob Klien and Stein's can be found at affordable prices. A 15% discount is offered to those with a theatrical union card. The affordable services include a makeover and lesson for $25, a facial for $30, and eyelash dying, waxing, manicures, and pedicures.
Mon.-Fri. 10 A.M. to 6 P.M., Thurs. till 8 P.M., Sat 10 A.M. to 5 P.M.

RICHARD STEIN SALON

768 Madison Ave. (65th &
66th Sts.)
879-3663

Richard Stein has developed his worldwide reputation by combining elegance and individuality with easy maintenance. He has expanded his operation with his Fleuremedy brand hair-care products—shampoo, conditioner, spritz, and pomade—which contain extracts of natural flowers and oils. There are also facials, manicures, makeup sessions, and waxing. Haircuts start at $55 and go up to a whopping $175 for an initial visit with the master himself.
Tues.-Sat. 9 A.M. to 5 P.M.

SUGA

This sleek, mirrored, white and gray salon, run by the renowned Japanese stylist Suga, concentrates only on hair

*115 East 57th St. (Park &
Lexington Aves.)
421-4400*

and nails. A cut by Suga is $150 and others start at $45 (not including shampoo and blow-dry).
Mon.-Sat. 9 A.M. to 6 P.M., Wed. till 8 P.M.

VIDAL SASSOON

*767 Fifth Ave. (58th &
59th Sts.)
535-9200*

This innovative hair salon for men and women continues to live up to its reputation as a source for excellent haircuts. Although its roots are in London, members of the team are not only from England, but also Germany, Nicaragua, and Spain, among other countries. High school students, children under 12, and airline stewardesses all receive a 30% discount. Others who are budget conscious can have their hair done by closely supervised cutters-in-training for a fraction of the regular fee.
Mon.-Sat. 8:30 A.M. to 5 P.M., Thurs. till 7 P.M.

HEALTH CLUBS

BODY BY JAKE NEW YORK

*160 East 56th St., 5th Fl.
(Lexington & Third Aves.)
759-5253*

Everything about this exercise studio exudes energy—from the lively hand-lettered signs announcing new classes to the bouncy, fit instructors wearing Body by Jake T-shirts. Although the trendy outfits of the clientele may indicate otherwise, this is not an aerobics studio. Instead, the focus is on non-impact (your feet don't leave the floor), calisthenic, and isometric exercises that leave your body lean and mean. All classes are led by a trained instructor who is guaranteed to motivate (the loud music doesn't hurt either), as well as an assistant who walks around the studio correcting form. In addition to this workout, there are yoga and stretch classes that improve flexibility and a weight room membership plan for just $25 a month, with unlimited use of their weights and exercise machines. Jake, by the way, does exist; owner Jake Steinfeld spends most of his time in L.A., where he serves as a personal trainer to such luminaries as Priscilla Presley, Steven Spielberg, and Margot Kidder.
Mon.-Fri. 7:30 A.M. to 7:45 P.M., Sat. & Sun. 9 A.M. to 4:30 P.M.

THE EXERCISE EXCHANGE

*236 West 78th St.
(Broadway)
595-6475*

The guiding theory behind this studio is that all bodies are not created equal, and there is no single "right" regimen— so the aerobic, stretch and tone, workout, and exercise classes incorporate the best from a variety of techniques, including yoga, Nickolaus, and Pilate. They teach exercise in such a way that you learn about and understand your body from the inside out. You'll learn correct positioning as well as your own limits and potential, enabling you to continue exercising correctly for the rest of your life. Jean-Paul Mustone, the director of this studio, has tried to eliminate as many of the excuses used for not exercising as possible. You won't be able to say you can't make the times, because he holds classes every day of the year except Christmas. Don't think you can afford to keep in shape? Think again! The prices are among the most reasonable in New York City, with discounts for college students and performing arts professionals. It costs $9 for a single class, $75 for ten, and $140 for 20. Now that's reasonable!

Mon.-Fri. 7 A.M. to 8:30 P.M., Sat. 9 A.M. to 4:30 P.M., Sun. 10 A.M. to 3:30 P.M.

EXERCISE PLUS

19 East 48th St., 4th Fl. (Fifth & Madison Aves.) 935-2677

Don't expect to find lots of svelte women in shiny leotards jumping around the studio. Instead, you'll see women on their backs, carrying an extra load (a baby), working out in a low-key but vigorous fashion. Exercise Plus programs are designed to help women keep in shape at precisely the time they tend to feel most out of shape. Emphasis is on abdominal strength and proper breathing to complement Lamaze techniques. Classes are divided into prenatal and postpartum groups, and in addition to the training, they are an excellent, supportive meeting ground for women to share their feelings about pregnancy and motherhood. Free babysitting on the premises enables new mothers to enjoy a carefree hour of exercise and fun. One month (eight classes) is $95, six months (50 classes) is $395, and one year (100 classes) is $600. There are also unlimited classes for $160 a month.

Mon.-Thurs. 9:30 A.M. to 7:30 P.M., Fri. 9:30 A.M. to 3:30 P.M., Sat. 10:30 A.M. to 1:30 P.M; closed Sat. in summer.

LOTTE BERK METHOD LTD.

23 East 67th St. (Fifth & Madison Aves.) 288-6613

Russian dancer Lotte Berk developed the method taught here to women only. It's based on strenuous movements to stretch and strengthen muscles, with particular attention on the abdominals. For women with lower back or posture problems, or women who just want to tone their bodies, these safe exercises extract the best from ballet, modern dance, yoga, and orthopedic theory. Individual classes or memberships available.

Mon.-Fri. 7:45 A.M. to 7:30 P.M., Sat. 10 A.M. to 1 P.M.

353

New York Health & Racquet Club

*110 West 56th St. (Sixth
& Seventh Aves.)
541-7200*

Members of the NYH&RC can use any of the seven locations to take advantage of the plethora of facilities, services, and activities offered by this expansive, complete club. Among the basic facilities are a pool, whirlpool, steam rooms, sauna, tanning booths, tennis, racquetball, international racquetball, and squash. The exercise equipment is equally varied, including Nautilus, Ergometers, Eagle Cybex, Kaiser-Cam, Lifecycles, Liferowers, and old-fashioned free weights. Each member is prescribed an individualized exercise regime that is constantly updated. One-on-one training is also available. There are also ongoing classes in calisthenics, karate, aerobics, low-impact aerobics, and ballroom and tap dancing. You can also attend a nutrition class, a quit-smoking program, or a weight-control seminar. Call the above number for other Manhattan locations.
Mon.-Fri. 7 A.M. to 10 P.M., Sat. & Sun. 10 A.M. to 6 P.M.

Sports Training Institute

*239 East 49th St. (Second
& Third Aves.)
752-7111*

The first thing you should know is that while STI is concerned with your health, it's not a club. The clients, mostly midtown business people, work one-on-one with personal trainers for 45-minute sessions, then shower and leave. No one hangs out; besides the exercise and locker rooms, there's no place to. STI is serious. To begin with, you can't be accepted without a physician's written clearance. Then you are evaluated by a staff member, 95% of whom have or are working toward a master's degree in exercise physiology. They compile your fitness profile and arrange a training schedule (three appointments a week are recommended) that emphasizes strength, endurance, power, flexibility, and aerobic training.
Mon.-Fri. 6 A.M. to 9 P.M., Sat. 10 A.M. to 6 P.M; closed Sat. in summer.

The Vertical Club

*330 East 61st St. (First &
Second Aves.)
355-5100*

The Vertical Club is one of the largest gyms in the United States, and certainly the largest facility in New York City. It has over 300 pieces of equipment, including Nautilus, Universal, Paramount, Kaiser, free weights, Lifecycles, and Stair-Masters. In addition to the largest indoor track in the city, The Vertical Club offers a swimming pool, whirlpools, steam and sauna rooms, squash, racquetball, tennis, massage, aerobics, a sun deck, tanning facilities, a juice bar, and a restaurant. Two types of memberships are available: executive, which includes everything, or a tennis membership exclusively for tennis players.

Mon.-Fri. 6 A.M. to 10:30 P.M., Sat. & Sun. 9 A.M. to 8:30 P.M.

SCENTS

CRABTREE & EVELYN

620 Fifth Ave. (49th & 50th Sts.)
581-5022

The East Side is fortunate to have a source for wonderful Crabtree & Evelyn toiletries, which are delightfully perfumed with herbs, flowers, and fruits. This boutique is crammed with powders, soaps, creams, toothpastes, handdrawn brushes, tins, and baskets. It also has a varied choice of comestibles, including jams, jellies, sauces (chutney, mustard), honey, spices, chocolates, cookies, biscuits, teas, and other gourmet items from the countrysides of England and Europe.

Mon.-Sat. 10 A.M. to 6 P.M.

JEAN LAPORTE

870 Madison Ave. (70th & 71st Sts.)
517-8665

Follow your nose, as the saying goes: In this small, meticulously kept shop, you're instantly bombarded by the combination of the French parfumerie's eau de toilettes. Jean Laporte's inspiration comes from the scents of flowers, fruits, woods, and spices, which he carefully combines into novel, subtle fragrances, such as Eau d'Oranger (néroli, orange, jasmine), Orchidée Blanche (a bouquet of iris, ambergris, honey, and vanilla), and Bois Epicés (spicy woods). Also sold are amber sachets, a unique terra-cotta amber ball, unusual contemporary jewelry, antique perfume bottles, and burning oils. The *Livre des Senteurs* (Book of Scents), containing eight small bottles of different scents, serves as an olfactory bible.

Mon.-Sat. 10 A.M. to 6 P.M.

Books

APPLAUSE THEATRE BOOKS

This comfy, spacious bookstore is tucked away in a sunken plaza. It offers a complete stock of all theater titles—plays, criticism, biographies, and how-to books. Theater magazines

*211 West 71st St.
(Broadway & West End
Ave.)
496-7511*

can also be found, and Applause Theater publishes its own line of plays and useful books for the actor. Also worth visiting is its sister shop, Applause Cinema Books, at 100 West 67th Street (787-8858).
Mon.-Sat. 10 A.M. to 8 P.M., Sun. noon to 6 P.M.

ARGOSY BOOKSTORE

*116 East 59th St. (Park &
Lexington Aves.)
753-4455*

What a pleasure it is to leave the surrounding 20th-century street scene for this store's Dickensian setting, exemplified by green lampshades, wood paneling, and old leather bindings. The rare and used books are organized by subject, and there's virtually everything imaginable. By appointment only, you can also purchase or browse through the oodles of letters and signed photographs in the autograph department, and see the selection of choice modern first editions.
Mon.-Fri. 9 A.M. to 6 P.M., Sat. 10 A.M. to 5 P.M.; closed Sat. Dec. to May.

BARNES & NOBLE BOOK STORE

*105 Fifth Ave. (18th St.)
807-0099*

Barnes & Noble is a great store for general book browsing, with its three million hardcovers, paperbacks, and new and used textbooks arranged in a huge space with lots of elbow room. Though Barnes & Noble's extensive medical and nursing department is famous, you'll also find engineering, business, reference, and craft books; computer books and software; high school and college outlines: and study aids. The Sale Annex across the street contains thousands of bargains—best-sellers, current fiction and nonfiction, children's books, paperbacks, publishers' overstocks and more, at well below list price. Call the above number for other store locations in the city.
Mon.-Fri. 9:30 A.M. to 9 P.M., Sat 9:30 A.M. to 7 P.M., Sun 11 A.M. to 6 P.M.

THE BIOGRAPHY BOOKSHOP

*400 Bleecker St. (11th St.)
807-8655*

This is the only bookstore in New York specializing in biographies, autobiographies, diaries, letters, journals, and travelogues. All the well-known titles are stocked here, as are the smaller and more obscure presses, university presses, and British and foreign imports. You can also buy black-and-white postcards of famous authors and fun paper doll cut-out books—for only $3, you can dress Pope John Paul II, Greta Garbo, Vivien Leigh, or Princess Di.
Tues.-Fri. 1 P.M. to 9 P.M., Sat. noon to 10 P.M., Sun. noon to 5:30 P.M.

DOUBLEDAY BOOK SHOP

724 Fifth Ave. (57th St.)
397-0550

From the outside, Doubleday doesn't have the allure of Rizzoli or Scribner's, but the store is unquestionably a reader's paradise, whether you are looking for something in particular or just looking. This enormous store stocks a fine, broad selection of hardcovers and paperbacks. The paperback fiction section is especially appealing, as it manages to highlight both contemporary novels and the classics. Browsers can move around here; there's lots of space between shelves and a wide staircase to take you to the basement and second floor. The glass elevator is a nice touch, calling your attention to the store's well-lit and extensively stocked space. Call the above number for other store locations in the city.
Mon.-Sat. 9 A.M. to midnight, Sun. noon to 5 P.M.

GOTHAM BOOK MART & GALLERY

41 West 47th St. (Fifth & Sixth Aves.)
719-4448

"Wise Men Fish Here" has been the motto of this bookstore for 65 years. Frances Steloff, who started the store with a $100 loan and a $100 Liberty Bond, is a legend in these parts. A strong opponent of censorship long before such opposition was fashionable, she helped launch the careers of such literary giants as D.H. Lawrence and Henry Miller by selling their books when no one else would. Unlike the modern-day bookstore, where titles are neatly categorized, Gotham Book Mart is often in a state of frenzy, but the staff knows their way around. Chances are if you request a title, they'll not only have it among their half-million collection, but they'll be able to effortlessly find it. Rare first editions can also be retrieved here. The gallery, with changing exhibits, is upstairs.
Mon.-Fri. 9:30 A.M. to 6:30 P.M., Sat. 9:30 A.M.to 6 P.M.

J.N. BARTFIELD BOOKS & GALLERY

30 West 57th St. (Fifth & Sixth Aves.)
245-8890

Visit one of New York's most fascinating book shops and peruse an incredible variety of antiquarian books. Fine bindings, rare books, and sets and singles of Dickens, Twain, Shakespeare, and other famous authors vie for your attention. You'll find color-plate books, paintings, atlases, first editions of course, and sporting books galore. The owners say they have the largest collection of "old worthwhile books"; we say it's worthwhile to make a trip here.
Mon.-Fri. 9 A.M. to 5 P.M., Sat. by appointment only.

KITCHEN ARTS & LETTERS

A store couldn't be more appropriately named; this is the cook's Rizzoli and Gotham rolled into one. There's even a kitchen in the back where authors sometimes hold demon-

1435 Lexington Ave. (93rd
& 94th Sts.)
876-5550

strations. The books are well organized by both subject
(wine, bread, pasta, etc.) and region. But it's more fun if you
don't know what you're looking for; that way you're likely to
come across the collection of old cookbooks and promotion-
al recipe booklets, which should be savored for the illustra-
tions alone. Don't forget to check the bulletin board on your
way out for an update on cooking news, announcements, and
events.
*Mon. 1 P.M. to 6 P.M., Tues., Wed. & Fri. 10 A.M. to 6:30
P.M., Thurs. 10 A.M. to 8 P.M., Sat. 11 A.M. to 6 P.M.*

LIBRARIE DE FRANCE
LIBRERIA HISPANICA

610 Fifth Ave. (49th &
50th Sts.)
581-8810

What was once a meeting ground for French tourists now
gives equal time to Spaniards. Stocking roughly one million
books in French, Spanish, and other non-English languages,
Librarie de France has one of the largest collections of
foreign language books in the United States. It also carries
dailies, periodicals, records, and calendars, and has a second
location at 45 Fifth Ave (673-7400).
Mon.-Sat. 9:30 A.M. to 6:15 P.M.

MADISON AVENUE
BOOKSHOP

833 Madison Ave. (69th &
70th Sts.)
535-6130

This is a serious bookshop for devoted fans of the printed
word. Current fiction and all that's new or important in art,
poetry, philosophy, and literary criticism can be found here.
The staff is knowledgeable and bends over backward to assist
you, whether it's to select a gift or merely find something on
the crowded second floor. The spindly spiral staircase is used
to hold the overflow of books, making the trip up or down a
somewhat scary experience. It's a book browser's delight; be
prepared to dawdle.
Mon.-Sat. 10 A.M. to 6 P.M.; closed Sat. in summer.

THE MILITARY
BOOKMAN

29 East 93rd St. (Fifth &
Madison Aves.)
348-1280

Where can you find over ten thousand titles covering every
aspect of military, aviation, and naval history? The Military
Bookman, of course! This is the only bookstore in New York
with books filed by war—from ancient battles right up
through Vietnam. The Military Bookman also deals in rare
and out-of-print books on such topics as Strategy and
Tactics, Armored Vehicles, and Espionage.
Tues.-Sat. 10:30 A.M. to 5:30 P.M.

THE RARE BOOK
ROOM

Once upon a time, Greenwich Avenue was filled, virtually
door to door, with rare-book stores. Today, Roger and
Irvyne Richards' Rare Book Room is the only one left on the

125 Greenwich Ave.
(Seventh & Eighth Aves.)
206-6766

block, and one of the few left in the city. Contemporary and 19th-century signed novels are the specialty. Also evident is an astounding selection of signed celebrities' old photographs, the prize of which is a 1912, pre-film photo of Charles Chaplin ($650). Contemporary authors include Joseph Heller, Gore Vidal, Graham Greene, Tennessee Williams, Truman Capote, Gertrude Stein, Ernest Hemingway, and more. There are a few copies of the first Webster Dictionary from 1828, that sell for $3,000. The oldest work in the shop is a Shakespeare reader, dated approximately 1648, for $10,000.
Tues.-Sat. 1 P.M. to 8 P.M.

RIZZOLI BOOKSTORE

31 West 57th St. (Fifth &
Sixth Aves.)
759-2424

You might want to put Rizzoli on your museum list. Plan to spend a lot of time in this sophisticated bookstore with its rich, wood-paneled walls, domed ceiling, chandeliers, and perfect displays. If the ambience doesn't transform you, the art section will. You'll also find European newspapers and magazines, classical, jazz, and new-age records, and an exquisite section of Penguin paperbacks. Anything you purchase here, even if it can be found at a hundred other bookstores, will feel special.
Mon.-Sat. 10 A.M. to 10 P.M., Sun. noon to 8 P.M.

STRAND BOOK STORE

828 Broadway (12th St.)
473-1452

As the best of New York City's used-book stores, Strand's selection is literally overwhelming. In addition to over one million used books, there are new books, some rare ones and—for half-price—reviewers' copies in mint condition. Shipments of brand-new books arrive daily, so it makes sense to "know thine author," as warns a sign here. In the basement are stacks (and more stacks) of yesteryear's bestsellers. On the main floor, books are arranged by topic. The best deals are on the tables in front.
Mon.-Fri. 9:30 A.M. to 9:30 P.M., Sat. 9:30 A.M. to 6:25 P.M., Sun. 11 A.M. to 5 P.M.

ZEN ORIENTAL BOOKSTORE

521 Fifth Ave. (43rd &
44th Sts.)
697-0840

Don't be discouraged when you walk into this store and realize that many of the books are in Japanese. Walk a little further and you'll find books in English on just about every aspect of Japanese society, from gardening to etiquette, as well as translated works by major Japanese authors. In the

back is a gift section with dolls, lamps, tea and sake sets, paintings, and stationery.
Mon.-Sat. 10 A.M. to 7 P.M.

Children

CLOTHES

AU CHAT BOTTÉ

903 Madison Ave. (72nd & 73rd Sts.)
772-7402

One of the most exclusive, tasteful, and ultra-expensive children's stores in the city, this is the place to buy that elegant, sophisticated, and very feminine dress your daughter needs for a party, or, perhaps, dancing school. You won't find these classic styles in any department store—frilly smock dresses (many of them French, Italian, and British imports) in cotton, silk, and even taffeta. The clothes are more suited for a stroll in the park than a romp through the playground. For newborns there's the exquisite Infants Room in the back—a perfect place to dress your up-and-coming debutante.
Mon.-Sat. 10 A.M. to 6 P.M.

BÉBÉ THOMPSON

98 Thompson St. (Spring & Prince Sts.)
925-1122

While many of the other children's clothing stores in this trendy, extravagantly priced neighborhood have recently closed, Bébé Thompson appears to be doing just fine. It's perhaps the choicest infants' store (sizes newborn to 6) in the city, carrying a wide variety of top-quality, adorable, original clothes and accessories for the impeccably dressed infant. You can pick up a Panama hat, a cotton bonnet, or Maud Frizon shoes and baby boots. Very SoHo prices.
Daily noon to 7 P.M.

CITYKIDS

130 Seventh Ave. (17th & 18th Sts.)
620-0120

This minute and absolutely meticulous store features upscale play and dress clothes for sophisticated little city slickers (size newborn to 12) at equally sophisticated prices. The best imports and domestic lines are represented here, but come

for the special items. A staff of in-house designers makes T-shirts, dyed cotton shorts, sweatshirts (with such New York City themes as yellow taxis and skyscrapers), wool collegiate jackets with leather sleeves, varsity sweaters, and more, much of which features either the Citykids name or its skyline logo. Almost half of the store is devoted to an imaginative, unique, and large selection of toys, knickknacks, and accessories.
Mon.-Fri. 11 A.M. to 7 P.M., Sat. 11 A.M. to 6 P.M.

KIDS KIDS KIDS

*436 Ave. of the Americas
(9th & 10th Sts.)
533-3523*

This small, new, fashionable, and very funky Village clothing store for young kids (infants to 6x) is as unpretentious as its owner, Carol Ray. "I'm the kissy monster," she coos as she makes funny faces while trying to find the best-fitting blue-and-white striped baseball cap she can for an infant in his stroller (who isn't crazy about trying on hats). The clothing here is original and adorable, ranging from sophisticated, European styling to a casual, funky look (a pair of black-and-mint-striped leggings with a matching black-and-mint pussycat T-shirt, handmade by a local artist). Nothing frilly or too fussy, and mostly reasonable prices.
Mon.-Fri. 11 A.M. to 6:30 P.M., Thurs. till 7 P.M., Sat. 11 A.M. to 6 P.M.

ONCE UPON A TIME

*171 East 92nd St. (Third
& Lexington Aves.)
831-7619*

This tiny store specializes in resale and antique clothing—but don't expect to find cheap, worn seconds here. Resale clothing for kids is a very good idea when it's properly done, and Ronnie Mann cleverly relies on a steady roster of multi-children mothers to bring her only the best names in infants' and children's clothing, all in good to excellent condition. She doesn't accept rips, stains, or Health Tex. Some items do show their wear (usually just a year's worth), but these are top brands at reduced prices: baby items from Klimmers, Baby Dior, Marese, Sophie, Guess, and Osh-Kosh, lots of adorable print and smock dresses, and such special items as Victorian christening gowns and a lovely assortment of antique quilts. New handmade crib quilts are sold here as well.
Mon.-Sat. 10 A.M. to 6 P.M.; closed Sat. in summer.

WICKER GARDEN

A grand store full of classic clothing for babies and children to size 10. Owner Pamela Scurry loves beautiful things and

1327 Madison Ave. (93rd St.)
348-1166

has filled her store with them. On the main floor, you can sit on pretty white park benches while your child tries on shoes from a large selection (from Stride Rite and Keds to their own line of dress and school shoes). Top-quality, mainly pastel infant layette clothing is found here, as are racks of frilly and very feminine party dresses. Even the playclothes are fine and delicate looking—no jeans here. Climb the winding staircase and you'll find a fairly expensive boys' line (size 2-10) that includes sailor suits, cotton sweaters with nautical themes, and preppy dress clothes combining navy or Madras-print blazers with khaki pants, a Dior button-down and a tie by Grant or Cardin. Prices range from (believe it or not) the very reasonable to the ultra expensive.
Mon.-Sat. 10 A.M. to 5:30 P.M.

TOYS

CHILDCRAFT

150 East 58th St.
(Lexington & Third Aves.)
753-3196

Childcraft has a longstanding reputation as "the" educational children's toy and craft store in the city. This place is two wide-open floors of play heaven. Alongside the endless assortment of top-quality wooden puzzles, arts and crafts supplies, musical instruments, pull toys, and games, you'll find some of the most fun, creative toys around. Pick up some amazingly authentic-looking rubber play food (from a Baggie full of cold cuts and cheese to a full-sized pineapple), or perhaps a vinyl animal nose or rubber pig hand puppet. And if you're a wooden block lover (those classic natural-colored blocks that get passed down from generation to generation), Childcraft has the best selection around.
Mon.-Fri. 10 A.M. to 5:45 P.M., Sat. 10 A.M. to 4:45 P.M.

DARROW'S FUN ANTIQUES

309 East 61st St. (First & Second Aves.)
838-0730

Established in 1964, Darrow's claims to be the first antique and collectible toy store in the world. It certainly houses one of the most comprehensive selections of antique toys on the East Coast. Darrow Sr. spent his lifetime entertaining and explaining to rapt audiences about the world of toys. Now in a brand new store, the second-generation Darrow carries on amid crowded aisles lined with a constantly changing panorama of games and toys that will recall your own childhood. The most popular items are jukeboxes, and comic characters like Dick Tracy, L'il Abner, and Popeye. A nice variety of memorabilia.
Mon.-Fri. 11 A.M. to 7 P.M., Sat. 11 A.M. to 4 P.M.

DOLLHOUSE ANTICS

1308 Madison Ave. (92nd & 93rd Sts.)
876-2288

If you think you cannot afford to buy your dreamhouse in Manhattan, you may be pleasantly surprised when you visit this store. With dollhouses starting at $95, you'll have lots of money left over for custom interior design and furnishings. Among the custom products offered are miniature wallpapers, light fixtures, and moldings. All merchandise, from ketchup bottles to couches, is on the scale of one inch to one foot, and all details are perfectly intact. For the do-it-yourselfer, dollhouse kits are also available.
Mon.-Sat. 11 A.M. to 5:30 P.M.; closed Sat.-Mon. in summer.

DOLLSANDDREAMS

1421 Lexington Ave. (92nd & 93rd Sts.)
876-2434

A hand-picked selection of dolls, doll accessories, and quality toys. You'll find treasures on every shelf of the store: expensive, one-of-a-kind collector dolls, handmade in Europe, fine children's dolls from Gotz of Germany, Sasha dolls, even the popular La New Born from Spain—a soft, extremely lifelike baby doll (black or white) with newborn wrinkles, diaper, belly-button bandage, hospital tag, and anatomically correct features. You can buy a sturdy, contemporary-style wood dollhouse and fill it with fabulous accessories. Order the *working* TV and radio (at, needless to say, hefty prices). All the houses can be expanded with balconies and garages; you can even put a stable and a corral full of horses out back to increase your property value.
Mon.-Fri. 10:30 A.M. to 6 P.M.

F.A.O. SCHWARZ

767 Fifth Ave. (58th St.)
644-9400

One of the grandest, most exciting, and unique stores in all of America, F.A.O. Schwarz has delighted even the most jaded city residents since it first opened in 1862, and a visit to the store's magical new home (just across from the old landmark site) is somewhat akin to a trip to Disneyland. There's an amazing 28-foot high animal clock tower that welcomes you in with a song (surrounded by such moving mechanical toys as the Little Engine That Could), and a cast of costumed characters (from a cavewoman to a mad scientist) is on hand for both your entertainment and to direct you around this tremendous, two-level store. Most of the new F.A.O. Schwarz is divided into individual, child-size boutiques, each with a clever name that reveals its special contents. Downstairs, you'll find Clowning Around, Toys of Extinction, and the hugest selection of stuffed animals we've ever seen, from the reasonably priced traditional teddy bear to an incredible, large-as-life giraffe ($2,500). Ride the glass elevator to the second, larger level and you'll find a kid-size

Ferrari (it'll hit 30 m.p.h. and costs just $12,500) and the most chic kid's clothes around. On Little Madison Avenue, the Learning Center has the newest in high-tech laser and video toys, or you can buy plain old Blocks By The Pound. Schwarz loves to cater to out-of-towners—it'll arrange for a personal shopper or will deliver large toys or gifts anywhere in the world. There are fine toys for every "child" (at every price) in this fantasyland.

Mon.-Sat. 10 A.M. to 6 P.M., Thurs. till 8 P.M., Sun. noon to 5 P.M.

FORBIDDEN PLANET

821 Broadway (12th St.)
473-1576

A science-fiction megastore. Kids of every age are sure to lose themselves in Forbidden Planet's vast selection (on two huge floors) of sci-fi comics, books, anthologies, magazines, toys, games, calendars, movie posters, and more. Upstairs you'll find stacks of fantasy, horror, and detective books, as well as hardcover and paperback science-fiction classics. Forbidden Planet is famous for having the largest selection of comic books in the city, and up here you'll find rack after rack of newly released comics, including Japanese and French comics and the currently in vogue, book-length "graphic novels" (more for adults). Downstairs you'll find old and vintage comics, neatly arranged by title and edition date. The toy selection downstairs is superb if you're a devotee of science fiction and fantasy toys; it contains all the hot, mass-market sci-fi toys, pet monsters, and wonderfully frightening horror masks and wigs. Another location at 227 East 59th Street (751-4386).

Mon.-Sat. 10 A.M. to 7 P.M., Fri. till 8 P.M., Sun. noon to 5 P.M.

GO FLY A KITE

1201 Lexington Ave. (81st & 82nd Sts.)
472-2623

This store has the best selection of kites in Manhattan, from trendy stunt kites (two-string acrobatic kites from $15 to $200) to an entire wall of handmade nylon kites in the brightest, most playful designs heralding anything from cuddly teddy bears to penguins relaxing under a beach umbrella. There are silk kites from China, paper kites from Japan, and plastic kites for inexperienced flyers. The store carries about 200 different types in all, along with a full range of kite-flying accessories (bags, tails, wind socks, string winders, etc.). It also sponsors a kite-flying festival in Central Park each spring. The handmade and imported kites covering the walls and suspended from the ceiling are soothing, colorful, and beautiful.

Mon.-Sat. 10 A.M.-6 P.M., Thurs. till 7:30 P.M., Sun. noon to 6 P.M.

IRIS BROWN'S VICTORIAN DOLL & MINIATURE SHOP

253 East 57th St. (Second & Third Aves.)
593-2882

This shop is so tiny it's easy to miss. But don't let the size fool you; it's a treasure chest filled with delicate porcelain Victorian dolls, child-scale furniture, dollhouses, and accessories, all of which encourages fantasy in both adults and children. Though the store is really too small to accommodate browsers, Iris Brown, a renowned expert on rare and antique dolls, will happily answer any serious inquiries. Prices are expensive.
Mon.-Fri. 11 A.M. to 6 P.M., Sat. 12:30 P.M. to 5:30 P.M.

THE LAST WOUND-UP

290 Columbus Ave. (73rd & 74th Sts.)
787-3388

The electronic age often has people yearning for days gone by, which explains in part the appeal of this place. If it can be wound up, it can be found here. The store's policy is to encourage you to live out childhood fantasies; there's a playpen where anyone is allowed to play on the premises. Whether it's roving eyes for $4, phantom feet that walk on their own for $3, a Betty Boop alarm clock for $25, or a musical chimp for $9.95, it'll wind up in this store. Two other locations at Herald Square and South Street Seaport.
Mon.-Thurs. 10 A.M. to 8 P.M., Fri., Sat. & Sun. till 10 P.M.

THE LAUGHING GIRAFFE

1065 Lexington Ave. (75th & 76th Sts.)
570-9528

If you walk into this store and find adults on the floor playing with toys, don't be alarmed—it's probably the owner and friends testing out the merchandise. Susan Crowley, formerly a teacher for 14 years, has a master's degree in education and really knows her stock, from both a practical and an academic standpoint. She sells everything from stuffed animals, board games, and building sets to classic children's books, yo-yo's, and the unforgettable Etch-a-Sketch. The emphasis is on creative, intelligent toys for children from one to nine years of age.
Sept. to May Mon.-Fri. 10 A.M. to 6 P.M., Sat. 10 A.M. to 5 P.M.; June to Aug. Mon.-Fri. 10 A.M. to 5:30 P.M.

LE BEAR BOUTIQUE

506 Amsterdam Ave. (84th & 85th Sts.)
595-2368

The only store in New York City devoted *exclusively* to teddy bears (O.K., there are a couple of stray animals too, like tiger puppets, but only one or two). There are bears absolutely everywhere, even hanging around in the painted wood trees.

You'll find all the big name bears here, from popular characters like Paddington and Smokey the Bear to Steiff collectibles and Gunds of every size (from about $25-$100), including the popular Bialosky Bear dressed in an aviator, skiing, camping, or clown outfit. A whole bunch of clever VIP bears from North American Bear live here, including Lauren Bearcall, Albeart Einstein, and Bearb Ruth. A store specialty is the beautiful selection of handmade, one-of-a-kind stuffed bears and bear puppets (ranging in price from $35 to $250) made by individuals all across the U.S.A. (including a minister from Massachusetts).
Mon.-Sat. 11 A.M. to 6 P.M.

LIONEL MADISON TRAINS/MADISON HARDWARE CO.

105 East 23rd St.
(Lexington & Park Aves.)
777-1110

This *mess* of a store (it looks like a tiny, worn, tacky hardware store, right down to its pink neon sign) is probably New York City's most famous establishment for serious train collectors. The store carries every conceivable train part or train diorama accessory you could ever need or want. You can find signal bridges, fire houses, evergreen trees, street lamps, station platforms, road signs, lots of track, an operating gravel dump conveyor, a Mobil gas sign, and even a mini Howard Johnson's. Most of the rare, impressive selection of antique metal and first-edition trains in the back of the store are for display only, but every collector should have a look. And not to worry—there are plenty of new trains for sale here, including top-of-the-line electric train sets by Marklin, Lionel, and LGB.
Mon.-Fri. 7:45 A.M. to 5 P.M., Sat. 8 A.M. to 4 P.M.;
closed Sat. July & Aug.

THE NEW YORK DOLL HOSPITAL

787 Lexington Ave., 2nd
Floor (61st & 62nd Sts.)
838-7527

Owner Irving Chais, one of a long legacy of doll doctors (the business was started by his grandfather in 1900), is as friendly and charming as his shop. Here you can revive your tot's favorite doll or stuffed animal, whatever its condition. As Chais puts it, "We've never lost a patient yet." Ask to see his own collection.
Mon.-Sat. 10 A.M. to 6 P.M.

NORA'S ARK

171 East 92nd St.
(Lexington & Third Aves.)
534-4660

A tiny, bright gem of a store with an extremely thoughtful, carefully chosen collection of toys, games, puzzles, craft items, and books for infants to pre-teens. Nora's Ark is frequently the first to carry that one-of-a-kind item that a child (and parent) can't resist. Some special items that are

sure to please include a children's pasta maker by_____
and a dinosaur mat that can be colored with mar._____
comes with a book about dinosaurs and a plastic dinosaur
toy). Most of the top-quality names in infant and children's
toys are represented here. Best of all, almost everything in
the store sells for under $25!
Mon.-Sat. 10 A.M. to 5 P.M., Wed. till 9 P.M.

PENNY WHISTLE TOYS

*132 Spring St. (Wooster &
Greene Sts.)*
925-2088

Everything at Penny Whistle is carefully selected and meant
to be "good for your child," but owner Meredith Brokaw's
high standards don't take one bit of the fun out of these toys.
There are neatly divided sections for science, robots, arts and
crafts, construction toys, ride-ons, costumes, plush dolls and
toys (from Madame Alexander to Gund and Steiff), dinosaurs, puzzles, games, magic tricks, pool toys (including a
23-foot-long sea dragon raft), sporting equipment, and
more. You can get a knickknack for under a dollar or an
entire Brio train set with accessories for about $425. You
won't find any war toys here, but you will find a lot of
imaginative, child-powered toys. There's another location at
448 Columbus Avenue (873-9090), and one on 1283 Madison Avenue (369-3868).
*Mon.-Wed. 11 A.M. to 6 P.M., Thurs.-Sat. 11 A.M. to 6:30
P.M., Sun. noon to 6 P.M.*

Clothes

MENSWEAR

DISCOUNT

BFO

149 Fifth Ave. (21st St.)
254-0059

Upon entering the brightly lit second floor, you are con-
fronted with bins and bins of shirts in all styles from all the
top designers—Givenchy, Perry Ellis, Calvin Klein, Valentino, Ralph Lauren, Yves St. Laurent—sold for up to 50% off
(and sometimes more) the average department store price. A
standard blue Oxford shirt sold for $45 elsewhere goes for
$16. One-hundred-percent silk ties by Ted Lapidus, Pierre

Balmain, and Fendi hang from the walls in many-colored splendor and sell for just $7.50. There is a small selection of sportswear (pullovers and cotton shirts) as well as belts, handkerchiefs, socks, and underwear. American suits range from $45 to $125, Italian suits average $225, and name raincoats, sportcoats, and overcoats are priced approximately 60% below retail. Who shops here? Says one salesman, "All the best informed men, from Brooklyn to Argentina."
Mon.-Sat. 10 A.M. to 5:30 P.M., Thurs. till 7 P.M.

SYMS

45 Park Pl. (Church St. & Broadway)
791-1199

Syms is a bargain-hunter's dream and a service-needer's nightmare. This no-frills department store sells highly discounted fashion for both men and women. There are designer suits, couture, famous-maker coats, shoes, underwear, ties, jackets, accessories, and kids' clothes. Go if you have time to dig. The price of an item starts out low and is lowered at regular intervals based on its length of time in the store. No credit cards—cash, check, or the Syms credit card only. The store is too big to ever seem crowded, but this City Hall location gets a little spooky on Saturdays.
Mon.-Sat. 8 A.M. to 7 P.M., Thurs. till 7:30 P.M.

READY-TO-WEAR & DESIGNER

ADDISON ON MADISON

698 Madison Ave. (62nd & 63rd St.)
308-2660

Addison on Madison is a little store with a catchy name that sells only shirts and related accessories. These shirts, 100% cotton and imported from France, come in only four variations: button-down, regular- or wide-collared, and French cuffed. In white, pastels, or subtle prints, these shirts are good-quality staples for any wardrobe. Also in Trump Tower, as is Addison on Madison for women.
Mon.-Sat. 10 A.M. to 6:30 P.M.

BIJAN DESIGNER FOR MEN

699 Fifth Ave. (54th & 55th Sts.)
758-7500

Bijan has created perhaps one of the finest retail establishments in the world. Once you are let in by the proper and impeccably mannered doorman, you enter a world of beige and white (Bijan's favorite colors), with a Baccarat crystal chandelier, polished brass banisters on the double staircases leading upstairs, and, with typical Bijan verve, a simple workman's ladder is painted white and draped with a mink throw large enough to be a bedspread. The clothes are displayed behind heavy lead-crystal doors, like jewels. Everything in the store, from suits, shoes, and ties to wallets and luggage, is designed by Bijan himself, and all of his fabrics

are exclusive. At this point his only product for women is a perfume (also available at the store).
Mon.-Sat. 10 A.M. to 6 P.M. by appointment only.

BROOKS BROTHERS

346 Madison Ave. (44th St.)
682-8800

One doesn't chance into Brooks Brothers, one is born into it. This store is the definition of prep. Nothing's ever quite in style here, so nothing is ever out of style either. Classic suits, Oxford shirts, polos—everything one needs for the office or a foxhunt. Brooksgate starts boys off on the right preppy foot, and there is an ultra-conservative women's line in the same boxy styles. Prices are moderately high; quality and service are very high. Another location at 1 Liberty Plaza (267-2400) across from the World Trade Center.
Mon.-Sat. 9:15 P.M. to 6 P.M.

BURBERRY'S

9 East 57th St. (Fifth & Madison Aves.)
371-5010

Burberry's classic trench coat offers just the right amount of status when the signature plaid lining peeks out when the coat is thrown casually over a blue-suited arm. This plaid is also found on scarves, umbrellas, bathrobes, even desk accessories. Burberry's carries complete, costly, and conservative lines for both men and women, all with the British flair for fine fabrics and exacting quality. Expect to pay for it.
Mon.-Fri. 9:30 A.M. to 6 P.M., Thurs. till 7 P.M., Sat. 9:30 A.M. to 5 P.M.

THE CUSTOM SHOP SHIRTMAKERS

115 Broadway (Wall St.)
267-8535

A store in the old English tradition of London's Savile Row, The Custom Shop specializes in men's custom-made suits and shirts in a large variety of fabrics. The made-to-measure shirts cost $32.50, a price based on the cutting of four shirts. Suits start at $395. You can also purchase ties, suspenders, cuff links, and ready-to-wear shirts.
Mon.-Sat. 8:30 A.M. to 5:30 P.M.

D. CENCI

801 Madison Ave. (67th & 68th Sts.)
628-5910

Que bello! D. Cenci can outfit the sophisticated man from shoes to shirts in its own line of Italian menswear. It's comfortable, although expensive, to shop here—the staff is friendly and the racks are full, a refreshing alternative to the snobby atmosphere prevalent on Madison Avenue. There's a nice selection of sweaters, as well as everything you can wear them with. Slimming, Italian-cut suits sell for $600 to $1,500.
Sept. to May Mon.-Fri. 10:30 A.M. to 7 P.M., Sat. 10:30

A.M. to 6 P.M.; June to Aug. Mon.-Fri. 10:30 A.M. to 6 P.M.

F.R. TRIPLER & CO.
300 Madison Ave. (46th St.)
922-1090

Tripler is a favorite shop of the very affluent. Whether updated, traditional, or formal, its men's clothing is of the highest quality. This is home to New York's largest assortment of both Hickey Freeman (suits, sportcoats, and topcoats) and Oxxford (the finest hand-tailored suits available). Top-notch personal service is standard, and the shop's alterations department is perhaps the best in New York City. *Mon.-Fri. 9 A.M. to 5:45 P.M., Sat. 9 A.M. to 5:30 P.M.*

PAUL STUART
Madison & 45th St.
682-0320

Shoppers are often struck by the quiet atmosphere and spacious interior at Paul Stuart—this is a place for serious shopping. The store offers its male customers an American look that is updated, traditional, and classic. The large staff gives plenty of assistance, and on hand is a coordinating consultant trained to create the look you're searching for. With its smart sportswear and dresses and elegant Japanese knits, Paul Stuart's much smaller women's department caters to the woman who doesn't have to wear a suit (although suits are available).
Mon.-Fri. 8 A.M. to 6 P.M., Sat. 9 A.M. to 6 P.M.

YVES ST. LAURENT MEN'S BOUTIQUE
859 Madison Ave. (71st St.)
371-7912

Yves St. Laurent's men's designs have a classic simplicity that befits the high prices. The store offers excellent service and plush surroundings to accommodate men who just can't be bothered with ordinary shopping. The primary-colored casual wear and the elegantly traditional suitings make this the store of choice for an older, monied clientele.
Mon.-Sat. 10 A.M. to 6 P.M.

TAILORS

DUNHILL TAILORS
65 East 57th St. (Fifth & Madison Aves.)
355-0050

Dunhill presents custom men's clothing for the American CEO after an English look in suits, sportswear, and formal wear. The shop's selection of polo shirts (in sea-island cotton and silk), cotton trousers, and sweaters are as elegant as they are casual. Dunhill sells the definitive navy blue, gold-buttoned blazer, but you'll have to get past the lovely ties first, which can prove difficult, even if you're not looking for one.
Mon.-Sat. 9:45 A.M. to 5:45 P.M.

SAINT LAURIE LTD.

897 Broadway (20th St.)
473-1000

Tired of mass-produced suits that seem to be programmed to lose their buttons the minute you leave the store? Looking for hand-tailored suits, but can't afford the airfare to Savile Row or Hong Kong? Relax. Saint Laurie is a merchant tailor offering hand-tailored suits at less than mass-market prices. Selling directly to the public, they've eliminated the middleman's markup. For under $300, Saint Laurie sells traditionally styled suits in traditional fabrics for both men and women. Visit before 4 p.m. on any weekday and you can see the tailors in action.
Mon.-Sat. 9 A.M. to 6 P.M., Thurs. till 7:30 P.M., Sun. noon to 5 P.M.; closed Sun. in summer.

TUXEDOS

A.T. HARRIS

47 East 44th St., 2nd Fl.
(Vanderbilt & Madison Aves.)
682-6325

This small, cluttered shop has been dressing men in traditional formal attire of the finest quality since 1892. In addition to tuxedos, dinner jackets, and tails, you'll find all the elegant accessories necessary for a night on the town, including silk top hats, white kidskin gloves, spats, waistcoats, and walking sticks (all for rent). Custom-tailored formal attire is also available. No wonder nine presidents have been outfitted here for weddings and inaugurations. Prices, luckily, are far from presidential: tuxedo rentals start at $80, which includes all accessories except shoes.
Mon.-Fri. 8:30 A.M. to 5:45 P.M., Thurs. till 6:45 P.M., Sat. 10 A.M. to 3 P.M. by appointment.

ZELLER TUXEDOS

201 East 56th St., 2nd Fl.
(Second & Third Aves.)
355-0707

A New York institution for rented formal wear, this showroom offers a unique salon atmosphere and a professional sales staff that can get you in and out in ten minutes. Of course, if you prefer, you can linger for a few hours until you find the perfect tuxedo from designers like Pierre Cardin, Luxiano Barbera, Windsor, and Padgett and Poole. All accessories are included in the price, which starts at $80; shoes are another $20.
Mon.-Fri. 9 A.M. to 7:45 P.M., Sat. 10 A.M. to 4:45 P.M.

SHOES

BALLY OF SWITZERLAND

Bally makes the kind of shoes you might expect from the Swiss. Noted for its sedate loafers in a few limited styles with little variation, Bally relies on lightweight leather

645 Madison Ave. (59th &
60th Sts.)
832-7267

construction, not as sleek as its Italian neighbors to the south, but not nearly as hard and clunky as the English. Some people think Bally shoes are classy and comfortable, while others consider them to be stolid and dull, but few demean the materials or the workmanship. As for the store itself, it's as interesting as the shoes. Men's only at this location; call the above number for other stores in the city. *Mon.-Sat. 9:30 A.M. to 6 P.M.*

BILLY MARTIN'S

812 Madison Ave. (68th
St.)
861-3100

It may be an East Coast operation, but Billy Martin's exudes Western style. Long an American classic, it has an authenticity unparalleled in the city. Even cast members of *Dallas* have been known to shop here for exotic boots and accessories. There's an outstanding selection of boots priced according to the quality of the leather; expect to pay as much as $850 for a pair of ostrich boots (in black, chocolate, honey, or chili) and as little as $210 for suede boots. You can also get Stetson and Cripple Creek hats. Everyone who walks in here walks out a dude.
Mon.-Fri. 10 A.M. to 6:30 P.M., Sat. 10 A.M. to 6 P.M.

CHARLES JOURDAN

Trump Tower, 725 Fifth
Ave. (56th & 57th Sts.)
644-3830

Charles Jourdan's women's shoes and ready-to-wear in sophisticated styles are never too dull or too daring, but always *très chic* in that particularly French way. Great men's shoes are found upstairs, and a small Seductra boutique on the garden level features a racier line of women's footwear. The staff is friendly, the store busy and bright, and the prices almost reasonable.
Mon.-Fri. 10 A.M. to 7 P.M., Sat. 10 A.M. to 6 P.M., Sun. noon to 6 P.M.

EL VAQUERO

908 Madison Ave. (72nd &
73rd Sts.)
737-8730

El Vaquero's window is a blaze of silver, white, and gold, not to mention lizard, metal, and jewels. Where else could you find gold lizard-patterned, high-top sneakers, or even more outrageous, silver-studded pumps? Made in Italy, these shoes are glitz galore.
Mon.-Sat. 10 A.M. to 6 P.M.

JOAN & DAVID

Joan & David's women's shoes are lovely. From classic pumps and long, lean flats to 40's-style lace-up boots, the

805 Third Ave. (50th St.)
486-6740

shoes are made with the finest leathers and the most attentive design. This is the only free-standing boutique (the other four Manhattan locations are tucked inside Ann Taylor stores, which are almost always crowded). This makes the Third Avenue shop a welcome relief—there is less of a mob to wade through and no wait at the register. If you're in the Hamptons, it's worth going the extra few miles to Amagansett to visit the Joan & David outlet, where these pricey shoes can be purchased at a substantial discount.
Mon.-Fri. 10 A.M. to 7 P.M., Thurs. till 8 P.M., Sat. 10 A.M. to 6 P.M.

MAUD FRIZON

49 East 57th St. (Park & Madison Aves.)
980-1460

Shoes as art, priceless and modern, is what you'll find at Maud Frizon: sky-high heels with exotic cut-outs, serpentine sandals, quilted flats. Textures, shapes, and colors are crafted into original designs that are as shocking as their prices. Some styles are truly outrageous, others more wearable, but all are interesting. If you can afford it, there are some nice looks and a lot of fun to be found here.
Mon.-Sat. 10 A.M. to 6 P.M.

ROGER VIVIER

965 Madison Ave. (75th & 76th Sts.)
249-4866

A number of special treatments distinguish Roger Vivier's shoes for women—heels are inlaid with metal and then mounted with silver or rhinestone bolts; some are finished in gold. There isn't a shoe here that stops short of being incredible. For a pair of perfect, seamless crocodile pumps, you'll pay close to $2,000. A pair of hand-cut leather mosaic pumps are hand-wrapped with silk thread to achieve an effect that even Dorothy's ruby slippers couldn't duplicate. All the shoes are for dress or evening, and they start at $225. Vivier also sells handbags and scarves.
Mon.-Sat. 10 A.M. to 6 P.M.; closed Sat. in summer.

SUSAN BENNIS WARREN EDWARDS

440 Park Ave. (56th St.)
755-4197

Shopping for shoes at Bennis & Edwards is a luxury. The owners are also the designers and, in typically autocratic style, they control every aspect of the production of their footwear. Both men's and women's styles come in classic and costly materials, such as alligator, ostrich, silk, satin, and suede. Most importantly, the quality of workmanship and the extraordinary details, colors, and patterns set these shoes apart.
Mon.-Fri. 10 A.M. to 6:30 P.M., Sat. 10 A.M. to 6 P.M.

373

WOMENSWEAR

DESIGNERS

COURRÈGES

520 Madison Ave. (53rd St.)
319-5766

Courrèges' modern looks are brilliantly displayed in this airy Itokin Plaza collection of shops. The shops here cater to a youthful and glamorous crowd, and Courrèges is the most upscale of the bunch. Lots of primary colors, neatly spun knits, and cool cottons make a perfect palette for these young, fashion-forward designs. It's a classic look made younger, bolder, and brighter than the uptown designers' styles.
Mon.-Sat. 10:30 A.M. to 6:30 P.M.

EMANUEL UNGARO

803 Madison Ave. (67th & 68th Sts.)
249-4090

Ungaro is (relatively) unintimidating and it has something for every woman—whoever they may be. Some of Ungaro's designs are perfectly styled—trendy and tailored in youthful cuts and classic fabrics. Other designs are strangely Miami-matronly—full-figured and boldly patterned in some less than pleasing florals and prints. The common elements are the Ungaro name and couture price tags. Try it—you might like it.
Mon.-Sat. 9:30 A.M. to 6:30 P.M., Thurs. till 7:30 P.M.

GIVENCHY

954 Madison Ave. (75th St.)
772-1040

Haute couture, heavy attitude, and sky-high prices sum up this designer boutique. Everything—from ga-ga gowns to signature silk scarves—is lovely to look at, intimidating to touch, and difficult to afford. Sit on a comfy brown chair while the staff displays a sampling of the wares, or browse through the stunning collection at your own leisure (or risk).
Mon.-Sat. 10 A.M. to 6 P.M.

GUCCI

683 Fifth Ave. (54th St.)
826-2600

One of the oldest Italian retail establishments in the U.S. and now a household name, Gucci is a department store for those who never look at price tags. For the wealthy and/or status-conscious, Gucci offers a style all its own—those interlocking G's and red and green Gucci stripes. For extra-special customers there's even a key that gives access to a private showroom.
Mon.-Sat. 9:30 A.M. to 6 P.M., Thurs. till 7 P.M.

KOOS VAN DEN AKKER

795 Madison Ave. (67th & 68th Sts.)
249-5432

Remember the collages you made in elementary school? Well, this designer from the Netherlands has taken that idea one step further, creating both off-the-rack and customized clothing for men and women. His designs are wild, combining colors and fabrics in ways you never thought possible to create a truly unique look. Tired of your old fur coat, or just can't decide which fur is right for you? Let Koos van den Akker create a new collaged fur coat for you. The Madison Avenue store specializes in custom work, while the boutique at 26 East 66th Street features Koos's ready-to-wear.
Mon.-Sat. 11 A.M. to 6 P.M.

MARTHA

475 Park Ave. (58th St.)
753-1511

Very few designer boutiques can beat Martha in the glamour department. Besides the luxurious salonlike setting, the old-money clientele, the attentive staff, and the models prancing about in the latest evening wear, Martha is the home of the perfect party dress. Short and crinolined, satin and seductive, beaded and extravagant—they're all here, and they're all flawlessly executed. See some of these frocks, and you'll try to think of an occasion to justify the extravagance. There's another store—models and all—at 725 Fifth in Trump Tower (826-8855).
Mon.-Sat. 9 A.M. to 6 P.M.

MISSONI

836 Madison Ave. (69th St.)
517-9339

Missoni is known for richly textured sweaters in lush wools and lusher patterns. Once seen, these are sweaters you'll lust after and must own at any cost. Though the sweaters are definitely the most popular items, this Italian designer also has a wonderful collection of suits and sportswear for both men and women.
Mon.-Sat. 10 A.M. to 6 P.M.; closed Sat. in summer.

NORMA KAMALI O.M.O.

113 Spring St. (Mercer & Green Sts.)
334-9696

One step into this SoHo boutique and you'll realize that as Norma Kamali has grown up, she's gone through some serious attitude changes. Previously her designs tended toward the ridiculously sublime—lighthearted, fun fashion for the young at heart. But the long, rectangular shop is currently filled with a more sedate look—navy blues, glen plaids, white linens, and basic black. Nonetheless, there's still a hint of her old humor in this refreshing new look: a skirt is slightly oddly pleated, a navy dress dramatically shaped, a white shirt unusually tailored. Most of the clothes

are wearable and almost affordable. Great lingerie and swimwear, too.
Daily 11 A.M. to 7 P.M.

SONIA RYKIEL

792 Madison Ave. (67th St.)
744-0880

These signature knits are simple and distinctive, which gives Rykiel a most loyal following. This modern Madison Avenue boutique offers a wide selection of knitted day and evening wear, and the racks are packed full; a ruffled gown refuses to stay within the confines of the space allotted to it.
Mon.-Sat. 9:30 A.M. to 6:30 P.M., Thurs. till 7:30 P.M.

YVES ST. LAURENT RIVE GAUCHE

855 Madison Ave. (71st St.)
988-3821

This archetypal designer's boutique is predictably elegant and surprisingly unintimidating. The daywear runs from the stylishly traditional to the downright matronly, but the evening clothes never lack for glamour. It's all very expensive, but the clientele is devoted to the quality intrinsic to the St. Laurent name.
Mon.-Sat. 10 A.M. to 6 P.M.

DISCOUNT

BOLTON'S

225 East 57th St. (Second & Third Aves.)
755-2527

For some reason, going to Bolton's is not like shopping. Women come to this discount store so regularly that it becomes part of the weekly routine. There's no high fashion here, just standard wardrobe staples. With prices this low, it seems silly not to buy that extra blouse or cotton sweater. There's usually a decent collection of linen clothing in the warmer months, as well as great wool sweaters in winter. Sales are frequent and worthwhile. Call the above number for other store locations.
Mon.-Sat. 10 A.M. to 6:45 P.M.

EMOTIONAL OUTLET

91 Seventh Ave. (16th St.)
206-7750

It's easy to get hooked on Emotional Outlet. Walk in and you're immediately offered wine, coffee, cookies, and a chair for your husband. But what's particularly nice about Emotional Outlet is its contemporary fashion for real women at real prices. It's a great place for "occasion" shopping—when you need an interview blouse or an outfit for Saturday's party. Sales are always superb, and the staff is friendly and, more often than not, honest with their opinions (only upon request). One warning for the shy: the dressing room is exactly that, one large room. Four locations in Manhattan.

Mon.-Fri. 11 A.M. to 8 P.M., Sat. 11 A.M. to 7 P.M., Sun. noon to 6 P.M.

FURS

FRED THE FURRIER

581 Fifth Ave. (47th & 48th Sts.)
765-3877

At Fred's you will not only find every fur, but fur everything. The choice of coats mixes Fred's own designs with many other major labels, including Andrew Marc, Chloe, Giancarlo Ripa, Blackgama, and Hudson Bay. Mink, sable, raccoon, fox, lynx, coyote, beaver, and many other furs are offered in both classic and contemporary styles, and there's a complete salon of fur coats for men. And for someone who wants fur in every aspect of their wardrobe, Fred has hats, mufflers, flings, ear muffs, sweaters, shawls, and lingerie made of or trimmed in fur. They will also do a major remodeling of your old fur or alter their new styles to fit your needs.

Mon. & Thurs. 10 A.M. to 8 P.M., Tues., Wed. & Fri. 10 A.M. to 7 P.M., Sat. 10 A.M. to 6 P.M., Sun. noon to 5 P.M.

FUR SALON AT BERGDORF GOODMAN

754 Fifth Ave. (57th St.)
872-8752

Sit and be served at the Fur Salon at Bergdorf's. Plush couches envelop you until the always-accommodating staff can bring you something delicious to slip on. As in the rest of the store, only the best and most fashionable are sold here. Be it Bergdorf's own line, Galanos, or Fendi, the styles are either timeless or fresh off the runway. And in true Bergdorf's tradition, no one who shops here cares one bit if it can be found cheaper somewhere else.

Mon.-Sat. 10 A.M. to 6 P.M., Thurs. till 8 P.M.

HARRY KIRSHNER & SON

307 Seventh Avenue, 4th Floor (27th & 28th Sts.)
243-4847

Making sure you absolutely love your fur coat is the staff's primary concern here. Their mission is one of matchmaking, not selling. As a result, the shop is low-pressure, congenial, and personalized without compromising style. Harry Kirshner & Son has developed an international reputation for workmanship over the years, and so can be trusted to alter, remodel, repair, and custom design, as well as store your coat during the summer months. Look out for the yearly pre-season sale, where you can find great discounts on the already reasonable prices, along with furs from top designers like Lanvin, Dior, Carol Little, Valentino, Nina Ricci, and Balenciaga.

Mon.-Fri. 9 A.M. to 6 P.M., Sat. 9 A.M. to 5 P.M.

MAXIMILLIAN

*20 West 57th St., 3rd Floor
(Fifth & Sixth Aves.)
765-6290*

You won't find the superb Maximillian furs anywhere but at its showroom. Maintaining one of the finest reputations for quality, style, and service, Maximillian makes half its coats to order. Storage, repair, cleaning, and remodeling services are also provided.
Mon.-Fri. 9 A.M. to 5 P.M.

REVILLON AT SAKS

*611 Fifth Ave. (49th &
50th Sts.)
753-4000*

Surrounded by the collections of all the high priests of designer fashion, the third-floor fur salon at Saks seems plain in comparison. The decor is bare and very brown—the furs, the carpet, even the petite couches for men to sit on while their wives and girlfriends model the exquisite furs. Most furs are Revillon's own label, but there are other big names available as well: Blass, Givenchy, and the like. It's all available much cheaper on Seventh Avenue, but here you can also find something fun to wear underneath your new fur, and you can charge it all on your Saks card.
Mon.-Sat. 10 A.M. to 6 P.M., Thurs. till 8 P.M.

RITZ THRIFT SHOP

*107 West 57th St. (Sixth
& Seventh Aves.)
265-4559*

The Ritz Thrift Shop has made a reputation for itself the world over by selling almost-new fur coats for both men and women. They offer a wide selection of styles and skins at prices ranging from $500 to $15,000. All coats are cleaned and will be altered free of charge.
Mon.-Sat. 9 A.M. to 6 P.M.

LINGERIE & HOSIERY

LEGGIADRO

*700 Madison Ave. (62nd &
63rd Sts.)
753-5050*

Young and not-so-serious, this stocking store has cubbyholes filled to the brim with legwear in parfait colors and a potpourri of designs, including stockings by Missoni, Cerruti, Elbeo, Hot Sox, and Leggiadro's house line. Seams, textures, tassels, and rhinestones enhance this youthful collection. Prices are reasonable, and the selection is huge—you'll find it impossible to leave with just one pair.
Mon.-Sat. 10 A.M. to 6 P.M.

LA LINGERIE

*Trump Tower, 725 Fifth
Ave. (56th & 57th Sts.)
980-8811*

Enter La Lingerie and you'll feel like you've entered Jane Seymour's boudoir or the set of an Anais Anais commercial. Sachets, dried flowers, and wicker baskets create an air of ultimate femininity, which is continued by the silk-lined velvet bra, panty, and garter sets, lacy teddies, satin tap pants, and naughty nightwear—all ultra-romantic, ultra-luxurious,

and (naturally) expensive. Buying lingerie is fun; buying it here truly sets the mood it is meant to be worn in.
Mon.-Sat. 10 A.M. to 5:45 P.M.

VICTORIA'S SECRET

34 East 57th St. (Park & Madison Aves.)
758-5592

Once upon a time this lingerie shop was just a mail-order business associated with The Limited. Then it became a boutique attached to the store. Finally, with the new 57th Street location, it has branched out on its own. Victoria's Secret has one of the best (and definitely the least expensive) lingerie and loungewear collections in town. Lacy petticoats, racy garters, silk panties, flannel nightshirts, romantic teddies, and cool cotton undershirts are all reasonably priced and meant to be worn. The professional staff will help hunt for those matching panties, search for the right size, and gift wrap anything, no matter how small.
Mon.-Fri. 10 A.M. to 7 P.M., Thurs. till 8 P.M., Sat. 10 A.M. to 6 P.M., Sun. noon to 5 P.M.

WIFEMISTRESS

1044 Lexington Ave. (74th & 75th Sts.)
570-9529

Buying lingerie doesn't have to mean choosing between cheap, tacky corsets and fabulously expensive, too-delicate-to-wear froufrou. Wifemistress falls squarely in the middle by catering to an above-average-income customer who wants very feminine, good-quality undergarments. Most of the bras, panties, and silks are imported from France and Italy; many of the cottons are made in Switzerland and Germany. It also carries bathing suits.
Mon.-Sat. 10 A.M. to 6 P.M.

READY-TO-WEAR

ANN TAYLOR

3 East 57th St. (Fifth & Madison Aves.)
832-2010

The flagship store on 57th Street carries not only Ann Taylor merchandise, but also edited selections from other designers. The end result is a shop full of tailored, casual sportswear that is basic to the American lifestyle. Nothing is too fancy or frilly, and everything is stylish (vs. preppy) and comfortable. Ann Taylor also carries Joan & David shoes, sensibly priced (but not cheap) and chic. Call the above number for other Manhattan locations.
Mon.-Sat. 10 A.M. to 6 P.M., Thurs. till 8 P.M.

BETSEY JOHNSON

Betsey Johnson's whimsical designs run the gamut from wild and outrageous to almost preppy conservatism: bubblegum-colored crinolines and bustiers, skin-tight

130 Thompson St. (Houston & Prince Sts.)
420-0169

stretchy dresses adorned with snaps, cheerful acrylic sweaters in silly patterns, floral print dresses cut long and boxy. It's kicky, odd, none-too-expensive, and a lot of fun. There's a definite adventure to be found here, as the strange mix of clientele peep in and out of the barely curtained dressing rooms in various stages of Betsey dress (and undress). Call the above number for other store locations.
Mon.-Sat. noon to 7 P.M., Sun. 1 P.M. to 6 P.M.

CHARIVARI

257 Columbus Ave. (72nd St.)
496-8700

Charivari means uproar, and this six-store fashion empire has consistently turned the rules upside down. One of the first to lay claim in the then-unfashionable Upper West Side, Charivari now has five stores between West 72nd and West 85th Street; three of them appear on consecutive blocks. Charivari is what today's fashion is all about. Armani, Kamali, Gaultier, Williwear, Byblos, and Kenzo, of course, are all featured now. But Charivari's success is based on the fact that it featured them *then*. It was one of the first retailers to venture into Japan, and those earlier discoveries are now fashion household names: Matsuda, Miyake, Yamamoto.
Mon.-Fri. 11 A.M. to 8 P.M., Thurs. till 9 P.M., Sat. 11 A.M. to 7 P.M., Sun. 1 P.M. to 6 P.M.

PARACHUTE

121 Wooster St. (Spring & Prince Sts.)
925-8630

Beware of a store with more empty space than merchandise —each item must be carrying more than its share of New York City's sky-high per-square-foot rents. Alas, this is the case with Parachute. The expensive clothing has that baggy, unisex, unicolor look. It's all actually quite wearable, although it seems ridiculous to pay such prices to look like that. The staff and the price tags can be intimidating, but stick to your guns, have some fun, and try the stuff on.
Mon.-Fri. noon to 8 P.M., Sat. noon to 7 P.M., Sun. 1 P.M. to 7 P.M.

POLO/RALPH LAUREN

867 Madison Ave. (72nd St.)
606-2100

Well-defined elegance is perfectly housed in one of the Upper East Side's most awe-inspiring buildings. While Mr. Lauren's clothing and accessories for men, women, and boys are available at several fine department stores, here you'll get the full scope. Special services include free alterations, personal shopping, and made-to-measure gentlemen's clothing.
Mon.-Sat. 10 A.M. to 6 P.M., Thurs. till 8 P.M.

VICTORIA FALLS

451 West Broadway
(Houston & Prince Sts.)
254-2433

Former actress Rena Gill started this store after years of people begging her to sell them some of the antique hats she collected and displayed in her home on Thompson Street. She finally opened Victoria Falls and has since branched out into antique Victorian blouses and dresses, jewelry, and her own line of day-into-evening wool, crepe, and linen suits, plus lingerie and blouses. You'll find a fusion of the Victorian era through the 30's and up-to-the-minute styles. Many fashion designers, artists, and actresses shop here for the hopelessly and wonderfully romantic (but not too fussy) clothes.

Mon.-Sat. 11 A.M. to 7 P.M., Sun 12:30 P.M. to 6 P.M.

YVES ST. TROPEZ

4 West 57th St. (Fifth &
Sixth Aves.)
765-5790

The name alone should clue you in on the clothes offered here. For those who can afford it, this store has the finest quality silk clothing in styles ranging from conservative to daring, but all in excellent taste. If you need a new cruise wardrobe for the QE II, or just a simple evening gown, you'll find it here.

Mon.-Sat. 10 A.M. to 6:30 P.M.

Department Stores

B. ALTMAN & CO.

361 Fifth Ave. (34th St.)
679-7800

B. Altman lacks the dazzle and glitter that have come to typify most other New York department stores, but to its staid clientele that is its strong point. Altman is serious and old-fashioned in both decor and merchandise. Quality is always high, and while there isn't much that's terribly exciting, there's much that is elegant. This is the perfect place to shop without distraction, even during end-of-season sales, which are among the best in New York.

Mon.-Sat. 10 A.M. to 7 P.M., Thurs. till 8 P.M., Sun. 11 A.M. to 5 P.M.

BARNEY'S

106 Seventh Ave. (16th &
17th Sts.)
929-9000

It's difficult to remember that Barney's is a full-scale department store—it's more like a large Charivari than a small Bloomingdale's. The young, chic, affluent crowd that shops here is in the know. They want to choose from only the

best and expect to pay for the quality, service, and designer names. It's all the top of the line, the cream of the crop —what's hot, what's in style, and what's selling. Barney's is especially strong in menswear, with clothes for boys, too, in sizes 4 to 20, but the smaller women's store is also exciting. Climb the spiraled stairs; each level offers the most forward-thinking fashion available today. Hot looks by Montana, Klein, Alaia, Miyake, Gualtier, Yamamoto, Fendi, Rykiel, Ellis, Kenzo, Matsuda—you name it, it's here. Don't forget that Barney's also has home furnishings—silver, bedding, china, gifts, linens, and even a bridal registry.
Mon.-Fri. 10 A.M. to 9 P.M., Sat. 10 A.M. to 8 P.M., Sun. noon to 5 P.M.

BERGDORF GOODMAN

754 Fifth Ave. (57th St.)
753-7300

Just as there is only one New York City, there is only one Bergdorf Goodman. In the same location since 1928, this grand store looms over the rest of Fifth Avenue, always one step ahead of its neighbors. Shopping here is truly a royal experience, with marble floors, crystal chandeliers, and the sound of water falling from a fountain that once flowed at the Long Island estate of the Vanderbilts. All the major names are here, innovative and conservative, including (among many others) Fendi, Angela Cummings, Barry Kieselstein-Cord, Issey Miyake, Azzedine Alaia, and Donna Karan. Many of these collections are created exclusively for Bergdorf's and can be found nowhere else in the U.S. The windows offer a glimpse into the world of the "haves." Stare at them long enough and you'll see yourself transformed into a modern-day prince or princess with perhaps enough money to step inside.
Mon.-Sat. 10 A.M. to 6 P.M., Thurs. till 8 P.M.

BLOOMINGDALE'S

1000 Third Ave. (59th St.)
355-5900

Bloomingdale's is not only a shopping experience, it's a shopper's heaven. The bazaarlike atmosphere of the main floor is enhanced by models and salespeople hawking perfumes, makeup, and other specials to customers weaving their way through the Casbah of cosmetic and accessory counters. In addition to the usual carnival, Bloomingdale's transforms itself each spring into another country; recent festivals have featured France, Italy, and the South Seas. Underneath all the glitz and showbiz, a veritable treasure trove of merchandise is to be uncovered by the stalwart shopper. Men are fortunate that their departments are relatively contained on the first and lower levels—women

must roam the upper floors hoping to stumble on one ot to seven shoe shops (depending on the ever-changing layou of the store) or the boutiques of Yves St. Laurent, Missoni, Sonia Rykiel, Ralph Lauren, and the current crop of Bloomie's young designer finds, plus furs and bridal ensembles. Then there are lots of objects, from furniture and home electronics to books and art supplies, along with all the attendant services to said possessions, such as decorating, cleaning, repair, and engraving, and, finally, a travel bureau so you can get away from it all once you get it home. If you wish to take something home for dinner, you can peruse the delicacies shop, which replicates, with comestibles, the madhouse on the upper floors. If all this sounds too much or too tiring, don't despair. Bloomingdale's has thoughtfully instituted a personal shopping service so your whims may be indulged at moment's notice without requiring more from you than pushing seven numbers on a phone (705-3375), and issuing your commands to a willing servant.
Mon. & Thurs. 10 A.M. to 9 P.M., Tues., Wed., Fri. & Sat. 10 A.M. to 6 P.M., Sun. noon to 6 P.M.

BONWIT TELLER

8-10 East 57th St. (Fifth Ave.)
764-2300

For years Bonwit's has clung to its identity as a boutique-style department store for women. Always more middle-of-the-road than its competition, Bendel's and Bergdorf's, Bonwit's has finally come into its own with the increase of working women who need tailored yet glamorous styles. Standard to the mix are Albert Nippon, Ralph Lauren, Anne Klein, and Liz Claiborne. Following suit, the shoe department also emphasizes a blend of classic and comfortable styles. Bonwit's continues to be an excellent source for colorful, but not punky, accessories such as scarves, bags, belts, and jewelry. But where the store has taken off in recent years is in its small men's boutique—look into it.
Mon.-Fri. 10 A.M. to 7 P.M., Thurs. till 8 P.M., Sat. 10 A.M. to 5 P.M., Sun. noon to 5 P.M.

HENRI BENDEL

10 West 57th St. (Fifth & Sixth Aves.)
247-1100

This is not a store for those lacking self-assurance. You must be able to move with Bendel's trend-setting clientele and know intimately the important names in fashion, accessories, cosmetics, and gifts. You'll pay handsomely for anything you buy (especially clothes), but you'll no doubt be repaid extravagantly in compliments. Bendel's has nothing that is not clever and avant-garde, and that goes for the decor, too. Even if you haven't the funds, take the time to wander into this wonderland. The first floor boasts not departments but boutiques that wind in and out of each other. Not everything makes sense, but it doesn't have to: Henri Bendel is concerned only with the spontaneous and hip—very hip. *Mon.-Sat. 10 A.M. to 6 P.M., Thurs. till 8 P.M.*

MACY'S HERALD SQUARE

34th St. & Sixth Ave.
736-5151

Macy's Herald Square is known everywhere as "the world's largest store"; it occupies nearly an entire city block. Serving the middle and upper-middle classes and resembling a zoo on Saturdays, Macy's is still the store for the basics, despite its occasional scuffed floors and painfully slow service. The show begins on the main floor, where a marble Art Deco interior dazzles the eyes more than the fine jewelry, elegant leathers, bright scarves, and chic cosmetics and fragrances. Climb a grand marble staircase up to the balconies and you'll find yourself browsing through two of Macy's most unusual boutiques: a branch of the Metropolitan Museum of Art Gift Shop, and an antique and estate gallery offering rare jewelry. Upstairs are the Little Shops, featuring for women the designs of Giorgio Armani, Anne Klein, Claude Montana, Calvin Klein, and others. There is a children's department, zippy and fun even for parents, and several floors devoted to items and furnishings for the home—linens, china, crystal, furniture, state-of-the-art electronics, and telephones. Housewares and gourmet delicacies are available in the Cellar, and if your timing's right, you may find the likes of Julia Child or Paul Prudhomme conducting a seminar in the test kitchen. And to really round out your day, there's a Glemby Hair Salon, a film developing center, an American Express Travel Service, and (why not?) a full-service post office.
Mon., Thurs. & Fri. 9:45 A.M. to 8:30 P.M., Tues. & Wed. 9:45 A.M. to 6:45 P.M., Sat. 9:45 A.M. to 6 P.M., Sun. 10 A.M. to 6 P.M.

SAKS FIFTH AVENUE

611 Fifth Ave. (49th & 50th Sts.)
753-4000

For those who can afford to choose, there's no other choice. Saks has become a byword for taste and elegance. This store does not aim to surprise its shoppers (they have been coming here too long for that); it simply offers impeccable clothing and merchandise for those who seem to know what they want before they arrive. The emphasis is on designer fashions, with the majority of floors devoted to women's clothing of the more luxurious variety. But the menswear floor is also terrific, with a contemporary section that is evolving

quite nicely. The cosmetics department on the first floor appears to be one of the most popular in the city, since it is bustling at the most unexpected hours. There are special boutiques (leather accessories, stationery, and gifts) on 49th and 50th Streets, a full-service beauty salon, a chocolate and food shop, and, of course, the Revillon fur salon.
Mon.-Sat. 10 A.M. to 6 P.M., Thurs. till 8 P.M.

Flowers

BOUQUETS À LA CARTE INC.

1110 Park Ave. (82nd St.)
289-8300

For over 20 years Bouquets à la Carte has been helping New Yorkers celebrate every type of occasion with baskets and bouquets of flowers (as well as a stunning array of other gifts). Send a "Get Well Quick" message with chocolate aspirin, ginger ale, chicken noodle soup, the morning paper, and flowers; or a "Happy Birthday" basket, which includes a custom-decorated birthday cake, confetti, Moet & Chandon Champagne, and balloons. The store also features such select gift items as Moustier and Limoge porcelain, crystal, Belgian chocolates, British and Italian silver, and out-of-the-ordinary gifts, like a Lucite cowboy hat filled with chili fixings, barbecue sauce, and down-home recipes.
Mon.-Fri. 8 A.M. to 7 P.M. Sat. 10 A.M. to 3 P.M.

RENNY

27 East 62nd St. (Madison & Park Aves.)
371-5354

When you proceed past the huge antique marble table covered with orchids that greets you, you'll have entered one of New York's most elegant and beautiful flower shops. Understated opulence is the theme at Renny, which creates lush, overstuffed arrangements of exotic and specially imported flowers. You can find sweet peas in January, French tulips, and the most exquisite arrangements of flowers and Champagne or flowers and chocolates. Renny also designs for parties, whether for ten or 2,000. Arrangements start at $35.
Mon.-Sat. 9 A.M. to 6 P.M.

RONALDO MAIA FLOWERS

Things are always changing in this shop—Mr. Maia is constantly in his upstairs studio designing new containers and baskets for flowers, along with glassware and candle and

27 East 67th St. (Madison Ave.)
288-1049

potpourri holders. Maia designs all the accessories to ensure a most exclusive look for his most exclusive clientele. In addition to flower arrangements, which start at $50, the shop offers one-stop service for those planning a reception or special function. Maia will find you a space, a decorator, furniture, china, and linen, and will also recommend a caterer. And if you're curious about what's going on in the studio, call ahead to arrange a visit.
Mon.-Fri. 9:30 A.M. to 6 P.M., Sat. 11 A.M. to 5 P.M. Closed Sat. in summer.

Food

BAKERIES

DAVID'S COOKIES

466 Ave. of the Americas (11th St.)
645-7749

David's Cookies are guaranteed to awaken dormant cookie monsters. Despite the onslaught of competitors, David Liederman's cookies are still in a class of their own—buttery and rich, with chunks of semi-sweet Lindt chocolate that will make any mouth salivate. Liederman says the most popular cookie is the chocolate chunk; in the ice creams, another part of David's repertoire, the vanilla chocolate chunk is reputedly New York's favorite. French baguettes, quite authentic with a hard crust and an airy inside, can also be purchased at most of the stores. Call the above number for other locations around the city.
Mon.-Thurs. 10 A.M. to 11 P.M., Fri. & Sat. 10 A.M. to 1 A.M., Sun. 11 A.M. to 10 P.M.

THE EROTIC BAKER

582 Amsterdam Ave. (88th & 89th Sts.)
362-7557

The Erotic Baker offers the most notable expression of the sexual revolution in the field of confectionery. Though it will take on the occasional "non-erotic" project, The Erotic Baker specializes in graphic representations of sexuality in cake and cream. Whether or not you find them erotic is your business, but enough people do so that The Erotic Baker suggests orders be placed a day or two in advance. Phone orders are accepted, and delivery is available.

Mon.-Thurs. 11 A.M. to 7 P.M., Fri. & Sat. 11 A.M. to 8 P.M.

ESS-A-BAGEL

359 First Ave. (21st & 22nd Sts.)
260-2252

Bagels are a part of New York's heritage. If you want to try the best New York has to offer, this is the place. (One client reportedly packed two suitcases of Ess-a-Bagels for his Alaska trip.) The small, bustling shop bakes the bagels on the premises, virtually guaranteeing that you can always get a hot bagel of any of the nine varieties: pumpernickel, pumpernickel raisin, cinnamon raisin, sesame, plain, onion, poppy seed, garlic, and salt. We recommend the many cream cheeses (vegetable, salmon) and the various spreads, particularly the whitefish salad.
Mon.-Sat. 7:30 A.M. to 10 P.M., Sun. 7:30 A.M. to 4 P.M.

KATHLEEN'S BAKE SHOP

155 East 84th St. (Third & Lexington Aves.)
570-1515

This small, sparkling-clean store proudly carries on a tradition that started when Kathleen King began selling cookies at her father's farm as a child. Kathleen is famous for her chocolate chip cookies (which are moist on the inside, crunchy on the outside, and full of big chips) and her apple crumb pie. She also bakes, among other delights, fruit pies, a sour-cream coffee cake, brownies, and banana and zucchini breads, as well as her famous Crutchley Cruller hearts. Prices are reasonable and the goodies delicious.
Mon.-Sat. 8 A.M. to 7 P.M.

LITTLE PIE COMPANY LTD.

410 West 43rd St. (Ninth & Tenth Aves.)
736-4780

For cheesecake, there's Miss Grimble's; for apple pie, there's the Little Pie Company. From just one flawless apple pie recipe, this store has built a business that sells an overwhelming variety of pies and cakes. The bakers utilize the many varieties of apples, use all fresh ingredients, and put tender, loving, homebaked care into all the goodies. Among the more popular items are applesauce carrot cake and cheddar-cheese crust-apple pie, but the sour cream apple walnut cake is the one to die for. They also make mouthwatering seasonal pies. (If you want a cranapple pie at Thanksgiving it's a good idea to reserve a month in advance.)
Mon.-Fri. 8 A.M. to 7:30 P.M., Sat. 10 A.M. to 7 P.M., Sun. noon to 5 P.M.

MISS GRIMBLE'S CHEESECAKE & BAKERY EMPORIUM

The classic vanilla cheesecake is Miss Grimble's pride and our joy, but there are variations to tempt the most traditional dessert lover: raspberry marble, vanilla-and-chocolate marble, lemon, orange, and hazelnut, to name but a few. The

305 Columbus Ave. (74th
& 75th Sts.)
362-5531

cakes are available in two sizes (seven and ten inches) and start at $12. The Texas pecan pie is not to be missed; drop by for a slice as part of your stroll along Columbus. For the truly decadent there are Grimble tortes, the most popular of which consists of layers of chocolate (crust, cake, cream, and icing) laced with Grand Marnier.
Mon.-Thurs. 9 A.M. to midnight, Fri. 9 A.M. to 1 A.M., Sat. 9 A.M. to 2 A.M., Sun. 9 A.M. to 11 P.M.

PATISSERIE CLAUDE

187 West 4th St. (Sheridan
Sq. & Sixth Ave.)
255-5911

Parisians living in New York satisfy their cravings for croissants at Claude's, an unpretentious and delightful small bakery that offers the best in French pastry. Besides sinfully buttery croissants, you can get brioche, éclairs, napoleons, fruit tarts, and an incredibly rich dark chocolate and almond layered square (all baked in the back). Claude also makes individual quiches with a light, flaky pastry and creamy cheese filling—if only they could set the standard for the rest of New York! The delicacies can be taken home or eaten at one of the few small marble-topped tables, where you can sit and watch the world go by, or, perhaps, talk to Claude. Stoic at first, he'll warm up to you in no time and make his way into your heart . . . and stomach!
Daily 8 A.M. to 8 P.M.

CANDY

ECONOMY CANDY

131 Essex St. (Delancey &
Rivington Sts.)
254-1531

Catering to both the glutton and the gourmet, this store has a formidable selection of dried fruits, nuts, hand-dipped chocolates, and candies. Many of the treats will take you down memory lane—chocolate babies and jawbreakers, to name a few. The selection is unprecedented, and the prices are 20% to 50% off suggested retail. The gourmet can also find coffees, spices, and mustards at reduced prices. A second location is at 108 Rivington Street.
Daily 8 A.M. to 6 P.M.

GODIVA CHOCOLATIER

The recent entry of other European chocolatiers in the New York market has not affected the popularity of that old standby, Godiva, whose chocolates are still manna to a

701 Fifth Ave. (54th &
55th Sts.)
593-2845

chocoholic. Open oysters (milk chocolate filled with hazelnut cream) and truffles (pure, creamy chocolate in a variety
of flavors dusted with cinnamon or cocoa) are the most
popular single purchases, while a pound or more of selected
chocolates cushioned in Godiva's famous jewellike golden
box is the most frequent selection for gift-giving. Other
locations at 560 Lexington Avenue (593-2845) and 85 Broad
Street (514-6240).
*Mon.-Sat. 10 A.M. to 6 P.M., Thurs. till 7 P.M., Sun. noon
to 6 P.M.*

LI-LAC CHOCOLATES INC.

*120 Christopher St.
(Bleecker & Hudson Sts.)
800-242-7374*

Since 1923, Li-Lac has been hand dipping chocolates in the
back of this small, pretty store—in a spacious, immaculate
kitchen, complete with the original marble table tops. You'll
find all the basic sticks, squares, drops, and slabs here, as well
as a new, too-cute line of chocolate typewriters, computers,
and the like. Favorites are the French assortment (a one-
pound, 50-piece selection for only $20) and the incredible
truffles—French, rum, Champagne, mocha, caramel cream,
Grand Marnier, amaretto and more. These treats are also
sold at Barney's at 106 Seventh Avenue.
Mon.-Sat. 10 A.M. to 7:45 P.M., Sun. noon to 7:45 P.M.

TEUSCHER CHOCOLATES OF SWITZERLAND

*620 Fifth Ave. (49th &
50th Sts.)
246-4416*

Truffles, truffles, and more truffles made of renowned Swiss
chocolate are flown in fresh from Zurich every week. The
specialty of the house is Champagne—a delicious blend of
fresh cream, butter, and chocolate with a Champagne cream
center that is dusted with confectioner's sugar. If you haven't
already put this book down and run off to go buy one, let us
add that you'll also find nougat, almond, walnut, kirsch,
orange, cocoa and solid milk-, dark-, and white-chocolate
truffles. And if you still haven't left, you don't have to: you
can order them by mail.
Mon.-Sat. 10 A.M. to 6 P.M., Thurs. till 7:30 P.M.

CAVIAR

IRON GATE PRODUCTS

*424 West 54th St. (Ninth
Ave.)
757-2670*

Make careful note of the address, because Iron Gate is
located on the second floor of a warehouse and there's no
sign out front. The interior is that of a somewhat seedy
shipping department, but the products Iron Gate offers are
all first-rate. Along with fresh imported caviar, Iron Gate

specializes in fish and fowl. The fish selection includes Scotch and Danish smoked salmon, smoked eel, smoked trout, and smoked whitefish. As for fowl, a wide assortment of smoked and fresh quail, pheasant, partridge, and squab are available. For those who make their own exotic pâtés, Iron Gate even carries two grades of fresh mullet liver.
Mon.-Fri. 9 A.M. to 4 P.M.

PETROSSIAN

182 West 58th St. (Seventh Ave.)
245-2214

Are you one of the very, very picky gourmands who crave caviar of firm grain and delicate flavor, with a hint of sea spray, and no coloring or preservatives added? Then you can relax. Petrossian is a direct importer of the finest Russian caviar—beluga, sevruga, or osetra, whichever you prefer. The boutique, located off the restaurant in a beautifully restored landmark building, also offers a host of other well-known Petrossian products: smoked salmon, foie gras, cassoulet, smoked eel. In addition to the exclusive caviars and high-quality food products, Petrossian also sells exquisite caviar servers and spoons. There is a second boutique in Bloomingdale's ground-floor delicatessen shop at 59th and Lexington (355-5900).
Mon.-Fri. 11:30 A.M. to 1 A.M., Sat. 5:30 P.M. to 1 A.M.

CHEESE & PASTA

CHEESE OF ALL NATIONS

153 Chambers St. (Greenwich Ave.)
732-0752

Every cheese you've ever wanted, and then some, are sold at reasonable prices, both retail and wholesale by the case. St. André is a bargain at $3.99 for a half pound, and there are daily reductions, such as Austrian Fontina for $2 a pound, or low-salt Edam for $2.50 a pound. Breads, crackers, oils, and hors d'oeuvres are sold as well.
Mon.-Fri. 8 A.M. to 5:30 P.M., Sat. 8 A.M. to 5 P.M.

IDEAL CHEESE SHOP

1205 Second Ave. (63rd & 64th Sts.)
688-7579

The name says it all. For many connoisseurs, this is New York's *only* cheese shop. There are hundreds of varieties, both domestic and imported; the assortment of the latter is unsurpassed. Goat cheese, triple crème, Stilton, Livarot—be extravagant, and round out your selection with a pâté and crackers. The salespeople, friendly and extremely knowledgeable, will sometimes call your attention to a product for which you haven't asked, and this is one place where you should take their advice.
Mon.-Fri. 9 A.M. to 6:30 P.M., Sat. 9 A.M. to 6 P.M.

LA MARCA CHEESE SHOP

161 East 22nd St. (Third Ave.)
673-7920

This tiny shop boasts more than 150 types of cheese. The owner, originally a partner in Dean & DeLuca, is a cheese connoisseur. All cheeses are aged on the premises. Custom-prepared trays are available, and a delectable pie—made from Gorgonzola and Mascarpone—is worth a try.
Mon.-Fri. 10 A.M. to 6:45 P.M., Sat. 9:30 A.M. to 6:15 P.M.

PASTA PLACE

163 First Ave. (10th St.)
460-8326

There are some places that native New Yorkers call their own, which they will only share grudgingly. Pasta Place is such a store. In not much more than a hole-in-the-wall is a wealth of riches for pasta aficionados. Fresh pastas change daily and include garden vermicelli, egg or spinach fettucini, gnocci, and spinach and cheese ravioli, starting at $1.50 per pound—the prices and quality can't be beat. Other goodies include homemade sauces by the pound, from marinara to pesto; freshly grated Parmesan cheese; and fresh homemade mozzarella for only $3.79 a pound. Try to shop in the early part of the day, as the selection diminishes by evening.
Mon.-Sat. noon to 7 P.M.

COFFEE & TEA

MCNULTY'S TEA & COFFEE CO. INC.

109 Christopher St. (Bleecker & Hudson Sts.)
242-5351

The aroma of coffee beans and fresh tea wafting through this store is sufficient grounds (as it were) to dissuade anyone from the "convenience" of instant. The store's old-fashioned interior transports you back in time to the days of the Boston Tea Party. The exotic origins of some of the merchandise will disintegrate the last of your resistance to these freshly roasted, caffeine-laden substances: places as far away as Timor and New Guinea are represented here on Christopher Street. The selection of teas includes rare Darjeelings and extra-fancy jasmine leaves.
Mon.-Sat. 11 A.M. to 11 P.M., Sun. 1 P.M. to 7:30 P.M.

PAPRIKAS WEISS IMPORTER

Right in front of this specialty food store are the items that gave this shop its start: 17 varieties of coffee beans from Hungary, Colombia, Vienna, Turkey, Italy, Kenya and Guatemala, all freshly roasted and custom ground. Next to

1546 Second Ave. (81st &
82nd Sts.)
288-6117

the coffees are 18 types of loose tea as diverse as Russian
Samovar and Prince of Wales.
Mon.-Sat. 9 A.M. to 6 P.M.

GOURMET GROCERIES

BALDUCCI'S

424 Ave. of the Americas
(9th & 10th Sts.)
673-2600

Balducci's has come a long way from the mom-and-pop
stand it once was. Still family-owned, this large emporium is
a gathering place in Greenwich Village, a neighborhood
feast for the senses. As you walk into this European-style
market you can almost taste everything. Balducci's is pleasantly crowded during weekday working hours with happy
shoppers filling their carts with every imported goodie
imaginable—biscuits, mustard, olive oil, mineral water,
cookies, and more. Customers chat with one another as they
sample the fresh array of cheeses and decide whether to
choose the homemade canneloni or the shrimp primavera.
By 5:30 P.M. the pace quickens as devotees race in to pick up
the main course before their dinner guests arrive. The
produce section is like a burst of spring in winter; year-round
mangos, asparagus, and strawberries brighten any winter's
day. There are gift baskets and mail orders, too. Enter at your
own risk around Christmas.
Mon.-Sat. 7 A.M. to 8:30 P.M., Sun. 7 A.M. to 6:30 P.M.

BLOOMINGDALE'S DELICACIES

1000 Third Ave. (59th St.)
705-2958

With an emphasis on name and display, Bloomingdale's
Delicacies is a culinary boutique that stresses packaged
samplers—Crabtree & Evelyn preserves, Petrossian bottled
cassoulet, Mediterranean fish soup, and so on. Unlike the
unimpressive meat and cheese departments, the selection of
prepared foods is extensive, though its tempting presentation
does not justify the outrageous prices. There are seasonal and
holiday displays, but much more fun, and the best reason for
shopping here, are in the in-store tastings, two or three of
which are always beckoning.
*Mon.-Thurs. 10 A.M. to 9 P.M., Fri. & Sat. 10 A.M. to
6:30 P.M.*

DEAN & DELUCA INC.

121 Prince St. (Greene &
Wooster Sts.)
431-1691

Since 1977, SoHo has been home to one of the finest
specialty food stores in New York. In this case, quality does
not rule out quantity—there's an in-depth selection in
almost every food category. Breads, for example, come from

12 different bakeries around the city, while even more sources (which will remain confidential) are responsible for the pastries. There are always about 200 cheeses in stock; selection depends on the season and availability from such countries as France, Spain, Belgium, Denmark, England, and Canada. And Dean & Deluca also carries 30 different varieties of coffee beans, including Sumatra, Mexican, Costa Rican, and Kona, the only American coffee (from Hawaii). Whatever you're buying, you can rest assured that owner Joel Dean has searched out the best for his Prince Street store. You can phone and have your order delivered almost anywhere.
Mon.-Sat. 10 A.M. to 7 P.M., Sun. 10 A.M. to 6 P.M.

FAIRWAY MARKET

2127 Broadway (74th & 75th Sts.)
595-1888

Even if you don't live in the neighborhood, the abundance of fresh produce should draw you here. About 45,000 customers each week will agree with us. Because Fairway does such an incredible business, prices are extraordinarily cheap. There are stacks of kiwis, cherimoyas, and cactus pears, as well as all sorts of cheeses. How to choose between the chèvres, beautifully displayed (on vine leaves, with charcoal, and in different shapes), and the American camembert, a recent addition to the store's *fromage* department? Throughout the market are homemade signs indicating the how-tos of vegetable care and offering mouth-watering, foolproof recipes for dishes from stuffed mushrooms to gnocci. There are also breads, grains, jams, vinegars, a deli section, and fresh fish.
Mon.-Fri. 8 A.M. to midnight, Sat. & Sun. 8 A.M. to 10 P.M.

GRACE'S MARKETPLACE

1237 Third Ave. (71st St.)
737-0600

It's heaven to be in Grace's produce section; you never have to dig out the best vegetable from beneath an avalanche of rotten ones, because they are all of excellent quality. This high standard is evident in every area of the store: everything is fresh and fully stocked. Following the pattern of her parent store in the Village, Balducci's, Grace's has compact food "boutiques" with offerings of bread, cheese, deli items, produce, and delicious desserts and European chocolates.
Mon.-Sat. 7 A.M. to 8:30 P.M., Sun. 8 A.M. to 7 P.M.

THE SILVER PALATE

This gourmet outlet has two kinds of customers: those who cook and those who don't. For those who do, The Silver

274 Columbus Ave. (73rd
St.)
799-6340

Palate carries an impressive range of its own bottled sauces, relishes, nut oils, and herb vinegars. For those who don't, this shop-in-miniature offers the famous Silver Palate cuisine already realized. Made on the premises with the freshest ingredients and a bit of zip, the entrées (honey curried chicken, roast veal with lemon caper mayonnaise, linguini with clam sauce) change daily. If you anticipate working late, portions can be reserved by phone. The Silver Palate also vends a selection of homemade salads, breads, and desserts, as well as flavor-coordinated picnic baskets.
Mon.-Fri. 10:30 A.M. to 9:30 P.M., Sat. & Sun. 10:30 A.M. to 7:30 P.M.

ZABAR'S

2245 Broadway (80th St.)
787-2000

Zabar's isn't merely a food store—it's a sideshow as well, particularly behind the counter, where the lox men know they're putting on a performance. Smoothly, they trim the smoked salmon, be it Scotch or Irish, Norwegian or Nova Scotian, before dolloping out a half-pound of herring salad for Number 79. Always get your numbers first (different numbers are necessary for the appetizing cheese and prepared-meat departments), then browse while you're waiting. Zabar's carries everything you've ever heard of, and much that you haven't, at exceptionally low prices. The aisles are loaded with coffees, teas, spices, preserves, mustards, chocolates, and breads. The store has the ambience of a subway car at rush hour, but to the local regulars—mostly Columbia academics, West End Avenue lawyers, and side-street creative types—it's home.
Mon.-Fri. 8 A.M. to 8 P.M., Sat. 8 A.M. to midnight, Sun. 9 A.M. to 6 P.M.

HEALTH FOOD

EARTH'S HARVEST TRADING CO.

700 Columbus Ave. (95th
St.)
864-1376

This store prides itself on carrying only the finest and freshest of natural food products. It has a large grocery section with such everyday food items as juices, cereals, pasta, and fresh bread, without the usual refined sugar or preservatives. It also sells bulk flour, grains, nuts, and dried fruits, along with vitamins, a good selection of books and magazines, and natural cosmetics (including the brands Weleda, Reviva, and Kiss My Face). Over 200 herbs are sold in bulk for both cooking and medicinal purposes; an herbal-

ist is on hand Monday through Friday to make recommenda-tions.
Mon.-Fri. 9:30 A.M. to 7:30 P.M., Sat. & Sun. 10 A.M. to 6 P.M.

THE HEALTH NUT

2611 Broadway (99th St.)
678-0054

This store's four well-placed locations eliminate many of the excuses used for not starting to eat more organically, with foods free of preservatives and refined sugar. East Side, West Side, uptown, or midtown, there's a Health Nut near you. The stores are well stocked with organically grown produce, meat, poultry, nuts, and seeds, as well as books and cosmet-ics. There is a special macrobiotic foods section with all the necessary grains and seeds. Visit the other locations at 1208 Second Avenue, 825 Second Avenue, and 2141 Broadway.
Mon.-Sat. 9:30 A.M. to 8 P.M., Sun. noon to 7 P.M.

INTEGRAL YOGA NATURAL FOODS

250 West 14th St. (Seventh & Eighth Aves.)
243-2642

Two things make this natural food store stand out from the others in New York City. First, it's affiliated with the Yoga Institute and therefore can keep you up to date on the latest course offerings in yoga and Eastern religions. Second, it's a strictly vegetarian store—no meat, fish, or eggs. What it does have is a large variety of bulk foods, from flour and rice to dried fruits and beans, with everything in between: vitamins, books, dairy products, and a health and beauty section for natural shampoos, conditioners, and toothpastes, as well as makeup. The highest standards are maintained. None of the products has sugar, fructose, or preservatives.
Mon.-Fri. 10:30 A.M. to 9:30 P.M., Sat. 10:30 A.M. to 8:30 P.M., Sun. noon to 6:30 P.M.

SPICES

PETE'S SPICES

174 First Ave. (10th & 11th Sts.)
254-8773

Pete's spices are incredible. This large store, cluttered with bins, boxes, and jars of every cooking ingredient from Wehani rice to calendula (marigold), will surely have the impossibly obscure ground seed you need for that Indian recipe. The store caters to caterers, restaurants, and ethnic cooks. The sales staff are knowledgeable and glad to help you with an ingredient and its significance, as well as teach him or her how to bake a simple (or a complicated) bread. Spices are imported from all over the world—South America,

Turkey, Spain, the West Indies—wherever the purest, best products are found. They also have a large selection of medicinal herbs, such benevolent herbs, spices, and teas like devil's claw, grains of paradise, and squaw vine, used in different countries for a variety of different traditional, folkloric, or superstitious purposes. Prices are low, especially when sold in bulk.

Mon.-Sat. 10 A.M. to 7:30 P.M., Sun. 12:30 P.M. to 5 P.M.

Gifts

ASPREY

Trump Tower, 725 Fifth Ave., 2nd Fl. (56th & 57th Sts.)
688-1811

Asprey is *the* place to find or create the perfect gift. In their own words, there is *nothing* that Asprey cannot do. You only need to visit the store to see the phenomenal collection of objects or talk with one of the enthusiastic, creative salespeople to see how wild your imagination can run. Among the items in New York's auxiliary to the 206-year-old London institution are desk sets, cigarette boxes, mother-of-pearl caviar servers, flatware, crystal, blankets, first editions of Mark Twain's *Tom Sawyer*, and fine men's and women's antique jewelry. In addition, you can have anything made in solid gold, silver, leather, and precious or semi-precious stones. Or you can have your favorite book bound by their own bindery, which uses the finest leathers and most exquisite end pages. In the same breath they will offer to make you a solid gold telephone or a saddle in crocodile; you only have to choose—and pay.

Mon.-Fri. 10 A.M. to 5:30 P.M.

HAMMACHER SCHLEMMER & CO.

147 East 57th St. (Lexington & Third Aves.)
421-9000

Hammacher Schlemmer's retail policy may be eccentric, but at least it is clear: its merchandise must either be the best at what it does or the only product that does it. The Hammacher Schlemmer Institute tests all the products before they are stocked, including those brought to the company by many Edisons *manqué*. Where else can you find an electric ice cream scoop for all those hard-to-dig creamy flavors? Or a bicycle mower that allows you to exercise while you trim the lawn? The lengthy placard descriptions beside

each item make browsing fun. As for the prices, there is a reason they are not displayed. Guess.
Mon.-Sat. 10 A.M. to 6 P.M.

TUSCANY GALLERIES

1001 Second Ave. (53rd St.)
593-0728

The unusual blend of *objets d'art* at this store means you can probably find the perfect present for the person who has everything. Whether it's a snow-filled glass paperweight, a goblet, or a musical cigarette box, an affordable notion can be found. There's virtually no rhyme or reason to the eclectic display, so the shopper must be willing to rummage. The back of the store holds a gallery featuring the work of Joy Gush, a well-known local artist.
Mon.-Sat. 11 A.M. to 7:30 P.M.

Home

CRYSTAL

BACCARAT

55 East 57th St. (Madison & Fifth Aves.)
826-4100

Baccarat has been the world's preeminent manufacturer of fine crystal for more than two centuries, and its superiority shows scant signs of abating. Founded in 1764 under the aegis of Louis XV, Baccarat deals in both decorative and table glass. The store's chrome-and-steel étagères hold sculptured crystal statuary, often of animals, alongside fine glasses, stemware, and decanters. In addition, the upper floor offers Ercuis and Christofle silverware, Caralene-Ravnaud china, and Les Etains du Manoir pewter.
Mon.-Fri. 9:30 A.M. to 5:30 P.M.

HOYA CRYSTAL GALLERY

450 Park Ave. (56th & 57th Sts.)
223-6335

Crystal that combines contemporary design, Japanese artistry, and innovative technology is on display here. Fumio Sasa, Hoya's design leader, guides a staff of ten artists in producing an award-winning collection that has been exhibited in museums throughout the world. It includes crystal art sculptures ranging from $500 to $30,000, plus an extensive selection of functional crystal: stemware, vases, bowls,

clocks, and gifts ranging from $50 to $500. Hoya's lead crystal is known for its purity, clarity, and reflective brilliance.
Mon.-Sat. 10 A.M. to 6 P.M.

STEUBEN GLASS

717 Fifth Ave. (56th St.)
752-1441

Steuben's beautiful, serene showroom is a museum as much as a retail store. At any time of day you'll find people admiring the remarkable design, quality, and craftsmanship of the crystal and glass sculptures, vases, and bowls that have made Steuben a household name internationally. Prices are far (very far) from cheap, but then again, when you buy a Steuben glass piece you join the ranks of royalty and foreign leaders: this glass has been chosen for gifts of state by every U.S. president since 1947.
Mon.-Sat. 10 A.M. to 6 P.M.

FABRIC

JERRY BROWN IMPORTED FABRICS

37 West 57th St. (Fifth & Sixth Aves.)
753-3626

It's hard not to get overwhelmed in this store—there are bolts and bolts of fabric in all colors, types, and patterns. Here you'll find only natural fibers and European imports. The ground-floor showroom displays the more casual merchandise; the upstairs—for which you need a sales escort—is the locale for the more elaborate fabrics: sequined and beaded lace, gold lamé. Warning: Only fabrics are sold here. For patterns and accessories you'll need to go elsewhere.
Mon.-Fri. 9 A.M. to 6 P.M., Sat. 9 A.M. to 5:30 P.M.

LAURA ASHLEY

714 Madison Ave. (63rd St.)
735-5000

Once again, here's that familiar English country print in wallpaper and other fabrics for the home. Unlike most, Laura Ashley wallpaper is actually paper (with vinyl backing), because nothing here, not even the wallpaper, deviates from the delicate.
Mon.-Sat. 10 A.M. to 6 P.M., Thurs. till 7 P.M.

MARIMEKKO

7 West 56th St. (Fifth & Sixth Aves.)
581-9616

Don't mistake this establishment for a Japanese store. "Marimekko" is Finnish for "Mary's little dress." Those who are already *au courant* shop at Marimekko for unique, artistic leisure clothing and fabrics designed in Finland. Although the styles are understated, the colors range from subdued to brilliant. Also available are brightly colored and patterned pillows and other Finnish-style home furnishings. *Mon.-Fri. 10 A.M. to 6:30 P.M., Thurs. till 7:30 P.M., Sat. 10 A.M. to 6 P.M.*

PARON FABRICS

60 West 57th St. (Fifth & Sixth Aves.)
247-6451

A well-stocked, organized store with every type of fabric imaginable and plenty of salespeople ready to help. Each bolt of cloth is clearly labeled with the fiber content and price. A few doors down, on the fourth floor, is Paron II (56 West 57th Street), where you'll find remnants of the same quality fabrics for 50% off the already reasonable original prices. *Mon.-Sat. 9 A.M. to 5:45 P.M.*

FURNITURE & BEDDING

CONRANS

Citicorp Center, 160 East 54th St. (Third Ave.)
371-2225

Conrans is a department store for city living, jammed with treasures for every cramped corner of a Manhattan apartment. Many a young professional can be seen filling up a cart with all the necessities to make his or her new place seem like home. This immense store carries all sorts of chairs, drafting tables, coffee tables, bed frames, and utility carts. An entire department has a complete collection of add-on shelving and closet organizers in primary colors. Then there are glasses in a million styles, inexpensive ceramics in a variety of mod pastels, vases, table settings, lighting, Marimekko fabrics, linens, and duvet covers—plus toys, desk accessories, prints, cookware, tote bags, and planters. Other locations around the city. *Mon.-Fri. 10 A.M. to 9 P.M., Sat. 10 A.M. to 7 P.M., Sun. 11 A.M. to 6 P.M.*

KLEINSLEEP

2569 Broadway (96th & 97th Sts.)
866-5300

Posturpedic, Maxipedic, Beautyrest, Correct Comfort, Perfect Sleeper—you'll find every kind of bed from all the name manufacturers at prices (especially during sales) that will let you sleep at night. Immediate delivery available. *Mon.-Fri. 10 A.M. to 9 P.M., Sat. 10 A.M. to 6 P.M., Sun. 11 A.M. to 6 P.M.*

SCANDINAVIAN GALLERY

Scandinavian Gallery has a great selection of modern furniture of high quality. You'll find sofas, loveseats, and sleepers in natural fabrics, subtle colors, and current styles (all

*185 Madison Ave. (34th &
35th Sts.)
689-6890*

reasonably priced in the $500-$700 range) along with attractive dining and bedroom ensembles, oak and teak shelving, tables, and stands. All the accessories featured in the displays are for sale—an eclectic array of lamps, sculpture, ceramics, and rugs.

Mon.-Fri. 10 A.M. to 7 P.M., Sat. 10 A.M. to 6 P.M., Sun. noon to 5 P.M.

KITCHENWARE

D.F. SANDERS

*952 Madison Ave. (75th &
76th Sts.)
879-6161*

Hi-tech housewares have been in vogue since the opening of MOMA's design collection. A lovely store filled with these functional *objets d'art*, D.F. Sanders has a good selection of well-designed pieces: everything is pleasantly graphic and completely practical. Perfect furnishings for modern spaces. Located in SoHo, too, at 386 West Broadway (925-9040).

Mon.-Sat. 10 A.M. to 6 P.M., Sun. noon to 5 P.M.

HOFFRITZ FOR CUTLERY

*331 Madison Ave. (42nd &
43rd Sts.)
697-7344*

Hoffritz made its reputation in cutlery, and you can still find an excellent selection of fine French, German, and Swiss kitchen knives here, in addition to carving sets, hunting knives, pocket knives, and literally hundreds of types of scissors. Indulge yourself in a pair especially designed for trimming beards, for instance, or ignore the implications and ask for the pair that cut double-knit polyester. Hoffritz also carries some fine upscale gift items: gold-plated flasks, imported electric shavers, handmade shaving brushes, and the like. Call the above number for other Manhattan locations.

Mon.-Sat. 9 A.M. to 6 P.M.

MACY'S THE CELLAR

*Herald Square, 34th St. &
Seventh Ave.
695-4400*

Although Macy's Cellar offers a good supply of packaged gourmet gift baskets, its real draw is the bountiful assortment of kitchenware and small household appliances. The selection of electric woks and waffle irons, for instance, is without rival. From pots and pans to place settings, Macy's offers many good buys, especially during the regular sales. Macy's carries most of the high-end brands, but don't be afraid to try The Cellar's own: they are usually excellent.

Mon., Thurs. & Fri. 9:45 A.M. to 8:30 P.M., Tues. & Wed. 9:45 A.M. to 6:45 P.M., Sat. 9:45 A.M. to 6 P.M., Sun. 10 A.M. to 6 P.M.

POTTERY BARN

117 East 59th St.
(Lexington & Park Aves.)
753-5424

The Pottery Barn is full of color, from its pastel china to its two-toned stemware. Actually, some of the china is also two-toned and a bit wild, but most of the stock is simple and quite reasonably priced. The selection of glassware is excellent, and there are a half a dozen flatware styles to choose from. As for plates, there is the aforementioned china, as well as a host of plastic alternatives. The Pottery Barn also carries such various and sundry household goods as flashy garbage cans, plastic picture frames, wicker baskets, and folding chairs. Call the above number for other Manhattan locations.
Mon.-Sat. 10 A.M. to 6:30 P.M., Mon. & Thurs. till 8:30 P.M., Sun. noon to 5 P.M.

ZABAR'S

2245 Broadway (80th St.)
787-2000

Legendary for its supply of foodstuffs, Zabar's has recently added an entire second floor of kitchenware, every bit as bracing as the first floor. One room is devoted entirely to pots and pans, from imported French copper to all-purpose aluminum, from fish poachers to woks. Another is filled with coffee makers, food processors, electric potato peelers, and portable meat slicers. A third houses even smaller doodads: chopping boards, folding wooden dish racks, egg timers, and the best garlic presses we've ever seen. All the items are very well priced, particularly the cutlery.
Mon.-Fri. 8 A.M. to 8 P.M., Sat. 8 A.M. to midnight, Sun. 9 A.M. to 6 P.M.

LIGHTING

LEE'S STUDIO

211 West 57th St. (Seventh Ave. & Broadway)
265-5670

If you're looking to light up your life—or desk, loft, bedroom, or stage—then a visit to this store is a must. Be warned, though: the interior is just as crowded as the window display, and you should be careful if you're accompanied by an active youngster or frisky pooch. The store has a warehouse feeling, with every available inch covered by lamps. But that means you're likely to find what you're looking for—besides lighting in all shapes, sizes, colors, and styles, there are also wall and desk clocks, ceiling fans, sleek phones, and Levolor shades. But first and foremost, both here and at the new store at 1069 Third Avenue, it's lamps,

lamps, and more lamps. It's also one of few Tizio distributors in New York City.
Mon.-Fri. 10 A.M. to 6:30 P.M., Sat. 10 A.M. to 6 P.M.

LET THERE BE NEON INC.

38 White St. (Church & Broadway)
226-4883

A vision of bright lights and big-city nights best describes this store, which claims to be the first and "by far the best" establishment to specialize in neon. It is known for artfully transforming customers' sketches, ideas, and hand wavings into neon novelties. Owner Rudi Stern says, "People call up with neon dreams and need the images realized within 24 hours." All this and more is possible. Prices start at $200.
By appointment only.

LINENS

ANICHINI GALLERY

150 Fifth Ave., Suite 524 (20th St.)
982-7274

Operating almost as a salon, the Anichini Gallery, owned and operated by two dynamic women, offers antique linens, lace, crafts, poetry and drama readings, musicals, and contemporary art exhibitions. A mixed bag, perhaps, yet the complete selection of hand-worked items provides unusual choices. There's a full range of bed and table linens from the 19th and early 20th centuries, along with beautiful antique blouses, capes, dresses, and shawls. Browse through the past to make a present (or your presence) more exciting.
Mon.-Fri. 9 A.M. to 5 P.M. by appointment only.

DESCAMPS

723 Madison Ave. (63rd & 64th Sts.)
355-2522

These bed linens, towels, and robes—all designed by Primrose Bordier and imported from France—are for those seeking a less traditional look. Whether floral or geometric, the patterns border on the painterly, in the modern sense. Even the whites and the solid pastels vibrate color. Descamp's baby linens are exquisite, though bolder than most. The terrycloth robes, sporty and vibrant, make wonderful gifts.
Mon.-Sat. 10 A.M. to 6 P.M.

D. PORTHAULT & CO.

18 East 69th St. (Madison & Fifth Aves.)
688-1660

Recognized worldwide as the finest French manufacturer of bed linens, Porthault actually invented the printed sheet. Not surprisingly, its trademark is a large floral print available on sheets and terrycloth towels, robes, and accessories.

Although many items are in stock, custom orders are welcome on all the 100%-cotton, -linen, and -silk merchandise. Porthault also manufactures children's clothing (up to size 8) in, of course, 100% cotton.
Mon.-Sat. 10 A.M. to 6 P.M.

FRETTE

787 Madison Ave. (66th & 67th Sts.)
988-5221

Indeed, this is the stuff that dreams are made on—a most uncompromising line of silk, linen, and cotton sheets that will lull you to sleep in luxury. The prices are as lofty as the look, but you won't, if you choose carefully, be replacing these pieces soon. You'll also find towels, terrycloth robes, and other items for the bath.
Mon.-Fri. 10 A.M. to 6 P.M., Sat. 10 A.M. to 5:30 P.M.

JANA STARR-JEAN HOFFMAN ANTIQUES

236 East 80th St. (Second & Third Aves.)
861-8256

Over the years, these two antique dealers have put together a huge inventory of fabulous table and bed linens. They are chosen from every imaginable country, and you'll marvel at the handmade lace and embroidery. The shawls, the jewelry, the hats, the canes, and the charming white dresses are all quite outstanding. White is the key word here, and removing the few spots one finds is an art perfected by the owners. Known for their unusual materials, they sell a varied range of curtains, linens, and things of yesteryear.
Mon.-Sat. noon to 6:30 P.M.

PRATESI

829 Madison Ave. (69th & 70th Sts.)
288-2315

Pratesi provides New Yorkers with an exclusive source of the world's finest Italian linens and lingerie. Although there are only two new collections a year, special orders are welcome. All sheets are 100% cotton and have a thread count of 320 per inch (by comparison, percale cotton, the best most department stores offer, is 220 per inch). Some of the most popular purchases include sheets, table linens, terrycloth robes, cashmere blankets, plush towels, and baby items.
Mon.-Sat. 10 A.M. to 6 P.M.

SCANDIA DOWN SHOP

1011 Madison Ave. (78th St.)
734-8787

Before starting your annual hibernation, why not stop by this store and pick up a luxurious down comforter that's guaranteed to keep you warm? In more types and combinations of down and feather than you thought possible (white Balkan goose down, grey duck down, white goose feather, etc.), Scandia Down's comforters are sold in sizes crib to king. In

addition to down comforters, they sell down pillows and robes, lap blankets, European linens, potpourris, and a small selection of imported beds. For a nominal fee, they also provide a washing and maintenance service (for Scandia Down comforters only). You'll pay more for a comforter here than you will at a department store, but you can be sure that the quality is worth it. The store makes an extra effort to clean the down and reduce the feather content—leaving you with a comforter that will last a lifetime (or two).
Mon.-Fri. 10 A.M. to 6 P.M., Sat. 10 A.M. to 5 P.M.

SILVER

JAMES ROBINSON INC.

15 East 57th St. (Fifth &
Madison Aves.)
752-6166

Originally from London, the Robinsons give special attention to the acquisition and display of Georgian- to Victorian-era silver. There are more hallmarks here than you can imagine. Place settings of intricate, beautiful patterns form an interesting collection; these table settings can be completed by choosing antique china and porcelain dinnerware. Table accessories—crystal candlesticks and the like—are plentiful, and if you'd like to complete the table by adorning the hostess's neck, there's lots of silver jewelry, too.
June to Aug. Mon.-Fri. 10 A.M.-4:30 P.M.; Sept. to May Mon.-Sat. 10 A.M. to 5 P.M.

JEAN'S SILVERSMITHS

16 West 45th St. (Fifth &
Sixth Aves.)
575-0723

Located in a sliver of a storefront somewhere between a nook and a cranny, Jean's has little choice but to stock its wares from floor to ceiling. As a result, this is not a store for browsing, nor should it be. Jean's specializes in American flatware. You've just inherited Grandmother's silver, and they haven't made that sort of salad fork since Taft? Jean's probably has it, and at a reasonable price, too. Need a set of goblets, a candelabra, or a tea service as well? They're also available, as are an abundance of platters. Everything is somewhat tarnished, but that's the sign of a real bargain, right?
Mon.-Thurs. 9:15 A.M. to 4:45 P.M., Fri. 9:15 A.M. to 3:45 P.M.

M. RAPHAEL OF LONDON

Established in London in 1911 and in New York in 1948, M. Raphael enjoys a solid reputation, and curator Henry Raphael is an internationally respected authority. The breadth of

1050 Second Ave. (55th St.)
838-0178

the shop's antique silver collection (English, Continental, American) is recognized on both sides of the Atlantic; many of the items date back to the 17th century. Excellent value here.

Mon.-Sat. 10:30 A.M. to 5:30 P.M., Sun. noon to 6 P.M.

S. WYLER INC.

713 Madison Ave. (63rd & 64th Sts.)
838-1910

If you're looking for silver or porcelain, or both, S. Wyler can offer you choice pieces, plus the expertise of the author of the definitive *The Book of Old Silver*. With a worldwide reputation built during 98 years in business, S. Wyler carries on the family tradition (via son Richard) of selling fine antique porcelain, silver, and Victorian *objets d'art*.

Mon.-Fri. 9 A.M. to 5:30 P.M.

TIFFANY & CO.

727 Fifth Ave. (57th St.)
755-8000

If they ever did serve breakfast at Tiffany's, silverware wouldn't be a problem. Located on the second floor of this grande dame of gilt (known best for its luscious jewels), the silver department veritably gleams. Once you've see the sterling omelet pan, for instance, it's hard to imagine why anyone who could afford it would use anything else. Strolling the aisles of glass display cases, one finds much that beckons, not the least of which are the museum-quality pieces interspersed with the retail items. The selection of flatware is handsome and costly, but after all, this is Tiffany's.

Mon.-Sat. 10 A.M. to 5:30 P.M.

Image & Sound

CAMERAS & FILM

DUGGAL

9 West 20th St. (Fifth & Sixth Aves.)
242-7000

Widely acknowledged to be the top processing lab in the city, Duggal does professional work at professional prices, handling everything from Kodak processing to custom color printing. You can rent a studio, get slides duped, and have your photos laminated and mounted.

Mon.-Fri. 7 A.M. to midnight, Sat. & Sun. 9 A.M. to 5 P.M.

47TH STREET PHOTO

67 West 47th St. (Sixth &
Seventh Aves.)
398-1410

Though 47th Street Photo's reputation as a cheap outlet for electronics and computers is largely undeserved, for mass-market 35-mm cameras it does have some of the best prices around. But if you don't know exactly what you want, stay away—service here can be as brisk as the sales. On the other hand, if you do know, and you're not interested in shopping around, this is probably your best one-stop. Excellent prices on film, too.
Mon.-Thurs. 9 A.M. to 6 P.M., Fri. 9 A.M. to 2 P.M., Sun. 10 A.M. to 4 P.M.

KEN HANSEN PHOTOGRAPHIC

920 Broadway (21st &
22nd Sts.)
777-5900

If classic cameras—Nikons, Hasselblads, Rolliflexes—make you drool, then make a pilgrimage to Ken Hansen, where you'll find an overwhelming selection. Think of it: 30 mint Leicas in a row. For Ansel Adams disciples there's an impressive large-format department, plus Hansen's peerless collection of bags and gadgets. This is not a discount house, but Hansen doesn't overcharge.
Mon.-Fri. 9:30 A.M. to 5:30 P.M.

LENS & REPRO

33 West 17th St. (Fifth &
Sixth Aves.)
675-1900

A family operation that deals exclusively in the most sophisticated professional equipment, Lens & Repro specializes in top-of-the-line studio fittings (strobes, tripods), which it rents as well as sells. As at Ken Hansen, you pay not only for product, but also for service. For instance, if you're on a shoot in Brazil and your equipment falls in the Amazon, you can trust Lens & Repro to have a replacement outfit helicoptered in.
Mon.-Fri. 8:30 A.M. to 5:30 P.M.

ELECTRONICS

THE AUDIO EXCHANGE

28 West 8th St. (Fifth &
Sixth Aves.)
982-7191

Probably the best place in the city to shop for used high-end stereo equipment, Audio Exchange is nothing if not thorough: it boasts an attentive staff, a well-appointed listening room, and a service department that carefully inspects then warrants all the used components, and even handles installations. You'll find good deals on everything from Carver to Tandberg, and on a wide range of peripherals, such as Grado

cartridges, Sennheiser headphones, and Monster Cable. Another location at 57 Park Place (964-4570).
Mon.-Fri. 11:30 A.M. to 7 P.M., Sat. 11:30 A.M. to 6 P.M.

HARVEY ELECTRONICS

2 West 45th St. (Fifth & Sixth Aves.)
575-5000

Though you can find a few medium-range components here, Harvey is basically high-end, both in image and inventory. While the discount houses have salesmen in sportshirts, Harvey's are in dress shirts and ties; the store's displays are no less neatly groomed. As for the equipment, all the big names are represented: Nakamichi, Bang & Olufsen, Yamaha, McIntosh. You see—and, more importantly, hear—everything before purchasing, unlike the electronics stores that display nothing and deliver your merchandise packed without your having inspected it. Regular prices are premium, but the sales are not bad. Harvey also maintains its merchandise with an in-house service department.
Mon.-Fri. 9:30 A.M. to 6 P.M., Sat. 10 A.M. to 6 P.M.

MIDTOWN AUDIO & VIDEO CENTER

150 West 28th St.
629-8633

Of Manhattan's discount electronics stores, Midtown is the least user-friendly, but it's also the cheapest. It's not that the salespeople are rude, it's just that nothing is on display—it's all boxed in a warehouselike storefront, so you have to know what you want. The best prices, of course, are cash only.
Mon.-Fri. 9 A.M. to 6:30 P.M., Sun. 11 A.M. to 5 P.M.

RECORDS

BLEECKER BOB'S GOLDEN OLDIES

118 West 3rd St. (MacDougal St. & Sixth Ave.)
475-9677

If Tower Records doesn't have what you're looking for, Bleecker Bob's probably will, especially if it's an import single. Hard-to-find albums, though, are still hard to find here, because the store's organization is somewhat eccentric: grouping is by genre rather than alphabetically. Don't let the maze discourage you, because the people at the counter know the location of every album, and if you're just browsing, the genre system might turn you on to a new band. Prices are consistently inconsistent, so search out the values (start with the clearance rack).
Daily noon to 1 A.M., Fri. & Sat. till 3 A.M.

J & R MUSIC WORLD

You don't need college calculus to figure out that J & R maximizes record price and selection. Though it can be

23 Park Row (Ann & Beekman Sts.)
732-8600

weak on independents and imports, J & R does carry a huge stock of back-catalog and reissue material, and it offers the best prices in town on current major releases. The Main Outlet at 23 Park Row houses rock, pop, and folk, as well as the audio and video hardware departments (better known for viewing than buying).
Mon.-Sat. 9:30 A.M. to 6:30 P.M.

RECORD MART

1470 Broadway (42nd St.)
840-0580

Calypso. Salsa. Samba. Reggae. Longing for these Latin and Caribbean beats but can't afford the time or money to go to the exotic destinations that gave birth to these sounds? Look no further. Record Mart, located in Times Square, the heart (and soul?) of New York, offers one of the largest selections of Caribbean and Latin American music in New York.
Mon.-Thurs. 9 A.M. to 9 P.M., Fri. 9 A.M. to 11 P.M., Sat. 9 A.M. to 10 P.M., Sun. noon to 8 P.M.

TOWER RECORDS

692 Broadway (4th St.)
505-1500

The 4th Street branch of Tower Records has more records, CDs, and tapes under its roof than any other store in the city. It even carries most of the independent labels, a great reason to shop here. Come for the spectacle, too: in addition to the regular in-store band promos, the customers and the cashiers all model the latest East Village looks. As a result, the Fourth Street Tower is where some of rock 'n' roll's many contradictions come alive: pink-haired fans of the Splat Cats ringing up Lionel Richie, Wayne Newton, and the Chieftains at $7.99 a pop. The Tower at 66th Street and Broadway has a large selection as well, but boy, is it boring in comparison.
Daily 9 A.M. to midnight.

Jewelry

COSTUME

CIRO OF BOND STREET INC.

The designs are fairly conservative—nothing is too big or too garish in this credible collection of costume jewelry. Simulated pearls are set simply and believably, and faux

711 Fifth Ave. (56th St.)
752-0441

diamonds and gemstones are perfectly scaled. Fancy addresses mark the seven Manhattan Ciro stores—proof that many people are faking it when putting on the ritz.
Mon.-Sat. 9:30 A.M. to 5:30. P.M.

QUALITY

A LA VIEILLE RUSSIE

781 Fifth Ave. (59th St.)
752-1727

Located next to the Sherry Netherland hotel and diagonally across the street from the Plaza, this boutique is a monument to the wonders of Russian craftsmanship. Long a landmark at this special corner, A La Vieille Russie displays a magnificent array of jewel-encrusted icons, glass, jewelry, and enamel that will dazzle your eye and dent your wallet. But go see the beautiful pieces anyway—a little dazzle never hurt anyone.
Mon.-Sat. 10 A.M. to 5:30 P.M.; closed Sat. in summer.

BUCCELLATI

Trump Tower, 725 Fifth Ave. (56th & 57th Sts.)
308-5533

Buccellati's Trump Tower store screams money. The surprisingly stark interior reveals an ornate collection of Italian design, crafted to be works of art by themselves with perhaps less thought to how they will look being worn. Big stones, thick chains, large pins—the look is expensive and showy, but undoubtedly elegant. There are some smaller pieces without the glitz and heavy price tags. Buccellati has a silver store at 46 East 57th Street that features an exquisite collection of silver goods of more traditional design.
Mon.-Sat. 10 A.M. to 6 P.M.; closed Sat. in summer.

BULGARI

Hotel Pierre, 2 East 61st St.
(Fifth & Madison Aves.)
486-0086

The house of Bulgari is one of the few privately owned family establishments that is as dedicated to important jewelry as it is to personal service. The New York branch of the Rome store is run by Nicola Bulgari, a grandson of the founder. From the moment you enter the brass-and-steel latticed doorway and are seated amid the recessed display cases, you are aware of the Bulgari difference. Bulgari's designs, originally inspired by the Art Deco movement, are today a skillful blend of the formal and the casual. Typical pieces are designed around antique coins or cameos, a Bulgari trademark. Also popular are the *trombinos*, domed-shaped rings set with one or two precious stones.
Mon.-Sat. 10 A.M. to 5:30 P.M.; closed Sat. in summer.

409

CARTIER

725 Fifth Ave. (52nd St.)
753-0111

The definition of good taste, Cartier is the only Fifth Avenue jeweler to openly display its wares—hence it is one of the hottest tourist spots on the street. Browse freely through the gift collection of exquisitely simple fine jewelry and signature watches—all items are set in crystal-clear glass cases for easy viewing. In a separate room on the first floor, there are elegantly set tables proudly displaying Cartier's silver, china, glass, crystal, and stemware. One can only dream about the lives of brides registered here. The store is immaculate, amazingly friendly, and justifiably expensive.
Mon.-Sat. 10 A.M. to 5:30 P.M.

HANS APPENZELLER

820 Madison Ave. (68th & 69th Sts.)
570-0504

Beautiful modern jewelry by this Dutch designer is lovingly displayed in glass cases so the light hits the pieces just so. Appenzeller jewelry is flawlessly fluid and pleasingly graphic. There are made-to-order bracelets to cling to your wrist, hammered earrings, wire mesh chokers, and smooth, rounded rings twinkling with baby gemstones.
Mon.-Sat. 10 A.M. to 6 P.M.; closed Sat. in Aug.

HARRY WINSTON

718 Fifth Ave. (56th St.)
245-2000

Harry Winston is famous for its giant gems and the giant celebrities who buy them. Quality and size are the trademarks of the rocks found here. This is the real stuff, the big time. What other fine jewelry store is closed the day before Mother's Day?
Mon.-Fri. 10 A.M. to 5 P.M.

WATCHES

TIME WILL TELL

962 Madison Ave. (75th & 76th Sts.)
861-2663

Although digital watches may be accurate, their excessive functionality has taken all the fashion out of wearing a watch. Re-enter the antique wristwatch. One of the most lovingly guarded collections of these timeless beauties can be found at Time Will Tell, a charming little shop that sells only antique watches. One of the knowledgeable staff will provide pertinent biographical data on whichever watch you're considering adopting. These little bits of history sell for $300 to over $30,000. (Functionality is cheap; collector's items cost.) Patek Phillipe, Vacheron & Constantin, Hamilton, and Paul Ditesheim are names of master craftsmen; don't expect Seiko, Pulsar, or Casio.
Mon.-Sat. 10 A.M. to 6 P.M.

WEMPE

*695 Fifth Ave. (54th &
55th Sts.)
751-4884*

Wempe offers a complete selection of contemporary watches and clocks, as well as fine European jewelry in both classic and contemporary styles. The extremely professional staff will work with you while you choose one of the many designs, or they will help you select any combination of precious stones to be worked into your own design—they offer a complete selection of stones and diamonds. There is also an on-site repair service for all Wempe items. *Mon.-Sat. 10 A.M. to 6 P.M.*

Leather Goods

BELTRAMI

*711 Fifth Ave. (55th &
56th Sts.)
838-4101*

Italians produce exquisite leather goods with style, and the Beltrami style is one of classic luxury. Men and women will find leather and suede coats (with and without fur), suits, and other clothes in glove-tanned leather. It also has shoes (most with matching bags) and complete sets of matching luggage. About 80% of the merchandise is designed by Beltrami; the remainder are exclusives from other Italian manufacturers. The staff is very obliging; if, for example, you see a black coat but would prefer the style in yellow, it will be their pleasure to make it up for you. *Mon.-Sat. 10 A.M. to 6 P.M., Thurs. till 7 P.M.*

BOTTEGA VENETA INC.

*635 Madison Ave. (59th &
60th Sts.)
319-0303*

This Madison Avenue store looks like the first floor of a department store, albeit an expensive one—umbrellas, hosiery, and scarves there, shoes here, and bags over there. The handbag collection is less formal and more colorful than other designer imports—woven leather is the trademark look, not repetitive initials. Some of the woven styles are available in interesting tri-color patterns—red, yellow, and orange or blue, green, and violet. The shoe department's selection is mixed—some styles are pretty and unusual, others dowdy and dull, but all are dazzlingly expensive. *Mon.-Sat. 10 A.M. to 6 P.M., Thurs. till 7 P.M.*

LANCEL

Luxurious leather or practical polyurethane with at least one signature Lancel "L" on the bag is what you'll find here. The shapes are elegant—neatly rounded or starkly squared, all

690 Madison Ave. (62nd
St.)
753-6918

bags subtly yet securely fastened. The look is similar to
Fendi, but the prices are slightly less. Lancel features a full
line of handbags, luggage, and accessories—from teeny
wallets to large leather trunks.
Mon.-Sat. 10 A.M. to 6 P.M.

LEDERER

613 Madison Ave. (58th
St.)
355-5515

The selection here is enormous—leather goods, handbags,
luggage, and accessories in an expansive array of styles—all
executed flawlessly with proper attention to detail. Hermes
and Chanel look-alikes sit next to exotic-skin treasures—
alligator, lizard, and crocodile bags, either classically plain or
extravagantly fancy, with jeweled or cameo clasps. Also to be
found are Hartmann luggage, a complete men's collection,
and an intriguing selection of authentic hunting gear. No
bargains, but prices are less than designer.
Mon.-Fri. 9:30 A.M. to 6 P.M., Sat. 10 A.M. to 6 P.M.

MADE IN THE USA

130 East 59th St. (Park &
Lexington Aves.)
838-5076

When shopping for women's leather clothing and outer-
wear, be sure to stop by here. This smallish store is teeming
with racks of jackets, coats, pants, and skirts in black or
colored leathers and plain or adorned styles. A recent visit
uncovered many of the same styles found at comparable
stores for one-third the price. The salespeople are very
helpful and friendly, especially if they think you're buying,
not browsing. Don't be bashful—if you don't see what you
want, ask one of the salespeople to check in the back. There's
a small selection of men's leather gear, too.
*Mon.-Fri. 9 A.M. to 7 P.M., Sat 10 A.M. to 7 P.M., Sun.
12:30 P.M. to 6 P.M.*

NORTH BEACH LEATHER

772 Madison Ave. (66th
St.)
772-0707

If you spot someone in a drop-dead leather outfit bought in
this country, odds are it came from North Beach Leather.
Here you'll find luxury leathers in ultra-high-fashion styles:
bolero jackets, bandeaux, full-zippered minis, strapless dresses, trousers, blazers, and jeans in jellybean colors or basic
black. It's all so fashion-forward that most of the outfits
seems like next year's styles. Prices are predictable but not
pretentious—in the $300-$500 range.
Mon.-Fri. 10 A.M. to 7 P.M., Sat. 10 A.M. to 6 P.M.

Rent A . . . /Where to Find

BABYSITTER

AVALON NURSE REGISTRY & CHILD SERVICE

*116 Central Park South
(Sixth & Seventh Aves.)
245-0250*

Open all the time, Avalon will send a reliable sitter to your house or hotel for a starting price of just $6 an hour, plus carfare, with a four-hour minimum (prices vary according to the age and number of children). In addition to babysitters, it can provide housekeepers, tutors, nurses, nannies, even hospital equipment. Whatever your situation, this business will help you to have fewer worries.
Daily 24 hours.

GILBERT CHILD CARE AGENCY INC.

*115 West 57th St., Suite 3R (Sixth & Seventh Aves.)
757-7900*

Finding a babysitter you can trust is not as difficult as you may have thought. This company has been in business for over 40 years and has built its reputation by word of mouth. The sitters are carefully interviewed; references are checked thoroughly. And best of all, the rates are surprisingly affordable: $5 per hour per child (which increases by 25 cents for each additional child), plus carfare and a 12% agency fee. Service extends to hotels with a four-hour minimum.
Mon.-Fri. 9 A.M. to 5 P.M.

COSTUME

ALLAN UNIFORM RENTAL SERVICE INC.

*112 East 23rd St.
(Lexington & Park Aves.)
529-4655*

Fancy yourself as Scarlett O'Hara or Rhett Butler? Maybe a 1920's flapper or gangster suits you better. These and 150 other costumes are waiting for you in this roomy loft on 23rd Street. Other favorites include Cleopatra, Zorro, clowns, the Easter bunny, and of course Santa Claus. The shop is family owned and operated, reliable, and extremely accommodating. Most costumes come with all accessories (tommy guns, wigs, snakes, etc.) and it also sells makeup. Prices are very reasonable ($30-$65 for 24 hours), and the stock is constantly being expanded.
Mon.-Fri. 9 A.M. to 5 P.M.; open Sat. in Oct.

ANIMAL OUTFITS FOR PEOPLE

252 West 46th St., 3rd Fl.
(Eighth Ave. & Broadway)
840-6219

You'll find a whole menagerie here, but not one of these animals will be breathing. This store rents animal, and only animal, costumes for adults. Many of your favorite animals you've seen on TV have come from this store: the six-foot lobster seen on the David Letterman show; the polar bear recently seen advertising a popular wine cooler. Keeping these two company are reindeer, tigers, lions, alligators, the classic gorilla, and even a cockroach or two (ubiquitous in New York). It rents only original creations, so you won't find the likes of Big Bird or Kermit the Frog. The minimum price is $75 for three days.
Mon.-Fri. noon to 6 P.M. by appointment only.

UNIVERSAL COSTUMES CO.

535 Eighth Ave., 21st Fl.
(36th & 37th Sts.)
239-3222

Dread Halloween or costume parties? Fear no more. You'll surely find a costume to your liking in Manhattan's largest costume rental shop for adults. There are racks filled with period clothes, animals, futuristic ensembles, and international garbs. What you don't see they'll make in the workroom. Prices start at $50.
Mon.-Fri. 9:30 A.M. to 5:30 P.M.

FURNITURE

CHURCHILL FURNITURE RENTAL

44 East 32nd St. (Madison Ave. & Park Ave. So.)
686-0444

Here you can get one piece or an entire package for homes, apartments, or offices. Churchill also has complete accessories, including lamps, pictures, carpets, mirrors, draperies, televisions, bed linens, china, and cookware. The huge selection includes styles that are contemporary, classic, and traditional; children's furniture, too. Short- or long-term leases are available, as well as a purchase-option plan, immediate delivery, and an interior design service.
Fri.-Sat. 9 A.M. to 7 P.M., Sun. 11 A.M. to 5 P.M.

HELICOPTER

ISLAND HELICOPTER

East 34th St. & the East River
925-8807

Island, in business for over 18 years, runs a large, diversified fleet of four- to 14-seat jet helicopters. It welcomes any kind of request, from airport runs to cinematography, personal, and sightseeing charters. Corporations may lease the helicopters or use Island's own courier service.
By appointment only.

HOUSEKEEPER

MAID TO ORDER
500 Park Ave. (59th St.)
223-4455

If you've brought everything with you on this trip but your personal help, this agency may be exactly what you need. The butlers are reliable and handy—you can hire someone who will press your clothes, shine your shoes, and drive your car; he (or she) can even serve as a translator. This business started with just a nucleus of five people; today the entire on-call staff of 50 to 60 people has been personally recommended by that original core group, so you needn't worry about the character of the employees.
Daily 5 A.M. to 8 P.M.

LIMOUSINE

BERMUDA LIMOUSINE INC.
537 West 20th St. (Tenth & Eleventh Aves.)
249-8400

Absolutely classic and not flashy, Bermuda's Cadillac limousines have transported distinguished American and European families, clubs, and corporations for over 45 years. Reasonable hourly, daily, weekly, and monthly rates. Both business and personal charge accounts are welcome.
Daily 24 hours.

CLASS ACT LIMOUSINE
2315 Twelfth Ave. (32nd St.)
491-5300

This ultimate limousine service considers the extraordinary to be normal. Standard features in each of the Mercedes, Lincoln, and Cadillac stretch limousines are an open bar, fresh flowers, color TV, VCR with a choice of 200 movies, 12-speaker stereo with a cassette library, fine crystal, solid and glass partitions, sensuous interiors, and elaborate custom controls. Service 24 hours a day; trips to anywhere.
Daily 24 hours.

SECRETARY

ALL-LANGUAGE SERVICES INC.
545 Fifth Ave. (45th St.)
986-1688

All-Language will translate and/or type your manuscript in any of 59 languages for $25 per page.
Daily 24 hours.

LNS TYPING SERVICE

"If we can read it or hear it, we'll type it," is Lori's motto, and they will type anything—business letters, manuscripts,

*317 East 75th St. (First &
Second Aves.)*
288-TYPE

financial reports, resumes, directories, at $2.50 per page,
with a $25 minimum.
Mon.-Fri. 9 A.M. to 5 P.M.

TV & VCR

COLUMBUS TV AND VIDEO CENTER

*529 Columbus Ave. (86th
St.)*
496-2626; 496-2627

With stores like this one, one need never buy another
appliance again. You can rent a TV—small or large screen—
a VCR, even an air conditioner for very reasonable fees.
Many brands are available; prompt delivery and installation
are free of charge, and any broken item is replaced immediately. No minimum or maximum time limits, either.
Mon.-Sat. 9 A.M. to 8:45 P.M.

VIDEO

CINE CLUB VIDEO

*201 East 42nd St. (Third
Ave.)*
818-1660

Becoming a member of Cine Club Video is more like
subscribing to HBO than joining a video club. Membership
fees are based on the number of tapes you wish to rent—$30
per month entitles you to three cassettes at all times. There
are no late fees, no rewind charges, no time constraints, and
no hassles. Checkouts and returns are tracked by optical
sensor for minimum waiting. There are over 7,600 titles to
choose from, a computerized catalog, a monthly newsletter,
and even low-cost VCR rentals. This concept is definitely
not for everyone, but it's perfect for diehard movie fans.
Mon.-Sat. 10:30 A.M. to 6:45 P.M.

RAREBIRD VIDEO

*482 Broome St. (Wooster
St.)*
334-8150

"Our selection of video is the most esoteric in this city,"
boasts owner Jack Morris of his five-year-old establishment.
His selection is also one of the largest. This small shop (the
basement is under renovation to provide twice as much
space) houses over 7,000 titles in rentals and sales, with
much variety in all genres: silent films range from slapstick
comedy to Louise Brooks favorites, black-and-white classics
from the original *Scrooge* to Bogie and Bacall, Disney films,
animated features, and the gamut of exercise tapes. Films in
the foreign section are both subtitled and dubbed, and there
are special divisions devoted to the careers of such masters as
Fellini, Kurosawa, Buñuel, and Bergman. Membership per
year costs $49.95 ($35 to renew), and each video costs $2.99

416

per night. Periodically there are showings of neighborhood artists' work. This is the only video rental store in SoHo and therefore has an established following that includes many of the local celebrities.

Daily 11:30 A.M. to 10 P.M., Sun. till 8 P.M.

YACHT

MANHATTAN YACHT CHARTERS

233 East 81st St. (Second & Third Aves.)
772-9430

This yacht charter company specializes in complete party planning for two to 600 people. An international boat brokerage firm with contacts all over the U.S. and the world, it'll put you in touch with a boat ready to fulfill your needs. That could mean a little red tugboat for a movie shoot or a luxury yacht for a once-in-a-lifetime wedding party. Menu planning, entertainment, and decorations can be arranged.

Mon.-Fri. 9 A.M. to 5 P.M.

YACHT OWNERS ASSOCIATION OF NEW YORK

225 West 34th St. (Seventh & Eighth Aves.)
736-6526

Relief is in store for those unable to deny the sailor in them. This association acts as a broker for 400 licensed captains in the New York area who charter their boats, which can accommodate two to 400 people. Perfect for all occasions: an intimate anniversary dinner, wild wedding bash, or glorious cruise to the Caribbean. Call them up for an appointment to see photos of the boats; they'll take you out to inspect the one that particularly impresses you. After that, mate, the rest is up to you.

Daily 9 A.M. to 5 P.M. by appointment only.

Sporting Goods

ATHLETE'S FOOT

16 West 57th St. (Fifth & Sixth Aves.)
586-1936

The Athlete's Foot has been around since the running and exercise craze was in its embryonic state. Today this establishment, the biggest of its kind, sports more than 20 different brands of sneakers. The variety of sizes and styles is unparalleled. If you can't decide which brand or style is right for your needs, turn to the staff. There are several other shops around the city; call the above number for their locations.

Mon.-Fri. 10 A.M. to 7 P.M., Sat. & Sun. noon to 6 P.M.

HERMAN'S SPORTING GOODS

135 West 42nd St. (Sixth Ave. & Broadway)
730-7400

Herman's dabbles in most sports but is particularly strong in tennis, golf, exercise equipment, and sportswear. The store carries all the name brands (Nike, Adidas, Reebok, New Balance), but itself is hardly chic—it looks more like an upscale Woolworth's. Shop here for reasonable prices and for convenience's sake. The service, if you get any, is terrible; the salespeople are often so misinformed that they become misleading. Look out for the regular sales. Call the above number for other store locations.
Mon.-Fri. 9:30 A.M. to 7 P.M., Sat. 9:30 A.M. to 6 P.M.

HORIZONTAL

336 East 61st St. (First & Second Aves.)
826-2992

The Horizontal, next door to the Vertical Club, appropriately offers the largest selection of bodywear in the city. The merchandise is divided into ten different departments that display the latest shoes, sports and active wear, tennis racquets, running gear, and everything else, from headbands to socks.
Mon.-Fri. 10 A.M. to 9 P.M., Sat. 11 A.M. to 7 P.M., Sun. 11 A.M. to 6 P.M.; closed Sun. in summer.

HUDSON'S

97 Third Ave. (12th & 13th Sts.)
473-0981

Ten years ago, Hudson's was known as one of the most complete outfitters in the city. Its slightly ratty, surplus-store atmosphere befitted its seasoned, outdoorsy clientele. When the outdoors became "in," Hudson's remodeled and expanded to a full block of storefronts. Since that time, the clothing selection has ballooned, while the stock of equipment has receded (and the price of what remains has risen). But the selection of sweaters, anoraks, raingear, and long underwear can save you a phone call to L.L. Bean.
Mon.-Thurs. 9:30 A.M. to 8 P.M., Fri. & Sat. 9:30 A.M. to 7 P.M., Sun. noon to 6 P.M.

PARAGON ATHLETICS

867 Broadway (18th St.)
255-8036

Paragon lives up to its name. It's simply the best sporting goods store around. No sport is too minor, no piece of equipment too superfluous for Paragon to stock it on one of its three sprawling floors. For every baseball glove at Herman's, Paragon carries four or five. And Paragon's excellence extends to its sales staff. Because the camping department is staffed with outdoorsy types eager to use their employee discount, most of the salespeople have first-hand experience with the merchandise.
Mon.-Fri. 10 A.M. to 8 P.M., Sat. 10 A.M. to 7 P.M., Sun. 11 A.M. to 6 P.M.

Tobacconists

FAMOUS SMOKE SHOP

55 West 39th St. (Fifth &
Sixth Aves.)
221-1408

This store has turned selling cigars into a very professional operation. The 1,000-square-foot humidor in the basement ensures that the cigars you carry home with you, priced 30%-50% off retail, are the freshest possible. It is a direct importer, hence the lower prices, and it offers such brands as Macanudo, Don Diego, H. Upmann, and Ramon Allones. *Mon.-Fri. 7 A.M. to 6 P.M., Sat. 8 A.M. to 2 P.M.*

PIPEWORKS AND WILKE

16 West 55th St. (Fifth &
Sixth Aves.)
956-4820

A true specialty shop for pipe smokers, Pipeworks and Wilke is New York's oldest pipe shop, first established in 1862. All the new pipes are handmade, carved in a workshop in Shaftsbury, Vermont, and start at $22.50; seconds cost $12.95, or three for $33. Antique pipes run up to $3,000. That they blend their own tobacco is obvious from the smell of the store; they also carry a small selection of tinned tobacco. In addition there's pipe paraphernalia and smoking books. The staff members smoke pipes themselves and work to develop a long-term relationship with their clients. Once a pipe smoker, always a pipe smoker. *Mon.-Fri. 9:15 A.M. to 5:30 P.M., Sat. 9:30 A.M. to 4:30 P.M.*

ARTS

Galleries

57TH STREET

BLUM/HELMAN

20 West 57th St. (Fifth &
Sixth Aves.)
245-2888

Irving Blum, a man of great erudition and charm, opened his first gallery, Ferus, in Los Angeles, which became legendary, exhibiting the best from both the East and West coasts. Among some of the exhibitions were Andy Warhol's first show in the United States, early exhibitions of Jasper Johns, Robert Rauschenberg, and Roy Lichtenstein, and an important but overlooked exhibition of the work of the late Joseph Cornell. Moving to New York some years ago, Blum formed a partnership with Joseph Helman and opened a gallery of great influence and international repute. Concentrating on contemporary "masters" (Ellsworth Kelly, Robert Moskowitz, and Lichtenstein), Blum/Helman has also developed a stable of younger American artists, including Bryan Hunt, John Duff, and Donald Sultan, whose work has had tremendous critical and popular success. The gallery therefore has a two-part function: promoting the new and giving added credence to the old. This serious, committed gallery always offers something of interest to gallery browser and collector alike.
Tues.-Sat. 10 A.M. to 6 P.M.

FITCH-FEBVREL GALLERY

5 East 57th St., 12th Floor
(Fifth & Madison Aves.)
688-8522

This small gallery, opened by Andrew Fitch and his wife, Dominique Febvrel, wasn't long in making its mark. It specializes in late 19th-century master prints and drawings (mainly European, but also some American and Japanese). Here's where you'll find Redon Bresdin, Max Klinger, and Belle Epoque artists. A gallery to be watched.
Tues.-Sat. 11 A.M. to 5:30 P.M.

GALÉRIE ST. ETIENNE

24 West 57th St. (Fifth &
Sixth Aves.)
345-6734

Galérie St. Etienne resembles a university library reading room, with its glass cases filled with prints and drawings and the salon-style hanging of its exhibitions. It specializes in Austrian and German expressionist prints and drawings by

such important historical figures as Gustav Klimt, Oskar Kokoschka, Egon Schiele, and Kathe Kollwitz, as well as European and American folk art, specifically Grandma Moses. The atmosphere here is one of reserve and scholarship. Co-director Hildegard Bachert is an authority on lesser-known artists of the period. Exhibitions are infrequent, but when undertaken, as with the works of Kollwitz and Alfred Kubin in 1982, they are first-rate and include intelligent, well-designed catalogs.
Tues.-Sat. 11 A.M. to 5 P.M.

SIDNEY JANIS GALLERY

110 West 57th St. (Sixth & Seventh Aves.)
586-0110

Sidney Janis, one of the great deans of the New York art scene, has been in business for more than 40 years. The list of exhibitions at both his old locale (6 West 57th St.) and the gallery's new location reads like a who's who in modern art: de Kooning (1952), Pollock (1952), Gorky (1953), Kline (1956), Rothko (1955), Guston (1959), Duchamp (1959), Kelly (1965), Leger (1948), Kandinsky (1948), Mondrian (1943), and Henri Rousseau (1951). Other exhibitions have displayed an originality and concern for scholarship worthy of any museum—and indeed, many works shown at Janis over the years have ended up in museum collections, the most impressive being the Janis personal collection, now housed in the Museum of Modern Art. Janis, like Alfred Stieglitz, has sought to bring the best of European and American art together in a setting that offers a cohesive aesthetic, and his exhibitions both establish and break historical precedent, no matter how unusual the concept might initially appear (as was the case with a major show of Brancusi and Mondrian in 1982, for example). Although he's in his early 90's, Sidney Janis remains an active dealer and member of the art community, and his gallery continues to be an inspiration and an asset.
Mon.-Sat. 10 A.M. to 5:30 P.M.

KENNEDY GALLERY

40 West 57th St.
(Broadway & Eighth)
541-9600

This gallery is entirely devoted to American art from the American Revolution up to the outbreak of World War II. The work shown, including that of the moderns, is by nature extremely conservative. Painters such as Charles Demuth and John Marin are shown for their pictorial qualities, yet the work of tougher, more experimental artists, such as Morgan Russel, Marsden Hartley, and Morton Schamberg, is not. The atmosphere is also decidedly conservative and restrained. A large gallery with rooms of hunting prints, naive oils, and the like, Kennedy—although one of the leaders in the field of indigenous American painting—is rather like a glorified antique shop. Nonetheless, it does show a group of important 20th-century American painters, including Demuth, Edward Hopper, Walt Kuhn, John Sloan, and Charles Burchfield. Despite its limitations, the quiet, older, more institutionalized sensibility at Kennedy is endearing.

Tues.-Sat. 9:30 A.M. to 5:30 P.M.

MARLBOROUGH GALLERY

40 West 57th St.
(Broadway & Eighth Aves.)
541-4900

Marlborough, at one time a veritable institution and one of the leading international galleries, has lost some of its glory, simply from age and competition; it also suffered in no small part from its involvement in the improper handling of the estate of the late Mark Rothko. Aside from these concerns, Marlborough maintains a high profile, particularly in London, exhibiting the work of major American and European painters, sculptors, and photographers, including Henry Moore, Francis Bacon, Kurt Schwitters, Barbara Hepworth, Oskar Kokoschka, Irving Penn, Brassai, and Helmut Newton; also exhibited on occasion are works by Rodin, Degas, and Renoir. Marlborough also represents a group of such contemporary artists as Reuben Nakian, Arnaldo Pomodoro, and Fernando Botero, whose work can best be described as inconsequential and whose reputations, let alone prices, are ludicrously inflated. The gallery itself is huge by midtown standards, yet dingy and unkempt—although it is the only gallery north of SoHo with an outdoor sculpture terrace. We have found the staff to be perfectly incompetent and uninterested when asked about particular prices in the gallery.

Mon.-Sat. 10 A.M. to 5:30 P.M.

PIERRE MATISSE GALLERY

41 East 57th St. (Second &
Third Aves.)
355-6269

Son of the great French Impressionist Henri Matisse, Pierre Matisse has been since 1932 the sole U.S. dealer for such major historical figures as Balthus, Chagall, Calder, de Chirico, Dubuffet, Giacometti, Miro, and Tanguy. M. Matisse's influence cannot be overestimated. During the late 1930's, when he first exhibited the likes of Chagall, Miro, and Calder, the Museum of Modern Art was still a fledgling, parochial institution. It was Pierre Matisse, along with such others as Sidney Janis and the late Julien Levy, who provided a forum for current trends in European painting and sculpture to be viewed firsthand, and made a case for modern European art when it was little known, let alone fashionable.

Today, Matisse mounts less frequent exhibitions, yet every two years or so he puts on a true blockbuster, such as the early Chagall paintings in 1977, and the new paintings by Balthus in 1980. To have lasted more than 50 years in a business that is nothing if not capricious is a testament to this legendary art dealer's unique commitment and unswerving vision.

Tues.-Sat. 10 A.M. to 5 P.M.; closed in summer.

ROBERT MILLER

41 East 57th St. (Second & Third Aves.)
980-5454

This is by far one of the most elegant galleries in New York, with an attention to detail bordering on the compulsive. Since opening his gallery seven years ago, Miller has offered a consistently exciting program of exhibitions with a group of gallery artists that includes Lee Krasner (the estate), Juan Hamilton, Jean Helion, Robert Mapplethorpe, Robert Graham, Louise Bourgeois, and Alice Neel (the estate). The gallery also exhibits fine and rare photographs (under the tutelage of Howard Read), a selection of fine classical antiquities, and the work of such modern American masters as Ralston Crawford, Marsden Hartley, and Georgia O'Keeffe. Robert Miller's urbane yet open demeanor, the pleasantness of the surroundings, and the competence of the staff make a visit to this gallery a joy.

Tues.-Sat. 10 A.M. to 5:30 P.M.

PACE

32 East 57th St. (Second & Third Aves.)
421-3292

Pace is one of the premier galleries in the world. It encompasses such disciplines as modern painting and scultpure, contemporary painting and sculpture, African and primitive art, fine art prints, photography, and an active publishing concern. But it is the vast holdings of modern and contemporary works that has secured the gallery its sizable reputation. Owner and director Arnold Glimscher has amassed an all-star list of major American and European artists, including Louise Nevelson, Lucas Samaras, Richard Serra, Agnes Martin, Robert Irwin, Isamu Noguchi, Chuck Close, Barry Flanagan, and the estates of Mark Rothko, Pablo Picasso (in part), and Ad Reinhardt. Recently Pace caused quite a stir in the art world by snapping up Julian Schnabel from Mary Boone's gallery and adding the venerable English painter Malcolm Morley and the hot young American painter George Condo to its already prestigious roster. Pace simply has the very best of just about everything and exhibits same with great intelligence and panache.

Tues.-Sat. 9:30 A.M. to 5:30 P.M.

UPTOWN

ACQUAVELLA GALLERY

*18 East 79th St. (Fifth &
Madison Aves.)
734-6300*

Acquavella occupies one of New York's most distinguished French neoclassical townhouses. Built in 1908 and modeled after an 18th-century Bordeaux residence, the building was once owned by Duveen Brothers, the celebrated art dealers who formed the greatest collections in the United States—those belonging to J. Pierpont Morgan, Henry Clay Frick, Andrew Mellon, and John D. Rockefeller, Jr. The interior is noted for its rusticated stone, black and white tiled floors, and monumental stairway. Acquavella, which acquired the building in 1967, exhibits 19th- and 20th-century American and European painting and sculpture, with a strong emphasis on the Impressionists. Major exhibitions in the past have included Degas, Modigliani, and Tanguy; all were accompanied by handsome, well-written catalogs.
Mon.-Fri. 10 A.M. to 5 P.M.; Sat. by appointment only.

LA BOETIE GALLERY

*9 East 82nd St. (Fifth &
Madison)
535-4865*

Owned and directed by Helen Serger, La Boetie specializes in art of the early 20th century, including Bauhaus, De Stijl, surrealism, Dada, and futurism. These individual and for the most part unrelated movements had a profound influence upon modern society, for they attempted to change the very nature of everday life through design, ideas, or the potentially revolutionary act of applying paint to canvas. La Boetie mounts one or two major exhibitions yearly; the gallery's facsimile exhibition of the Nazi's "Degenerate Art Exhibition" of 1937, for example, was one of major historical importance, reproducing in great detail the works of Otto Dix, George Grosz, Max Beckmann, and others condemned by the National Socialists under Adolf Hitler. Pieces shown are primarily works on paper, but a few paintings and sculptures are also on view. La Boetie offers a wealth of important historical material from one of the richest and most influential periods in the history of art.
Tues. to Sat. 10 A.M. to 5:30 P.M.

COLNAGHI GALLERY

Colnaghi recently celebrated its fifth anniversary in New York; in London, it celebrated its (almost unbelievably)

21 East 67th St. (Fifth & Madison)
772-2266

227th. During its renowned tenure, Colnaghi has become one of the most important galleries for and appraisers of old master English paintings and drawings; sculpture, furniture, and works of art from the 16th to the 19th centuries; and European paintings and drawings from the 16th to the 20th centuries. It is indeed a marvel to walk into a commercial gallery and find paintings by the likes of Tintoretto, Bronzino, Canaletto, Vermeer, Rembrandt, Van Eyck, and Titian for sale—at fabulous prices, no doubt, but nevertheless available. Steeped as it is in the grand European tradition of art dealing, Colnaghi's atmosphere is decidedly reserved and intended for the serious collector. Casual viewing or browsing is of course allowed, but certainly not encouraged to any degree, though the staff is gracious. Major exhibitions, such as "Discoveries from the Cinquecento," are accompanied by lavishly produced catalogs. Although Colnaghi focuses its attention primarily on the works of old masters, it also exhibits and places the works of such important 19th-century artists as Courbet, Corot, and Rousseau. A gallery experience not to be missed.
Mon.-Fri. 10 A.M. to 6 P.M., Sat. 11 A.M. to 5 P.M. during exhibitions.

BARRY FRIEDMAN

1117 Madison Ave. (84th & 85th St.)
794-8950

Barry Friedman's appetites are both voracious and catholic, to say the very least. His gallery is devoted to certain art movements of the late 19th and early 20th centuries, including the Vienna Secession, Art Nouveau, the pre-Raphaelites, French and German symbolism, and Neue Sachlichkeit (or new realism of the 20's and 30's). Artists shown include Gustave Moreau, Fernand Khnopff, Edward Burne-Jones, Christian Schad, and Tamara de Lempicka. Friedman also collects and exhibits the finest in furnishings and objects, featuring the work of this and the last century's greatest designers: Hoffman, Reitveld, Bauhaus, Breuer, Moser, the Russian avant-garde, Mallet-Stevens, and others. Highly recommended.
Mon.-Sat. 10 A.M. to 6 P.M.

M. KNOEDLER AND CO.

19 East 70th St. (Fifth & Madison Aves.)
794-0550

Knoedler is an internationally established and recognized gallery housed in yet another imposing Upper East Side townhouse. The gallery's aesthetic emphasis rests in three major areas: Italian, Flemish, and German old masters; the Impressionists; and 20th-century American painters, includ-

ing Adolph Gottlieb, David Smith, Frank Stella, Richard Diebenkorn, and Robert Motherwell. The old-master department is open by appointment only and is in most cases reserved for those who are known to the gallery and are serious collectors. With its broad yet well-defined range of interests and its abundance of curatorial talent, Knoedler remains one of the world's leading art concerns.
Tues.-Fri. 9:30 A.M. to 5:30 P.M., Sat. 10 A.M. to 5:30 P.M.

SERGE SABARSKY

58 East 79th St. (Park & Madison Aves.)
628-6281

Sabarsky is this country's major dealer and authority on German expressionism. Many important names are featured here: Egon Schiele, Max Beckmann, Oskar Kokoschka, Paul Klee, Leon Kirchner, George Grosz, Otto Dix, Franz Mare. Sabarsky no longer has exhibitions, which is a great loss for New York, since he was able to borrow the best examples of artists' work from museums, private collections, and institutions. Memorable exhibitions have included one-man shows of Dix, Schiele, and Emil Nolde, all within the last three years. A scholar of great repute, Sabarsky was instrumental in bringing the work of this period to the greater attention of the public at large, which, even as late as the 50's, regarded German expressionism with surprising disinterest.
By appointment only.

DAVID TUNICK GALLERY

12 East 81st St. (Fifth & Madison Aves.)
570-0090

The preeminent print dealer in the world, David Tunick exhibits only the finest material in the most elegant surroundings. Walking into the gallery may be likened to entering the house of Dior in Paris for an exclusive, private showing. Located in a beautiful townhouse just off Central Park, Tunick is filled with period furniture, dark rugs, and mahogany-lined viewing rooms, all replete with old master prints and rare, limited modern prints that are second to none and include only first strikes. Among the old masters shown are Durer, Rembrandt, Tiepolo, and Piranesi. The moderns include Beckmann, Kirchner, Picasso, and Toulouse-Lautrec, as well as a strong American group including Whistler, Sloan, Marsh, and Stuart Davis. The inventory is extensive, as is the list of published material that accompanies exhibitions. Tunick is only for the serious collector; simple browsers are either frowned upon or merely ignored. We recommend calling ahead for an appointment. *Mon.-Fri. 10 A.M. to 5 P.M.*

WILDENSTEIN

19 East 64th St. (Fifth & Madison)
879-0500

Founded in Paris in 1877, Wildenstein is undoubtedly one of New York's poshest commercial art enterprises. Their forte has always been, and still is, French Impressionist paintings. They either have or can get their hands on the best, and if you are willing to pay the price, they might be able to acquire your chosen painting for you. The owner, Daniel Wildenstein, produced a catalog on Claude Monet's paintings, an attestation to the gallery's longstanding commitment to scholarship, which today is represented by a wonderfully varied and select handful of historical exhibitions. A recent show titled "Sarah Bernhardt and Her Times" featured a panoply of paintings, sculpture, photograhic documentation, furniture, objects, all directly and indirectly pertaining to Sarah Bernhardt's life. The very definition of gentility and erudition, Wildenstein is not to be missed.
Mon.-Fri. 10 A.M. to 5 P.M.

SOHO & VICINITY

MARY BOONE

417 West Broadway (Spring & Prince Sts.)
431-1818

If Castelli is the most prestigous contemporary art gallery in the world, Mary Boone is certainly the most fashionable, and hence the most visible to the public. The gallery became the focus of international attention in the early 80's via two of its American painters, the young, talented, outspoken, and prodigious Julian Schnabel and David Salle. Although Boone later lost Julian Schnabel to the Pace Gallery, she has since added to the lustre of her stable by adding Brice Marden and Eric Fischl, as well as art media darlings Sherrie Levine and Barbara Kruger. All styles are displayed here, elegantly and with great care. The gallery has also exhibited a variety of important European artists, originally shown in the Cologne Gallery run by Michael Werner, Ms. Boone's husband. Some of these include Georg Baselitz, Markus Lupertz, and Jorg Immendorff, along with expatriate James Lee Byars. The prestige and influence of this galllery cannot be overestimated, and though it has been severly criticized on occasion for fueling the already overstoked fires of art-world hype, Mary Boone has weathered the storm very well indeed.
Tues.-Sat. 10 A.M. to 6 P.M.

LEO CASTELLI GALLERY

420 West Broadway (Prince & Spring Sts.)
431-5160

The most prestigious gallery for contemporary art in the world. For the past 30 years Leo Castelli has exhibited a group of primarily American artists who have become the acknowledged masters of our time. Jasper Johns, Robert Rauschenberg, Frank Stella, Andy Warhol, Roy Lichtenstein, and many others had their beginnings at Castelli and remain with him to this day. Castelli's influence on art since the end of World War II cannot be underestimated. What is shown here inevitably takes hold and is soon in the forefront of modern paintings and sculpture, beginning with such important movements as abstract expressionism, pop, minimalism, and more recently the new wave of figurative painting. A landmark. There's another gallery location at 142 Greene St. (431-6279); Castelli Graphics is at 4 East 77th St. (288-3202).
Tues.-Sat. 10 A.M. to 6 P.M.

DIA ART FOUNDATION NEW YORK EARTH ROOM

141 Wooster St. (Houston & Prince Sts.)
473-8072

THE BROKEN KILOMETER

393 West Broadway (Spring & Broome Sts.)
473-8072

The Dia Art Foundation, a nonprofit foundation funded by the de Menil family, maintains four permanent exhibition spaces in the greater SoHo area. Works are commissioned or owned by the foundation and are exhibited in a setting that is more akin to a museum than to a conventional commercial gallery. The spaces are well maintained and staffed, and comprehensive printed information is offered on each work.

The most striking of the four exhibits are the two installations by Walter de Maria, the first being the New York Earth Room—14 tons of dark, verdant earth filling a 3,600-square-foot gallery up to earth level. The leveled dirt is balanced against a typical SoHo gallery space: white walls, ceiling columns, track lights, and so on. This extraordinary sight, coupled with its pungent odor of damp earth, is a wonderful study in contrast to the ex natura quality of most art galleries.

De Maria's Broken Kilometer comprise 500 highly polished solid brass rods arranged in five parallel rows of 100 rods each; the distance between each rod increases from the beginning of the row to the end, so that the last, barely visible rows of the rods seem to recede into nothingness. Housed in a large ground-floor gallery with high ceilings and diffuse natural light, this large piece (45 feet wide by 125 feet long) is lit by stadium lights, which activate the highly polished surface of the rods. The overall effect is one of precision, clarity, and tranquility—a beautiful, if not stunning, achievement.

Dia is planning to open a spacious permanent exhibition

space at 548 West 22nd St. in the Chelsea area (989-5912). In a building located in a primarily industrial and warehouse neighborhood, the foundation will mount a few select, large-scale exhibitions, the first being a tripartite show of the work of Blinky Palermo, Imi Knoebel, and Joseph Beuys. The facility will also house works from the foundation's extensive permanent collection.

GAGOSIAN

521 West 23rd St. (Tenth & Eleventh Aves.)
807-0807

After closing a once-active and progressive gallery in Los Angeles, Gagosian opened an impressive space in New York with a group of blockbuster exhibitions. Located in Chelsea, Gagosian is well off the beaten track, but it's more than worth the effort to get there. Recent exhibitions have included a retrospective of works on paper by Cy Twombly, the early black and white paintings of Robert Rauschenberg, the abstract landscapes of Willem de Kooning, Susan Rothenberg's horse paintings, and the oxidation paintings of Andy Warhol. Exhibitions are not always scheduled to immediately follow one another and they tend to run for different lengths of time; a phone call in advance is strongly advised. Although the gallery does not represent artists per se, one can usually find examples of work by such artists as Richard Artschwager, Frank Stella and Donald Judd. Two well-known private contemporary art dealers, Peder Bonnier (627-2720) and Perry Rubenstein (206-7348), also maintain semi-public spaces in the building, offering a variety of American and European work. Phoning in advance is recommended.
Tues.-Sat. 10 A.M. to 6 P.M.

PAT HEARN GALLERY

735 East 9th St. (Aves. C & D)
598-4282

The last of the important galleries left in what was once a thriving hotbed of activity in the art world (the East Village), Pat Hearn seems intent upon remaining in the often-daunting reaches of "Alphabet City," while her colleagues, such as Jay Gorney and Massimo Audiello, have moved westward. The gallery is beautifully done and, though perilously close to Avenue D (the very eastern end of the island of Manhattan), bears little or no traces of the rougher edges common to the Lower East Side. All is clean and light, and the gallery's stable of artists, especially painter Philip Taaffe, is admirably chosen. The gallery has also mounted a number of interesting, unconventional group shows in recent months, usually featuring works of lesser-known American and European artists in new and penetrating contexts.
Wed.-Sun. 1 P.M. to 6 P.M. and by appointment.

SONNABEND

420 West Broadway, 3rd Floor (Prince & Spring Sts.)
966-6160

Illeana Sonnabend, former wife of Leo Castelli, has devoted herself to contemporary art with a zest equal to that of her ex-husband's (and for as many years) and has a gallery whose reputation is near his equal. In light of recent, difficult events in the art world, this is a remarkable achievement. Sonnabend represents some of the most talked-about and coveted young American artists working today, including Terry Winters, Carroll Dunham, Jeff Koons, Ashley Bickerton, Peter Halley, and Meyer Vaisman. Much of this work is new and very controversial—Sonnabend has never shied away from controversy and a certain aesthetic audacity, even when it was distinctly unfashionable. Certain artists long associated with the gallery, such as Barry LeVa, Mel Bochner, and John Baldessari, existed in comparative obscurity because their work is more conceptual and therefore "difficult." This sort of work has enjoyed a renaissance lately, due in part to changing trends, but also to Sonnabend's unflagging support for these artists. Other artists of note represented here include young American painter Robert Yarber and a number of important Europeans: Jannis Kounellis, Gilber & George, and Bernd and Hilla Becher. One of the most consistently engaging and provocative galleries in New York.
Tues.-Sat. 10 A.M. to 6 P.M.

SPERONE WESTWATER

142 Greene St. (Houston & Prince Sts.)
431-3685

Sperone Westwater boasts a high-powered, immensely successful group of American and European artists. Although somewhat small by SoHo standards, the gallery is an important one. Having achieved a great deal of attention in the early 1980's by hosting the very first U.S. exhibitions of "the three C's," Sandro Chia, Francesco Clemente, and Enzo Cucchi, the gallery has continued to have a very rich schedule. Notable exhibitions have included those of Bruce Nauman, a true American genius; Gerhard Richter, one of Germany's most outstanding and prolific postwar painters; and Blinky Palermo (a.k.a. Peter Heisterkamp), who died tragically at the age of 37. American Susan Rothenberg, the highly regarded painter of mysterious images, has recently joined the gallery, further adding to its already substantial international presence.
Tues.-Sat. 10 A.M. to 6 P.M.

Museums

America has gone art crazy. Several years ago there was a new gold rush, this time for "The Gold of Tutankhamen." Then, in 1980, a million people—7,000 a day—jostled for places in line to see the Picassos at the incredible retrospective organized by the Museum of Modern Art. The "Treasures of the Vatican" show was no less spectacular.

These events no longer attract only aesthetes and connoisseurs. Nowadays, almost every new exhibition draws the same teeming, anonymous crowds that fill a ballpark or wait three hours to see a film. New York, like Paris, is now a city of "exhibitionists." There's something disquieting about this frenzy, whipped up by advertising, a hunger for the "not-to-be-missed" exhibition or event. But New York's appetite for art seems insatiable, and you must be ready to stand in line and elbow (and be elbowed) to attend any exhibition of the slightest importance. You should keep this in mind when planning your museum visits: don't be stingy with your time when devising your schedule.

There are more than 50 museums in New York, obviously of unequal interest. We will introduce you to the most famous ones first, and then to a few others, which are not indispensable but are by no means without interest.

MAJOR ART MUSEUMS

GUGGENHEIM MUSEUM

Fifth Ave. and 89th St.
360-3500

It looks like a French brioche stuffed with a 400-yard spiral ramp. It has provoked myriad jokes (the museum should supply sea-sickness pills with each entrance ticket; it's the architect's revenge on the artist; etc.), and was the source for many arguments between Solomon Guggenheim and his architect, Frank Lloyd Wright, which were aggravated by accounts in the press and the opinions of the Urban Planning Commission. In fact, the design and construction process took so long that the multibillionaire patron of the arts had been dead for two years before the snail-shaped museum that bears his name finally opened its doors in 1951.

After an elevator ride to the top, you begin the descent of this long, reinforced-concrete spiral—a brilliant creation that allows you to test your cardiovascular conditioning and the endurance of your calves while feasting your eyes on the treasures displayed. The museum owns, and exhibits in rotation, some 5,000 modern paintings, sculptures and drawings. The collection, which is both high in quality and intelligently planned, is dominated by the collections of Kandinsky (close to 180 canvases); Mondrian's abstract work; cubist paintings by Juan Gris, Georges Braque and Picasso; works by Paul Klee, Marc Chagall, Picabia, Michaux, Max Ernst and more; as well as pieces by such important contemporary American artists as Jackson Pollock and Robert Rauschenberg. The Tannhauser collection, which became a part of the museum in 1965, is of an earlier period and includes 75 pieces (masterpieces, many of them) by Renoir, Cézanne, Van Gogh, Degas, Pissarro, and Picasso (from his "Blue" period).

It would be unfair not to single out the museum's cafeteria, situated on the ground floor. The food is not only attractively presented, it is actually edible, thus affording the establishment a unique position in the otherwise lugubrious landscape of New York museum restaurants.
Wed.-Sun. 11 A.M. to 4:45 P.M., Tues. till 7:45 P.M.

METROPOLITAN MUSEUM OF ART

Fifth Ave. and 82nd St.
535-7710

The biggest art museum in the United States is one of the most dangerous in the world. Visitors risk artistic apoplexy and cultural embolism—or at least leaving with severe indigestion. Everything you might ever want to see is here—and then there's more. The visitor floats with ecstasy, but gradually dizziness sets in, and soon he or she is swaying on tired feet, and ends up waving the white flag, wishing dire misfortune on the authors of those guides that enjoin, "The Metropolitan—a full day or nothing."

Three hours, 12 minutes, 28 seconds—that is our absolute record. Of course, one does what one can, but if you want our opinion, anything over two and a half hours borders on the foolhardy. Above all, never enter with the intention (unless you're feeling suicidal) of roaming at random through these endless floors, halls, and galleries. A wiser course consists of first finding out what is to be seen. There's usually a temporary exhibition, and as they are generally of great beauty, they are a splendid reason for one's first trip to the museum. Then, since one exhibition will probably not have brought you to your knees, treat yourself to a stroll through the American Wing's 20 rooms, which are, with the Astor Court (an exquisite re-creation of a 16th-century Chinese garden courtyard), among the Met's latest grand achievements. There are more stunning masterpieces to be seen in other sections, but when you're in the lap of modern America, why not discover its past as well? Displayed in a gigantic greenhouse are innumerable pieces of furniture from the 18th and 19th centuries, paintings by both näif and professional artists, stained glass from the Belle Epoque, western bronzes, and Tiffany glass, all shown in natural settings. The message is a sound one. Until recently, America had stuffed its museums with the past of other cultures; but America, too, is a civilization with a past. So much for a first visit: and afterwards?

We must leave that up to you. A large descriptive board at the museum entrance indicates which sections are open at what times. Try not to miss the permanent gallery (the Sackler Gallery) of Assyrian art, with a spectacular display (in a different part of the museum) of the remains of the Egyptian temple at Dendur. (The Egyptian section is, after those at the Cairo Museum, the Louvre, and the Berlin Museum, the biggest in the world.) You should also trot off to the galleries filled with Impressionist masterpieces— you've seen them in reproduction, but here they shimmer before your eyes. Then lose yourself in the Lehman Collection, a series of rooms crammed with 18th-century paneling, French furniture, and Italian, Flemish, and French paintings, tapestries, and magnificent classical drawings.

The latest giant addition to the Met is the Lila Acheson Wallace Wing, which houses the Iris and B. Gerald Cantor roof garden.

Try to make time another day to visit the galleries of Asian and Islamic art, the 15 or so rooms with reconstructions of interiors of European châteaus and mansions (the exquisite Cabris mansion at Grasse and a marvelous Louis XVI storefront from Ile Saint-Louis in Paris, among others), or the overwhelming section of medieval art. Don't overlook the ground-floor boutique, either, where in addition to numerous art books there are excellent reproductions and all sorts of attractive objects that make reasonably priced gifts. *Tues. 9:30 A.M. to 8:45 P.M., Wed.-Sun. till 5:15 P.M.*

MUSEUM OF MODERN ART

Here too, the Rockefeller Foundation distributed its magical manna to make MOMA into one of the most exciting museums in the world. Created in 1929 to introduce the

11 West 53rd St. (Fifth &
Sixth Aves.)
708-9400

public to the Paris School, it later broadened its scope considerably, aiming to present not only all the most important currents in modern art, from French Impressionism to American abstract expressionism (via German expressionism, Dadaism, and surrealism), but also to follow all facets of contemporary art, including architecture, photography, cinema, and furniture. In addition to its permanent collection, it displays a variety of temporary exhibitions, such as its incredibly successful Picasso retrospective, which proved the museum to be too small and resulted in the undertaking of a three-year expansion program. Movies are shown regularly in the afternoon, free to visitors, and art lovers can catch their breath in the cafeteria on the first floor in the new building.
Thurs. 11 A.M. to 6 P.M., Fri.-Tues. till 6 P.M.

WHITNEY MUSEUM OF AMERICAN ART

945 Madison Ave. (75th
St.)
570-3676

This granite and concrete blockhouse, the work of Marcel Breuer, looks like a truncated pyramid. It was opened in 1966 to house the excellent collection of contemporary American painting and sculpture amassed since 1930 at the instigation of Gertrude Vanderbilt Whitney, herself a sculptor. It now contains over 6,000 works, most from the 20th century, and there are fine temporary exhibits. The Whitney's midtown branch is in the Phillip Morris headquarters on 42nd St. across from Grand Central Station, and there's a new branch in the Equitable Center (see below).
Tues.-Sat. 1 P.M. to 8 P.M., Wed. till 5 P.M., Sun. noon to 6 P.M.

WHITNEY MUSEUM AT EQUITABLE CENTER

787 Seventh Ave. (52nd
St.)
544-1000

This exhibition center, the Whitney's latest branch, has a sculpture court open to the public and a gallery that has varied exhibitions of fine art, architecture, and design. In addition to permanent galleries for full-scale traveling exhibitions, Equitable has some of the most extraordinary public (or corporate) spaces in the city. These public areas, including the restaurant, Palio, contain artworks commissioned by Equitable by such noted artists as Roy Lichtenstein, Sandro Chia, Scott Burton, Barry Flanagan, Thomas Hart Benton, and Paul Manship.
Mon.-Fri. 11 A.M. to 6 P.M., Thurs. till 7:30 P.M., Sat. noon to 5 P.M.

OUTSIDE OF MANHATTAN

BROOKLYN MUSEUM

Eastern Parkway near
Washington Ave., Brooklyn
(718) 638-5000

This massive fin-de-siècle building (since enlarged) stands at the northeast entrance of a vast botanical garden, remarkable in particular for its reconstruction of a 16th-century Japanese garden. Though not a cheery place, it houses an excellent collection of African, Oceanic, and native American cultural artifacts, and if you're interested in Egyptian art, pay the place a visit. The Brooklyn Museum also houses an exquisite collection of sculptures, bas-reliefs, small bronzes, ceramics, and jewelry dating from the predynastic period until Ptolemaic and Coptic times. Their temporary exhibits are usually quite interesting.
Wed.-Mon. 10 A.M. to 5 P.M.

OTHER MUSEUMS

AMERICAN CRAFT MUSEUM

40 West 53rd St. (Fifth &
Sixth Aves.)
956-3535

This small, relatively new museum presents often interesting exhibitions devoted to costume and contemporary applied arts.
Tues. 10 A.M. to 8 P.M., Wed.-Sun. 10 A.M. to 5 P.M.

AMERICAN MUSEUM OF NATURAL HISTORY

Central Park West and
81st St.
769-5000

This immense, pompous hodgepodge is populous on Sundays with large families and Boy Scout troops. The miles of cabinets display global fauna and flora, from prehistory on, including a 90-foot-long Fiberglas blue whale. The Gardner D. Stout rooms show off a vast ethnographical collection from Asia and the Middle East, but the museum could be more rigorous in its organization.

The museum also offers free hour-long "Highlight Tours" and two films, *Grand Canyon: The Hidden Secrets* and *Cronos. Grand Canyon* is shown daily at the Naturemax Theatre ($3.50 for adults and $1.75 for children), and the two are shown as a double-feature on Friday and Saturday. You might also visit the Hayden Planetarium, where presentations on astronomy are given in the Guggenheim Space Theater. On the whole, though, these are less successful than those at the Reuben H. Fleet Space Theater in San Diego.
Daily 10 A.M. to 5:45 P.M., Wed., Fri. and Sat. till 9 P.M.

THE AMERICAN NUMISMATIC SOCIETY

Broadway and 155th St.
234-3130

What do Herodotus, George Washington, and Caesar have in common? Their faces are all artfully engraved on various bronze, silver, and gold discs, expertly displayed in the American Numismatic Society. Ring the doorbell and you will be ushered into vaulted rooms where currency spanning the period from its invention to the inflationary present can be seen. Two special exhibits trace the evolution of American currency and international medals and decorations.
Tues.-Sat. 9: A.M. to 4:30 P.M., Sun. 1 P.M. to 3 P.M.

THE CLOISTERS

Fort Tryon Park (190th St. & Riverside Dr.)
923-3700

Overlooking the Hudson, beyond the Washington Bridge, lies the admirable collection of medieval art presented by the Metropolitan Museum, with the financial assistance of the Rockefeller family. Whole buildings are exhibited, and rooms from such monasteries as Saint-Guilhem-le-Désert have found sanctuary in the New World. These marvels, to which are added stained glass, tapestries, and sculptures, are presented with great style. Even the gardens are works of both beauty and scholarship.
Tues. to Sun. 9:30 A.M. to 5:15 P.M.

COOPER-HEWITT MUSEUM

Fifth Ave. and 91st St.
860-6898

The Carnegie Mansion provides a sumptuous setting for this permanent collection of European furniture, wallpapers, porcelain, glassware, antique textiles of every possible origin, bronzes, wrought iron, and silverware, along with a rich selection of drawings and architectural and decorative prints. This fascinating museum also presents temporary exhibits of the highest quality. Asleep for years, the museum is presently experiencing a renaissance.
Sun. noon to 5 P.M., Tues. 10 A.M. to 9 P.M., Wed.-Sat. to 5 P.M.

FRICK COLLECTION

1 East 70th St. (Fifth & Madison Aves.)
288-0700

On the ground floor of this Louis XV-Louis XVI-style mansion, built in 1913 for industrialist Henry Clay Frick, awaits an exceptional collection of European paintings—Bellini, Rembrandt, Holbein, Velasquez, Vermeer, Fragonard, Boucher, Claude Lorrain—shown as they were intended to be, in the living rooms and boudoirs of a (very grand) private house. The Frick Collection is a characteristic example of the (good) taste of an American tycoon in the robber-baron years who grew passionate about art and took

good advice in acquiring it.
Sun. 1 P.M. to 6 P.M., Tues.-Sat. 10 A.M. to 6 P.M.

THE HISPANIC SOCIETY OF AMERICA
Broadway and 155th St.
690-0743

This exhibit of Iberian (Spanish and Portuguese) painting, sculpture, and decorative arts is located in the center of the Audubon Terrace. The interior courtyards and galleries contain items of art and archaeology from the earliest Spanish civilizations to the present (including colonial America), but the most interesting art pieces are paintings by such masters as El Greco, Goya, and Velasquez.
Tues. to Sat. 10 A.M. to 4:30 P.M., Sun. 1 P.M. to 4 P.M.

INTERNATIONAL CENTER FOR PHOTOGRAPHY
Fifth Ave. and 94th St.
860-1777

This center possesses a rich collection of works by the greatest photographers of the 20th century. Its exhibitions are always of interest.
Tues. noon to 8 P.M., Wed.-Fri. noon to 5 P.M., Sat.-Sun. 11 A.M. to 6 P.M.

JEWISH MUSEUM
Fifth Ave. and 92nd St.
860-1888

This small, very active museum devoted to Jewish art and culture (manuscripts, coins, textiles, paintings, pottery, and so on) often presents provocative exhibitions. A little while ago Andy Warhol's "Portrait Gallery" (the likes of Einstein, Freud, Kafka, the Marx Brothers) caused much controversy in the press.
Sun. 11 A.M. to 6 P.M., Mon.-Thurs. noon to 5 P.M., Tues. noon to 8:00 P.M.

MUSEUM OF THE AMERICAN INDIAN
Broadway and 155th St.
283-2420

Probably the most complete collection of Indian culture anywhere in North, South, or Central America. A very clear presentation provides enormous amounts of information concerning the native peoples, whose self-evident artistic talents are highly valued by collectors. Located in the beautiful Audubon Terrace complex, you'll find an astonishing number of Indian treasures, from jewelry to weapons to costumes.
Tues. to Sat. 10 A.M. to 5 P.M., Sun. 1 P.M. to 5 P.M.

MUSEUM OF THE CITY OF NEW YORK
1220 Fifth Ave. (103rd St.)
534-1672

This absolutely fascinating museum, located in a handsome neo-Georgian building, contains remarkable models of New York's early development and of interiors throughout the centuries. There's a delightful collection of toys and dollhouses, John D. Rockefeller's bedroom from the 1880s, puppets, and an audio-visual presentation on the history of

New York.
Sun. and holidays 1 P.M. to 5 P.M., Tues. to Sat. 10 A.M. to 5 P.M.

NEW YORK HISTORICAL SOCIETY
Central Park West and 77th St.
873-3400

A visit to this museum agreeably rounds out a tour of the previous one. Here are superb collections of antique toys, New York silverware from the 18th and 19th centuries, and 19th-century furniture, as well as portraits, carriages, and nearly all of John James Audubon's marvelous watercolor originals (433 of 435) for his *Birds of America.*
Tues.-Sat. 10 A.M. to 5 P.M., Sun. 1 P.M. to 5 P.M.

Music & Dance

New York is without doubt the dance and music capital of the world, where the concert-goer is frequently forced to choose from the myriad performances offered on any given night. The real problem is not simply deciding what to see, but deciding what you can afford to miss. Your choices may range from the debut of a young soloist at the acoustically spectacular Carnegie Hall to a sublime performance of George Balanchine's 1934 ballet *Serenade,* danced by the New York City Ballet at Lincoln Center's State Theater.

There is no height of the season on New York's cultural calendar, just changing seasons. In the fall and winter, Avery Fisher Hall houses the New York Philharmonic; come summer, it plays host to the breezy Mostly Mozart Festival. And beginning in 1988, the month of June will bring the biannual New York International Festival of the Arts. Chamber music, modern dance, classic opera—from the established to the experimental, all have their forums in the city that is home to one of the largest populations of professional dancers and musicians in the world. Not surprisingly, most of them live on Manhattan's Upper West Side, within walking distance of Carnegie Hall and Lincoln Center, and are easily identified by pulled-back ballerina hairstyles and turned-out feet or, depending on their calling, violin cases and tuxedos in the early afternoon.

For musicians, the New York debut is still a portentous event, the stage upon which international careers are launched—or cut short. Not only does New York introduce dozens of new faces each season, but it also gives audiences many occasions to welcome back the famous "old friends" they have come to know well over the years. Verdi, Wagner, and Mozart are to be heard at the Metropolitan Opera House, and brand-new modern operas, with titles such as *Nixon in China,* are to be seen, heard, and discussed at the Brooklyn Academy. Everyone, from former child prodigies like Yehudi Menuhin and current prodigies like the Japanese violinist Midori to contemporary and avant-garde composers, converges on New York, where, no matter how obscure or offbeat the production, there always seems to be an audience that's willing.

In finding your way through New York's dance world, it's important to know that the terms "downtown" and "uptown" apply more to orientation than geography. Uptown implies a more established artist and audience; downtown suggests that the art and audience are less restricted —anything goes. Or, as David White, experimental dance's chief producer, put it, "Uptown is learnable; downtown is ideas and inspiration, which are born instead of learned." New Yorkers pride themselves on discovering new artists, and the so-called downtown dance scene is a good place to go speculating—you'll have to wade through a lot of work that will forever be in progress, but when you do happen upon a wonderful performer, you'll have the advantage of seeing them up close, at the start of their rising careers, and in an intimate setting. And you don't always have to go to a small theater to see a young choreographer's work: The big ballet companies have lately been inviting several modern choreographers, like Mark Morris and Karole Armitage, to create works for them. European choreographers have also been drawing more focus in New York, and many have developed enthusiastic followings, particularly Pina Bausch of Germany and Maguy Marin of France. If you prefer seeing dance in a different setting, check out the various dance events strutting about town that are sponsored by such groups as Dancin' in the Streets and the waterfront-based Art on the Beach.

TICKETS

Though you may be initially overwhelmed by the choices to be made, a careful glance at the listings and recommendations—some annotated by critics—in *The New York Times, The Village Voice, The New Yorker* magazine, and the "Cue" section of *New York* magazine will help you whittle down your selection. In their Friday editions, the major local papers list the weekend's goings-on in their entertainment sections, and the Friday and Sunday *New York Times* often give advance notice of major concerts, so you may want to buy a copy a few months ahead of your visit to ensure getting tickets for popular concerts. Or write to the theater for a schedule of performances and then order by mail. Remember: The best seats for major companies and orchestras regularly sell out. In the city, tickets are available through most Ticketron (399-4444) and Telecharge (239-6200) outlets.

Although the prime seats for stellar dance and music events can be costly—at the Met they range from $50 to $95 for the Parterre and $45 to $75 in the Orchestra—inexpensive tickets are available if you're willing to stand or sit high up in the area dubbed "the Gods" (called so because you can just about touch the ceiling). Standing-room tickets, which go for about $6 in Family Circle or $9 in the Orchestra, are available at 10 A.M. Saturdays for performances Saturday through Friday. You can also cut costs by buying an obstructed-view seat at the Met or State theaters. The best concerts, of course, are not always the most expensive; indeed, tickets to many of them can be had for a song (or a nominal fee) including those given by the Metropolitan Opera on Central Park's Great Lawn, those in the elegant Frick Museum on Sunday afternoons in summer, or in the city's many churches. You should also try such small companies as the Light Opera Company of Manhattan, known as LOOM, which presents fine Gilbert and Sullivan operettas throughout the year at its small theater in Manhattan.

Keep in mind that "Sold Out" rarely means unavailable, it just means you have to work a little harder. Your best bet is to go to the theater one hour before curtain time and look for anxious subscribers hoping to sell their extra tickets at the door. If you find yourself awaiting a late companion before the performance, simply leave the ticket at the box office in an envelope with the latecomer's name on it. The box office usually stays open for a half hour to an hour after the curtain goes up.

For half-priced tickets to many performances, be sure to check out the Music & Dance Booth in Bryant Park at 42nd St. and Sixth Ave. (382-2323), tickets may include those for Lincoln Center and Carnegie Hall. Open daily from noon to 7 P.M. (hours do vary), the booth takes cash and travelers checks only and adds a modest service charge.

LINCOLN CENTER

The central shrine of highbrow culture in New York, Lincoln Center is the country's largest performing arts center, and certainly among its most flourishing. Located at 64th St. and Broadway, the imposing complex was built in the 1960's by several leading American architects, Philip Johnson among them, and has been responsible in large part for the revitalization of New York's Upper West Side, the area north of Columbus Circle, now lined with numerous restaurants. The major halls of the complex—the State Theater, the Metropolitan Opera House and Avery Fisher Hall—are rarely dark; flags above the Center's front steps announce the resident of each house, which may well range from the New York City Opera to the Bolshoi Ballet to the Kool Jazz Festival. During intermission, be sure to step out onto the balcony of the theater you're visiting to watch the audiences doing likewise across the way.

Despite its grandeur, Lincoln Center offers a number of free events throughout the year, including concerts at the cozy Bruno Walter Auditorium in the Library of the Performing Arts; at the Damrosch Park bandstand on the south side of the Met; and at the Juilliard School, where every Wednesday afternoon student prodigies give recitals. A guided one-hour tour is an excellent way to sample Lincoln Center's diversity. (Call 877-1800 ext. 516; tours run daily from 10 A.M. to 5 P.M.)

During the warmer months, you can dine at the outdoor cafe beside Avery Fisher Hall, grab an ice cream cone or capuccino at the concession stand, or catch one of the many free performances in the plaza sponsored by Lincoln Center Out-of-Doors. The plaza's main fountain is not only a favored rendezvous point but a lovely brown-bag lunch spot and ideal vantage point for people-watching. For daily information, call the concert hotline at 877-2011 after 9 A.M. The Lincoln Center Park and Lock Garage has room for 750 cars and never closes. Enter on West 62nd or West 65th Sts.

METROPOLITAN OPERA HOUSE

362-6000, 799-3100 (backstage)

Plush and stately (some say gaudy) the Met remains the crown jewel of Lincoln Center. With 3,800 seats, it is the largest of the Lincoln Center's three main halls. Signature Chagall tapestries hang in the lobby facing the plaza, red carpets cover the sweeping staircase, and crystal chandeliers inside the hall rise before each performance to a gold-leafed ceiling, never failing to evoke a gasp from the audience.

Opening nights draw a decidedly well-heeled and expensively appointed crowd, though people like to dress up every night for the Met. Completed in 1966, it is home to the Metropolitan Opera and the luminous voices of the opera world. Beginning in May, it welcomes the American Ballet Theater onto its stage, which, under the direction of Mikhail Baryshnikov, has been increasingly spotlighting its younger, mostly American, dancers. Since his defection in 1972, the Russian-born Baryshnikov, known as Misha, has been called the world's greatest male dancer, though in recent years his appearances have been seriously curtailed due to a chronic knee injury. ABT's programs range from such tireless 19th-century classics as *Sleeping Beauty* to contemporary works by young choreographers. Come summertime, the Met Opera gives an occasional performance in the cities' parks, and the Opera House begins importing international ballet companies, including the likes of the Royal Ballet, The National Ballet of Canada, the Bolshoi, and Rudolf Nureyev's Paris Opera. (Yes, he still dances!) Ticket prices for opera and the big ballet companies rival those of Broadway. For a backstage tour of the Met that lasts one-and-a-half hours, call the Metropolitan Opera Guild (582-7500).

Box office open Mon.-Sat. 10 A.M. to 8 P.M., Sun. noon to 6 P.M.

NEW YORK STATE THEATER

870-5570; New York City Ballet charge, 870-5570; New York City Opera charge, 307-7171

Home to the New York City Ballet and the New York City Opera, this 2,779-seat theater was designed by Philip Johnson and Richard Foster in 1964, with recommendations solicited from choreographer George Balanchine and Lincoln Kirstein, the co-founders of City Ballet, one of the world's great ballet companies. Since Balanchine's death in 1983, the company, under his successors, Peter Martins and Jerome Robbins, has tried to uphold the legacy of the Balanchine repertory—celebrated for its plotless works and the speed and design of its choreography—and to extend its classical tradition. The company presents its winter season from November to February and its spring season from April to June. Just as it did under Balanchine, City Ballet bills itself as "starless," meaning no advance casting lists are published. Each season brings a new work by Robbins or Martins and, of course, those incomparable Balanchine classics. To appreciate the patterns of Balanchine's ballets, try the seats at the top of the house, which offer a particularly revealing vantage point. In December, City Ballet's performances of the *Nutcracker* are an annual fixture and the hottest Christmas tickets in town.

From midsummer through the fall, the New York City Opera, led by former diva Beverly Sills, offers opera at half the price of Met tickets, but certainly not at half the value. The company accents American singers. Keep in mind that there is no aisle down the middle of the orchestra, so get seats near the end of the row or in the upper rings if you don't want to climb over people.

Box office open Mon. 10 A.M. to 8 P.M., Tues.-Sat. 10 A.M. to 9 P.M., Sun. 11:30 A.M. to 7:30 P.M.

AVERY FISHER HALL
874-2424, 874-6770 (to charge)

From mid-September to May, this 2,700-seat hall is home to The New York Philharmonic, the oldest symphony orchestra in the U.S., and, under Zubin Mehta's baton, one of the most vital. Originally called Philharmonic Hall, Avery Fisher was renamed to honor the patron who gave $10 million to redo the hall's poor acoustics, which were largely remedied in 1976 when the hall was considerably reconstructed. Tickets cost from $7.50 to $30, but you may want to sit in on one of the Philharmonic's 22 morning dress rehearsals open to the public (usually on Thursdays) throughout the season for only $4. (All rehearsals begin at 9:45 A.M. Call for dates.) In June, the Kool Jazz Festival moves in, followed by the popular Mostly Mozart Festival, which offers exceptional programs at still-modest prices. Since its inception in 1966, the festival has presented more than 40 different chamber ensembles and over 60 conductors and 85 pianists, including Peter Serkin and Alicia de Larrocha.

Box office open Mon.-Sat. 10 A.M. to 5:45 P.M. (or 15 minutes after start of performance), Sun. noon to 5:45 P.M.

ALICE TULLY HALL
362-1911, 874-6770 (to charge)

Snuggled in Lincoln Center's Juilliard School building, the intimate 1,096-seat Alice Tully hall is blessed with what are said to be the best acoustics in the complex. A wonderful setting for chamber music, it is home to the Chamber Music Society of Lincon Center, which holds court here from October through May. In late September, the toney New York Film Festival screens the latest movies; call well in advance for tickets, as they are hard to come by. For a glimpse of tomorrow's musical fixtures, check out the Juilliard student orchestra, as well as the free Wednesday afternoon concerts at 1 P.M. given during the school year by fledgling virtuosos.

Box office open Mon.-Sat. 11 A.M. to 7 P.M. or showtime, Sun. noon to 6 P.M. or showtime.

JUILLIARD SCHOOL CONCERT OFFICE

144 West 66th St.
(Broadway)
874-7515, 874-0465

The Juilliard School, one of the premier performing arts conservatories in the world, regularly showcases the diverse talents of its students in both the 277-seat C. Michael Paul Hall and the Juilliard Theater. At the latter, the School of American Ballet, the wellspring of the New York City Ballet, holds its annual workshop production in late May or early June. If you're up for some of the finest dancing in town and a sneak preview of the next generation of ballet stars, put your bid in for tickets early; they go quickly. Call or write the School for American Ballet, 144 West 66th St. New York, New York 10023, 877-0600.

GUGGENHEIM BANDSHELL

Damrosch Park
877-1800

Located on the southwest corner of Lincoln Center, the bandshell features free concerts in the summer, from rock music to opera, with frequent performances by the Guggenheim Band.

NEW YORK PUBLIC LIBRARY AT LINCOLN CENTER

111 Amsterdam Ave. (64th & 65th Sts.)
870-1600

If you consider yourself a dance, music, or theater lover, be sure not to bypass this terrific library, certainly among the best performance-arts research centers in the world, and in the case of its dance collection, the best. Chances are that performance you've always lamented missing can be found on videotape in the third-floor dance library.
Hours vary.

BRUNO WALTER AUDITORIUM

111 Amsterdam Avenue
(65th St.)
870-1630

Located in the center's Library of the performing arts, this 212-seat hall has held free recitals, concerts, and other performances for the past 20 years. Concerts are planned every weekday at 4 P.M. and Saturdays at 2:30 P.M. Recent programs have ranged from a four-hand piano concert to a soprano and pianist performing show tunes by George Gershwin, George M. Cohan, and Irving Berlin.
Hours vary.

OTHER CONCERT HALLS, DANCE & MUSIC SPACES

Not only does New York boast diverse attractions, but it also has countless settings in which to see them. Auditoriums, concert halls and lofts come in every size imaginable; the smaller the theater, the more intimate the atmosphere and the lower the admission fee. At some of the fringe theaters, you may find yourself sitting in a hard-backed chair or on the floor, but such spartan amenities give these places their character. If it's jazz you're seeking, you'll find everything from the standards and the blues to fusion and beyond at any one of the city's numerous jazz clubs, ballrooms and lofts (see Nightlife). And in the dark, smoky nightclubs that gave them their start, you can still catch such jazz greats as Sarah Vaughan and Dizzy Gillespie. Check the *Village Voice* for weekly listings. The following is a sampling of New York's infinite variety of music and dance venues.

CARNEGIE HALL

Seventh Ave. at 57th. St.
247-7800

An acoustical paradise, this 2,800-seat hall prompts rapturous praise. "It is a building built more by music than by man," declared Yehudi Menuhin. "It's the queen hall of New York," said Isaac Stern. For performers, a Carnegie Hall debut is the ultimate rite of passage, and sometimes a most unusual one: Yehudi Menuhin was 11 years old at his 1927 debut (the concertmaster had to tune the child's violin because his hands were too small). A year after his own debut, pianist Vladimir Horowitz said, "I played louder, faster, and more notes than Tchaikovsky wrote." Tchaikovsky himself conducted on the hall's opening night on May 6, 1891; since then, the house that industrialist Andrew Carnegie built (in an area that was then a suburb) has surveyed several chapters of musical history. Those who have claimed its stage include Arturo Toscanini, Gustav Mahler, Duke Ellington, Billie Holiday, Judy Garland, and Isaac Stern and Jack Benny in their only known duet performance. The Beatles made their New York debut here, and even the funeral of the great impresario Sol Hurok was held in this hall. Many non-musical greats have also left indelible impressions, including dancer Isadora Duncan, actress Sarah Bernhardt, and statesman Winston Churchill, who lectured on the Boer War.

Carnegie Hall was scheduled for demolition in the early 60's when the New York Philharmonic, its regular attraction, left it for the new Philharmonic Hall (now Avery Fisher). When violinist Isaac Stern led the fight to save it, the city took over, and a nonprofit corporation was set up to run it. In 1986, Carnegie Hall underwent a $50-million facelift to restore it to its original splendor, resulting in a revamped lobby and backstage area, mended masonry, new grand staircases, improved dressing rooms and plumbing, new seats, floors, and carpets in the main hall, and a renovated recital hall, now called Weill Recital Hall.

There is a concert here practically every night of the week, ranging from a solo recital by Luciano Pavarotti to Klaus Tennstedt conducting the London Philharmonic in a performance of Mahler's *Symphony No. 1.* A limited number of student and senior-citizen discount tickets (about $5) go on sale in the lobby between 6 P.M. and 6:30 P.M. the evening of the performance (between 1 P.M. and 1:30 P.M. for matinees).

BROOKLYN ACADEMY OF MUSIC

30 Lafayette Ave., Brooklyn
(718) 636-4100

Despite the fact that most Manhattanites deplore the thought of leaving the borough, a good many don't hesitate to make the trek to BAM, where some of the most innovative and unlikely programming in dance, music, and theater is showcased. In the fall, the splashy Next Wave Festival pays tribute to the avant-garde, with an eclectic array of solo and collaborative performances by emerging American and international artists, who in the past have included performance artist Laurie Anderson, choreographers Mark Morris and Pina Bausch, and composer Philip Glass, whose 1972 opera *Einstein on the Beach* got a full-blown revival here in 1985. Of its three theaters, the 2,100-seat Opera House is the largest and most elegant. During the intermission, you'll never be bored watching the parade of fashion-conscious patrons, whose costumes are often as colorful as those on stage. The oldest performing-arts institution in America (Anna Pavlova and Enrico Caruso stopped here), BAM also hosts the home concerts of the Brooklyn Philharmonic under the baton of Lukas Foss, as well as many local and touring dance companies, such as Twyla Tharp Dance and the Central Ballet of China. The Academy recently purchased and completely refurbished the nearby Majestic Theater, opening it with director Peter Brook's nine-hour epic, *The Mahabharata.* Don't go to BAM hungry; your choices of places to eat nearby are limited. BAM is a short subway ride to Brooklyn; take the IRT nos. 2, 3, 4, or 5 or the D, B, R, or N trains to the Atlantic Ave. stop. The less daring can always opt for a cab.

CITY CENTER THEATER

131 West 55th St. (Sixth & Seventh Aves.)
246-8989

Built in 1923 as a Shriner's temple, this Moorish-style Manhattan dance mecca underwent a major renovation a few years back to improve its ground floor and sight lines. (Still, you should try to avoid the extreme side seats.) The first rows of the over-reaching balcony are particularly good. Many of the leading national and foreign modern dance companies hold seasons here, including, the Joffrey Ballet (which is also based in Los Angeles), the Alvin Ailey American Dance Theater, Dance Theater of Harlem, and the troupes of Merce Cunningham, Paul Taylor, Lar Lubovitch, and Trisha Brown. Maguy Marin's company debut here in 1986—her dancers performed *Cendrillon* (Cinderella) wearing baby masks—caused such a stir that it was brought back a few months later.

THE JOYCE THEATER

175 Eighth Ave. (19th St.)
242-0800

The former Elgin movie theater in lively Chelsea has been redesigned into a charming, 474-seat Art Deco theater for smaller dance and regional theater companies. The American Theater Exchange is held here every summer; the rest of the year is devoted to seasons by the resident Feld Ballet, as well as to those by Karole Armitage, Lucinda Childs, Molissa Fenley, and Garth Fagan. After the theater, sample one of the many funky restaurants in the neighborhood.

MEEKIN CONCERT HALL

Abraham Goodman House, 129 West 67th St. (Broadway & Amsterdam Aves.)
362-8719

One of the city's newest recital halls, the intimate Meekin seats 457 and offers varied concert series of chamber music, early music, Jewish music, original instruments, and new music. The Mendelssohn String Quartet and the Boston Camerata are regular guests.

KAUFFMAN CONCERT HALL

92nd Street YM/YWHA, 1395 Lexington Ave. (92nd St.)
427-4410 (information); 996-1100 (to charge)

There is not a bad seat in this warm, burnished-woodpaneled theater, which features some of the most interesting programming in the city and draws a particularly eclectic and discerning audience. In a subdued, unpretentious atmosphere, you can savor first-rate performances of chamber and orchestral music as well as those by such individual artists as Yo Yo Ma and Sherrill Milnes. The Guarneri, Juilliard, and

449

Tokyo String Quartet regularly perform here, as does the New York Chamber Symphony, the Y's resident group, which is conducted and directed by Gerard Schwartz. During the Christmas season, the Chamber Symphony performs Bach's *Brandenburg Concerti,* with a special champagne performance on New Year's Eve. The Hall, however, is not only filled with music: throughout the year, its celebrated Poetry Center (established in 1939) offers readings by such literary lions as Isaac Bashevis Singer, Salman Rushdie, Nadine Gordimer, and Milan Kundera. There are also lecture series by critics, composers, historians, and policy makers.

THE GRACE RAINEY ROGERS AUDITORIUM

Metropolitan Museum of Art, Fifth Ave. and 82nd St.
570-3949 (information)

Located in the galleries that house the Met's world-class Egyptian collection, the 700-seat Auditorium offers a number of concert series of vocal, chamber, and early music. Several notable chamber ensembles play here, including the Beaux Arts Trio and the Guarneri Quartet. Lecturers on art history, dance, and music are given throughout the year by noted scholars.
Box office open Tues.-Fri. 1 P.M. to 4 P.M. Sat.-Sun. 11 A.M. to 4 P.M.

TOWN HALL

123 West 43rd. St. (Sixth Ave. & Broadway)
840-2824

Here you'll find a mixed bag of performances with a focus on classical, jazz, folk, and polycultural music events. The singers and comedians who have recently sold this place out hailed from Brazil, Russia, and Poland. (Popular in their own countries, many of these performers may be a tad obscure to New Yorkers.) Classical music ranges from concerts by the Philharmonia Virtuosi to a modern composers series. A former drawing card was an all-male opera company that performed in drag.

CENTRAL PARK BAND SHELL

Central Park, 72nd St. & Central Dr.
860-1335

Once one of the city's more neglected outdoor concert spaces, this bandshell has been transformed into a showcase for contemporary performers by Summerstage, a two-month summer festival of free jazz, opera, dance, and new music that began in 1987.

THE PROMENADE

Battery Park City

Set along the shore of the Hudson River, the Promenade regularly features jazz and popular music concerts during warmer weather.

WINTERGARDEN

*One World Financial
Center, 200 Liberty St.
945-2600 (for information)*

Scheduled to open in April 1988, this 120-foot-high, glass-enclosed complex will house the only palm trees in New York (16 of them). Its additional feature is its planned roster of performances by both emerging and established dance and music artists, from the Harlem Boys Choir to American Ballroom Theater.

DANCE THEATER WORKSHOP

*219 West 19th St.
691-6500*

A wonderful place to scope out the latest in new art, DTW has become the downtown dance world's center of incubation under the guidance of its director, David White. Many dancers and would-be choreographers, impatient with the long apprenticeships they may have to serve in the bigger companies, strike out on their own with a DTW debut, and some continue to return after they have moved on to bigger houses like BAM. The perimeters of the performing area change from show to show, and often the performers engage the audience in very direct ways. You may get glimpses of works in progress or see multi-media performances like the recent New-Wave puppet revue, in which an Ivory Snow bottle and baby shoes were meant to represent a schoolteacher and her pupils. You can expect the unexpected here. DTW recently added 11 P.M. shows on weekends to slot in more work.

THE KITCHEN

*512 West 19th St. (Tenth
& Eleventh Aves.)
255-5793*

Founded in 1971 as a space for video art, The Kitchen quickly established itself as an important venue for major innovations in music, performance art, and dance as well. Though it has gone through several changes of locales, it is now housed in a former ice house and film studio on the far west side of Manhattan. Everything from new music from Japan to new theatrical performance pieces are showcased in The Kitchen's two large, open rooms. (It also has a video viewing gallery.) "For many artists," says its director, Barbara Tsumagari, "we provide their first serious, well-produced performance opportunity in New York, in a context of interest in the art iself, not the audience." See for yourself.

P.S. 122

*150 First Ave. (corner of
9th St.)
477-5288*

This public-school-turned-performance-space (hence P.S.) near the East Village offers evenings of mixed, small-scale performances of dance, music, performance art, theater, and comedy. Shows are held either on the second floor, in a long room with risers and chairs that doubles as a rehearsal space, or in the downstairs gymnasium. Well-known New York artists who got their start here include Ethyl Eichelberger, known for his one-man rendition of *King Lear* with music, and playwright Eric Bogosian. Audiences are decidedly downtown and hip, and tickets are cheap: from $4 to $8.

FRANKLIN FURNACE

112 Franklin St. (West Broadway & Church Sts.)
925-4671

Franklin Furnace ranks high among the city's most popular purveyors of performance art. Established in 1976, it also features monthly installations of largely non-commercial art. Laurie Anderson got her start here.

LA MAMA E.T.C. AND LA MAMA ANNEX

74 East 4th St. and 66 E. 4th St., respectively
254-6468

The seeds of this hothouse of experimental theater, music, and dance were sown 25 years ago by Ellen Stewart, the mama of its namesake, and today, it's still thriving and is as exciting as ever. The programming is eclectic and international in flavor.

Theater

To most people, theater in New York mistakenly means Broadway. While it certainly offers some of the finest home-grown and imported theater around, Broadway is by no means the only show in town—nor is this theater-packed area off Times Square the only place to find first-rate actors and playwrights. If you fancy innovative American drama or something with an experimental bent, you should look beyond, to the city's hundreds of smaller theaters. Since Broadway shows have become astronomically expensive to produce—between $3 and $5 million for a musical and $1 and $2 million for a drama—prudence rather than luck has been the hallmark of the Broadway roster. Shows with state-of-the-art sets and wide box-office appeal prevail, though fine dramas occasionally get their due. In recent seasons, the trend has been toward Neil Simon plays, revivals of sure-fire hits and blockbuster musicals, these days largely imported from London. *Les Miserables* (known to NYC theater-goers as "Les Miz") opened in March, 1987 with $11.2 million in advance ticket sales, while in the 1987-88 season, *Cabaret* returned after a 21-year absence from Broadway, and *The Phantom of the Opera*—yet another bonanza for composer Andrew Lloyd Webber—settled in for a long run.

In fact, musicals now account for more than three-quarters of total box-office income, and the public's appetite for them has helped push Broadway out of its much-publicized slump of recent years.

The theater is where most actors declare their hearts to be, and the Broadway (and Off-Broadway) stage is where you'll find some of the biggest names in film and television plying their trade. In seasons past, Dustin Hoffman played Willy Loman in *Death of a Salesman,* Kevin Kline took on *Hamlet,* and William Hurt and Sigourney Weaver starred in *Hurlyburly,* directed by Mike Nichols.

The very mention of Broadway summons expectations of extravagance, spectacle, and polish. These expectations are often dashed when first encountering the porn shops, blinding neon signs, and questionable street life surrounding New York's theater district (the area between 41st and 53rd Sts. bounded by Sixth and Eighth Aves). Nevertheless, many of the 37 Broadway houses are elegantly appointed historical landmarks that are rich in theatrical lore. (When perusing your program, be sure to check the page devoted to the history of your particular theater.) And if it's theatrical history you want to sample, don't overlook Shubert Alley, a narrow walkway between 44th and 45th Sts. west of Broadway that is named for the three brothers, all of them producers and theater owners, who, in the early part of the century, began the Shubert organization, one of the two biggest theater owners on Broadway today (Nederlander is the other). You may also want to check out Sardi's, that celebrated thespian watering hole, where caricatures of both the famous and the near-forgotten paper the walls.

Before you start scurrying about for theater tickets, do a little advance homework. First, read a smattering of reviews to get a consensus of opinion on the show you want to see. *The New Yorker* is a good source for snappy capsule reviews and more expansive critiques of Broadway head-liners, as are the Friday and Sunday editions of *The New York Times, New York* magazine, and the weekly *Village Voice.* A good review, particularly in *The New York Times,* can set a show on a long-running course and often makes seats hard to come by; a pan, however, can leave a show shipwrecked overnight.

For news about the city's theater, dance, and musical events, try NYC/On Stage, the new 24-hour information service provided by the Theater Development Fund, a nonprofit group that helps boost audience attendance. A recorded message will give you performance descriptions, locations, ticket prices, schedules, and advice on how and where to purchase your tickets. In the city call 587-1111; outside the city, call (800) 782-4369.

Broadway is very pricey, with musicals running up to $47.50 for orchestra seats and straight drama ranging from about $15 to $37.50 a seat. To secure seats in advance for hit shows, you can write to the theater, but make sure you enclose a certified check or money order for the proper amount, a list of alternate dates, and a stamped, self-addressed envelope. A simpler route is to call and charge your tickets to a major credit card; they will be waiting for you at the box office prior to the performance, but remember to bring your credit card for identification. (The credit-card services will charge you an extra $2.50-$2.75 per ticket.) Try Telecharge 24 hours a day at 239-6200 or Chargit from 10 A.M. to 8 P.M. at (800) 223-1814; in the city dial (516) 227-3600. You can also buy tickets at one of the many computerized Ticketron outlets in the city. For the most convenient location, call 399-4444. Remember that weekend performances are more expensive and more in demand.

If you come up short at the box office, tickets for sold-out shows may be available at a commercial ticket agency, such as Golden & LeBlang's (1501 Broadway, between 43rd and 44 Sts., Room 1814, 944-8910). Its commission varies from $2 plus five percent of the ticket price if sold at the window to $2 plus a hefty 18 percent of the box office price if charged to a credit card over the phone. The hours are 8 A.M. to 8 P.M. Monday-Saturday, 9 A.M. to 6 P.M. Sunday. If you're staying at a major hotel, chances are the concierge can whip up something for you at short notice, though at additional cost.

If you're willing to join the (sometimes very long) queue and perhaps brave the elements, you should not overlook the Times Square TKTS booth at Broadway and 47th St., one of three kiosks run by the Theatre Development Fund. (Broadway celebrities announce the booths' various hours on a recorded message, dial 354-5800.) For a charge of $1.50 per ticket, half-price tickets to Broadway and Off-Broadway plays are available for the day of performance ONLY. Secure your place early if you want decent seats, and bring the current theater listings in case your first three choices sell out (a sign at the front of the booth tells you what shows are still available). The booth is open from 3 P.M. to 8 P.M. Monday-Saturday; from 10 A.M. to 2 P.M. for Wednesday and Saturday matinees; and from noon to 2 P.M. on Sunday. Traveler's checks and cash are the only methods of payment accepted. Shorter lines can be found at the TKTS satellite booth in the lobby of the World Trade Center. For

Broadway tickets, the hours are 11 A.M. to 5:30 P.M. Monday-Friday and 11 A.M. to 3:30 P.M. Saturday. Tickets to Off-Broadway evening performances are sold from 11 A.M. to 1 P.M. Monday-Saturday. For Wednesday, Saturday, and Sunday matinees, tickets may be purchased the day before the performance from 11 A.M. to closing.

If stalking the streets hasn't worn you out, you may want to try standing-room tickets which are are available for about $10 at some of the Broadway houses, either in advance or on the day of the performance. Another option is to try "Twofers"—tickets that entitle you to buy two seats for the price of one. Twofers are usually available for shows that are not packing them in every night, which means they are either in previews, in an extended run, or not very good. If it's a long-running show, its unlikely you'll catch the original cast. To get these tickets, try the front desk at your hotel, the cashier's booth at many restaurants, or the offices of the Visitors' Bureau, 2 Columbus Circle (59th St. and Eighth Ave., 897-8222).

Off-Broadway is not a geographical demarcation—it's an umbrella term that refers to the city's smaller, not-for-profit theaters where new plays are tested, classics are revived, promising talent is discovered, and some of the theater's finest actors, directors, and playwrights converge. Many of the plays that eventually make it to Broadway are first performed Off-Broadway; in fact, Broadway often looks to the fringe for its future productions. Among the many plays that started here and moved to Broadway are such Pulitzer Prize winners as *A Chorus Line, Sunday in the Park with George,* and *Crimes of the Heart.* (If you see these shows early on, you'll have the luxury of seeing first-rate theater up close and at nearly half the price of Broadway.) Keep in mind, however, that not every show aspires to Broadway, and some are better experienced in intimate settings. Since productions here cost much less to mount, Off-Broadway is much more open to experimentation. Not only are the houses smaller, but the minimum wage for performers is lower than on Broadway, where performers work under an Equity (actors' union) contract. As a result, Off-Broadway gives new talent a venue—playwrights like Eugene O'Neill, Edward Albee, Samuel Beckett, and Sam Shepard and once-struggling actors like Geraldine Page, Meryl Streep, and Al Pacino all looked to Off-Broadway for their first important showcases.

There are several theaters and established repertory companies that can be counted on to produce significant work, including some of the many repertory companies along Theater Row, the stretch of former porno movie houses on the south side of 42nd St. west of Ninth Ave. that was converted in the late 1970's into a compound of theaters and restaurants. Here you'll find such companies as Playwrights Horizons (where the Stephen Sondheim musical *Sunday in the Park with George* was developed), the Harold Clurman Theater, and the Samuel Beckett Theater. These theaters now have a common box office called Ticket Central, which is open from 1 P.M. to 8 P.M. daily. Call 279-4200 for credit card reservations.

Be sure to check the Circle Repertory Company (where Lanford Wilson's plays were first produced), The Roundabout, Provincetown Playhouse, the Negro Ensemble, the Manhattan Theatre Club, the Hudson Guild, the Lucille Lortel, Circle in the Square, the American Place Theatre, and, of course, Joseph Papp's Public Theater near Astor Place. Papp is one of the city's leading producers, and his Public Theater, also known as the New York Shakespeare Festival, premieres some of the most vital theater in the city. Meryl Streep, Robert De Niro, and Kevin Kline are among the actors who have shone in the Public's productions. (You can get half-price tickets at the box office on the day of performance, but go early—lines can be long.) Come summertime, the New York Shakespeare Festival moves outdoors to Central Park's Delacorte Theatre. Free Shakespeare in the Park, presented most evenings through early September (usually one month per production), is a summer ritual for most New Yorkers. Tickets are dispensed to those in line at 6 P.M., though you should get there in the late afternoon armed with a book, blanket, and picnic basket.

Don't overlook the two recently revived theaters at Lincoln Center, the Vivian Beaumont and the smaller Mitzi E. Newhouse, where in past seasons works by such leading American playwrights as David Mamet, John Guare, and Arthur Miller were produced. "Good plays, popular prices" is their slogan—one that might readily be applied to Off-Broadway itself.

Since there are many more actors in New York than there are theaters—your young waiter is almost certain to be an aspiring Olivier— diverse showcases have sprung up around the city to display their wares. In the Village and TriBeCa, churches, lofts, and schools frequently play host to the fledgling star. Off-Off-Broadway is devoted to innovation, which means that just as you stand a good chance of happening upon something inspiring, so you may also endure something dreadful. Check the listings and keep your eyes out for posters announcing inventive theatrical experiences. The most reliable are to be found at the Performing Garage in SoHo, where the wonderfully eclectic Wooster Group performs, La Mama E.T.C. (Experimental Theater Club), an avant-garde, international venue, and the Squat Theater, a repertory group that mixes the mediums of theater and film, as well as at St. Clement's Episcopal Church and the Minetta Lane. Bear in mind that imagination and a sense of adventure are helpful assets when combing the outer reaches of New York theater.

SIGHTS

EXPLORING THE CITY

Awonderful—and frustrating—fact about New York is that there's always something new to see and do. First-time visitors usually head straight for the Statue of Liberty, the tall buildings, and Rockefeller Center, but New York is much more than that. It's a city of very distinct neighborhoods, each with its own flavor and character. It's also a city where you can indulge all your interests—the arts, architecture, fashion, finance, and nature, too. Even those who live here can always get to know New York better, and see it through new eyes. Take off on foot, guide in hand, and discover your own personal tour, or choose one of the packaged ones we've listed and visit some of New York's terrifically unique attractions. Take time to go off the beaten path, and you'll experience this intriguing city on an intimate, human scale.

Amusements

BRONX ZOO

Fordham Rd. & Bronx River Pkwy., the Bronx
367-1010

Adults and kids alike will be fascinated by a visit to one of America's largest and most innovative zoos, home to more than 3,800 animals. With 265 acres to cover, it's a good idea to take one or more of the guided tours (available March to Oct.). The Safari Tour train ride (adults $1.25, children $1) and Skyfari tram (adults $1, children 75 cents) provide good overviews of the park, and the Bengali Express monorail (adults $1.25, children 75 cents) gives visitors an exciting glimpse at wildlife in the zoo's natural habitat, Wild Asia (it's the only way you can see Wild Asia; look for gazelle, elephants, tigers, antelope). There's plenty to see on foot, as well: the World of Birds, complete with simulated jungle and rain forest; the World of Darkness nocturnal animal exhibit; and, of course, the reptile and monkey houses. *March to Oct. daily 10 A.M. to 5 P.M., Sun. 10 A.M. to 5:30 P.M. (Nov. to Feb. till 4:30 P.M.). Adults $3.75, children $1.50 March to Oct.; winter rates $1.75 and 75 cents respectively. Tues.-Thurs. optional donation. Parking $3.*

CONEY ISLAND

Surf Ave., Brooklyn

Its glory days are long past, but Coney Island still attracts up to a million visitors on summer weekends. The beach, though crowded in good weather, is wide and pretty, and a few of the attractions remain—the old Cyclone roller coaster, the original Nathan's hot dog stand, the boardwalk. Nearby are reminders of a more elegant time, including the skeleton of the famous 1939 World's Fair parachute jump.

INTREPID SEA-AIR-SPACE MUSEUM

Intrepid Sq., Pier 86, Twelfth Ave. & West 46th St.
245-0072

Here's an impressive look at military hardware in an authentic environment—the aircraft carrier U.S.S. *Intrepid*, veteran of World War II, Vietnam, and NASA recovery missions. The museum portion features films (on the history of the *Intrepid* and the Medal of Honor) and a large collection of airplanes and weaponry, but just as interesting is the opportunity to explore the massive carrier itself.
Wed.-Sun. 10 A.M. to 5 P.M. Adults $4.75, children $2.50.

NEW YORK AQUARIUM

Surf Ave. & West 8th St., Brooklyn
(718) 266-8500

Just east of the Coney Island boardwalk is a lively collection of 20,000 sea creatures, including sharks, whales, dolphins (on view only in the summer), seals, sea turtles, electric eels, and—everyone's favorite—penguins. Watching them all at play and then strolling among the indoor tanks can't help but make you feel cool and relaxed.
Daily 10 A.M. to 4:45 P.M. Adults $3.75, children $1.50.

SOUTH STREET SEAPORT

Water St. (Peck Slip & John St.)

Yes, it's "touristy" in the manner of other urban commercial developments, but South Street Seaport is one of the classiest projects of this type, with dozens of fashionable shops, gourmet food stores, and restaurants housed in restored buildings. Similar to Boston's Quincy Market and Harbor Place in Baltimore, South Street Seaport, another in the Rouse Corporation's series of landmark restorations, is long on the hard tourist sell and short on the history. Eat, drink, and spend as much money as you can is the real theme of this attractive waterfront development at the tip of New York Harbor, and there are endless opportunities for both, from the tourist shops to the enclave of restaurants situated on the third floors of both main buildings. The food ranges from good to the worst abominations of so-called ethnic fare, so wander around and investigate before you choose. Among the more notable snacks you'll find frothy egg creams, great barbecued ribs and grits, garlicky falafel, and great hot fudge sundaes. You can walk it all off as you stroll along the harborside. Visitors may explore a museum gallery and ships, including the square-rigger *Peking* (1911), the *Ambrose Light*

Ship (1908), and the fishing schooner *Lettie G. Howard* (1893). The museum is open daily year-round (call 669-9424 for the exact hours, as they vary; adults $4, seniors $3, children $2). From May to September, the schooner *Pioneer* is available for harbor sails (669-9416).

STATEN ISLAND FERRY

Foot of Whitehall St., next to Battery Park
806-6940

At 25 cents, it's the cheapest ride in town, and one of the best, with gorgeous views of the Statue of Liberty, Ellis Island, and the Manhattan skyline. The trip to Staten Island and back takes only an hour and is a refreshing way to rest your feet and escape the crowds.

Landmarks

BROOKLYN BRIDGE

From Frankfort St. & Park Row in Manhattan to Cadman Plaza, Brooklyn

The most famous and best-loved bridge in New York is this graceful mix of stone and steel. A marvel of engineering, its Gothic arches have inspired artists, poets, and joke-tellers for more than a hundred years. If weather permits, take time to walk across the wooden pedestrian path—the view of the city and East River through the bridge's graceful web of steel cables is unforgettable.

BROOKLYN HEIGHTS PROMENADE

Just across the Brooklyn Bridge, Brooklyn

You'll love this romantic view of Lower Manhattan's sky-scrapers, the Brooklyn Bridge, and the Statue of Liberty. But a trip to the promenade is also a good excuse to explore the charming residential streets of Brooklyn Heights, popular since the nineteenth century for being close to, and yet removed from, the city. Some of America's best writers have called this neighborhood home, including Walt Whitman, Herman Melville, Thomas Wolfe, Arthur Miller, and Norman Mailer.

CATHEDRAL CHURCH OF SAINT JOHN THE DIVINE

Amsterdam Ave. & West 112th St.
316-7540

Though only two-thirds finished, this massive Episcopalian church ranks as the world's largest Gothic cathedral, with a floor area greater than Notre Dame and Chartres combined. Begun in 1892, the all-stone cathedral is actually a mixture of Byzantine-Romanesque (the apse, choir, and crossing, built first) and French Gothic (the nave and western facade). World War II put a halt to construction, but efforts to

complete the cathedral's 294-foot-high towers resumed in 1979. The work is slow, since each tower will need 12,000 stones, all carved with the same tools and methods used on the great medieval cathedrals. Visitors can watch apprentice craftsmen, many of them neighborhood young people, at work in the cathedral stone yard. Inside, a cluster of eight 130-ton granite columns frame the sanctuary opposite the 40-foot-wide rose window. Smaller details—the marble pulpit, a set of Barberini tapestries, and the seven apsidal chapels—are equally memorable.
Daily 7 A.M. to 5 P.M.

THE CHRYSLER BUILDING

Lexington Ave. & 42nd St.

This Art Deco monument symbolizes the romance of the city to many New Yorkers. And no wonder—the stainless-steel sunburst spire, which resembles the 1929 Chrysler radiator grill, gleams on sunny days and adds a distinctive sparkle to the skyline at night. Built into the façade are many automotive-inspired touches, most notably gargoyles fashioned after 1929 radiator caps. The lobby, decorated in African marble and chrome, is full of delightful surprises, including wood-on-wood inlayed wood elevators and a painting of the building itself on the ceiling.

ELLIS ISLAND

New York Harbor
269-5755

From 1892 to 1954, millions of immigrants passed through the halls of these Neoclassical/Byzantine brick and iron buildings, currently being restored. Accessible by ferry (from Battery Park and Broadway), Ellis Island is especially meaningful to those whose ancestors arrived here, but the now-silent buildings are evocative to anyone interested in America's "melting pot" heritage.
Tentatively scheduled to reopen in 1988.

EMPIRE STATE BUILDING

Fifth Ave. & 34th St.
736-3100

It isn't tallest in the world anymore, but the Empire State Building is still the most famous skyscraper ever built, and a potent symbol for New Yorkers—tall, elegant, and exciting. A trip to its 86th floor outdoor observatory and 102nd floor enclosed viewing area should be one of your first stops in the city. The view (50 miles on a clear day) is dazzling, of course, and it's also a good way to get your bearings. If possible, go twice—at night, the city glitters below you like a romantic fairyland. The Empire State's five-story base blends in so well with surrounding buildings that passers-by never feel overwhelmed by its height. The lobby contains a Guinness World Records Exhibit Hall that is especially popular with kids (open Mon.-Fri. 9:30 A.M. to 5:30 P.M., weekends till 6 P.M.; adults $3, children $2; 947-2339). *Observation deck daily 9:30 A.M. to midnight. Adults $3.25, children $1.75.*

FLATIRON BUILDING

23rd St. & Fifth Ave.

This building on the triangle where Broadway crosses Fifth was supposed to be called the Fuller Building, but it looked so much like a flatiron that the name stuck. Built in 1902, the limestone-clad Flatiron was one of the city's first steel-frame buildings.

FULTON FISH MARKET

South St. bet. Fulton St. & Peck Slip

When Sinatra sings about "the city that never sleeps," he could be referring to the Fulton Fish Market, where thousands of pounds of fresh seafood are bought and sold each day before the sun rises. It's truly something to see, as sellers load bags of oysters and clams and icy boxes of fish onto vans headed for supermarkets, restaurants, and fish stores in the metropolitan area. Early risers who come downtown to take in this fishy ambience can join the dealers for breakfast at Carmine's Bar and Grill at the corner of Front and Beekman Streets.
Daily 4 A.M. to 7:30 A.M.

GRAND CENTRAL TERMINAL

42nd to 46th Sts. bet. Lexington & Vanderbilt Aves.

Most of the half-a-million people who pass through the concourse at Grand Central every day don't have time to look up and admire its 125-foot-high vaulted ceiling twinkling with the constellations of the zodiac. Lighted ads and an enormous color slide (from Kodak) distract a bit from the grandeur, but the concourse remains a magnificent space.

GRANT'S TOMB

Riverside Dr. & 122nd St.
666-1640

High above the Hudson sits the white granite mausoleum of Ulysses S. Grant, commander of the Union Army during the Civil War, and President from 1868-76. In truth, Grant isn't buried here (as the old joke would have it). He lies entombed here—above ground—beside his wife, Julia, in a nine-ton black marble sarcophagus centered in an open crypt (modeled after Napoleon's tomb at the Hôtel des Invalides in Paris). The interior rotunda and exterior terrace and stairs are all quite stately, but the best part of a visit to Grant's Tomb is relaxing on the colorful (make that slightly garish)

mosaic tile benches surrounding three sides of the building. Designed by community residents in 1973, they are a flowing, free-form series of city scenes, animals (look for Mickey Mouse), automobiles, and more. The effect is refreshing and fun.
Wed.-Sun. 9 A.M. to 4:30 P.M. Admission free.

NEW YORK PUBLIC LIBRARY

Fifth Ave. & 42nd St.
340-0849

Eighty-eight miles of books are shelved in New York's beautiful Beaux Arts library, one of the five largest libraries in the country. Book lovers will want to visit the huge reading room on the third floor; everyone else can lounge on the steps between those famous marble lions, Patience and Fortitude, and watch the throngs hurry by.
Mon.-Wed. 10 A.M. to 9 P.M.; Thurs.-Sat. 10 A.M. to 6 P.M.

NEW YORK STOCK EXCHANGE

20 Broad St. (Wall St.)
656-5167

Interested in money? If so, you'll be fascinated by this glimpse of capitalism in action, as 3,000 people scurry around the paper-covered floor of the Stock Exchange. Before entering the third floor viewing gallery, you can hear a short explanation of stock tables, the workings of the market, and the activities of those frantic people on the trading floor. Don't expect to see ticker-tape machines—transactions are recorded electronically, and most of the hubbub takes place around TV screens.
Mon.-Fri. 9:20 A.M. to 4 P.M. Admission free.

PIERPONT MORGAN LIBRARY

29 East 36th St. (Madison Ave.)
685-0610

Pierpont Morgan *père* actually lived in a separate building on this site, one that was demolished when the library was expanded. This structure was originally built to house his and his son's splendid collections. Lively exhibits and a wonderful gift shop lift the gloom and deep-seated ennui that sometimes sets in when visiting the place where some of the richest of the super-rich had fun indulging in their avarice for rare books, incunabula, manuscripts (both literary and musical), drawings, etc. A favored item: the pair of lapis lazuli columns in the rotunda (ask a guard the way).
Tues.-Sat. 10:30 A.M. to 5 P.M., Sun. 1 P.M. to 5 P.M. Closed in Aug.

RIVERSIDE CHURCH

Riverside Dr. & 122nd St.
222-5900

Some of the loveliest views of the city can be seen from atop the 21-story tower of Riverside Church, home of the world's largest carillon. You may even feel like a character in a Hitchcock movie as you climb the final twisting steps among the 74 bells (the largest weighs almost 41,000 pounds; the smallest, about 10). A few of the carillon bells peal on the hour, but it's more fun to actually watch the instrument being played by expert carillonneurs, who press wooden levers with their hands and feet in a small cabin in the sky. Concerts are given at noon on Saturdays, and on Sundays at 3 P.M. The church itself was built by John D. Rockefeller, Jr. in 1930 from a design inspired by Chartres cathedral. From the outside, the nave is dwarfed by the 400-foot tower, which isn't surprising considering the steel columns and beams required to support 20 floors of offices and 100 tons of carillon.

Church open daily 10 A.M. to 4 P.M. Tower open Mon.-Sat. 11 A.M. to 3 P.M., Sun. 12:30 P.M. to 4 P.M.; admission to tower 25 cents.

ROCKEFELLER CENTER

48th to 51st Sts. bet. Fifth & Sixth Aves.

That distinctive "New York" feeling you'll get at Rockefeller Center does not just derive from the hordes of office workers and tourists surrounding you—it also comes from the wonderful mix of limestone-covered buildings, open spaces, and acres and acres of underground shops and restaurants. In fact, Rockefeller Center, built in the 30's by John D. Rockefeller, Jr., on land leased from Columbia University, may be America's most successful piece of urban design.

Begin your exploration of the area by strolling through the Channel Gardens, named for their location in the Promenade between the British Empire Building and La Maison Française (Fifth Ave. between 49th & 50th Sts.). You'll feel yourself drawn to the famous bronze and gold-leaf statue of Prometheus, which presides over the equally famous skating rink in winter, and an outdoor cafe in summer.

Rising majestically above Prometheus is the 70-story RCA building, home (at least as this writing) of NBC-TV. The lobby of "30 Rock," as New Yorkers call it, is decorated with murals representing *American Progress* by José Maria Sert. Guided tours of NBC's studios begin here (Mon.-Sat. 9:30 A.M. to 4:30 P.M., Sun. 10 A.M. to 4 P.M.; no children under 6; $5.50; 664-7174) and you can inquire about tickets for TV show tapings at the information desk in the center of 30 Rock. Tickets for *Saturday Night Live* and *Late Night with David Letterman* must be ordered well in advance by writing to NBC Tickets, 30 Rockefeller Plaza, New York, NY 10112; standby tickets may be available (664-3055).

Each of the thirteen original Rockefeller Center buildings

contains Art Deco touches, many have roof gardens, and all are accessible through the vast underground passageways. (Note especially the view of St. Patrick's Cathedral and the statue of Atlas as seen from the underground escalator in the International Building, Fifth Avenue at 51st Street.)

Rockefeller Center's jewel is Radio City Music Hall, the Art Deco showplace that seats almost 6,000 people. Everything is glamorous here: the grand staircase and chandeliers (among the largest in the world) in the foyer, the mural-covered restrooms downstairs, and, of course, the Rockettes, who perform precision dances and high kicks at Music Hall stage shows several times a year. Backstage tours are available (Mon.-Fri., call 541-9436 for reservations and times; $3.95).

STATUE OF LIBERTY

The American Museum of Immigration, Liberty Island, New York Harbor
269-5755 (ferry)

The most famous statue in the world survived the hoopla surrounding her hundredth birthday in 1986 with dignity intact. Even jaded New Yorkers get a lump in their throats at the sight of Liberty's torch shining from 305 feet up in New York Harbor. You can get a good view of sculptor Frédéric Bartholdi's copper-clad masterwork from the Staten Island Ferry, as well as on the ferry that goes to Liberty Island (45 minutes one-way). If time permits, do take an hour or so to explore the island—the statue's size is most apparent when you're standing at the base. An elevator (providing it's working) takes you to the top of the 154-foot pedestal, which houses the American Museum of Immigration; hardier souls can then climb 171 spiral staircase steps (12 stories) to the crown for a bird's-eye-view of New York.
Daily 9 A.M. to 4 P.M. Ferry leaves from Battery Park. Year-round tours run every hour on the quarter hour in the summer; winter times vary. Ferry admission adults $3.25, children $1.50; statue admission adults $1, children free.

TRINITY CHURCH

Broadway & Wall St.
602-0800

An imposing presence at the base of Wall Street, the original Trinity Church was built back in 1696. The current sooty black building, constructed in 1846 of dark red sandstone, is actually the third Trinity Church to stand on this site. The adjoining cemetery dates back to 1681, and is filled with famous folks, including Alexander Hamilton, Robert Fulton, and William Bradford. Workers in the financial district often sit in the coolness of the churchyard to enjoy a (relatively) quiet lunch.
Mon.-Fri. 7 A.M. to 5 P.M.; Sat. & Sun. 8 A.M. to 4 P.M.

UNITED NATIONS

First Ave. bet. 42nd & 48th Sts.
754-7539 (tours)

The familiar modern buildings of the United Nations (1947-53) still look impressive, especially as juxtaposed with the glass-covered U.N. Plaza across the street. A visit to the U.N. takes you literally out of the country; though in Manhattan, the complex lies in international territory. Proof —postcards mailed here will bear a U.N. postmark. The complex's designs were selected by an impressive group that included Le Corbusier, Oscar Neimeyer, and Wallace K. Harrison.

The U.N. tour is extremely popular, but you won't see much unless the General Assembly is in session (mid-Sept. through Dec.). Do take special note of the beautiful Léger murals on the Assembly Hall walls. On your own, you can walk through the carefully groomed U.N. gardens, see the Chagall stained glass window, the Apollo 14 moon rock, and the model of Sputnik I in the lobby of the General Assembly building. Free tickets to General Assembly sessions and meetings of the various U.N. councils are available on a first-come, first-served basis half an hour before the meeting that day (usually 10:30 A.M. & 3:30 P.M.) at the main information desk (754-1234). You'll be able to listen in with earphones in English, French, Spanish, Chinese, Arabic, or Russian, the official languages of the U.N.

Lunch with a view of the East River in the delegates' dining room. It's open to the public (Mon.-Fri. 11:30 A.M. to 2:30 P.M.), but again, unless you're a group, it's first come, first served. Wonderful souvenirs from around the world are on sale in the basement, tax-free, along with U.N. stamps.

Guided tours every 20 minutes daily 9:30 A.M. to 4:45 P.M.; call for information on foreign language tours. Adults $4.50, children $2.50, no children under 5.

WORLD TRADE CENTER

Two World Trade Center, 107th Fl.
466-7397

Though the most recent King Kong seemed to like them, these giant twins aren't particularly interesting to look at, but the view from a quarter mile up is spectacular. Weather permitting, you can even go outside on the 110th floor rooftop, the world's highest outdoor promenade, for a truly heart-stopping look at the Wall Street skyscrapers (they look so small!), the Statue of Liberty, New York Harbor, and the rest of the city, even past the George Washington Bridge way uptown at West 178th Street.

Daily 9:30 A.M. to 9:30 P.M. Adults $2.40, children $1.35.

Neighborhoods

The following is by no means an all-encompassing list, but for a tourist wanting a taste of what's quintessentially New York, these are the four areas not to miss.

CHINATOWN
Mott & Pell Sts.

Arrive hungry, because Chinatown means delicious, inexpensive eating (don't be put off by the hole-in-the-wall look of many of the restaurants). It's also fun to window-shop for fans, tea sets, jade, ivory, and other souvenirs as you make your way down the narrow streets. Kids and kitsch-lovers will enjoy a visit to the Chinese Museum at 8 Mott Street, which features tic-tac-toe playing chickens (daily 10 A.M. to 10 P.M.; adults $1, children 50 cents; 964-1542). Nearby, at 64 Mott, is the Eastern States Buddhist Temple of America (daily 9 A.M.-8 P.M.). When you're ready for dessert, walk north on Mott to Grand Street, and enjoy a pastry and cappuccino in *Little Italy*. There aren't any tourist attractions per se in the neighborhood, but there are plenty of sidewalk cafes where you can sit, talk, drink, and be merry, before picking up some Italian goodies to take home.

GREENWICH VILLAGE
14th St. to Houston St.

Many New Yorkers feel so passionate about the Village that they claim they never feel comfortable north of 14th Street. Greenwich Village is, indeed, a world unto itself—a maze of streets so convoluted that West 4th crosses West 12th, where echoes of Bohemia on MacDougal Street are just steps away from the modern buildings of New York University, and high rises co-exist with quiet blocks of brick and stone row houses. Take time to wander around this fascinating neighborhood, beginning at Stanford White's Washington Square Arch at the base of Fifth Avenue. Note the Greek Revival homes once occupied by Edith Wharton, Henry James, William Dean Howells (all at No. 1), and John Dos Passos (No. 3) on Washington Square North (the stables behind them are now MacDougal Alley and Washington Mews), then walk south on MacDougal Street, past the historic Provincetown Playhouse and Minetta Tavern, to Bleecker Street. From there, go west and let yourself get lost in the web of streets lined with quaint shops, restaurants, antique dealers, and every type of dwelling (especially picturesque: Grove, Gay, Morton, and Jane Streets). The *East Village* (east of Broadway, especially lower Second Avenue) has a funkier air; the hippies of the 60's have been replaced by young punk artists of the 80's, who co-exist with the traditional enclaves of Ukrainians and other ethnic groups.

SOHO
Canal St. to West Houston St.

Between Chinatown and Greenwich Village is the city's artist community, SoHo (for south of Houston—pronounced *HOWston*). It's an area of spooky-looking cast-iron architecture, originally built for industry but converted into studio lofts by artists in the 50's and 60's. Galleries, restaurants, and trendy shops make the area a must for art lovers; branching out from West Broadway and Spring Street, you can visit some of the galleries listed in the Arts section, then pick up a chic outfit or some jewelry and spend the evening dining in the area. Southwest of SoHo is an even newer artistic neighborhood with yet another acronym name, *Tribeca* (for the triangle below Canal Street).

TIMES SQUARE
Broadway & Seventh Ave., 42nd to 47th Sts.

By day, it looks seedy and uninviting; by night, there's plenty of excitement left on the Great White Way. Named for the newspaper that for years was headquartered on the southern end (the *New York Times* has since moved up to West 43rd Street), Times Square, which is actually shaped more like an hourglass, is the hub of the city's theater district as well as its more X-rated amusements. The giant Mariott Hotel at Broadway and 45th (1985) marked the beginning of a controversial movement toward redeveloping the area. A number of large office buildings and hotels have been proposed, but opponents fear that the special honky-tonk quality of the neighborhood could be lost.

Parks & Gardens

BROOKLYN BOTANIC GARDEN
1000 Washington Ave., Brooklyn
(718) 622-4433

Though much smaller than its sister garden in the Bronx, the 50-acre Brooklyn Botanic Garden is well worth a visit for delights like its Japanese Garden (open April-Oct. 11 A.M.-4 P.M.), Shakespeare Garden, herb garden, and America's oldest and probably largest collection of bonsai trees. In springtime, the blossoming cherry trees are just as pretty as

Washington, D.C.'s; in June the rose garden comes vividly to life. There's also a fragrance garden for the blind with Braille markers, and a whole new conservatory opening in 1988.

Tues.-Fri. 8 A.M. to 6 P.M. (4:30 P.M. in winter); Sat. & Sun. 10 A.M. to 6 P.M. (4:30 P.M. in winter). Free.

CENTRAL PARK

West 59th St. to West 110th St. bet. Fifth Ave. & Central Park West

Believe it or not, Central Park was once 843 acres of swampland. For more than a century, it has been the heart of the city, a truly democratic place where New Yorkers can escape their apartments and office cubicles to fly kites, jog, skate, play checkers, ride horses, have a romantic row on the lake, or simply stare at the sky in their own peaceful corner. The design, by Frederick Law Olmstead and Calvert Vaux, brilliantly combines open vistas, meadows, and small bodies of water with woods, hills, and thousands of trees. Remarkably, the maze of pedestrian paths, bridle paths, and cross-town roads only rarely intersect—a series of tunnels, arches, bridges, and sunken roadways keep all forms of traffic moving, yet separated.

Each visit to Central Park reveals new treasures, new views, new areas to explore. Among the highlights: The charming Gothic Revival Dairy at 65th Street in the center of the park doesn't sell milk anymore; it's now the Visitor Information Center, a source of free maps, exhibits, slide shows, and Ranger tours (397-3156 for information). Just below the Dairy is the newly refurbished Wollman Memorial ice skating rink (open in winter; 517-4800 for information); to the west is every child's favorite attraction, an antique merry-go-round (daily 10:30 A.M. to 4:30 P.M., till 5:30 on weekends; in winter open Sat. & Sun. only, weather permitting; 879-0244 for information). More treats for young parkgoers: a children's petting zoo at Fifth Avenue between 65th and 66th Streets (daily 10 A.M. to 4:30 P.M.; 10 cents), and climbable statues of Alice in Wonderland and the Mad Hatter at the elliptical Conservatory Water, above the entrance at 72nd Street and Fifth Avenue. In the summer, children can hear stories every Saturday at 11 A.M. at the statue of Hans Christian Andersen.

On springtime Saturdays, model yacht enthusiasts hold races in the Water. To the west is the lovely Central Park Lake, where you can rent rowboats at the Loeb Boathouse ($6 an hour with $20 refundable deposit; daily 10:30 A.M. to dusk; 517-3697 for information) or simply watch the action from Bethesda Terrace, lovingly restored by landscape architects and stone craftsmen. With its majestic fountain, the terrace anchors the northern end of Central Park Mall, a formal promenade lined with giant elms and statues. Street performers vie for attention near the Mall's large band shell, home to a variety of concerts in warm weather.

West of the lake, near Central Park West and 72nd Street, is Strawberry Fields, a two-and-one-half-acre garden dedicated to the memory of John Lennon, who lived in the Dakota apartment house across the street. Some 25,000 strawberry plants nestle among flowers, trees, and exotic plants, many donated by other countries. Rising from the eastern bank of the lake is a heavily wooded section of the park known as the Ramble. Birdwatchers and gay couples frequent this area; because it is so overgrown and contains dozens of easy-to-get-lost-in paths, we'd advise you not to explore the Ramble alone.

Just behind the Metropolitan Museum of Art is the park's best picnic area, the Great Lawn. Hundreds of thousands of New Yorkers gather here on summer evenings to hear free concerts by the New York Philharmonic and the Metropolitan Opera, and rock fans have enjoyed performances by Simon & Garfunkel, Diana Ross, and others. Theater lovers gather on the great lawn every summer as well, lining up for free Shakespeare-in-the-Park performances at the Delacorte Theater (861-7277 for information). On the hill above the theater stands Belvedere Castle (1869), once a weather station, and now an education center. The view from the castle is terrific in every direction.

If you're a jogger, you might want to join the hordes who circle the reservoir located above 86th Street. As you clock your mile and a half, you can discreetly watch for celebrity runners like Madonna and Jackie O. Bridle paths also ring the reservoir; experienced riders may rent a horse and English saddle from the Claremont Riding Academy (175 West 89th St.; weekdays 6:30 A.M. to 10 P.M., weekends till 5 P.M.; $25 an hour; 724-5100).

When exploring Central Park, use common sense—unless you're attending an organized event, stay out after dark.

GRAMERCY PARK

Lexington Ave. bet. 20th & 21st Sts.

Though you can't stroll inside—Gramercy Park is the city's last surviving private park, for use by area residents, who have a key—you'll be charmed by this model of a nineteenth-century London square. The west side is composed of a lovely row of red brick town houses with intricate ironwork porches. The south side includes the National Arts Club, once the home of New York governor Samuel Tilden, and the Players Club, founded by actor Edwin Booth in 1888. (A statue of Booth as Hamlet stands in the center of the park.)

NEW YORK BOTANICAL GARDEN

Fordham Rd. & Bronx River Pkwy., the Bronx
220-8700

For instant relaxation in a gorgeous natural setting, spend a few hours walking among the azaleas, magnolias, and rhododendron in the world-famous Bronx Botanical Garden, located just north of the zoo. You'll see hundreds of flowers, trees, and herbs from around the world, plus a 40-acre hemlock forest, rock garden, and pine grove. The jewel of the 250-acre garden is the beautifully restored Enid A. Haupt Conservatory, a domed glass pavilion built in 1901. Inside are simulated deserts, a waterfall, an orangery, coconut palms, orchids, and many more goodies to delight you. *Daily 10 A.M. to 5 P.M.; conservatory open 10:30 A.M. to 5 P.M. Admission free; conservatory $2.50, free on Sat.*

PROSPECT PARK

Grand Army Plaza, Brooklyn

Once was not enough for the Olmstead-Vaux team that created Central Park. This Brooklyn landmark, another masterwork, includes a large lake, meadows cut with paths and streams, a small zoo, and a variety of arches, pavilions, and bridges, all designed to follow the area's original landscape. In fact, because Olmstead and Vaux had a freer hand here than in Central Park, they were happier with the result. The entrance is at the impressive Grand Army Plaza, which includes a monument to JFK and a triumphal arch dedicated to Union Army soldiers and sailors.

RIVERSIDE PARK

Riverside Dr. to the Hudson River bet. 72nd & 145th Sts.

It isn't large enough to be a real oasis in the manner of Central Park, but Riverside Park provides a peaceful slice of green for West Siders. Notable along the park's three-plus miles are the 79th Street boat basin, where a number of houseboats are parked (there's a short promenade for waterside strolling), and the Soldiers' and Sailors' Monument at West 89th Street. Adding interest to the park are its varying levels; it shows old railroad lines at one point, then juts down to the Henry Hudson Parkway.

WASHINGTON SQUARE PARK

Base of Fifth Ave.

You'll see it all in this former potter's field—musicians and magicians, aging hippies, NYU students, elderly chess players, neighborhood kids, and more than a few drug dealers. In good weather, all forms of humanity gather in Washington

Square Park, the center of Greenwich Village. There's nothing pastoral about it, but you'll encounter an interesting cross-section of New York life here.

Tours

BY AIR

ISLAND HELICOPTER

Heliport at 34th St. & the East River
683-4575

Here's the most dramatic way to see the city, with a chance to come face to face with the Statue of Liberty and peek inside the top floors of the World Trade Center. Five choices of flights range in length from six minutes to 40 minutes. Best bets: the flight over the financial district to the Statue of Liberty ($40), or the same one plus midtown and Central Park ($50). Photographers will love it.
Daily 9 A.M. to 9 P.M. $30-139 (two-person minimum per flight).

BY BOAT

CIRCLE LINE

Pier 83, West 43rd St. & Twelfth Ave.
563-3200

The Circle Line tour—a three-hour ride literally around Manhattan—is a terrific way to get a new perspective on the city as you ride under the great bridges, note the differences in terrain (upper Manhattan looks almost rural!), and take in the great skyscrapers and luxury riverside apartment buildings. An experienced guide points out the major sights, shares bits of gossip, and tells corny jokes. Most New Yorkers have never taken the Circle Line, but it's their loss—save the trip for a pretty afternoon when you're really exhausted. Take a picnic basket along and enjoy!
Year-round, departures from 9:45 A.M. to 3:15 P.M. Adults $12, children $6.

HUDSON RIVER DAY LINE

Our favorite time of year to take this all-day trip up the Hudson is in September, when the weather is cooling off a bit and the leaves are just about to start turning gold. You'll

Pier 81, West 41st St. &
Twelfth Ave.
279-5151

cruise north as far as Poughkeepsie, with stops at lovely Bear Mountain State Park and at the Military Academy at West Point. If you choose to stay on the boat to West Point, a sightseeing tour of the U.S.M.A. costs a few dollars extra; otherwise, you can spend four hours exploring Bear Mountain, lunch and swim there, then wait to be picked up on the boat's return trip.

Late May to mid-Sept., Wed., Thurs., Sat., & Sun. Adults $18, children $9. Departs 9:30 A.M., returns 6:30 P.M.

THE PETREL

Battery Park
825-1976

Sailing on a 35-passenger, 70-foot yawl—it's an unusual, fun way to spend a lunch hour, happy hour, or, for romantics, a starry night. For lunch you'll need to bring your own, but you can buy sodas or drinks at the cash bar. Sails are around the Upper Bay and last between one-and-one-half and two hours; they'll take you around the Statue of Liberty as long as wind and weather permit.

April to Oct., times vary. Lunch sails $7.50, evening sails $10-17.

THE PIONEER

South Street Seaport, Pier 16 (off Fulton St.)
669-9400

This 102-foot schooner takes two- and three-hour cruises in warm weather. Charters are available as well (a mere $975 for three hours, or $800 for two) and you can invite your friends for a ride.

May to first week in Sept., Mon. & Tues., 3 P.M. (also 6 P.M. starting mid-June), Thurs.-Sun. noon & 3 P.M. (also 6 P.M. starting mid-June). $16 for a two-hour ride, $21 for three hours.

BY BUS

If time is short or you're not keen on walking everywhere, consider a bus tour of the city. You'll cover a lot of ground and learn more about New York from the multilingual guides than most of the natives know. The companies listed here offer a variety of tours, including lower Manhattan, uptown, all the major sights, and some boat tours. Prices vary, so give a call, shop around, and compare. Some possibilities are: Campus Coach, 545 Fifth Ave., 682-1050; Crossroads Sightseeing, 701 Seventh Ave., 581-2828; Gray Line Sightseeing, 900 Eighth Ave., 397-2600; Manhattan Sightseeing Tours, 150 West 49th St., 869-5005; New York Big Apple Tours, 22 West 23rd St., 691-7866 (regular tours in French,

German, Spanish, Italian; private tours for ten or more available in English); or Short Line Tours, 166 West 46th St., 354-5122.

SPECIALTIES

BACKSTAGE ON BROADWAY

228 West 47th St.
575-8065

Theater buffs will be enthralled by a 60- to 90-minute tour of a current Broadway show. A theater pro takes you backstage to explain how the magic really happens. Early reservations are a must.
Mon.-Sat. 10:30 A.M. Adults $6, students $5.

DOORWAY TO DESIGN

1441 Broadway, Suite 338 (41st St.)
221-1111;
(718) 339-1542

A professional interior designer will give you a behind-the-scenes look at top furniture and fabric showrooms, antique dealers, artists' studios, and private townhouses. A similar tour is offered for the fashion houses and design studios on and off Seventh Avenue.
By appointment only. $20-25 for a half-day program; longer tours available.

FEDERAL RESERVE BANK

33 Liberty St. (William St.)
720-6130

After you've visited the stock exchange, where fortunes are made and lost, drop by the Federal Reserve Bank to see a real "piggy bank" and ogle at the $165 billion in the gold vault. Also included in the hour-long tour are the security and cash counting departments.
Mon.-Fri. 10 A.M., 11 A.M., 1 P.M., & 2 P.M. Free admission, reservations required a week in advance.

HARLEM SPIRITUALS, INC.

1457 Broadway, Suite 1008 (41st & 42nd Sts.)
302-2594

Harlem's jazz age comes to life again in a fascinating nighttime tour every Thursday, Friday, and Saturday. After a traditional soul food dinner, you'll visit a cabaret and hear some good jazz or rhythm & blues (7 P.M. to midnight; $60 including dinner and cocktails; you'll be picked up afterwards). If you prefer a daytime visit, consider a rousing "Spirituals and Gospel" tour held every Sunday from 8:45 A.M. to 12:45 P.M. ($25), which culminates at a Baptist church service. A more complete tour of this historic neighborhood is available on Tuesday and Thursday from 9 A.M. to 1:30 P.M. ($32), with a soul-food lunch included.
Sun. and weekday tours leave from Short Line tour office, 166 West 46th St.

HOLIDAYS IN NEW YORK

152 West 58th St. (Sixth & Seventh Aves.)
765-2515

Holidays arranges personalized tours of New York neighborhoods, shopping districts, or art galleries with multilingual private guides who escort you by taxi or chauffeured car. The company also offers a four-hour Harlem Sunday Gospel Tour ($25) with church service, museum, soul-food lunch, and a walk in the neighborhood included.
$25 per hour plus expenses.

HORSE-DRAWN CARRIAGES

Central Park South & Fifth Ave.

For many visitors, a trip to New York wouldn't be complete without a romantic carriage ride through Central Park. Carriage rentals are available at the southeast corner of the park near the Plaza Hotel.
$17 for first half hour, $5 for each quarter hour after that.

INSIDE NEW YORK

203 East 72nd St. (Second & Third Aves.)
861-0709

For the clotheshorse in the crowd, there's a tour of the studios of famous designers and furriers, plus the chance to shop for designer fashions at wholesale prices. Multilingual guides cover the hottest spots on Seventh Avenue. Art tours around SoHo and the Lower East Side are also available.
Times vary; tours by appointment. $20 and up (groups only).

SCHAPIRO'S WINERY

126 Rivington St. (Essex St.)
674-4404

Find out how kosher wine is made and sample "the Wine You Can Almost Cut with a Knife," then browse through the food booths in the large Essex Street Market.
Sun. 11 A.M. to 4 P.M. Admission free.

SINGER'S TOURS

130 St. Edward's St., Brooklyn
(718) 875-9084

Lou Singer, 61, also known as "Mr. Brooklyn," loves showing people around his city. Give him a call to reserve a place on one of his personalized tours of Brooklyn or Manhattan: "Waterfront Brooklyn," "Fabulous Flatbush," "Noshing on the Lower East Side," "Historic and Architectural Brooklyn," "Little Old New York," and many more. Lou, a great talker, escorts you in a bus or minibus he drives himself.
By appointment only. $25.

WALKING

ART TOURS OF MANHATTAN

Whether you're seriously interested in art, or simply curious, take a private tour of artists' studios, galleries, and museums with a Ph.D. as your guide. And if you're looking to buy that

76 Library Pl., Princeton, NJ
228-1637;
(609) 683-0881

perfect piece for your home, an art consulting service is available for an additional fee.
Morning, afternoon, and evening tours. $25-45.

MUNICIPAL ART SOCIETY

457 Madison Ave. (50th St.)
935-3690

This preservation-minded civic group conducts tours of different neighborhoods around the city. Knowledgeable guides share a wealth of information about architecture, city planning, and history. A free one-hour tour of Grand Central Station is given every Wednesday at 12:30 P.M. (meet under the huge Kodak sign in the concourse).
April to Oct., Sat. & Sun. Times vary; call for reservations. $8 members; $12 non-members.

MUSEUM OF THE CITY OF NEW YORK

1220 Fifth Ave. (103rd St.)
534-1672

Take a four-hour exploration (with lunch break) of a particular neighborhood's historical, cultural, and sociological history, led by one of the Museum's urban historians.
Mid-March to May & late Sept. to mid-Nov., Sun. 11 A.M. to 3 P.M. Non-members $10; members $6; children, students, & seniors half-price.

NEW YORK WALK-ABOUT

c/o Lister Travel Service, 30 Rockefeller Plaza
582-2015 (weekdays);
(914) 834-5388 (evenings & weekends)

Most of the walkers on these informative tours are New Yorkers eager to learn more about the evolution of their city. About 25 different tours are offered (one or two per weekend), including "Millionaires' Row—New York's Gold Coast," "Greenwich Village—Echoes of the Past," and walks through Chinatown/Little Italy, the Lower East Side, and Brooklyn Heights. Occasionally, there's a Saturday afternoon tour of SoHo or a Saturday evening tour (10 P.M. to 1 A.M.) entitled "Nocturnal New York."
March to July & Sept. to Nov., Sun. 11 A.M. & 2 P.M. $6.

92ND STREET Y

1395 Lexington Ave.
427-6000

The Y has long been a leader in sponsoring unusual walking tours, often with celebrated guides like historian Kate Simon. Three or four tours are offered per weekend with subjects as varied as Jewish Harlem, the East Village, a "mystery tour," a day in Irish New York, and a tour of Coney Island.
Year-round; most tours on Sun. $8-25.

BASICS

At Your Service

SAFETY

Common sense is your best security in New York city. No matter what neighborhood you're in, it's safest to be aware of what's happening around you at all times. Wear your jewelry but don't flash it, and certainly don't go onto the subway with it in full sight. If you take the subway at night (and lots of good people do) make sure to wait for your train in a well-lit area near the token booth. The parks are beautiful, so stroll through them if you like, but never at night and never alone in isolated areas, no matter what the time. If you know where you're going and look and act sure of yourself, you can spend a wonderful, crime-free holiday in New York.

FOREIGN EXCHANGE

It's still difficult to walk into the average bank and get foreign money changed. Many banks require you to have an account at the branch with which you wish to do business before they'll exchange your money. Not to worry, though—there are many international banks that gladly provide this service, along with some companies that do nothing but foreign exchange. Of these, two of the best are Bank Leumi Trust Co. of New York, 535 Seventh Ave., 392-4000, and Deak New York Inc., 630 Fifth Ave., 757-6915.

INFORMATION

Emergencies (ambulance, police, fire), 911
Special Events, 566-4074
Time, 976-1616
U.S. Customs, 466-5550

U.S. Passport Office, 541-7700
Visitors' Bureau, 397-8222
Weather, 976-1212

Getting Around

AIRPORT TRANSPORTATION

BUSES

Carey buses (718-632-0500) depart for Kennedy from five Manhattan locations: 125 Park Ave. near Grand Central Station, Port Authority between Eighth and Ninth at 42nd St., the Hilton Hotel near Rockefeller Center at 53rd and Sixth Ave., Sheraton City Squire at Seventh Ave. and 51st St., and Marriott Marquis at Broadway and 45th. There's also an express bus from Grand Central to the Pan Am Shuttle at La Guardia. The buses run every 30 minutes from the stations, from 5:45 A.M. to 1 A.M.; every 20 minutes from the hotels, from 5:45 A.M. to 10:45 P.M. The price is $8 to JFK and $6 to LGA.

Abbey Transport (201-961-2535) provides bus service between Newark and the major hotels in Manhattan, on both the east and west sides of town. Service runs from 8 A.M. to 11:30 P.M. The trip takes 30-45 minutes and costs $12. (Some hotels charge a supplemental service fee.)

If you're operating on a strict budget, try the Transport of New Jersey buses from the Port Authority Bus Terminal (41st St. and Eighth Ave., platform 39). You won't find a better price unless you walk or ride a bike. The 24-hour service is $5.

HELICOPTER

For an unparalleled view of Manhattan, and for the fastest trip possible to the airport, New York Helicopter's (800-645-3494) 10-minute ride to JFK can't be beat. Flights depart from 34th St. and the East River. The price is $58 one way, with departures every half hour from 2 P.M. to 7:30 P.M.

TAXIS

New York taxis have had a recent fare increase, so the cost for getting to the airports from the city can be shocking, especially if you're leaving during rush hours. Allow yourself plenty of time to make your flight; the ride should take about one hour to Kennedy and Newark and 30 to 40 minutes to La Guardia. Average prices, according to the New York Taxi Commission (869-4110): midtown to La Guardia, $20, to Kennedy, $30, and to Newark, $30, plus a required $10 to be added to the meter fare. This includes tips and tolls, which must be paid by the passenger.

TRAIN TO THE PLANE

If you don't mind a one-and-a-half hour trip from midtown to your airline terminal, this is the way to go. The price is reasonable ($6.50), and you simply take the special subway that starts at 57th St. and Sixth Ave. and goes downtown to the airport, where an express bus will take you and your bags to your terminal. The stations serviced by the JFK Express are: 57th St. at Sixth Ave.; Rockefeller Center; 42nd St. at Sixth Ave.; West 34th at Sixth Ave.; West 4th St.; Chambers St.; Broadway-Nassau; and Jay St.-Borough Hall (Brooklyn). For additional information, call (718) 330-1234.

AUTO RENTAL

If you're the kind who enjoys dodging—potholes, taxis, bicycles, jaywalkers, delivery trucks—then you may be the brave soul who'll want to rent a car in Manhattan. You'll find the rental companies at the airports as well as in the city. Summer weekends are the most difficult times to find a car, so reserve well in advance. The major companies are Avis (800) 331-1212; Hertz (800) 654-3131; and National (800) 328-4567.

BUSES

Buses are a good, albeit slow, form of reasonable transportation around the city. If you ride them during non-rush hours, you'll get a seat and can enjoy sightseeing through Manhattan for just $1, the cost of a token (exact change required). Call (718) 330-1234 to find out about special cultural and shoppers' buses.

FINDING STREETS

Manhattan is one of the simplest big cities in the world to find your way around in. North of the Village, most of the streets make up a logical criss-crossing grid, with numbered streets running east-west and avenues (Park, Madison, Fifth) running north-south. From the Village on down to Wall Street and Battery Park, however, you'll need help finding your way through the crooked maze of streets. Check with our map in this guide; if you need more detailed information, pick up a "Flashmaps" guide—almost all bookstores carry them. Tip: Fifth Avenue divides the east and west sides of the city, and east-west blocks are about twice as long as north-south blocks. If you can, call your destination to find its cross street and, if necessary, directions.

LIMOUSINES

Limousines come in all sizes and colors, and all offer comparative services at competitive prices. Some of the best choices are Bermuda Chauffered Limousine Service, 637 West 20th St., 249-8400; Class Act, 2315 Twelfth Ave., 491-5300; and Carey Limousine, 517-7010.

SUBWAYS

If the tracks aren't being worked on or the trains being diverted to another route because of water main problems, the subway is the fastest way to get around in the city and its boroughs. It is by no means luxurious traveling, but for the money ($1) you can't beat it.

TAXIS

Taxis are a necessary evil in this city. They're expensive, often in ill repair, and sometimes downright uncomfortable, especially when their springs are broken and you're bumping around on the potholed Manhattan streets. But on the up side, they're a dime a dozen in most areas, except during rush hour and pre-theater hour, when you really need them. Be sure any taxi you take is a licensed medallion cab; then, if you run into problems, you can contact the Taxi Commission at 869-4110. It'll cost you $1.15 just to enter the taxi plus 15 cents per eighth of a mile. If the traffic flows, you can expect to pay about $9, including tip, for a midtown to SoHo ride; about $4, plus tip, from midtown to the Upper East Side; and about $3, plus tip, for a simple crosstown ride.

RADIO TAXIS

There are many to choose from, and most will arrive 10 to 15 minutes after you've phoned. Some of our favorites are Skyline, (718) 482-8686; All City, 796-1111; and UTOG, 741-2000.

TELEPHONE NUMBERS: TRAINS & BUSES

Amtrak Penn Station, 736-4545
Long Island Railroad, Penn Station, (718) 454-5477
Metro North, Grand Central Station, 532-4900
New York Transit Authority, (718) 330-1234
Port Authority Bus Terminal, 564-8484

Goings-on

By now you know that New York is a city that never rests, no matter what the season. The following is a list of some of the major events that take place throughout the year. For more detailed and up-to-the-minute information, visit or call Visitors' Information at the New York Convention and Visitors' Bureau, Two Columbus Circle, 397-8222, or the Information Center at Times Square on 42nd St. between Broadway and

Seventh Ave. (walk-in information only). They are both open Mon.-Fri. 9
A.M.-6 P.M., Sat. and Sun. 10 A.M.-6 P.M.

JANUARY

National Boat Show (mid-Jan.), Jacob Javits Center; 216-2000.

Winter Antiques Show (mid- to late Jan.), Seventh Regiment Armory,
Park Ave. at 67th St.

Greater New York International Automobile Show (late Jan.), Jacob
Javits Center; 216-2000.

FEBRUARY

Westminster Kennel Club/Westminster Dog Show (mid-Feb.), Madison Square Garden; 563-8300.

MARCH

St. Patrick's Day Parade (March 17th), Fifth Ave. from 44th to 86th
Sts.; 397-8222.

APRIL

Ringling Bros. Barnum & Bailey Circus (April and May), Madison
Square Garden; 563-8300.

Easter Parade (Easter Sunday), Fifth Ave. from 49th to 59th Sts.;
397-8222.

Cherry Blossom Festival (late April), Brooklyn Botanic Garden; (718)
622-4433.

MAY

Washington Square Art Show (Memorial Day weekend and first two
weekends in June), University Place; 982-6255.

Rose and Orchid Show (late May), New York Botanic Garden, the Bronx; (718) 220-8777.

City beaches open (late May).

JUNE

Guggenheim Concerts (mid-June to early Aug.), Damrosch Park, Lincoln Center and Seaside Park in Brooklyn; 867-8290.

Metropolitan Opera/New York Philharmonic free concerts (all month), city parks; 755-4100.

Museum Mile (mid-June), Fifth Ave. from 82nd to 105th Sts.; 722-1313.

Kool Jazz Festival (late June and July), locations vary; 877-1800, 787-2020.

Belmont Stakes (Triple Crown, mid-June), Belmont Park, Queens; (718) 641-4700.

JULY

Shakespeare in the Park (July and Aug.), Delacorte Court, Central Park; 535-5630, 598-7100.

American Crafts Festival, Lincoln Center; 677-4627.

Mostly Mozart Concerts (July and Aug.), Lincon Center; 874-2424.

AUGUST

Lincoln Center Out-of-Doors Festival, Lincoln Center Plaza; 877-1800.

U.S. Open Tennis Championships (Aug. and Sept.), Flushing Meadows, Queens; (718) 271-5100.

SEPTEMBER

New York Philharmonic season opens, Avery Fisher Hall, Lincoln Center; 874-2424.

Washington Square Art Show, University Place; 982-6255.

New York Film Festival, Lincoln Center; 362-1911.

OCTOBER

Start of ice-skating season at Rockefeller Center; 757-5731.

Thoroughbred racing opens at Aqueduct Racetrack, Queens; (718) 641-4700.

NOVEMBER

Macy's Thanksgiving Day Parade (last Thurs. of Nov.), Central Park West from 77th to 34th Sts.; 560-4495, 397-8222.

Virginia Slims Women's Tennis Championships (mid-Nov.), Madison Square Garden; 563-8300.

DECEMBER

Christmas tree lighting at Rockefeller Center; 397-8222.

Nabisco Masters Tennis Championship (early Dec.), Madison Square Garden; 563-8300.

MAPS

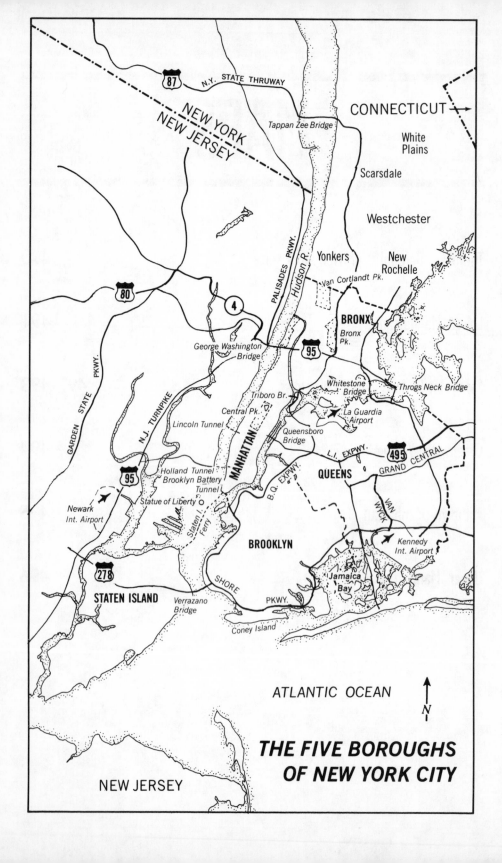

THE FIVE BOROUGHS
OF NEW YORK CITY

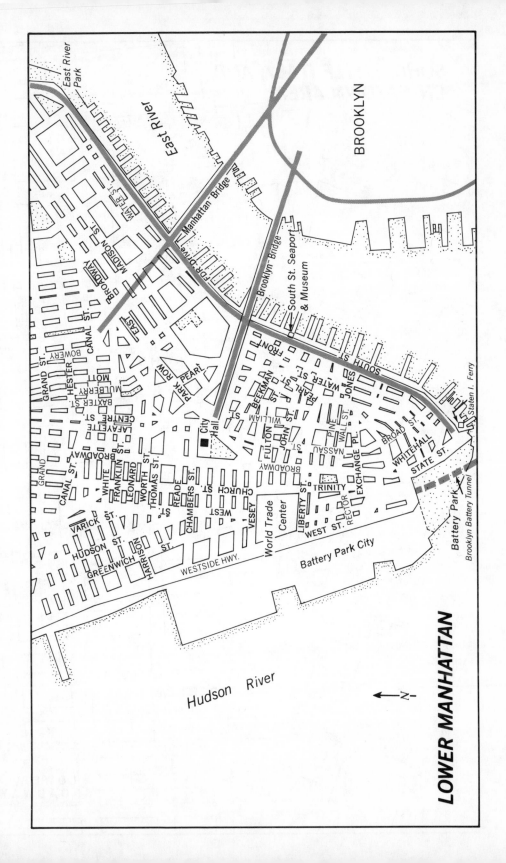

LOWER MANHATTAN

SOHO, LITTLE ITALY, AND CHINATOWN AREA

BLEECKER STREET

WEST HOUSTON STREET

LAFAYETTE STREET

KING STREET

CHARLTON STREET

VANDAM STREET

SPRING STREET

HUDSON STREET

VARICK STREET

AVENUE OF THE AMERICAS

SULLIVAN STREET

THOMPSON STREET

PRINCE STREET

SPRING STREET

MERCER STREET

BROADWAY

CROSBY STREET

SOHO

WEST BROADWAY

WOOSTER STREET

GREENE STREET

BROOME STREET

CANAL STREET

HOWARD STREET

DESBROSSES STREET

VESTRY STREET

LISPENARD STREET

LAIGHT STREET

GREENWICH STREET

WALKER STREET

HUBERT STREET

WHITE STREET

BEACH STREET

N. MOORE STREET

FRANKLIN STREET

FRANKLIN STREET

TRIBECA

LEONARD STREET

To Brooklyn Battery Tunnel

HARRISON STREET

JAY STREET

WORTH STREET

LAFAYETTE STREET

**L O W E R
B R O A D W A Y**

THIRD STREET

LOWER EAST SIDE

SECOND STREET

FIRST STREET

STANTON STREET

RIVINGTON STREET

ELIZABETH STREET

MULBERRY STREET

LITTLE ITALY

SUFFOLK STREET

CLINTON STREET

NORFOLK STREET

ORCHARD STREET

LUDLOW STREET

To Williamsburg Bridge →

KENMARE STREET

DELANCEY STREET

CLEVELAND PLACE

MOTT STREET

BOWERY

CHRYSTIE STREET

FORSYTH STREET

ELDRIDGE STREET

ALLEN STREET

ESSEX STREET

GRAND STREET

N

CENTRE STREET

BAXTER STREET

HESTER STREET

MONROE STREET

CHINATOWN

E. BROADWAY

HENRY STREET

BAYARD STREET

PELL STREET

DIVISION STREET

MADISON STREET

Chatham Square

WORTH STREET

Kimlau Square

To Manhattan Bridge →

PARK ROW

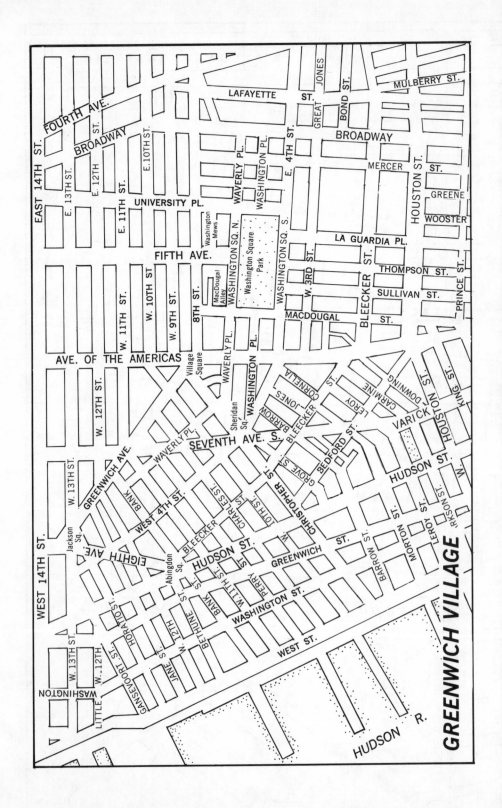

GREENWICH VILLAGE

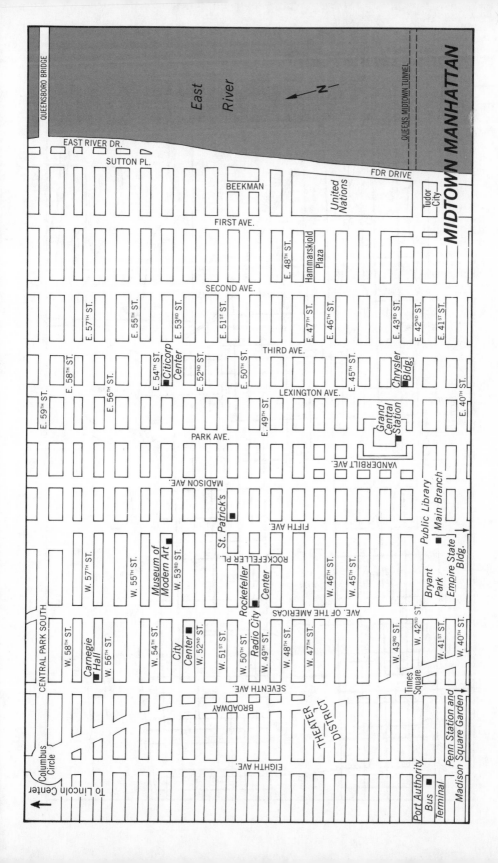

Upper Manhattan

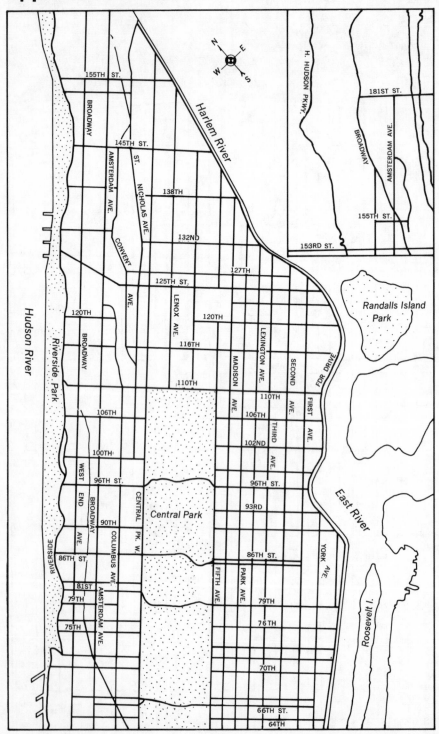

INDEX

C

D

E

M

Q

R

S

T

U

V

W

Y

Z

MORE GAULT MILLAU "BEST" GUIDES

Now the series known throughout Europe for its wit and savvy reveals the best of four major U.S. cities—New York, Washington, D.C., Los Angeles, and San Francisco. Following the guidelines established by the world-class French food critics Henri Gault and Christian Millau, local teams of writers have gathered inside information about where to stay, what to do, where to shop, and where to dine or catch a quick bite in these key locales. Each volume sparkles with the wit, wisdom, and panache that readers have come to expect from Gault Millau, whose distinctive style makes them favorites among travelers bored with the neutral, impersonal style of other guides. There are full details on the best of everything that makes these cities special places to visit, including restaurants, diversions, nightlife, hotels, shops, the arts—all the unique sights and sounds of each city. These guides also offer practical information on getting around and coping with each city. Filled with provocative, entertaining, and frank reviews, they are helpful as well as fun to read. Perfect for visitors and residents alike.

Please send me the books checked below:

☐ The Best of Los Angeles $14.95

☐ The Best of San Francisco $14.95

☐ The Best of New York $14.95

☐ The Best of Washington, D.C. $14.95

PRENTICE HALL PRESS
Order Department—Travel Books
200 Old Tappan Road
Old Tappan, New Jersey 07675

In U.S. include $1.50 shipping UPS for 1st book, 50¢ each additional book. Outside U.S., $2 and 50¢ respectively.

Enclosed is my check or money order for $ _____

NAME _____

ADDRESS _____

CITY _____ STATE _____ ZIP _____